# FROM TREATIES TO RESERVES

# FROM TREATIES

# TO RESERVES

The Federal Government
and Native Peoples in Territorial Alberta,
1870–1905

D.J. HALL

McGill-Queen's University Press
Montreal & Kingston • London • Chicago

ISBN 978-0-7735-4594-6 (cloth)
ISBN 978-0-7735-4595-3 (paper)
ISBN 978-0-7735-9768-6 (ePDF)
ISBN 978-0-7735-9769-3 (ePUB)

Legal deposit fourth quarter 2015
Bibliothèque nationale du Québec

Printed in Canada on acid-free paper that is 100% ancient forest free
(100% post-consumer recycled), processed chlorine free.

McGill-Queen's University Press acknowledges the support of the Canada
Council for the Arts for our publishing program. We also acknowledge the
financial support of the Government of Canada through the Canada Book
Fund for our publishing activities.

**Library and Archives Canada Cataloguing in Publication**

Hall, D.J. (David John), 1943–, author
From treaties to reserves: the federal government and Native peoples
in territorial Alberta, 1870–1905/D.J. Hall.

Includes bibliographical references and index.
Issued in print and electronic formats.
ISBN 978-0-7735-4594-6 (cloth). – ISBN 978-0-7735-4595-3 (paperback). –
ISBN 978-0-7735-9768-6 (ePDF). – ISBN 978-0-7735-9769-3 (ePUB)

1. Native peoples – Alberta – Government relations – History – 19th century.
2. Native peoples – Alberta – Government relations – History – 20th century.
3. Indian reservations – Alberta – History – 19th century.
4. Indian reservations – Alberta – History – 20th century. I. Title.

E78.A34H34 2015      971.23004'97      C2015-905249-1
                                        C2015-905250-5

This book was typeset by Interscript in 10.5/13 Sabon.

To Adeline

For unwavering support
and uncompromising honesty

# Contents

Contents

# Acknowledgments

As every author knows, many personal debts are accumulated, and new friendships made and old ones strengthened, during the long journey of producing a manuscript. I am grateful to the late John Eagle for many discussions of this book in its early stages over several years; and to Rod Wilson, who, over numerous lunches, patiently and engagingly broadened my understanding of Native peoples, and acted as a sounding board for many of my ideas. Merrill Distad, Dale Gibson, Ted Binnema, and Don Smith all read early drafts of the manuscript, pointed out many errors, made many thoughtful suggestions, and always left me encouraged. I acknowledge my debts to them at numerous points in the text and endnotes. I take full responsibility for any errors, omissions, or other shortcomings. I also mostly profited from the comments of anonymous readers, and the book is better for that process. Thanks as well to Lorie Huising, whose technical expertise proved enormously helpful, and to Maurizio Yamanaka, for drawing the maps.

I have always learned much from teaching, from having to clarify my ideas for students, and from the stimulation of discussion, debate, and even dealing with student assignments. I miss that in retirement, but want to acknowledge two groups in particular: the fine graduate and senior undergraduate students who studied aspects of Native and early Alberta history with me at the University of Alberta in 2009; and the wonderful classes of outspoken, frank, and enthusiastic seniors with whom I engaged each May in the Edmonton Life-Long Learners' Association program over several years, also at the University of Alberta. Students rarely know how fruitful these interactions can be for their instructors.

Mark Abley, of McGill-Queen's University Press, believed in this work and guided me through the approval process with enormous patience and wisdom; I cannot say how much I have appreciated him. Production of a book is a team effort for the publisher, and I am grateful to all who have contributed in their various ways. In particular, I acknowledge Ryan Van Huijstee, Jessica Howarth, Joanne Pisano, Filomena Falocco, and Jacqui Davis.

Finally, thank you from the depths of my heart to Adeline, whose love and unshaking conviction of the value of my work have been the rock upon which I have depended over these many years.

# A Note on Terminology and Spelling

Terminology with reference to Canada's Native peoples is fraught with difficulty and controversy. "Indians," the oldest term,[1] is a colonialist designation of mistaken identity, but it has stuck mainly because (as in India itself) the diverse languages and cultures of Native peoples could provide no single word that could have widespread acceptance. It is often unclear whether the term connotes only status Indians (those with treaty rights, mostly on reserves), or whether it includes non-status Indians as well. Still, the term continues to be widely used by Indians themselves, and by many scholars who write on related matters. In the period addressed in this book it not only was the term most widely employed, but also had legal significance; I have used it to refer to those Native peoples who white people of the day termed "Indians," both status and non-status. I also use "Native peoples," which may have a wider meaning (depending upon context) and may include the Metis.

Some prefer the term "aboriginal peoples," though it too carries problems of ambiguity and differentiation, and I do not use it in this book. Less useful is "Amerindians," a word intended to distinguish between the Indians of India and those of the Americas, and extensively used in the United States. Despite its adoption by a few distinguished Canadian scholars, such as Olive P. Dickason, most historians of Canada's Native peoples have avoided it, and I have tried to minimize its use in the present work. "First Nations," though widely used, even preferred, since the 1980s, seems to me anachronistic when applied to the past, when it was unknown; there is also frequent uncertainty as to whether it includes only status Indians, or all Indians, or Metis, or all groups together. It has been widely adopted by many of Canada's Native peoples, and increasingly by scholars writing on the subject and in legal documents. Nevertheless, for clarity, I lay it aside.

Even "Metis" carries mixed messages. In the mid-nineteenth century and later, the term was spelled "Métis" and usually denoted persons of mixed French and Native ancestry; many still prefer that spelling. To refer generally to people of mixed Native and non-Native parentage, the common term in English during the period studied herein was "half-breed" or "half-breed," which has such disparaging connotations that it is now socially unacceptable. Yet it was the common term throughout the period of this book, and so it appears in a number of quotations. I have tried otherwise to use "Metis," which toward the end of the period was coming to have a more generic application than only to those with some French blood and according to Gerhard Ens is generally used among Metis today.[2]

## REFERRING TO THE INDIANS OF TREATIES 6 AND 7

Indians in the period under review usually used the tribal names, but white people did so very rarely. I have endeavoured to use tribal names where feasible, but popular English names come up regularly in the documentation and in some contexts it makes sense to use them.

The Nizitapi (Blackfoot)[3] culture embraced by Treaty 7 (1877) in what became southern Alberta had three principal identity groups who all spoke the Blackfoot language and gathered on three separate reserves. The American component in Montana, known as the South Piegan, is on the Blackfeet Indian reservation. The Canadian groups, by their tribal names followed by their official and popular names during the period, are the Siksika (Blackfeet), Kainai (Blood), and Piikani (or Pikunni, or Peigan). Of these, the Kainai still frequently use "Blood" to refer to themselves, and still have a Blood Tribal Council.

The Tsuu T'ina, related linguistically to the more northerly Beaver tribe, were officially and popularly known as the Sarcee (or variously Sarsi, Sarci, or Sirsi).

Bands of Stoneys were encompassed in Treaties 6 and 7. They are related to the Assiniboine (a common term in the nineteenth century, meaning "people who cook with stones") or Sioux from further south and east. Variant spellings in the documents include Stonies or Stonys (both of which the Stoneys today regard as erroneous). Those in the western part of Treaty 7 call themselves "Iyarhe Nakoda"; a common current term is "Mountain Stoney." They regard the term Assiniboine as an imposition of outsiders.[4] Stoneys in both Treaty 6 and 7 refer to themselves as Nakoda or Nakota, meaning "the people." The term Stoney still has legitimacy and is widely used.

Most Indians in Treaty 6 were Cree, a word still widely used and accepted. There also were some Stoney Nakota Sioux bands in Treaty 6, popularly called Assiniboine in the nineteenth and early twentieth centuries.[5] Other names – Iroquois and Chipewyan (the latter variously spelled; member of the Dene Nation) – remained largely unchanged. Note that even bands identified as other than Cree had a significant mixture of Cree blood and culture, for intermarriage among bands was common.

A case of particular interest is the agency known in the period under review as Bear Hills, Peace Hills, and – from the 1890s onward – Hobbema (the name of a Dutch painter, chosen by William Van Horne of the Canadian Pacific Railway). Since 1 January 2014, "Hobbema" has been replaced with "Maskwacis," the Cree term for Bear Hills.[6] In this book, I use the term(s) most appropriate to the time under consideration, and acknowledge that Maskwacis has a deep cultural resonance for today's Indians.

What becomes confusing is the fact that government officials, government documents, the popular press, and even Indians themselves referred to bands by a variety of names with little consistency: by location or by chief (usually the current chief, though sometimes by an influential earlier chief), and occasionally by both location and by chief. Because orthography varied widely with respect to Indian names, and because sometimes a chief was known by more than one name (usually an Indian name and an English name, but sometimes by more than one), and because some bands came and went, it requires great care to sort them out in government records. In some cases, for example, the same band may be referred to by different names (or spellings) within the same annual report, or (more frequently) in different years. For instance, the Samson Cree band (later the Samson Cree First Nation) was just as often referred to as the Sampson band. The James Seenum band was also known as the Pakan band (following an alternate name for Seenum) and as the Whitefish Lake band. The fact that many bands were of mixed Indian descent (for example, Cree and Stoney), or of mixed Metis and Indian descent, can also create confusion. Government reports, especially in the first decade or so after the treaties, are often inconsistent in their reporting of any given band's Indian identity. In this book, I have tried to use what I understand to be the most common tribal referent, but cannot guarantee that everyone will agree with my choices.[7] Note, too, that the names of twenty-first century bands are not always a reliable guide to those of the late nineteenth century.

### REFERRING TO WHITES

Finally, the problem arises of terminology for non-Native Canadians. Noel Dyck contends that the term "whites" "has today virtually disappeared from official or polite use."[8] That may be true for the multicultural Canada of the late twentieth or early twenty-first centuries, but in the period under review Natives and non-Natives commonly used it. The word reflected both a "racial" and a cultural distinction, and legally differentiated non-Native from Native peoples. In the context of the time, non-Native people of colour in western Canada were very few in number and mostly marginalized; during the period covered by this book they had almost no perceptible influence on shaping the dominant prairie culture, for which they mostly remained stereotyped outliers. Beyond its legal meaning, the term white in popular usage was a more restrictive social construction than it later came to be: in racist late-nineteenth century non-Native society, it also frequently excluded many southern and eastern Europeans, Jews, and even Irish. Despite its difficulties, I often have employed the term white because it was relevant to the period.[9]

Finally, some prefer the term "settlers" for all who did not have Native ancestry, because it identifies people by who they are rather than who they are not.[10] I find that problematic for this study because the term had a much narrower, more specific meaning during the time and in the place of this study. Some scholars of Native peoples' history employ "newcomers," but this too has by no means been universally adopted.[11]

### NOTES

1  Another old term, "savages," derived from the French *sauvages*, is no longer acceptable, though I have not altered it when it appears in a very few quotations in this book. The term Indian generally is understood to exclude Metis and Inuit.

2  Ens, "Metis Identity, Personal Identity and the Development of Capitalism," 174n2.

3  I follow Carter and Hildebrandt in using Nizitapi, though "Niitsitapi" is also common. Another form is "Niitsitapilsinni," meaning "real people": see The Blackfoot Gallery Committee, *The Story of the Blackfoot People*.

4 The terminology is further clarified at www.stoneynation.com. The three First Nations today are the Bearspaw, Chiniki, and Wesley. On the Sharphead band, see www.anishinabe-history.com/first-nation/paul.shtml.

5 See, for example, the Alexis First Nation website (www.alexisnakotasioux.com).

6 *Edmonton Journal*, 2 January 2014, A3. The first and last syllables are emphasized; the "c" in the last syllable has a "ch" sound, and the syllable rhymes with "lease."

7 Anyone interested in more detail on the problems of transliteration and translation from Native languages might usefully begin with Wolvengrey, "On the Spelling and Pronunciation of First Nations Languages," 113–25. Of special relevance to the Alberta case are 114–17 (Cree) and 119–21 (Dakota, Lakhota, and Nakoda).

8 Dyck, *What Is the Indian "Problem,"* 9. See this work for a fuller discussion of these matters.

9 I do acknowledge that "whiteness" studies is a relatively new and developing field of investigation that calls into question any simplistic notions of a "white race." A fine introduction to evolving cultural constructions of whiteness is Painter's *The History of White People* – chapters 10 to 15 are particularly germane to understanding notions of a white race in North America and Europe during the period examined in the present volume.

10 Asch, *On Being Here to Stay*, 8–9.

11 For example, Axtell, *Natives and Newcomers*; Trigger, *Natives and Newcomers*.

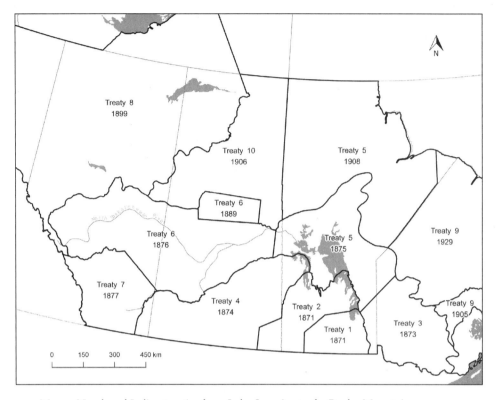

Map 1 Numbered Indian treaties from Lake Superior to the Rocky Mountains

All maps drawn by Mauricio Yamanaka. Note that historical reserve boundaries on maps may not correspond precisely to current reserve boundaries.

Map layers based on information available through GeoBase (Aboriginal Lands of Canada, Canadian Geographical Names, Canadian Geopolitical Boundaries, National Hydro Network, and National Road Network), now accessible through www.geogratis.gc.ca, and through the National Weather Service (Rivers of the US), accessible at http://www.nws.noaa.gov/geodata/catalog/hydro/html/rivers.htm. Map of Treaty 7 reserves and Montana reserves adapted with permission from R.B. Morrison and C.R. Wilson, eds., *Native Peoples: The Canadian Experience*, 2nd ed. (Oxford University Press Canada, 1995), 386.

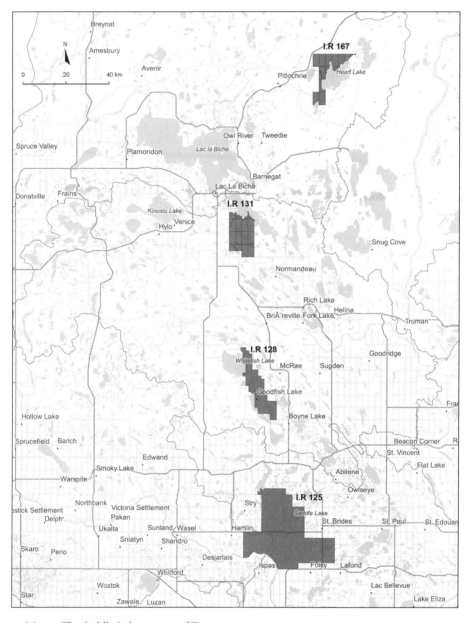

Map 2 The Saddle Lake agency of Treaty 6

IR 125: Combines Saddle Lake and Blue Quill (formerly IR 127) reserves
IR 128: James Seenum reserve
IR 131: Beaver Lake reserve
IR 167: Heart Lake reserve

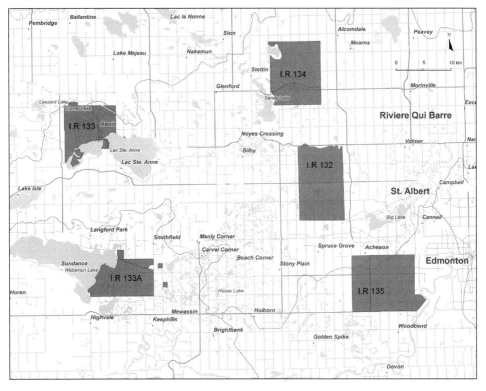

Map 3 The Edmonton agency of Treaty 6

IR 132: Michel Callihoo reserve

IR 133: Alexis reserve

IR 133A: White Whale Lake (or Paul) reserve

IR 134: Alexander reserve

IR 135: Enoch (Tommy la Potac), or Stony Plain reserve

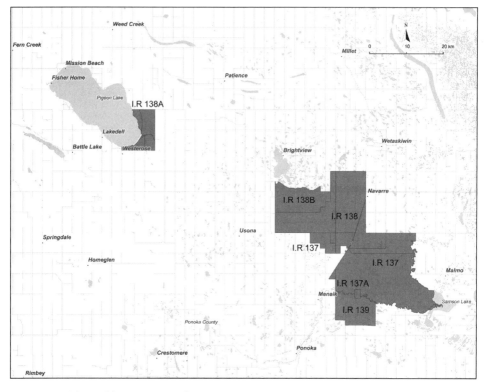

Map 4 The Hobbema agency of Treaty 6

IR 137 & 137A: Samson reserve
IR 138: Ermineskin reserve
IR 138A: Pigeon Lake fishing limit for Hobbema
IR 138B: Addition to Ermineskin reserve
IR 139: Bobtail (or Muddy Bull, or Montana) reserve

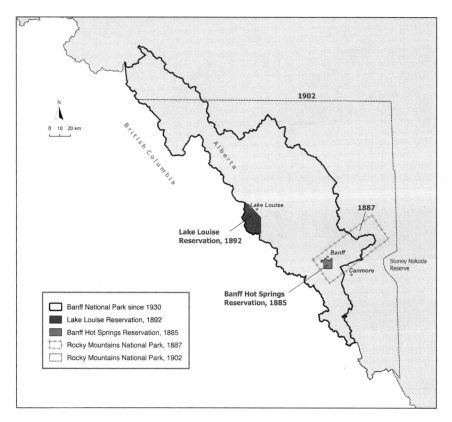

Map 5 Changing boundaries of the Rocky Mountains National Park

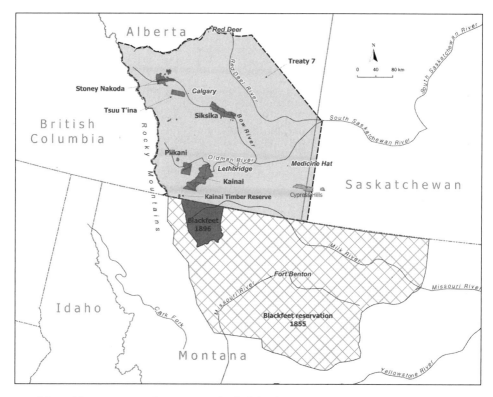

Map 6 Treaty 7 area and reserves, with Blackfeet lands in Montana.
The Stoney Nakoda designation comprises IR 142 (Bearspaw), IR 143 (Jacob),
and IR 144 (Chinitci) reserves.

Adapted with permission from R.B. Morrison and C.R. Wilson, eds., *Native Peoples:
The Canadian Experience*, 2nd ed. (Oxford University Press Canada, 1995), 386.

# FROM TREATIES TO RESERVES

I profoundly believe in the difference between history and memory; to allow memory to replace history is dangerous ... Without history, memory is open to abuse. But if history comes first, then memory has a template and guide against which it can work and be assessed.

Tony Judt, *Thinking the Twentieth Century*

# Prologue

In this book, I examine the policies of the Canadian federal government with respect to the Native peoples of territorial Alberta between roughly 1870 and 1905. I present a case study in the broader history of relations between Native peoples and whites in Canada. A basic premise is that the two sides that attended the treaty process of the 1870s were products of profoundly different cultural experiences and had widely disparate expectations. They therefore had quite divergent understandings of what the treaties meant.[1] These differences had significant implications for the nature and implementation of government policies, and for Indian responses to those policies, during the early years of reserve settlement.

The Indians who signed Treaty 6 in 1876 and Treaty 7 in 1877, for their part, faced increasingly dire circumstances and desired a permanent accommodation with the dominion that would ensure their physical and cultural survival. Most immediately, that meant starvation relief, medical aid, and the continuing right to hunt and fish in their traditional territories; it also meant guaranteed reserves where they would receive aid in beginning a more settled agricultural life to supplement (but not replace) their traditional lifestyle, and where their children would receive some schooling. Evidence from elders suggests that they envisaged a kind of kin relationship with newcomers in which they would be respected and supported as necessary, and would share the resources of the region. Elders believe that the treaty process was about not surrendering their lands, but sharing them.

Her Majesty's Canadian government – the other party to the treaties – thought, in contrast, that the treaties' principal objective was to acquire full title to the land in preparation for its peaceful occupation by white settlers, for a stipulated price. The secondary goal was to enable Indians to survive by transforming them from hunter-gatherers to settled, self-supporting agriculturalists or pastoralists, educating them, and preparing them for assimilation into the wider Canadian society. The government negotiators and officials believed that, at the treaty talks, Indians had indicated they accepted, and even desired, fundamental change. In the medium term, the government aimed for a settled, educated Indian population similar to that of central Canada, especially that of western Ontario. In the long term, its ultimate purpose was Indians' full citizenship and assimilation as individuals into the dominant culture, rather than their survival as members of collectivist indigenous cultures. There was little new in this. Neither Confederation nor the treaty-making process had changed the government's basic Indian policy goals, about which there was widespread consensus among Canada's political and other elites.

However, consensus on ends did not mean agreement on means. Indian policy was highly politicized. Specific policies and their economic cost were regularly contested. Incompetence, corruption, inconsistency, and tight-fistedness severely marred the often chaotic-seeming process. Interestingly, most of the policies deployed in the prairie West – including establishing reserves, encouraging Indian agriculture, and attempting various approaches to schooling – derived from policies employed in pre-Confederation Canada. These very policies, ironically, had then been criticized for their lack of success. But that experience did not lead the government to look for new departures in the West. The government never managed to think very far outside the box it had built for itself over many years; like most entities in most historical eras it was confined by its past, and its policies can be read in part as an extended series of footnotes and annotations to what went before.

When Indians in western Canada objected to and resisted many of the policies, the government tended to assume that they were lazy, refractory, more primitive than those of central Canada, and too ready to take advantage of public welfare. Officials also believed that Indians were reneging on the treaty commitment to abandon their past and embrace a new future. Indians, for their part, felt betrayed by the government, which allowed hunger to persist, seemed unable to limit rampant disease on reserves, imposed an alien education system, and moved increasingly to restrict both their traditional lifestyle and off-reserve activities. They experienced not the partnership they had envisaged, but subordination and control. So the government did not entirely have its own way: Indians' resistance, the particular environments of the Alberta reserves, and the exigencies of the local economies forced significant modifications in the application of the government's policies in the quarter century or so after the treaties were signed.

In recent decades, Indians' view of the true meaning of the treaties, shaped and reinforced by oral traditions, has become the dominant version of what took place in the 1870s. The treaty commissioners thus are portrayed as having understood and even to some degree shared the Indians' perception of the process and terms, only to subsequently betray this mutual agreement of peace and kinship. At the risk of over-simplification, there is a tendency to view the story as one in which strong, independent, sovereign Indian nations lived mostly peaceably and responsibly until the 1870s on the abundant bounty of nature, and came as equals to discuss a mutually beneficial plan for sharing the prairie region with the Crown's representatives. The men and government whom the Indians had trusted not only turned out to be greedy, careless, and corrupt, but also colonized, subordinated, and impoverished a people who soon were starving, diseased, and dying on reserves. Indians, despite all, managed to resist at least some of the government plan and survive. The government of the later nineteenth century thus has, in many accounts, become an irredeemable villain. In the present account, I contend that this approach in turn distorts understanding of the government's policy and actions, and argue that the story is in fact much more complex.

To look at the past through the lens of the present is both natural and to some extent unavoidable. The twentieth century saw a revolution in notions of human rights. It saw the acceptance of an inherent moral equality and dignity not only of individuals but also of cultures. The rise of Indian activism, the Charter of Rights and Freedoms, and court decisions all contributed to a rethinking of the past. However, these new perspectives were, by and large, beyond the experience, culture, or worldview of those who in the late nineteenth century developed policies that affected Canada's Indians. The dominant society imputed the degree of dignity and value attached to individuals and cultures, and Indians usually fell near the bottom of that scale. Prevailing social values largely framed what governments could or would do. A principal goal of this book is to re-examine federal policies in light not of what in hindsight we wish had happened, but of what it was possible for the government to do, given the political, environmental, social, economic, and legal context of the day.

For example, Canadians of the second half of the nineteenth century had a worldview dramatically different from those of a century or more later. They came to the prairie West as unapologetic imperialists and colonialists, approaches later condemned. For nineteenth-century Canadians, it seemed unarguable that land needed to be "possessed" and "improved," and Indians "civilized" (in the white understanding of those terms). They shared what one writer describes as Europeans' "confidence in their unique command of progress," which led to a "disconcerting arrogance ... towards other cultures."[2]

To offer a different example, few, if any, in the nineteenth century imagined that physical environment might be a significant factor in determining whether a society transitioned from hunting and gathering to settled agriculture. Lack of such "progress" was taken instead to be prima facie evidence of a people's inherent inferiority.[3] In other words, the fault for this perceived failure lay with the people themselves; that their circumstances might have framed their lifestyle and worldview received little consideration. Racist theories pointing to purported inherent characteristics that accounted for a given people's progress or lack of it abounded, and underlay the assumptions of policymakers and the public alike. Those who so admired their own material progress were unable to advance very far in their tolerance and acceptance of cultural differences.

Canadians of the nineteenth century also shared a mixture of other ideologies that in part shaped policies toward Native peoples. On the one hand, Canada was a liberal hegemonic state that accepted the superiority of individualist, assimilationist, and capitalist values; on the other hand, it also was the inheritor of a traditionalist, paternalist, and sometimes collectivist Tory tradition. Unsurprisingly, these conflicting ways of thinking, along with contradictory attitudes toward Native peoples, contributed to policies that often were internally inconsistent.[4]

Canadians shared a long European heritage of prejudices when contemplating Native peoples. In *The Conquest of America: The Question of the Other*, Tzvetan Todorov examines, among other matters, the conflicted attitudes of the Spanish of the late fifteenth and early sixteenth centuries with respect to the "otherness" of the Native peoples they encountered. Some saw Indians as people with the potential to be like themselves, which they presumed desirable. Others often saw Indians as so far removed from their understanding of civilized human beings as to justify regarding them as at best semi-human and thus relegated to an inferior, even slave, social status. Stephen Greenblatt puts the notion well, with reference to the early sixteenth century: "Such was the confidence of this [European] culture that it expected perfect strangers ... to

abandon their own beliefs, preferably immediately, and embrace those of
Europe as luminously and self-evidently true. A failure to do so provoked impatience, contempt, and even murderous rage."[5] If Canadians
of the nineteenth century had long since rejected notions of murderous
rage and slavery, puzzlement regarding Indians' perceived alterity, and
the question of what to do about it, still provoked many similar contra-
dictions. These remained unresolved during the period covered in this
book. Assimilating Indians to the cultural norms of white society and
encouraging them to accept Christianity, a process then termed civilizing, seemed, to many, obviously beneficial. At the same time, there always
were others who doubted Indians' ability to be civilized.

Civilization was a culturally specific notion.[6] In the Canadian West, it
included taking up a fixed residence; demarcating individual plots of
land; pursuing agriculture as the core of economic activity and as the
molder of social values; replacing Native religions or spirituality (called
"superstition") with some form of Christianity; learning the basics of
speaking, reading, and writing English or, less frequently, French; obey-
ing Canadian law; and dressing like whites with pants and short hair for
men and boys and dresses for women and girls. The wider purpose of
civilization, as Edward H. Spicer perceptively puts it, was "the release of
the individual from the limited sphere of kinship status to the vastly
expanded role of citizen."[7]

In Canada, the goal of this process was called enfranchisement. Indians
were encouraged to embrace these standards individually and move
from social and legal inferiority to full equality, citizenship, and integration. Few adopted this course, but those in the nineteenth-century prairie
West received less encouragement to do so than those elsewhere in the
country. Ambivalent about prairie Indians to begin with, officials soon
began to treat them differently than other Canadian Indians, concluding
that they were too primitive to handle the level of local reserve government that was intended elsewhere in the country to promote notions of
responsibility and citizenship. Instead, officials decided that even movement off reserves had to be limited and controlled. Nowhere in Canada
was the government's abiding ambivalence about Indians, and its consequences, more evident than in the prairie West.

My primary purpose in this book is to address the government's
Indian policies, but I also endeavour to fairly represent and analyze
Indians' perceptions of, and responses to, those policies. Relevant evidence includes Native oral tradition (the recorded and transcribed
evidence of elders), as well as autobiographical memoirs and other

treatments of aspects of the Indian historical experience. These illuminate aspects of how the Indians understood the treaties of the 1870s, and their relationship with the Crown. The elders' contribution is crucial to understanding the culturally distinctive Indian view of the treaty relationship and of the terms of the treaties. (Of course, whites' appreciation of the relationship and terms was equally culturally distinctive.) This evidence also illustrates how, at a very basic level, the two sides substantially failed to understand one another.

The cultural differences were profound. Canadian officials' individualism mostly could not comprehend Indians' collectivism, and vice versa. Whites thought of right and wrong in terms of individual responsibility, innocence, and guilt, and Indians thought in terms of honour, shame, and social relationships. Canadians were imbued with Western notions of chronological time as the most logical way to understand sequences of events; Indians, generally, had a more cyclical view of life, and perceived the sequence of events and their relative importance in very different ways. Words, promises, and relationships: the two cultures, including their respective languages, apprehended all differently. Such nuances, and many more, were largely lost on most Canadians in the nineteenth century. They usually were dismissed as the gap between civilized thought and primitivism: Indian views were not given an inherent and equal legitimacy.

In itself, this should not necessarily connote some sort of corrupt or cruel intent on the part of government. Olive P. Dickason put it well in 1991 when she remarked that it is important to keep in mind that the men who framed and carried out what in retrospect are considered repressive policies "were not just individuals with queer [peculiar] ideas; most were representative of their times. Many of them were sincerely dedicated to Amerindian welfare and actually believed they were acting in the Amerindians' best interests. They accepted the prevailing idea that peoples could be regulated into a cultural conformity that the dominant society considered acceptable. Today such a notion appears at the very least quaint, but fifty years ago it was not considered arguable."[8]

Undeniably, there were broken promises, some government policies were ill considered and had tragic results, and there is much to criticize. By 1905, the government had not achieved its main Indian policy goals as set out in the 1870s. It nevertheless did accomplish some things, laid some groundwork for the future, and modified several policies in face of the evolving realities of the prairie West. Sometimes this was to the Indians' advantage, and other times it was not. In the period as a whole, the government went far beyond what it understood the literal terms of the treaties in many areas to require, including agricultural assistance, famine relief, health care, and education (though in the early part of the reserve period its response too often was laggardly, stingy, and corrupt). This will startle those who see the record as one of unmitigated failure to fulfill treaty obligations, of parsimony, of misjudgment, of incompetence, and of bad faith. Outcomes certainly were mixed at best, often disappointing, and too frequently tragic. Nevertheless, over nearly three decades the government came to accept, reluctantly, that treaty obligations that it had originally hoped would be transitional and temporary had become permanent, costly, and obligatory. This result was, at least in part, due to Indians' determination to ensure their cultures would somehow survive, to retain their identities and shape their future, and to insist on their understanding of the treaty arrangements while the world as they had known it crumbled around them.

It is important to emphasize that Native peoples, both within and between bands and tribes, did not have a single common experience, nor did they have a single response to government policies. This was partly because they came from different tribal, linguistic, and cultural traditions. Like Canadians, they had a variety of attitudes, both collectively and individually. Many cooperated and complied with the new regime, while others resisted it. Some farmed willingly, some reluctantly or half-heartedly, and some refused and looked to alternative ways to survive. Still others exhibited all these attitudes over time. Some willingly sent their children to the schools, and some did not. Some sought out white medical care, some saw it as a possibly useful adjunct to Indian methods, and some refused any of it, including vaccination for smallpox. Some broke the law, and some brought lawbreakers to the police. Parallels to all these attitudes could be found among whites. However, in the process, Indians also forced the government to make accommodations in a great many areas, which contributed to the difference in policies or applications between 1905 and twenty-five or thirty years earlier. These Indians were not assimilated after a short transitional period, as the government expected in the 1870s, and did not quickly become wholly self-sustaining. The reserve system allowed their cultures to persist and helped them to assert at least some influence over the nature and pace of change.

MIXED MESSAGES: A CASE IN POINT

On 15 July 1870, the Dominion of Canada assumed title to the region formerly known as Rupert's Land and the North-Western Territory. It borrowed £300,000 from the British government to partially compensate the Hudson's Bay Company (HBC) for the loss of its monopolistic lease upon this large portion of its fur-trade empire.[9] Under British law, ultimate title to the land resided in the Crown. The British transferred the funds to the company and then, happy to shed the responsibility, assigned control of the land to the dominion. The land still was Crown land, but now under the control of Her Majesty's Canadian government. The tiny first iteration of the province of Manitoba, centred on the confluence of the Red and Assiniboine Rivers, also was inaugurated on 15 July 1870, but the Canadian government reconstituted the rest of the region as the North-Western Territory.[10] This transaction was a huge step toward achieving the young dominion's ambition to become a transcontinental nation.

Gradually, in the fall and winter of 1869–70, news of the transaction spread among the Indians of the North-Western Territory. Rumour had it that the HBC had sold the land to Canada. How could this be? As far as the Indians were concerned, the HBC had never owned the land and therefore had no right to sell it. If Canadians wanted to use the land, surely they first needed to talk with its indigenous occupants.

From the outset, therefore, there were two conflicting assumptions. Canadians knew that they had satisfied British legal requirements to gain ultimate title to the land. Indians understood nothing of this, but they knew they had occupied the land for uncounted generations. The story, however, was never so simple. The Canadians also knew, but had not yet communicated, that British law recognized an aboriginal right in the soil; in all the negotiations with the British leading to the transfer of land, they acknowledged that Indians would have to be consulted and compensated for loss of that right.

As well as hearing about the alleged land sale, Indians had certainly heard about the tumultuous events at Red River in 1869–70. The Metis of that region had forced the Canadians to postpone from 1 December 1869 their intended control of the land, and in effect to negotiate terms of entry into the West. Out of that came the creation of Manitoba, some guarantees therein for the bicultural (French-English) nature of the community, and limited land concessions. The Canadians sent out a lieutenant governor, Adams Archibald, to get the new province up and running, and to govern the North-Western Territory from Fort Garry with an appointed council. As soon as Archibald arrived in Manitoba the local Indians demanded a treaty, but he put them off. He also had to cope with a Canadian militia sent to give substance to Canadian authority, yet openly dismissive of Metis and Indians. What on earth did all this portend for the future of Native-newcomer relations? What did Canada intend? Would the newcomers voluntarily seek treaties? If so, on what terms? These were important issues for Indians who had witnessed the American treaty processes with their promises made and broken, the American Indian wars, and the inexorably expanding western settlement frontier.

Yet the Indians of the prairies almost certainly had no idea of the Canadians' even more basic, if rarely directly expressed, assumptions. Because the land had been owned by the British Crown, all the peoples of the region were already deemed British subjects, not independent, sovereign peoples. Equally important for understanding the impending Native-newcomer interaction were prevailing British and Canadian assumptions about Metis and Indians. For many, these local peoples were invisible, or nearly so. The West was widely described as unpopulated virgin land crying out for (white) settlement and development. For others, Native peoples were all too visible: inferior, backward, and impediments to progress. Even in central and eastern Canada, after over two hundred years of exposure to Europeans, most people did not consider Native peoples to be the equal of whites, even if others nevertheless held out hope for civilizing them. Moreover, the government believed it had a legal, moral, and humane responsibility to them because they were regarded in law as minors and wards of the state. The government intended to establish its authority in the West, enforce the law, and enquire about Native peoples' needs prior to negotiating with them, but it already had a pretty clear idea of where they stood under Canadian law.

Canada had been ambivalent about assuming responsibility for the West. It was supposed to be the country's patrimony, its guarantee of growth and future greatness, as the American West was proving to be further south. But for a country with a small population, heavy indebtedness, no meaningful military, and great demands for infrastructure in the original provinces, taking over the West was an intimidating prospect. In 1865, John A. Macdonald, one of the leading proponents of Confederation, remarked that he would "be willing, personally, to leave that whole Country a wilderness for the next half century." His preferred solution was for the British to create a Crown colony from the HBC's lands, in effect assuming the cost of holding it in trust for Canada until the new dominion was ready to take over. The British refused, and Macdonald realized that Canada would have to act to pre-empt aggressive American expansionists who were eyeing the region.[11] But Canada still hoped to move at a measured, affordable pace in the West.

At the beginning of the 1870s, the Native peoples of future Alberta were in the midst of several serious problems that placed them in a much weaker position than that of even two or three years earlier. A smallpox epidemic in 1869–70 had devastated their population. A starvation fall and winter followed in 1870–71. Bison, the main food source for Plains Cree and Nizitapi, were rapidly disappearing from the northern reaches of their traditional range. So too were fur-bearing animals, a serious problem for those dependent upon the fur trade to acquire necessary supplies. Ranging over much of the region were well-armed, unscrupulous American traders who destructively plied Indians with whiskey. These difficulties exacerbated intertribal tensions and risk of warfare. Indian leaders thus faced extraordinary pressures as they contemplated their futures. Canadians presented both a possible threat and a potential source of badly needed aid.

It was in this context that in April 1871 four chiefs and some of their followers – representing the Plains Cree who dwelled between Forts Carlton and Edmonton – decided to take action together. Wikaskokiseyin (Sweet Grass, the leading Cree chief in the area), Kehewin (the Eagle), Nee-ta-me-na-hoos (Little Hunter), and Kis-ki-on (Short Tail) wanted to convey a message to the government of the Dominion of Canada, which, they had heard, had assumed control of the region. Their chosen intermediary was William J. Christie, chief factor for the Saskatchewan district of the HBC, headquartered at Fort Edmonton. The intended recipient of their petition was Lieutenant Governor Archibald, representative of the Canadian government, at Fort Garry. Their petition, dated 13 April 1871,[12] consisted of four main points.

First, they welcomed Archibald to the West, and offered their friendship. They addressed him as "Great Father," and wanted to establish a brotherly relationship, or a kin relationship, with him and the other newcomers. They invited Archibald or a representative to come and talk with them.

Second, they objected to the HBC's sale of the lands to Canada; Rupert's Land and the North-Western Territory had not been the HBC's to sell. The lands were Indian property and were not for sale.[13]

Third, they wanted the government to understand the desperate poverty of their people following the smallpox epidemic and the equally terrible starvation winter. They noted their impoverishment resulting from the fur shortage. They asked for provisions for famine relief, and for the means to pursue agriculture – animals, tools, implements, and instruction – so that they could sustain themselves when traditional means failed.

Fourth, they wanted the new government to exclude the unscrupulous American whiskey traders from the region and to maintain peace within it. The alcohol trade and intertribal warfare were destabilizing their society.

The petition amounted to a call for a treaty (though they did not use the word) with the newcomers – a negotiated, supportive kinship of mutual respect. They likely envisaged it as being solemnized in the fashion of the fur-trade ceremonies, resulting in a relationship with the newcomers similar to that developed with the HBC. Despite their objection to the HBC's land sale, the chiefs seem to have been open to discussing how, or on what terms, the newcomers might be permitted access to the lands. They knew that their traditional way of life could not alone sustain them much longer, and that the newcomers were rich enough to be able to provide famine relief, knowledgeable enough to help them transition to agriculture, and strong enough to provide a more secure social and political framework. It was, in sum, a petition that asserted Indian ownership of the land, but that affirmed friendly intent, acknowledged real need, and extended an invitation to discuss a closer, mutually beneficial relationship.

The petition did not arrive in Red River as a stand-alone document, however. Christie provided a cover letter and a memorandum that set out his interpretation of the situation and contextualized the petition. The purpose of the Indians' visit, he noted, "was to ascertain whether their lands had been sold or not, and what was the intention of the Canadian Government in relation to them." Many rumours had been circulating, and they wanted to hear the facts of the case from Christie. Presumably, he affirmed the sale as fact. He did reassure them that the government would send commissioners to treat with them, and that "Canada, in her treaties with Indians [of central Canada], heretofore, had dealt most liberally with them, and that they were now in settled houses and well off, and that I had no doubt in settling with them the same liberal policy would be followed."[14] Note that although Wikaskokiseyin said that the Indians did not want to sell their lands, Archibald and Canadian officials probably construed Christie's remarks to suggest that they were open to a treaty along the lines of those negotiated earlier in central Canada, which Canadian authorities understood to have involved land surrenders.

Christie claimed that he satisfied the Indians, but it appears that he was somewhat unnerved by their demanding demeanor, which evidently conveyed a message to him that was quite different from the restrained and mostly friendly tone of their message to Archibald. He apparently felt under duress when he complied with their insistence upon supplies and presents for "them, their immediate followers, and for the young men left in camp." To have failed to do so, he believed, would have meant "the beginning of an Indian war." Christie also warned the government that "the buffalo will soon be exterminated."[15] Consequent starvation would inevitably lead to Indian unrest, and a high risk they would seize supplies from HBC posts and settlements, unless the government fed them. There were no means to maintain law and order; he reported that he had publicly announced the new ordinances of the North-Western Territory's council prohibiting trade in alcoholic beverages and the use of strychnine, but without power to enforce the laws, it was a useless exercise.

Moreover, the chiefs evidently were concerned that the unruly militia[16] the Canadian government sent to Red River following the 1869–70 resistance might be used for more aggressive purposes with respect to the Indians of the plains. Christie assured them that if troops were sent to the Saskatchewan country, they would be there to protect all parties and to maintain law and order. He also fretted that if gold were discovered in the region, as it had been in Montana, there could be a breakdown of law and order comparable to that on the American frontier. The government's highest priorities, therefore, should be provision of a means to impose law and order, and negotiation of a treaty with the Indians of the Saskatchewan District.[17]

Despite his mixed ethnic heritage and years spent living among or near, and trading with, Native peoples, Christie conveyed a message considerably different from that of the chiefs, one probably more troubling to the government. The chiefs focused on relationship building and an agricultural future, while Christie portrayed an unstable frontier and emphasized the need to maintain the law and establish order and the importance of a treaty. They worried about the resumption of intertribal conflict, and he worried about the pillaging of settlers and HBC posts. They challenged the legitimacy of the HBC's purchase of the land; he assumed that the dominion government had a right and duty to act in the region, even prior to any treaty. Thus, while Christie apparently intended to reinforce the chiefs' message of urgency of government action, and although he noted that the chiefs said "they would welcome civilization" (which likely meant something different to them than to him), he arguably framed his comments in a way that detracted from what the chiefs intended to convey. His message was not necessarily their message.[18]

Christie naturally also represented the perspective of the HBC, which desired a stable, predictable climate for trade. Whether or not Indians considered the sale of the lands to be legitimate, they recognized that the HBC no longer had authority, and that Canada was the new power to address. Therefore, more than ever, the HBC operated on the sufferance of what Christie regarded as a dangerously unstable Native population until such time as the Canadian government was able to impose law and order, which explains the anxious tone underlying his cover letter and memo. He not only was forwarding a message, but also was a translator, recipient, and interpreter of it. The message that he sent was much more than what the chiefs probably thought they were sending. In fairness to Christie, the demanding actions of the chiefs and their followers conveyed a message that arguably was not the same as the words of their petition.

How, then, was the message received in Red River? Archibald arrived in Manitoba in the late summer of 1870, and found himself situated amidst a numerically dominant mixed-blood population (many of whom recently had challenged the authority of the Canadian government, with some success), a local Native population expressing grievances and demanding a treaty, and a Canadian militia force contributing to unrest in the larger population at least as much as it underpinned the local government's authority. It is unsurprising that Archibald felt he was walking a tightrope on the edge of a restless volcano.[19]

The messages from Fort Edmonton in 1871 seemed far less pressing than the situation at Fort Garry, and contained little that was new from Archibald's perspective. The government understood the aboriginal right to the land to mean a right to live off the land by traditional methods, not outright ownership. The treaty process, which Archibald was about to engage in with the Manitoba Indians, really meant offering a consideration to the Indians, in return for which they would give up that right and permit white possession of, and peaceful access to, the land. This was by no means the establishment of a supportive kinship in return for access to Indian-owned land as the chiefs envisioned. At any rate, the process of treating with all the Indian bands of the West would, Archibald knew, reach the Saskatchewan country in due course. It was good to know that Indians wanted assistance in taking up agriculture:

that was what government had done for those in central and maritime Canada, what had been promised in some American Indian treaties, and what the government intended to encourage in the West. This was not a surprise, nor did it seem especially urgent. The chiefs likely saw their request for agricultural assistance as indicating a desire to supplement their traditional way of life; Archibald, by contrast, almost certainly saw it as expressing a willingness to abandon the hunting and gathering lifestyle that the Indians themselves acknowledged could no longer sustain them.

As to the offer of friendship, for Archibald that would have been filtered through Christie's report that he had had to pacify the Indians with presents and supplies, and his implication that they remained dangerously unreliable. The lieutenant governor likely agreed that it was indeed unfortunate that the Indian had suffered so much from the scourges of smallpox and starvation, but government in those days worked to respond to crises more than it did to prevent them. It was already doing what it could to vaccinate Native and non-Native people. The region still lacked the infrastructure to allow the government to acquire or move large quantities of supplies into the area at short notice. The issues raised needed to be, or were being, addressed after a fashion, but crises came and went. From a distance, one might well assume that in the interim life would go on as it always had for Indians, who were habituated to living life on the edge.

The reception of the messages from the four chiefs and Christie was further complicated by an event of which they would have been unaware when the messages were sent. On 17 April – just four days after the chiefs' message was dated – the federal government passed an order-in-council to appoint Wemyss Mackenzie Simpson as Indian commissioner. Archibald had requested that someone be appointed to look after Indian matters in the West, and particularly to commence the treaty process. The government even appointed Simpson an officer in the militia, so that he could wear a uniform to impress Indians as "having the Queen's authority." When the message from the chiefs and Christie arrived at Fort Garry, Archibald referred it to Simpson without much comment. After a failed attempt to negotiate a treaty with Indians between Lake Superior and Manitoba, followed by successful negotiation (with Archibald) of Treaties 1 and 2 in and around Manitoba itself, Simpson finally forwarded the message to Ottawa in November. Essentially he appended it to the end of a lengthy report concerning the 1871 treaty negotiations and other Indian matters. There he suggested (following

Christie's language) that a treaty with the Indians of the Saskatchewan District was pressing, and left the documents to speak for themselves. The way that he reported the matter took all the urgency out of the documents, which were duly printed without comment in the annual report of the Indian Branch of the Department of the Secretary of State for the Provinces.[20]

This incident constitutes a classic case of how the message sent was not necessarily the message received, and how a message could simply be lost in the dark hole of bureaucracy. Setting aside the problem of translation, for we cannot know whether Christie's summation of the chiefs' concerns was wholly accurate, there are the matters of Christie setting the message in a particular context, of its reception by a beleaguered lieutenant governor who was anxious to hand off the Indian file, of the complex pressures of negotiating treaties and other matters in the Manitoba area, of the message's reception in an Ottawa bureaucracy in which it generated little attention, and of the near indifference of officials and bureaucrats who came to the matter of Indian administration with a set of assumptions and priorities that were substantially at variance with those of the Indians in the remote prairies.

This case was a precursor of much that was to follow with respect to Indian policy. When Native leaders wanted to communicate with government, their messages were subject to some loss of cultural meaning in translation; more was lost when they were interpreted and contextualized by the agents, farm instructors, or police chosen as intermediaries; and they were received by officials or bureaucrats who had other priorities and little feel for local reserve conditions. Of course, the same process operated in reverse.

One of the recurrent themes of the period addressed in this book is that the government and Native peoples only partially comprehended one another. Both words and actions meant different things to each party, which in turn occupied different cultural spaces. Even when good will appears to have been intended, the respective sides seemed on many occasions to talk right past one another. Each operated in a particular cultural context, each harboured different values and expectations, and frequently neither really heard what the other was trying to communicate, especially at the level of wider purposes and ultimate goals.

# PART ONE

# Framing Federal Indian Policy, 1870–77

# 1

# Shaping Canadian Indian Policy

Canadians understood that ultimate title to Rupert's Land and the North-Western Territory had been vested in the British Crown – perhaps since 1670, and certainly without contest since the conclusion of the Seven Years' War in 1763. They also understood that the dominion inherited that title – and the right and duty to govern – when the land was transferred in 1870.[1] Moreover, Canada presumed that the Indians of the region already were subjects both of Canada and of Her Majesty's Canadian Government (the Crown), as were all Indians and whites of central and Maritime Canada,[2] whether or not a treaty had been negotiated with them. The dominion assumed that, along with its other laws, its existing Indian laws, policies, and policy goals would be immediately applicable to the newly acquired West. The treaties thus were not viewed as a necessary precursor to the exercise of Canada's authority, but as a particular kind of agreement between the Crown and some of its subjects.

This may surprise, or even shock, those who presume Indians were sovereign and negotiated with the Crown as equals. They tend to assume that the appropriate context for appreciating the nature and meaning of the treaties lies largely in the relationship and patterns of negotiation that evolved between white and Indian populations in the region in the two centuries preceding 1870. Elucidating the Indian context for the treaties has proven essential to comprehending the Indian perspective.[3]

However, there also was a distinctly British-Canadian understanding of what was going on in the making of the treaties that was considerably at variance with the Indian perspective, and was as deeply culturally rooted. Accepting Indian forms of negotiation in order to secure a treaty did not alter the underlying Canadian outlook or purposes. For Canada, the treaties were framed within and became part of an existing, if still evolving, structure of Indian policies and laws. Government negotiators and policymakers in the latter half of the nineteenth century did not have the understanding of Indian culture, beliefs, and assumptions that is now readily available. They could not have shared the conclusion of the courts of the latter half of the twentieth century that eons of Indian occupancy of the land trumped the Crown's ownership claims; such a position would have been unthinkable in the 1870s. Equally, many other aspects of white culture and law were never explained to Indians, mostly not out of malice, but because much in any culture goes unsaid. Each side made many assumptions about the essence of human nature and good faith, and about what the other understood. In fact, they often did not understand each other at all.

Indians near Hudson Bay had been exposed to white fur traders since the late seventeenth century. By the mid-nineteenth century, the Indian relationship with the Hudson's Bay Company across the prairie and parkland region was established. The HBC acknowledged Indians' possession of the land, at the very least in the sense that they occupied the land, that they derived their living from it, and that negotiation with them was required to gain reliable and peaceful access to it. Of necessity, the HBC accepted and adapted many Indian diplomatic customs in the fur trade, and negotiated trading and social relationships with them. Out of this arose a somewhat paternalistic responsibility for a limited level of welfare: Indians received some provisions, medical supplies, and other assistance when required and available. Accordingly, a measure of mutual respect, even obligation, developed between Indians and fur traders, and this cumulative history greatly influenced Indians' anticipation of their relationship to Canadians and to the British Crown.[4]

In 1870, Canada's Indian policies and purposes were rooted in its history, not that of the former HBC territories. Dominion officials, while negotiating treaties with the Indians of the northwest over the next seven years, tried to reassuringly employ some of the same forms and even some of the same people associated with the HBC and the fur trade. Yet Canada's underlying purposes pre-existed these negotiations, and were fundamentally at odds with prairie Indians' past experience. The HBC's primary interest had been the fur trade, its primary labourers were Indians, and it mostly wanted to preserve the environment and relationships that produced furs. Moreover, practically speaking, the HBC had limited powers to impose its will on the more numerous Indian population. Indians perceived the HBC mostly as beneficent and supportive of, rather than a challenge to, their traditional way of life.[5] Canada's intentions for the region, by contrast, were radically transformative: settlement, agriculture, production of natural resources, and ultimately integration with a transcontinental dominion economy and beyond to a transoceanic imperial economy. It anticipated that in the near future the white population would be overwhelmingly dominant, and it developed its policies with that expectation at the forefront. The Indian population would have to adapt, or be transformed, accordingly. The differences appear very stark in hindsight.

At the time, all this was much less clear. Canada in the mid-1860s felt ill-prepared to assume control over the HBC territories. Events thrust the West upon the young dominion too soon, for the government was preoccupied with other issues. The governance model that shaped politicians' thinking about the region initially was that of the crown colony,[6] and – tragically – the issue of the Indians' fate in the West was mostly incidental to Canadians' objectives in acquiring the region.

## THE IMPLICATIONS FOR NATIVE PEOPLES OF THE RED RIVER RESISTANCE

The Red River Resistance of 1869–70 had important results not only for the Metis of Red River and for national politics in Canada, but also for Indians in the North-Western Territory. The Metis forced the dominion government to negotiate terms for Canada's entry to the West. They won important concessions, including the creation of the province of Manitoba and guarantees for their culture with respect to French/ English bilingualism and dual Roman Catholic and Protestant school systems. They also gained a promise of secure tenure for their traditionally laid out plots of land, and a further concession of land for Metis children in acknowledgement of their ancestry.[7] The Metis did not expect to avoid the tide of settlement sweeping across the North American plains, but they did want to protect their culture and, through a provincial government they would initially control, to mitigate the domination of the province.

The most obvious lesson for Native peoples, both from the Red River Resistance and from the experience of American Indians, was that whites must be pressed to negotiate before they arrived in overwhelming numbers. Handled carefully, they might be induced to provide needed aid and security, and perhaps even guarantees for some continuation of traditional ways.

However, there were other, less immediately obvious lessons. First, the tiny size of the new province was the Canadian government's attempt to limit the area to which the changes embedded in the Manitoba Act would apply. Canada reconstituted the remainder of the region, from Manitoba west to the Rocky Mountains, as the North-West Territories; here, the government anticipated that its intended policies would hold sway unimpeded. Second – a point crucial for understanding government policy – Metis failed to gain provincial control of Crown lands. Manitoba was the only province in Canada in the nineteenth century to be deprived of this control, essential for creating conditions conducive to the survival of Metis culture and for drawing revenue from its lands. Third, when the government created Manitoba, decided to retain control of Crown lands and resources, and committed to recognizing Metis land claims and to providing land for Metis children, it was acting upon its belief that it, or the Crown, held title to the lands and could make commitments with respect to them prior to any negotiation with the Indians of the region.[8]

Events would show that the Canadian government regarded the negotiations with the Red River Metis to be of a very different order than treaty negotiations with Indians. Metis had developed a strong identity as a separate people, occupied a different rung on the social ladder, and had a number of leaders and spokespersons who were comparatively educated and articulate in at least one, if not both, of Canada's official languages.[9] The terms of the agreement were embodied in an act of Parliament, the Manitoba Act, and were mostly not a mystery to the Metis. By contrast, the government tended to regard Indians as primitive, as wards of the state, and as in need of "civilizing" if they were to avoid dying out altogether. It did not regard treaties with Indians as of the same significance as an act of Parliament.[10]

### UNFOLDING DISASTER IN THE WESTERN PRAIRIES

At the same time that the Red River Metis were debating their future and forcing the Canadian government to negotiate and to create Manitoba, the Indians of the future Alberta were attempting to flee the devastation of the most recent major epidemic of smallpox to sweep through their region. The impact for the Nizitapi in the Southwest was at least as, if not more, serious than it was for the Cree. There had been several previous plagues (1781–82, 1801, and 1837–38); each had been a crushing catastrophe. Hugh Dempsey reports that in the last of them, the Nizitapi "suffered some 6,000 casualties, or almost two-thirds of its members."[11] The disease spared no sector of the population. Modern-day North Americans, largely isolated from catastrophic epidemics on this scale, can scarcely comprehend not only the emotional impact on individuals, families, and bands of such vast, sudden, and ill-understood losses, but also the destruction of social structures.

A digression is called for in order to set the context for the events of 1870 and following. James Daschuk shows that Indian societies in the future Canadian plains and parkland had long lived on a knife-edge with respect to survival. For well over a century, and perhaps longer, many diseases – tuberculosis, scarlet fever, measles, and influenza – ravaged them regularly. Smallpox lingered, though it was less dramatic than the virulent, catastrophic epidemics. Epidemic and persistent disease wiped out some Indian populations and allowed others to become dominant and take over their territories. Indeed, according to Daschuk's evidence, population loss due to disease was higher in the century prior to 1870 than it was after the region became part of Canada. Disease, moreover, weakened people, rendering them less able to hunt or gather food and contributing to starvation. But starvation and poor health were also the product of rapidly fluctuating weather patterns during the Little Ice Age, and of the fur and hide trade's excessive pressure on food and fur resources. The result was intense rivalry and warfare as Indians competed for food and trading goods.[12] Daschuk's evidence largely undermines the myth that Indians enjoyed peace, prosperity, and good health that whites destroyed; this was simply not the case.

Yet during the roughly three decades after the devastation of the 1830s, the Nizitapi and Cree recovered considerably. Their environment and food supply remained sufficiently robust despite measurable decline, though survival was always challenging. By the 1860s, whites regarded the Nizitapi as prosperous, proud, arrogant, and even dangerously war-like.[13] The Cree were, perhaps, less secure. All were about to enter a perfect storm of negative circumstances.

The most dramatic of these circumstances – the last smallpox epidemic – began in the late summer of 1869, when some American travellers who had contracted smallpox were quarantined on a Missouri River steamboat that stopped at the mouth of the Milk River to unload cargo. There, a member of the Piegan[14] slipped aboard the boat and stole an infected blanket from one of the patients. In the cruel words of a contemporary Montana account, the disease spread "like wildfire" among the Indians of the region, "sending them to perdition in quicker time than bullets and bad bread could do the work."[15] By the time the epidemic had spread from Montana to Canada and run its course, over 1,000 Piikani and over 600 each of the Kainai and Siksika had perished, and the Tsuu T'ina were reduced from fifty to twelve lodges.[16]

The 1869 epidemic occurred in a context very different from the previous three. The region that in 1905 would become central and southern Alberta had, in the late eighteenth and early nineteenth centuries, been a distant, somewhat isolated part of the HBC's hinterland. The Nizitapi, for example, had for years made the trek to the HBC forts at Rocky Mountain House and Edmonton to trade furs, bison hides, horses, and pemmican for a variety of metal and cloth household goods, as well as traps, weapons, and hunting and fishing equipment. This trading network was based on rivers flowing to Hudson Bay, allowing the HBC to maintain a monopoly, or at least dominance, in the region. However, in the 1840s and 1850s American traders began to exploit the Missouri/Mississippi River system and challenge the HBC's monopoly from the south. They spread into British territory and set up accessible trading posts in Nizitapi territory; alternatively, Indians could travel south to trade at Fort Benton in Montana Territory.

While this did give Indians convenience and more trading options, these changes were accompanied by a destructive assault on the fauna and people of the region. By the 1870s, American industrial demand for bison hides accelerated the already massive slaughter of the animals, with many tens of thousands of animals from Canadian and American herds being shot each year. Whites, Metis, and Indians all participated and reaped quick, short-term profits. At the same time, American whiskey traders had no compunction about debauching Native peoples and then impoverishing them. Thus the smallpox epidemic occurred just as the animal upon which so many of the plains peoples relied for food, clothing, shelter, and tools was being pushed to the brink, and when Native peoples were unable to seriously resist the wanton exploitation of the well-armed American free traders. Indeed, the first mass starvation after the union with Canada occurred in the winter of 1870–71 not among the Nizitapi, but among the Cree farther north: bison no longer came into their region, at least not in significant numbers, and other game and fur-bearing animals had been largely wiped out.[17] Canada in 1870 thus assumed authority for an extremely needy region in which it was, for the time being, almost powerless to either exert control or provide assistance. Within a generation or two, Indians went from being confident occupiers of a vast region with sufficient resources to facing an uncertain new future they had not chosen. They were determined to try to secure their survival and to have a role in shaping how that future would unfold.[18]

## CANADA EXERCISES AUTHORITY

Canada's assumption of authority in Rupert's Land and the North-Western Territory in 1870 carried significant implications for Indians. Section 91 (24) of the Constitution Act 1867 gave the federal government responsibility for Indians and Indian lands throughout the dominion. Both before and after 1870, Indians of the West were held to be subjects of the Crown: in 1873, for example, Secretary of State Joseph Howe asserted that, with or without treaties, "the Indians of the North West are still subjects of the Queen and are bound to obey the laws."[19] Canada's Indians, including those in the North-Western Territory, also were regarded as legally wards of the state. The Canadian government's action with respect to Red River, and to Rupert's Land generally, demonstrated its underlying assumption that it had received from the British the ultimate title to the land, and that it could legislate for the region and its peoples without any worry that it might not have the authority to do so.[20] In 1869, in anticipation of the transfer, the federal government passed An Act for the Temporary Government of Rupert's Land and the North-Western Territory when United with Canada, usually referred to as the Temporary Government Act, in anticipation of the transfer.[21] The government renewed the act on a more permanent basis in 1871 specifically to apply to the territory.[22]

Moreover, beginning in 1870, the federal government created a form of local government for the North-Western Territory: a federally appointed lieutenant governor (until 1876 also the lieutenant governor of Manitoba) who, together with a federally appointed local council, was to govern under direction from Ottawa and pass, under delegation of certain power from Ottawa, necessary local laws that did not violate the provisions of the Constitution Act, 1867. In October 1870, one of the first acts of this local authority was to ban the importation or sale of alcoholic beverages throughout the territory.[23] That it did not have the means to enforce the ban was immaterial; the point is the assumption that the federal government and the North-West Council had authority to legislate for the region prior to any treaty talks with Indians. In the same month, Lieutenant Governor Adams Archibald sent William Francis Butler on an expedition to report on conditions in the territory between Manitoba and the Rocky Mountains. Archibald also assumed the right both to direct Butler to engage in preventive health measures (vaccination for smallpox) for Indians and whites, and also to appoint him a justice of the peace empowered to enforce Canadian and territorial law throughout the North-West Territory.[24]

In the spring of 1873, several of the leading Metis in the North-West Territory sent a petition to the next lieutenant governor, Alexander Morris, outlining several concerns. It is interesting that their last, seemingly least important point was the one that Morris seized upon to emphasize his authority. They wrote, "as there are no laws made as yet for this country, we go on as heretofore. We make a law, and that law is strong, as it is supported by the majority." Morris responded:

> You are in error when you suppose that there are no laws in force in the North-West Territory. The laws of England are in force here, and the administration of the territories has been confined to me as Governor and to a Council appointed by the Crown, which is now composed of eleven members ...
>
> The criminal laws of the dominion have been extended to the North-West, and a severe law prohibits the sale of intoxicating liquors therein.
>
> Magistrates will be appointed for the carrying out of these laws and a police force will be kept up to maintain order and prevent crimes and offences against our people.[25]

Thus Morris emphasized that Canadian law applied to the territory prior to any negotiation with the local people, and that the law was about to be enforced. In his view, laws made in the old ways had no legitimacy.

A further example of lawmaking in advance of treaties was the land survey. In the summer of 1869, before the transfer, the federal government had planned to implement a square survey in the West similar to that adopted in the United States to facilitate homesteading, and it prematurely sent surveyors to Red River to begin to prepare the way for incoming settlers, a major factor in precipitating the Metis resistance of that fall. In the spring of 1871, the federal government formally adopted the land survey system, and the first surveyors were on the job in Manitoba in July, before any treaty had been negotiated. The Dominion Lands Act of 1872 confirmed this policy.[26]

In these years, the federal government undertook other laws and activities affecting the West without prior agreement with the Indians of the territory, including the international boundary survey (really a joint British-American endeavour with Canadian participation), the establishment of the North-West Mounted Police (1873), the creation of the Department of the Interior (1873), the North-West Territories Act (1875), the Indian Act (1876) and its antecedents, surveys for telegraph communication and railways, as well as activities of the Geological Survey.

As early as 1873, perhaps taking a leaf from Riel's book, some Native people farther west briefly stopped the Geological Survey, apparently to try to force Canada to negotiate a treaty.[27] It was not a major interruption, for the survey did continue in other areas. In 1875, some Cree moved more forcefully to stop the telegraph, railway, and geological surveys, not because they wanted to keep out the Canadians, but to try to bring the government to treaty negotiations and determine mutually beneficial terms for using the land. The government, however, never doubted its ultimate right to act in these areas, with or without Indian assent.

While Canada assumed authority over the region and its peoples before negotiation with them, the dominion government evidenced but scant knowledge of Indians, or of how to begin to address its obligations to them. In 1870, Archibald was instructed to establish friendly relations with them, and report on "the course you may think most advisable to pursue, whether by treaty or otherwise, for the removal of any obstructions that may be presented to the flow of population into the fertile lands that lie between Manitoba and the Rocky Mountains." He was also to report on Indians of the North-Western Territory, "their numbers, wants and claims, the system heretofore pursued by the Hudson's Bay Company in dealing with them," and suggestions for their protection and "improvement of their condition."[28]

### FROM CHAOS TO ORDER

On 17 May 1873, a group of wolfers[29] was camped on the Teton River in Montana Territory, within a day's journey of Fort Benton on the Missouri River, when a Piegan war party rode off with nineteen of its horses. The wolfers did not know the thieves' identity, but were determined to recover their property and seek revenge. A posse of twelve

heavily armed men set out to follow the trail, but after three days heavy
rains wiped out remaining traces. They decided to go to the Cypress
Hills, in British-Canadian territory, where whiskey traders had established a couple of forts. A camp of American Northern Assiniboine
Indians located there clearly did not have the horses. The wolfers proceeded to one of the forts and spent the day drinking. The nearby Indians
were also apparently drinking, though they presented no threat to the
wolfers. On 1 June, without provocation, the wolfers decided to "clean
out" the Indian camp. One local trader, Abel Farwell, was friendly with
the Indians and attempted unsuccessfully to get the situation resolved
peacefully. The wolfers instead opened fire, killing as many as twenty-six
Assiniboine. A wounded Indian killed one wolfer and was in turn quickly
dispatched. The wolfers also seized a few Assiniboine women, took them
to their camp, and repeatedly raped two of them.[30]

The Cypress Hills Massacre, as this tragic episode became known, had
an electric effect on Canadian public opinion. Canadians deemed this
kind of brutal lawlessness characteristic of the American West, but it was
not supposed to happen in British territory. The primitive state of communications is revealed in the fact that the Canadian government did
not learn of the incident until the beginning of September 1873, and
then from the American government. Happily, it had a solution almost
immediately to hand, for on 30 August it had passed an order in council
to implement a new police force.[31]

A police force for the West was the product of a lengthy gestation. In
1869, Macdonald responded to initial reports of the Red River Resistance
with ruminations about creating such a force modelled on the Royal Irish
Constabulary, with mounted riflemen organized as a police rather than
a military force. Although policing was a provincial power under the
Canadian constitution, the North-Western Territory remained under
federal control, and so required a federal force to maintain law and
order. Still, establishment of such a force had not appeared urgent once
the Red River Resistance was resolved in 1870.[32] From the citadels of
power on Parliament Hill, the West appeared reasonably peaceful and in
no immediate need of more active governance.

Appearances were deceiving. "Out of sight, out of mind" seemed to
apply to the situation in the southwestern North-Western Territory
between 1870 and 1873, inasmuch as most Canadians seem to have
been blissfully unaware of the sad trend of events there until the Cypress
Hills Massacre. Fort Benton, established in 1847 at the head of naviga-
tion on the Missouri River in Montana, had become by the mid-1860s

the metropolitan centre that most influenced the portion of the territory from the Rocky Mountains east at least as far as the Cypress Hills and north to the Bow River.[33] That strategic location made it faster and cheaper to import goods to the region from the south than via the HBC's northern river trade routes. Without effective Canadian law enforcement, the international boundary and the prohibition against importing alcohol were meaningless. The thirst for profit led not only to the massive and wanton slaughter of bison each year, but also to the slaughter of many other animals for their pelts on an unprecedented scale. A particular case was the almost industrial-scale killing of wolves by men regarded as inhabiting the bottom of the social scale, who would kill bison and lace the carcasses with strychnine, sometimes killing two dozen or more wolves with a single carcass. According to Dempsey, by 1874 the trade in wolf pelts was almost as valuable as that in bison hides, with some trading posts receiving as many as four thousand pelts in a season.[34] This trade also led to conflict with Indians, who not only resented that the strychnine killed their dogs, but also regarded the wolves as their property.

Even worse was the trade in alcohol. Indians seemed unable to resist the firewater, and traded their possessions readily for it – bison hides, fur pelts, even their valued ponies and sometimes the clothes off their backs. Beyond impoverishing themselves, they would commit crimes, stealing horses, cattle, or other goods to trade for it. Worse still, they also frequently attacked one another when drunk, killing and maiming family members, friends, and foes. They might lie down to sleep off the effects and simply freeze to death. Some Indians turned to alcohol to salve their grief after the devastation of the 1870 smallpox. Writes Dempsey, "by the winter of 1871–72, the focus of the Blackfoot people had shifted from warfare, hunting, and family life to alcohol."[35] Chiefs lost their authority, and social and family structures broke down in many instances.[36] Few whites seemed to care, and when men such as the wolfers sometimes killed several Indians at a time, it was simply disregarded.[37]

Upon hearing of the Cypress Hills Massacre, Macdonald agreed that the police force had become necessary, but he was disposed to train it in Ontario and send it west in the spring of 1874. Morris's persistent, anxious demands finally changed his mind, and he agreed to send 150 men to Fort Garry to train over the winter and be ready in the spring to take action. The men arrived at the beginning of November, just before freeze up, and also just before the 5 November 1873 defeat of the Macdonald government in Ottawa over the Pacific Scandal. Prime Minister Alexander Mackenzie, Macdonald's parsimonious Liberal successor, had never been much of a believer in the proposed police force. However, he was deeply concerned by the reports of unrest and lawlessness in the West, and finally in the late winter of 1874 he relented and agreed to provide a full complement of 300 men to bring law and order to the furthest reaches of the prairie region.[38] British-Canadian law in the North-Western Territory was to move from theoretical construct to practical reality.

The government construed the police force a boon to Indians, and to some extent Indians agreed. One of the duties of a liberal-democratic government is to ensure a reasonably stable and safe environment for its people. The benefits for Indians were not unmitigated, as time would show.

## MARKING AND POSSESSING
## THE NORTH-WEST TERRITORIES

In September 1872 a British and an American survey party met at Pembina on the Manitoba-North Dakota border to commence an official survey of the international boundary from the Lake of the Woods west along the forty-ninth parallel to the Rocky Mountains. Because it had international implications, and because Canada was still colonial in status, the British had to be in charge of what otherwise would be viewed as a Canadian interest. Relations between the United States and any part of the British Empire remained a British responsibility – or potential liability, should trouble arise. However, Canada asserted itself by agreeing to pay half the cost of the commission, and (after the first two British choices turned down the apparently dubious honor) the British accepted a Canadian recommendation for chief commissioner, Captain Donald Roderick Cameron, the British son-in-law of an influential federal politician from Nova Scotia, Sir Charles Tupper.[39]

The American party was accompanied by a substantial military escort for protection from Indians, though the British-Canadian side deemed this unnecessary. The survey was a considerable project, and it must have made some impression on the Indians. According to one account, in 1873 on the British-Canadian side alone some 230 officers and men were employed – some to locate and survey the boundary and construct stone cairns and earth mounds to mark it, but many others to assist with provisioning and supplies. By 1874, 210 oxen, 114 horses, 55 ponies, and 112 wagons and carts were at work along the line.[40]

Incidents with Indians were few, and most often involved individuals helping themselves to stores in supply depots along the line intended for the survey crews. Generally, reports indicated that Indians were friendly. Once the party encountered a small group of Nizitapi who were said to have wanted nothing more than for whites to put the whiskey traders "out of existence, for they are robbing them – getting all their ponies, etc."[41] They were about to get their wish.

Just what effect did the international boundary survey have on Indians at the time? Very little, it would seem. It must have appeared that whites had laboured mightily to bring forth, if not a mouse, just a series of widely spaced mounds and concrete monuments along an arbitrary imaginary line across the prairie. The line bisected the vast territory across which the bison and Indians from time immemorial had moved, and continued to move, essentially unobstructed. In 1873 and 1874, the surveyors encountered a few substantial bison herds, as well as Indians and Metis travelling freely to or from the hunt. Only gradually during the decade did the boundary begin to assume significance and become the "medicine line" that wondrously stopped pursuing authorities on either side of the forty-ninth parallel. Yet the same line that could provide refuge also began to divide peoples and the regional economy as each nation-state began to assert its authority.[42]

In 1873, the government asserted its authority in another way: it created the Department of the Interior, charged with administering land policy under the Dominion Lands Act of 1872, including surveys and the various categories of land set aside for homesteading, railways, schools, and the HBC, as well as supervising the settling of intending farmers on the land.[43] The land policy, adopted prior to the treaties, underlay the dominion's position in the treaty negotiations. The government offered Indians 160 acres per family of five in 1871 – the same amount it offered homesteaders. A quarter-section farm was thought to be substantial, given the agricultural technology of the era, and it was assumed that almost all Indians would wish to become farmers. Although the government subsequently increased the amount of land per Indian family, the starting premise was that Indians should be treated on the same basis as whites. The reserve was considered a base for settlement and agriculture, and an area for cultural transition and reformation, not preservation.

If the surveys had little direct impact on Indians in the 1870s, the arrival of the North-West Mounted Police in October 1874 to assert Canadian authority produced an immediate and obvious effect. That May the minister of justice, A.A. Dorion, told officers of the force that the role of the police would be to preserve British-Canadian law and order, stopping "lawless American traders" from dealing in liquor and disrupting Indians' regular lives. It was their task to represent Canadian sovereignty, impose order, and maintain the principles of justice.

Dorion also was clear that the police were to act on their own in suppressing the liquor traffic, and were not to seek the aid of Indians as allies. The police were to act as a separate and distinct authority. Moreover, presents distributed to Indians were to conciliate them, but "were not intended as an expression of political or social equality." One historian, B.J. Mayfield, argues that this shows that the Indians of the West, even before the treaties, were regarded as being in the same state of wardship as those of central and eastern Canada.[44] It does indicate something of the mindset with which the Canadian government approached treaty making. Besides distributing gifts, there were two ways in which the police quickly established a positive relationship with the Nizitapi: they apprehended whiskey traders and stopped the traffic; and they assured them that they did not come to take their land, but that the government would talk with them at a later time about the matter.[45]

Mayfield contends that the Nizitapi were willing to accept a state of "cooperative co-existence" with the police if, in addition to stopping the liquor traffic, they would protect them from the incursions of other tribes and stop horse theft.[46] The request for protection makes sense, given the growing competition for depleting food resources; that to curtail horse stealing does not, because the Nizitapi themselves continued to steal horses at least until the late 1880s, after which the activity became more sporadic.[47] The immediate end of the liquor traffic impressed the Indians, who evidently were concerned that the police might leave once that task was accomplished. Late in 1874, Assistant Commissioner James F. Macleod reported, "all that have come to see me invariably ask how long are we going to stay. Their delight is unbounded when I tell them that I expect to remain with them always."[48]

The police began to construct Fort Macleod, and the sense that personal security was more or less assured led to settlement around the fort first by some Metis families and then by a few white farmers, while the stability and opportunity to market to the police encouraged at least one rancher to bring in 700 cattle. This created unease among the Nizitapi, who Macleod had promised would not lose their land without an agreement with the government.[49] It is unlikely that Macleod would have seen these developments as a contradiction, since the land occupied by the fort, the farms, and even a few ranches would have seemed but a small fraction of the vast region occupied by Indians; the force in any case needed supplies and a place to live, and any concerns could be addressed before long at treaty talks. If the HBC could build forts and farm around them, surely there ought to be no problem for the police, who arguably provided an equivalent benefit to Indians, to do so. Yet Indians had not granted permission for any of this. Was it a precursor of what was to come, of promises made and easily broken? A treaty, they hoped, would place matters on a better foundation.

Meanwhile, the government also reorganized Indian administration. It moved its Indian branch from the jurisdiction of the secretary of state for the provinces to the Department of the Interior from 1873 to 1880, when it received full departmental status as the Department of Indian Affairs.[50] In many ways, however, the difference was cosmetic. It mostly remained under the authority of the minister of the interior, who was charged with administering land and settlement policy in the North-West Territories; this simply guaranteed that Indians would be administered in the context of policies that prioritized settlement.[51]

## THE INDIAN ACT AND ITS ANTECEDENTS

The Indian Act, passed in 1876 by the Liberal Mackenzie government, provided the framework for administration of Indians and Indian lands in Canada. It did not mark a departure; it was mainly a consolidation of various laws developed and in force over many years.[52] It eventually became both a focal point and a symbol for critics of Indian policy, who reviled it as embodying a set of objectionable social and governmental attitudes and policies toward a subordinated and oppressed people. Ironically, in the nineteenth century, it was thought to be in Indians' best interests.

All people were held to be subjects of the Queen, but that did not mean that all were equal under the law. Relatively few of the Queen's subjects held full voting and citizenship rights: usually white men over twenty-one years of age who owned or rented a prescribed amount of property. Generally speaking, poorer men, almost all women, persons of colour, many Metis, unenfranchised (that is to say, nearly all) Indians, and minors were proscribed in various ways from exercising full British citizenship rights. However, Canada's Indian legislation, now subsumed in the Indian Act, took the process much further, defining who was (and therefore who was not) an Indian. That is, it viewed Indians as a separate "race," supposedly identifiably different from and inferior to all others in society. It set out many of the parameters within which Indians were to lead their lives, seeking to protect them and their lands in prescribed ways; but it also established a process by which Indians could achieve full citizenship rights and put their Indian status behind them, a principal goal of government policy. Contrary to what often is said about this legislation, the government did consult with representative Indians of central Canada about the consolidation, and Mackenzie told the House of Commons that "whatever had to be done with the Indians must be done with their consent."[53]

The process that eventually led to the Indian Act of 1876 began much earlier. While the province of Canada had achieved responsible government in respect of internal, domestic affairs by the end of the 1840s, the British retained control of Indian policy until 1860. Originally, as a matter of colonial and military policy, the British had related to the Native peoples of the lands they colonized in many respects on a nation-to-nation basis, and as having much the same rights under the law as whites. Indians had enjoyed considerable self-government and control of culture change.[54] But by mid-century the British wished to turn over responsibility for Native peoples to the reluctant colonial authorities, and supported a number of colonial laws that imposed restrictions and regarded them as subjects of domestic policy. In 1850, Canadian legislation defined and protected Indian lands, as distinct from Crown lands, in Lower Canada; it also provided an early definition of who was legally considered an Indian.[55] Exemption from taxes on Indian lands was provided for Indians and those married to them. In 1851, the legislation became more restrictive, as whites who lived among Indians and white men married to Indian women were excluded from Indian status – an early differentiation between "status" and "non-status" Indians.[56] In 1857, the government formalized the goal of integrating Indians into the larger society with the Gradual Civilization Act, presented by the then-attorney general for Upper Canada, John A. Macdonald. Its purpose was to enfranchise Indians (that is, grant them the vote, ownership of a plot of land, and full status as British subjects) when they met certain qualifications. They must be male, at least twenty-one years of age, literate and orally proficient in one of Canada's official languages, "sufficiently advanced in the elementary branches of education and ... of good moral character and free from debt." Some who were not literate, but who could speak an official language, manage their own affairs, and be deemed virtuous could also be enfranchised. Such individuals were to receive a patent for up to fifty acres of reserve lands, a sum of money, and the vote and equality of status as British subjects. As they ceased to be wards of the state, they would lose status as Indians. All this was held to be an honour, but it was one that, to the dismay of the government, few Indians chose to seek.[57]

Prior to Confederation, Indian administration in Canada had been quite decentralized. After 1867, according to Douglas Leighton, "growth of centralized authority over its Indian clients became the Department's hallmark." The intention, he notes, was to introduce "the Ontario system of Indian administration to the Canadian west."[58] In 1868, the dominion government placed Indians and their lands under the secretary of state for the provinces. In 1869, it passed a more coercive Enfranchisement Act. One innovation with continuing significance was a so-called blood quantum provision: in order to share in annuities or other money paid to Indians, a person had to have a minimum of one-quarter Indian blood. Another provision disqualified Indian women married to non-Indian men, and their offspring, from collecting annuities – the so-called marrying out rule. Finally, the 1869 legislation required that chiefs, or chiefs in council, maintain roads and public buildings on reserves, as municipal councils were required to do in white communities, or the government would do it for them and charge the cost to the band. Reserves continued to be seen as the places where Indians would undergo the transition to civilization.[59]

The Indian Act, 1876, maintained most previous assumptions, policies, and goals. The first foundational principle was that, in law, there were two categories of people: Indians, and whites (all others). The second principle was that Indians were classed as minors, and therefore as wards of the state.[60] Superintendent General David Laird, when introducing the bill, stated, "the Indians must either be treated as minors or as white men." His deputy, Lawrence Vankoughnet, wrote in August 1876, "the legal status of the Indians of Canada is that of minors, with the Government as their guardian." A third principle was that wardship ought to be temporary. As Laird put it, "the interests of the aborigines and of the State alike require that every effort should be made to aid the red man in lifting himself out of his condition of tutelage and dependence and that it is clearly our wisdom and our duty, through education and every other means, to prepare him for a higher civilization by encouraging him to assume the privileges and responsibilities of full citizenship. In this spirit and with this object the enfranchisement clauses in the proposed Indian Bill have been framed."[61] Most of the act, therefore, was concerned with defining who was an Indian, with setting out the moral and legal responsibilities of the government in managing the lives of its Indian wards, and with encouraging them along the path to full enfranchisement.

It was assumed that, as minors, Indians could not responsibly manage many aspects of their lives. Reserves were held by the Crown in trust; they were free from taxation, but could neither be mortgaged nor seized for debt. Indians' lands could only be disposed of by the consent both of a majority of adult band members and of the superintendent general. Proceeds from any sales were held in trust by the Crown, though up to 10 per cent could be distributed in cash to members of the band concerned. Timber and mineral resources on reserves were likewise protected. One change made in 1876 with respect to Indian lands was introduction of a policy of surveying reserves into individual plots and providing location tickets to individual Indians to promote the idea of private rather than common property. This policy had some antecedents in the American policy of giving plots of land on reservations to individuals. It also paralleled in a limited way the idea behind homestead regulations for whites: if an Indian suitably improved the land over a three-year probationary period, and demonstrated that he could use it productively, he would be eligible for enfranchisement and title to his land.[62] John Tobias contends that this amounted to a policy to rid the country of reserves. That is, as each Indian became enfranchised and gained title, the reserve would diminish by that amount. Once all were enfranchised, no reserves would remain.[63]

A few other examples illustrate aspects of government policy. The act overrode traditional approaches to band government, and provided incentives for bands to adopt a government-determined elective system. Chiefs and councilors were to be elected for three-year terms and the government could depose uncooperative chiefs.[64] The earlier provisions that required chiefs and band councils to emulate the functions of municipal governments continued; they had to maintain roads, ditches, fences, schools, and other public buildings on the reserve, as well as provide primary care for the sick and disabled. This too was intended to prepare Indians for integration into Canadian society. It is true that most of the provisions for elective and municipal forms of government on the reserves were never implemented in the prairie region during the period discussed herein. However, that was because the government subsequently decided that the Indians of the region simply were not prepared for that level of responsibility. In the mid-1870s, the distinction that would result in administrative policies for the prairie Indians different from those that prevailed in central and eastern Canada and British Columbia had not yet been made.

The assumption that the Indian Act would apply as it stood was reflected in comments made by treaty commissioners at Treaties 6 and 7. Herein lay the basis of a major misunderstanding between the government and treaty commissioners on the one hand, and the Indians on the other: the government assumed that its Indian legislation operated prior to the treaties, framed them, and formed the context within which they would be interpreted; the Indians negotiating these treaties had never heard of that legislation, considered the treaties to be primary, and came to consider the Indian Act as either subordinate to the treaties or an illegal imposition.

When did the prairie Indians become legally minors or wards of the state? At least in recent decades, Native peoples generally have held one of two main positions on the matter. Both positions contend that before the treaties the Indians of the region were independent and sovereign. One holds that with the treaties the Indians agreed to live under Canadian law, under conditions specified therein. The other holds that under the treaties they never surrendered their sovereignty or their land; instead they permitted whites to use the land, except for the reserves, under specified conditions and with specified benefits for Indians. From this perspective, the Indian Act and its antecedents also constituted an illegal imposition on Indians.

The discussion that follows, therefore, is from the perspective of British and Canadian law. Wardship was not a result of the Indian Act of 1876, for that status applied to Indians well before Confederation.[65] There was no question, under British-Canadian law, that Indians of the former HBC territories were subjects of the Crown and that responsibility for them passed to Her Majesty's Canadian government on 15 July 1870. But were they wards of the state prior to negotiation of a treaty relationship and its obligations upon the state? Can the HBC providing supplies and medical care to needy Native peoples, for example, be construed as the acknowledgement of moral and legal responsibilities to people who had become dependent upon it, and who had such rights as dependent or minor subjects of the Crown?[66] Even after Confederation, the case is not entirely clear. Canadian law was held to apply in Manitoba and the North-Western Territory from July 1870, but there was a complication with respect to certain laws respecting Indians. The act of 1868, which placed governance of Indians under the secretary of state for the

provinces, carried forward from the pre-Confederation era a rather limiting definition of Indians. Part of this definition required that they
belong "to the tribe, band or body of Indians interested in [Indian] lands
or immoveable property," which amounted to saying that part of being
Indian required belonging to a tribe or band that had to be associated
with a reserve. In the spring of 1874, when the government decided to
legislate to resolve some outstanding problems in Manitoba and British
Columbia and remove any doubt that Canada's Indian legislation
applied there, it also addressed the fact that in most of the North-Western
Territory there were no "Indian lands" – that is, no treaties had been
negotiated nor reserves established. The government eliminated any
ambiguity about the application of legislation in relation to the Indians
by giving officials discretionary authority to apply the provisions of acts
of 1868, 1869, and 1873 to the Indians of the territory, even in the
absence of treaties or reserves.[67]

Did this legal anomaly leave the wardship status of Indians in limbo
until 1874? It is possible to argue that from 1867 the dominion government had assumed a moral and legal duty with respect to the Indian
subjects of the Crown within Canada's borders, including those of the
North-Western Territory from July 1870. If the legal anomaly noted
above leaves the question in doubt, the legislation of 1874 ensured that
laws concerning Canada's Indians applied to the North-Western
Territory (and predated Treaties 4 to 7). From this perspective, the
treaties were about defining aspects of the terms of the moral and
legal obligations toward wards, not about the status of wardship
itself. That is, wardship preceded, rather than resulted from, the treaties.
Alternatively, some might argue that Indians did not consent to Canadian
law, or to the status of legal minors, until they assented to the treaties.
Nevertheless, when the NWMP began operations in the region in the fall
of 1874, neither it nor the government had any doubt that Indians
already were legally minors, albeit minors whom circumstances dictated
be treated with respect.

## TREATY POLICY

The Indian Act of 1876 and its predecessors formed the framework
within which policies, including treaties, were developed. The Indians of
the West in the 1870s, however, were mostly unaware of this legislation.
They had not been consulted about it, and even if it had been brought to
their attention they likely would not have agreed with much of it, for it

represented a world and values alien to them. It was instead the treaties, in the making of which they were central participants, that defined for them the agreement under which they consented to white settlement and laws.

Both Indians and Canada understood at the outset that negotiation and agreement must precede substantial Canadian possession and use of the land, though they did not necessarily have the same thing in mind.[68] Canada's approach was shaped by law, especially its Indian legislation, and by past practice. Additionally, the government sought advice from those familiar with the negotiating, gift exchange, and ceremonial aspects of treating with Indians in connection with the fur trade.[69] Indians' approaches were also shaped by their experiences with whites in the fur trade and otherwise since the seventeenth century, by what they knew of the experience of American Indians,[70] by their own customary laws, and by the traditional ways to settle intertribal disputes. Also, as Canada and Indians signed treaties, each became part of the framework of subsequent treaties. By the time Treaties 6 and 7 were negotiated, the pattern was ingrained.

Only occasionally hinted at in most of the treaty negotiations was the inexorably expanding North American settlement frontier. It was never a matter of whether settlers would arrive in large numbers, but of when and under what conditions. No government could prevent the process altogether. Perhaps the most dramatic example of the failure of such an attempt occurred between 1763 and 1783. The Royal Proclamation of 1763, considered immensely important subsequently as establishing Indian rights under British law, attempted to control the settlement of the trans-Appalachian West and to establish an "Indian territory" in which white settlement would largely be prohibited. By 1783, white migration and the American Revolution had exploded these restrictions. Eighty years later the frontier, supplemented by railways, was broaching the trans-Mississippi West and Minnesota Territory, and expansionists in Canada West (the future Ontario) were demanding annexation of the HBC territories for settlement. By 1870, the frontier was south of Manitoba, with American annexationists eying the potential of the North-West Territories. The treaty negotiations could not be isolated from this context and, despite appearances on the ground, a great disparity in power separated the two parties.

Another factor not well discussed at the treaty negotiations was that, deeply rooted in the English understanding, Native peoples did not own or possess the land. They instead occupied it, roamed over it, and derived their living from it. True owners, in that same understanding, would establish permanent dwellings, carry on agriculture and pastoralism, and define the boundaries of their plots with surveys, fences, hedges, and the like. They would labour to "improve" the land and enhance its productivity. The treaties, therefore, were about compensating Indians for the loss of their traditional way of life, and opening the country to those who would truly own it and develop it.[71]

For Indians, by contrast, ownership lay more flexibly in collective occupation from time immemorial. The land gave them their living. The treaties were about sharing the land and its resources in return for a relationship with the newcomers and guarantees for future support as needed.

Still, the Canadians were bound by law, tradition, and a particular sense of justice to negotiate with Indians. The roots of the English concept of treaties as agreements with respect to land rights underwent a lengthy evolution. According to Patricia Seed, as late as the seventeenth century the English term "treaty" meant any written agreement, "as opposed to speaking, or gesturing, or participating in a ritual," between two or more persons. Thus, in the English tradition, a treaty was a written document; for Indians, a treaty comprised oral commitments, sealed by ritual and ceremony. In the eighteenth century, written treaties were employed in acquisition of land from Indians, by which the English compensated them in return for permanent title to the land. Indians' resistance sometimes resulted in coercion or threats from the authorities before the treaty was signed. Under British law all title to land devolved from the sovereign, and treaties were negotiated and signed by representatives of the Crown or government; therefore "such accords constituted the most secure legal title to native lands under English law." Another major reason for having the Crown negotiate land purchases with Indians, says Seed, was to ensure state control of the distribution of so important an economic asset to its subjects and citizens, obviating squabbles over land rights among colonists or settlers.[72]

Canada's approach flowed from these and other premises under British law. There never was any question in the minds of the British and Canadian governments, and of HBC officials, that ultimate title to British North America lay in the British Crown by right of "discovery," of occupation and exploitation, and of conquest.[73] The fact that Indians occupied and lived off the land did not give them full title, but what the courts later defined as "a personal and usufructuary right, dependent upon the good will of the Sovereign." This right to "absolute use and enjoyment of their lands" could only be alienated to the Crown.[74] In a sense, then, the treaty negotiations from the government perspective were partly, or even mainly, about determining the price at which Indians would be willing to alienate their ancestral rights.

The Royal Proclamation of 1763 forbade individuals to purchase land from Indians, stipulating that only the Crown or government could negotiate the surrender of Indian title to the land, and that this must be done openly and with the consent of the Indians concerned. While the lands granted to the HBC had been specifically excluded from the provisions of the proclamation, both Canada and Great Britain recognized during the negotiations for the transfer of Rupert's Land and the North-Western Territory that the underlying principles of the proclamation would apply in this region: Canada acknowledged in December 1867 that it would have to consider and settle "any claims of Indians to compensation for lands required for purposes of settlement," such terms to be "in conformity with the equitable principles which have uniformly governed the British Crown in its dealings with the aborigines."[75] Thus from the beginning Canada was committed to treating with the Indian population of its new territories; previous practice constituted the template for future negotiation. From the Canadian perspective, this meant compensating Indians for loss of their title or, to put it another way, for loss of their right to live off the land in their traditional way, so that whites could possess and settle the land peacefully. Canada in effect expected to complete its right of full, unimpeded ownership of the land to which the British had already granted it ultimate title.

Indians did not view the situation in the same way. Over the previous two hundred years, as they saw it, they had allowed fur traders to access the region for a price, periodically renegotiated as an exchange at fur-trading, relationship-establishing ceremonies; they did not believe that in so doing they had surrendered any title to their land to the HBC or the British government. Today Indian elders assert that in the 1870s the only thing that Indians conceded to whites was a right to access and use the land for a price and subject to certain conditions. From this perspective, the treaties were about how the land might be shared for mutual benefit. Indians pushed for treaties because their circumstances were increasingly tenuous and they needed aid to survive in the new context.

Neither side operated from a position of strength. The formerly feared Indians of the 1850s and 1860s were by the 1870s seriously weakened by disease, alcohol, warfare, and the demise of the bison and other animals.[76] They were anxious for help, but not so weak as to be willing to

open the region to whites at any price. It is difficult to conceive of the
Nizitapi welcoming a police force in the 1850s; however, in the 1870s
they accepted the small numbers of NWMP, which were effective in the
drastically changed circumstances.

The Canadian government also was weak economically and militarily.
Under the Confederation agreement, it assumed the accumulated public
debt of the constituent provinces; it also committed to heavy expenditures to hold the new country together, most notably the construction of
the Intercolonial Railway to link the Maritimes with central Canada.
The government, as seen, had to obtain a loan from Great Britain just to
secure Rupert's Land, and it certainly had no capacity to put an army in
the field to back up its Indian policy as the Americans had done. In 1871,
to persuade British Columbia to join Confederation, the Macdonald
government, perhaps rashly, committed to constructing an all-Canadian
railway to the Pacific within ten years, an obligation that the Mackenzie
government from 1873 complained was ruinously expensive. Rupert's
Land in the meantime was remote and communication difficult until
completion of the railway in the mid-1880s. Moreover, in 1873 the
dominion sank into a depression along with the rest of the Anglo-
American world. Canada's capacity to act swiftly, generously, and deci-
sively with respect to Indian treaties in the 1870s was very limited. Its
strength was potential, lying in the looming, irresistible approach of the
settlement frontier.

Past treaty-making experience shaped Canada's approach. Three treaties with the Indians of the upper Great Lakes – the so-called Robinson
Huron and Robinson Superior treaties of 1850, and the Manitoulin
Island Treaty of 1862 – were bare bones compared with what would
follow in the West in the 1870s. They provided for reserves, the boundaries of which were spelled out; for an initial payment or gratuity (a kind
of signing bonus); for a small annual payment or annuity; and for off-
reserve hunting and fishing privileges.[77] Limited as the written treaty
terms appear, the government was flexible, and went well beyond these
terms in providing support to Indians. John L. Taylor notes, "there was
precedent in old Canada for every significant item which came to be
included in the western treaties," including those in respect to agriculture, education, and hunting and fishing supplies.[78] In these early treaty
negotiations, Indians had high expectations about what they wanted to
receive for their land, based on prices paid elsewhere in Upper Canada
and in the United States south of the Great Lakes. Commissioner William
B. Robinson held firm for a lower price, noting, "the lands now ceded

[north of the Lakes] are notoriously barren and sterile" – that is, unsuited to agriculture.[79] Relating perceived value of the lands to the price to be paid was part of the government's argument in negotiations from Treaty 1 onward.

Both the Canadian government and the prairie Indians would have also been familiar with the provisions of the American treaties of the 1850s with the Nizitapi, among others. For example, the Fort Laramie Treaty of 1851 provided for 320 acres of reservation land for each adult male Indian; for seeds, implements, and instruction for intending farmers; for a cow and a yoke of oxen for each farm; for a suit of clothing for every man each year for thirty years, and cloth for clothing for women and children; for annuities of ten dollars for each man, or twenty dollars if he settled down and farmed; and for Indian lands to be held free from white settlement. While the 1851 treaty involved numerous Native American nations, the 1855 treaty was specifically with the Nizitapi and Gros Ventre peoples. The annuities and other promises of 1851 were replaced with the following: the federal government agreed to provide goods totalling $350,000 annually for ten years, and to spend an additional $15,000 annually on schools and agriculture; Native Americans committed to allegiance to the United States, to remain within the confines of a very large reservation that was meant to allow them to hunt and roam as well as to farm, to try to control horse raiding and cease warfare, to allow American citizens to pass through reservations unmolested, to surrender to authorities any Indian accused of a crime against a white, and, finally, to not cross into British territory.[80] It is highly likely that these American treaties shaped how the prairie Indians in Canada envisaged the terms of a treaty, and thus influenced some of the treaty discussions and provisions.[81]

When instructing the Canadian commissioners about to enter the treaty process in 1871, Howe noted that the government's objective was to secure right of passage for people travelling from what is now Thunder Bay to Manitoba, and such lands for settlement as "may be susceptible of improvement and profitable occupation." But the cash-starved and parsimonious government directed the commissioners to obtain the lands as cheaply as possible, certainly for no more than twelve dollars per family of five. "In fixing this amount," warned Howe, "you must not lose sight of the fact that it cannot fail to have an important bearing on the arrangements to be made subsequently with the tribes further West."[82] In this he was prescient: Indians would regard the provisions of one treaty in most cases as a basic starting point in the next negotiation.

This was why government negotiators arrived at the treaty talks with a
draft treaty in hand, which has annoyed some subsequent commentators. The negotiations, even at Treaty 1, were never de novo; they followed precedent and were intended to set a common pattern for
negotiation across the prairie region. Howe also viewed the treaties as
business propositions, not as an opportunity to develop relationships.

The language used in the treaty negotiations reveals much. The treaty
commissioners portrayed themselves as representatives of the Queen.
This almost certainly meant something different to them than to Indians.
They were appointed by, and represented, Her Majesty's Canadian government. As Victorian gentlemen, they clearly had great respect for the
*person* of the Queen, and for the monarchy generally. As politicians, they
knew what it meant to be a privy councillor (or member of the Cabinet),
formally an advisor to the monarch. In practice, the government carried
on its business and generally informed the monarch (or, in Canada's
case, the governor general as the Queen's representative) about what it
was doing; the ability of the monarch, or governor general, to influence
policy was exceedingly limited.[83] They understood that the monarch, in
treaty negotiations, was a stand-in for the government, and that the government undertook treaty obligations on behalf of the Canadian people,
not the person of the monarch. The monarch also represented an institution meant to govern disinterestedly on behalf of all citizens of the country including minorities, even if it had little practical power to do so, and
which was not beholden to the changing popular moods that so preoccupied politicians.

For Indians, in contrast, the "Queen," the "Queen Mother," or the
"Great Mother" appears to have connoted a distinct, benign person, a
great chief with ultimate authority and with whom it was possible to
form a kinship relationship, and the treaty commissioners were understood to be empowered to make commitments to her Indian "children"
on her behalf. On occasion an Indian spokesperson would refer to the
government, but how they understood the term is not very clear.[84]

The government negotiators referred to the Queen setting aside lands
for reserves as a gift for her Indian children, stressing both the Queen's
generosity and ultimate ownership of the land; they never referred to
reserves as land that belonged to Indians by right. Similarly, when the
government offered gratuities, annuities, seed grain, animals, implements, or even uniforms for the chiefs, it offered them as the Queen's
generous gifts, her bounty and benevolence, not as compensation for
Indians giving up their right to traditional use of the land in favour of
settlement and agriculture.

Many writers accept that Indians attached great religious significance to the ceremonies, including the dances and stroking of the pipe, which preceded the actual negotiations. Whites, in contrast, did not.[85] When the commissioners mentioned the Great Spirit, it was almost always to say, in effect, that God intended that everyone should share the land which He created, and that He intended that those who could use it most efficiently – obviously Europeans – should be its prime occupiers and users. When the Bible stated that God gave humans dominion over all the earth, and told them to go forth and multiply, the meaning was very clear to the nineteenth-century white mind, and it included the idea that dominion meant possession, development, and improvement.[86] Still, it is curious that at these ceremonies whites did not invoke God in a particularly religious way. In their own society, there usually were prayers, or even full-scale religious services, invoking God's blessing before important events. Apparently none of this happened at the treaty talks, despite the fact that there were both Protestant and Roman Catholic clergy present – mostly, it turned out, to help translate and to reassure and persuade Indians that it was in their best interests to accept the treaties. If services were held, it was because the treaty talks went over a Sunday when secular work could not be conducted, and they were no different than taking the sabbath off while on the farm or trail, holding services, and resting the animals. They had neither greater religious significance nor significance for the treaties themselves.

Peter Erasmus, who had training as a clergyman and was the Metis translator employed by both the Cree and the government at Treaty 6, commented correctly on the "deep significance to the tribes" of the preliminary ceremonies; but, he added, "few people realize that those so-called savages were far more deeply affected and influenced by their religious beliefs and convictions than any comparable group of white people, whose lip service to their religion goes no deeper than that."[87] What he missed, however, was that while many of the white negotiators were deeply religious men, for them negotiating a treaty was not a particularly religious occasion. It was possible to show respect for Indians' religious sentiments without sharing or fully understanding them. Other whites, of course, were simply bemused by that which they did not comprehend and deemed primitive superstition.[88] One culture readily separated religious from secular issues; the other saw them as irrevocably one.

Treaty 1 of 1871, covering roughly the original small province of Manitoba, began a pattern of negotiation that proved important through Treaties 6 and 7. It is scarcely surprising that the government's initial offer to the Indians "consisted only of reserves and a small cash gratuity and annuity."[89] (Gratuities, an initial payment for signing, were proposed at three dollars per person, and annuities were to be fifteen dollars per family of five, or in proportion, payable in cash or equivalent goods.) The pattern was based on what had transpired earlier in the province of Canada. The negotiations soon reached an impasse, for the 160 acres of land offered per family of five would not permit Indians to continue traditional hunting and fishing, and without assistance the expected conversion to a settled, agricultural lifestyle would fail.

Part of the impasse perhaps arose from Indian expectations based on the precedent of the American treaties of the 1850s. Within the confines of the very large Blackfoot reservation in Montana, for example, Indians were supposed to be able both to carry on their traditional hunting and gathering, and to take up their 320-acre farms. They were to live, whether farming or hunting, entirely within the reserve. In the much smaller, distinctly limited Canadian model, by contrast, the reserve was a place for settlement, permanent residence, and transition to agriculture, but Indians could roam beyond its boundaries to hunt, fish, and gather on lands that whites did not require for other purposes. The American model was likely far more familiar to Canadian prairie Indians than that of the Robinson treaties in Upper Canada.[90]

At any rate, Indians took initiative and asked for agricultural implements, animals, and schools. (They were fairly familiar with these items. Some of them had farmed on St Peter's band lands, and they had seen established farming communities in Metis settlements. Missionaries had operated schools among them. These provisions were also included in the US treaties.) The commissioners readily assented, as the government had long provided such items for Indians in central Canada where they were not a treaty requirement, and the logjam was broken. That these promises did not appear in the written treaty has been viewed as carelessness at best or intentional deception at worst – either is possible, but neither is likely. In his 3 November 1871 report to Ottawa on the negotiations, Commissioner Wemyss Simpson itemized these promises,[91] and there is reason to believe that had they been promptly and generously fulfilled, their omission from the text of the treaty might have been of far less moment. Unfortunately, the Ottawa officials chose to interpret the treaty narrowly, and ignored the so-called outside promises that were integral to the Indians' understanding of it.[92] Indians' protests forced the government to amend the treaty in 1875,[93] and the experience led Indians in subsequent negotiations to question the government's integrity and to insist that all oral promises must appear in a final written treaty.

That Indians should – and wanted to – be transformed into farming peoples was an underlying assumption of the government's approach to the treaties. They feared for their future, according to Morris, and were "tractable, docile, and willing to learn." He advocated that Indians should be induced "to erect houses on their farms, and plant their 'gardens' as they call them, and then while away on their hunts, their wives and children will have houses to dwell in, and will care for their patches of corn and grain and potatoes. Then, too, the cattle given them will expand into herds."[94]

A few other points that arose in connection with Treaty 1 affected subsequent negotiations. One is that Archibald stated that the Queen "wished to place her red subjects on the same footing as the white," and indeed he believed that, with the bounties, he offered them more than white settlers would receive.[95] The government offered Indians reserves based on 160 acres per family of five, which was as much land as it offered to homesteaders.[96] This was believed in the 1870s to be a generous amount of land for viable farming. It was larger than the 80- or 100-acre farms that were common in rural Ontario, and that were also provided for in the Huron, Superior, and Manitoulin treaties. There were obvious differences from white farms: Indians could not own the land outright, or dispose of it, unless they became enfranchised and gave up Indian status, so it was tribal and not individual land. Moreover, white settlers from 1871 had a right to purchase under certain conditions a second, usually contiguous, 160-acre plot (called a pre-emption), while Indians did not. Still, Archibald was explicit about the government's intentions, stating:

> These reserves will be large enough, but you must not expect them
> to be larger than will be enough to give a farm to each family,
> where farms shall be required. They will enable you to earn a liv-
> ing should the chase fail, and ... you must not expect to have
> included in your reserve more of hay grounds than will be reason-
> ably sufficient for your purposes in case you adopt the habits of
> farmers. The old settlers and the settlers that are coming in, must
> be dealt with on the principles of fairness and justice as well as
> yourselves. Your Great Mother knows no difference between any
> of her people.[97]

Prior occupancy conferred no advantage.

Archibald also insisted that the Indians determine who would speak for them and have the power to commit them when signing the treaty.

This was in part because some Indians asserted that those who had signed the earlier Selkirk Treaty of 1817 had not had the right to do so. "For some time," wrote Archibald, "a doubt has existed whether the Chief, nominally at the head of the Indians of the Indian settlement, possessed the good will and confidence of that Band." This was a change for bands that could bring all or most of their members to treaty talks, and that expected leaders who conducted the talks to report back to, discuss with, and represent the opinions of the entire band. But the government wanted the certainty of dealing with an authorized leader whose signature on the treaty document would be binding.[98]

Thus Treaty 1, especially when the outside promises are taken into account, established a pattern: reserves to encourage settlement and agriculture;[99] assistance in getting started in the new way of life; a school on each reserve; a promise of some continuing hunting, fishing, and gathering rights; exclusion of alcoholic beverages from the reserve; and a promise from the Indians to maintain a peaceful relationship with "Her Majesty's white subjects." Treaty 1 also spelled out the area surrendered by Indians, and set out roughly where each reserve would be located. This, Archibald told them, was their opportunity to secure land and other benefits before the anticipated hordes of settlers descended. Treaty 2, covering an area to the west and north of Treaty 1, also was negotiated in 1871, essentially on the same terms as Treaty 1 but with less controversy.

Treaty 3 of 1873 covered the region between Lake Superior and Manitoba; it was crucial for a secure all-Canadian transportation route from the Great Lakes to the prairies. The Indians of the region appreciated the value of their lands and resources, and negotiations were difficult. The result had significant implications for future treaties. Partly because agricultural land was scarce, and Indians would require a larger territory to live in the traditional way, the government greatly expanded the formula for creating reserves to 640 acres per family of five. It increased the gratuity to twelve dollars per capita, and annuities to five dollars. It wrote the right to hunt and fish, subject to some limitations, into the treaty, and promised $1,500 annually for ammunition and twine. It promised agricultural and other implements, seed grain and potatoes, oxen and cows for those who decided to farm. Salaries (twenty-five dollars for chiefs and fifteen dollars for up to three subordinate officers per band) and suits of clothing for chiefs and headmen were also included. The commitment to obey the law, maintain the peace, and act as good subjects of the Queen was spelled out in much more detail than in Treaties 1 and 2. J.R. Miller points out that the ceremonial and ritual aspects were also significantly more pronounced.[100]

The Ojibwa of the Treaty 3 area have been characterized as "hard-nosed bargainers,"[101] and the improved terms, compared with Treaties 1 and 2, indicate that they enjoyed some success. But they had to confront equally hard-nosed bargainers in Morris and fellow treaty commissioner S.J. Dawson, who also achieved some important successes. The Indians attempted to present a solid, united front, but Morris perceived underlying divisions and exploited them to get a treaty. Chief Mawedopenais made some firm pronouncements about Indian ownership of the land, and he and other Indians at various points claimed mining, timber, and water rights in the entire region. Morris maintained the British-Canadian position concerning ownership of land and resources. Indians, he stated, would only secure mineral rights on their reserves. When the Indians questioned the government's right to take wood for steamers on the rivers and lakes of the region, Dawson contended it "was a right which ... was common to all Her Majesty's subjects ... Wood on which the Indians had bestowed labor was always paid for; but wood on which we had spent our own labor was ours." Morris added, "wood and water were the gift of the Great Spirit, and were made alike for the good of both the white man and red man." When Mawedopenais said that the tribes had already chosen the areas they wanted for reserves, Morris demurred and indicated that further negotiation with surveyors would be required, though Indian desires would be accommodated as far as possible. When Mawedopenais objected to land having already been surveyed for the HBC where he wanted his reserve, Morris stated that the rights of the company had to be respected as well as those of the Indians. Once more, Indian claims had no priority.

Finally, Morris stated, "I wish you to understand we do not come here as traders, but as representing the Crown, and to do what we believe is just and right." He was making an important distinction between fur-trade and treaty negotiations. Though they shared the outward trappings of the fur-trade ceremonies, the discussion at hand was different: Morris represented "the Queen's government," and the negotiations included an assertion of government primacy and authority. When Mawedopenais extended his hand, he said, "I hold fast all the promises you have made, and hope they will last as long as the sun goes round, and the water flows, as you have said." When Morris took his hand, he replied, "I accept your hand, and with it the lands, and will keep all my promises," committing to a permanent friendship.[102] The contrasting emphases express much. Morris made concessions at the edges, ones that did not infringe upon the government's core rights and goals.

Dawson reported that the Indian leaders had deliberated at length over the provisions of the treaty and asked him for fuller explanations of "certain passages." Prior to signing the treaty, he insisted, "they comprehended perfectly the nature of the obligations into which they were about to enter, that the surrender of their territorial rights would be irrevocable, and that they were to stand forever afterwards in new relations to the white man." He also reported that the chiefs themselves stated as much "with great solemnity to their people."[103] Thus, the commissioners believed they had done everything possible to ensure that Indians understood and accepted the land transaction embodied in the treaty.

One remaining point arising from the Treaty 3 talks must be noted. At a particularly difficult juncture in the negotiations, the chiefs had retired to consult with four prominent Metis, after which they returned to the talks disposed to accept the treaty. Mawedopenais told Morris, "I wish you to understand you owe the treaty much to the Half-breeds." Morris replied, "I know it," and went on to praise the Metis men for "their cordial support."[104] It is interesting, therefore, that when the chief asked that the Metis families who lived with the Indians "should be counted with us, and have their share of what you have promised," Morris refused. Relying on the Red River precedent, and knowing Canadian law, he stated that the Metis "must be either white or Indian.[105] If Indians, they get treaty money; if the Half-breeds call themselves white, they get land." He promised to refer the matter to Ottawa, recommending that the Metis families "be permitted the option of taking either status as Indians or whites, but that they could not take both."[106] This problem, and this distinction, would crop up in future treaties.

The negotiation of Treaty 4 of 1874, covering most of present-day southern Saskatchewan, was notable mainly for the intense bitterness some of the Indians expressed about the HBC allegedly selling their land without their consent in 1870, and insistence that they, not the company, should have received the payment.[107] But an expression of anger is what it remained: it resulted in no change to the basic structure of the treaty. The provisions in fact were much the same as those of Treaty 3, including the formulas for reserves, gratuities and annuities, schools, hunting and gathering rights, and agricultural assistance. Soon it was apparent that the provisions for agricultural support were insufficient and had to be supplemented, and this realization would influence the demands of

Indians negotiating Treaty 6. It perhaps is worth noting that government officials, to say nothing of the public, considered 640 acres per family of five to be an absurdly large land grant, far beyond the capacity of most experienced farmers to cultivate given the technology available in the 1870s.[108] Because the prairie region was so vast, it seemed a minor issue at the time and a cheap way to buy future peace, but within twenty years attitudes changed significantly.

The innovation in Treaty 4 lay on the government side, in what Miller terms a "blanket extinguishment clause." The treaty not only stated, as in previous treaties, that Indians would "cede, release, surrender and yield up" to the government of Canada and the Queen "all their rights, titles and privileges" in the area of land specified as surrendered, but also added that they surrendered all rights "to all other lands whatsoever situated within Her Majesty's North-West Territories, or any of them, to have and to hold the same to Her Majesty the Queen and her successors forever."[109]

Treaty 5 of 1875 covered the area north of Treaties 1 and 2, including the northern part of Lake Winnipeg and the lower Saskatchewan River basin. This area was not immediately vital for settlement, but it was vital for transportation. The Saskatchewan River, along with the North Saskatchewan and South Saskatchewan further west, was the main route for moving goods into and out of the fertile belt where most settlement was expected to take place. No railway reached Edmonton, for example, until 1891, and even then it was from Calgary. Not until the early twentieth century did a railway parallel the North Saskatchewan River. Treaty 5 therefore was strategically important. However, it marked a clear setback for Indians in the region, since the government not only got them to settle for reserves based on the Treaty 1 formula (160 acres per family of five), but also significantly reduced their annuity payments.[110] Needless to say, the Indians of the future Treaty 6 region took their starting point as Treaty 4, not Treaty 5.

CONCLUSION

By 1876, the dominion government had established a pattern of negotiating treaties with prairie Indians. If many of the trappings of the ceremonies had roots in, and parallels to, those between fur traders and Native peoples, the assumptions underlying the government's understanding of the treaties, and the promises made, were rooted in pre-Confederation practice and principles of British law. From the government perspective, the first five numbered treaties remained fundamentally the same, varying only in details. They were between the government and Indians (excluding Metis). The government (Queen) possessed ultimate title to the land, and Indians did not, despite their assertions to the contrary. The treaties were about land surrenders (that is, surrender of aboriginal title in the land), compensation to permit peaceful white settlement, and the means (reserves, assistance, education, and so forth – all as grants from the Queen's bounty) to ensure that Indians had the opportunity to adapt, transform, and thrive in the new circumstances. The experience of negotiating Treaties 1 through 5, and the provisions of those treaties, in turn framed the negotiation of Treaties 6 and 7. The government presumed that, while there might be some regional variation according to local circumstances, the basic design and logic of the treaties was established.

For the government, moreover, the treaties were framed by a broader set of assumptions about Canada's purposes in assuming control of the prairie region, as well as about the Indian population and its ultimate fate. Canada entered the prairie West determined to supplant the Indian population.[111] Perhaps Indians thought the treaties were about sharing the land, but the government did not. It was confident that Canadians and immigrants could use the land more efficiently and intensively to enrich themselves and to feed and supply themselves and others. As federal authorities saw it, Indians represented a passé way of life and needed to give way to others who could realize the region's potential as God had intended. Canadians believed that their Indian policy would be peaceful and more humane than the aggressive destructiveness of the Americans. Yet it remained coercive: it gave Indians the opportunity to adapt and assimilate, but insisted they change. This was to be the first important step in putting Indians on a secure path to a transformed future.

Canada further believed that it had not only purchased the region from the British and HBC, but also inherited a region to which British-Canadian law already applied. It did not hesitate to pass numerous laws to administer the region and prepare it for the arrival of a white settlement population, or to apply Canadian criminal law as well as laws affecting Indians specifically – all without negotiation with the Indian population, who were in any event considered wards of the state. Nor did the government see any difficulty with providing police to enforce the laws. These assumptions underlay its approach to the treaty-making process.

Indians, by contrast, had no idea they were considered wards, nor did they think they were selling their land. They were anxious about the future, given the worsening food shortages, the prevalence of disease, the inexorable advancement of the settlement frontier in the United States, and the HBC's apparent abandonment of its established role not only in trade, but also in community support. Indians saw the treaties as a way to secure not only their physical survival, but also their culture and future in rapidly changing circumstances, by establishing a strong relationship with the newcomers and by sharing access to their land. They accepted that change was coming, but they wanted to maintain as much of their traditions as they could for as long as they could, while adjusting to the new realities.

# The Paradox of Agreement and Mutual Incomprehension: Treaties 6 and 7

Having negotiated five treaties within four years, the Canadian government at last moved in the late summer of 1876 to come to terms with the Indians in the vast portion of the fertile belt north of Treaty 4 and west from Treaty 5 almost to the Rocky Mountains, the future central Saskatchewan and Alberta (Treaty 6). It then completed the process in 1877 (Treaty 7) for the southern portion of the future Alberta. The northern half of the future province of Alberta (along with parts of Saskatchewan, British Columbia, and the North-West Territories) was addressed much later, in 1899 (Treaty 8).[1] In the first part of this chapter, I focus on the negotiation and terms of Treaties 6 and 7, which affected most of the future district of Alberta. In the second part, I reflect on the treaties and examine some of larger contextual and interpretive issues, as well as some misconceptions, that are essential to understanding the subsequent development of policy, and responses to it, in the post-treaty or reserve era.

PART I

*Treaty 6*

Despite the fear of intertribal warfare expressed in the Cree petition of April 1871, the Cree and Nizitapi made a formal peace later that year at the Red Deer River and the threat receded. Neither side could afford to continue fighting given the devastation of the smallpox epidemic, the effects of the whiskey trade, and the shrunken bison herds. The most important aspect of the peace was to permit the bison hunt to continue for both sides without conflict.[2] Two violent episodes in 1873, between the Piikani and Crow tribes, and the Cypress Hills Massacre, were much smaller in scale than the Cree-Nizitapi wars and did not affect the peace of 1871.[3]

Yet any appearance of improvement in the situation in the western plains was deceiving. Discontent was widespread. It took five long, hard years after 1871 to bring the government to the bargaining table at Forts Carlton and Pitt in 1876, despite both Indian unrest and demands and also angry letters from Lieutenant Governor Alexander Morris to hasten the process.[4] Intertribal peace may have been achieved, but the other elements of crisis portrayed by the chiefs in 1871 did not improve. The bison herds continued to shrink. The starvation of 1870–71 was repeated during the winter of 1873–74: according to a report from Victoria on the North Saskatchewan River, many Indians were again reduced to eating their "horses, dogs, buffalo robes and in some cases their snow shoes and moccasins," before succumbing and dying.[5] By 1874, bison no longer frequented the eastern prairies either, and officials feared spreading famine and open conflict unless action was taken to conserve the animals and provide relief supplies. Thus the Cree demand for guarantees for famine relief at the treaty negotiations in 1876 was a product of heart-rending experience.[6] Native frustration at the government's inaction boiled over in the summer of 1875. Taking a leaf from Louis Riel and the Metis at Red River in 1869–70, they halted construction of the telegraph line between Winnipeg and Edmonton, and stopped the Geological Survey and the survey of the Pacific railway line (all of which they had previously tolerated), "on the grounds that they would not permit such trespassing until a treaty was completed."[7]

The tactics got the government's attention. It hastened to employ Rev George McDougall to travel among the various bands, informing them of the government's intention to treat with them the following summer and offering presents. He estimated that he had visited approximately 4,000 Indians, and reported, "though [they] deplored the necessity of resorting to extreme measures, yet they were unanimous in their determination to oppose the running of lines, or the making of roads through their country, until a settlement between the Government and them had been effected." In 1875, the Cree message to the government was not "Get lost," but "Get serious! We need help now."

McDougall also noted that the treaty provisions they sought included prohibition of alcoholic beverages in their country, prohibition of the use of strychnine, and strict punishment for "all parties who set fire to our forest or plain." They further requested "that our chiefships be established by the Government. Of late years almost every trader sets up his own Chief and the result is we are broken up into little parties, and our best men are no longer respected."[8] In other words, they wanted the government not only to negotiate with them, but also to impose order in an increasingly unstable environment.

The negotiation of Treaty 6 took place, as promised, at Fort Carlton on the lower reaches of the North Saskatchewan River in late August 1876, and at Fort Pitt, upstream on the North Saskatchewan and west of Battleford, in early September. The treaty covered the region from almost the western boundary of present-day Manitoba, taking in mainly the North Saskatchewan River drainage basin north from the Red Deer River and following it west to the foot of the Rockies. Though HBC officers recommended holding negotiations at Edmonton and the Victoria settlement, neither of the sites of negotiation lay in present-day Alberta, which was inconvenient for some of the Cree, Stoneys, and others in the western portion of the treaty area. However, a majority of them were covered by subsequent adhesions to the treaty between 1876 and 1878.[9]

On 18 August, according to Morris, he and his fellow commissioners (W.J. Christie and James McKay, both Metis), escorted by the North-West Mounted Police, "proceeded to the Indian camp [at Fort Carlton] ... The Union Jack was hoisted, and the Indians at once began to assemble, beating drums, discharging fire-arms, singing and dancing." After a half-hour of this, they began "the dance of the 'pipe-stem,'" and presented the pipe to Morris and his colleagues to stroke with their hands. This, Morris understood, meant, "in accordance with their custom we had accepted the friendship of the Cree nation."[10] It was partly that, of course. But it also was a religious ceremony that had a deeper meaning for the Cree. It involved a solemn commitment that "only *the truth* must be used," and commitments made in the presence of the pipe "must be kept."[11]

Following the precedent of earlier treaty negotiations, the commissioners presented a basic offer that they viewed as consistent with past practice: the relinquishing of all aboriginal rights and title to the lands in the specified treaty area, apart from reserves; the right to continue to hunt and fish on unoccupied lands; a gratuity to each person for signing; payment of annuities to each band member in perpetuity, together with specified clothing, medals, and flags for chiefs and councillors; setting aside of reserves, based on a formula of 640 acres per family of five, on which they were to live and pursue agriculture, and which could not be disposed of without their consent; provision of agricultural implements, oxen, cattle, and seed grain; schools; and prohibition of "intoxicating liquor" on reserves. In return, Indians agreed to a major change in their way of life, and to acting as law-abiding, peaceable subjects of the Queen.[12]

Some younger, more radical Cree wanted to resist the treaty, but the senior chiefs – Mistawasis and Ahtahkakoop – prevailed. The imminent disappearance of the bison had to be faced. Said Mistawasis: "the Great White Queen Mother has offered us a way of life when the buffalo are no more." Ahtahkakoop argued that his people had no more power to stop the influx of whites than they had to prevent a plague of locusts, and "surely we Indians can learn the ways of living that made the white man strong." They both recommended accepting "the Queen's hand," that is, taking treaty and creating a relationship with whites.[13]

They nevertheless reshaped the offered terms. They were skilled, informed negotiators who brought their own highly qualified translator, Peter Erasmus,[14] to the talks; they also insisted on receiving the government offer in writing, having it read to them, and making their own counter-proposals in writing to minimize misunderstanding.[15] NWMP officer Sam Steele, who was present at the negotiations, recalled that Erasmus "stood at the end of the table facing [the Indians], his position graceful and dignified, his voice deep, clear and mellow, every word distinctly enunciated."[16]

Sparks were struck by Poundmaker, outraged that the governor proposed to give them only 640 acres of land for each family: "This is our land! It isn't a piece of pemmican to be cut off and given in little pieces back to us. It is ours and we will take what we want."[17] Though many Indians approved of this passionate outburst, Morris – seemingly shaken – still conceded nothing on the size of land grants. He patiently explained, "unless certain lands were set aside for the sole use of the Indians, the country would be flooded with white settlers who would not give the Indians any consideration whatever." In Erasmus's opinion, Morris's simple and sincere approach gradually impressed and persuaded his audience.[18]

However, the Cree persuaded the commissioners to grant "more agricultural implements, livestock and wagons than in previous treaties." They also negotiated three new provisions: $1,000 each year for three years to assist in the transition to agriculture, assistance in the event of "famine or pestilence," and a "medicine chest" to be kept at the home of every Indian agent.[19]

The last two demands, and the importance the Cree attached to them, were not only the product of the recent years of starvation and epidemic disease, but also have a longer-term context. In 1857, a select committee of the British Parliament was established to consider matters related to the possible renewal of the HBC monopoly. It heard many witnesses, both supporting and opposing the company's interests. A.S. Morton summarizes parts of the testimony:

> Sir George Back testified that on his expeditions he had seen Indians who "must have starved without the aid of the Hudson's Bay Company." The Indians "seemed always to feel that they could fall back upon the clemency and the benevolence of the white man at any extremity; that as long as he had anything to spare in his store the Indian was certain to be relieved." Dr. John Rae, was asked about a statement of Sir George Simpson's that every trading establishment was in fact an Indian hospital. He replied: "Wherever we act as medical men our services are given gratuitously. We go to a distance if the Indian is at a distance, and have taken him to a fort, and he is fed and clothed there. And it is no uncommon thing to hear the old Indians, when unfit for hunting, say, 'We are unfit for work; we will go and reside at a fort.' That is the ordinary feeling which prevailed in the country."[20]

The HBC did not maintain a qualified doctor all the time at any given fort, let alone every fort, and it could not accommodate every ill or aged Native person. However, the testimony speaks to the relationship that had evolved between the HBC and the Native population: Native peoples apparently saw the HBC as a kind of patron, or alternatively as kin, with the obligation to assist when and as needed. If so, it also probably speaks to the kind of relationship the Cree thought they were entering into when Canada agreed to include these provisions in the treaty.[21] From their perspective, the company's responsibility toward them was being transferred to the government of Canada, the new power in the region. They wanted formal recognition of this in the treaty, especially as they had not received assistance (apart from some smallpox vaccinations) from the government during the previous six years. Just what the Canadian negotiators understood of these expectations and their implications is unclear.

The Cree of Treaty 6 were knowledgeable about previous treaties and had the benefit of an interpreter who spoke their language well. They understood that the written text was crucial to the newcomers, and McKay and Erasmus, who assured the chiefs that everything promised in the oral discussion was included in the written document, read and explained the entire text of the treaty to them before they signed it.[22] It seemed as though every reasonable effort had been made to ensure a common understanding, and reports of the proceedings suggest that both parties thought that they had found a mutually acceptable ground in August and September 1876, despite some fears and misgivings on the part of the Cree.

Misunderstanding indeed began to emerge quickly in the years after the signing, often because of unspoken assumptions on each side. For example, oral tradition claims that the Cree understood that the treaty allowed whites to use the land outside reserves for agriculture to a depth (from two inches to two feet, depending upon which elder is telling the story) necessary for that purpose. Whites, however, understood a land surrender in much more sweeping terms: it included water, fish, subsurface rights, forests, animals, and so forth. The Cree assumed that because whites had not asked for these items specifically, they were excluded from the treaty;[23] whites assumed that because they had not specifically been excluded, they were included. Whites assumed a surrender meant the end of aboriginal title outside the reserves; the Cree assumed they retained the title, and were permitting whites to use the land in a specified manner. Whites assumed the other treaty provisions were to be fulfilled only to the letter of the law, as cheaply and infrequently as possible. The Cree assumed a spirit of generosity and flexibility would prevail.[24]

## Treaty 7 (1877): The Government Approach

David Laird was an imposing figure. Known to the Indians at Blackfoot Crossing as "the tall White man," he was said to be six feet, four inches tall and he sought to conduct himself with honesty and seriousness of purpose in all areas of his life. Andrew Robb describes him as "sober, pious, high-minded, energetic, and capable," acting "always with the conviction that he was on the side of right and progress."[25] Elected to the House of Commons in 1873 as a Liberal from the brand-new province of Prince Edward Island, he was named minister of the interior and superintendent general of Indian Affairs when the Mackenzie Liberal government assumed office in November. His appointment was odd, for he knew little about the West or its peoples and had been cool to its integration into Canada. He quickly set about getting some first-hand knowledge, however, participating in the negotiation of Treaty 4. Curiously, despite his responsibility for the West, he appears not to have been involved in the drafting of, or the debate on, the North-West Territories Act of 1875.[26] In October 1876, shortly after the passage of the Indian Act, Mackenzie asked Laird to become the first lieutenant governor of the North-West Territories,[27] perhaps finding in his devoutly Presbyterian colleague qualities of character – "stern morality, caution, and devotion to duty" – that he wanted modelled in the western country.[28] It was Laird, clad in the colorful full-court regalia of a representative of Queen Victoria, who presided with NWMP Commissioner James F. Macleod over the negotiation of the last of the prairie treaties in September 1877. Whatever else they thought or came to believe about Treaty 7, Indians reportedly respected Laird as a man of his word: "the man whose tongue is not forked."[29]

Macleod had already established his reputation among the Indians. Directing NWMP operations in the southwestern prairies since October 1874 from a base at Fort Macleod, he had mostly eliminated the ruinous whiskey trade and depredations of the whites, maintained peace among the various tribes, and formed strong relations with leaders such as Crowfoot of the Siksika and Red Crow of the Kainai.[30] Born in Scotland, Macleod came to Canada as a child with his family in 1845. He trained as a lawyer, but also was interested in the militia and pulled political strings to go to Red River under Col Wolseley in 1870, remaining in the West until 1872. In 1873, Prime Minister Macdonald offered him an appointment as superintendent and inspector in the NWMP, then being established, and by 1876 he had risen to commissioner.[31] The relationship of trust established between police and Indians over the previous two years was decisive in persuading the uneasy Nizitapi and others to treat with the government.[32]

Originally, the government planned to hold the negotiations at Fort Macleod. Crowfoot demurred, insisting upon Blackfoot Crossing on the Bow River, in the midst of his own territory, about ninety miles northeast of the fort. Neither whites nor other tribes were happy with this change, but they reluctantly accepted. Security was not an issue for whites; indeed quite a few wives of officials, women from as far as Edmonton and the mission at Morleyville, and "the whole white population of Fort Macleod" turned out for the ceremonies.[33] Changing the site did, however, present a logistical problem. The government had a large party of its own to move to the crossing with supplies and food for themselves as well as supplies, gifts, and food for the assembled Indians. After Laird, who journeyed from Battleford, had rested at the fort for a few days, an advance NWMP party accompanied a substantial train of wagons to

Blackfoot Crossing. Two days later, the remainder of the police accompanied Laird to the meeting site. The lieutenant governor was struck by the location, where an easy ford could be made of the clear, rapid waters of the river. He reported:

> There is a beautiful river bottom on the south side of the river. It extended about one mile back from the river, and is some three miles in length. The river, as far as the eye can reach, is skirted close to the water by a narrow belt of cotton-wood and other trees.
>
> When I surveyed the clear waters of the stream, the fuel and shelter which the wood afforded, the excellent herbage on hill and dale, and the Indians camped in the vicinity crossing and re-crossing the river on the "ridge" with ease and safety, I was not surprised that the Blackfeet were attached to the locality, and desired that such an important event in their history as concluding a treaty with Her Majesty's Commissioners should take place at this spot.[34]

The government negotiators arrived with a colourful troop of 108 police in their red uniforms, 119 horses, and two 9-pounder guns.[35] From the beginning the government believed, as Adams Archibald put it bluntly just prior to the negotiation of Treaty 1 in 1871, that "military display has always a great effect on savages, and the presence, even of a few troops, will have a good tendency."[36] From 1876, the NWMP replaced the militia at these ceremonies, but the intent was the same. Of course the small police force in 1877 was but a corporal's guard compared to the nearly 4,400 Indians, many probably well-armed, camped at the crossing.[37] One of the police present at the event, Cecil Denny, recalled the kaleidoscope of sound, movement, and colour:

> There must have been at least a thousand lodges in camps on both sides of the river ... They were plentifully supplied with meat, having only just left the large buffalo herd down the stream to the east. Their horses, herded day and night, covered the uplands to the north and south of the camp in thousands. It was a stirring and picturesque scene; great bands of grazing horses, the mounted warriors threading their way among them, and, as far as the eye could reach the white Indian lodges glimmering among the trees along the river-bottom. By night the valley echoed to the dismal howling of the camp's curs, and from sun to sun drums boomed from the tents. Dancing, feasting, conjuring, incantations over the sick,

prayers for success in the hunt or in war, all went to form a pan-
orama of wild life vastly novel and entertaining, and seen but once.
Never before had such a concourse of Indians assembled on
Canada's western plains; never had the tribes appeared so con-
tented and prosperous.

In addition to the Siksika, Kainai, Piikani, Tsuu T'ina, and Stoney
Nakoda present to negotiate, there were, observed Denny, "many Crees
... drawn by curiosity to the treaty ground," Metis hoping to capitalize
on gratuity or annuity payments, and white traders from both north
and south especially interested in obtaining buffalo robes and offering
horses.[38] While the main purpose of the gathering was to arrange the
treaty, there were numerous sub-plots as trading and sacred ceremonies
intermingled; as many tribes, some of whom neither liked nor trusted
one another, and who competed for the same food supply, were in close
proximity and had to work together; and, moreover, as differences
played out within tribes between those who supported and opposed
the treaty.

Regrettably, existing accounts of the treaty discussions are frustratingly fragmentary in their coverage of what actually was said. Laird,
for example, reported, "the Commissioners [Laird and Macleod] met
the Indians at two o'clock on Wednesday [September 19]. An outline
was given of the terms proposed for their acceptance." The commissioners then told the chiefs to think over the terms with their people
and return the next day. When they reassembled, "we further explained
the terms outlined to them yesterday, dwelling especially upon the fact
that by the Canadian Law [Indian Act, 1876 and its antecedents]
their reserves could not be taken from them, occupied or sold without
their consent." They were assured of "their liberty of hunting over
the open prairie ... so long as they did not molest settlers and others in
the country."[39]

The Toronto *Globe* reported more details, but still gave only a very
abbreviated account of Laird's speech. The Great Spirit who made all
things, he said, allowed the Queen to rule "over this great country and
other great countries," and "made the white man and the red man brothers."[40] He spoke of the evenhanded introduction of law and order
through the NWMP, bringing stability to Native life. The Great Mother
also had decided to try to prevent the destruction of the bison.[41] The
treaty was offered, as it had been to other Indians over the past few

years, to enable them to live "in some other way" – i.e., farming or ranching – because "the buffalo will probably be all destroyed."[42]

In some important respects Treaty 7 paralleled Treaty 6, including the surrender of land, the formula for creating reserves, the blanket extinguishment clause, hunting rights, gratuities, annuities, implements, and an annual appropriation for ammunition, along with medals, clothing, rifles, and extra payment for chiefs and minor chiefs or councillors. But the written text also departed from Treaty 6. It stipulated that the government would pay teachers' salaries rather than maintain a school on each reserve. It did not include the three-year transition payment, the medicine chest, or the promise to provide emergency relief. It promised Indians specified numbers of farm animals, but if they chose to raise crops, they would receive fewer animals along with appropriate equipment and seed. Finally, reserve boundaries were spelled out as the Indian leaders requested (though, at Indians' insistence, they subsequently changed). Despite these differences, Laird told the assembled Indians, "the Queen wishes us to offer you the same as accepted by the Crees [in Treaty 6]. I do not mean exactly the same terms, but equivalent terms, that will cost the Queen the same amount of money."[43] In practice, the government would also provide transitional aid, medical aid, and emergency relief as though they had been written into the treaty.

The government's approach to offering animals in the treaties was well established by Treaty 7. According to Morris, it deliberately limited the number granted, and was "not bound to extend the number. This was done advisedly, by the successive Governments of Canada, and the Commissioners, acting under their instructions; for it was felt, that it was an experiment to entrust them with cattle, owing to their inexperience with regard to housing them and providing fodder for them in winter, and owing, moreover, to the danger of their using them for food, if short of buffalo meat or game." The government believed, furthermore, that Indians would always ask for more if they thought it would consent, and wanted them to understand that any increase "should be, not as a matter of right, but of grace and favor, and as a reward for exertion in the care of them, and as an incentive to industry."[44]

The chiefs mulled over the proposals with their people and returned to meet again with the commissioners. They were not overjoyed at the government's offer. They acknowledged the benefits of peace and stability resulting from the NWMP's presence. They pointed out, however, that Canada's offer was much less than that the United States had made to

Native Americans, though they acknowledged that it would be acceptable if made in perpetuity, rather than being quickly phased out as in the United States.[45] The Canadian government offered an initial gratuity of twelve dollars per head, and annuities "forever" of twenty-five dollars for each chief, fifteen dollars for specified numbers of minor chiefs, and five dollars "to every other Indian of whatever age." Payment was to be made "to the heads of families."[46] Button Chief (also known as Medicine Calf), war chief of the Kainai, thought that the annuities should be set at fifty dollars for each chief and thirty dollars "for all the others, men, women, and children." He also wanted compensation for the timber hitherto used by whites in the district, noting its rapid depletion.[47] Laird responded with what he thought was humour: "On the contrary, I said, if there should be any pay in the matter it ought to come from the Indians to the Queen for [the expense of] sending them the Police. Hereupon, Crowfoot and the other Chiefs laughed heartily at the Blood orator of the day."[48]

Evidently Button Chief articulated another hope of his people: that the government and the NWMP would prevent others – most notably the Cree and Metis – from entering and hunting in traditional Nizitapi lands. Since the advent of the NWMP, these competitors had exploited the bison without fear of Nizitapi reprisals. Laird refused: "the Crees and Half-breeds ... were the Great Mother's children as much as the Blackfeet and Bloods, and she did not wish to see any of them starve." They would only be prohibited from reserve lands.[49] The seemingly fair policy of placing all on an equal footing thus could work against the Nizitapi with respect to protecting their traditional, and limited, food supply.

Language and other cultural issues significantly impaired full understanding of the treaty terms and purposes. Difficulties related to the interpreters' competence were a greater issue at Treaty 7 than at most previous numbered treaties. Laird acknowledged that the commissioners' first interpreter, Kiaayo ko'-si (Bear Child, or Jerry Potts), was unsatisfactory, but believed that problem had been solved by hiring James Bird, who "has been many years among the Piegans and Blackfeet, and is a very intelligent interpreter." Further, the Nizitapi had selected their own interpreter, Jean-Baptiste L'Heureux, who "also rendered good service in this respect." The terms of the treaty nevertheless were "interpreted to the Indians"; eventually they accepted them, especially when Crowfoot, after long deliberation, assented.[50] Macleod then spoke with each tribe to determine where they wanted their reserves. To try to avoid future problems, Laird took pains to determine that the chiefs who signed the treaty were approved by their people to do so. Over fifty chiefs and councillors marked their sign ("X") or touched the pen as the mark was made on their behalf. Macleod stated, in part: "The Chiefs all here know what I said to them three years ago, when the Police first came to the country – that nothing would be taken away from them without their own consent. You all see to-day that what I told you then was true."[51] Gratuities were paid, the police band played "God Save the Queen," and the artillery fired a few celebratory rounds.

The deed was done, and in good faith – or so Laird, Macleod, and the government believed. For the government, the most important provision in Treaty 7, as in its predecessors, was the surrender of aboriginal title, ensuring peaceful settlement of, passage through, and exploitation of the resources on and in the treaty area: "The said Indians have been informed by Her Majesty's Commissioners that it is the desire of Her Majesty to open up for settlement, and such other purposes as to Her Majesty may seem meet, a tract of country, bounded and described as hereinafter mentioned." The consent of "her Indian subjects inhabiting the said tract" had been sought "to make a treaty ... so that there may be peace and good will between them and Her Majesty ... and Her Majesty's other subjects." Thus "the Blackfeet, Blood, Piegan, Sarcee[,] Stony and other Indians inhabiting the district ... do hereby cede, release, surrender, and yield up to the Government of Canada for Her Majesty the Queen and her successors forever, all their rights, titles and privileges whatsoever to the lands included within the following limits." It also stated that the "said Indians ... shall have the right to pursue their vocations of hunting throughout the tract surrendered ... subject to such regulations as may, from time to time, be made by the Government of the country ... and saving and excepting such tracts as may be required or taken up from time to time for settlement, mining, trading or other purposes" by the government or authorized persons. The remainder of the treaty spelled out the obligations on both sides resulting from the surrender, and set out reserve boundaries.[52]

Yet, despite the outward good humour and celebratory optimism of the day as signatures were at last affixed to the document, an underlying uncertainty lingered, especially for Indian leaders. A vignette reported by Oblate missionary Father Constantine Scollen is illustrative. At the signing ceremony, an ambivalent Crowfoot had refused to touch the pen when the "X" was inscribed opposite his name. About a year later, he asked Scollen what it meant to "touch the pen." Scollen told him it was equivalent to a signature on the document, and binding. Already

displeased with what he viewed as the government's laxity in fulfilling
the terms of the treaty, Crowfoot brightened at the thought that perhaps
the treaty was not binding upon him. Scollen quickly disabused him –
Crowfoot had accepted a gratuity in 1877 and an annuity in 1878 under
the treaty, which bound him to its terms. "I dare say," added Scollen,
"after all the old gentleman [Crowfoot] still had his own opinion."[53]
This episode not only shows the significant gap between the two sides'
understanding of what was entailed at the signing ceremony, but it also
likely profoundly affected Crowfoot's attitude toward the implications
of accepting anything further from the government.

### The Obverse Side of the Coin: Indians Approach Treaty 7

Isapo-Muxika was the most famous figure on the Indian side of the
Treaty 7 negotiations. Born into the Kainai tribe, his father was killed
when he was a young boy and his mother subsequently remarried a
Siksika. Thus he was Siksika by adoption. He demonstrated leadership
skills early, was involved in many battles with other tribes, and was
wounded several times. He received his name, Isapo-Muxika, after one
of these battles. Because he was friendly with white fur traders and
missionaries, often against the wishes of many in his tribe, he became
well-known in the white community, albeit by Crowfoot, the English
translation of his name. One factor in his achieving eminence was that
he survived the smallpox epidemic, which carried off several other able
chiefs. Another was his unusual ability to look to the long term: he recognized, for instance, that cooperation with the NWMP likely would be
of greater benefit than harm, since the police could stop the perpetual
intertribal conflict and whiskey trade that were killing so many of his
people.[54] Though within his tribe he was one of two head chiefs, the
police treated him as the true "leader of the entire Blackfoot nation."
At the same time, he understood that leadership among his people
depended upon diplomatic skills, on consultation and persuasion.[55]
Getting Indians to gather at Blackfoot Crossing for treaty talks would
not have happened without his insistence, prestige, and cooperation. At
the same time, Isapo-Muxika himself was filled with conflicted feelings
and foreboding about that very process. Were Indians securing their
future, or selling their birthright for the proverbial mess of pottage?[56]

A close contemporary of Isapo-Muxika was Mékaisto, or Red Crow,
of the Kainai tribe. His early prestige derived from reckless daring as a
young warrior; unlike Isapo-Muxika, however, he was never wounded

or injured in the many battles in which he participated. Like the Siksika
chief, he succeeded to leadership partly because the smallpox epidemic
carried off many chiefs, including his father. His reckless abandon was
worsened by heavy drinking, which led to tragedy in his personal life: his
wife was accidentally killed in one drunken brawl, he killed his brother
in another, and killed two other drunken men in a third. Hugh Dempsey
writes, "the shock of these troubles turned him from a reckless warrior
into a strong but conservative leader."[57] Mékaisto believed in cooperation with the police and whites, though less openly than Isapo-Muxika,
but only reluctantly supported meeting at Fort Macleod for discussions
with the government officials in 1877. The fort was fairly central for all
the tribes, and very convenient for the Kainai; according to Dempsey,
"he was so angered by the change of location [to Blackfoot Crossing]
that he was prepared to boycott the whole proceedings."[58] He gave in to
persuasion, but he arrived late and not in a good mood.

The Indian population of the southwestern prairie region was restless
and troubled. Scollen, who had laboured as a missionary over a period
of at least fifteen years, mostly with the Cree, but also among the
Nizitapi, reported in 1876 that the formerly "proud, haughty, numerous" Nizitapi had of late "fallen into decay" and were "utterly demoralized as a people." [59] He attributed the decline to the advent of the liquor
traffic, and to the smallpox epidemic. He had lived among the Nizitapi,
establishing the first Oblate mission in their territory, near the future
Fort Calgary, in 1873, and reported, "it was painful ... to see the state of
poverty to which they had been reduced. Formerly they had been the
most opulent Indians in the country, and now they were clothed in rags,
without horses and without guns." Then the NWMP – "their salvation"
– arrived, stopped the whiskey trade, and enabled them to recover significantly. The Nizitapi acknowledged the benefit of "the Red Coats,"
but Scollen believed that beneath this appreciation they feared "the
white man's intention to cheat them" and were "extremely jealous of
what they consider their country." No one, "white men, Half-breeds, or
Crees," was previously allowed to remain long in Nizitapi country, and
the whiskey traders had only been able to establish themselves because
of superior rifles. The police who chased out the traders were believed
by the ambivalent Nizitapi to be there also "to protect white people"
from them. As evidence of the state of things, Scollen pointed out that
farmers were settling around Fort Macleod and Fort Calgary. The
Nizitapi thought that "this country will be gradually taken from them
without any ceremony."[60]

Not explored by Scollen was the other major concern of all prairie Indians: the rapid decline of the bison. On his way to Blackfoot Crossing, Laird noted that most days his party saw bison, but in small herds with few calves, and that they saw many carcasses, from many of which even the hide had not been removed. He concluded, "the export of buffalo robes from the territories does not indicate even one-half the number of those valuable animals slaughtered annually in our country."[61] Indians were even more keenly aware of this than the lieutenant governor, and if they seemed prosperous and well-fed prior to the treaty negotiations, such perceptions were deceiving.[62] Well before the treaty, Isapo-Muxika had been realistic about the future, stating, "We all see that the day is coming when the buffalo will all be killed, and we shall have nothing more to live on, and then you will come into our camp and see the poor Blackfeet starving ... We are getting shut in, the Crees are coming into our country from the north, and the White men from the south and east, and they are all destroying our means of living."[63] In 1876, newspapers reported that the Nizitapi had to kill their prized horses for food.[64] Some bands missed the 1877 treaty talks because they had gone south to hunt, while others who attended were hungry and anxious to leave to seek out remaining buffalo herds in order to lay in supplies for the coming winter.[65]

Many Indians faced internal dissension over what to do about the white population. Some favoured uniting to confront and demolish the threat. They saw the Europeans in the region as still small in numbers and vulnerable. Seven years earlier, the Piegan had lost two hundred warriors in battles with the US army, and in 1870 over 170 peaceful Piegan were slaughtered by an American army contingent under Major Eugene M. Baker. Moreover, the Indians at Blackfoot Crossing knew that in 1876 the Sioux had annihilated General Custer's army forces at Little Big Horn. They also were angry that the US government had flouted its treaty agreements in the northern plains states and territories. Chief John Snow of the Stoney Nakoda writes, "at that time, numbers were on our side. If the various tribes of the western plains and the Rocky Mountain region had confederated at this point in history, they would have had enough strength and more than enough warriors to wipe out all the white settlers then in the area."[66] At the same time, notes Snow, "our medicine men, chiefs and elders had heard by moccasin telegram" of the waves of Europeans descending upon the eastern shores of the continent, described as being like "ants on a hill."[67] Any Indian victory would be Pyrrhic, and would in the long run bring down the wrath

of the whites, who then would dictate the terms of the future relationship. That Sitting Bull and the Sioux had fled to Canada's Cypress Hills
to escape the US army's revenge for Little Big Horn was not lost on
Canada's Indians. The wisdom of, and respect for, the elders prevailed
over the passion of youth, but by no means easily.[68]

Despite deep doubts, Indians were ultimately persuaded to enter negotiations with the government by two groups of whites for whom they
developed a degree of trust: the NWMP and the missionaries. Isapo-
Muxika, though thankful in many ways for the police presence, had also
been mistrustful of them, and not simply because their even-handed
application of the law often worked against the Nizitapi's interests. The
police had assured the chiefs that no land would be taken from them
without their permission, yet had established Forts Macleod and Calgary
without discussion. Rev John McDougall, a Wesleyan Methodist missionary from Morleyville, wrote in 1875 that Indians were "quite indig-
nant" that Fort Calgary "was being placed, as they said, right in the path
of the buffalo," impairing access to their principal food supply. "What
right," they demanded, "had the white man at this time to establish centres without the government conferring first about it with the Indians?"[69]
These forts, in turn, attracted settlers whose farming exacerbated the
problem. Missionaries, especially Father Albert Lacombe and McDougall,
who worked closely with Indians and gained their trust, persuaded them
that it was in their best interests to negotiate with the government. In the
years after the treaty, many Indians felt betrayed and bitter. There was
a Siksika legend that "when Big Knife [Lacombe] died, he had a black
dot on his heart ... because he was not honest with the Indians about
what they would lose if they made treaty."[70] Snow is scathing in his
comments about McDougall.[71] These men, and the NWMP, stand
accused of representing themselves as primarily concerned for Indian
welfare, only to be discovered subsequently to have been agents of the
government, imbued with enthusiasm for white settlement and economic
development. It must be said that both missionaries and police perceived
the situation differently, and would have been shocked to find their
actions construed in this way.

In 1875, Isapo-Muxika called together chiefs of the Kainai, Piikani,
and Siksika, and they produced a petition to Morris. They noted the
promise that "the Government, or the white man, would not take the
Indian lands without a Council of Her Majesty's Indian Commissioner
and the respective Chiefs of the Nation" and that whites had "already
taken the best location and built houses in any place they pleased" where

Indians hunted. Moreover, they noted that Metis and Cree were hunting year round "in the very centre of our lands." Intriguingly, they stated, "the land is pretty well taken up by white men now." They wanted an early meeting with the commissioner, and a stop put to settlement "till our Treaty be made with the Government." The exception to the exclusion of whites would be the NWMP and missionaries, "for we are much indebted to them for important services."[72] A preliminary meeting never took place, and the government moved directly to treaty negotiations in 1877.

### Considering Oral Tradition

Much is made of memory's importance and reliability in a traditional oral, or non-literate, culture. Indians' perceptions of the meaning of the treaty commitments rest heavily on their oral traditions. How to weigh such evidence along with traditional documentary sources is a challenging question. For many decades after the treaties the written record was viewed, particularly by whites, as primary; in the last twenty years or so, some have asserted that the oral record must be primary, and that the written record is useful only insofar as it does not contradict Indians' accounts.[73] Such an assertion is arguably extreme. Certainly oral memory is an essential part of the historical record, but it too must be understood for what it is, and must be as subject to critical evaluation as is the traditional documentary record.

John Tosh usefully distinguishes between oral history (the memory of recent events, usually not going back more than one or two generations) and oral tradition ("narratives and descriptions of people and events which have been handed down by word of mouth over several generations"). This "body of knowledge" becomes "the collective property of the members of a given society." Both, he notes, demonstrate "how non-élite communities construct and modify cultural meaning over time."[74] James V. Wertsch, who has studied collective memory, notes, "the memory of individuals is fundamentally influenced by the social context in which they function." The collective memory that emerges "is part of complex processes such as the negotiation of group identity." This, in turn, takes primacy over factual accuracy.[75]

Oral history and tradition also constitute performance, and performance is adjusted, however subtly, to context.[76] In other words, oral tradition evolves over time according to circumstances, and the selection, construction, and reconstruction of facts are intended to convey culturally relevant truths. The stories of cultural tradition are handed down, says Tosh, "because they hold meaning for the culture concerned. In the last resort, the traditions are valued not for themselves, but because other more important things depend on them."[77] Or, looked at another way, the historical record may be constructed and understood quite differently in oral and literate cultures.

Written documents are fixed, can at best constitute only a partial representation of the truth concerning the past,[78] and are subject to different interpretations depending upon individual authors and readers, new evidence, changing circumstances, and purposes. Oral traditions, also at best only partial representations of the past, are less fixed until written down and are more adaptable to changing circumstances and needs, so that they may focus on or bring out different aspects of the truth of the past. Both require careful analysis and interpretation. Historical "truth" is neither singular nor fixed in either case.

Dempsey views this issue still differently. He is sympathetic to the Indian perspective on the treaties, but still is critical of many modern elders' claims in their oral traditions. He notes that some have better memories than others; they are not all of equal quality or validity. He also believes that some claims in the oral record are part of "religious and historical revisionism," and a "case of Indians perceiving their history as they would like it to have been, rather than as it was." Along this line, and speaking of a Mi'kmaw case in Nova Scotia, William Wicken observes, "the story told has often been shaped [more] by what was needed than by what was."[79]

It is natural for oral tradition to evolve according to circumstances. But when it is written down – a tendency that increases as the society itself becomes less oral and more literate – it becomes "fixed," hence no longer "performed," and the now-written text becomes authoritative. It is not insignificant that much of the Indian oral tradition concerning treaties was written down in the period of renewed Native activism and radicalism of the 1970s and after. Thus the seemingly remarkable unanimity of elders' memory arguably represents a consensus on the nature of their story and the causes of the problems they then faced. Moreover, many of the elders whose memories were recorded had been to school and were no longer the product of an exclusively oral culture. Literacy may subtly affect how one thinks about orality, and how and what one chooses to commit to a permanent record.

The question indeed needs to be raised about whether Indian cultures were purely oral at any point from the 1870s onward. By the time the treaties were negotiated, numerous Indians (though still a small minority) had received some education and understood what written texts were about. It was not accidental that the Indians insisted that Wemyss Simpson write down the "oral promises" of Treaties 1 and 2 in 1871, or that they insisted that the written text of subsequent treaties be read to, and discussed with, them. They knew white memories depended on written texts. But the written text of the treaties and treaty negotiations, read and interpreted to the Indians present at the negotiations of 1876 and 1877 and readily available to later literate Indians in the form of the written vellum texts provided to each signatory band, in turn arguably influenced the elders' oral tradition.[80]

Moreover, arguably Indians' emphasis as they remembered the treaties in the immediate post-treaty period differs from their emphasis now – not because the modern recollection is necessarily erroneous, but because memory emphasizes different things in different contexts. For example, Indians in the late 1870s and 1880s were mostly concerned about treaty promises with respect to such matters as relief supplies, agricultural equipment, and freedom of movement off reserves. In the modern era, they focus more on treaty rights concerning peace, land, and sovereignty.

### The Indians' Evidence

The oral tradition of the Treaty 7 elders, committed to print in the later twentieth century, contains few additions to the specifics provided in Morris's book on the treaties. These elders understandably lament the absence of the words of many, or even most, of the chiefs who spoke during the negotiations, but they do not provide much to fill in the gaps. Their emphasis instead is on Indian perceptions of what actually took place, the larger meaning of the treaty, process, and problems of translation and comprehension. The most fundamental of these perceptions, important in the late twentieth century, are (a) that Treaty 7 was a peace treaty between parties who were equals; and (b) that it definitely was not a surrender of aboriginal title to the lands.

Typical of the notion that a peace treaty was negotiated is the statement of Kainai elder Louise Crop Eared Wolf:

> Our people's concept of the treaties is entirely different from the non-Native's point of view. Treaty, or *innaihtsiini*, is when two powerful nations come together into a peace agreement, both

parties coming forward in a peaceful, reconciliatory approach by exercising a sacred oath through the symbolic way of peace [i.e., smoking the pipe and exchanging gifts] ...

To further explain, Indian people's concept of treaty is one of creating a good and lasting relationship between two nations who at one time were at war with one another.[81]

The treaty, she claims, as does Wallace Mountain Horse, was analogous to treaties the Kainai entered into "with the Crows, Sioux, Crees, and other tribes."[82] The Stoney elders also maintain that they were called "to gather at Blackfoot Crossing to make a peace treaty." Snow records, from Stoney elders, that a chief asked Laird what the "real meaning" of the treaty was. Laird was said to have responded, "to make peace between us ... I am willing to pay you money if your put down your rifle and make peace with me." To Hilda Big Crow of the Tsuu T'ina, "a treaty is a contract of peace with the government; Treaty 7 was a peace treaty."[83]

Others see it as more than a "contract of peace with the government," and believe that one of its purposes was "to stop the Indians from killing each other, and to put an end to the disruptions caused by liquor."[84] Peace was to be not merely between Indians and whites, but also between tribes. This is confirmed by several elders, including Pat Weaselhead, whose father was a boy present at the negotiations; Camoose Bottle of the Kainai; and Annie Buffalo of the Piikani.[85]

The arrangement regarding land, according to the elders, was not a surrender but instead permission for whites to use the land subject to certain conditions. The Siksika understood that whites were to be allowed "to use the land to the depth of a plough blade. As Chief Calf put it, 'Today, we only loan out one and two feet. White men could dig post holes for the fences. The ground underneath we did not loan out.' One foot was for planting, another foot for post holes."[86] Ben Calf Robe, another Siksika, heard from the elders who had been at the treaty negotiations: "They agreed to make peace, but they didn't say anything about selling the land." This went for sub-surface minerals, water, trees, animals, birds, or fish: "The Old People didn't get asked to sell these things."[87] Reportedly, some Stoneys even believed the treaty was not very important: "If the land for growing wheat was all they [whites] wanted, there was no problem."[88]

Parenthetically, if true, it must be stated that this interpretation implies a rather selective memory on the part of the Indians negotiating the treaty. Treaty 7 was not an isolated event: other treaties, both in the United States and in Canada, as well as white activities in the American and Canadian West, preceded and framed the context of the 1877 treaty negotiation. In fact, some of those at Treaty 7 had witnessed the 1855 treaty with the Blackfoot in Montana, and probably others; they had seen the repeated seizure of reservation land granted to Montana Indians in 1855, and the ongoing desire of American whites for land for agriculture, timber, and minerals had been abundantly clear.[89] Other treaties before 1877 on both sides of the line had consistent and readily apparent consequences with respect to the land. The Geological Survey in Canada, which the Cree had stopped, made it clear that whites intended to use the land for purposes additional to farming. Whites also had long engaged in mining, hunting, fishing, and gathering. The Nizitapi, Stoney, and Tsuu T'ina of the future southern Alberta did not live in a cocoon. They were intelligent, experienced, and informed. They had an extensive context within which to understand the meaning of the treaties.

Nevertheless, if one accepts at face value the elders' interpretation, it underlines the problem of mutual incomprehension at the negotiation. One factor was cultural: each side had a different understanding of what a treaty entailed. Another was language: problems of translation, and the fact that many of the legal and spatial concepts in the English-language text of the treaty did not have precise equivalents in Native tongues. Sadly, neither side came to the Treaty 7 talks well prepared in this regard. One translator, Kiaayo ko'-si, was from Montana and of Kainai and white parentage and had spent time with the Kainai and Piikani; Blackfoot was his first language, and he only learned English from his second adoptive father after the age of five. He spent much time living or trading with various Indian tribes and developed a working knowledge of their customs and several of their languages. In 1874, his language skills and knowledge of the Nizitapi enabled him to introduce James Macleod to Isapo-Muxika and Mékaisto, among others, and act often thereafter as a scout and interpreter. But while Kiaayo ko'-si was competent in Blackfoot for everyday purposes,[90] he was a dismal failure at Blackfoot Crossing. His English skills were inadequate for understanding the legal language of the draft treaty, considerably compounding the problems of translation.[91] He was also inebriated much of the time. With respect to Kiaayo ko'-si's approach to translation, Dempsey relates the story that once a group of starving Indians came to Fort Macleod, where "the chief ... kept up a constant tirade for several minutes. Potts, sitting quietly, made no attempt to translate." At last, Macleod asked what the chief was saying. Kiaayo ko'-si's laconic response: "He wants grub."[92] Kiaayo ko'-si was well known for such pithy summaries of long Indian orations, and it seems likely that his translations of English speeches into Blackfoot were of much the same nature. For the treaty talks, far more detail and nuance obviously was essential. His incompetence led the chiefs to demand he be replaced.[93]

His successor James Bird, a former whiskey trader, had the virtue of not being intoxicated. He was fluent in Blackfoot, though his skills have since been denigrated, probably unfairly.[94] The Nizitapi wanted their own man, and asked Jean L'Heureux to serve as interpreter. He had been expelled from studies for the priesthood in Quebec because of allegations of immorality, but he headed west, where he passed himself off as a priest and lived among the Nizitapi. His Blackfoot evidently was good (though according to one source he comprehended the language far better than he spoke it), and he understood the requirements of translation at Blackfoot Crossing better than Kiaayo ko'-si, but English was not his first language and his ability to translate the high-level terminology accurately is debatable.[95] Scollen, an Oblate, spoke Cree quite well, and knew enough Blackfoot to help translate for Isapo-Muxika. John McDougall was fluent in the Cree language from his time among them near Edmonton, but had yet learned little Assiniboine, the language of his new Stoney charges.[96] As a result, the Nizitapi, Stoneys, and Tsuu T'ina had to conduct at least some of the discussion in Cree – a second language for them, but the lingua franca of the fur trade.[97]

A related issue for the Stoneys was the government preference for a single spokesperson despite the fact that the three bands each had chiefs who considered themselves equals. The government favoured Chiniki, who spoke both Stoney and Cree and who generally got on well with McDougall. Ultimately Bearspaw and Kichipwot (also known as Jacob Goodstoney), the other two chiefs, signed in addition to Chiniki.[98] But the treaty negotiations of September 1877 masked divisions among the Stoneys about whether the treaty was desirable. Moreover, many of them were not present, but were off in their traditional hunting grounds in British Columbia and the Kootenay Plains.[99]

Then there was the issue of conveying British legal and spatial concepts in Native tongues. It was unclear to many Indians "how the land was to be partitioned."[100] There were no equivalents for "cede," "surrender," "mile," "square," and "title," among other terms. Wilton Goodstriker comments dryly, "these difficulties with interpretation and terminology would have made for a trying day, and it is no wonder

several of the interpreters resorted to intoxicants. Today we would like
to ask the most proficient Blackfoot speakers to translate the entire text
of those talks, but so far there is no one able to do so."[101] That granted,
even under the best of circumstances anyone translating from one language to another finds that some words and phrases in one may not be
precisely rendered in the other, and even the most accomplished translators sometimes have to resort to circumlocution and a variety of imagery
to convey essential concepts. This problem is compounded when dealing
with radically different languages and cultures.

The other major factor leading to mutual incomprehension is simply
that each side came to the talks not only from different cultures, but with
different priorities and different ideas of what was involved. The meaning that any person or group attaches to a given text or process varies
according to context, intent, and perception. Simply because one side
perceives the process from a given perspective does not necessarily mean
that the other side, with a different understanding, is wrong, dishonest,
or duplicitous. Moreover, subsequent experiences also colour recollection of the process or text.

The Indian side was deeply troubled about what it should do. Perhaps
it was a peace treaty but, if so, the peace needed to be underpinned by a
relationship, binding on the government, to enable them to survive, even
flourish, under radically changing circumstances. With the bison disappearing before their eyes, they were going to have to learn to live off the
land in a very different way. That they did not fully apprehend what
these changes might mean was to be expected. But they, like all Indians
who had made treaties since 1871, knew that they needed means to
begin to forge a different life: farm implements, seed grain or cattle and
other animals, and farm instruction, as well as education for their children. Much of the chiefs' initial response to the terms of treaty addressed
these issues. Button Chief spoke of "large bags of flour, sugar, and many
blankets." Eagle Tail mentioned "flour, tea, tobacco and cattle, seed and
farming implements." Bearspaw wanted "provisions and money ... as
much as possible." Old Sun asked for "cattle, money, tobacco, guns, and
axes," and an end to whites' use of poison (for wolves).[102] Tsuu T'ina
elder Clarabelle Pipestem recalled that her people "entered into the
treaty for peace as well as for food and tools, livestock, education, medication, and freedom from taxes." Tom Heavenfire, another Tsuu T'ina
elder, held "that the treaty guaranteed 'ammunition money every year,
like the medicine chest'" and annuities. To that list, Maurice Big Plume
added "government protection." Most of these points were included one

way or another in the government offer, so the elders' tradition adds little in terms of specific provisions. The major contribution of these recollections is with respect to Indians' overall understanding of the treaty's purpose.[103]

The issue of security received as much attention. The NWMP's arrival had transformed Indians' lives. Isapo-Muxika put it bluntly: "If the Police had not come to the country, where would we be all now? Bad men and whiskey were killing us so fast that very few, indeed, of us would have been left today. The Police have protected us as the feathers of the bird protect it from the frosts of winter." Button Chief, in an oft-quoted line, said that the police had ended the liquor traffic: "I can sleep now safely. Before the arrival of the Police, when I laid my head down at night, every sound frightened me; my sleep was broken; now I can sleep sound and am not afraid."[104] A sound, peaceful sleep meant much to people who had suffered through the stresses experienced over the previous decade.

Experience with the police, who thus far had mostly kept their promises, predisposed Indians to accept the treaty. A relationship had evolved out of experience since 1874. Could that relationship be reliably assured in the future? In other words, would the government keep its promises? That was what troubled Isapo-Muxika as he mulled over the proposal. He and Mékaisto discussed the offer at length. Then they consulted with their respective chiefs. Isapo-Muxika apparently also discussed the matter with Pemmican, a respected elderly shaman, who eventually offered his reluctant and regretful approval. Isapo-Muxika's was the most influential voice among his people, and the decision-making weighed heavily upon him. After long deliberation in his lodge, he emerged, rode around the camp, and then spoke: "The reason I took much time to come out, I was thinking about what is going to take place. You know the White man is not being honest with the promises he is making to take care of you. I feel sorry for my children. They will no longer be able to live as they please. They will be restricted from everything."[105] This pessimism may have resulted in part from his assessment of the experience of Native Americans. He may have mistrusted Laird and Macleod, or he may have seen that they could not guarantee the future. Despite this, he signed the treaty, in effect concluding that change was inevitable and had to be accepted. Some of the Piikani heard him say: "All of you people, you have given up. The reason why I haven't given up [is that] in the future our way of living is going to change. We will no longer live our nomadic way of moving around. Away in the future there will be no more hunting or living from the earth." To reject the treaty and revert to war, as some wanted, "would be sad for the children of the future."[106]

Isapo-Muxika's words finally persuaded the reluctant chiefs to sign the treaty, partly because he reflected the fears of many, and partly because he articulated what they did not want to believe about the future but knew was true. He was more than a master politician, for his people recognized that there was no artifice in him. His agony was their agony. He embodied them, and spoke for them.

Mékaisto provides a somewhat different perspective. According to his biographer, Dempsey, he and most of the other Kainai chiefs "attached no great importance to the treaty." The treaty, says Dempsey, "called upon the chiefs to envision a life without buffalo, without nomadic camps, and without freedom. It was simply beyond their comprehension."[107] Mékaisto believed that in exchange for letting whites into the region, "the Queen would furnish [his people] with plenty of food and clothing ... every time they stood in need of them." He trusted Macleod and Laird, and accepted Isapo-Muxika's decision, agreeing to sign. But, notes Dempsey, he "had no clear grasp of the land aspects of the treaty" and did not understand it to mean giving up the traditional nomadic life of his people.[108] Perhaps. However, Garrett Wilson notes that one of the traders present at the negotiations, Charles Conrad of the I.G. Baker Company in Fort Benton, also was a friend trusted by Mékaisto. Conrad apparently "studied the treaty terms and conferred with Red Crow. Both agreed that 'it treated the Indians fairly, protected their rights, and was as good as they would get.'"[109] Mékaisto's subsequent actions provided leadership to settle on the reserve and commence farming.

PART 2

*Reflections on White and Indian Perceptions*
*of the Treaties and the Treaty Process*

Indians and whites did not always have a common understanding of the treaty process and its outcomes. Cultural differences often were such that, in Dempsey's opinion, "two people could be talking to each other without each person really understanding what the other meant." This was certainly the case with aspects of the treaty negotiations. When Indians "encountered something they did not understand," he writes, "they were usually too polite to say anything. As a result, the person speaking to them assumed they were fully aware of any consequence of the discussion."[110] Whites were just as disinclined to seek clarification of Indian statements.

This matter raises the question of just what is implied in the historical record, which states on several occasions that the treaty provisions were read to Indian leaders, often at their request, and were explained to them. Some have argued that this means Indians understood the treaty provisions; others point out there is no indication of precisely what was explained, or how.[111] Keeping in mind Dempsey's point, it seems unlikely that white explanations always provoked incisive questioning on the Indian side, or that all uncertainties were clarified. It seems more likely that government officials and translators such as like Morris, Christie, Erasmus, and McKay told the assembled chiefs what they thought they wanted or needed to know based on their understanding of Indian concerns. Even if men of both Indian and white ancestry and with Native language skills, such as Christie, Erasmus, and McKay, had had special insight into Indian culture and honestly wanted to do their best for the Indians, they themselves were not fully Indian and occupied a very different social, cultural, and occupational space with inevitably different perceptions. At the same time, it would be unjust to assume the chiefs were passive recipients of these explanations, given the number of issues they raised that are recounted in the written record. There must have been some give and take.[112] There equally had to be a large element of mutual trust.

Indians tend to regard the treaties as treaties of peace and, because of the sacred ceremony attached to the negotiations, as permanent and inviolable. According to Kainai elder Louise Crop Eared Wolf, "the exchange of gifts" sanctions an "agreement which can never be broken," and the smoking of the sacred pipe "is similar to the non-Native's swearing on the Holy Bible." The treaty was intended to create "a good and lasting relationship between two nations who at one time were at war with one another." Wallace Mountain Horse, also of the Kainai, recalled that they had frequently been at war with the Crow and Cree, but "we made treaty with them and to this day we are still on friendly terms with one another. There's no way a treaty that has been made can be altered."[113]

While there are multiple examples of this view, questions may be raised about it. Before 1871, peace treaties were about ending intertribal wars and creating the conditions for peace in more or less traditional and mutually understood circumstances. These solemnly negotiated peace treaties were violated when it seemed advantageous – for example,

when parties wanted to access or protect food resources, or to enact
revenge. Dempsey's 2010 study, *Maskepetoon*, is replete with examples
of Indian peace treaties made and violated from the 1820s through to
the peace of 1871.[114] And even that "peace" was not much different
than that of the earlier treaties. The Cree-Blackfoot treaty was also violated: the Cree repeatedly raided horses from the Kainai, considered acts
of war, and Mékaisto and other chiefs in the early 1880s requested that
the government and the NWMP intervene to prevent retaliation and the
outbreak of active conflict. Arguably, only decades later did the 1871
treaty take on the retrospective aura of permanence and inviolability. It
seems the treaties between the Kainai and Cree in 1871 and Kainai and
Crow in 1873 did not collapse into open conflict not because of sacred
promises, but because of the intervention of Department of Indian
Affairs officials and the NWMP.[115]

If the numbered treaties of the 1870s were thought of as peace treaties, it was likely in the sense of preventing rather than ending conflict. If
so, they were about maintaining peace in face of impending massive
change. Another important difference between the numbered treaties
and the intertribal peace treaties is that the latter had a more common
cultural nexus, while the former were between culturally disparate parties with different objectives and a higher risk of misunderstanding.

There also were differences about what ownership of land entailed.
Indians objected to the HBC's sale of their lands, which they believed
that neither the Queen, nor the HBC, nor any whites had ever owned.
They could hardly conceive that one could "own" land, at least in the
British sense of ownership, any more than one could own the air or the
water. If one *could* own land, it was clear to them that they, collectively,
had the primary right of ownership. For them, ownership related to the
territory over which Indian nations roamed to sustain themselves, and
which they could defend; their territorial boundaries remained highly
flexible and – to whites – ill defined.

Of necessity, Indians lived in harmony with, and according to the
bounty provided by, nature. Hunting and gathering required living in
groups of limited size and following a nomadic or semi-nomadic lifestyle. It inhibited the population growth and social or institutional developments that agriculture had necessitated and sustained in other parts
of the world. According to Cynthia Stokes Brown, traditional hunter-
gatherer societies typically had pretty good health, and "archaeologists
now believe that changing to domesticated food may have represented a
decline in the quality of diet, and certainly it meant an increase in the per

capita workload." Agriculture, then, was harder work than hunting and gathering, and only was acceptable when population pressures and declining food supply forced a change. Brown also asserts, "in statistical terms, one hunter-gatherer needed about ten square miles of favorable territory to collect enough food to live. One square mile of cultivated land, however, could support at least fifty people. Hence agriculture could support a human density fifty to a hundred times greater than hunting and gathering could."[116]

Whites, bound by their agricultural worldview and the need to feed and supply a rapidly expanding population, could not conceive of land in its natural state as productive; it had to be settled, enclosed, culti vated, and "improved." In this lay the English notion of land ownership. Roaming, hunting, and gathering did not confer ownership. By not using the land intensively, the Indian population was wasting its potential. Simpson told the Saulteaux at Fort Garry in 1871 that the road to wealth – which he assumed they wished to follow – "is not to trust to the wild grasses for raising cattle and horses, but to fence in the land, cultivate it, and thus get far more easily abundance of hay for their animals." Archibald put it even more baldly: "God ... intends this land to raise great crops for all his children, and the time has come when it is to be used for that purpose."[117] Just as Indians invoked the Great Spirit to affirm and seal their understanding of the treaties, so too did whites see their different and ultimate purposes, enabled by the treaties, as God ordained.[118]

Intertribal territorial disputes were frequently over access to resources – most often bison, in the cases of the signatories to Treaty 7 and the Plains Cree, but also other animals hunted for food and furs. They may not have fully grasped British-Canadian concepts of ownership, but they understood that under the treaties their traditional lifestyle would be gradually restricted as white settlement increased. While they hoped the government could protect the bison and even see them recover, most chiefs saw agriculture and a more settled way of life as inevitable, at least providing a necessary supplement to hunting and gathering. The price for their agreement to live in peace with the white settlers was government help to transition and survive.

A frequent theme in Indians' oral tradition is the notion that mines and forests were not mentioned in the treaty discussions, and thus were not granted to the newcomers. This too needs to be addressed. In the Treaty 3 area, Indians wanted compensation for trees whites had used in the past, which they received,[119] but after the treaty was negotiated

whites were able to make free use of the forests without additional compensation, except on reserve lands. All parties understood that was
included. As noted in the discussion of Treaty 3, the commissioners
made it clear that Indians would have rights to natural resources only on
reserves, an underlying principle of each treaty. With respect to the lands
of Treaties 6 and 7, employees of the Geological Survey had drilled near
Fort Carlton, but stopped when Indians objected; whites also had mined
coal at Edmonton without apparent opposition. The Siksika had stopped
miners in their area, and demanded compensation for timber used by
the police and other settlers. Also, they frequently visited the northern
American plains and foothills and were certainly aware of what whites
were doing with respect to mining and forestry further south. In other
words, by the time Indians came to treaty talks, they had seen that whites
intended to use the land for more than simply agricultural purposes. It
probably never occurred to the government officials that Indians would
not comprehend that surrendering land included subsurface and water
rights, as well as the flora and fauna that grew on the land or in the
water, because that was assumed in British-Canadian law. Perhaps the
most important point is that mining was specifically mentioned in
the talks at Treaties 6 and 7, and lumbering was mentioned in Treaty 6,
as activities whites might pursue, along with settlement, that would
eventually restrict Indians' traditional lifestyle.[120]

Indians of the nineteenth century perhaps regarded themselves as
autonomous, if not sovereign. The reality is that neither British-
Canadians nor Americans so regarded them. In the United States, they
were regarded as nations from the 1820s until at least 1871, but only in
a very restricted sense.[121] Such status did not confer any advantage.
Quite the reverse: nation-to-nation treaties meant that either side could
legally abrogate or alter the treaties at will, which the US government
did repeatedly. Moreover, nation-to-nation treaties were not justiciable:
that is, Native Americans could not take the government to court over
violations of treaties to which it was party. Thus, while Indians thought
of themselves as autonomous, they had a considerable disadvantage.[122]
Autonomy, as opposed to sovereignty, conferred a greater advantage
under the British system in the nineteenth century: Indians were regarded
as subjects of the Crown, and contracts between Crown and subjects
were in fact justiciable.[123]

Earlier, during the fur-trade era, Indians' autonomy appeared to
be acknowledged through the ceremonies with traders that created
and renewed alliances; this could be taken to imply some right of

possession. Traders were in Indian territory on sufferance, and gave gifts both during the trading ceremonies and for use of the Saskatchewan River.[124] But any latent notions of sovereignty, or even autonomy, were challenged with the arrival of the NWMP. The police assumed that they represented an existing overarching authority within which, with or without treaties, Indians were subjects. Initial Indian concerns about the police presence before the treaties – because they appropriated a limited amount of land and resources – were allayed to some extent as they imposed British-Canadian law and order and peace in a manner Indians at first accepted as impartial. The police helped to transform the theoretical status of Indians as subjects of the Crown into a more practical, visible reality. The treaty process, as understood by whites in the nineteenth century, in turn produced an agreement between Crown and subjects, not Crown and sovereign nations. Indians did not object to being called the children or subjects of the Great Mother by police or at treaty talks, perhaps because to them that represented acceptance and equality, despite an implied subordination. As the police, missionaries, and treaty negotiators understood it, Indians accepted that they were subjects of the Queen (as were whites), and therefore subject to her laws and not sovereign. However, whites did not assume that they and Indians shared the same status or rank. They had for some time regarded Indians as inferior and incapable of managing their own affairs, whether in the economy of the fur trade or in the impending era of settlement agriculture.[125]

For their part, Indians interpreted terms used in the treaty negotiations such as "mother," "brothers," or "children" differently than did whites. Jean Friesen observes, "an Indian perspective would suggest that in the Indian world kinship was the idiom through which reciprocal obligations were invoked in alliances," and that "*exchanges* were always embedded in some kind of kinship pattern whether real or fictive." Kinship provided the basic terms of the exchange or alliance. To them, therefore, "in using such language the treaty commissioners were accepting an implied moral responsibility of greater proportions than they realized."[126] Whites saw Indians' acceptance of themselves as the Queen's children as an acceptance of her superior rank and authority; conversely, no one spoke of whites as children of the chiefs. For Indians, entering into a relationship with the Great Mother carried with it an expectation of receiving care, as a mother generously provides for her children.[127] Whites would have argued that children properly would mature into self-sustaining adulthood.

Each side in the talks had different perceptions about how the other understood the future. What the government negotiators seem to have heard was that Indians wanted to settle down, learn to work (i.e., farm), receive initial help in doing so, and have their children educated. Indians after all had seen farms operated by whites and Metis near forts and settlements, and had been exposed in a limited way to schooling prior to the treaties. A few in the Treaty 6 area of the future Alberta had engaged in some farming.[128] There would be a transition period, but it would surely be short. The government believed that it had extended the hand of friendship and had made a firm and realistic commitment to assist Indians in their transition to a brighter, cheerier future. A hand up, to it, did not mean an obligation to provide perpetual handouts.

Yet this scarcely represented the mood of the Indians. For them the future was opaque, and gloomy at best. They were divided as to the wisdom of accepting the treaties, but were unsure about the alternative.[129] Who was to know if the particular terms of a treaty were good? What they most wanted, needed, and believed (or at least hoped) they had secured through the treaty process was an economic relationship and a sacred commitment that they would be treated as kin, supported, and supplied with what was needed in changing circumstances in the future. Many of the details were almost certainly less important to Indians in 1876 and 1877 than a generous and supportive partnership into the indefinite future that would enable them to retain the essence of who they were.

Especially in the last half-century or so, some Indians have asserted that their ancestors in the 1870s were sovereign peoples negotiating solely with the Imperial Crown and not with the government of Canada. This notion is important in law and politically in the present day, and is vital to understanding how many Indians view the treaty relationship. However, it would have been incomprehensible to Canada's treaty commissioners, and to the government of the late nineteenth century. Officials' references to the Queen were intended as metaphor; none would have understood that they represented the Queen personally.

To bolster their argument, some Indians claim that the Canadian government was never mentioned in the treaty negotiations, which were conducted solely in the name of the Queen. That claim does not withstand close examination. The government was in fact mentioned several times, although the details of how it functioned likely were obscure. As early as 1871, the Cree chiefs referred to it when they sent their petition to Archibald.[130] At the Treaty 6 negotiations, Poundmaker stated that he wanted "the advice and assistance of the Government."[131] Moreover, the government was mentioned specifically and repeatedly in each of the treaties from Treaty 3 to 7, documents that were read and explained to Indian leaders.

That issue aside, the treaty commissioners never would have understood or accepted that they in fact were direct emissaries from, or authorized representatives of, Queen Victoria herself. For them the Queen was the personification of the state. The commissioners were appointed by, and derived their authority from, the federal government of the Dominion of Canada – Her Majesty's Canadian Government. Each lieutenant governor had been a federal politician, and both Morris and Laird referred to having been members of, and to consulting with, or having been sent by, the Queen's councillors (i.e., the cabinet) in Ottawa. The governor general represented the Crown (and in the 1870s was regarded as the only true representative of it in Canada), but was subject to the direction of the Canadian government as the Queen was to the British government. The governor general appointed every lieutenant governor on the dominion government's recommendation. These officials reported to the federal government, and in the 1870s were regarded more as servants of that government than as representatives of the monarchy.[132] This was especially the case in the North-West Territories, which was directly under federal jurisdiction, and where the lieutenant governor's principal duty was to carry out federal policy. Even if, for the sake of argument, the lieutenant governor during the treaty negotiations was exercising a different role and in some way was construed to be a representative of the monarch, Queen Victoria was a constitutional monarch who could not exercise powers, or conclude treaties, independently of her government.

Though internally self-governing for over twenty years, in the 1870s Canada was regarded internationally as a British colony. The dominion had no power to treat with sovereign nations, nor did it have any desire to do so.[133] Canadians were happy to be subjects of the British Crown, and assumed that the Native population of British North America enjoyed the same status. Indians had become a matter of internal, domestic administration in British North America prior to Confederation. The post-Confederation numbered treaties were understood, therefore, to be a matter of internal, domestic policy, negotiated with the Indians of Canada by the government of Canada on behalf of the people of Canada. Legally, Indians had not sovereignty but acknowledged rights, and it was these that the treaty process was expected to address. The treaties, therefore, were certainly sui generis – but to Canadians they were internal administrative agreements, contractual or covenantal, between the Canadian government ("the Crown") and some of its subjects, thus fulfilling the commitment made when the British transferred Rupert's Land to the dominion. Parliament did not ratify them, although they were referred to the governor general for approval. There is no indication that Queen Victoria was even aware of the treaty process, or that her British government had any interest – let alone involvement – in it beyond ensuring that the Canadian commitment to treat with Indians was included in the transfer agreement of 1869. These treaties were of a very different order than international treaties.[134]

Thus the idea that in the treaty process of the 1870s sovereign Indians were negotiating directly with the Queen, who had the power to dictate policy to her Canadian government, is an interesting later development but bears no resemblance to how the treaties were understood by officials or government in the late nineteenth century. It was that contemporary understanding that shaped the government's policies with respect to post-treaty Indian affairs.

Prior to 1870, the Canadian government had not given much serious thought to the requirements of the treaty process beyond what had been done in the Robinson and Manitoulin Island treaties. Even in 1867, Canada assumed that the British would negotiate with the western Indians prior to transferring the HBC's lands. As late as October 1868, the British shared that expectation: "Indian Reserves ... will be made by Her Majesty's Government ... before the Company's territory is transferred to Canada."[135] Yet by the following March the date for Canadian takeover – 1 December 1869 – had been advanced, and the resultant memorandum of agreement included the statement, "It is understood that any claims of Indians to compensation for lands required for purposes of settlement, shall be disposed of by the Canadian Government in communication with the Imperial Government."[136] The document did not assume Indian sovereignty, only compensation for loss of the right to use the land, as had been British practice in Canada long before the new dominion assumed control of Indian policy.[137]

In practice, the "communication with the Imperial Government" envisaged in 1869 became some communication with the HBC and use of some former HBC employees as treaty negotiators in some of the numbered treaties. This was mainly because they were thought to have expertise in dealing with Indians, not because they were expected to guide Canadian policy. Macdonald reportedly told Sir Stafford Northcote of the HBC that "Indians ... are the great difficulty in these newly civilized countries." While they had been a problem for the Americans, he thought "the Hudson's Bay Company have dealt with the Indians in a satisfactory way. The policy of Canada is also to deal with the Indians in a satisfactory manner." The prime minister planned to have HBC officials at the various fur trade posts hand out the annuities once the treaties had been negotiated, because they "are known to these Indians," and it would "keep the Indians in good humour." Plainly, Macdonald had little conception of the importance to Indians of the annual ceremony as regular symbol of renewing a relationship. To deduce from this that "Macdonald intended no departure from the relationship that the HBC had established with First Nations," as one work asserts, is at least open to question.[138] The policies embedded in Canada's Indian legislation, in wardship leading to assimilation, and in the treaty relationship were fundamentally different from the HBC-Indian relationship in the fur-trade era. The notion that Canada intended merely to continue HBC policies makes sense only in the most general terms of maintaining peaceable relations. The bases of Canada's very different policies for the future were already in place.

Canada's purpose was to get Indians settled on reserves, to open the land to white occupation, and then to transform and absorb the Indian population. In 1871, the deputy superintendent general wrote, "the Acts framed in the years 1868 and 1869, relating to Indian affairs, were designed to lead the Indian people by degrees to mingle with the white race in the ordinary avocations of life."[139] Canada's goal in the West from 1870 did not turn out quite as planned. With hindsight, the reserve system established under the treaties, and the status of wardship long practiced in Canada and confirmed in the 1876 Indian Act, can be seen to have inhibited rather than encouraged this process. However, in the 1870s the government expected that as Indians grew accustomed to agriculture and settled life, and as they were educated in the schools and converted by Christian denominations, they naturally would wish to give up their Indian status and embrace the rights of full British subjects in Canada.

## CONCLUSION

In the 1870s, the Indians of Canada's prairies and parklands dreamed their culture would survive and even be renewed. The Canadians, for their part, dreamed of a mainly agricultural territory adding to the prosperity of the entire nation. Yet the Canadians had only vague ideas about the requirements to achieve that dream. At the outset, government thinking about how to secure peaceful possession of the land, and how to proceed afterward, was largely imagined within the central Canadian pre-Confederation experience, and out of a desire to avoid the experience of tragic conflict with Native Americans that accompanied the settlement frontier in the United States. The process of negotiating treaties over six years took the government into new territory, figuratively as well as literally. Indian persistence resulted in treaties that became more generous in details than the government had originally envisaged, but remained essentially unchanged both structurally and in their fundamental principles from Treaty 1 to 7. Nor did the process produce much change in the larger goals of Canadian Indian policy. That policy was predicated upon transforming Indians, not preserving their culture and lifestyle. Canadians understood the treaties to be a significant step underpinning that process.

Sarah Carter and Walter Hildebrandt write that the treaties "meant the profound diminishment of the land base, economies and many of the basic freedoms of First Nations," while permitting the white settlement, economic development and exploitation of the prairie region.[140] The implication is either that none of these things would have occurred without the treaties, or that the treaties somehow could have been instruments to sustain and secure the old ways. However, the Indians' land base, economies, and freedoms were compromised before the treaties. They knew that the old ways already were not sustainable without change, and that the advancing frontier of white settlers would not be halted. The treaties, in part, were an acknowledgement of that reality. The incoming tide was about to transform the region. Therefore, the plans proposed in the treaties and accepted (if understood differently) by both sides – settlement on reserves, education, managed change – at least constituted an effort to confront the inevitable and mitigate the impact. How these hopes and commitments would unfold in practice remained to be seen.

Such problems only became apparent in the future. Meanwhile there was hope and optimism. In September 1877, the negotiations at Blackfoot Crossing came to a cheerful close:

> The chiefs presented an address to the Commissioners, expressing the entire satisfaction of the whole nation with the treaty, and to the way in which the terms had been carried out. They tendered

their well-wishes to the Queen, the Governor, Col. McLeod, and the Police Force. They ... said that it was their firm determination to adhere to the terms of the treaty, and abide by the laws of the Great Mother. Potts, the interpreter at Fort McLeod, said he never heard Indians speak out their minds so freely in his life before.

In reply, the Lieutenant-Governor said he was much pleased to receive this address from the Chiefs of the great Blackfeet nation, which in fact was to the Great Mother, as the Commissioners were merely acting for her, and carrying out her wishes. He was certain she would be gratified to learn of the approval of the Chiefs and their acceptance of her offers. In return the Great Mother only required of them to abide by her laws.

Macleod concurred, and promised to continue to be the Indians' "friend" and to do what he could for their welfare. He added: "You say that I have always kept my promises. As surely as my past promises have been kept, so surely shall those made by the Commissioners be carried out in the future. If they were broken I would be ashamed to meet you or look you in the face; but every promise will be solemnly fulfilled as certainly as the sun now shines down upon us from the heavens."[141]

There seems no good reason to think that Morris, Christie, and McKay in Treaty 6 and Laird and Macleod in Treaty 7 bargained other than in good faith, even if they and the Indians understood some things differently.[142] They all shared the intense emotion, passions, enthusiasms, intensity, and commitment of those days together. It was, however, mostly up to others to carry out the terms of the treaty: men who had not been there, who had not shared the experience, the give and take, the uncertainties, and finally the trust that went into making and signing that document. Many of Isapo-Muxika's deepest fears would be realized. It would not be long before Macleod would have wished to hide his face from those whom he addressed that sunny September day.

Such, at least, is a widely accepted view of the treaties and subsequent history of Indian-white relations. That there is much merit in it must be acknowledged. And yet the truth of the matter is not so simple. The sense that Indians and whites had reached a clear understanding and lasting friendship at the closing ceremonies for Treaty 7 masked substantial underlying differences about the meaning of the treaty process and commitments, and what actually had been achieved. Subsequent events and changing circumstances would soon challenge some assumptions, and reveal underlying attitudes, of treaty negotiators on both sides. A case in point: consider the peroration of Alexander Morris's 1880 essay on the Indians with whom he had recently treated: "And now I close. Let us have Christianity and civilization to leaven the mass of heathenism and paganism among the Indian tribes; let us have a wise and paternal Government faithfully carrying out the provisions of our treaties, and doing its utmost to help and elevate the Indian population, who have been cast upon our care, and we will have peace, progress, and concord among them in the North-West."[143] Among whites, Morris was one of the most sympathetic to and optimistic about Indians, but this was not the discourse of a man who regarded them as equals.

Hon. Alexander Morris, here as minister of inland revenue,
was a government commissioner negotiating Treaties 3 to 6
and author/compiler of *The Treaties of Canada with the Indians*
(1880). Library and Archives Canada/Topley Studio fonds/
PA-025468 (MIKAN 3476623).

William J. Christie, inspecting chief factor for the HBC's
Saskatchewan District, ca. 1860. He was headquartered at
Edmonton (1858–72) and served as a government commissioner
for Treaties 4 and 6. Hudson's Bay Company Archives, Archives
of Manitoba HBCA 1987/363-E-700-C/94 (or N15853).

Chief James Seenum of the James Seenum band signed Treaty 6
and thereafter remained a strong spokesman for his people, and
loyal to the government in 1885. Provincial Archives of Alberta
B 1056.

Chief Ermineskin, of one of the Bear Hills (now Maskwacis) Cree bands, is pictured here in 1884 with Matthew McCauley, later the first mayor of Edmonton. Provincial Archives of Alberta B 1047.

Hon. David Laird, minister of the interior, was a commissioner
at Treaty 7, served two terms as Indian commissioner, and
worked hard to implement his understanding of the treaties.
Library and Archives Canada, Topley Studio fonds/ PA-025478
(MIKAN 3476755).

James Farquharson Macleod of the NWMP famously won Native peoples' loyalty, was a commissioner at Treaty 7, and later served as a magistrate and judge. Glenbow Museum Archives NA-23-2.

Isapo-Muxika, a prominent Siksika chief, signed Treaty 7 with
very mixed feelings but generally supported cooperation
with whites. Provincial Archives of Alberta P-129.

Crowfoot

Mékaisto, a leading Kainai chief, signed Treaty 7 and, convinced that the bison would not recover, led his people to accept a settled life on the reserve. Provincial Archives of Alberta B 1054.

Stamixo'tokan (also Chula), a prominent Tsuu T'ina chief, signed Treaty 7 and later proved a staunch defender of his people and their reserve lands. Provincial Archives of Alberta P-109.

John Chiniki, chief of a band of Stoney Nakoda, signed Treaty 7 but controversially participated in delineating reserve boundaries without consulting chiefs of other bands. Glenbow Museum Archives NA-662-1.

Peter Erasmus, a Metis guide, trapper, farmer, entrepreneur, teacher, and government servant over a long life, was also a capable linguist and acted as a translator at Treaty 6. Provincial Archives of Alberta B 976b.

Kiaayo-ko'si (better known as Jerry Potts) was a Metis guide and interpreter who introduced Isapo-Musika and Mékaisto to the NWMP, but was a failure as a translator at Treaty 7. Glenbow Museum Archives NA-1237-1.

PART TWO

# Implementing the Treaty Commitments
# in the District of Alberta to 1905

# 3

# The Reserve Era to 1905: An Overview

The Canadian government deliberately set out to deal with Indians in a manner different from that of the US government. Partly, of course, this resulted from a practical need to avoid armed conflict. However, Canadians also tended to assume that as inheritors and exponents of what they believed was the superior British way of doing things, they would indeed be more sensitive and honourable in upholding their promises. The task of government officials, wrote Prime Minister Sir John A. Macdonald in 1880, must be "the carrying out of all treaty stipulations and covenants in good faith and to the letter."[1] This was not as straightforward a matter as it first seemed. Officials and Native peoples understood those commitments quite differently, as the early reserve era would demonstrate. Beyond these misunderstandings, however, many additional problems arose from what J.R. Miller describes as the government's "bumptious," "insensitive," and seemingly incompetent approach to administration.[2]

One of the government's basic assumptions was that Canada's major treaty commitment in return for unobstructed title to western lands was to help Indians transition from hunting and gathering to settled agriculture. The ultimate hope was that they would embrace the values of the individualist, acquisitive capitalist society of which they were expected to become an integral part. A related understanding was that Indians actually wanted to make this change and would support an active and rapid transition.

The government in the 1870s did not plan for a large permanent administrative structure because it believed that within two or three years, or perhaps ten years at most, it could dispense with farming instructors as Indians turned to the new way of life and became individually and communally self-supporting on the reserves. Indian Commissioner Edgar Dewdney told Native leaders gathered at Fort Walsh in 1879, "if they would only make up their minds to settle down, I was sure that in two or three years they would be independent and have plenty to live on, without begging from the Government." A year later, he told Macdonald, then superintendent general, that "in another year I think a few instructors might be dispensed with in some districts where the Indian reserves are in good working order, and they can be placed in a new reserve where the Indians are not so far advanced."[3]

That is, just as in white society where people were constituent parts of self-supporting families, communities, and municipalities that provided primary care for one another, including the sick, disabled, and elderly, so too would Indians share these values and rely little on the government. Politicians in 1880 would not have conceived the extent of the bureaucracy in place a quarter-century later to administer Indian Affairs, nor that a treaty commitment for emergency famine relief and a medicine chest would become a heavy, ongoing welfare expense. Despite the evidence of 1879, government officials and Indians also appear to have believed that the bison and other game animals would recover enough, at least in the short term, to ease the Indians' transition and the government's burden for relief. That did not occur, and the government was stunned at the demands a starving and weakened people placed on its limited resources (see chapter 4 in this book). In this chapter, I outline the administrative structure of Indian Affairs as it applied to the prairie West, and particularly to Alberta. I also sketch aspects of the band and reserve structure, and population development, over the period from the treaties to 1905, to provide a framework for the themes in subsequent chapters.

## ADMINISTRATIVE STRUCTURE

At the apex of government administration was Indian Affairs, headed by the superintendent general, which from 1880 was a separate ministry and cabinet post.[4] Indian Affairs was a branch of the Department of the Secretary of State for the Provinces (1867–73), and then of the Department of the Interior (1873–80) before it became a separate department in 1880, though it normally still fell under the minister of the interior, who also was superintendent general of Indian Affairs.[5] The superintendent general dealt with major policy matters and legislation, and with patronage appointments – which included most of the "outside service" (officials in the field, as opposed to the "inside service" bureaucrats in Ottawa) who carried on the administration in the West. Patronage also governed awarding government contracts for equipment, supplies, transportation, construction, medical attendance, and so forth. Even after Macdonald ended his direct responsibility for Indian Affairs, the prime minister might at any time choose to exert influence in policy or patronage matters. It also was to the prime minister that the North-West Mounted Police usually reported, and it was he who dealt with their deployment and other police-related matters that influenced the governing of Indians.

The chief civil servant was the deputy superintendent general: he ran the department from Ottawa, and interpreted and implemented legislation and policy.[6] In practice, he also was tremendously influential in shaping legislation; most of the time the responsible ministers trusted his advice. The deputy was, moreover, the principal gatekeeper with respect to expenditure, and most deputies were in accord with and willing to impose the government's parsimonious expectations.[7] They were responsible for Indian administration across the country, but because of the great expense associated with the region covered by the numbered treaties, the prairie West tended to receive a greater proportion of attention than the deputies might have wished. Most of them had little direct experience with western Indians, and therefore limited sympathy; but considerable experience in the exceptional case of Hayter Reed seems only to have produced greater rigidity, as I will show in subsequent chapters.[8]

The chief official on the ground in the West was the Indian commissioner, a position created in 1873.[9] The commissioner travelled throughout the treaty region; received correspondence from agents, farm instructors, and police; and formulated recommendations for his superiors in Ottawa. Because each also was a high-level patronage appointment, they not only corresponded with the deputy superintendent general, but directly with the superintendent general. Brian Titley sums up the Indian commissioner's task as "to put in place and render workable the apparatus of containment implicit in government policy. The assertion of State authority over Native communities was the fundamental aim." Titley quotes Dewdney as declaring in 1884 – a year of considerable unrest – that Indians must accept "the supremacy of the white man and the utter impossibility of contending with his power."[10] In the seven or eight short years since the treaty negotiations, government thinking had moved far away from any notion of

real partnership, let alone kin relationship, envisaged by Indian signatories to Treaties 6 and 7.

When Macdonald and the Liberal-Conservative Party returned to
power in 1878, the prime minister, in his capacity as superintendent
general of Indian Affairs, sought the advice of then-Commissioner David
Laird, his most experienced man on the ground and former treaty commissioner, as to what structures would be necessary to carry out treaty
obligations and the Indian Act's requirements. Laird recommended
appointing "permanent agricultural instructors," each of whom might
have charge of as many as three or four bands where reserves were
grouped closely. He suggested five instructors for Treaty 4, eight for
Treaty 6, and two for Treaty 7. This, he thought, would obviate any
necessity for "Indian sub-Agents," leaving the very few agents with the
task of paying annuities and supervising the farm instructors, then envisaged as the main reserve-level officials, and expenditures. With respect to
agents, it is perhaps worth noting that in 1878 there was but one, M.G.
Dickieson, for the whole of Treaty 6, and that Col. Macleod of the
NWMP acted as agent for Treaty 7.[11] (It is useful to keep this in mind
when interpreting the terms of Treaty 6 that provided for a medicine
chest to be kept at the Indian agent's house, which in Dickieson's case
would have been in Battleford and therefore of little use to Indians in
most of his jurisdiction.) There is nothing to indicate that the government in the early post-treaty years envisaged the larger number of agents
later in operation. Nevertheless, the task of overseeing the whole of
Treaty 6 was so obviously impossible for a single person that in 1879
Dewdney restructured it to have three agents: Palmer Clarke in the eastern end, Col. James G. Stewart in the western end (future Alberta), and
W.L. Orde, who also acted as superintendency clerk, in the centre at
Battleford.[12]

Macdonald was disposed to follow much of Laird's advice, at least at
first. Accordingly, Indian bands were grouped into "farming agencies,"
with a farm instructor for each. In 1880, for the Treaty 7 area, there was
one such instructor for each of the Stoney, Siksika, Piikani, and Kainai
(the Tsuu T'ina were disputing their reserve location), and two supply
farms were established, at Pincher Creek and at Fish Creek near Fort
Calgary. For Treaty 6's future Alberta section, there were three farm
instructors: one for six bands in the district of Bear Hills/Pigeon Lake,
one for four bands in the Lac la Nonne/Rivière Qui Barre area, and one
for three bands in the Saddle Lake district. A position for a fourth farm
instructor for bands in the region of Whitefish Lake/Lac la Biche was

unfilled. The Indian agent, Stewart, was based at Edmonton and supervised the farm instructors and twelve or fifteen bands.[13] However this skeletal structure was devised at a time when many reserves had not yet been surveyed, when some Indians were contesting the boundaries that had been surveyed, and when most of the Indian population still pursued a traditional lifestyle a good deal of the time. The government had distributed agricultural implements and farm animals from as early as 1878, but there were regular complaints of shortages that hampered attempts at farming.

By 1905, much had changed. Most reserves were well established, and a majority of Indians generally resided on them. Agriculture and some traditional and non-traditional economic activities in large part sustained them (albeit still with considerable government aid), and a majority of Indian children were in school for at least part of their childhood. In addition to the Indian commissioner, there were three inspectors of Indian agencies and reserves for Treaties 4, 6, and 7. Within the district of Alberta there was one agent for each of five reserves in Treaty 7, and three agents, each in charge of several small reserves, in Treaty 6. There were four or five medical officers for the district, to say nothing of other physicians paid to respond to health concerns; in 1880 there had been no medical officers specifically for Indian Affairs, though NWMP surgeons (three or four at most for the whole of the North-West Territories) did their best to meet needs. In 1905, each agent headed a separate staff, which usually included a couple of farm instructors, an interpreter, sometimes a clerk and issuer of goods or rations, several stockmen for reserves that focused on raising cattle, and sometimes a teamster. There was a small hospital staff (mostly nursing sisters) on the Kainai reserve. Rather than living at a distance, officials (except for physicians) were required to live on a reserve. In total, there were approximately fifty officials at the agency or reserve level in the district of Alberta in 1905.[14] None of this is related to staffing or inspection of schools,[15] nor does it cover the number of officials required to secure and distribute supplies and goods to the reserves, or the bureaucrats who oversaw matters from the commissioner's office or Ottawa, or the number of NWMP required to maintain security and peace between Indians and whites, or contract employees such as physicians.

The division of the North-West Territories into districts in 1882 gradually had an impact on "Indian administration." Indian policies devised by the federal government, and by the Department of Indian Affairs (created in 1880), applied either across the country, or at least across the prairie region. The major DIA administrative divisions at first were treaty areas, but from 1882 the new district of Alberta included the western portion of Treaty 6 and all of Treaty 7. The Alberta portion of Treaty 6 was usually administered from Edmonton, although occasionally the Saddle Lake district was included in the inspectorates centred at Battleford. Within a few years after 1882, however, the new district boundaries in the North-West Territories provided a political-geographic framework for the provision of government services, including Indian Affairs.

Finally, it is important to consider department policy with respect to developing a measure of reserve self-government. In 1868, Ottawa, as part of its policies to lead Indians to assimilation and enfranchisement, legislated the creation of elective band councils, limited to three-year terms, with a view to encouraging Indians to manage local, internal affairs. The policy was systematized, expanded, and revised repeatedly in subsequent iterations of the Indian Act, as well as the Indian Advancement Act of 1884, though usually without much interest from Indians themselves. Deputy Superintendent General James Smart wrote in 1897, "the department's policy has ... been gradually to do away with the hereditary and introduce an elective system, so making ... these chiefs and councillors occupy the position in a band which a municipal council does in a white community." He noted with some disappointment that the provisions "have not been taken advantage of as speedily or extensively as could have been desired." The government decided to be more proactive, and by the end of the 1890s imposed the policy on almost all bands in Ontario (except for Treaty 3), Quebec, and the Maritimes.[16]

As for the treaty Indians from Treaty 3 in western Ontario to the district of Alberta, the government generally believed that they were too primitive to be trusted with elective institutions. When the treaties were signed in the 1870s, a number of officials assumed that the provisions of Canada's Indian legislation would apply in the West as well as elsewhere, as will be seen. By the early 1880s, Dewdney concluded that only one band in the entire region, the St Peter's band in Manitoba, might be given an elective council, though he feared that the chief might correctly understand that elective institutions constituted a threat to his authority.[17] Despite some suggestions that other bands might be included in subsequent years, attitudes hardened after the rebellion of 1885, and Reed as Indian commissioner and deputy superintendent general then quashed any progress in this direction. Reed wanted to end the old system of hereditary chiefs and headmen altogether, but instead of adopting elective institutions he wanted to place bands directly under departmental control, which he thought would be "one of the strongest aids towards the destruction of communism and the creation of individuality." During Reed's time in office, he tried to eliminate traditional forms of band governance, not only to encourage individuality, but also to make Indians more amenable to government direction and ultimate assimilation. Despite a few elections on the reserves, by and large Reed's policy for western Indians "was defeated by the resistance of the Indians to it and their persistence in maintaining some form of tribal political organization."[18]

Thus, the government's stated policy and legislation provided that Indians on reserves should have the equivalent of elective municipal institutions to learn democracy and responsibility for their own internal affairs. Yet the government then hedged the policy, especially in western Canada, because it did not trust Indians to make good choices: such elections as were permitted were supervised, the government could (and did) remove elected chiefs and councillors, and government officials supervised policies devised by tribal councils. The parallels to teacher-supervised high school class president or student council elections are remarkable: western Indians were mostly treated like children who could not be trusted and whose every act was subject to intrusive supervision. One result appears to have been that Indians increasingly mistrusted officials. As late as the 1940s when officials belatedly tried to promote the elective council system, they found in Alberta "little evidence that the Indians desired to adopt the three-year elective system."[19]

## NATIVE POPULATION AND RESERVES

Determining with any precision the Indian population that took treaty in 1876 and 1877 is notoriously difficult. It is clear, for example, that when it came time to pay out annuities many persons from the bands that signed the treaties were absent, and were likely off hunting or fishing.[20] Other bands that subsequently took adhesions had, in a few cases, not been informed of the treaty talks, or were too far away to make travel to a central treaty site practicable. There was confusion about who was to be included in the treaties and who was not, especially with respect to the Metis population. Indians also manipulated official counts to collect more annuity money.[21] Officials were aware of many of the problems, but it would take some time to begin to establish any kind of accurate figures. In 1881 in Treaty 6, annuities were paid to thirty chiefs,

105 headmen, and 5,121 Indians. Probably less than half of these lived in the future district of Alberta. In Treaty 7, payments went to six chiefs, twenty-three headmen, and 2,960 Indians.[22] These population figures are low, probably in part due to the fact that many were hunting in the United States at the time of payment.

One of the first reasonably reliable population indicators was the 1884–85 census of the North-West Territories. It showed a total population in the district of Alberta of 15,533; of these, 9,418 (over 60 per cent) were "Indian" and 1,237 (about 8 per cent) were Metis.[23] In 1901, the date of the last census of the district of Alberta, the total population had reached 65,876. This included 5,620 Indians (8.5 per cent) and 3,686 Metis (5.6 per cent).[24] That the Indian population declined significantly, both in absolute numbers and as a proportion of the population, while the Metis population nearly tripled, cannot be doubted. Yet this change likely is only partly attributable to birth or mortality rates and more accurate counts; it also owes much to the desire of many Metis who had taken treaty, and therefore who in 1884–85 had been classed as Indians, to reclaim Metis status. Still, to note that the Indian and Metis population dropped from over two-thirds of Albertans in 1884–85 to about 14 per cent in 1901 shows that their relative marginalization in the early twentieth century is understandable, if regrettable.

Despite the confusion over numbers, no part of Canada's population was more regularly counted, studied, and analyzed by the government than the Native peoples. Annual departmental reports provide census numbers for each band, though particularly in the early years the mobility of a still semi-nomadic population made accuracy difficult, as did band membership fluctuations. In some cases, bands changed names, amalgamated, divided, or disbanded. In at least one case, that of the Passpasschase band near Edmonton, the government questioned the band's legitimacy, obtained a somewhat dubious surrender, and sold its land, most of its members either having left treaty or dispersed to other bands.[25] Still, because the government, as part of its treaty obligations, had to provide annuities to all Indians who had entered the treaties, and because it had to exercise vigilance in handing out provisions and supplies to bands, accurate records were essential.

The Treaty 6 bands in the district of Alberta were administered in three groupings, known as agencies, each at first comprising six or seven small or medium-sized bands. In turn, these were referred to sometimes by location and sometimes by the chief's name. To further confuse the issue, chiefs were often known by more than one name, or by their

Indian name or its English translation, and each name could be subject to a range of spellings in written records. By 1886, these agencies settled down to four to six bands each, though their composition and location continued to fluctuate in succeeding years. What follows, therefore, is a very rough characterization.

The Saddle Lake agency (known as the Victoria agency in the early years, after the eponymous settlement and HBC fort in the vicinity where it was first headquartered) in the north-east included the Saddle Lake (also known as Little Hunter, or Onchaminahos), Blue Quill (sometimes referred to as Egg Lake – later Whitford Lake – in the early years), James Seenum (also known as Pakan, or Whitefish Lake), Lac la Biche (Peesayses, variously spelled), Muskegawatick (also known as Wahsatenow or Wasatnow, or Bear Ears), Chipewyan (Heart Lake, today part of the Dene Nation), and Beaver Lake (or Kequanum) bands. Except for the Chipewyan band, these bands were mostly Cree or mostly Metis, and the Lac la Biche band was wholly Metis.[26]

The Edmonton agency included the Enoch (Tommy la Potack or Stony Plain), Alexis (or Joseph), Michel (or Michel Callihoo), Alexander, and Iron Head or Paul (White Whale Lake or Lake Wabamun, and a branch of Alexis) bands, as well as a small group known as Orphans at St Albert. Of these bands, the Enoch and Alexander bands were Cree; the Michel band was Iroquois or Iroquois/Cree; and the remainder were mostly Stoney Nakota Sioux (usually then called Assiniboine or Stoney). South of Edmonton, the Hobbema agency (also known earlier as the Bear Hills agency and then for a few years as the Peace Hills agency) comprised the Samson, Ermineskin, Louis Bull (Muddy Bull), Sharphead, and Montana (or Bobtail or Little Bear) bands. Most in the Hobbema agency were Cree, but the Sharphead band was Stoney (Assiniboine).

Treaty 7 is more straightforward: it comprised larger bands and reserves in five agencies. Three of these were members of the Nizitapi: the Siksika, the Kainai, and the Piikani. The remaining two were the Tsuu T'ina and the Stoney Nakoda, which for much of the 1880s and 1890s were administered as a single agency.

Tables 3.1 to 3.7 present problems that cast doubt on their consistency and accuracy in detail. Much is unexplained with respect to census fluctuations. However, the overall picture seems reasonably reliably represented, and some patterns emerge. For one thing, there is greater consistency in the last decade represented than in the first, which suggests some systematized data collection, but also fewer bands closing and merging. With the exceptions of the James Seenum band in the Saddle

Table 3.1  Population, selected years, Saddle Lake (or Victoria) agency, Treaty 6[1]

|  | 1886 | 1890 | 1895 | 1898 | 1902 | 1905 |
|---|---|---|---|---|---|---|
| Saddle Lake | 78 | 112 | 91 | 121† | 133 | 138 |
| Blue Quill | 47 | 27 | 87 | 101 | 110 | 109 |
| James Seenum | 279 | 307 | 312 | 328 | 331 | 331 |
| Lac la Biche (Peesayses) | 16 | 17 | 19 | 18 | 16 | 10 |
| Antoine (Chipewayan of Heart Lake) | 82 | 88 | 69 | 66 | 70 | 80 |
| Muskegwatic or Wahsatenow | 48 | 41 | 23* | – | – | – |
| Beaver Lake (Kequanum) | 130 | 108 | 100 | 109 | 99 | 94 |
| Agency total | 680 | 700 | 701 | 743 | 759 | 762 |

\* Merged with the Saddle Lake band in 1894.
† Includes Wahsatanow

Table 3.2  Population, selected years, Edmonton agency, Treaty 6

|  | 1886 | 1890 | 1895 | 1898 | 1902 | 1905 |
|---|---|---|---|---|---|---|
| Enoch | 140 | 181 | 148 | 124 | 122 | 123 |
| Michel | 88 | 75 | 79 | 82 | 97 | 89 |
| Alexander | 220 | 203 | 219 | 187 | 190 | 173 |
| Alexis/Joseph | 211 | 158 | 145 | 137 | 147 | 144 |
| Iron Head/Paul (branch of Alexis at White Whale Lake) | not given separately | 55 | 137** | 145 | 147 | 152 |
| Orphans (St Albert) | not given | 11 | 8 | 6 | 5 | 1 |
| Agency total | 659* | 683 | 736 | 681 | 708 | 682 |

\* Includes the Passpasschase band of 191 persons. The band ceased to exist by 1890; most members were discharged from treaty and some joined the Enoch band.
\*\*Includes Sharphead population, merged from Hobbema.

Table 3.3  Population, selected years, Hobbema (or Peace Hills) agency, Treaty 6

|  | 1886 | 1890 | 1895 | 1898 | 1902 | 1905 |
|---|---|---|---|---|---|---|
| Samson | 275 | 305 | 285 | 332 | 320 | 356 |
| Ermineskin | 172 | 133 | 173 | 172 | 166 | 165 |
| Louis Bull/Muddy Bull (Pigeon Lake) | 95 | 71 | 56 | 66 | 71 | 78 |
| Cheepoostequahn (Sharphead Stoney, Wolf Creek) | 200 | 91 | 2* | – | – | – |
| Bobtail/Montana (Little Bear) | 101 | – | 2 | 57 | 52 | 56 |
| Agency total | 843 | 600 | 513 | 627 | 609 | 655 |

*Merged with Iron Head/Paul band in Edmonton agency.

Table 3.4  Total population, selected years, Treaty 6 bands in the district of Alberta

|  | 1886 | 1890 | 1895 | 1898 | 1902 | 1905 |
|---|---|---|---|---|---|---|
| Aggregate totals | 2,182 | 1,983 | 1,950 | 2,051 | 2,076 | 2,099 |

Table 3.5  Population, selected years, Treaty 7 agencies

|  | 1886 | 1890 | 1895 | 1898 | 1902 | 1905 |
|---|---|---|---|---|---|---|
| Siksika | 2,147 | 1,827 | 1,267 | 1,099 | 942 | 842 |
| Kainai | 2,241 | 1,983 | 1,427 | 1,291 | 1,253 | 1,204 |
| Piikani | 932 | 924 | 781 | 658 | 530 | 499 |
| Tsuu T'ina | 341 | 914* | 236 | 227 | 203 | 205 |
| Stoney | 633 | – | 576 | 581 | 661 | 652 |
| Treaty total | 6,294 | 5,648 | 4,287 | 3,856 | 3,589 | 3,402 |

*Combined figure for Tsuu T'ina and Stoney; breakdown not provided.

Lake agency and the Samson band in the Hobbema agency, the bands and reserves in Treaty 6 are much smaller than those in Treaty 7. The population of Treaty 6 generally was more stable than that of Treaty 7, which declined 46 per cent from 1886 to 1905, including 20 per cent in the last decade of that period. Within Treaty 7, the Stoney population remained relatively steady while others shrunk significantly. In 1905, Indians in the bands that had been included in the district of Alberta from 1882 to 1905 totalled 5,501, according to Department of Indian Affairs figures, down slightly from the 5,620 recorded for the 1901 census.[27]

It is helpful to know the size and location of Indian reserves, and the band numbers, which serve as identifiers in many DIA documents. Names, areas, and locations in tables 3.6 and 3.7 appear as set out in the original DIA document.

### LOOKING FORWARD

Part 2 of this book is a mostly thematic examination of federal-Indian relations in territorial Alberta during the first quarter-century or so of the post-treaty reserve period, and of federal efforts to provide a managed transformation of Indians, as well as Indians' compliance or resistance. In chapter 5, I survey Indian economies, on and off the reserves, and consider the extent to which the agricultural experiment was successful. In chapter 6, I examine how the government's plan to incorporate formal education – which Indian representatives had asked for at treaty talks – into the civilizing process worked out in practice. In chapter 7, I explore the ways in which the government tried, and often failed, to meet its legal and moral responsibility, and Treaty 6 obligation, to provide its wards with medical care. In chapter 8, I assess the early development of the ongoing friction over hunting and fishing rights between Indians, who understood the treaties to have guaranteed hunting and fishing rights, and the government, which maintained that this never was an unfettered right. Finally, in chapter 9, I explore Indians' relationship to the police and justice system.

First, however, I consider the years immediately following the treaties, a period of transition to reserve life, but also one of tragedy and stress. In these years, both the government and Indians began to explore just what the commitments made in 1876 and 1877 were to mean in practice, when Indians and whites had to take the measure of one another under new and mostly unforeseen circumstances. Above all, the two sides began to discover just how differently each had understood the treaty commitments of 1876 and 1877.

Table 3.6  Schedule of Alberta Indian reserves, Treaty 6, 1902[2]

| Band | Name | Area (sq. miles) | Location |
|------|------|------------------|----------|
| 125 | Pakan, Little Hunter, Blue Quill | 115.00 | Saddle Lake |
| 125A | Cache Lake (adjoins 125) | 14.00 | Saddle Lake |
| 127 | Blue Quill (included in 125) | relocated | Saddle Lake |
| 128 | James Seenum | 17.50 | Whitefish Lake |
| 132 | Michel Callihoo | 40.00 | near Edmonton |
| 133 | Alexis | 23.00 | Lac Ste Anne, near Edmonton |
| 133A, 133B | White Whale Lake | 32.70 | Lake Wabamun, near Edmonton |
| 134 | Alexander | 41.00 | near Edmonton |
| 135 | Enoch (Stony Plain, Tommy la Potac) | 30.29 | near Edmonton |
| 136 | Passpasschase | surrendered/sold, 1888 | near Edmonton |
| 137 | Sampson | 61.50 | south of Edmonton |
| 138 | Ermineskin | 61.50 | south of Edmonton |
| 138A* | Pigeon Lake | 7.75 | south of Edmonton |
| 139 | Bobtail's | 31.50 | south of Edmonton |

*A fishing limit was provided on Pigeon Lake for the exclusive use of members of bands included in the Hobbema agency.

Table 3.7  Schedule of Indian reserves, Treaty 7, 1902[3]

| Band | Name | Area (sq. miles) | Location |
|------|------|------------------|----------|
| 142 | Bear's Paw (Stoney) | 109.00 | near Morleyville |
| 143 | Jacob (Stoney) | | |
| 144 | Chiniquay (Stoney) | | |
| 145 | Tsuu T'ina | 108.00 | near Calgary |
| 146 | Siksika | 470.00 | Gleichen, east of Calgary |
| 147 | Piikani | 181.40 | near Macleod |
| 148 | Kainai | 546.76 | near Lethbridge |
| A | timber limit for 148 on Belly River | 6.50 | south of the Kainai reserve, in present-day Waterton Park |
| B | timber limit for 147 | 11.50 | west of the Piikani reserve |
| C | timber limit for 146, Castle Mountain | 26.50 | west of the Rocky Mountain Park |

Note: Timber limits were provided for reserves that had within their boundaries little or no timber suitable for building, fencing, and so forth. The Siksika never found the Castle Mountain timber limit to be of any use.[4] Apparently they surrendered it in 1892,[5] so it is unclear why it was still listed in 1902.

Notes to Tables 3.1 – 3.7

1  CSP, 1887, #6 (DIA), 254–56; 1891, #18 (DIA), xlii; 1895, #14 (DIA), 79; 1896, #14 (DIA), 366–67; 1899, #14 (DIA), 424–25; 1903, #27 (DIA), pt. 2, 80–85; 1906, #27 (DIA), pt. 2, 75–82. The same sources apply to tables 3.1 to 3.5.
2  CSP, 1903, #27a (Schedule of Indian Reserves in the Dominion; Supplement to DIA Report), 18. Orthography and terminology as in original.
3  CSP, 1903, #27a, 19.
4  See Armstrong et al., The River Returns, 94–95, 413n15.
5  Canada, Indian Treaties and Surrenders, vol. 3, 91–92.

# 4

# The Unravelling of a Relationship:
# The Troubled Transition to Reserve Life

The extinguishment of the Indian title in the soil in Manitoba and the Northwest Territories has added largely to the burdens of the country. The traditional policy of Canada towards the Indians has been ever such as to secure the confidence and good will of the Indian population; but it has wholly failed in training the Indians to habits of industry and self-reliance. A new departure in our Indian policy at an early day is absolutely necessary, a departure which will enable the country to look forward with some confidence to a period when the annuities may be commuted, the Indians enfranchised, and the special guardianship of the state terminated.[1]

Such was the opinion in 1878 of David Mills, minister of the interior and superintendent general of Indian Affairs: the numbered treaties entailed upon the dominion a series of onerous, costly obligations. The government's hope for an early termination of its recently contracted commitments contrasted sharply with the views of the government officials and the Indian leaders who had met at Forts Carlton and Pitt in 1876, and at Blackfoot Crossing in 1877. There each side had envisaged a long-term relationship, though with significant differences. The Indian leaders thought they had a permanent engagement that would support their peoples and cultures. Setting aside for the moment the basic issue of title to the land, the government officials thought the treaties were about protecting and supporting Indians through a process of change, leading to their becoming self-supporting and ultimately enfranchised. They understood that this would require both significant up-front costs and a long-term commitment. By contrast, the ink was barely dry on Treaty 7 before the cash-strapped Mackenzie government bemoaned the expense to which it was now committed. It looked forward to implementing policies that would push Indians into a rapid, short-term transformation and assimilation. The reserve system, the annuities and assistance, the obligations of wardship: it regarded them all as a temporary, if costly and necessary, transitional phase. This revealed much about the assumptions underlying future policies and administration. What the government regarded as for the ultimate good of the Indians (and the beleaguered national treasury), the Indians regarded as a betrayal of trust.

### MUTUAL DISAPPOINTMENT

Sir John A. Macdonald was superintendent general from 1878 to 1887, so his attitude concerning Indians was critical in shaping policy in the early reserve era. He thought it important that he as prime minister should hold the portfolios central to western development, but Indian issues seldom occupied his full attention.[2] In this role he was, in the words of his biographer Richard Gwyn, an "erratically engaged dictator."[3] His prejudices, moderate for the day, nevertheless came through when he addressed the House of Commons in May 1880:

> Whenever there is an Indian settlement the whites in the vicinity are very naturally anxious – when they see the slovenly, unfarmer-like way in which the Indian lands are cultivated especially if the lands be very good – to get rid of the red men, believing, and perhaps truly, that the progress of the locality is retarded by them, and that the sooner they are enfranchised, or deprived of their lands, and allowed to shift for themselves, the better. I dare say it would be better. If the Indians were to disappear from the continent, the Indian question would cease to exist. But we must remember that they are the original owners of the soil, of which they have been dispossessed by the covetousness or ambition of our ancestors. Perhaps, if Columbus had not discovered this continent – had left them alone – they would have worked out a tolerable civilization of their own. At all events, the Indians have been great sufferers by the discovery of America and the transfer to it of a large white population. We are bound to protect them ...
>
> The general rule is that you cannot make the Indian a white man. An Indian once said to myself: "We are the wild animals; you cannot make an ox of a deer." You cannot make an agriculturalist

of an Indian. All we can hope for is to wean them, by slow degrees absorb them or settle them on the land. Meantime they must be fairly protected.[4]

This from the man who had sponsored the Gradual Civilization Act of 1857, and whose government was about to spend hundreds of thousands of dollars annually in the effort to turn Indians into farmers, proclaiming on the one hand that it could not be done, and on the other that it could and must be done quickly. His personal choice as Indian commissioner, Edgar Dewdney, declared optimistically in 1879 that Indians would not need farm instructors – still envisaged as the principal reserve-level officials – for more than a few years. Yet Macdonald by 1880 seemed to recognize that it would be a far longer process. He cautioned those who imagined that the Indians of the Northwest would soon resemble those of central and eastern Canada: "You cannot judge the wild nomad of the North West by the standard of the Indian of Ontario." He added, "we hope that the Indians will now settle down; but Indians are Indians, and we must submit to frequent disappointments in the way of civilizing them."[5] He would have ample occasions on which to express his disappointment.

However, if disappointments are mostly related to failed expectations, Indians had many more occasions to be disappointed in the government. From being treated with respect at the treaty negotiations, and from believing that whites would partner with them during the period of difficult change, they soon faced hunger and even starvation. Rations were frequently of substandard quality and insufficient quantity. Clothing was in short supply,[6] as were the implements and animals needed to farm successfully. Constantine Scollen, Oblate missionary, commenting in the spring of 1879 on the recent months of rampant starvation among the Nizitapi, angrily asserted that this state of affairs was a bitter disappointment and a betrayal of the Indian understanding of their agreement with the government: "They hoped that it [Treaty 7] simply meant to furnish them with plenty of food and clothing and particularly the former every time they stood in need of them."[7] Even the police, who had seemed in the 1870s to guarantee the equal application of the Queen's law, eventually became agents of intimidation and enforcers of inequality. Misunderstandings concerning the meaning and promises of the treaties added to the difficulties on both sides. Indian appeals to the government fell on deaf ears, were dismissed as provoked by agitators, or were refused as unjustified complaints.

## HUNGER

Initially, not yet comprehending Ottawa's real purposes, the Siksika were tolerably satisfied with Treaty 7. Whether in Canadian or American territory, they found an adequate supply of food in the fall of 1877, and the initial treaty payment, or gratuity, of twelve dollars per person allowed purchase of new blankets and guns, and more horses. Under Isapo-Muxika's leadership, they went into their winter camp, anticipating that snow on the prairies would drive the bison west toward the foothills where Chinook winds normally kept grass uncovered. But the winter of 1877–78 was unusually mild. The snows mostly did not come, and did not stay long, and prairie fires ravaged the open rangeland. Such bison as remained in Canada stayed north and east of Cypress Hills in present-day Saskatchewan, forcing the Siksika, along with the Kainai and Piikani, to trek eastward into proximity with other bison-hunting peoples – Cree, Assiniboine, Sioux – all searching for a very limited number of animals. Though the supply was enough to meet immediate needs in 1877–78, the pressure on the herds was excessive and the bison could not last much longer.[8]

When it signed Treaty 7, the government believed that if hunting were controlled there would be sufficient bison for as many as ten years to help meet Indian nutritional needs during the transition to agriculture.[9] Indians seemed to share that hope, expecting that they would be able to pursue life much as before but with a safety net, a treaty relationship that was supposed to guarantee the Queen's support in the event of shortages. The abrupt and widespread collapse of bison and other game in the winter of 1878–79 came as a shock to both sides, despite frequent predictions over the previous decade from both Indians and whites. Some of the Indians in Treaty 7 began to drift south to Montana in search of the remaining herds; others remained in Canada and tried to subsist on nearly depleted supplies of elk, deer, and antelope, and then on prairie populations of small game. According to Hugh Dempsey, "rabbits, mice, moles, porcupines, badgers – anything with meat on its bones was eaten, no matter how rank." As the Plains Cree had done in 1873–74, the Nizitapi ate many of their dogs and horses, and even stewed leather goods in search of nourishment. The presence in the Treaty 7 area of nearly a thousand desperate and destitute Cree also seeking food only made matters worse.[10]

The hunger of that desperate winter and the summer of 1879 was not entirely the result of poor governance. Officials on the ground, including

Lieutenant Governor David Laird, Dewdney, and the police, advocated a strong response to the emergency, and Dewdney ordered large amounts of cattle and food supplies, anticipating that the Indians would have to be fed in the winter of 1880, but supplies were scarce, distant, and costly to purchase and transport. He commended the efforts of Isapo-Muxika to restrain the understandably radical tendencies of younger tribesmen.[11] J.S. Dennis, deputy minister of the interior, noted the "most distressing" conditions among the western Indians, particularly reports that in the spring whole families, and even one entire small band, had died of starvation. He thought "the conduct of the suffering Indians" to have been "most admirable," but feared that desperate people soon would resort to desperate measures.[12]

And so the treaty relationship began to unravel. Bob Beal and Rod Macleod observe that, whatever the ultimate causes of the demise of the bison, Indians saw a causal connection between the advent of the government, the signing of the treaties, and the disappearance of their main source of sustenance: "they believed, not unreasonably, that the government owed them a living, regardless of the formal arrangements." The government did not see it that way.[13] Almost everyone agreed that an urgent response to the immediate crisis was essential, but the government also believed the long-term solution lay in encouraging or prodding Indians to farm to support themselves. In the treaty negotiations, it had promised to provide food for three years, once the Indians had settled on reserves, at the end of which it expected they would be fairly self-sufficient in agriculture.[14] Beyond that, it believed food relief should be limited in quantity and period of availability: enough to prevent starvation, but not enough to encourage dependency. Officials imagined that hungry Indians would have incentive to work harder to feed themselves and their relatives. Success in this endeavour would generate pride as a farmer rather than as a hunter, and would redefine Indian masculinity. Arguably, that was what the government believed it owed Indians in this relationship: the opportunity in changed circumstances to be progressive and successful, and to take pride in being self-sustaining.

Despite appearances, the government did make some effort to meet its treaty obligations with respect to food and farm implements. In the 1877–78 reporting year, it imported via the North Saskatchewan River, and distributed to the bands in the western division of Treaty 6, some 6,000 pounds of flour, 154 of tea, 203 of sugar, 94 of tobacco, and 3,419 of pemmican. It also distributed ploughs, harrows, whippletrees, trace chains, scythes, snaiths, hay forks, axes, hoes, spades, and sickles to most bands. Some bands received saws and saw files, wagons, carts, horses, oxen, augers, and seed wheat, barley, oats (very little), and potatoes.[15] Many bands had settled on reserves (as yet mostly unsurveyed), reportedly beginning to farm with a will. However, Laird found that most were "absolutely destitute of food" in the spring of 1878; rather than being inspired to work harder, they were too feeble to farm unless provisioned. Moreover, the James Seenum band had a poor crop as a result of drought: "I fear they will have no produce to dispose of next spring. The same, I fear, may be said of every other Band in the Territories."[16]

Laird hoped that the scarcity of game would require Indians to "turn their attention to tilling the soil or raising stock to enable them to live." The government, he contended, must "adopt early and energetic measures to prepare them for the change in their mode of living and sustaining themselves and families," teaching and assisting them to farm and raise cattle. Of course, this would necessitate discouraging "the use of the tent and wigwam," and encouraging settlement in permanent dwellings and adoption of the lifestyle "of the White man." Laird further recommended that reserves be "subdivided into lots," and that "each head of a family should receive a location ticket, covering the land to which he is entitled."[17] Within the confines of the reserve, each Native man would become an individual property occupier.

A partisan appointee of the late Liberal government, Laird resigned as commissioner early in 1879. His successor, Dewdney, was a Conservative and good friend of Macdonald, whose party had won the federal election in the fall of 1878. Macdonald and his officials took Laird's parting advice seriously. They instructed Dewdney to establish fifteen farming agencies across the West, as well as two supply farms that would produce food and seed grain for Indians, and also teach them to farm. In addition, he was to distribute food at Forts Macleod and Walsh to stave off starvation.[18]

The initial relief supplies for the Treaty 7 area in 1879 (twenty-eight head of cattle, 1,500 pounds of flour, 100 pounds of sugar, as well as tea and tobacco), which mostly had to be purchased from the Americans at Fort Benton, were inadequate.[19] Dewdney was startled to see formerly strong, healthy people now "quite emaciated" and so weak they could scarcely work. Reports from Indian agents, the NWMP, priests, civilians, and Indians poured into government offices to warn of the impending crisis of starvation. The government wavered. Its every inclination, in accordance with its understanding of the treaty discussions, was to refuse to supply Indians until they were settled as intending farmers upon reserves. It also wanted to establish that relief supplies were to be only of an emergency and exceptional nature, not a result of any presumed treaty right to ongoing and regular aid. Yet Macdonald acknowledged that the government might have to feed Indians until they became self-sustaining. Certainly the sick and aged required ongoing support; others must "prove to be in earnest in endeavouring to become self-subsisting." If they did not work, there would be no food.[20]

Having insufficient supplies to distribute, Dewdney suggested to Isapo-Muxika that he seek bison in the United States, substantial numbers of which were being reported, and late in 1879 the chief had no choice but to take Dewdney's advice and lead his people into Montana (though he left the sick, disabled, and elderly to be fed at Fort Macleod).[21] The presence of thousands of Canadian Indians caused resentment among Montana Indians, fear among American settlers, anger among ranchers, and frustration for the US army. The army escorted the Indians back to Canada, only to have them return in search of food. Moreover, bad as the situation was, it quickly became worse. Whiskey traders in Montana welcomed the exploitable population, which readily traded meat, buffalo robes, and horses for firewater. Some even prostituted their women.

Almost totally destitute, with many dying of starvation and of diseases such as measles and mumps, worsened by malnutrition, and realizing that the bison supply was effectively destroyed, the Siksika finally decided to return to Fort Macleod in the spring and summer of 1881 to seek government rations. They walked the trail north, for they had few horses left, and many more died en route. A reported 1,064 reached the fort, but "at least one thousand members of the nation in Canada perished" between 1879 and 1881.[22] In those years, they realized that a familiar way of life also had effectively perished. The survivors seemed like exiles in their own land.

Farther north, in the Treaty 6 region, shortages were just as severe. James Green Stewart, of St Paul parish in Manitoba, became the Indian agent at Edmonton in the fall of 1879. The following summer he told the superintendent general, Macdonald, that even though he had exceeded his instructions with respect to how much he could expend on rations, it really was not so much if the amount were divided by the total number of the destitute. Looked at this way, he had only given "a small portion to each sufferer." He continued:

I may well call them sufferers, for I have never seen anything like it since my long residence in this country. It was not only the want of buffalo, but everything else seemed to have deserted the country; even fish were scarce. Fur-bearing animals, from which the Indians might have supplied themselves with clothing etc., were not to be had. In some cases some hunting might have been done, but the poor people were naked, and the cold was intense, and remained so during the whole winter; under these circumstances they behaved well, and no raids were made on anything here. They ate many of their horses, and all the dogs were destroyed for food; in fact, everything was tried and failed. In our assistance the strictest economy was practised, and unless the Indians had been allowed to die, or to help themselves to the settlers' cattle (neither of which ways would have brought much credit to anybody concerned), we could not have got through with less. We fully hoped that in the spring, wild fowl and fish would have been plentiful, but owing to the continued bad weather, few of either of these sources of provisions were available.[23]

W. Anderson, Stewart's successor in 1881, observed "there were many sick and destitute old men, women, widows, orphans, &c., about Fort Edmonton" who required relief. His solution was to set up a soup kitchen. Though "the Indians were prejudiced against it," he found it was "greatly appreciated and proved a most economical method of furnishing relief." So successful was the idea that he directed farm instructors at the Peace Hills and at Rivière-Qui-Barre to emulate him to relieve "local distress among the aged and weak."[24] It was also briefly adopted in the Victoria (later Saddle Lake) agency.

Badgered by opposition claims of extravagance in supplying Indians with rations, Macdonald and his officials reduced the amounts by half, and even three-quarters, to try to force the Indians to work harder at raising crops. He noted, "when they fall into a state of destitution we cannot allow them to die for want of food. It is true that Indians so long as they are fed will not work." Rations accordingly were withheld "until the Indians are on the verge of starvation, to reduce the expense."[25]

Brutal as this story is, and traumatic as the loss of their way of life was for the bison-hunting plains Indians, it was not the whole story of the Indians of the district of Alberta after the signing of the treaties. Some, like the Stoneys of Treaty 7, had formerly taken bison when available, but were able to compensate at least partially for their loss by hunting other game and fish in the foothills and mountains. Indians in Treaty 6 who lived in woodland or parkland areas initially managed a bit better on traditional forms of subsistence, though some of these too were on the verge of extermination. Indeed, many saw little change in their way of life, except for the annual treaty payments and the periodic appearance of an Indian agent.

Officially, the government wanted all Indians in the treaty areas to become self-sufficient agriculturalists. In practice, it came to realize that not all lived on land with much agricultural potential, and that some could survive with a traditional lifestyle and not require supplies and rations while others could make a living from a variety of occupations. The government was much more concerned with getting Indians whose circumstances had changed radically, or who lived in areas that were near the projected railway or otherwise likely to attract white settlement, to settle down and support themselves as farmers or ranchers, or through other non-traditional means.

Noel Dyck argues that the government itself was the main reason its agricultural policy did not achieve its goals, because in encouraging Indians to hunt and fish (to avoid the high costs of provisioning them), they were often off the reserves and not ploughing land or planting, cultivating, and harvesting crops to maximum productivity. While government officials in Ottawa believed "farming activities should always take precedence over hunting," Indians were receiving mixed messages, and their "experience as hunters did not lead them to the same conclusion" as the officials. Another example of mixed messages was Macdonald's idea that Indians should be employed as construction workers on the Canadian Pacific Railway to offset food costs, which also took them off reserves and away from their farms. Dyck moreover points out that when Indians asked for grist mills to produce flour from their wheat, the government took three years to determine the cheapest way to provide them, so that "Indians in the western portion of Treaty Six were left over a hundred miles away from the nearest grist mill."[26]

The problems were complicated because the government insisted on centralized control of purchasing of supplies (thus maximizing patronage opportunities, as well as centralized control of expenditures, for contracts for supplies and their transportation), so it took months longer than it should have to get implements, animals, and food. When they did come, they were too often inadequate in quantity and of poor quality. Many Indians who wanted to work were unable to do so because of the want of tools, and then government blamed them for wandering off the reserves to hunt or fish, or for depending upon its food supplies. Some farm instructors were so occupied with their own farms, or so unsuited to working with Indians, that they provided little direction. Government officials also tended to impatience when Indian farmers did not succeed in wheat farming, despite the fact that the growing season in the parkland of Treaty 6 or the foothills of Treaty 7 was frequently too short for the varieties of wheat then available; Indians tended to prefer barley, which was more reliable. When they did produce a surplus, Indians found that there was no market for it, so that they could not use it to purchase supplies such as bacon, tea, tobacco, and clothing.[27] In other words, from the beginning they faced considerable impediments – many the result of government policy – to success as grain or mixed farmers.

ANNUITIES AND RATIONS

On occasion, especially in the first post-treaty years, Indians could manipulate some things to their advantage. One obvious example was at annuity payments, when they were dealing with officials who were not familiar with them. Hobbema elder Lazarus Roan said in 1974 that he had heard stories from a relative who, as a child of seven, had witnessed the treaty signing:

> The first time the treaty payment was made, each person received twelve dollars [gratuity], and then the children, boys and girls, were loaned to others: "We would change clothing and appearance before we would sit next to a woman. She then would have a family of about eight or ten children." He also stated that there was never a question of name nor age. The only question they asked the woman was "Are these all your children?" The woman would say yes and she would then receive her money.[28]

The Siksika told researchers in the 1940s that at annuity payments after the treaties, some of them found that by changing from a Hudson's Bay blanket to a buffalo robe and using a different name, they could dupe government officers into granting them more than one payment.[29] Many of the Kainai apparently collected annuities for some years on both sides of the international boundary, and considered it "their right to do so since they had roamed over the entire area." Others declined to take annuities, and still others collected them only intermittently.[30]

Small wonder, then, that annuity lists are not always reliable population reports, especially in the early years. Moreover, officials frequently arrived to make annuity payments in the summer when many Indians were away hunting. Band membership was often loose, especially as people would move from one band to another. Metis sometimes moved from taking treaty to withdrawing from bands to take scrip or to pursue a more independent lifestyle as trappers, hunters, or traders. Moreover, it seems likely that births would be reported in order to collect the annuity, but that deaths would not be immediately reported if a deceased relative could be claimed to be away hunting so that their annuity might still be received. The government moved fairly quickly to limit fraud by employing devices such as a ticket system that prevented switching children or collecting at more than one band's annuity payments. The new system reduced the number of names on the list and effected considerable savings.[31]

For Indians, the time of the annuity payments each year became an opportunity to air their grievances – which might include complaints about a farm instructor, the quantity or quality of supplies, and so forth – before officials. The payments also became a reaffirmation of the treaty relationship: they saw the money paid by the government as a renewal, however imperfect, of that commitment and those promises.[32] This impression was reinforced because the government undertook to feed the people who assembled for annuities, as it had during treaty negotiations. For example, in preparation for annuity payments in 1878 to members of Treaties 4 and 6, the government spent over $40,000 on provisions, which included tea, coffee, tobacco, pipes, sugar, syrup, pemmican, dried meat, beef, oxen, bacon, flour, biscuits, beans, potatoes, oats, and sundries, as well as freighting costs and the expenses of driving cattle to the various meetings.[33] This was in addition to the expenses of officials and a North-West Mounted Police presence. If the supplies were late, Indians might refuse to receive the annuities until they arrived. Officials also learned to withhold supplies to secure Indian cooperation, for example in conducting a census of each household.[34]

One of the most noticeable themes of Canada's Indian administration in the West is the constant harping of the government, opposition, and press on the need to be tight-fisted. They thought this concern reasonable, since over 70 per cent of the Department of Indian Affairs budget was spent on prairie Indians, who comprised about 25 per cent of all Canadian Indians. Many of these costly ongoing expenditures related to

fixed treaty obligations, such as the annuity payments and accompanying ceremonies. Eventually the government reduced expenditures for
items such as food and gifts by paying the annuities on Indians' home
reserves, rather than at some more central location with a more elaborate ceremony. "Emergency" relief, which Indians viewed as a treaty
right, turned out to be a continuous and even higher annual expenditure.
Farm animals and implements provided for in the treaties were by no
means one-time expenditures, to say nothing of seed grain, farm instructors, demonstration and supply farms, and so forth. Add to this the cost
of schools, medical supplies and personnel (and eventually hospitals),
and police and the justice system, and it must have seemed to government, and to many whites, that Indians were pampered, costly, and milking the system.

Reinforcing these government and public attitudes was another serious economic depression, which began in the last quarter of 1882.
Canadian exports plunged, and the federal government's surplus at
the beginning of the decade turned into a deficit for several years.
Retrenchment was the order of the day by 1883, and Indian Affairs was
not spared. Deputy Superintendent General Lawrence Vankoughnet
toured the western agencies that year and concluded that significant cuts
were possible. He believed that agents had been too generous in handing
out rations and in other ways, and therefore initiated what G.F.G. Stanley termed "wholesale dismissals of clerks, assistants and other employees of the Department in the North-West, and a stricter supervision over
the issue of rations to the Indians." At the Battleford Industrial School,
pupils' rations were slashed from 1.5 pounds of beef per day to one-
quarter pound. Often quoted is Stanley's observation that "the Government's policy could be summed up in six words: feed one day, starve the
next."[35] Furthermore, starvation was not merely a consequence of government stinginess – it sometimes was a deliberate policy instrument to
subordinate recalcitrant Indians to the government's purposes, while
provisions could reward approved behaviour.[36]

## RESERVES

The original, rather complex, provision for reserves that was written in
to Treaty 7 followed Isapo-Muxika's plan to have the Siksika, Kainai,
and Tsuu T'ina nations secure contiguous reserves, and thereby a very
large presence, along the north side of the Bow River and part of
the South Saskatchewan (to the confluence of the Red Deer River),

beginning twenty miles above Blackfoot Crossing and thence eastward nearly two hundred miles in a strip averaging four miles wide. Curiously, it also provided that a similar strip one mile wide on the south side of the river would be part of the reserve for a period of ten years, at which point it would cease to be reserve land, without compensation; this strip of land specifically excluded a coal seam about five miles below Blackfoot Crossing.[37]

This planned reserve was never implemented in its original form. By 1878, the Kainai and Tsuu T'ina decided that they wanted separate reserves more clearly in their traditional territories. Nothing could be done to survey the reserves until Indians had exhausted the idea of the bison hunt,[38] so it was 1880 before Chief Mékaisto of the Kainai walked government officials over the area he had chosen: traditional wintering grounds southwest of present-day Lethbridge, bounded by the Belly, Oldman, and St Mary Rivers. Mékaisto was determined to show leadership in accepting change, building the first house on the reserve, and supporting the establishment of a church and a school. Not all the Kainai were so willing, but eventually poverty and hunger forced them to join Mékaisto's followers and accept reserve life.[39] In 1879–80 the Piikani reserve was surveyed, and in 1883–84 the Tsuu T'ina reserve and a drastically reconfigured Siksika reserve were demarcated. By this point the CPR was mostly constructed to Calgary, and other land in the area had been surveyed so that the reserve lands were spelled out in terms of numbered townships rather than natural landmarks. The Siksika reserve would be just south of the CPR, the Bow River would run through it with Blackfoot Crossing near its centre, and it had a much larger profile to the south of the railway than originally planned.[40]

Controversy surrounded the selection of the Stoney Nakoda reserves. These Indians comprised three main bands: the Bearspaw (Chief Bearspaw), the Chiniki (Chief Chiniki), and Jacob's (Chief Kichipwot) bands. The Stoneys believe they were an afterthought in Treaty 7, which was mainly a treaty with the Nizitapi; indeed, they believe they should have been asked to sign an adhesion to Treaty 6, since much of the territory they traditionally occupied was a part of it. In truth, however, their traditional territory ranged from the American borderlands and the Highwood River in the south, through Morley in the Bow Valley, and north to the Bighorn-Kootenay Plains (this last area on the upper reaches of the North Saskatchewan River was only included in Treaty 8). Each of the bands occupied one of these foothill-mountain regions most of the year, though they often wintered together in the Morley region. Chief

Bearspaw expected a reserve to the south, and Chief Kichipwot expected one in the Kootenay Plains region, but they found themselves consolidated in Morley, apparently because of the influence of the missionary John McDougall. The Stoneys saw their three bands as having the same separateness of identity and legitimacy as the three Blackfoot-speaking nations that received individual reserves of their choice.[41]

When the government surveyor arrived in 1879, the only persons with whom he consulted appear to have been McDougall and Chief Chiniki, who seems to have undertaken to speak for all Stoneys even though he lacked authority to do so. The other chiefs were away hunting with their bands. The result was three contiguous reserves, often viewed as a single reserve, near the Methodist mission at Morleyville. The reserves were poorly located for agricultural purposes, as the government would soon recognize. Moreover, even the surveyor, John Nelson, acknowledged, "when the survey was made many of these Indians wished to have the reserve at the Dog Pound or Red Deer River." Members of Jacob's band insist they were promised "land at the head of the Saskatchewan River in the mountains" when Treaty 7 was negotiated.[42]

There also were moments of tension about surveys at other reserves as Indians realized just how limited reserves would be based on one square mile per family of five, compared to what they imagined they would possess to permit them to hunt and fish as before. The tension usually dissipated when they understood their treaty right to hunt, fish, and gather beyond the reserve boundaries. A more significant area of dispute concerned the population count on which the reserve size calculation would be based. By the time reserves were surveyed, bands were often significantly smaller than when they signed the treaties, and surveyors typically based their calculations on the numbers present at the most recent annuity payments. Still, most of these disputes were solved with some diplomacy.[43] In the opinion of one scholar who examined this process, although the government was admittedly slow to complete the surveys, "government officials acted honorably in the designation of reserve lands." He also concluded that, on the whole, Indians received all the reserve land to which they were entitled, and in some cases even more. He found that the surveyors "usually included areas with valuable woodland and hay lands in the reserve – resources that the Indians would appreciate only in later years."[44]

In Treaty 6, however, there was one particularly troublesome case: that of the Passpasschase band.[45] In 1877, Chief Passpasschase and his headman and brother, Tahkoots, signed an adhesion to Treaty 6, and

202 members accepted treaty payment (as did the bands of Chiefs Alexis and Alexander at the same time). From there, the story becomes complex. The members of the band were mostly Metis, many of whom (or their forebears) had moved from Lesser Slave Lake to the Fort Edmonton region in the 1850s, where they traded, hunted, and worked for the Hudson's Bay Company. They were regarded as unreliable, troublesome, and even dangerous; Tahkoots, also known as "The Murderer," was believed to have killed a number of Tsuu T'ina and Siksika who had come to trade at Edmonton, thus exacerbating enmity between the peoples. Some Edmonton bands (Passpasschase, Alexis, Alexander) were trying to farm with wooden treaty implements such as spades, hoes, and ploughs without much success, and the hunt was still vital to their continued subsistence. The collapse of the bison herds, however, brought many Cree and Assiniboine to Fort Edmonton for food, and they too hunted and depleted the game upon which the Edmonton bands had relied. The government soon distributed flour, pemmican, and meat at Edmonton and Fort Saskatchewan, but the few local officials, who had only limited quantities of food to meet the unexpected demand, were still unable to provide an adequate response.

In 1880, the government finally sent a surveyor to establish reserves for the various bands, but the situation had changed since 1877. Many Passpasschase band members had left to pursue a living elsewhere while even more joined, so that 241 received annuity payments in the summer of 1880. The band wanted its land located on the south side of the North Saskatchewan River, directly across from Fort Edmonton, but some would-be settlers had established claims there. Tension arose. Not only were there conflicting land claims, but the settlers resented the fact that the Indians received large quantities of expensive supplies (which the government agents purchased from the HBC) without seeming to do any productive work.

After Passpasschase was induced to agree to the location of the reserve boundaries four miles further south than he desired, the survey commenced. On the same day, Inspector T.P. Wadsworth came to pay annuities to the band, but Passpasschase chose to make extensive demands before he would accept payment. After two days of this, Wadsworth decided to call his bluff and went to the north side of the river, where he began to pay a new band. What he called the Edmonton Stragglers included eighty-four members from Passpasschase's band who were anxious not to lose their payments.[46] Wadsworth told the surveyor to measure Passpasschase's reserve based on its now lower population figure. Moreover, he told the Stragglers that they would not have any land set aside for them. (Most were Metis who later, in 1885–86, took scrip to settle their aboriginal title.) When Passpasschase realized that the reserve would be much smaller than anticipated, he angrily halted the survey, and Dewdney informed the band that the survey might never be completed. This would have violated the treaty provisions, and after much procrastination and intrigue the survey of a forty-square-mile reserve was completed in 1884 on land that decades later would be a large part of south Edmonton. It turned out that the Passpasschase reserve would be very short-lived.

What did "reserve" mean to Indians in the 1880s? Without reserves, and promises that they would be permanent and inviolable, there could have been no treaties in the 1870s. Yet as the reserve era began, questions surrounded them. Indians had witnessed American incursions into, and appropriation of lands on, supposedly sacrosanct Indian reservations: could Canadian treaty promises of secure tenure be trusted? Additionally, they might have sensed that the government expected reserves to be places for transition and civilization from which they would be assimilated into white society. The language of the treaty negotiations was about transition and change, not preservation. It was only as Indians lived on reserves that the full meaning evolved, and some measure of confidence emerged – confidence that secure tenure was their right[47] and that reserves were home. When they believed that everything else had been torn away, reserves came to be a link with their past, their culture, and their traditions. Herein lay community, identity, language, kinship, and sacred symbolism. Here was the base from which they could resist the government plan, and on which they could preserve their identity as Indians.[48]

## DETERMINING "WHO IS OR WHO IS NOT AN INDIAN": THE CASE OF THE METIS

In the 1860s, many Metis moved from Red River to join settlements at Lac la Biche, Lac Ste Anne, and St Albert (mostly French and Catholic Metis), and near Saddle Lake (mostly English and Protestant Metis), in search of a better economic future. Some great herds of bison were still accessible in their range as far north as the North Saskatchewan River, and were critical to the Metis for food and other necessities, as they were to Indians.[49] The settlements were also close enough to the parkland and boreal forest that the Metis could hunt and fish; maintain traplines; and engage in trade, freighting, and other work for the HBC. Some farmed on a small scale. There also was a cultural logic in their move, because it was Cree territory, and a majority of Metis in the future Alberta had Cree ancestry and kin relationships. Others were of Ojibwa (Saulteaux), Assiniboine (Stoney), or Iroquois ancestry, who usually lived in peaceable relations with the Cree.[50]

The Cree even had a specific term for Metis: *Otipemisiwak*, meaning "free people" or "the people who own themselves."[51] This status of being an independent people who were not tied to permanent employment with the HBC, were free to live where they wished, and could take up such activities as they wished, was crucial to the Metis identity in the nineteenth century. It was an important differentiation between them and Indians, though one not always clearly and consistently maintained.

The story was different with the Nizitapi, who had been the implacable enemies of the Cree since the early nineteenth century. They saw the Cree as encroaching upon bison and territory they regarded as their own.[52] Indeed, Nizitapi hostility to interlopers, regardless of origin, helps to explain why it often was difficult to secure Metis guides for missionaries and explorers who wished to traverse Nizitapi land, as well as the relative paucity of Metis with Nizitapi ancestry.[53]

Life remained something of a struggle for the Metis of this region. In the early 1870s they, as well as some Metis from Red River and some local Cree, established winter camps to hunt bison for both food and hides. However, the animals were increasingly scarce. Many people were near starvation for much of the winter, and they also suffered heavy losses of oxen and horses. Profits were usually marginal. Not only did the bison no longer appear so far north, but by 1877 and 1878 they were scarce even further south, ending the winter hunts.[54] Yet these same Metis hunters opposed the 1877 ordinance restricting the bison hunt, and appealed to Laird at the treaty talks that year to relax the law. The lieutenant governor assured them that enforcement in the first year would not be rigorous; in 1878 the ordinance was repealed. By that time, there were few bison left anywhere to protect, and the robe trade had essentially died out.[55]

Metis, however, had a broader purpose in their petition to Laird in 1877: they were nearly destitute, and appealed for government aid in the form of farm implements and seed, which they knew their Indian relations were receiving. In reply, Laird told them he could not grant their wish, but would pass the request on to Ottawa authorities with a favourable recommendation. He was pleased they wished to settle down and farm, and until they were self-supporting, they would have under the "buffalo" ordinance "the privilege of hunting buffalo three months every autumn," enabling them "to lay in a winter's stock of provisions" – which he surely knew was an increasingly empty hope. Laird concluded with an assurance, "the Government feel a kindly interest in your welfare, and it is because they desire to see you enjoying the full franchise and property rights of British subjects, and not laboring under the Indian state of pupilage, that they have deemed it for the advantage of half-breeds that they should not be admitted to the Indian treaties."[56]

Only two years before, Bishop Vital Grandin of St Albert had written a lengthy, impassioned appeal to the government for support for Metis needs. He denounced those who portrayed the Metis as "a barbarous people, incapable of culture." Such a perception, he argued, was mistaken: the Metis indeed wanted to farm, but implements such as ploughs were very scarce, and were excessively costly when available. They were cultivating fields of potatoes with only "sticks, fire-hardened, and yet we are not disheartened." Moreover, the church remained the sole support for a half-dozen schools in the North-West Territories, as well as three orphanages, all serving mainly Metis children. Additionally, the church was the only institution that attempted to look after "the blind, the deaf and dumb, the lame and idiots." Grandin wanted funding for agriculture, the schools, and orphanages, along with land grants for Metis. He secured a grant of $300 from the minister of the interior to assist in maintaining the school at St Albert.[57]

Given their desperate circumstances, it is scarcely surprising that many Metis in the Treaty 6 area decided to seek treaty status based on their Indian ancestry. Freedom would mean little if it led only to starvation. Thus several bands of "Indians" who adhered to the treaty were partially or predominantly Metis. According to Gerhard Ens, individual Metis entered the treaties "both as a strategy of survival and because they had relatives in the various bands that took treaty."[58] As seen, under the Indian Act of 1876, a person legally was classed either as white and a full British subject, or as an Indian and a ward of the state. Metis were forced to make a choice, often determined by practical reasons: in taking treaty, they assumed an Indian identity, with its financial and other benefits; a few years later, when the government offered them scrip to extinguish their Metis title, many left the treaty and resumed a Metis identity instead. Thus they had what Ens terms an "instrumental" or a "situational" identity.[59]

Yet the legal situation was not as clear as the government suggested. Under the Manitoba Act, 1870, an aboriginal title for Metis had been recognized: Manitoba Metis were entitled to a land grant because of their Indian ancestry, and because they had lived off the land as had the Indians.[60] Many Metis in the future Alberta had left Manitoba well before 1870, but many more Metis in the North-West Territories had left during the 1870s, prior to receiving any of the land or scrip to which they were entitled in that province. Would their claims be recognized beyond Manitoba? Would the government extend the right to all Metis?

These questions were in the air when the treaties were negotiated in 1876 and 1877. For example, in 1876, government agents went to pay annuities in the Treaty 4 area in present-day southern Saskatchewan; there they found "half-breeds who wished to join Bands and draw money as Indians." Agent M.G. Dickieson asked them whether "they had ever belonged to 'any particular Band,' or had recognized any Indian as their Chief. They replied in the negative, and informed me their desire was to form a Band, distinct from the Indians, and under a Chief of their own." Dickieson told them that, under the Indian Act, they could not. The Metis then chose to present themselves as members of bands being paid annuities, and even claimed to be Indians, not Metis. The agent asked them to swear that their fathers were Indians, which they refused to do, and he declined to pay them. But he also recognized that this was a very unsatisfactory situation, pointing out in his report that a number of treaty Indians who were being paid annuities had white fathers but had always lived and been recognized as Indians. Others had mostly, but not always, followed the Indian way, while yet others of similar background were closer to the white way of life. The question, he stated, was "where shall the line be drawn to decide who is or who is not an Indian?" The law was unhelpful and inconsistent, and Dickieson found himself paying some in a family as treaty Indians, while refusing brothers, sisters, or even parents of these individuals. He drew a strict line based on his understanding of the law, and later discovered that most of the Cree and Assiniboine chiefs approved of his decision, as they did not want Metis arbitrarily added to their bands.[61]

But that was only one example. In a different case, at Fort Walsh the same year, Inspector J.M. Walsh of the NWMP found that Indians arrived with a set of demands that had nothing to do with annuities; one was that "the Half-breeds be admitted to the treaty, and receive the same payment as themselves; they regarded them as their brothers of the plains, and were not inclined to part company with them now." Walsh told them he was not permitted to grant their request, because the government believed some Metis had taken land scrip in Manitoba, and now wanted to "be paid both ways." He told them they could apply through him to the minister, indicating their willingness to give up any claim to land and be subject to the same laws as all treaty Indians.[62]

In 1878, Laird advised the government that the uncertain situation was increasing dissatisfaction among Metis in the territories, and that it was time to put them on the same basis as those in Manitoba with respect to land claims. Laird did not want to admit more Metis into the treaties; indeed, he recommended that the law be amended to permit Metis who had entered treaty to leave it, if they repaid gratuity and annuity money they had received, the enticement being the opportunity to receive scrip. Laird pointed out the problematic example of the Lac la Biche band members who had taken treaty in 1876. The chief and all members of the band were Metis. Trouble arose in 1877 at payment of annuities when a number of band members' relatives showed up wanting to be admitted as band members to receive annuities. The presiding official had declined to pay any who were not on the 1876 list, and Laird pointed out to the new Conservative government that there would be a widespread Metis movement into the treaties if a precedent were set by accepting these claimants. The Lac la Biche chief complained directly to Laird about the injustice of the exclusion. Laird replied that, because the treaty commissioners had not understood that the chief was Metis, they had erred in admitting him in the first place, and Laird did not intend to compound the error unless he heard otherwise from the government.

This moved the government belatedly into making its policy clearer. Dennis commented, "I do not think it at all politic, if any other course can be adopted by which half-breeds can be satisfied, that persons of this class should be treated with and paid as Indians." His superior, Macdonald, noted his agreement. The government thus decided to encourage Metis to leave the treaties, and to forbid any more from entering them.[63] In 1880, it amended the Indian Act to exclude any Metis who had "shared in the distribution of half-breed lands" both from the provisions of the act and also from the treaties. It provided as well, following Laird's advice, that any Metis "who may have been admitted into a treaty shall be allowed to withdraw therefrom on refunding all annuity money received by him or her under the said treaty," or that such person would suffer "a corresponding reduction" in whatever land or money script to which they might be entitled.[64]

## METIS POLICY AND FEDERAL INDIAN POLICY

The growing agitation over land rights recognition among Metis at Prince Albert and Batoche has been well documented as part of the background to the North-West Rebellion of 1885.[65] Less well known is the fact that in 1880 a group of Metis from the Edmonton area also petitioned for land on the same basis as applied in Manitoba, complaining that delays in addressing the matter meant that land they desired or claimed by prior possession was being withheld as a result of the surveys or was being priced out of their reach.[66] At any event, early in 1882 the beleaguered prime minister acknowledged at last that the government needed to meet the demands of the Metis of the North-West Territories "reasonably,"[67] meaning that he accepted they had a legitimate claim to compensation for their aboriginal title. But what was this to mean in practice?

In 1878, Dennis, who had had some direct contact with western Metis in the 1870s, wrote a memorandum based on that experience claiming there were two classes of Metis. One was primarily nomadic and dependent upon the bison hunt. The other was found in settlements such as Edmonton, St Albert, Lac Ste Anne, and Saddle Lake, had permanent houses and undertook some farming, but still engaged in some hunting and gathering and depended upon the annual bison hunt for survival. (He had not yet grasped that the demise of the bison was contributing to the existential crisis of the territorial Metis.) He thought Metis "very little better able than are the Indians to take care of themselves," and therefore believed they "have, as natives, as good a right to the protection of the Government as the Indians." He proposed three ways to do this:

1 Essentially, give them Indian status, regard them as wards of the government, make a treaty with them, "and look forward to their remaining for many years in their present semi-barbarous state."
2 Issue scrip to each individual, "and then let them take their chances of living or starving in the future."
3 Give them inducements to settle and farm, "especially to raise cattle."

He thought the first alternative would be acceptable to neither the government nor Metis. The second he considered likely to be a disaster:

based on the Manitoba experience with issuance of scrip, it would be rapidly wasted, and once the bison were extinct, "we would find ourselves face to face with a formidable, nomadic, semi-savage element which would prove a standing menace to the peace and prosperity of the Territories."

Dennis was trying to steer the government toward his preferred third option. He supported the territorial government's recommendation to give Metis non-negotiable scrip that they could only use to purchase land, allowing them to take up land wherever they wished. He also would allow for some aid in the form of agricultural implements and seed to actual settlers. To contextualize Dennis's concern, in 1878, Canada was trying to cope with a significant group of Indian refugees from the United States – mostly Sitting Bull's band at Cypress Hills – who were thought potentially destabilizing. Thus Dennis argued policies "should be adopted to cultivate and maintain relations with our Indians and half-breed populations, calculated to attach them to us, and to convince them that the Government is desirous of fulfilling its obligations to them in the utmost good faith." He proposed that supporting them in adapting to farming, cattle raising, and especially "the mechanical trades" would help them to survive independently after the demise of the bison, to be emancipated from "tribal government," and to merge "into the general community."[68]

Out of this, Dennis produced a recommendation that bore fruit, though not quite in the form he anticipated. He contended that industrial schools should be established for Metis and Indians, and that they would be a force for stability in the West. Macdonald quickly picked up on the idea, and asked Dennis to write to a failed Conservative candidate in the late federal election, Nicholas Flood Davin, appointing him a one-man commission to investigate the industrial school model. Because the schools were subsequently implemented as Indian industrial schools (see chapter 6 in this book), it is often forgotten that Dennis emphasized the Metis issue when he first framed the idea for the prime minister. Davin's commission was to "make a report upon the subject of industrial schools for the education of Indians and half-breeds," and included Dennis's rationale. Accordingly, Davin's March 1879 report was "on Industrial Schools for Indians and Half-Breeds."[69] He did pick up the idea of Metis as key to addressing the western situation: "The mixed-blood is the natural mediator between the Government and the red man, and also his natural instructor." That mediatory role, in his mind, justified educating them at the industrial schools along with the Indians.[70]

Initially Macdonald was open to Dennis's suggestion for a more generous, proactive, and constructive policy toward the Metis (outside the treaties), but he soon changed his mind. Some initial responses to Davin's report, when circulated, were very cool to government funding of industrial schools.[71] Dennis resigned in 1880, removing an influential advocate for action. By the time industrial schools were introduced in 1883, the government did not intend to support the education of Metis children. The few who did attend such schools were either supported by the Church or able to pay fees. By the latter part of 1882, the dominion was heading back into a depression. The cash-starved government restrained Indian Affairs expenditures, and was not going to begin spending to educate children to whom it had no legal obligation.

The land issue remained and could not be ignored much longer. Yet it presented a dilemma. Land or money scrip in Manitoba had ended up mostly in speculators' hands with little or no permanent benefit or legacy to the Metis, especially if compared with the inalienable Indian reserves. The lack of a base for community, stability, and future economic growth was of great concern to both government and church officials. Early in 1885, the government announced essentially that it would extend the Manitoba policy to the North-West Territories: all Metis resident in the territories on 15 July 1870 (the same date as in Manitoba) would be entitled to participate in the land or money scrip grant, and a Half-Breed Land Claims Commission would be established to carry out the policy. It would prove to be a flawed policy with significant implications for Indian bands as well as for Metis. But it was announced near the height of tensions between the government on the one hand, and Metis and Indians on the other; the outbreak of hostilities delayed its implementation.

### GRIEVANCES, UNREST, AND RESISTANCE

These tensions did not develop spontaneously. Rumours of unrest had circulated since the signing of the treaties as police, missionaries, Indian agents, farm instructors, and others had reported the human suffering and barely suppressed anger. Indian leaders had pleaded with officials, and petitioned Ottawa officialdom without result. Ottawa seemed to believe that a firm hand would keep Indians in line, and that trouble only arose because soft-hearted, if not soft-headed, police and agents were too generous and led western Indians to believe the government might cave in to persistent pressure. However, being penny wise proved pound foolish. Indians had many legitimate grievances. Flour and tea, often handed out as rations, could not compensate for bison or other protein.[72] Beef and bacon were sometimes substituted, but were in limited supply and frequently of poor quality. As malnutrition and illness ravaged reserves, Indians were angry that agents had supplies in storehouses that they would not – often under direct orders from Ottawa – distribute. The government spoke of the need to grow food, but often did not provide implements and farm animals on schedule or in sufficient quantity or quality. Some Indian agents, farm instructors, and police were as humane, sympathetic, and flexible as possible under the circumstances – indeed, some were fired for their generosity. Others, however, were rigid, arrogant, and heartless – infuriating and alienating Indians, but too often commended and promoted by Ottawa.

Warning signs were everywhere as Indian threats and violent incidents increased. In 1880, the Cree at Bear Hills (later Hobbema) threatened to seize food supplies by force. In January 1883, Chiefs Ermineskin, Bobtail, and Samson wrote a desperate appeal to Macdonald, noting "our dire poverty, our utter destitution," asserting they had only survived because of "the charity of the white settlers who are not bound by treaty to help us," and concluding, "our widows and old people are getting the barest pittance, just enough to keep body and soul together, and there have been cases in which body and soul have refused to stay together on such allowance." Consequently, the treaty promises seemed to them "meaningless." They wondered whether there was a plan to annihilate their people gradually, and warned, "the motto of the Indian is 'If we must die by violence let us do it quickly.'"[73] Receiving no response, in July 1883 the Bear Hills Cree marched to Edmonton to confront the agent, who told them they would only receive food back on the reserve. They seized the agent, and only released him when the HBC provided food from its store on promise of repayment when annuities were paid. The NWMP helped defuse the situation by providing additional supplies. Beal and Macleod note, "after a victory dance, the Indians went home."[74] True, but they were learning that only firm and decisive action would produce results.

Several incidents demonstrated increasing Indian willingness to stand up to the NWMP. In 1882, at Blackfoot Crossing, the police attempted to arrest Bull Elk, a minor chief who had allegedly fired at a white man. The Siksika were determined to protect him, and surrounded the police contingent. The incident appeared at first to have been resolved by negotiation with Isapo-Muxika, who secured Bull Elk's release with a promise that he would stand trial. The Siksika rejoiced in what appeared to be a victory.[75] Unhappily, the police returned in force to seize Bull Elk despite the more or less trumped-up nature of the charge against him, and broke Isapo-Muxika's trust in their fairness.[76] In 1884, Indians at Crooked Lakes, east of Alberta, defied a police force of about forty when they tried to arrest Yellow Calf, who had allegedly assaulted a stubborn agent and seized (or stole) desperately needed food supplies.[77]

All this was fuel for the fire that burned in the hearts of many prairie region Indians – especially the young men who chafed under the new way of life. The older men had proven their manhood and earned respect in the buffalo hunt, horse stealing, war, and the ceremonies and rituals that were an integral part of the nomadic, hunting-gathering way of life.[78] Angry but resigned to the new way, members of the older generation had their identities, memories, stories, and songs. Members of the younger generation naturally were frustrated: what identity, what future would be theirs? What outlet would there be for their energies or anger? Moreover, what kind of leader would repeatedly submit to broken promises, starvation, humiliation, and slow, painful annihilation by malnutrition and disease?[79]

Indians had long known that unity of purpose and action could enable them to pressure the government more successfully. The government was determined to prevent such solidarity from getting off the ground. It feared an alliance between Sitting Bull's Sioux (in the Cypress Hills area, 1877–81) and the Nizitapi and Cree, though historic differences and competition for scarce resources between these groups prevented the idea from going very far.[80] It undermined Cree Chiefs Big Bear, Piapot, and Little Pine as they tried to create an Indian territory for all the plains nations, in part by settling Piapot and Little Pine and their bands in different parts of Treaty 4. Big Bear resisted treaty until starvation forced his hand, and he agreed to adhere to Treaty 6 and settle near Frog Lake in 1883. However, he remained committed to united action, hoping with other Cree chiefs up to early 1885 to convene a Treaty 6 council that would include bands from the district of Alberta as well as the district of Saskatchewan – plans aborted by the North-West Rebellion that spring.[81]

The North-West Rebellion was principally a Metis rebellion, and calls to join in were mainly resisted by the Indians of the territories.[82] Louis Riel had been pushing for Metis and Indians to unite against the government, though they had differing agendas and little record of mutual confidence. For some years, Riel had lived in exile in Montana as a consequence of events associated with the Red River Resistance of 1869–70.

That resistance resulted in the creation of the province of Manitoba in 1870, and in recognition of some bilingual, educational, and land rights in the provincial constitution – rights intended to benefit the mixed-blood community, but which did virtually nothing for Native peoples in the new province. The Indians of the prairie West had sought to protect their rights in treaties with the Queen, in which the Metis role (apart from functioning as translators) was mostly peripheral and self-interested. In other words, neither Riel personally nor Metis generally had a record of seeking to protect Native peoples' interests, and indeed they had been active competitors for scarce bison in the 1870s, taking hides in commercial quantities and destroying the animal on which plains Indian cultures depended.

The years after 1870 produced deception and delay in settling the land rights of the Manitoba Metis. The Metis grew to distrust the government. Many also moved to the banks of the North Saskatchewan near Prince Albert and Batoche to establish their community anew.[83] They were angry with the government's procrastination and insensitivity, but hoped that, as in 1869–70, Riel could get its attention. He promoted the idea of united Native action to recapture the North-West Territories for Indians and Metis, and tried to engage Isapo-Muxika's support in 1880, while the latter was in Montana, and again in 1881. Isapo-Muxika declined, convinced that war with whites was foolhardy.[84] Still, when Riel agreed to return to Canada in the summer of 1884 to aid the cause of the Saskatchewan Metis, he had not given up on the idea of united resistance to the federal authorities.

This is not the place to follow the main events of the North-West Rebellion of 1885, all of which occurred in the district of Saskatchewan. It began with the Metis defeat of a significant force of NWMP at Duck Lake, near Prince Albert, on 26 March 1885; continued in April and May with confrontations between the Canadian militia (hastily rushed into the field) and the police on the one hand, and the Metis and some Indians who supported the cause on the other; and ended in May and June with the capture or surrender of Riel, some of his colleagues, and many Indian leaders.[85] The rebellion did affect Alberta, however, and its consequences were very real for the Native peoples – including Metis – of the district. It is important to recall that Indian chiefs virtually all opposed supporting Riel; that the Metis coerced some Saskatchewan bands into supporting the cause; that many Indians who did support the cause were often linked by blood or marriage to the Metis; and that the remaining Indian participants did not constitute an organized resistance to the government.[86]

The fighting in 1885 took place well north of the almost-completed CPR, which had reached Calgary in 1883. Most of the line was available to distribute troops and supplies from central and eastern Canada across the southern part of the territories. Major General Frederick D. Middleton, the officer commanding the Canadian forces, devised a three-pronged movement of troops north from the CPR to engage the rebelling Metis and Indians, commencing from Qu'Appelle and Swift Current in Assiniboia, and from Calgary in the district of Alberta. The last of these was commanded by the eccentric Major General Thomas Bland Strange who, having retired from the British Army, took up horse ranching in Alberta near the Siksika reserve in the early 1880s. Bilingual and happy to take command of a group of French-Canadian militia, he was ordered to proceed north from Calgary to Edmonton, and then east down the North Saskatchewan River to approach the fighting from the west.[87]

The militia were a great relief to white Albertans. Those in or near Edmonton felt isolated, vulnerable, and frightened – they heard about the police defeat at Duck Lake, after which the telegraph service failed. Isolation facilitated rumour-driven terror. Did this portend a general Indian uprising? They heard that at the Saddle Lake agency, which was mostly Cree and sympathetic to the Cree in Saskatchewan, members of the Blue Quill and Little Hunter bands on 3 April had seized a local farm instructor who had refused their demand for an ox to eat and for other supplies, and had raided the storehouse.[88] Some individuals from the Saddle Lake reserve had gone east to join forces with the Big Bear or Poundmaker bands. The James Seenum band, and many of the Blue Quill band, remained loyal.[89] Meanwhile, south of Edmonton at Bear Hills, excitement about the police defeat was rapidly rising and Chief Bobtail had asked other Edmonton-area bands whether they would support Poundmaker, with whom the Bear Hills bands had a close connection. Frightened whites, including government officials, fled for Edmonton, leaving Father Constantine Scollen, the Oblate priest assigned to the district, to negotiate with the local Native peoples on 9 April, when he pointed out the long-term risks of joining the rebellion. The older chiefs agreed with him, but some younger Native people still headed east to join the rebel forces. On 11 April, the *Edmonton Bulletin* informed its readers fearfully, "when the Indians around Edmonton will rise would appear now to be only a matter of days."[90]

Open conflict was avoided in Alberta, but it was, note Beal and
Macleod, "an uneasy peace." Officials had warned the Native peoples in
no uncertain terms of the consequences for rebellion. At the same time,
officials believed it would have taken little encouragement to tip the
scales in favour of rebellion. Indian Agent S.B. Lucas told Dewdney that
if the Bear Hills Native peoples were "joined by Indians from Battleford,
the Blackfeet or Stonies from Lake St Ann's," they would rise. In fact, the
only band in the Treaty 6 region of Alberta that Lucas felt fairly certain
would remain loyal was that at Whitefish Lake, which had in the past
resisted overtures for united action from Poundmaker and Big Bear.
"I have no confidence in the promises made by Bears Hills band," he
wrote, "Ermine Skin admits that he cannot even control his men."[91]
With a virtually indefensible fort and the nearest NWMP detachment
nineteen miles distant at Fort Saskatchewan, many Edmontonians feared
the worst. They sent a messenger to Calgary for military help, and called
on the NWMP under Inspector Griesbach to defend Edmonton in the
meantime. Efforts were made to repair the old fort, two brass cannon
were mounted, little-used arms were tested, and a system of patrols was
established. Whites from all around the Edmonton region scurried in to
seek what protection might be offered. Near the end of April 1885, the
fright of a few weeks was relieved when Strange and his troops arrived;
he left a small company when he headed east, where in late May he
would engage the Cree rebels at Frenchman Butte, a short distance down
the North Saskatchewan from Fort Pitt.[92]

A great irony was that overwhelmingly the Native peoples had no
intention of rising in rebellion, and made every effort to convey this, but
were not believed. Alberta Native peoples were mostly puzzled at the
fright that had seized the whites, and apprehensive about how the government would respond in wake of the troubles. Having heard rumours
that Fort Edmonton had fallen and that the usual supplies would not
be forthcoming, some young men at Hobbema seized supplies from
the abandoned HBC post and from some homes abandoned by fleeing
whites. Within a few hours, the chiefs persuaded them to return what
they had taken, and thereafter no more trouble occurred.[93]

The only other significant incident in the Treaty 6 area in Alberta
occurred on 26 April at Lac la Biche, as a result of messengers from Riel
and Wandering Spirit asking local Cree and Metis to seize the local HBC
post. They did so with great abandon, grabbing all the available merchandise, food, and fur, and then vandalizing the building and its remaining contents.[94] It seems to have been a brief moment of mob psychology

that remained local and produced neither injuries nor fatalities, nor any increased tendency to rebel.

In the Treaty 7 area, there was near "mass hysteria" among whites,[95] despite less danger of actual uprising. At first the news of Duck Lake excited the Siksika and Kainai, and whites rushed to take refuge in Fort Macleod, realizing that nearby Native people significantly outnumbered them. There were, however, divisions within the bands. Some, mainly younger warriors, were anxious to make common cause against their white enemies. Older leaders, such as Mékaisto and Isapo-Muxika, were more cautious. They still saw the Cree as their real enemies, and if the whites and the Cree wanted to fight, so be it. Yet others appear to have been willing to fight with the whites against the Cree and Metis. The local government agents also wisely increased beef and flour rations to the Treaty 7 Siksika, Kainai, and Piikani, on the belatedly acknowledged principle that satisfied stomachs were less likely to go to war. Overtures from the Cree were rejected, and Isapo-Muxika opportunistically sent Macdonald a declaration of loyalty to the Queen, "whatever happens." For a federal government stressed by the demands of fighting the rebels in Saskatchewan, the declaration was a welcome affirmation from the western chief most favourably regarded by the Canadian public; Isapo-Muxika's message was duly publicized and sent on to the Queen. Yet local officials and missionaries such as Father Lacombe, who for some years had been suspicious and critical of the Siksika chief because of his resistance to government educational and agricultural policies, were more grudging in their praise, believing that his sentiments were more political opportunism than heartfelt loyalty. Isapo-Muxika's request for a small amount of ammunition to enable the Siksika to defend themselves against the Cree was summarily denied. Trust on either side went only so far.[96]

## AFTERMATH

The dénouement of the 1885 North-West Rebellion did not shed much lustre on the government. Riel was convicted of treason, and hanged in November, with long-lasting political results for the nation. Some Metis and Indian leaders fled to the United States for asylum, but the government rounded up dozens more, including Big Bear and Poundmaker, and tried them under charges that ranged from murder and treason-felony to arson and property crimes.[97]

Stonechild and Waiser argue that far fewer Metis than Indians were brought to trial despite the greater numbers and culpability of Metis involved in rebellion; that in effect Indians were tried in kangaroo courts that had little interest in the truth and were determined to produce convictions quickly and cheaply; and that all this was deliberately orchestrated by a government determined to dominate Indians by blaming them for the rebellion when it knew that most Indian leaders had consistently counselled against participation and had repeatedly declared their loyalty and adherence to treaty promises, and that most Indians who did participate were coerced by Metis at rifle point. The government argued that by participating in rebellion the Indians had violated the treaties, which in turn justified abrogating many of their treaty rights.[98] Although the serious rebellious activity was confined to the district of Saskatchewan, and almost no Alberta Indians were brought to trial (seemingly none faced any serious charges), government retribution applied to all prairie Indians. Where property damage had occurred, the chiefs were held responsible for not controlling their people, and the entire band suffered. The government did not attempt to understand Indian social and political structures and customs, or the practical limits of any chief's influence.

Indians in the North-West Territories faced three major consequences. First, the government (modestly) rewarded those who had remained loyal during the outbreak[99] with increased rations, agricultural implements, farm animals, and the like. It also made much of those Indian leaders who had encouraged loyalty, taking them on a train trip to central Canada where they were photographed and fêted. By contrast, it punished bands responsible for property damage and withheld their annuities to recover costs. In 1886, Dewdney referred to it as a "policy of reward and punishment":

The policy of rewarding those who proved faithful and depriving the rebels of their annuities has worked admirably. This latter course, which should be continued – at any rate, until they have paid for the property they wantonly destroyed – affords a most effectual means of keeping alive in the memories of those, only too ready to forget, the certain consequences of such misconduct as that of which they were guilty, and as they are provided as they were before with food and clothing, the temptation to commit outrages is removed.

Again, the amount of kindness which they receive, allows them to hope that, by continuing to behave themselves, they may, through time, recover their lost position.

Another good result of this policy, is to be found in the fact, that, owing to the rewards of the loyal having taken the form – to a great extent – of presents of cattle, the herds, which were so unfortunately destroyed last year, are in a fair way to recover their proportions.[100]

Second, the government determined to pursue even more rigorous centralization of policy making, and a more aggressive approach to acculturation and to halting traditional practices such as dances. Third, it illegally and unilaterally imposed a system requiring any Indian who wished to leave a reserve to have a pass signed by the local Indian agent, and it sought the support of a very reluctant N W M P in enforcing the new system.[101] This also was a product of the need to reduce the risk of confrontations between Indians and increasing numbers of white settlers, ranchers, and traders.

These policies were developed at least partly in response to popular pressure. Macdonald certainly knew how to trim his sails when a tempest threatened. In 1878, he had been fairly optimistic about how quickly change would result from a well-ordered policy in the Northwest, and was more sympathetic than most in Ottawa to Indians' plight. Gwyn claims, rather too generously, that Macdonald was without prejudice with respect to Indians; that he knew Indians better than any other federal minister with the same responsibility in Canadian history; that he acknowledged they were "the original owners of the soil," dispossessed by avaricious whites; that Indians had "certain inalienable rights"; and that assimilation was improbable.[102]

A good indicator of how pressures reshaped Macdonald's attitude arose during debate in 1885 with respect to his Electoral Franchise Bill. It had long been one of Macdonald's objectives to give the federal government control of a uniform franchise and voting mechanisms across the dominion (along with the attendant patronage), rather than relying on variable provincial laws. He had proposed such legislation in 1870, and again in 1883 and 1884, always without success. In 1885 he was determined to see the matter through. Among other things, he advanced the then-radical notion of the vote for women, at least for widows and spinsters, but backed off in face of vigorous opposition. He also successfully proposed the vote for Indian men with the same property as required for eligible white men – for which Gwyn praises him – and was prepared to put his prestige as prime minister and superintendent general on the line to see the matter through. However, in the course of the debate, which took place against the background of the ongoing North-West Rebellion, a differentiation emerged between his attitude to Indians of the Northwest and to those of central Canada. In 1872, Macdonald flatly opposed extension of the franchise to Indians,[103] but by 1885 he had rethought his position. He introduced the legislation on 19 March, exactly one week prior to the battle of Duck Lake; the second reading took place on 16 April, and discussion of the Indian clause in committee began on 24 April, after the government had rushed troops west to deal with the rebellion. Thus the context raised the emotion of the debate. When asked on 30 April who would be a qualified Indian voter, Macdonald seemed remarkably generous: "an Indian who is qualified would have a vote if he is a British subject. If an Indian has an income of $300 a year, he will have a vote the same as any other person." This would apply to Indians on reserves, not only those few who were formally enfranchised, and would include Indians of the Northwest:

Mills: "Poundmaker and Big Bear."
Macdonald: "Yes."
Mills: "So that they can go from a scalping party to the polls."[104]

Macdonald realized that giving the vote to Indians, who at the time were widely believed to have revolted against the government, murdering whites, was not going to fly. He shortly revised his position, declaring, "the Bill can in no way apply to the savage nomads of the North-West." By implication, Poundmaker and Big Bear no longer met the standards to vote. Indians who qualified were "Indians of the old Provinces, where they are educated and have been under a civilizing process for years and years, where they have schools, where they can read and write." He thought that Ontario Indians, "as a rule, can read as well as the white man."[105] Macdonald had begun with the intention of making the vote available without distinction across the dominion to all Indian men who qualified in the same way as white men; the events in the Northwest in March and April 1885 forced him to qualify his proposal, and make it clear that Indians of the Northwest were unsuited for the vote.[106] This typified the hardening of attitudes of official Ottawa toward Indians of the Northwest.

The rebellion over, getting Indians to settle down and accept agricultural life seemed even more urgent. The government firmly believed that settled Indian farmers would be much less likely to endanger the peace than a nomadic, insecure, and hungry population. Settlement, moreover, was the necessary precursor to effective education and permanent change among Indians.

The post-treaty period of adjustment in the North-West Territories included at least one more phase that significantly affected several bands, mostly in the Treaty 6 area. With the rebellion over in the summer of 1885, the dominion government sent its Half-Breed Scrip Commission to the territories to offer scrip to Metis to extinguish their title to land. However, the commission was empowered only to deal with Metis who could demonstrate their residency in the territories on 15 July 1870; since many either had no documentation or had entered after 1870, the policy was fundamentally unjust. The North-West Territories government passed resolutions in 1887, 1888, 1889, and 1893 to demand that the federal government recognize the right of all Metis born before 1885, but to no avail. Ottawa refused to modify its policy.[107] The commission also was directed not to recognize claims of any man who took up arms against the government in 1885, and widows and children of any killed in action against the government were prohibited from inheriting the claim (though they might have legitimate rights in their own persons). In many cases, the commission was unable to make such determination, and such claims were reserved.[108]

In 1885, therefore, the commission recognized the claims of some 797 Metis heads of families and children in the district of Alberta, of which 631, or 79.2 per cent, made their claim in the Treaty 6 area, and the rest in the region of Treaty 7. Over 92 per cent of the Treaty 6 claimants lived in the area of St Albert/Edmonton/Fort Saskatchewan. Almost 90 per cent took money scrip rather than land scrip.[109]

A major goal of government policy in 1885 and 1886 was to encourage Metis who had taken treaty to leave and extinguish their land claim with land or money scrip, and this appears to have been wildly successful. To make this option attractive, the government changed the regulations. Metis who had previously left the treaty and had previous annuities deducted from their scrip were reimbursed for the deduction, while new applicants could leave the treaty without any obligation to repay their annuities. The *Edmonton Bulletin* was delighted with the resulting stream of applicants: "By freeing themselves from the treaty they relieve the government of a considerable charge and heavy responsibility and enroll themselves in the ranks of the workers instead of the drones, to which they formerly belonged."[110] Ironically, so attractive was the opportunity to many Metis that it unexpectedly caused public consternation out of fear that suddenly many destitute Metis, hitherto

supported on reserves by the federal government, would be impoverished and dependent upon local whites. The commissioners therefore
were directed that Metis who "lead the same mode of life as Indians are
not to be granted discharges from Treaty."[111] Nevertheless, many Metis
applied to be released from the treaties, and were accepted. Deputy
Minister of the Interior A.M. Burgess commented in his report for 1886
that "a large proportion of the claims of last season were made by Half-
breeds who had formerly ranked as Indians, and had been in receipt of
annual payments and other treaty privileges through the Department of
Indian Affairs. Great care was taken that only such Half-breeds of this
class as were likely to be able to maintain themselves were permitted to
sever their connection with their respective bands."[112]

The commission sessions in 1885 were only the beginning; in 1886,
the flow increased. Speculators, happy to pay a discounted rate for Metis
scrip, employed Metis runners to encourage "as many Indians as possible to seek discharges from the Treaty." Those reluctant to leave the
treaty were mocked, told they were "slaves," and reminded that everything that they had belonged to the government. Without instructions,
scrip commissioners had to accept applicants who applied according to
prescribed form. According to Kenneth Tyler, "since the only evidence
required was that of sworn statements by friends to the effect that the
applicant was of mixed blood, few Indians had any difficulty in 'proving'
that they were entitled to be considered 'half-breeds.'"[113] Although they
were supposed to be informed that the decision to leave treaty and accept
Metis status was irrevocable, many of the applicants appear to have
believed they could re-enter the treaty at any time.

Chaos best describes the atmosphere at the commission hearings of
1886. Officials at Hobbema stopped granting discharges on 1 July, but
by then Chief Bobtail, most of his followers, and large numbers from the
Samson and Ermineskin bands had received discharges. The commissioners then moved to Edmonton where, according to one account, they
found the entire membership of the Passpasschase and Enoch bands
camped in anticipation.[114] In all, in 1886 some 667 claims were accepted,
at least 300 of which were leaving treaty. It has been calculated that "in
1885 and 1886 almost 43 per cent of the Treaty Indians in the Edmonton
Agency lost Indian status by conversion." Certainly some full-blooded
Indians were allowed to convert. Moreover, accusations have been made
that there was a measure of outright corruption by speculators, and possibly on the part of some government officials.[115] Obviously, such rapid
loss of numbers affected the bands' social and economic structures.

However, a significant portion of the Treaty 6 bands remained Metis by ancestry; some had been refused permission to convert, and others preferred to retain a treaty Indian identity.

This part of the story concludes with the sad fate of the Passpasschase reserve. After much agonizing, almost all withdrawals from the Passpasschase reserve were allowed in 1886, though the persons who converted found to their dismay that they were not permitted to settle on the reserve lands; eventually they mostly migrated to areas north and east of Edmonton. Only ten men remained to receive annuities on the reserve in 1886. In 1887, most of these members moved and were absorbed into nearby bands. In 1888, the government found three members of the band to sign an instrument of surrender of the Passpasschase reserve.[116] Only four years had passed since the reserve was surveyed. The case was the first major surrender of Indian reserve land in the prairie region, in a process of dubious legality; more land surrenders would occur after 1896.[117]

It is ironic that the first surrender occurred so soon after the end of reserve surveys in the district of Alberta.[118] Yet it somehow typified the changed relationship between Indians and newcomers since signing the treaties in 1876 and 1877. The Indians saw the perceived promise of trust and sustaining kinship betrayed amid starvation, inadequate supplies, unreasonable expectations, and coercion. Government and officials often – though not always – stereotyped Indians as wild, lazy, too willing to live off unearned rations rather than supporting themselves, and more responsive to the big stick than to gentle persuasion. By 1885, the impression was entrenched that the Indians of the Northwest were more primitive and intractable than those of other parts of Canada and required different governance. Officials with these impressions were convinced they knew what was good for Indians, beginning with agricultural settlement and formal education. They had narrowed the definition of who could qualify as a treaty Indian, and reduced their numbers. They had begun to reduce rations and services. But Indians found ways to survive and maintain their identities, to resist and reshape policies, and in this they were abetted by at least some sympathetic officials. The story was by no means black and white.

# 5

# "Making Men of Them": Economic Activity

I am impressing the Indians with the importance of these valuable spheres of labour ... that learning to be farmers and stockmen will make men of them and give them the best education.

W.S. Grant, Indian agent, Hobbema agency, 1902[1]

To be fully human and fully a "man" in the English tradition meant to farm the land as God intended.[2] In the government's policy framework, only Indians who had learned such habits of labour could be considered "civilized" and eligible for enfranchisement and assimilation.[3] The reserve was intended to foster this process, to protect Indian people as they settled down and adapted to an agricultural lifestyle.[4] Reserve life was intended to be temporary, but also transformational, as Grant indicated. "Real men" ploughed fields and rode the range on a ranch; "primitive" hunter-gatherers did not qualify. Quite obsessed with defining masculinity in a world of rapid change, Victorians also believed that white men from cities and towns who hunted for sport in the wilderness, or rode a horse in the militia or police, were truly masculine;[5] ironically, Indians who hunted for a living or rode a horse in the wilderness were savages, wild, uncivilized, and less than completely masculine. Victorians found it difficult to comprehend Indians' entire traditional lifestyle as an occupation, and according to John Sutton Lutz, "trapping, hunting and fishing were considered to be the opposite of work."[6]

Victorian thought concerning the importance of farming went much further. As scholars of the day reflected on the agricultural revolution in history, they came to believe that farming was the step in human progress that made civilization possible. Graeme Baker, in his study of how and why foragers became farmers in early human history, notes that in the nineteenth century it was believed that turning to "farming allowed people not just to settle down and live in one place, but above all to own land and create surplus – the first steps to property ownership and capitalism that were the hallmarks of civilization ... Farming, it seemed clear, was the seminal moment in the story of human progress when people first began to use culture to take control of nature." These same scholars argued that the great advantage that farming had over hunting or herding was that it increased the time available "to do things other than simply seek food to survive." It "increased opportunities for self-improvement."[7]

Turning from foraging to farming (which in prehistory could take hundreds, or even thousands, of years) required a major change in the way people thought about themselves and their relationship to their environment. Notes Baker: "Prehistoric foragers probably saw themselves as part of the cosmos, along with the animals they hunted and the plants they gathered. It is argued that, once people became farmers, their cognitive world had to shift profoundly from a sense of belonging to and being part of the wild to 'acculturating' it as it became something to control and appropriate rather than be part of."[8] During the late nineteenth century in western Canada, many Indians were in a difficult transition state, caught between their traditional world view insofar as they continued to be hunters and gatherers, and the world of settled farming on reserves, where officials pressed them to transform into individualistic proto-capitalists.

Most Department of Indian Affairs officials thought of the transition in more simplistic terms. Farming was held to shape character. Deputy Superintendent General James Smart commented in 1898:

> Cultivation of the soil necessitates remaining in one spot, and then exerts an educational influence of a general character. It keeps prominently before the mind the relation of cause and effect, together with the dependence upon a higher power. It teaches moreover the necessity for systematic work at the proper season, for giving attention to detail, and patience in waiting for results.
>
> It inculcates furthermore the idea of individual proprietorship, habits of thrift, a due sense of the value of money, and the importance of its investment in useful directions.[9]

Whether for whites or Indians, the ideal was that a man should labour to provide food, clothing, and shelter for himself and his family, and aspire gradually to acquire goods, property, and an improved standard of life. Surely one's faith would deepen as one worked the farm and experienced the gifts of God the Creator – the meeting of one's quotidian needs and increase of one's material possessions – through diligence, sobriety, honesty, and reliability. Social values were generated and regenerated through rooted engagement with the soil, family, and a like-minded community.

Farming always was a more complex and communal undertaking than idealists portrayed; the independent, wholly self-sustaining yeoman farmer was a myth, not a reality. Successful farming required, besides good land and diligent labour, access to supplies, financial and other supports, markets, and transportation. Especially in its early stages, establishing a prairie farm frequently necessitated access to external work opportunities to supplement the small or unreliable farm income. It also required both experience with and local knowledge of soils, climate, and markets, whether to produce grain and garden crops or to raise farm animals. Reserves varied from rangeland in the south best suited to cattle to land suited to mixed farming to land with relatively limited agricultural potential. Not all crops were suited to every region. Some reserves also incorporated a variety of physical features not all suited to farming, such as heavy clay soils, semi-desert terrain, the thin soils of the foothills, or swamp.

Particularly in the early years, off-reserve markets for farm produce were small, restricted, or inaccessible. Only in 1883 did some reserves along the Canadian Pacific Railway gain limited access to railways.[10] In 1891, the railway reached from Calgary north to Edmonton, and south to Macleod and Lethbridge. In 1897–98, the Crowsnest Pass line was built west from Lethbridge. Branch lines were built from these trunk lines in many places, but not until late 1905 did another east-west line – the Canadian Northern Railway – reach from Saskatchewan to Edmonton. In other words, throughout the period a number of reserves north and west of Edmonton, and to the east in the Saddle Lake agency, never had close access to a railway to import or export goods. Given a choice, most white homesteaders only settled where the railways ran or were anticipated to run in the near future. Indian farmers on reserves did not have such options, and had little influence on railway routes. Some markets for Indian products and services existed by the 1880s in southern Alberta, though rather less extensively to the north, where freighting and sales of furs and fish were the main options in a very small white market. Economic opportunities for Alberta Indians were thus limited, but they were also diverse, and farming or ranching were by no means the only ways to make or enhance a living.[11]

Despite the difficulties, there is no doubt that the government intended a primarily agricultural future for Indians. This was unsurprising in a nation that was still mostly rural, and that derived many of its values from agriculture. Meanwhile, Indians derived most of their values from their hunting and gathering economy; the few who had done some farming viewed it as supplementary to fishing, hunting, and trapping. Now they were expected to focus on settled agriculture, embrace its value system, and view their traditional economy as at best supplemental.

Indian farmers faced most of the same challenges as white homesteaders in the West: crops ill-suited to the climate, lack of appropriate techniques for dryland farming, few farm storage facilities, and a string of natural disasters – drought, hail, fire, frost, insect pests, and crop diseases, most obviously. Indian farmers had some advantages compared to whites. They had no financial outlay for land, while white homesteaders had the expense of proving it up, or even of purchasing land if it was not designated for homesteads. The government, at least initially, provided Indians with implements, wagons, farm animals, seed for grain and root crops, and farm instructors.[12] (Later in the period, Indians were often able to afford to purchase many implements that they used both individually and collectively.) Indians could, in a number of cases, log their own timber from reserved berths or woodlands on reserves. Lands on reserves in excess of immediate needs could be leased to ranchers (in the south) or for timber (in the case of forested lands). Some reserves in Treaty 7 had coal seams that could bring in extra income, or reduce fuel costs on the reserves.

Indians also faced serious constraints, however. They did not have freedom of choice in many matters. The government prevented them from taking the risk of mortgaging their land, or using it as collateral. It determined or heavily influenced how much they planted, what they planted, where they planted, whether and to whom they could sell produce or lease land. Similarly circumscribed was freedom to slaughter animals for food, or to sell them. Once reserves were surveyed, Indians were usually unable to move elsewhere, whereas whites could and did abandon unproductive farms. In other words, Indian farmers were officially denied the right to freedom of choice, to take risks and learn by trial and error, and to accept independent responsibility. However, Indians did find ways in many cases to exercise agency over their living and economic arrangements. They often were not by any means as passive and obedient as the government would have liked. The numerous onerous restrictions which Indians faced, including efforts to limit both movement and marketing off reserves, would not have been tolerated by, or imposed on, whites. As in so many other aspects of their lives, their work was inspected, measured, quantified, and evaluated in intrusive detail each year.

In 1990, Sarah Carter published an influential study of government policy with respect to Indian agriculture, focusing on four agencies in Treaty 4 in eastern Assiniboia (today Saskatchewan). In it, she argues that Indians were usually more committed than the government to an agricultural future, that they had taken the initiative with respect to agricultural provisions in the treaty negotiations, and that government was far more a hindrance than a support to their success in farming. Indians, she contends, wanted to farm, but they resisted the government's assimilationist goals. She pointed out that United States and Ontario Indian farmers had exhibited a pattern of initial success following establishment on reserves, followed by stagnation or decline, and that government policies exacerbated a similar pattern on prairie reserves. She argues in particular that the seemingly eccentric Indian commissioner (1888–93) and deputy superintendent general (1893–97) Hayter Reed, who tried to force Indians into a pattern of peasant agriculture without modern equipment as a stage in evolution toward civilization, was an unmitigated disaster.[13]

Reed's name has become a byword for extreme government arrogance and incompetence.[14] Ironically, he actually reflected then-current ideas on social development from the leading anthropological thinkers of his day. In 1872, for example, Hodder Westropp wrote: "It appears as if there were but one history for every separate people, one uniform process of development for every race, each passing through successive phases, before attaining its highest social development. These successive phases are the rude and barbaric, the hunting, the pastoral, and the agricultural, corresponding with, and analogous to the stages of infancy, childhood, youth, manhood in the individual man. This sequence is invariable in man, as an individual and collectively."[15]

In 1892, Reed offered the following rationale for his policy:

Suppose ... that an Indian confine his operation to a single acre. From this he should, in an ordinary year raise, at a moderate computation, some eighteen bushels of wheat (where this can be successfully grown) which, after making all necessary deductions, will give him nearly, if not quite, five bags of flour.

Assisted by his family there is nothing to prevent his planting a portion of a second acre, with roots and vegetables, sufficient to supplement his flour to the degree of making it last for a good portion of the year.

Add to this the product of a cow or two, and the man has made a long stride towards independence.

Yet this is commonly accomplished by peasants of various countries, with no better implements than the hoe, the rake, cradle, sickle and flail.

The necessary use of these instruments can never be acquired if Indians be encouraged to contemplate the performance of their work by such labour saving machinery as can rarely be obtained and kept in repair entirely from their own resources.

He bemoaned Indians' tendency to bypass the necessary developmental stage of physical work by taking advantage of labour-saving machinery. Yet his ideas were out of touch with reality. Naturally, Indians saw no reason why they should not be able to use technology readily available to their white neighbours. Moreover, virtually nowhere in any year in the district of Alberta did wheat production on any reserve approach Reed's "moderate computation" of eighteen bushels per acre.

Reed conceded that stock-raising was likely to be more successful in Treaty 7, but only belatedly had the government begun to develop plans to encourage it.[16] He proposed that Indians sell some of their ponies and use the money for stock, "but unless some one from the east can be found with capital to purchase the ponies, the idea cannot be carried out." In other words, the department would not provide the funds to carry out the government's treaty obligation, perhaps on the assumption that stock supplied years earlier in a failed experiment had fulfilled that obligation.[17]

But this made no sense. First, for many years the government exceeded the treaties' limited stipulations to support agricultural activity on reserves with seed grain and potatoes, farm instructors, and so forth, even when all the evidence showed that such activity was mostly futile in the Treaty 7 region. Second, withholding cattle meant in part that many Indians were unable to feed themselves, thus creating a heavy annual financial commitment to providing rations to support Indians on their reserves – an expense the government regularly bemoaned. Whatever the case, Reed's belated proposal to encourage stock-raising was based on a small success with the Piikani, who in 1892 possessed 119 cows, 4 bulls, 141 oxen, and 121 "young stock." By contrast, there were in that year still no cattle on the Siksika reserve and only thirteen oxen on the Kainai reserve.[18] Although the Laurier government removed Reed in 1897,[19] Carter finds that his legacy persisted to some extent among department bureaucrats.

All intending agriculturalists in this period had to cope with particular climatic conditions. Settlement of the Canadian prairies took place just at the end of the Little Ice Age, when slightly cooler global temperatures produced generally shorter growing seasons than those in the twentieth century. Indeed, according to Alwynne Beaudoin, "the mid-nineteenth century stands out as being the coolest interval in the last 400 years." She claims, moreover, "the past few hundred years stand out as being among the coolest and wettest in post-glacial time," especially in the parkland and boreal forest, a reality that affected the judgment of nineteenth-century explorers and scientists with respect to the arability of the so-called fertile belt. Nonetheless, periods of drought that were common in the region still occurred, especially (but not only) in the south. Beaudoin asserts that, in fact, "drought has been part of the environment on the Prairies for most of the last 10,000 years." Drought, then, is "the norm, not the exception" – a reality government officials and early settlers were not predisposed to admit.[20]

## AGRICULTURAL PROVISIONS IN TREATIES 6 AND 7

The government commissioners arrived at Fort Carlton to negotiate Treaty 6 in 1876 with a draft based on Treaty 4 of 1874, during the negotiation of which Indians had successfully expanded the list of agricultural implements and farm animals to be supplied; two years later, at Forts Carlton and Pitt, Indian leaders had little trouble negotiating a further expansion of the list, as both sides recognized that even the revised Treaty 4 provisions had proven inadequate.[21] Alexander Morris expressed surprise at the Crees' "great ... willingness" to commence farming, and recommended that the government provide the implements and cattle "without delay." He declined a request to include in the treaty a requirement for farm instructors, but recommended that the government provide such instruction anyway – a suggestion David Laird also promoted.[22] The Treaty 7 negotiations the following year appear to have produced little discussion of the agricultural provisions, except that the government gave Indians the option to receive cattle for ranching, or to receive much the same provisions for implements, seed, and animals as in Treaty 6.[23]

The commissioners left the negotiations satisfied that Indians' willingness to settle on reserves and pursue farming indicated a desire to embrace fundamental change. In his examination of the transition from foraging to farming in prehistory, Baker notes it is probable "that in many instances foragers were attempting to *preserve* their way of life at a time of stress rather than deliberately seeking to *transform* it."[24] Although prehistory was a very different context from late nineteenth-century Alberta, there is every reason to believe that Baker's observation applies in both periods, and that therefore there was between the white and Indian negotiators of 1876–77 a case of mutual incomprehension.[25]

## MACDONALD'S DISAPPOINTMENT

When Sir John A. Macdonald resumed office as prime minister and superintendent general of Indian Affairs in 1878, he was initially somewhat optimistic about the prospects for his Indian policy in the West, and willing to be flexible in implementing it. He thought Indians of the Northwest ought to be able to learn to farm as successfully as those of Ontario and Quebec. Undoubtedly they would require encouragement to settle on reserves and take up agriculture. There were likely some nomadic tribes "incapable of settling down to such pursuits." Such Indians "should be induced to become herdsmen, and have flocks and herds,"[26] in accordance with the contemporary belief that pastoralism was normally a precursor of cereal agriculture. This suggests that Macdonald thought Indians' ability to farm was more related to the perceived character (the extent to which an inherently wild nature was modified) and state of development (degree of nomadism) of a given tribe than it was to matters of climate, soil, and the like.

Within a few years, the government admitted that in Manitoba and the North-West Territories many Indians remained indifferent farmers, and still supported themselves largely through traditional hunting, fishing, and trapping, as well as labour for various white businesses, entrepreneurs, and farmers. Agriculture remained the long-term goal, but the government found it advantageous to be relieved of the burden for rations and aid. As a case in point, faced with reserve land largely unsuited to agriculture, the Stoney Nakoda invested some effort in raising cattle, yet supported themselves principally by hunting, trapping, labouring in support of the CPR's construction, and cutting timber for sale. The government considered them essentially "self-supporting."[27]

Yet by 1887 Macdonald was, on the whole, frustrated at the lack of agricultural progress among Indians of the Northwest. His irritation was only partly a result of the North-West Rebellion – it also owed much to accumulated disappointments over the decade since the signing of Treaty 7. Defending his policy in the House of Commons, he asserted:

Why, an Indian who is healthy is a strong man, and just as able to work as a white man. The white man goes up to the North-West and works for his living. What does the Government do? The Government gives the Indian a reserve, he has lands reserved for him, he has seed grain given to him, he has implements of husbandry given to him, he has cattle given to him in order to plough his land, he has everything requisite to start in the successful cultivation of the land. The white man goes there and has to furnish all these things for himself. But because these Indians are too lazy to work, they eat the cattle instead of ploughing with them, they throw themselves upon the provisions they have a right to get, they eat the seed grain, and then they say they are starving, and they won't work, and they are made the object of sympathy by people who do not know anything about them. Those are the real facts. The reserves are carefully chosen, the Indians are consulted in the selection of the reserves, the Indians are carefully taken care of ... [On] the whole, I say that the administration of Indian affairs in the North-West has been exceedingly successful ... [T]he administration of Indian affairs in the North-West has been careful, has been humane, but has been firm, and whatever complaints have been made it is because that firmness did not suit the lazy, indolent Indians set up by interested parties who desire to have confusion instead of peace and order.[28]

Small wonder that he gave up the DIA portfolio that year.

Macdonald's statement reflects a basic change in attitude and a sense of betrayal. At the treaties it had seemed to officials that Indians were anxious to change their ways, embrace their new life, and work hard to succeed in it. Yet despite all their advantages (as he saw them) and all they had received, Macdonald believed they had proven lazy and ready to leech off whites. Far from being committed to becoming self-sustaining, preparing for enfranchisement, and seeking to embrace white society, Indians were proving recalcitrant, devoted to traditional ways, and likely to be a permanent problem for the government. That the government had created many of the problems, exacerbated others, and – from an Indian perspective – itself betrayed the spirit of the treaties was not part of the government's analysis.

## ECONOMIC ACTIVITY IN THE TREATY 6 REGION OF ALBERTA

### Early Agriculture at Whitefish Lake

Henry Bird Steinhauer, an Ojibwa reverend from Canada West, arrived at Whitefish Lake in 1857 to open a Methodist mission among the Cree.[29] His main goal was to Christianize them, but he also began to train them to read and write Cree syllabics and introduced basic farming skills. Agriculture was primitive, given the absence of most tools and work animals, but he taught Indians to cultivate potatoes and turnips using fire-hardened sticks to dig holes for planting. Using a wooden plough, he prepared some small plots of land for barley, the grain crop best suited to the short northern growing season. By the later 1860s, according to Peter Erasmus, most of the Indians at Whitefish Lake engaged in at least some farming because vegetables could supplement their diet and because they found "that a little grain fed to their ponies on winter trips increased the stamina and strength of their animals." The soil was so rich, recalled Erasmus, that the effort expended produced "big returns." The vegetables provided balance and reliability to the traditional diet, and the farming contributed to a change in the Indians' lifestyle. Erasmus noted that some had built log residences they occupied part of each year.[30]

What emerged by the 1870s was an approach to farming that mostly supplemented the Indians' traditional diet. The experience of Elizabeth Barrett, who arrived in 1875 to teach in the mission school, confirms the point. She found that locally grown produce still consisted of potatoes, turnips, and barley ("I like barley bread very well"), as well as "excellent butter of our own manufacture." Some other foods were imported ("a little flour, occasionally is a treat, rice and raisins, sugar, tea, salt, and spice constitute about the slim total"), and the rest was standard country fare ("buffalo meat … also moose meat, venison and bear. Wild fowl and eggs are also very plentiful at the proper season").[31] Whitefish was another staple.

It was not surprising, therefore, that James Seenum, chief of the Cree band at Whitefish Lake, informed the treaty commissioners at Fort Pitt in 1876 that he had begun to farm some years earlier. Chief Factor William Christie of the Hudson's Bay Company had encouraged him with the gift of a plough, a pit saw, and a grindstone. Having no horses, Seenum and members of his band pulled the plough themselves, but it now was broken. They also had "pulled up roots and used them for hoes." His people wanted to farm, appreciated the importance of growing grain and vegetables, and wanted new implements "as soon as possible."[32] He was almost certainly requesting assistance to enhance his band's traditional lifestyle and diet. He likely had little interest in changing a system that was working reasonably well. The treaty commissioners likely thought he was saying that his people, unusually, had had some farming experience, had seen its benefits, and were anxious to alter their traditional lifestyle by embracing agriculture more fully.

Whites tended to dismiss Native agriculture. George M. Grant, for example, stopped at Fort Victoria on the North Saskatchewan in 1872. Near the HBC trading post and Methodist mission house he saw a Metis settlement, interspersed with the tents of numerous Cree and some Metis farms: "The [Metis] farming is on a very limited scale, as the men prefer hunting buffalo, fishing, or freighting for the Company to steady agricultural labour, and neither farming nor gardening can succeed well, when the seeds are merely thrown into the ground in spring, and the ground is not looked at again till autumn, when everything is expected to be ripe and ready for ingathering."[33] He saw hunting, fishing, and freighting as diversions that were far more attractive than the hard, steady work of proper farming. Metis or Indians who farmed like this could not be taken seriously as farmers. Even a later historian, John Milloy, states, "mission agriculture remained no more than gardening."[34]

It appears that the James Seenum band mirrored to some extent what it saw at the Metis settlement near Victoria in the patterns of farming combined with other work and in the establishment of semi-permanent residences. When he wrote to his supporting mission society in Ontario, Steinhauer was anxious to demonstrate progress and delighted to point out that the Cree had "neat houses, gardens, schools and domestic animals." They were, he said, beginning to adopt European modes of dress, and he claimed that most of the adult members of his congregation (by this time, probably former pupils of his school) were able to read available Cree translations of the Scriptures and hymns and arrived at services with their Bibles and hymnals. So there was change, albeit quite gradual, and agriculture was contributing to it. Indians still hunted, gathered, and trapped nomadically part of the year, but they also had a core settlement with farm produce to which they regularly returned. ·

## *The Reserve Economies of Treaty 6*

The Whitefish Lake case, though of interest, appears to have been unique, or nearly so, among Indians of the future district of Alberta in the 1870s.[35] By the end of the territorial period, in 1905, the picture had changed, though not completely and not entirely in the way the government had envisaged twenty-five or thirty years earlier. The government had hoped that Indians would settle on reserves, that insofar as possible every able-bodied man would occupy and farm an individual plot of land, and that the reserves would be mostly self-sufficient, with a large proportion of Indians well on the way to acculturation and enfranchisement. By 1905, at one extreme, some bands still lived almost wholly in the traditional way, while at the other extreme, some bands were largely committed to agriculture and had significant numbers of individuals who farmed their own plots of land. The reserve economies were mostly quite mixed, and bands derived much or most of their income off reserve, either from traditional hunting, fishing, gathering, and trapping or from paid employment. Still, no Treaty 6 band was truly self-sufficient,[36] and most depended to varying degrees on government rations and other assistance. In certain instances economic differentiation meant some Indians were wealthy enough to employ others, while some were extremely poor. Such disparity, however, appears infrequent. Indeed, the Indians' tendency to share food and goods with one another, and belief they only needed to work hard enough to purchase necessities rather than to accumulate individual wealth, frustrated officials through the end of the territorial period.

Three bands in the Saddle Lake agency never made a serious attempt at settled agriculture before 1905. The Lac la Biche (mostly Metis), Beaver Lake (Cree), and Heart Lake (Chipewyan) bands were distant from settlement and markets for agricultural products, and were situated to take advantage of abundant opportunities to hunt, fish, engage in the fur trade, and work for the HBC or other whites as opportunity arose. The Indian agent apparently saw the latter two bands only at the annual treaty payments, when they appeared at Lac la Biche.[37] It is possible, but far from certain, that their active outdoor life may have left them reasonably healthy,[38] and their small numbers and nomadic lifestyle made it impracticable to establish schools among them.

Three of the bands in the Edmonton agency followed a similar pattern, using their reserves as a base. The Alexander (Woodland Cree), Alexis (Stoney Nakota Sioux), and Paul (related to Alexis) bands each had a few dilapidated houses and other buildings and raised a few cattle, but strongly preferred to hunt, fish, and trap. Field crops were minimal, though they put up some wild hay for winter feed for their animals. These bands derived much of their income from furs and selling fish to whites.[39]

The Alberta Treaty 6 bands that were closest to being self-supporting with regard to food were those at Hobbema, especially the Samson, Ermineskin, and Muddy Bull bands. Located in the southern part of the Treaty 6 region, this agency had above-average quality of land for crops, hay, and grazing,[40] and a slightly longer growing season than those farther north. This agency faced different challenges from most of Treaty 6. The Calgary-Edmonton railway ran through it from 1891, and the land surrounding the reserve was quickly settled. This laid it open to more outside influence, and meant Indians had to travel some distance from their reserves to find unoccupied lands suitable for traditional pursuits. But it also meant a nearby market for Indian labour (in land clearing or agriculture), fish caught at nearby Pigeon Lake, lumber and shingles from the reserve sawmill, and beef raised on the reserve. There also was a strong market for local muskrat pelts. By 1905, more than 72 per cent of Hobbema's economic production was generated from the reserves, mostly through agricultural activity. They were the only reserves in Treaty 6 where that was the case: in the others, most economic production was still generated off-reserve in 1905.[41]

Significant agricultural progress also occurred in the Whitefish Lake, Saddle Lake, and Blue Quill bands in the Saddle Lake agency, though there was little development of grain farming. Where reserves in the Hobbema agency, for example, produced some wheat, it remained a negligible crop (about 500 bu. in 1904) north of the North Saskatchewan. Barley production declined compared with the early years, possibly because imported wheat flour became competitively available. Oats production remained light, and so did vegetable and garden crops. Raising animals was the dominant activity: dairy and beef cattle, along with some hogs, sheep, oxen, and horses. Wild hay for winter feed was the main "crop" produced on the reserves. Inspectors were pleased to see well-constructed houses, outbuildings, and fences on the Saddle Lake reserves. Nevertheless, the Indians of these reserves not only continued to provision themselves off-reserve in the traditional ways, but they also sold fish, meat, and berries to whites, worked as freighters for the HBC, and even did some small-scale furniture manufacturing. Over 55 per cent of their economic activity came from activities other than agriculture. By 1905, some members of each band were still at best only partially settled, and preferred to spend most of their time in a traditional lifestyle. Nevertheless, many members lived most of their lives in fixed abodes, and most of their children received at least some formal schooling.[42]

Two Edmonton agency bands, Enoch and Michel, merit some attention. Enoch, the larger of the two, was located fairly close to Edmonton. While it had some of the best farmland in the agency, its population was relatively small (126 in 1904) and not very cohesive. Its numbers had fallen in 1885–86 when many Metis left the treaty, and by 1905 only about fifteen families were operating farms. The three largest were twenty, fourteen, and eleven acres, while others were much smaller and five operated only "market gardens." Some band members raised cattle or worked a reserve sawmill. Others made and sold moccasins and beadwork. Many worked off-reserve on steamboats or as rafters on the North Saskatchewan and Athabasca rivers or on other northern lakes and rivers. Yet others sought employment as wage labourers in or near Edmonton.

The remaining reserve was the Michel band of Iroquois and Metis (ninety-four persons in 1904), a few miles west of St Albert. Despite good agricultural land, band members often preferred to work off-reserve. Men and teams of horses were employed for railway survey crews, while others lived in the forest to hunt and trap. The agencies inspector, J.A. Markle, was especially impressed with this band because a few had become prosperous mixed farmers without a farm instructor or ration house. During his 1904 inspection, he "found Louis Callihoo's team out in the field at work on a summer-fallow, a reasonably large crop of all varieties of grain, fowl in the barn-yard, sheep in the paddock, pigs in the sty, cattle feeding on the hillside, implements for all farming uses in an open shed, a cream-separator in the dairy, an organ in the living room of the house, and other evidences of prosperity and good management, even to the week's wash out on the line to dry soon after the noon hour on a Monday – the afternoon on which I called. On a later date I saw Mrs Callihoo at St Albert delivering butter and eggs to her customers." He hoped that this Arcadian vision of an independent farmer prospering would set an example.[43] However, though Chief Callihoo evidently was respected, most others did not choose to follow where he led.

From the earliest days of reserve settlement, the government promoted individual farming. It was a policy embodied in the Indian Act, and after the treaties officials from the deputy superintendent general and Indian commissioner down through the ranks advocated for it. Surveyors demarcated not only reserve boundaries, but also individual plots of land. Farm instructors were expected to show Indians how to grow grain and root crops and develop gardens. They also taught Indians to save some grain for seed the next season (though many consumed it and counted on seed grain from the government for the next year), to grind the remainder into flour, and to store root crops to carry them through the winter. The government was so anxious to demonstrate the success of this policy that almost annually from the early 1880s to 1895 it published tables listing individual farmers on prairie reserves, areas cultivated, and the types and yields of crops. In general, compliance with this policy was noticeably greater among bands in Treaty 6 than in Treaty 7. The exceptions were those bands with highly persistent traditional lifestyles.

Government figures for 1895 constitute a useful example. Grain crops were good in the Edmonton and Hobbema agencies, and weak at Saddle Lake. Potatoes were a strong staple crop in all agencies. Horses, cows, and oxen were common to all, but in 1895 sheep and hogs were found only in the Edmonton agency. Saddle Lake reported no gardens, but they were widespread at Edmonton and Hobbema. In the entire Treaty 6 area, only the Enoch and Michel bands grew turnips, and only Michel grew carrots; potatoes remained the main root crop at Saddle Lake and Edmonton, but were marginal at Hobbema. Total areas under cultivation remained tiny, around 0.06 per cent of reserve lands. Individual farms were very small. A few farms had cultivated as many as twenty or thirty acres, but most ranged from one to six acres. Farm implements and vehicles, mainly consisting of ploughs, harrows, carts, and wagons, and other machinery (fanning, threshing, and mowing machines, and reapers) were decidedly scarce.[44]

Statistical tables could only convey so much. For example, the farmers listed were invariably the registered male land owners, but women and other family members were likely also involved with the farming, especially the gardens, root crops, and cows. There also was a varied commitment to farming. Numerous plots were planted simply to please the agent or farm instructor. Many Indians did not remain to cultivate, weed, and water their gardens and root crops during the growing season, but headed off-reserve to hunt, fish, gather, and engage in other more profitable economic pursuits, or to attend a sun dance. Farm animals were left in the care of a few aged band members while most other members were away. The statistics do not show why some members did not plant, while others planted but did not harvest, crops. The reasons might range from willful refusal to bad health or physical infirmity to drought, crop diseases, or infestations of grubs or pests. Sometimes agents reported the latter reasons. The statistics also obscure the fact that, despite official discouragement of the practice, many Indians preferred to live in villages in clan or extended family groupings rather than in isolated dwellings on individual farming plots. During the period under review, very few Indian farmers could support themselves and their families from agricultural proceeds, and so they relied on traditional means to feed themselves and on non-traditional opportunities for income. The government's statistics, helpful and informative to a point, are far from a reliable indicator of Indians' agricultural progress.

## ECONOMIC ACTIVITY IN THE TREATY 7 REGION OF ALBERTA

The reserves of Treaty 7 present quite different problems from those of Treaty 6. Not one was suited to predominantly grain farming, given the strains of grain then available and the sparse understanding of dryland farming techniques. Even mixed farming was challenging for most. The climate was mostly arid, and drought years were frequent. Except where the valleys of rivers and streams broadened into river flats and benchlands, productive layers of soil on the majority of reserve lands were generally shallow, quickly exhausted, and moisture depleted when cultivated. In most winters, warm and drying chinook winds from the west and southwest periodically broke up the periods of cold weather, melting snow cover and exposing the abundant prairie grasses. This attracted bison herds in the past, and in the 1880s attracted ranchers looking for cheap, reliable, and accessible feed.

The Kainai and Siksika reserves lay within the western portion of the Palliser Triangle, which included the southeastern quadrant of Alberta and angled southeast across present-day Saskatchewan to the southwestern corner of Manitoba. In the 1850s, John Palliser and Henry Youle Hind concluded that the region was too arid to support agriculture, and that even if the far western portion was not included in later definitions of the dry belt, intensive farming there would always be a challenge.[45]

Economically, Fort Benton had dominated the region since the mid-1860s, but the arrival of the CPR in 1883 began a reorientation of the Alberta economy, tying the region into the east-west transcontinental economy developing under the federal government's National Policy.[46] This affected the Treaty 7 reserves, along with the rest of the region. In 1883, the CPR proceeded west along the northern edge of the reconfigured Siksika reserve, near the Tsuu T'ina reserve, and through the Stoney Nakoda reserve. By the early 1890s, the railway extended north to Edmonton and south to Fort Macleod and Lethbridge, where it drew close to the Kainai and Piikani reserves. In 1897–98, the Crowsnest Pass line ran through the Piikani reserve. Under federal law, rail companies could, with compensation, take whatever land they required to run lines through otherwise sacrosanct reserves. Companies consulted Indians very little, and compensation for loss of land and damages remained negligible. While Indians benefitted from ready transportation and access to cheaper supplies in greater quantity and variety, they were angered at lines that bisected their reserves, often caused prairie fires, and killed many of their animals. After protests, the CPR provided more compensation for land and damages and began to fence off its main line, although that in turn caused new problems.[47] Certainly, the railways meant that Indians in Treaty 7 experienced more intense exposure over a longer period to white settlers and ranchers than did most in Treaty 6 during the period under review.

The railways facilitated Indian interaction with urban centres in the region, but in most cases reserves were near such centers anyway. The Tsuu T'ina reserve was almost a suburb of Calgary. The Piikani reserve was near Macleod. The Kainai reserve was also within easy distance of Macleod and close to Lethbridge, and the Mormon settlement at Cardston emerged on its southern boundary. The Siksika and Stoney Nakoda reserves were further from large settlements, but were on the CPR main line. Such access to urban centres facilitated selling, buying, and bartering goods, and sometimes opportunities for labour, but it also facilitated alcohol and prostitution.

The Treaty 7 reserves were located on the ranching frontier, and by the mid-1880s each was bordered by one or more large leases. The Kainai reserve was almost surrounded by the original closed leases of 1882, except for a portion of its eastern boundary – notably, the Cochrane ranch was directly across the Belly River along the southern half of its western boundary. The Piikani reserve was surrounded by leases, including the Walrond ranch. The Tsuu T'ina reserve was touched by the British-American ranch to the north and another lease to the south. The eastern end of the Stoney reserve was also surrounded. Even the Siksika reserve, somewhat to the east of the major ranching area, saw leases to its north, south, and west.[48] One advantage of the concentration of leases was that the DIA had to accept that the Treaty 7 reserves were in ranching country and that pushing mixed farming or grain growing was mostly futile. However, a major disadvantage was that ranchers habitually overstocked their lands and expected to access the fine grazing lands on the reserves, which they often believed were "wasted" under Indian ownership. Ranchers also regularly, if often unjustly, accused hungry Indians of stealing and consuming their cattle. Settling such disputes occupied much of the North-West Mounted Police's time in the area.

Finally, the Treaty 7 region has benefitted from more extensive scholarly examination of its economic history than has the Alberta portion of Treaty 6.[49] Paul Voisey's study of the Vulcan area[50] – more or less at the district centre, with the Kainai reserve to the south, the Siksika to the northeast, the Piikani to the west, and the Tsuu T'ina to the northwest – is an outstanding treatment of regional agriculture and community building. Voisey would likely be cautious about applying the findings of his microstudy more widely, given, for example, that soils, rainfall, and climate generally vary within the region, and that the reserves constitute a different social and economic situation from that of the white Vulcan community. Moreover, it was only in 1904 that Vulcan was founded in what had been ranching country, and Voisey therefore covers a period in which dry and wet cycles, among other conditions, were not necessarily identical to the quarter-century before 1905. In any event, rainfall varied unpredictably from year to year: Voisey notes that at Lethbridge, average annual rainfall from 1905 to 1935 was 15.6 inches, but it ranged from 25 inches in 1916 to 7.5 inches in 1918. The average in Calgary during the same period was 16.6 inches. Moreover, he points out that rainfall varied greatly within a season, sometimes not falling when required for plant growth, sometimes in cloudbursts that ran off the land quickly, and often evaporating rapidly in the dry and windy climate.[51]

But the delay in settlement is of interest, since the railway had gone through in 1891, and settlement normally followed the railway. To be fair, the Vulcan district was between fifteen and forty miles east of the railway, and the towns that had developed along the line (Claresholm, Nanton, and High River) originated as much to serve ranchers as aspiring farmers. Still, not only does the delay in developing grain farming indicate the strength of the idea that this was ranching country in the quarter-century after 1880, but it also reflects the need for suitable crops and farming techniques before cereal agriculture could be pursued successfully. One example is that the growing season for Red Fife wheat, the common wheat strain during the territorial years, often was longer than the number of frost-free days in the region; not until 1911 was the more suitable Marquis wheat introduced. Moreover, dryland farming techniques were ill understood until well after 1905.[52] It is curious, therefore, that the government did not begin seriously to promote raising cattle on reserves until the mid-1890s, and – at least during the territorial period – never stopped promoting grain, root vegetable, and garden produce production on the reserves despite years of discouraging or disastrous results.

Statistics for 1904–05 demonstrate the difference between Treaty 6 and 7 reserves. The Kainai produced no grain or root crops whatsoever; the other Treaty 7 agencies had almost negligible amounts of barley and some potatoes, and the Siksika and Tsuu T'ina grew small amounts of carrots and turnips. The Kainai, Siksika, and Stoney Nakoda reserves had fair amounts of hay. Yet all the Treaty 7 reserves had significant herds of horses and cattle. Predictably, they had relatively few ploughs and harrows, but more mowers, horse rakes, and wagons. The Stoney Nakoda was the only reserve in Treaty 7 that still earned almost half of its income from hunting and trapping.[53] By contrast, all Treaty 6 reserves that reported agricultural activity produced some grain, and in most cases more root and garden crops than any Treaty 7 reserve. Mixed farming dominated Treaty 6, while Treaty 7 had mostly converted to ranching. The outlier was the Stoney Nakoda reserve, which combined raising cattle with hunting and fishing. Indians in both treaty areas conducted extensive off-reserve activity.

One other indicator common to both treaty areas was the nature of reserve housing and farm structures. If these are a measure of progress, Alberta Indians lived in relative poverty in 1905. By this time, many white farmers were moving beyond their original sod huts, shanties, and log dwellings. Government statistics show not a single frame house in any Treaty 6 agency in Alberta or on the Stoney Nakoda reserve; housing in these places was all classed as log dwellings or shanties. The Tsuu T'ina reserve had one frame house, the Kainai three, the Siksika eight, and the Piikani twenty-one, but Indians on each still lived predominantly in log dwellings. In other words, with a few exceptions, Indians were using the same housing after twenty or twenty-five years on the reserves. There was not a single barn on any Alberta reserve, though there were quite a few horse and cattle stables and other shelters as appropriate.[54] Inspectors reported that many houses, fences, and other structures were so dilapidated or unsanitary as to be of little value. Note that in this period, the government was not responsible for Indian housing. It made suggestions and recommended upgrades, but Indians had to acquire materials and perform the labour to construct, repair, upgrade, or replace their dwellings. Generally they elected not to do so.

## The Kainai Reserve

The futility of the bison hunt and the starvation winter of 1879–80 led Chief Mékaisto to conclude, "God has taken all the game away." It was time to accept the necessity of a new way of life. He moved his lodge to the reserve and there constructed a log dwelling.[55] Others followed his example. By early November 1880, Agent Norman Macleod reported, "the Indians have forty houses nearly ready for occupation. They are building fireplaces in them. 'Red Crow' has built himself a comfortable house, and I have [arranged] ... to put a door and window into it for him, so as to encourage him."[56] Mékaisto and his followers accepted a settled future, undertaking the hard labour of cutting and preparing timber for the houses, and quickly mastering the necessary carpentry and construction skills.

Macleod and Inspector T. Page Wadsworth had anticipated far more trouble. They arrived at the Kainai reserve in May 1881 evidently concerned they would face reputedly fierce warriors set to resist change. They were surprised by what they found. "Perhaps the conduct of these Indians is too good to last," a skeptical Macleod wrote, "but certainly it was most gratifying to witness their docility and attempts of industry, their wish to be shown how to work, their desire to have a house of their own, &c."[57] Indians already occupied sixty-three houses. Considerable confusion arose, however, as many hundreds more Kainai returned from the United States that spring and summer and simply erected lodges around the more permanent dwellings. Within a few weeks, Macleod observed, the population of the reserve increased from 800 to 3,300, greatly disturbing the spring planting and straining the food supply. The latecomers also brought measles and scarlet fever, which spread rapidly and resulted in "great mortality among their children." Amazingly under the circumstances, all reports indicated, "the Indians are quiet and well disposed, and are eager to go to work," only being hampered by the scarcity of implements.[58]

The new reserve, the largest in Canada, stretched southwest from near the future city of Lethbridge to a southern border about fourteen miles north of the international border. It was bounded on the west by the

Belly River, on the north by the Oldman River, and on the east by the St Mary River, and comprised 547.5 square miles, or almost 352,000 acres, mostly "splendid grazing land." Land suited to intensive agriculture was limited, and such farming as was undertaken tended to be mostly in or near the river valleys, which were more sheltered and better watered than the higher plateau between the rivers. Indian settlement remained mostly scattered along the rivers on the margins of the reserve, though most concentrated on flats and benchlands of the Belly River near the confluence with the Kootenai (later Waterton) River.[59]

The DIA arranged to have over one hundred acres of land broken, but agriculture was difficult because the many hundreds of horses used the new fence posts to alleviate the common "prairie itch," destroying the rail fences and ruining the crops. The horses also stripped the prairie bare of grass near the Indian settlements.[60] Wadsworth appealed to Ottawa for more oxen and for a farming instructor for each of the communities.

The Kainai were not a united people. Mékaisto was willing enough to adapt to the new ways, but other chiefs and their followers were resistant, and only a minority of the band looked to Mékaisto as leader and had followed him to the reserve in 1880. When larger numbers arrived on the reserve in 1881, the rivalries continued. Macleod reported that some of the younger newcomers had "a spirit of mischief" and jealousy – or what in a later era would have been termed either resistance or vandalism – that they exercised against those already settled, as "fences were torn down at night and their gardens robbed."[61]

The government was still figuring out its agricultural policy. Its initial plan of 1879 had included establishment of "home farms" or "supply farms" operated by whites near Pincher Creek and Calgary to supply some of the needs of the population for food and seed during the transition to reserve agriculture. The plan entailed providing farming instructors to develop demonstration farms on the boundary of the reserves, and to guide and advise new Indian farmers. By the early 1880s, this system was largely discredited: it was patronage-ridden and in many respects a demonstrable failure.[62] The supply farms could not produce enough food or seed to meet demand. Reserve farms too often were staffed with many friends of the government who lacked the skills to relate to the Indians, and who were so preoccupied with getting their demonstration farms up and running that they were unable to provide leadership on the reserve. They also faced the same problems of climate, drought, frost, pest, and so forth that all other farmers encountered.

They had to adapt to a farming situation that was quite different from what they had known in Ontario or even the eastern prairies. In the early days, most of them also had administrative duties (doing what agents later did, including supply distribution on reserves) for which they were unsuited.[63]

Wadsworth, for his part, contended that the farm instructors should be on the reserve "to work with and for the Indians." If the demonstration farms were maintained it should be mainly to ensure an annual supply of seed grain. Many Indians were disinclined to turn over a portion of their crops to the agent or farm instructor to be stored as seed for the next season, even when they were compensated with the equivalent amount in flour.[64]

Most Indian farming on the Kainai reserve until the 1890s consisted of small gardens in the river valley, mainly between posts at Slideout and Standoff. In this context, the one crop Indians could readily produce in surplus quantities in the mid-1880s was potatoes. Agents attempted to control sale of potatoes to the surrounding community to try to ensure the Indians received a fair price. However, the market was tiny and the supply large, driving down prices; Agent William Pocklington reported that a couple of Indians had sold two eighty-pound bags to some whites for a total of twenty-five cents. He was delighted to negotiate a contract in 1885 with the NWMP for 20,000 pounds at one cent per pound. The Indians delivered the potatoes within half a day, indicating both their capacity to carry out the work and the amount of their surplus. When Pocklington urged them to plant even more, they replied, "What is the use, as we have lots in our cellars that we cannot sell, and more than we can eat."[65] Indians' desire to sell their surplus to generate income, which would enable them to buy other needed goods, showed that they embraced principles of the capitalist economy when given the opportunity, and that they understood the necessity of engaging with the broader regional economy. At the same time, they showed a natural reluctance to grow food that exceeded their own need and market demand.

From the earliest days on the reserve, the government encouraged the Kainai to settle on individual eighty-acre plots of land, erect their own houses and other buildings, and farm the land individually rather than collectively. In the 1890s, the square survey reached the reserve and plots were marked out.[66] In 1893, the DIA reported that about 140 Kainai were farming individual plots. Almost all had potatoes and garden crops. The most popular grain crop was oats, with just over 181 acres producing 940 bushels, or about 5.4 bushels per acre. Only five acres total were sown to wheat, yielding twenty bushels.[67] The small-scale farming produced minuscule yields, and few, if any, farmers were self-sustaining. In the early stages of agriculture in the river flats in the 1880s, however, there were too few oxen, usually government owned, available for ploughing up the land, and so the Indians began to use any of their horses suited to the purpose. Indian ponies were traditionally a symbol of wealth and prestige and most were not draft animals, yet Indians were willing, when able, to secure and use them for farm work.

In 1885, Pocklington listed sixteen Indians who ploughed and harrowed their own plots of land and planted crops under his supervision.[68] One, Striped Dog, a minor chief, not only put in four acres of oats, but also helped others who were without suitable horses. These Indians, Pocklington reported, "worked well and willingly, notwithstanding reports to the contrary." When it came to fencing, he admitted surprise at their efforts in erecting "a fence that would do credit to a white man."[69] Not only was his remark racist and condescending, but agents and farm instructors seemed to clutch at any straws of evidence, however ephemeral, of Indian "progress." They overrated examples of Indians who appeared to take to this kind of farming; the reality was that most of the Kainai did not do so seriously in this period. As a case in point: by 1893 no one named Striped Dog was listed among the farmers, but there was a Striped Wolf (possibly the same person) who was cultivating only a quarter-acre of potatoes with no ascertainable harvest.[70]

The region endured frequent drought.[71] An early example was in 1886, which also had extreme heat. Pocklington wrote, "weeds were really about the only things that did grow." He reported that crops were "a complete failure," with potatoes "about the size of marbles," and the little grain useful only for fodder. The following winter was "the most severe I ever experienced." In 1887, potatoes appeared promising, but cutworms destroyed turnips and other garden crops. That year no turnips or barley were harvested, very little wheat, and less than a third of the amount of potatoes of two or three years earlier. Oats were more successful. Statistics show Indians then possessed about 2,000 horses; fifteen oxen were government property and on loan for spring and fall work, but they remained the responsibility of the farm instructor. No cattle were shown in the statistics, but a slaughterhouse was constructed on the reserve to process fresh beef purchased from nearby ranchers.[72]

The DIA continued to provide seed potatoes or seed grain when the reserve or demonstration farm supply was inadequate. A fairly predictable story unfolded in each year's annual report: the hopeful efforts of the Kainai, the farm instructor, and the agent to grow grain, root, or garden crops were frustrated by drought, pests, frost, and the like. A crop usually was harvested, but in quantities so small, or in condition so poor, as scarcely to justify the effort put into it. No matter how diligently they worked in such impossible circumstances, the Kainai could never be the successful peasant farmers that Reed deemed a desirable part of their development. The situation was doubly difficult because as long as the Kainai could not raise enough to feed themselves, the government had a large ongoing commitment to support them with rations – a reality that continued through to 1905.

The Kainai made considerable use of their timber limit. In 1896, the agent reported that twice in the past year they had gone to cut "a large number of saw-logs" and many "dry logs" to use for houses, stables, sheds, and corrals. When run downstream, the river "seemed full of timber for miles." At the sawmill he observed fifty wagons employed "from morning to night, each Indian getting his logs piled up ready for sawing." Enduring cold weather and the frigid water of the mountain stream, Indians laboured with willingness and determination.[73]

The year 1894 marks the beginning of an important change in Kainai reserve history: two Kainai decided to take up a government offer to trade horses for heifers. With the arrival of the cattle, the ranching era began.[74] Agent James Wilson carefully selected men able to care for the cattle, because initial success would be essential to the future of raising stock on the reserve: "From the first the Indians recognized them as their own property, bought with their horses, and like most white people took better care of them than if they had been obtained for nothing. The first issue consisted of fifty head of heifers, and the following year one hundred more were purchased, and these have now [1896] increased to two hundred and ninety-one." By 1896, most Indians desired cattle. Wilson reported that they were careful about wintering the cattle, and that over two years only one yearling heifer had died – and that because of accident rather than neglect.[75] No white-run ranches in the district could have surpassed this record.

What lay behind this shift? The government, after all, had promised the Kainai cattle rather than agricultural equipment or seed grain in Treaty 7. According to Pete Standing Alone, it had provided cattle in 1883, after the Kainai settled on the reserve. But it apparently construed the cattle as a loan, and wanted to take all the calves until the loan was discharged. (This approach may have been because of a white conviction that Indians needed to prove their capability as pastoralists and to care for the animals and grow the herds rather than consume them.) The Kainai, in contrast, regarded the cattle as their property under the terms of the treaty. However, they also thought milking a cow was "distasteful" and the consumption of milk likely "to make people as stubborn and contrary as the animals it came from." They were inclined to slaughter the animals for food in face of shortages, or to use them as "payment for Medicine Bundle transfers or Society membership fees." The government concluded that the Kainai were not going to raise cattle in the approved way, and in 1884 and 1885 sold off those that remained.[76]

In 1893, the nearby Piikani made $935 selling beef, or 57 per cent of their total earnings that year. By contrast, the Kainai did not make anything from selling animals or agricultural products (nor did the Siksika), but they did make about $550 selling hay, $2,659 from freighting and labour, and $300 from hunting; total earnings were $3,559.89.[77] By the early 1890s, many of the Kainai had a different appreciation of cattle than they had a decade earlier. They had seen the Piikani's success and the profits from nearby white ranching, cut and hauled wild hay from their lands under contract to the ranchers, leased some reserve lands to ranchers for grazing, some of them had worked for the ranchers, and consumed many of the cattle purchased from ranchers.

The government saw the thousands of horses on the Kainai reserve as a nuisance, and offered to trade one heifer for one horse. The small beginning of 1894 grew quickly, though the Indian agent controlled the animals' slaughter or sale. By 1905, the Kainai reportedly possessed over 3,000 horses, and over 6,100 cattle; of these, 2,695 were classed as "milch cows" and only 371 as steers.[78] The government encouraged the cattle industry on the reserve by purchasing beef rations necessary to feed the people from the Indian farmer-ranchers, giving them credit at the agency; with this credit, individual Indians were able to purchase wagons and farm implements and other goods at an unprecedented rate. The government also invested frequently in purchasing thoroughbred bulls – 135 of them in 1905, consisting of Shorthorns, Herefords, and Galloways – and stallions (eleven in 1905) to improve the herds.

Concerning the horses, the inspector noted that the number of "matured mares" would require about forty stallions. Because most Indian-owned stallions were of inferior quality, "several hundred of their mares are yearly bred to very inferior sires, and in this way the Indians lose opportunities for gaining thousands of dollars every year more than they now do from the sale of surplus horses." However, it is not clear that Indians always shared the DIA's enthusiasm concerning the government-supplied stallions, which were often Clydesdales – desirable for farm work, but not very glamorous.[79]

Unsurprisingly, the Kainai owned few ploughs and harrows in 1905, but many mowers, horse rakes, wagons, carts, and draught sleighs. Their agricultural equipment and vehicles were valued at almost $43,000. To put this into perspective, the Siksika owned the next largest quantity of equipment in the Treaty 7 area, valued at $12,760, and the entire Saddle Lake agency had equipment valued at under $18,000.[80] The total value of Kainai livestock was almost $195,000, considerably above that of the Siksika (almost $113,500), and roughly five times the worth of any agency in the Alberta portion of Treaty 6.[81] An indicator is total income, including off-reserve income: the Kainai earned $90,600 in 1905, compared to the Siksika's $40,500 and lesser amounts for other Alberta tribes or bands.[82] Thus, even allowing for their larger population, the Kainai appear to have become within a decade the most prosperous of all Indians in Alberta.[83]

Even so, the government still supplied an enormous quantity of rations to the reserve each year. In 1904, this amounted to 337,883 pounds of beef, 3,293 pounds of bacon, 191,400 pounds of flour, 35,883 pounds of beans, and 805 pounds of tea. Only eighteen families, representing about ninety people, supplied their own beef. The government tried to reward Indians who raised their own beef by paying a premium of 1.5 cents per pound more than they offered to those receiving free rations.[84] It provided extra rations to encourage Indians to take on approved productive work on or off the reserve, but it also withheld rations from those who left without permission or who attended a sun dance as a means of exerting control. Many Indians resented this, and believed, as Pete Standing Alone put it, "since the white man had deprived them of their land and livelihood, he owed them rations on a permanent basis."[85]

The Kainai accomplishment was extraordinary in light of the fact that health conditions were dire throughout the period of study. In 1881, there were 3,146 Indians on the Kainai ration list. By 1889, the population was 2,129, a reduction of over 32 per cent; in 1904, it was 1,204, a further decline of almost 43.5 per cent.[86] Put another way, in 1904 the population was 38.3 per cent of that in 1881. Many might have lost hope, given such a heavy mortality rate over a quarter of a century. The Kainai responded with resilience and flexibility.

The Kainai not only vigorously defended their reserve territory from external encroachment, but also understood that their future prosperity

and growth depended on adapting to, and engaging with, the surrounding community. Keith Regular points out that the Kainai had a long history of adjusting to changing economic and climatic circumstances, and
of working within an extensive trading network. Thus the diversification
that took off in the 1890s fit into a historic pattern: some Kainai worked
at logging off the reserve, at freighting both on and off the reserve, and
at carrying mail, mining coal from the deposit on the reserve, interpreting and scouting for the NWMP, and day labour for ranchers, farmers,
and nearby townspeople.[87]

Coal, mined at the eastern extremity of the reserve, was limited in
quantity and not top quality, but satisfactory for most heating purposes.
Mining, notes Regular, "was solely a Native operation, jealously guarded
by the Bloods, and the only non-Native participation was in an advisory
capacity." They sold coal at Fort Macleod in the 1890s, and to the Galt
mining company at Lethbridge. More importantly, they supplied coal to
the agency and schools on the reserve.[88]

The reserve produced large quantities of hay, but demand frequently
outstripped supply. A large portion of the reserve was tied up in grazing
leases for neighbouring ranches, and in meeting the needs of reserve animals. Beyond immediate grazing requirements, livestock required hay
through the winter. In addition, the NWMP constantly required significant amounts of hay for its horses, contracts for which the Indian agents
regularly competed (individual sales were prohibited). At the time contracts were signed it was difficult to determine what quantity and quality
would be available, for no one knew how much would grow in the coming season, or how demand might affect price. Reserve hay was available
in sufficient quantity, and with sufficiently cheap labour for cutting and
delivering it, that it affected prices in the southern Alberta market. The
Kainai withheld hay when it was to their advantage. They also developed a reputation for fulfilling contracts reliably and quickly.[89]

The Kainai were major players in the freighting business in southern
Alberta, demonstrating dependability and undercutting white labour
rates. Over fifty teams, many of four horses, were available for contract
by the turn of the century. They carried coal, lumber, and other freight
between Lethbridge, Fort Macleod, and Cardston, to NWMP posts in the
region, and to local ranches and farms. Agents made every effort to get
the reserve freighters the best contracts and prices. They also, despite
official department policy, acquired the latest machinery so Indians
could compete effectively. Whites, of course, complained that Indians

had unfair competitive advantages, and could offer services for rates at which whites could not profit.[90]

Late in the territorial period, a new opportunity arose for Kainai labour: sugar beet farms just east of the reserve, near Stirling and Magrath. Begun in 1903, the labour-intensive sugar-beet industry was predicated on irrigation and the availability of willing Indian labour, including women and children. The work was back-breaking, dirty, and often cold and wet, and was deemed to be labour no white person would wish to undertake, especially for the wages offered. It began with planting in April, followed by thinning in June, regular cultivating and weeding, and harvest in November. The Kainai occasionally did not appear on the farms when they could find better-paying alternatives, but they were reliable and worked long, arduous hours. Again the agent discouraged sugar beet companies or farmers from negotiating directly with individuals for their services, because generally he could secure better rates in a contract. As it turned out, the timing of the new work usually did not disrupt other Kainai economic activities, though children might be pulled from school for a few weeks at crucial times. In 1905, the Kainai were paid at least $12,000 for their sugar-beet-related work.[91]

The sugar-beet industry was a prime example of what was rendered possible by irrigation, which promoters believed could turn the arid Palliser Triangle into verdant cropland. Small-scale irrigation projects in the region dated back as far as the late 1870s and early 1880s, and received a boost from the Mormon settlers at Cardston after 1889. In the 1880s, the US government attempted to introduce irrigation on the Blackfeet reservation in Montana; insofar as it was intended to encourage agriculture, it was an unmitigated failure, but construction of the works provided several years of almost the only paid employment available to the Montana Native Americans. The Canadian government only began serious planning for large-scale irrigation works in 1894, and it was not until the end of that decade that major work was undertaken. Almost certainly the Kainai and Siksika reserves would have been second-stage beneficiaries of this endeavour, but ironically the works east of the Kainai reserve were just being completed when one of the region's infrequent wet cycles began, and the problem became too much water, rather than too little. By 1905 the government was no longer planning for significant crop irrigation on the Kainai reserve, but instead hoped to use irrigation to increase the capacity of the land to handle grazing animals through more feed and water access.[92]

Not much attention is given in most of the departmental reports to women's role in the economy. In 1896, however, the agent noted that women performed "a considerable amount of work ... in the way of making moccasins for themselves and families, and in tanning robes for white people in the district." He added that many made "very good bread," that those who had cows made butter, and that some "did washing and house-work for the settlers in the immediate neighbourhood."[93] Thus the women, too, seized opportunities to participate in the regional as well as the reserve economy.

By the end of the territorial period, the growing white communities around the Kainai reserve were increasing pressure on the government for greater transportation access. They demanded roads through the reserve for ready access between towns and to resources. In 1899, for example, the DIA granted a road allowance to facilitate access from Cardson to the St Mary River. Wilson assumed the new road would replace two existing ones, but "the White settlers considered all three roadways necessary," even though they were of no use to the Kainai.[94] When Indians fenced off one road on the reserve in 1899, settlers complained about inconvenience and hindrances to mail delivery. Regular reports, "despite the fact there was clear trespass on the reserve, the DIA recommended that the fence be removed to grant unimpeded movement across the reserve. However, the DIA determined that the Government of the Territories could not secure road access without the consent or surrender of the Bloods."[95] It is hardly surprising, given this record, that after 1905 whites demanded the surrender of parts of the reserve, and that the Kainai withheld consent.

The improving Kainai economy depended in large part on their freedom to move somewhat freely off the reserve. Indian agents could not control all the off-reserve activity, and many entrepreneurial Indians contracted their services individually for short-term labour. Thus, at least some income was not accounted for in the official reports.[96] In a sense, then, even if the Kainai did not all become successful farmers, many accepted the capitalist system within which they were situated and with which they interacted extensively. The government assisted and facilitated many aspects of such economic success, but Indians also went beyond the government-approved way of life.

Finally, any picture of the state of the Kainai in 1905 must take into account the fact that the government still provided significant rations because the people were far from self-sufficient and such wealth as existed was unevenly distributed. The Kainai were dependent, and received levels of welfare support that white elderly, indigent, and disabled people could not yet access in comparable degree. Whether or not it was a treaty right, it was grudging, and as a long-term practice it undermined Indian morale. In addition, with so much white settlement in the district, liquor consumption on the reserve increased. The agencies inspector, who seemed to find the problem greater here than on other reserves, lamented that twenty years earlier it had been much easier to identify, arrest, and punish those who sold liquor to Indians; now convictions were rare, and the only limit on Indians' alcohol consumption appeared to be their ability to pay for it.[97]

## The Siksika and Piikani Reserves

In the early 1880s, Macdonald waxed enthusiastic about the Siksika. He praised Isapo-Muxika (whom he called "Chapo-Mexico") as in his opinion the ablest of Indian chiefs in western Canada because of his ability to persuade his supposedly warlike followers to be "loyal." The Siksika reportedly had nothing but "expressions of good will toward the Government," and claimed to be satisfied with their treatment. Macdonald played on a stereotype at odds with established facts: "This is the more gratifying when it is remembered that within less than half a decade, these Indians were continually on the war path, having been regarded as the most warlike Indians in the Dominion. They have now settled down to peaceable pursuits, almost every family having its house and farm or garden in connection therewith, and taking pride in growing crops and storing them away for use in winter."[98]

In truth, the Siksika experience had many parallels with that of the Kainai. They struggled to adapt to the new life, and their record as farmers was far from the idyllic picture portrayed by Macdonald. Most were not interested in farming, and for good reason: often the labour proved futile. Their principal on-reserve occupation by 1905 was raising stock and securing winter hay for their animals, though as with the Kainai, this was a relatively recent development. Many Siksika had other occupations, and engaged with the surrounding community as ranch or farm hands, freighters, or domestics. Some also laboured in a coal mine on the reserve. The agent, H.E. Sibbald, reported in 1905 that most Indians were willing to work for cash "to supply ... their present needs," and added that they seemed uninterested in amassing wealth. He also reported, "we have now, three Indians who, with their families, are entirely self-supporting, and twenty families on the semi-self-supporting list, so that we hope in time to have all the able-bodied men who have taken cattle, on the total self-support list, so that gratuitous rations will only be required for the old and infirm."[99]

This difficulty of persistent dependency went back many years on the reserve. A few Siksika began with small gardens in 1881, and more started the following year, producing as much as 100,000 pounds of potatoes in 1882, as well as some turnips and a small barley crop, under the supervision of a white farmer. This output had led to Macdonald's optimism. But the experience actually did not encourage farming, for they had to turn the hard soil with a few spades using their moccasined feet, which would have been painful, and they only cultivated with hoes. Eventually the government provided a few simple ploughs, but ploughing was difficult because, apart from a few DIA-owned oxen they had no draft animals of their own, as their horses were neither trained to nor strong enough for the work. Moreover, at first some chiefs had religious objections, believing that ploughing the fields was "going against the earthly beings."[100]

Complicating the situation was the fact that it was difficult to persuade the Siksika to accept cattle individually. Isapo-Muxika, perhaps jaundiced by his experience in 1877–78 following the treaty, had warned his people not to go this route: "If you accept cattle, the government will soon conclude that it is not necessary to continue the ration system and then you will be obliged to gain your own livelihood." One study explains, "free cattle [in the early 1880s] were often refused, not because their economic value was questioned but because accepting them implied an obligation to the agent. Every Blackfoot knows that a gift is given with great display of generosity, but it always carries with it an expectation of future return." Indeed, in some cases, refusal was a deliberate act of resistance.[101] As with the Kainai, in 1894 the government began to trade cattle for Indian ponies, but though Isapo-Muxika had died in 1890 his ideas continued to be influential, creating friction when some band members accepted.[102] Within a few years, however, several Siksika owned substantial numbers of cattle.

Inspector Markle, who previously had been the Siksika agent for some years, reported that when he had begun as agent, only 600 head of cattle had been held individually, and the government in 1901 had distributed 430,000 pounds of beef and similarly large amounts of bacon and flour. That year, he instituted a "work or starve" policy. In the 1904 fiscal year, Siksika farmer/ranchers owned 2,860 cattle, and the government had distributed only 145,318 pounds of beef and reduced amounts of other foodstuffs.[103] Markle tried to ensure that rations went only to the elderly or weak, but found to his frustration that such persons also used the supplies to feed their able-bodied relatives and so themselves never had enough.

As evidence of progress, Markle cited the case of Old Woman at War, who ten years earlier had traded ten horses for ten heifers: "He now owns more than one hundred head and has sold during the intervening period about twenty-five head, realizing therefor in the neighbourhood of $1,000 and he is now a self-supporting individual, i.e., he receives no beef, flour or other assistance from the government." Markle, typically, disparaged even this "success," reporting that Old Woman at War had not been "allowed to misdirect his earnings for liquor, not during the past five years at least; if he had been so allowed he would, no doubt, still be on the free ration list and finding fault with the government for giving him so little."[104]

The Siksika, like the Kainai, availed themselves of opportunities to earn income on and off the reserve, opportunities that multiplied after 1906 when the Gleichen and other surrounding areas were more intensively settled. Still, even before 1906 they had worked as farm and ranch hands, freighters, and domestics. They were able to market coal and hay off the reserve.[105]

The Siksika began to resent the authority represented by the Canadian government, the CPR, and the NWMP. The government had bungled the beginning of agriculture on the reserve. In 1883, when the reserve boundaries were being redrawn to accommodate the CPR route, it had tried to claim the coal seam, and Indians refused to cooperate until the government backed off. There were constant, usually not very successful, battles with the CPR for compensation for damages. In 1893–94, the government planned an irrigation ditch on the reserve to help overcome the dry conditions, but it did not provide shovels until late in the season, did not provide boots at all, and expected the digging to take place in November, when the days were short and cold and the soil hard. At about the same time there was a struggle with the government and CPR over a plan to run water pipes over reserve lands from the Bow River to the CPR station at Gleichen without Indian approval. In 1903, the government wanted the Siksika to lease some reserve land to nearby ranchers for grazing, but traditionalists defeated the proposal, having seen overgrazing on other Indian reserves and desiring to ensure sufficient pasturage for their own horses and cattle.[106]

Markle thus was building on a heritage of friction when he imposed his "work or starve" policy, cutting rations to all able-bodied Siksika. He believed they had had enough time and opportunity to learn to support themselves. Indians did not quite see it that way. To them, after a quarter-century of receiving them, rations were a treaty entitlement.[107] They also had years of failed attempts to farm on a reserve mostly unsuited to it. Markle himself confessed that hail, low prices, and some years of "light crops" had discouraged Indians who attempted to grow grain: "They found that a great deal more money could be gained, with considerable less work, by putting up hay for nearby ranchers than farming for themselves. With them, as with whites, it is a question of dollars and cents, and I do not know that I have good reasons for censure."

Many of the Siksika, as well as many other Indians in the district of Alberta, still preferred to live in tents or teepees during the warmer months, but had permanent winter dwellings. Some of the latter, in Markle's opinion, were excellent – the best had "papered walls, carpeted floors, mounted iron beds with springs, mattresses, sheets, blankets, pillows and shams and spreads thereon, together with an assortment of furniture of one kind or another." Others were fairly good, and quite a few were "entirely too small for the number who reside therein." Part of the problem, he admitted, was the need to purchase wagons, mowers, rakes, harness, and so forth, which left little money for building materials to improve the houses. The band had also expended funds to construct a vat for dipping cattle (essential to prevent the spread of certain diseases) and to fence more of the reserve land.[108]

The Piikani reserve contained some of the best watered, treeless grazing land in Alberta. In the midst of chinook country, grazing for most of the year was usually feasible. Agent J.H. Gooderham noted in 1905 that horse and cattle raising was the principal occupation of the people, and that the potential for farming had been little developed. He observed that white farmers around the reserve had begun to grow winter wheat and other grains, and hoped the Piikani would emulate them. The Crowsnest Pass railway bisected the reserve in 1898, and constructed two sidings there. Easier transportation, access to consumer goods, and movement of beef were to some extent offset by how many cattle the trains killed or injured, and by the fact that cattle were able to wander off the reserve at the breaks in the fences caused by the railway line. The CPR, however, erected fencing along its line to minimize these problems. Indians realized almost $6,500 from beef sales; Gooderham noted that all that profit was expended "in lumber, wagons, saddles, harness, wire, mowers, rakes, and other implements, food, clothing, stoves, furniture and cooking utensils." In the spring of 1905, Indians branded 441 calves, and expected another seventy or eighty at the fall round-up. They also earned other income from working a sawmill and freighting lumber.

Markle again mixed condescension with praise when he commented, "the Indians of this agency, on the whole, are well housed, many of them have excellent dwellings, from an Indian's point of view at least." He wanted to show Indians were progressing as individual farmers, noting, "almost every head of a family now owns a wagon, mower, rake, harness, fairly good work-horses and a dwelling very well furnished." Gooderham, by contrast, spoke of improvement as a collective achievement, both in terms of both farming and improvement of buildings. For example, he noted, "building new houses, stables and corrals and repairing old ones are going on continually and with noticeable improvement; and as we have plenty of lumber of all grades from our saw-mill at a cost of very little per thousand feet, the old log shanty with flat, mud roof is gradually disappearing and will in a short time be a thing of the past."[109]

## The Tsuu T'ina Reserve

Elizabeth Churchill notes that the Tsuu T'ina reserve was not suited to farming: "only fifty-two percent of the soils on the reserve fell into the Canadian Land Inventory Classes 2 to 4 for agriculture." The reserve had no Class 1 (excellent) and very little Class 2 land. In fact, "only 9,700 acres [under 14 per cent] of the total reserve lands were suitable for agriculture and most of these fell into the category of 90 frost free days or less." It was, however, suited to grazing. The Tsuu T'ina were stock-raisers who also farmed, and they supplemented their income working for nearby ranchers. By 1904, the reserve was properly fenced, and the Indians earned income grazing some 3,000 horses and cattle for nearby ranchers, in addition to over 500 of their own animals. By 1905, they were able to purchase all their farm implements – binders, mowers, rakes, wagons, ploughs, and the like – out of their earnings, and the agent noted "self-reliance and progress" were more in evidence as they took increasing interest in the farming and ranching. Government rations had been cut significantly since 1897, so that Indians received the equivalent of 0.75 pounds per day; not only was this cheaper for the government, but in Agent A.J. McNeill's condescending view it "tended to make the Indians more self-reliant and industrious and consequently more easily handled. Besides, the Indian is more healthy, as no doubt he suffered before from over-feeding and lying around in his camp – they now get more exercise and have something to live for."[110]

Churchill found that morale on the reserve in the 1880s had been low. Chief Bullhead reportedly said in 1885, "now the buffalo is gone we hang our heads[,] we are poor." Discouraged men were only induced to work with tea or tobacco. Beyond limited attempts to farm, other economic activities in the decade included hauling dead and fallen timber from the reserve to sell in Calgary or to nearby settlers. Oxen were used to plough land and transport goods for sale. The Tsuu T'ina also worked for wages (their only source of cash) or barter. Notes Churchill, "labourers ... could secure a degree of independence in this manner. Wages were put to immediate use in purchasing meat, blankets, heating oil and clothing," benefitting both themselves and the Calgary district economy.[111]

In the 1880s and 1890s, when Reed's eccentricities held sway, government policy undercut the reserve economy. Mechanization of agriculture, including purchase of machinery, was discouraged: "Indians were not trusted with new machinery. Harvesting was often performed by outside labourers. This substantially reduced the Indian earnings." The agent for the Tsuu T'ina told the DIA that Indians could earn six times the usual amount if they could harvest hay themselves. Most hides of animals slaughtered on the reserve for rations were sold to outsiders, as was the policy elsewhere; Indians were permitted to keep enough leather to make footwear, but not for other traditional clothing.[112] A small but telling example of the insensitivity of DIA policy-making occurred in 1895, when the department gave Bullhead a cow in hope that he would set an example for his reserve with respect to dairying. But the elderly Bullhead was not a man of means, even though the government gave him gifts of tea and tobacco to enhance his prestige, and he "had no one to milk for him except his aging wife and he was unable to purchase the pails and pans necessary for milking."[113]

Officials tended to conclude that when the Tsuu T'ina hauled wood and hay to sell in Calgary whenever they wanted money, undertook wage labour for cash, or hunted rather than undertaking the day-to-day responsibility of raising cattle or farming, they were being lazy. They reported that in the early twentieth century the Tsuu T'ina were more committed to stock-raising than in the past, a few farmed, "and the majority of them grow a patch of potatoes and cultivate a garden." The Indians reportedly were well housed, and the inspector noted improved sobriety (probably as a result of a constant police presence): "It is only a very few years since one or more of this band were in the guard-room at Calgary almost constantly; now this happens only occasionally."[114]

A by-product of the government policy was the emergence of a kind of reserve class system. The government viewed most Tsuu T'ina as indifferent farmers, but there were a few who were doing well, and who were building themselves bigger and better houses and purchasing finer furnishings. These individuals were favoured by the government when jobs were available to work on agency buildings or fences, "thereby sustaining their income differential from other workers." The government saw this as developing individualism and rewarding the industrious.[115] The income of most Tsuu T'ina, however, was inadequate: despite government efforts to cut back, between 1904 and 1906 nearly all still received daily rations, except for children enrolled in the boarding school. Like other Indians, many had long since concluded that rations constituted a treaty right.[116]

It can appear as though little progress was being made. But a different perspective was provided in 1897–98 when McNeill reported "a number of tourists, both American and European, visited the reserve at different times during the year," exhibiting an interest "in the red man and his life on the reserve. Many were surprised to find him engaged in farming, and so far advanced in the ways of the white man. They expected to see him the same as depicted in the Fenimore Cooper novels a century or two ago."[117] Stereotypes died hard.

## The Stoney Nakoda Agency

Three contiguous reserves (Wesley, formerly Jacob Goodstoney; Chiniki; and Bearspaw) made up the Stoney Nakoda agency near Morleyville. The soil was very poor, the climate dry, and the growing season short, so it was unfavourable to agriculture. It did have grasslands suitable for grazing, and Indians had herds of cattle and horses. Living in the foothills of the Rockies, the Stoney Nakoda had ready access to hunting and fishing resources, which they exploited extensively.[118] They earned income by cutting and delivering logs to a sawmill; providing and loading firewood, posts, and rails on train cars at the Morleyville station; and transporting large quantities of firewood to a lime kiln at Kananaskis. They also sold furs and beadwork to tourists at Banff. Early in the twentieth century, some of them apparently spent time working for ranchers near Fort Macleod, indicating that their extensive travelling off reserve was not only for hunting.[119]

A major change for the reserve was the ending of rations in 1904, except for provisions for the elderly and disabled. Markle reported that, prior to 30 June 1904, the Stoneys had never supplied "their own tables with meat [i.e., beef as opposed to game]. They expected – and in fact realized their expectations in this respect – the department to purchase their beef cattle and issue the beef therefrom back to them gratuitously." The result of the change was that in 1904–05 Indians contributed over 16,000 pounds of beef to their own support.[120]

Indian Agent Fleetham optimistically suggested that stock raising would become the "principal industry" on the reserve, and that any Indian who so desired could look forward to being self-sustaining as a result. The reality was that even before 1905 the unequal distribution of wealth was noticeable among the Stoney Nakoda. As a whole, they were said to have the lowest per capita income of the Treaty 7 tribes, and there were reports of food shortages among the elderly. At the same time, "the bulk of wealth among the Stoneys, chiefly in the form of cattle, was controlled by approximately twenty members of the tribe."[121]

Certain problems affected the Stoney Nakoda more than other Indians. The CPR's construction and operation in the Bow Valley and through the Rockies from 1883 onward scattered and killed game animals on their reserves and in their traditional hunting territory.[122] The creation of Rocky Mountains National Park, and conflict with sport hunters, created great difficulties.[123] Finally, the reserves contained waterways with the potential to generate hydroelectric power, and to operate water-powered mills, which attracted the attention of white developers. An application to secure rights to reserve lands around Horseshoe Falls reached the DIA in 1903. While some of the younger Indians were interested in the profits to be realized, Chief Chiniki and his family were resistant and the project did not proceed prior to 1905. In 1907, a price was negotiated and 1,000 acres were alienated from the reserve.[124]

## CONCLUSION

What the government and Indians heard at the treaty negotiations in 1876 and 1877 seems to have been more or less what they wanted to hear. Not least was this true with respect to the purpose and future of reserves and the reserve economies. The government thought it heard Indian chiefs accept that their traditional lifestyle was, or shortly would become, no longer viable; that a settled agricultural life on reserves was their future; and that their requests for implements, animals, and instruction indicated a commitment to change. The treaty commissioners agreed to the provision for famine relief; although Ottawa officials initially cringed at the potential cost, they imagined that the famines of the 1870s would be rarely repeated as Indians learned to feed themselves more reliably and sought to become self-supporting through agriculture. The government was tone-deaf to the implications of Indians' insistence upon a treaty right to continue to hunt, fish, and gather on unoccupied lands beyond the reserve boundaries, as it considered such activity to be a short-term, transitional supplement to agricultural production. Above all, it tended to view its experience with Ontario Indians – perceived as generally law-abiding, self-supporting, respectful, and cooperative – as a template of what might be hoped for within a generation or two in the new prairie West.

Indians, in contrast, appear to have begun with the premise that the foundational principles of the treaties were peace, a fraternal relationship, and mutual respect. They wanted a way to continue to live, and to do so *as Indians*, in a world of already devastating change. Reserves would be a permanent, secure, and inviolable base, and agriculture would be a valuable supplement to their lifestyle, while the right to hunt and fish seemed to be a guarantee that they could maintain tradition indefinitely. When they thought of independence and responsibility, it was within that context, and was more collective than individual. The treaty was a promise not only that they could continue to be Indian, but also that assistance would be available when necessary. Change was inevitable, but they and the government anticipated very different outcomes.

By the end of the territorial period in 1905, Alberta's Indians had diverse economies. In the far north of Treaty 6, to the west of Edmonton, and in the foothills and mountains west of Calgary, some Indians were able to maintain a good deal of their traditional ways. Some raised cattle and farmed minimally, while finding enough of their traditional diet to sustain themselves much of the time; they also could generate income from furs and wage labour. They maintained some of their nomadic life, were thought to be fairly healthy, and by 1905 only the Stoney Nakoda faced serious opposition to their hunting and gathering lifestyle. These bands might seem to exemplify the government's failure to implement its "civilizing" policies, but in fact the government's priority lay in using reserves to isolate and transform Indians whose ancestral territory lay in the prime settlement areas. If bands on the margins wanted to embrace the government program, that would be fine; meanwhile, especially in the case of those in the northern and western areas of Treaty 6, they caused relatively little expense or anxiety.

The government envisioned Indians running individual, self-sustaining mixed farms, with grain (mostly wheat, with some oats and barley), root crops (potatoes, but also carrots and turnips), and vegetable gardens, along with a few milk and beef cattle. Sheep, hogs, and poultry were absent from all but a few Alberta Indian farms in this period. The available strains of wheat, farm machinery (or lack of it), and farming techniques, combined with the Alberta climates and soils, meant that this idyllic vision was difficult to realize in the territorial years. By 1905, the vision was closest to realization on some farms in the Hobbema and Saddle Lake agencies, with a few individual cases, such as on the Michel and Enoch reserves, in the Edmonton agency. But these relative success stories were a distinct minority. Survival for Indians necessitated some continued hunting, gathering, and trapping, as well as engagement in the surrounding communities selling produce, merchandise, and labour.

All this off-reserve activity presented a problem for the government plan: it took Indians away from their farms and animals, sometimes for extended periods. If daily milking and feeding of cattle and weeding, cultivating, and irrigating gardens and root crops was supposed to instil discipline and responsibility, other activities such as the sun dance, extended or distant contract labour, or long hunting expeditions seemed more pressing, profitable, or congenial. Some Indians adapted to the farm routine, but many did not. Railways, ranches, and white farms and settlements all encroached on isolation and provided both opportunity and diversion.

The Nizitapi agencies and the Tsuu T'ina in Treaty 7 also marked a different outcome than the government intended. On the positive side, provision had been made in the treaty for cattle instead of agricultural implements and seed. The government finally began to provide the cattle in the mid-1890s, and by 1905 all these agencies had farmer/ranchers who enjoyed some success and profitability. The government cut rations, except for the elderly and disabled, and generally was optimistic about the future. But apparent success obscured some problems. First the legacy of the long period when the government had tried to force grain and root crop farming on these reserves with little success and at great human cost (to say nothing of the resultant friction between Indians and government) was a damaging one. Second, these reserves depended heavily on the off-reserve economy, in which Indians were not respected as equals and would experience discrimination. Third, prosperity was unequal in the cattle economy, and a relative few on each reserve controlled most of the wealth while many others remained impoverished. This pattern somewhat emulated the white ranching industry (the inequities of large and dominant ranchers versus small ranchers, and of ranchers versus farmers), but marginalized Indians confined to living on reserves had fewer alternative opportunities than smaller ranchers and farmers elsewhere. The ideal of every able-bodied Indian working a self-sustaining farm was not reality.[125] Eighty-acre farm plots were not suited to a ranching economy.

By 1905, the government's original goals seemed distant. Very few Indians were self-sustaining, and many were demoralized and lived in unhealthy, impoverished conditions. However, estimating success or failure involves other considerations. The comparison ought not to be between the unsatisfactory conditions in 1905 versus some idyllic pre-treaty Arcadia. Even if whites could have been withdrawn from the region at the end of the 1870s, the already serious depletion of bison and other food resources would have left the plains peoples in ever-worsening destitution and starvation. That was the reality of life for thousands of Indians prior to the treaties and reserves, and was why they desperately wanted the government to make a treaty. Plainly and simply, they needed help.

No government could have denied the advance of the North American settlement frontier, which occurred in the West far more rapidly than had been the case in central Canada. The loss of land for the traditional Indian ways of life took only about a generation in the fertile belt and southern prairies. The cost to the government for massive annual relief expenditures, farm supports in the form of everything from seed grain to animals, and continuing instruction for in many cases well over twenty years considerably exceeded anything the treaty commissioners anticipated. The government had to face the consequences of its heavy moral and legal responsibilities, and soon in effect extended indefinitely the three-year transition expenses of Treaty 6, along with other assistance. It pressured Indians to take up farming quickly, but it faced continual criticism for the high levels of expenditure, particularly for relief. It simply had to encourage Indians to hunt, gather, and seek off-reserve opportunities as a means of mitigating its obligations. The situation was in some ways chaotic, and the government's policies were too frequently inconsistent, ill considered, and harshly administered. As chapter 9 will show, attempts to restrict Indians' movement off reserves were regularly frustrated by the essential importance of such activity.

Focusing too much on the treaties as a guide to what government policy should have been can be misleading. As noted in chapter 1, the overriding legislation within which Treaties 6 and 7 were negotiated and under which administration was carried on was the Indian Act. It embodied at least three fundamental notions: that Indians' legal status was differentiated from, and generally subordinate to, that of whites; that Indians were wards of the government, which had corresponding moral and legal responsibilities; and that the goal of government policy was to lead the Indians to enfranchisement or full status as British subjects and erase Indian identity. Status Indians on reserves were a legally differentiated class of people for whom the federal state had moral and legal responsibility. They were managed, regulated, and rendered dependent. This is one key to understanding the failures of government policies: the very reserves that were supposed to help Indians transition from Indian status to responsible citizenship were administered in ways and with assumptions that undermined that goal.

The other key lies in the Indians themselves. By 1905, most lived for at least part of the year in permanent dwellings on the reserves, and life for most was radically different than it had been thirty years earlier. They adapted, though not necessarily according to the government's plan or schedule. Many learned the basics of farming, which would serve them in future, but they also learned that there were other ways – often more reliable, congenial, and traditional – to earn a living. They had learned to resist the government's straightjacket, maintaining their language and many customs, syncretizing the new and old ways in manners that worked for them, and often quietly ignoring the pass system and directives from agents and police. They also learned that the new system, including the ration system, could work for them in other ways, and they expected government to provide for the elderly and disabled in their communities. Some of this the government expected, at least when it came to those who were adolescents or adults when the treaties were signed; its other great hope for transforming Indian culture lay with influencing children through the education system.

# 6

## Of High Hopes and Dismal Failure: Transforming the Children

We have little or no imagination for comprehending the evil that originates in our desire to do good, to serve God, to help our neighbors, to make the world a better place.

Eugene H. Peterson[1]

The extermination of the past – by design, by neglect, by good intention – is what characterizes the history of our time.

Tony Judt[2]

So it was with Canada's policy for educating Indian children. The ends of saving their souls, of "raising" them from presumed savagery to the "blessings" of Christian and capitalist civilization, of preparing them for the full rights of British subjects: all justified, to missionaries, teachers, and politicians, a school system now widely reviled as an immoral, outrageous colonialist blemish upon the story of Indian-white relations in Canada. It attempted to erase the past – the Indian identity – to create a fresh, mostly assimilated future. The redemptive notion of rebirth, of casting off the old and becoming new, was a familiar one to Christian society. How was it that people who believed their intentions to be good and humanitarian could be so deceived about what their institutions and policies actually wrought? While acknowledging its failings, was the record as uncompromisingly negative as it usually is portrayed? Were there any benefits to be found alongside the blemishes?

### CONTEXTUALIZING THE TREATY COMMITMENT

Attitudes to Indian education cannot be understood apart from attitudes to children and to education in the white community.[3] Neil Sutherland,

an authority on the history of childhood, argues that in the 1870s and
1880s – just when Indian schools were being established in western
Canada – Canadians had little sense of childhood as a separate stage of
development with special emotional and other needs. Children, rather,
were viewed as potential adults, resistive and refractory, who through
discipline, education, and example could be shaped into responsible,
hard-working, and moral adults.[4] They were often viewed as economic
assets, valued for their labour. Thousands of British orphans or abandoned children were brought to Canada in this period as indentured
servants, placed mostly in rural homes, and expected to learn the discipline of work, as well as receiving some opportunity for formal education in their younger years. The work experience was held to be at
least as important as any classroom training. For some the experience
was positive; for many others, it involved abuse, alienation, and emotional distancing. But complaints were usually disregarded or down-
played in light of powerful lobbies and assertions about all the good
being done for the children.[5] So it would be when it came to schools
for Indian children.

By the mid-1890s, new ideas were becoming popular – ideas that paid
more attention to children's emotional and physical needs, but that were
part of the social reform movement demanding state intervention in a
range of previously private individual or family activities. The public
health movement in particular began to see the school, rather than the
home, as the best place to improve and "save" children.[6]

To turn to the treaty commitment to schooling, note that Treaties 6
and 7 do not share the same education clause. Treaty 6 of 1876 stipulated, similarly to previous numbered treaties, "Her Majesty agrees to
maintain schools for instruction in such reserves hereby made, as to her
Government of the Dominion of Canada may seem advisable, whenever
the Indians of the reserve shall desire it." A year later, Treaty 7 provided,
"Her Majesty agrees to pay the salary of such teachers to instruct the
children of said Indians as to her Government of Canada may seem
advisable, when said Indians are settled on their reserves and shall desire
teachers." The change was not explained, but is not negligible: Treaty 6
provided for schools on reserves, and Treaty 7 did not.[7] Treaty 6
addressed maintaining schools, but Treaty 7 addressed paying teachers,
which can be construed as somewhat different obligations. Both provisions gave the government substantial discretionary authority, but committed it to providing some level of formal education for settled treaty
Indians. In fact, the Treaty 7 provision fell closer to actual practice with

respect to schools on or near reserves in the post-treaty era.[8] Note that neither treaty specified day schools, despite later assumptions that they did. What did each side understand these clauses to mean?

In Canada, a commitment to some measure of publicly funded elementary education for whites had slowly been adopted over the three decades prior to Treaty 6. The nature and purposes of such education, and the extent of government support, had been (and remained) the subject of considerable debate. Taxation of ratepayers (property owners) to support schools in Canada West under the Common School Acts of 1846 and 1850 at first was widely resisted at the local level, and only gradually did the schools become universal. A school act of 1846 also was permissive at the local level for Canada East, and it took until 1876 before all of Quebec accepted taxation for schools.[9] In 1852, Prince Edward Island was the first British North America colony to pass a universal tax for free schools. Nova Scotia did not follow suit until 1865, and in New Brunswick taxation for local schools remained permissive rather than compulsory at the time of confederation.[10] Note too that, while the provincial governments provided limited grants for schools, the bulk of the funding came from local ratepayers and fees. For example, at the birth of the province of Alberta in 1905, rural school districts obtained 68 per cent of their revenues from local property taxes and 27 per cent from provincial government grants.[11]

With respect to Indian schools, John S. Milloy records that in the 1840s and 1850s in Canada West a number of Indian bands were open to contributing "one quarter of their annual treaty payments for an education fund." Two boarding schools[12] opened as a result, and "operated as a partnership. The government provided a yearly grant toward the lodging, clothing, and education of the children. The [Methodist] church supplied the teachers, supervisors, and necessary equipment."[13] The experience of central and eastern Canada must have influenced how the federal government conceived of the treaty commitment for education in the North-West Territories.

Public funding of education in Canadian society was about much more than making reading, writing and arithmetic accessible to the general public: it led to centralized government control, common curricula and standards, educational requirements for teachers, and inspectors to ensure maintenance of standards – all with the purpose of socialization (conformity) as well as academic education. According to J. Donald Wilson, Egerton Ryerson, the principal figure behind the mid-century educational reforms in Canada West, "looked on the school as a vehicle for inculcating loyalty and patriotism, fostering social cohesion and self-reliance, and insuring domestic [i.e., social and political] tranquility."[14] Publicly funded schools, then, were about instilling commonly accepted values, or about developing citizens, as well as inculcating a common body of knowledge – about forging unity out of diversity, to use a well-worn phrase. That the provinces controlled education under the constitution of 1867, and that they differed on the details of those values, did not alter these fundamental purposes of nineteenth-century schools. When the federal government assumed constitutional responsibility for Indians under the Constitution Act, 1867,[15] it included their education. Federal politicians shared the assumptions of their provincial counterparts: schools were the means by which Indian children could be assimilated into the dominant culture, and by which they could be socialized as well as academically educated. While the specifics of the nature and appropriate cost of the school system were still open to debate, federal officials almost certainly assumed that, as in the case of provincial education systems, the government would not bear the full cost. In this case, however, churches and their supporters would take the place of the local ratepayers in shouldering a portion of the financial burden, as they had done in the case of Indian education in central and maritime Canada before confederation.[16]

By confederation, Canadians had developed certain racist assumptions about Indians' education.[17] One was that they were mostly incapable of being "raised" to "the social and political level of their white neighbours."[18] If the goal of Indian education was assimilation, therefore, it meant acquisition of the ability to function in a self-supporting and independent manner, but, by implication, likely as a kind of underclass. Could that be achieved through day schools on the reserves? Many had their doubts. Some believed that boarding schools were best for training boys in agriculture and trades and girls in domestic arts and science.[19] Schooling for Indian children in central and eastern Canada had involved many church-run day schools, subsidized by government grants, and their success was held to be limited. Experiments with boarding schools began during the 1830s in hope of providing an effective alternative, but even before confederation they too had been judged a failure – in large part, it was believed, because the reserve conditions to which graduates returned tended to vitiate the schools' efforts.[20] In other words, by confederation Canadians had experimented with a variety of approaches to Indian education, with murky results. Yet these early efforts would influence federal Indian education policy in western Canada.

It is well to remember that, at least in the first two or three decades after confederation, over 40 per cent of school-age Indian children across the country were not enrolled at any school, absentee rates were extremely high, and day schools provided the educational experience for a great majority. In 1891, the superintendent general reported that, of over 13,000 school-age Indian children in Canada, only about 6,200 were enrolled in day schools, just over 1,000 in industrial schools, and around 300 in boarding schools. Average attendance at day schools was around 50 per cent, while that at boarding and industrial schools was about 73 per cent and 82 per cent, respectively.[21] Thus, on average on any given school day in Canada in 1891, around 55 per cent of enrolled Indian children attended – an acceptable figure for the era. Attendance at white schools was similar. Though 1891 figures have not been located for the North-West Territories, average attendance at white schools was 51.9 per cent in Manitoba and 54.8 per cent in British Columbia. Attendance in urban schools was also much better than in rural schools. In this context, attendance at Indian schools was very respectable for a system only recently established.[22]

After confederation the government hoped that Indian schools might succeed in western Canada. The region's experience with schools began in the future province of Alberta as early as 1842, when Rev Robert Rundle went to Lesser Slave Lake and endeavoured to teach Cree children to write a catechism in their own language, as well as offering other instruction. The Roman Catholic Sisters of Charity arrived at Lac Ste Anne in 1859 to care for the sick, aged, and orphans, and also operated a school; in 1863, they moved to a more central location at St Albert. In 1862, they opened a similar facility at Lac la Biche, where there had been a Roman Catholic mission for some years. A Catholic school opened at Fort Edmonton in 1862 to serve the children of English-speaking Metis and Hudson's Bay Company servants. Meanwhile, the Methodists began a mission and education work at Whitefish Lake in 1857, where Rev Henry Bird Steinhauer ran a school. At Victoria (later Pakan) in 1862, they opened another school attended by Metis, Indian, and some white children. Rev John McDougall started a mission at Pigeon Lake in the 1860s and a school at Morleyville in 1873. Still another Methodist school briefly operated in Edmonton in 1874–75.[23] Some of these schools even taught children to read and write in Cree, along with the basics of English or less frequently French.

In 1873, Chief Factor Christie and other HBC officials from Edmonton visited the Whitefish Lake school and were impressed with the children's accomplishments in "reading, writing and spelling, geography, arithmetic, and Bible history." In 1876, the federal government agreed to pay an annual subsidy of $300 to one or two approved schools with an average attendance over the year of at least thirty pupils.[24]

It might seem that schools mixing Indians, Metis, and white children would be a way to achieve the government's assimilationist goals. However, the government did not intend to assume ongoing financial responsibility for children other than those for whom it had both constitutional responsibility and a treaty obligation. After the North-West Territories Act passed in 1875, federal authorities assumed that the local government would soon be responsible for non-Indian (including Metis) education in the region.

How did the Indians understand the school provisions in the treaties? Their exposure to education, as with agriculture, suggested it need not interfere radically with their traditional way of life. Children voluntarily attended school when a band was living near one and if their parents encouraged it, but they usually travelled with their bands to hunt, trap, fish, and gather. Teachers (often the missionaries) had to adapt their schedules to Indian rhythms. For a short time, Father Albert Lacombe had tried to travel with the peripatetic Indians to maintain a greater continuity of instruction, an example other Oblates emulated.[25] That could not be, and was not, a long-term solution. Still, Indians' experience of the white education system before the treaties had been benign: schooling had been adapted to some extent to their needs, generally did not remove children from their families, and often involved instruction of Indian alongside Metis and white children.

Elizabeth Barrett arrived from Ontario in 1875 to teach at the mission school at Whitefish Lake. She struggled to learn Cree, concluding that the language was essential for a teacher or missionary, inasmuch as "the people love and cling to their mother tongue, and are not likely to soon permit the English [language] to take its place. Several who understand English will not speak a word of it, if they can possibly avoid doing so." The Cree appreciated her efforts to speak their language: "There seems to be implanted deep in the Indian nature, a quiet though stubborn and most persistent determination to retain their own habits and customs."[26] Too few later teachers would be so perceptive of, or sympathetic to, the people among whom they chose to work.

During the 1876 treaty negotiations, schools were little discussed. The draft treaty already provided for them. M.G. Dickieson, who was present at the negotiations at Fort Pitt in 1876 and subsequently became an

Indian agent, reported that only one band, from Little Touchwood Hills, broached the subject, apparently because one of its members had been educated at the St John's School in Manitoba. Dickieson told them "that so soon as they had a suitable building erected for a school house, a teacher would be provided and paid, and further that I had no doubt help would be given them by the Government in the way of materials if the Department saw that they were making efforts to erect a school-house, and were striving to secure the education of their children."[27] It was an interesting interpretation of the Treaty 6 provision, one that presumed Indians would take initiative and build the school, while the Department of Indian Affairs would subsidize it with materials and pay for a teacher. The government apparently did not disagree with Dickieson's interpretation, and authorized an expenditure of one hundred dollars toward building a schoolhouse on one reserve, a case that Superintendent General Edgar Dewdney in 1880 requested become a policy.[28] At Fort Carlton in 1876, when Indians requested "missionaries and school teachers," Alexander Morris replied that the churches provided missionaries, not the government. He reiterated the promise "that when you settled down, and there were enough children, schools would be maintained."[29] At Blackfoot Crossing in 1877, David Laird said, "as soon as you settle, teachers will be sent to you to instruct your children to read books like this one (the Governor referred to a Bible), which is impossible as long as you move from place to place."[30] When Dewdney toured the region and met with various Indians in 1879, he reported "almost all" bands "expressed a wish to have schools erected on their reserves, to educate their children."[31]

Walter Hildebrandt and Sarah Carter point out that Treaty 7 Indian leaders did not want white Canadian culture to replace their traditions: "They wanted their schools to be on reserves and did not want their children to be taken from their homes and families or to be punished for speaking their own language. The Blackfoot Confederacy, Tsuu T'ina and Stoney leadership wanted their children to be taught skills that would allow them to participate in the new economy of the West, rather than to be taught obedience or to despise their parents' way of life."[32] If so, it was another case of mutual incomprehension. Were schools not intended, government officials might have asked, to socialize and assimilate their pupils?

Indians did not rule out boarding schools, though they still wanted them on reserves. John Buffalo, an elder of the Ermineskin reserve, recalled, "when [Chief] Ermineskin took up his own reserve, he met with the priest to inform him that he wanted a school within his reserve. He told the priest that he wanted a boarding school and the priest helped him ... The government provided food, clothing, and accommodation for sleeping; that is how the children were being educated."[33]

## THE EARLY DEVELOPMENT OF THE SCHOOL SYSTEM

Between the signing of the treaties and the mid-1880s, a system with three kinds of schools for Indian children emerged: day schools on the reserves (the cheapest to run), boarding schools (housing pupils, usually on or beside reserves in this era, and running several times the per-pupil cost of day schools), and, by 1883–84, a few industrial schools (housing pupils, removed from reserves, and the most costly). All were run by religious denominations (mainly Roman Catholic, Methodist, and Anglican, and rarely Presbyterian). The department provided a subsidy, and gradually grew more rigorous in establishing a standardized curriculum,[34] annual inspections, and accounting of pupils and expenditures. The government did almost everything relating to Indian education as cheaply as possible. It limited grants for teachers in day schools to $300 per annum per school (ten dollars per pupil to a maximum average daily of thirty; this soon became twelve dollars per pupil to a maximum daily average of twenty-five); the rate remained unchanged even after 1905. Sometimes the government contributed to the cost of textbooks; equipment; or materials for construction, renovations, or repairs, but it was parsimonious and inconsistent. Schools thus lived on a financial knife edge, since religious denominations were unable to contribute enough to the cause. Corners were cut everywhere. Enrolment at boarding schools was usually limited by grant size (by the end of the period, about seventy dollars per pupil to a fixed maximum number), and pupils and staff had to work hard just to keep such schools afloat.[35]

Yet at every turn the opposition in Ottawa and critics in the press castigated the government for alleged extravagance. For example, beginning in 1896 and regularly thereafter, Frank Oliver, newly elected Liberal MP for Alberta and supposedly a Laurier supporter, demanded to know why the government spent over $300,000 per year to educate fewer than 1,000 Indian pupils in the North-West Territories, when the entire federal subsidy to the territorial government for all its responsibilities was but $242,000, out of which it had to provide grants to white schools for 10,000 students. Furthermore, hardly anyone thought the expenditure on Indian children was good value.[36] The government could justify the expenditures, but Oliver reflected popular opinion.

By 1880 there were two Roman Catholic boarding schools in the future Alberta, at St Albert and Lac la Biche, both of which received government support. In the early years, these schools were sometimes described as industrial or semi-industrial because they taught trades and domestic skills along with the regular curriculum.[37] "Indian" pupils at the former comprised twenty-eight boys and thirty-one girls, with an average attendance of forty-five; at the latter, seven boys and twenty-two girls, with an average attendance of twenty-two.[38] It is by no means clear that in these early years all pupils were treaty Indians. The St Albert school also operated as an orphanage, and Dewdney reported that thirty-one pupils were orphans who were fed, clothed, and housed at the school, and accordingly were expected to help out, the boys on the farm and the girls with various domestic chores. Some pupils almost certainly were day students. The St Albert school had qualified for the maximum $300 annual grant since 1876. Yet Church officials claimed that the actual cost per pupil was closer to one hundred dollars per annum, which meant a large deficit in operations, even at a school where the teachers were clerics or nuns sworn to poverty who received nothing beyond room, board, and clothing.[39] The children who farmed were meant both to learn skills for their futures and to serve the schools economically – a necessity for their survival. Church officials also noted that their resources, both human and financial, were further stretched because the mission and school also served as a hospital where the injured and ill sought treatment; many were turned away because there was no place to put them. The government paid doctors for medical attendance, but – at least in the early years – seemed to accept the work of nursing sisters as free labour. Concerning other schools in 1880, a Methodist school and orphanage had for several years operated at Morleyville, and Anglican schools operated for the Piikani and Kainai.[40]

Although agents in the field pushed for day schools on reserves as quickly as possible, the government was reluctant, claiming, "the Indian day school is ... under the best of circumstances, attended with unsatisfactory results." It cited irregular attendance, parents' unwillingness to insist on attendance, and "the frequent absence of many families from the reserves while fishing, hunting and berry picking." Indians often saw no reason for schooling to interfere with normal life, and the department instructed teachers "to adapt the periods of vacation to the time when the Indians will be absent from the reserve." But this could only be a temporary expedient: "The Indian youth, to enable him to cope successfully with his brother of white origin, must be dissociated from the prejudicial influences by which he is surrounded on the reserve of his band." That meant boarding schools, "whereat Indian children, besides being instructed in the usual branches of education, will be lodged, fed, clothed, kept separate from home influences, taught trades and instructed in agriculture." Officials believed that experience in Ontario, British Columbia, Manitoba, and the North-West Territories demonstrated the superiority of the boarding or industrial model.[41]

In the twenty-five years after 1880, day schools declined but did not disappear. However, the expansion of boarding schools and the introduction of industrial schools significantly changed the educational vision ·of the 1870s. Some bands remained too small and/or nomadic for a day school to be viable, and often the only educational option available to children from these bands was a distant boarding or industrial school. Despite later claims that reserve day schools were what the Alberta Indians wanted, many parents did not consistently send their children when such schools were available, even when the Indians themselves had constructed them. Undoubtedly some teachers were mediocre and underqualified, but even the best were frequently discouraged by their pupils' poor and irregular attendance.[42] It is difficult to detect any correlation between the quality of teaching and regularity of attendance at day schools. Indian cultures took some time to adapt to fixed buildings, a somewhat alien curriculum, strict methods of instruction, and the expectation of regular attendance. Moreover the benefits of an education modelled on the white system were not always immediately apparent.

Children simply may not have wanted to attend school, and Indian culture inclined parents not to force the issue.[43] Moreover, while Indians asked for schools when negotiating treaties, formal education was not a child-rearing priority compared, say, to learning to hunt, fish, gather, and prepare traditional food. White farm children were also often kept from school for priorities such as seedtime and harvest, or for childcare.[44] Eventually, the government introduced compulsory attendance laws; regrettably, they were more strict for Indian than for white children. But such laws meant that authorities concluded that getting most children to attend school regularly would require a stick as well as a carrot.

It is interesting, therefore, that boarding schools on or near reserves, despite their manifold problems, appealed to many Indians: children in these schools were fairly accessible to parents; they were fed, clothed, and housed in addition to being taught; and often lived in better conditions than they would have on reserves. Least popular by far were industrial schools, intentionally located some distance from reserves; these were expensive for the government to support, had the highest aspirations for the pupils, and yet perhaps were the greatest failures. Despite their later reputation, it must be remembered that many Indian parents, at least in the period under review, chose not to send their children to industrial schools, while others did.[45]

## THE SCHOOL SYSTEM AT THE END OF THE 1880s

After a decade of effort, DIA officials were confirmed in their belief that day schools could not produce rapid change. Indian children needed to learn "the mechanical arts," agriculture, and "domestic economy," wrote Dewdney in 1889, all of which were best learned in boarding or industrial schools.[46] Indeed, by 1888, DIA opinion had shifted against the day-school model.[47] One study claims these schools were characterized by "generally inadequate schoolhouses, educators and curricula" and that Indians' reactions to them were "apathy or hostility." Although the DIA tried to improve the facilities and inspection, there was no upgrading of teacher qualifications, no training program to prepare teachers for the special challenges of Indian schools, and no salary increases. Indeed, Prime Minister Sir John A. Macdonald declared in 1889, "very high educational requirements are not required for an Indian teacher. If he speaks English and Indian, and teaches the children to read and write the cipher, that is about all there is required. You cannot get men of high attainment to go into these schools at all, and $300 has been sufficient to obtain the description of teacher required for these Indian schools."[48]

At the end of the 1880s, many day schools were nevertheless still in operation. In the Saddle Lake agency there were four such schools, three Protestant and one Roman Catholic, with a second Catholic school scheduled to open in 1891 on the Blue Quill reserve. The Protestant school inspector observed that the agency contained about 140 children of school age, "but as they are on seven different reserves, four of which average only forty-two souls each, it is difficult to extend educational privileges to all." If his estimate is near correct, about fifty or sixty children in the agency were not even registered in school, though among those registered attendance was fairly good compared to other agencies. No schools existed for the Wahsatanow, Beaver Lake, or Chipewyan bands, all of which were small and maintained a semi-nomadic lifestyle.

As for the Lac la Biche band, its seventeen members resided in the town of that name; twelve were Metis who wanted to be discharged from the treaty. They had no reserve and received no government assistance beyond annuities.[49]

When inspector Albert Bétournay visited the boarding school at Lac la Biche in November 1891, he found nine Indian children (four boys and five girls), as well as fifteen white and Metis children (for whom the government normally took no financial responsibility). Some Indian children likely came from bands other than that at Lac la Biche, such as Beaver Lake. The school received the full $300 per annum for twenty-five treaty Indian students (twelve dollars per pupil), although it had nowhere near that number. Sometimes the DIA referred to it as an industrial school, which by normal standards it was not; furthermore, the industrial school formula provided for a grant of sixty dollars per pupil, by which standard it was underfunded. Whatever the financial case, the inspector cheerfully suggested that living and learning in proximity to white and Metis children helped Indian children more rapidly master English and other schoolwork.[50]

The Edmonton agency had both a Presbyterian and a Roman Catholic day school on the Enoch (Stony Plain) reserve, and one Roman Catholic school on the Alexander reserve. When the inspector arrived at the Alexander school on 14 November 1890, he found present only three pupils out of seventeen, as most were hunting and fishing with their parents. The band asked for a boarding school, the attraction of which was that children could remain housed, fed, clothed, and educated in their parents' absence. At Stony Plain, the Protestant school had burnt down in 1888, but the church had undertaken to rebuild and also to construct a building to house school boarders. At the Catholic Stony Plain school, which met in the Roman Catholic church, the inspector found that of thirty-eight school-aged Catholic children on the reserve, only twenty-five were enrolled, and only eleven were present when he appeared. Neither the Alexis nor the Michel Calahoo bands had schools on their reserves, so children were sent to nearby boarding schools.[51]

Also in the Edmonton agency was what the inspector referred to as the St Albert industrial school and orphanage.[52] It was bilingual in French and English, and the inspector was impressed with what he found:

Both the French and English languages are taught, and amongst various subjects taught I may mention reading in the fifth reader, and all the elements of grammar in both languages, free translation at sight from English into French and French into English, History of Canada in French and History of England in English, geography, arithmetic, composition, correspondence, elements of physiology, &c. The pupils are graded as follows: seven in first standard, fifteen in second standard, six in third standard, twelve in fourth standard, seven in fifth standard.

Moreover, the pupils learned to make their own clothing by hand, to say nothing of the usual household and farming chores. The inspector claimed the dormitories and other facilities were spacious and well ventilated, the children had a large playground, and only one pupil had died in a recent influenza epidemic (a disease often catastrophic among Indians). The DIA paid for fifty of the sixty pupils; ten older girls "have not been disposed of yet and in the meantime help the reverend Sisters a great deal." After age twelve, boys were not kept at the school, but were "transferred to the Roman Catholic Mission and employed on the farm." All in all, despite a smaller subvention from the government than the larger industrial schools received, the St Albert school "compare[d] very favourably with them."[53]

Reports in 1890 about the Peace Hills schools were not encouraging. In the summer, adults hunted and their children accompanied them. In the winter, attendance improved at the day schools on the Samson and Ermineskin reserves, with some parental encouragement, but the Louis Bull band lived at Pigeon Lake that winter, and on the Sharphead reserve the school did not even open.[54] The agent claimed that despite seeing some progress among children while in school, "outside of the schoolroom they do not seem to know any more than those that have never attended, with the exception of the girls who have been taught sewing and knitting, in which they are becoming very proficient and useful."[55] The Protestant inspector, J. Ansdell MacRae, reported nothing significant about the schools. The Catholic inspector arrived in November 1890 to find the only Catholic school, the Ermineskin, temporarily closed. Still, he noted, "this school has never been at any time very successful on account of the apathy of the Indians."[56]

At the Treaty 6 schools in 1889–90, average total attendance was 171 out of 317 on the rolls, or about 54 per cent – about 44.5 per cent if excluding the industrial/boarding schools at St Albert and Lac la Biche with close to compulsory attendance. This rate is a little lower than the national average attendance, but not dramatically so.[57] School administrators and inspectors also complained that many Indian children were not even registered, but without more information it is difficult to assess why.

Among the Treaty 7 schools at the end of the 1880s, the intended showpiece was the Roman Catholic industrial school near High River, known as St Joseph's Industrial School or as Dunbow. Authorized by the government in 1883 and opened in October 1884 under the leadership of Lacombe and the Oblates, it was one of three original true industrial schools in the North-West Territories, the others being further east, at Qu'Appelle (Roman Catholic) and Battleford (Anglican).[58] Located fairly centrally in the Treaty 7 area, St Joseph's was expected to attract children from the Siksika, Kainai, Piikani, and Tsuu T'ina reserves. Macdonald stated at the outset that the High River location was intentional, "as it is sufficiently far from any Reserve to prevent the Indian parents from resorting too frequently to the school, which would tend to interrupt the children in their studies."[59]

The children were to receive a considerable level of education, both academic and practical. Brian Titley notes that industrial schools were intended to initiate pupils "into the social and occupational patterns of white life. Punctuality and obedience – so vital for effective functioning in the capitalist economic system – were instilled in a relentless program of behaviour modification." A form of military discipline and uniforms was strictly imposed,[60] perhaps unsurprising in a society that regarded military training as a way to turn recalcitrant youth into responsible adults. Macdonald stated that this institution's purpose was "the education in the ordinary branches of learning and the instruction in industrial pursuits as well as the moral and social elevation of the Indian children who may be privileged to attend it." Educated in English, taught white customs, trained in agriculture or skilled trades (for boys), or domestic arts such as cooking and sewing and maintaining a household (for girls), graduates were expected to be able to make their way in white society, or to have homesteads to enable them to farm and establish families on their own plots of land like settlers, setting a transformative example to other Indians.[61] They would move from dependency to independence, from being wards of the state to fully enfranchised citizens.

The reality was disillusioning. The government devised its plan without consulting the Indians, and unsurprisingly not many Indians were willing to turn their children over to the government, on a more or less permanent basis for several years, to have them alienated from their people. In fact, when he presented his 1883 annual report to Parliament, Macdonald noted Indians were reluctant "to have their children separated from them, but doubtless, time will overcome this obstacle, and by commencing with orphans and children who have no natural protector, a beginning can be made, and we must count upon the judicious treatment of these children by the principals and teachers of these institutions eventually to do away with the objections of the Indian parents to their children being placed under their charge."[62]

Both government and school wanted to get the children when they were young and malleable; most of the few children the school secured in the early years were older, less pliable, and more fractious. In his first annual report, written in July 1885, Lacombe reported it was "a most difficult task" to recruit suitable pupils, as "we have to deal and contend, not only with the parents and guardians, but, I may say, with the whole reserve." At first they were able to recruit only a few orphans, and boys who were fifteen to eighteen years old; the latter came, Lacombe suspected, only because it was "a very comfortable way of getting through the winter months."[63] Lacombe's frustration, and astonishing lack of empathy for the Indians, probably led to his being replaced as school principal.

However, his attitude that the Indians were unable to make wise decisions about their children and needed to be coerced was common among church and school officials. Dewdney offered that the DIA should "obtain entire possession of all Indian children after they attain to the age of seven or eight years, and keep them at schools of the industrial type until they have had a thorough course of instruction, not only in the ordinary subjects taught at public schools, but in some useful and profitable trade, or in agriculture, as the aptitude of the pupil might indicate he was best fitted for." Such a policy would hasten the end of "the Indian question." Failing that, he believed that formal education of Indian children ought to be compulsory. For the time being, however, the government did not force parents to surrender their children to the schools.[64]

At the launch of the industrial schools in 1884, Dewdney, then Indian commissioner, noted that the start-up costs would be high, "but I can see no reason why after that time they cannot be self-supporting, or nearly so, in everything except the salaries of the principals and assistants, by the profits to result from the farming, stock-raising, and trades taught."[65] Although Macdonald did not much use this rationale, it represents the views of one highly placed official who was anxious to reassure critics troubled by the cost of the project. However, the relative expense of industrial schools always remained very high.

For the year ending 30 June 1890, Principal E. Claude, OMI, reported that thirty-six boys and sixteen girls attended St Joseph's Industrial

School. Of the children, nineteen were Nizitapi and thirty-three Cree.[66] With respect to health matters, a doctor visited the school thirteen times, conducted seventy-two consultations, inspected new pupils, wrote forty-five prescriptions, and diagnosed about ten cases of tubercular illness (scrofula, consumption, and tuberculosis), and a scattering of cases of influenza (two), sore throat (three), bruises (six), caries of the knee joint (one), deafness (three), bronchitis (three), frostbite (one), and another forty cases described as "slight complaints." One child died during the year from consumption; this death reflected the high rate of the disease in the Indian community at the time.[67] An 1892 report noted that between 1884 and 1892, St Joseph's admitted 156 pupils. By 1892, ten of these were dead – a number that, while tragic, would have likely been at least as large had the children remained on the reserves, where overall mortality rates during the same period were much higher. Regular attendance of pupils by a doctor was in accordance with best practices of public health in the late 1880s.[68]

With respect to academic learning, the children were fairly evenly distributed across the five approved levels or standards, which was rare among Alberta schools. Of the older boys, six received instruction as farmers, six as carpenters, and six as shoemakers; other children engaged in "ordinary fatigue" or duties. On the farm, despite a general drought that year, the school harvested twenty-five bushels of oats, fifteen of wheat, 500 of potatoes, 2,000 of other vegetables, and four tons of hay. It also possessed three horses, one bull, ten cows, thirteen calves, two oxen, one ram, thirty-two sheep, and thirteen lambs. The agricultural statistics show an emphasis on feeding the school as well as training the children. The work done in the shoemaker's shop was estimated at over $1,000, including making moccasins, boots and laces, and ox harnesses, as well as mending boots and harnesses. The carpenter shop generated almost $2,300, including construction projects, furniture, renovations, repairs, and painting projects. Indian Commissioner Hayter Reed noted that the shop's work went beyond the school itself, as the carpenter and boys worked on the Siksika reserve "most creditably," and some boys were sent unsupervised to aid in construction on the Stoney reserve at Morley. The girls produced almost $200 worth of clothing and other sewn and knitted goods, as well as mending clothing.[69] The coal burned by the school was purchased from the Siksika reserve.[70]

The farming and other statistics reveal something of how St Joseph's, to remain viable, depended on the labour of its children. To secure full government funding by maintaining an enrolment of fifty children who met the criteria demanded active recruiting. But the resulting $3,000 grant did not meet the full costs of room and board for the children, teachers, and support staff. It might be argued that "free" schooling, room, and board were not so free if the value of child labour is taken into account. However, the model in the minds of the government and administrators was that of the farm family, in which children contributed as age, strength, and gender roles allowed. When a white farm child went to school, the expected labour at home did not disappear: there still were chores before and after school, and sometimes school work had to be set aside altogether for seed time and harvest. Children learned, and were socialized into, their agrarian lifestyle and gender roles in the home and on the farm. Boarding schools acted in loco parentis, and so were not seen as exploitative. They had purposes in addition to academic learning.

Other schools in the Treaty 7 area were on or near reserves. Attendance was poor, as was the quality of reporting. Some trends nevertheless emerge. On the Siksika reserve, the agent reported that neither the Church of England schools nor the Catholic school were well attended, despite a few individuals like Running Rabbit, a minor chief, sending their children to the latter school. A Miss Brown, according to the agent, had opened a school for girls, but also met with poor attendance.[71] One of the continuing difficulties affecting attendance was that the Indians moved to another part of the reserve during the summer "for change of feed for their horses."[72] When the Catholic inspector visited the reserve, he learned that of ninety children who could attend the school, only ten did so, and his examination of them "was not very satisfactory." The teacher was able and well-intentioned, but low and irregular attendance vitiated his efforts.[73]

The inspector found a similar situation on the Piikani reserve: "The Indian parents do not care to send the children to [the day] school, and the children do not care to attend." In July and August of 1888, to try to adapt the school to Indian needs, the Catholic fathers in charge of it went to where the Indians were camped for a sun dance, erected a tent, and held a daily school there. Of course such solutions could not be long-term. Some Piikani children had been sent to St Joseph's industrial school rather than the local day school, but the parents of three of these boys soon missed them and brought them home.[74] Neither the day school nor the industrial school seems to have been attractive to the Piikani.

On the Kainai reserve, there was a bit more cause for optimism. The agent, William Pocklington, wrote that the Episcopal school at Red

Crow's village had the best attendance, and that "the children are active and are getting on fairly well." The Catholic school at Running Wolf's village was also well attended with "noticeable" progress, benefitting from the fact that "the Rev Père Legal is a most painstaking teacher, and his knowledge of the [Blackfoot] language is of great assistance to him in making explanations." He was pleased to observe that both these schools opened and closed with prayer. Pocklington found that the Methodist school was located farther from those it was intended to serve, and because they still were inclined to move about, attendance was irregular. The Church of England recently had opened a second school, at Bull's Horn's village, with a teacher appointed directly from England. He noted "the children attending these schools are provided with a luncheon on school days, of soup, alternated with boiled rice and biscuits." In their homes, the wives of Episcopal teachers and missionaries also taught knitting and sewing to girls with materials supplied by the DIA.[75]

Mike Mountain Horse, who attended school on the Kainai reserve in this period, recalled the difficulty for the missionaries of interesting "indifferent and even rebellious young natives in their studies." He continued, "All of us children attending these day schools would show up with painted faces, wearing breech cloths and blankets, and teacher would give us one biscuit of hardtack to insure our attendance for the next day ... We passed our time in drawing pictures on our slates, anything that suited our fancy to portray. Some drew a man in war paint dancing; others drew a warrior on horseback chasing buffalo." The children were mischievous and proficient at annoying the teachers. Sometimes when they got their biscuit they tried to run away, so the teacher had to chase after "the obstinate one and pull him into the schoolhouse." Such, he noted, "were the problems our teachers had to contend with in their work among us in early days." The behaviour fitted in with the tribal culture. Mountain Horse remembered that his childhood was typical: "We spent time playing, running and jumping. We ran about as wild and free as the birds, the young ones naked, and all of us scantily clad. Only when winter came did we don heavier clothing."[76]

F.A. Cornish, a Tsuu T'ina Indian agent whose duties also included the Stoney reserve, reported in 1889–90 that the Indians had erected a new day school of log walls on the Tsuu T'ina reserve, but the problem of low and irregular attendance at day schools persisted on both reserves. Progress was claimed for the few who attended regularly, and the teachers actively promoted the schools. Attendance at the McDougall

Orphanage and Boarding School on the Stoney reserve was better, and children learned to farm and raise stock.[77]

By the end of the 1880s, there was only modest progress in education in the Treaty 7 area. The chiefs may have supported the idea of schools at the treaty talks in 1877, but later their people evinced little interest. As with Treaty 6 schools, even teachers who spoke the relevant language and had at least a modicum of familiarity with the culture seemed to make little difference. Many Stoneys moved freely off the reserve, and many Nizitapi moved around within their larger ones, so the settled life-style and regular habits upon which the white approach to education depended were still not fully established among the Treaty 7 peoples. It remains to be seen how the situation changed after another decade and a half of effort.

## THE SCHOOL SYSTEM BY 1904–05

By the end of the 1904–05 school year only six Indian day schools remained in the district of Alberta.[78] They never had been the principal focus of the government's Indian education endeavor because they were deemed ineffective. Over the years some had closed, while others had become or been replaced with boarding schools on or beside the reserves. Those that remained were struggling and, to judge by their high absenteeism and low academic achievement, generally pretty unsuccessful.

Take the case of the Methodist school on the Paul reserve at White Whale Lake. It began in 1893 and was meant to teach carpentry, gardening, and domestic skills in addition to academic subjects. But in 1897 its well-liked missionary teacher was appointed principal of the Red Deer Industrial School, and the day school's attendance suffered as a number of parents moved their children to follow. When inspector J.A. Markle visited the Paul band school in 1904, no children showed up. Of twenty-five school-age children on the reserve, twenty-two were enrolled, but average attendance was reported as "three and one-half." Markle found the school building in poor repair, but the teacher and missionary willing enough to complete them if the necessary materials were provided. In a study of the school, Ruby Bird attributes the low interest to the distance of many pupils' homes from the school and lack of transportation; the lack of warm clothing in winter; the ongoing traditional lifestyle, which frequently took children out of school; and the lack of incentive to settle down to the routines of agriculture and formal education.[79]

In September 1904, Markle visited the Louis Bull school at Hobbema, where he found three boys and four girls present, all struggling with Level 1 work; it had an average daily attendance of three. He also went to the Samson school, where the average attendance in the previous year was slightly over four, though thirty potential Indian pupils lived fairly close and twenty-eight of those were registered. Twelve non-Indian children, belonging to the agent, clerk, interpreter, and resident missionary, also attended. The teacher told the inspector that these other children had a positive effect on learning for Indian children, but the low Indian attendance suggests otherwise. At the Saddle Lake agency, attendance was poor at the Whitefish Lake and Goodfish Lake schools, and the former lost its teacher during the year.[80] In general, despite the earnest efforts of qualified teachers, morale was poor.

Experience with day schools continued to demonstrate that neither Indians nor the government really wanted them. At one level, Indian coolness to the schools can be understood in practical terms. Mere location of a school on a reserve did not mean it was accessible to pupils, who might live up to several miles away and who usually had to walk if they did not have access to a horse. Many Indian families were too poor to clothe the children warmly in cold weather; even adequate footwear could be a problem. Malnutrition and disease undermined attendance. There also were other disincentives. Teachers, though usually formally qualified by the end of the period according to white standards, also usually were unfamiliar with the language and culture of the children, and found the intercultural challenges difficult and isolating. Many only lasted a year or two; those who lasted five or six were relatively unusual, unless they were combining the roles of teacher and missionary.

At another level, the nature and goals of the schools were fundamentally alienating to Indian culture. The mission schools prior to the treaties were different in many respects from what followed after 1880. Most earlier schools taught children to read and write in their own tongue first; the goal had been to enable them to read scripture and sing hymns in their own language, though many went beyond that. Teaching English or French remained important, but learning literacy first in their own tongue, or alongside the second language, was culturally more sensitive. By most accounts, the early schools accommodated the cycles and customs of Indian life, not only as to when they were operating but with respect to matters like flexible start times and irregular attendance. The later schools were not what many Indians of the 1870s had expected when they signed the treaties. They were more aggressively transformative in purpose, and alien in language, discipline, and curriculum. For education to work in any society, there needs to be a consensus on its necessity, purposes, and methods, but these were different in Indian and white societies. This was another case of mutual misunderstanding at the time of the treaties: the idea of schools meant something different to each party.

Launched in 1883–84 with fanfare and high hopes, industrial schools proved expensive to run and often dismal in outcomes. They had become a highly visible target for the opposition and other critics of governmental expenditure. Allegedly they aimed too high, benefitted too few, and harmed too many. This attitude was reinforced when the Liberals, who for years had questioned the spending on the schools, assumed power in 1896. The new deputy superintendent general, James A. Smart, warned in 1897 of the problem of over-educating Indians: "To educate children above the possibilities of their station, and create a distaste for what is certain to be their environment in life would be not only a waste of money but doing them an injury instead of conferring a benefit upon them."[81] Of course many Indians believed that the schools were doing their children "an injury," and definitely were not "conferring a benefit," but for very different reasons.

There were three industrial schools in 1904–05 in Alberta, at Calgary, Red Deer, and High River. Of these, the newest and (in Milloy's opinion) least successful was St Dunstan's at Calgary, which opened in December 1896 but closed in 1907 after several years of declining enrolment.[82] The school was originally intended to be Anglican, and retained that church's flavour: an Anglican clergyman was principal, it had religious exercises including opening and closing with prayer, and Roman Catholics would have regarded it as a Protestant school unsuitable for Catholic pupils. However, the Anglicans found they could not afford to run the school with the limited government subsidies, so the school became government-run, officially non-denominational, and the name was dropped in government reports. It became known simply as the Calgary industrial school, and was the last industrial school created in Canada.

The Calgary industrial school was located about 4.5 miles below Calgary along the Bow River, on land that proved inferior for agriculture, had poor drainage, and was subject to flooding. The government paid for the building, but it was constructed as cheaply as possible, with unhappy consequences. Having the bathroom and laundry in the basement, for example, not only was inconvenient, but also permitted "steam

and heat and moisture [to] ascend throughout the whole house." Because
no girls were admitted, the boys did the scrubbing, laundry, washing and
ironing, baking, and meal preparation assistance. "Each takes his turn,"
wrote Principal George Hogbin, "so that all are learning how to do these
things, and if when they leave here they do not do those things themselves they will at least be able to tell their wives how to do them." The
boys also were expected to do all the carpentry repairs on the facilities,
and to raise crops – turnips, potatoes, carrots, beets, parsnips, and other
garden produce – along with milking and feeding livestock. Undoubtedly
classroom work received something less than normal attention.[83]

Nevertheless, Mountain Horse, who was one of the Calgary Industrial
School's 1905 graduates, had very positive memories, recalling the
school as a "great educational centre [that] taught its pupils carpentry,
farming, printing and the bakery trade. These proved very useful to
many of the students who graduated." He had particularly enjoyed
sports at the school, and was captain of the soccer team.[84] Another of its
former pupils, Ben Calf Robe, commented that despite the school's defi-
ciencies it was better than the conditions on the reserves. Hugh Dempsey
also has a generally positive view of the school and its involvement of
the pupils in the Calgary community.[85]

The school drew most of its students from Protestant Siksika, Kainai,
Piikani, and Tsuu T'ina boarding schools, and the inspectors generally
found that they made good progress in examinations. However, the story
of the school ultimately is rather sad. Recruiting and retaining students
was increasingly difficult; the inspector noted that when he visited in
summer 1904, twenty-seven pupils were registered, but by the time of
his report a year later, thirteen had been discharged. As with other industrial schools, Indian parents mostly resisted sending their children there.
Moreover, while it had expected to draw from Protestant pupils on the
Siksika reserve, the Anglican boarding school was reluctant to act as a
feeder, as every student sent to Calgary meant loss of the per capita government grant.

The main building, despite its fine-looking sandstone exterior, was difficult to heat, and the atmosphere seemed to breed an unusual incidence
of disease. In the decade since 1896, commented Markle, ninety-four
boys had enrolled, but fourteen had since died[86] (whether of disease
contracted at the school is unknown). Four of these deaths were among
the sixteen pupils who graduated in carpentry. By 1905 the school no
longer had a carpentry instructor, so it no longer taught industrial skills
apart from farm work. In fact, it had become little different from many

boarding schools, except that it was far from the reserves and was, per capita, more expensive to operate.[87]

How much of a failure was the Calgary school? In the most detailed available study, Joan Scott-Brown acknowledges many serious problems, but also notes that quite a few later leaders of Indian communities had attended the school. Perhaps the most prominent was James Gladstone, who became a successful rancher, was for years president of the Indian Association of Alberta, and was the first Indian senator. Scott-Brown also holds that the school enabled the children to function in English, and to cope better with white society than they might have otherwise.[88]

The Red Deer Industrial School opened in 1893, was larger, and was not closed until 1919. Its difficulties stemmed first from underfunding. Amid high hopes, the government had funded industrial schools fairly generously during the decade after 1883, at least in retrospect. But the Red Deer school was established just when the departmental discouragement with industrial schools, along with a renewed economic depression, was leading to austerity: per capita grants were limited, and payments for other purposes were reduced. For their part, the Canadian Methodists were stretched too thin, having assumed a heavy burden for missions in Asia and among prairie immigrants, meaning that their Indian schools were a smaller priority.[89]

However, the school's problems also arose from poor management. Its first principal, Dr John Nelson, was a brutal disciplinarian; after an investigation into complaints, he was fired in 1895. His successor, Rev C.E. Somerset, a former Methodist missionary, was gentler and expanded the facilities, but could not maintain discipline to the point that some staff and students felt themselves under siege by certain unruly older pupils; he was let go in 1903. His replacement, Rev J.P. Rice from Toronto, another rigid disciplinarian, tried to effect necessary reforms and upgrades, but he soon ran the school into serious debt and was let go in 1907. Unsurprisingly, the school experienced high rates of desertion by pupils. Facilities were sub-standard and poorly maintained. The department repeatedly refused requests for funds to construct a separate infirmary for ill students, and high rates of illness and mortality resulted. Thus, during much of its first decade the Red Deer school was by no means a safe place for pupils or staff. All these things made recruiting pupils and teachers difficult. After a teacher seriously injured a student in 1895, Reed issued a general directive forbidding anyone save the principal of an institution from imposing corporal punishment, adding, "corporal punishment is considered unnecessary as a general measure of discipline and should only be resorted to for very grave offenses and as a deterrent example."[90]

Concerning the poor health conditions, one study in 1993 claimed that, of sixty-two pupils admitted between 1893 and 1895, one-third either died at the school or within a decade of leaving it. A report in 1900 for Superintendent General Clifford Sifton claimed, "of the 66 students discharged [to that time], 26 were doing well, 5 had turned out badly, 12 were dead, one had been transferred to another school, 4 were in ill health, and 18 were lost sight of." When Rice arrived in 1903, "the sight of the ragged ill-kempt and sickly looking children was sufficient to make me sick at heart." Milloy notes, "enrollment was down due to deaths, the removal of children by their parents, and because [according to Rice] the 'sanitary conditions of the buildings are exceedingly bad.'"[91]

Located just west of Red Deer on the Red Deer River, the school was about forty miles from the nearest Indian reserve, at Hobbema. It owned about three-quarters of a section of high-quality land, and had grazing rights on over 1,000 additional acres. In 1905, its capacity was ninety pupils; it had eighty-nine at the start of the 1904–05 school year, and eighty-one by the end. Still, this suggests some recovery from the situation reported by Milloy. Students spent either the morning or the afternoon in the classroom, and the rest of the day at other duties. The boys mostly kept busy with farm work, though five were learning carpentry. The girls all learned "housework, dairying and sewing, and some attention is given to fancy-work." A number of pupils were trained in vocal and instrumental music, and put on a "musical and literary entertainment" for the people of Red Deer during Christmas week. Despite a smallpox scare in the fall, efforts to improve health conditions paid off, and by the end of the year Rice reported that students' health was better than ever and the school's drug bill was less than half that of the preceding year.[92] Academically, Markle had no criticism to offer of student achievement, except for the relatively trivial matter that they were timid in replying to questions and needed to speak up more.[93]

In her study of the Red Deer Industrial School, Uta Fox is more sympathetic to the administrators and finds more positive features than other historians. Underfunding forced administrators to over-expand the agricultural activity, and to require more work from pupils, to try to make ends meet, even if in so doing they actually ran up the deficit. She acknowledges the difficulty in some years of recruiting pupils, attributing it to the distance from home, overworking of pupils, the reputation for corporal punishment and poor health conditions, and a failure to consider parental input. Between 1893 and 1895, twelve out of fifty-two students originally enrolled had deserted the school. Yet she also notes that when the Louis Bull day school closed, parents sent their children to Red Deer. She finds, moreover, that the school was supported by the Methodists of Saddle Lake. Apparently when Nelson took some pupils to Saddle Lake and parents saw their dress, comportment, and English ability, a number reversed their intention to withdraw their children, and eight new pupils were enrolled. Looking over the history of the school, she concludes that, despite its shortcomings, many students emerged with life skills in agriculture, domesticity, and literacy; some furthered their education at Alberta College; and several later became prominent leaders of Alberta Indians. While for many pupils the experience was a failure, and possibly traumatic, for some it had decided benefits.[94]

Titley also finds that the Red Deer Industrial School failed to prepare students for integration into white society, and for living in specially designated farming colonies for graduates of industrial schools. Most pupils simply returned to reserve life. But Titley, like Fox, also concludes that many probably benefitted from their experience:

> For the 185 students who passed through the school between 1893 and 1903, the average stay was 4.78 years and the average standard achieved on leaving was 3.38. The latter figure represented roughly six years of elementary schooling. It should be borne in mind that many students had already received some education before entering Red Deer. When all factors are considered, this level of education compares favorably with what the average non-Indian rural prairie child was receiving at the time … Undoubtedly, many graduates acquired a good basic education as well as some industrial and domestic skills. Whether, however, this was adequate compensation for the negative self-image and cultural loss that accompanied this process, it is difficult to say. One can only surmise that individual responses to the experience varied greatly.[95]

The third industrial school in Alberta in 1905, St Joseph's Industrial School at High River, was not only the oldest but also generally the best run. Its declared capacity was 125 students, but it seldom reached three-quarters of that figure.[96] It was the only Catholic industrial school in Alberta, so it recruited students from among Treaty 6 and 7 Catholic day and boarding schools. Younger children had class all day, but older children spent half days in class and then engaged in farm work and other tasks. Markle acknowledged that this hampered academic learning, but then noted that in the opinion of "those who have had opportunities to study the Indian question ... the youths of the present Indian generation are likely to be better citizens if they can be taught how to work and imbued with a willingness to do it, in preference to gaining their livelihood by leaning on others, than to start out on life's journey with a literary education."[97] He did think the teaching was good and that the students were making satisfactory progress.

By this time, the DIA expected all schools to report on how they provided recreational opportunities and healthful physical activities. St Joseph's principal, Rev Father A. Naessens, provides a typical example: "Every day two and a half hours are set aside for recreation, and one-half day each week is devoted to healthful open-air games. The boys play baseball and football. Their favourite winter sport is hockey. The girls amuse themselves during play-time at croquet, basket-ball and other exercises."[98] By 1905, St Joseph's had become a sizeable complex. Girls and boys were housed and instructed in separate buildings. Beyond dormitories and instructional areas, the facilities included a chapel and areas for food preparation and consumption, a workshop, a lumber shed, a bakery, stables, a granary, a piggery, numerous other outbuildings, and extensive fencing. Constructing and maintaining or replacing these structures was a substantial and costly task.

With respect to farming, Naessens had reason for pride. The school had numerous horses, cattle, pigs, and poultry, and won first prize for stall-fed cattle at the Calgary stock show. The pupils and farm instructors also produced a significant crop of oats, as well as some barley, wheat, potatoes, turnips and mangolds, and hay. Sales of produce and livestock raised $2,663 for the school.[99]

Early in its history, St Joseph's Industrial School had its share of difficulties: it was hard to recruit students from among the Nizitapi and Tsuu T'ina, and many ran away, were taken by their parents, or deserted at the time of the Riel uprising in 1885. Health issues plagued it, like all boarding schools. Finding an appropriate approach to discipline, and a case of sexual abuse, all tainted its reputation. Yet, it persevered and improved, so that in a comprehensive, sometimes scathing report on Indian schools in 1908, it was one of the few to be commended, as "splendidly conducted ... neat and clean."[100]

Available information does not always provide a full breakdown of where pupils in various schools came from, though there are a few clues.

In 1894, for example, the superintendent general, T. Mayne Daly, told the House of Commons that at the Elkhorn, Manitoba, industrial school, "we have Blackfeet, Piegans [sic] and Bloods, removed about eight hundred miles from the influence of their parents and their early surroundings." Daly did not indicate numbers, nor did he say whether Alberta children also attended other distant schools, such as that at Qu'Appelle in Assiniboia.[101] Still, his statement suggests that enrolment figures for the Alberta schools may not convey the full picture of educational involvement of Alberta Indian children.

Criticisms of industrial schools are noted below. Suffice it to say here that at least some critics found a sympathetic ear in the Laurier government after 1896, and that limiting expenditure on industrial schools while focusing on boarding schools on the reserves became a major policy goal.[102] The latter institutions were a sort of compromise between the failed day schools and the costly, problem-ridden, and failure-prone industrial schools. Boarding schools had mostly acceptable enrolments and regular attendance, and were significantly cheaper than industrial schools. They were located on or near to reserves, which made it easier for Indian families to visit their children. Children were clustered in the lower grade levels, but that was not uncommon in rural white schools (though arguably boarding school conditions should have produced better academic results).

Turning, then, to boarding schools, the Roman Catholic Blue Quill school was by 1905 the only such institution in the Saddle Lake agency, having absorbed the Lac la Biche school. It produced sufficient potatoes and other vegetables to meet its needs from about six acres of cultivated land. Boys were taught to supply fuel, bake their own bread, and care for farm animals, "without neglecting ... to keep their own rooms in order." Girls were "trained in habits of neatness and industry in the kitchen and laundry, also in sewing and general housework." Léon Balter, the principal, stated, "the program of studies provided by the department is faithfully followed," and he assured officials the school also worked hard "to instil into the minds of the pupils their duty towards God and man."[103] Almost all students came from the Blue Quill and James Seenum bands, and totalled in the mid- to high thirties. The inspector, W.J. Chisholm, found that discipline was maintained by a system of medals, buttons, or ribbons for merit "in application to duty, for obedience, politeness and piety, as well as for proficiency in certain subjects, such as arithmetic and writing."[104] Overall, he considered the academic performance very good to excellent. He reported the girls were trained "with the greatest care" in household duties. He noted agricultural pursuits were only modestly successful "and contribute but little toward the revenue of the school." This perhaps was not surprising, as Balter had no one in charge of agriculture among the sizeable staff.[105] The school, unsurprisingly, ran a deficit: total expenses for the year came to just over $3,700, of which government grants equalled about 57 per cent.[106] From the government perspective, the important fact was that, based on thirty-six pupils, the cost per student for room, board, clothing, and education was $103.36, substantially below the per-student costs of industrial schools.[107]

The report from the Ermineskin school at Hobbema was much the same. Markle reported that the pupils were "clean, well dressed, under the complete control of the teachers and recited their lessons very correctly and in audible tones. An examination of this kind would satisfy any one." He found no cases of illness, and the pupils had been in satisfactory health for some time.[108] Markle also noted that twenty-eight pupils were from the Hobbema agency, twenty-one were from the Edmonton agency, and one was listed as non-treaty.[109] That a majority of the students came from the Hobbema agency makes sense, but there is no clear explanation as to why so many would come from the Edmonton agency when the St Albert school was closer and both were Roman Catholic. The Enoch agent observed that there was active competition for children: the reserve was "diligently canvassed for pupils by the principals of the different boarding and industrial schools," so that "no children of school age are neglected."[110]

The other boarding school in the Treaty 6 region, and by far the largest, was the St Albert school; it also was the only such institution not on or bordering a reserve. Total enrolment in 1905 was 150, so the seventy-one treaty pupils constituted less than half the total. Most remaining pupils were Metis, and not eligible for the government grant. The unusually large school was well staffed. Besides Rev Sister Dandurand, the principal, there were fourteen other Sisters of Charity, a brother in charge of the boys, four brothers in charge of farming, stock, and agricultural instruction, and a full-time bandmaster. The entire student body was required to join the band and choral program, and during the ceremonies in September 1905 to inaugurate the new province of Alberta, the school musicians performed for the prime minister and other dignitaries.[111] The older boys were trained in larger-scale farming operations with the help of several hired men: not only were they expected to partake in farming, gardening, and stock raising, but they were taught to repair implements, harness, and fellow pupils' shoes. Because the school raised sheep, the girls were taught to card, spin, weave, and knit in addition to other usual skills. The school reported very good health, no epidemic diseases, and much attention paid to sanitary conditions and ventilation.[112]

In the Treaty 7 area, there were eight boarding schools located on or near the reserves: two each (Catholic and Anglican) at the Kainai, Piikani, and Siksika reserves, and one each at the Tsuu T'ina (Anglican) and Stoney Nakoda (Methodist) reserves. Almost all had to contend with the inefficiency of having to maintain facilities built to a capacity above actual attendance. The government in 1905 paid seventy-two dollars per pupil to a set maximum enrolment at such schools.[113] Pupils thus were valued in part for the grant money they represented, and schools competed for them. School administrators had no compunction about attracting students from day schools, but in turn resented the industrial schools that often took their best pupils. This could lead to bizarre situations, such as a case at the Tsuu T'ina school where a boy who had contracted scrofula was kept on in hope that his health would improve. It did not, and according to the principal, "he was allowed to go home finally, as we had more than the per capita grant allowed for."[114] It appears as though, had the school needed the money, the student would have been kept at school regardless of his health.

Still, taking the eleven boarding schools in Alberta together, there were 427 pupils registered in 1904–05, with an average daily attendance of over 90 per cent. From the government perspective, these children not only received regular supervised instruction, but also were housed, clothed, fed, and could access better medical services than on reserves. Such schools, with enhanced staffing, could provide a greater variety of informed instruction, both academic and practical, than was possible in single-teacher reserve day schools.

Several aspects of the inspector's reports on the Treaty 7 schools merit note. One was the condition of school buildings. At the St Paul school on the Kainai reserve, for example, Markle found that the boys' dormitory needed replacement, as "the one in use is dark and dismal and unfit for habitation." At the Old Sun's school on the Siksika reserve, the ill-constructed building was subject to drafts and impossible to heat properly during cold weather. The dormitory was erected on poorly drained land, foundation timbers were set in soil rather than on stone, and the building was unsanitary, leading to serious health problems among the pupils. At the McDougall Orphanage, the boys' bathroom was in a state of disrepair and unfit for use, the roof of a dairy/storeroom had collapsed, and other buildings were not properly cleaned or maintained. The reports implied not that any of this was a government responsibility, but that it was a failing of the school administrators and denominations. Markle made the connection between poorly constructed, maintained, and cleaned facilities and bad health; he did not make the connection that at least some of the problem lay with inadequate resources. Instead, he assumed that otherwise adequate resources were inefficiently used.

An often-forgotten problem in connection with the schools' financial difficulties is that, just like farmers in general, they were afflicted by climate, pests, crop diseases, and the like. These problems often appear in the school principals' reports. The result could be devastating for school budgets, planned around a certain return from crops, gardens, and livestock. In 1904, for example, the entire crop at the Tsuu T'ina school was lost to hail, and drought greatly reduced expected crops at St Joseph's. The inspectors commented less frequently on these matters, the department usually seemed little interested, and compensatory resources frequently were not supplied.

Markle's reports suggest that he held a severely practical and limited view of proper education. He listened to pupils read and recite material, and judged them on the accuracy, confidence, and clarity of their pronunciation and of their responses to his questions. He looked at samples of their written work, apparently more interested in neatness than content. He examined the cleanliness of schools and dormitories, and looked at the gardens, fields, animals, sewing, and knitting as evidence of students' progress. He was, however, unimpressed with the remarkable achievement of the senior pupils at the St Paul school in reciting a very long poem, "The Prairies," by American poet William Cullen Bryant:

> I am impressed with the idea that it is repugnant to a majority of the Indian youths to be compelled to commit a long poem to memory. Indian children have a comparatively short school life and to my mind, these short periods should be used to lay a foundation of knowledge that is most likely to be of practical benefit when they return to their reserves, to be either farmers or farmers' wives, and not to burden their minds with long poems that will in no way assist them to provide bread and butter for themselves.

His cold and prosaic response must have been demoralizing for the pupils and their proud teacher, Miss Wells, who was described by her principal, Gervase Gale, as very able, "thorough and painstaking."[115]

The years of high rates of illness on the reserves and in the schools were reflected in the emphasis on sanitation, ventilation, fresh air, regular baths, and outdoor exercise. At the Roman Catholic school on the Kainai reserve, reportedly "recreation is taken three times a day, after each meal. Football, swimming, fishing, shooting with bows and arrows, swinging and skating, are the favourite pastimes of the boys. The girls, too, have different little games, besides swinging, playing ball and skipping. Boys and girls have each their own playground," and were always supervised.[116]

By the end of the territorial period, the government was heavily committed to boarding schools. Sifton told the House of Commons in 1904 that under his administration, "We have substituted [for industrial schools] a less elaborate system; a system of what we call boarding schools where a larger number of children can for a shorter time be educated more economically and generally more effectively. What we desire to do is not to give a highly specialized education to half a dozen out of a large band of Indians, but if possible to distribute over the whole band a moderate amount of education and intelligence, so that the general status of the band would be raised."[117] By 1905, the twenty-four Alberta schools of 1889–90 – the majority day schools – were reduced to twenty-one. Eleven of these were boarding schools, as opposed to three industrial and seven day schools, so there is no doubt as to the change wrought by government policy.

What proportion of Indian children in the Treaties 6 and 7 portions of the district of Alberta were attending school by 1904–05? The answer is neither simple nor straightforward. The annual Indian census showed 885 children between ages six and fifteen. Of these, 759 (almost 86 per cent) were registered in school. Of those registered, over 56 per cent were in boarding schools, over 26 per cent in industrial schools, and just 17 per cent in day schools. According to the census, the majority of Indian children in the district of Alberta had some exposure to formal schooling in 1905.

However, the reality is more complicated. For example, the government paid grants for children in boarding and industrial schools up to age eighteen, and how many of those registered fell into the age group sixteen to eighteen is unclear.[118] The number likely would be fairly small, because Indian children, like most white children, tended to leave school long before age eighteen and often as early as twelve. Moreover, actual day school attendance was less than one third of those registered, though not a consistent third on any given day. How to calculate this in terms of meaningful school attendance is unclear. It seems fair to suggest that boarding and industrial schools, despite their manifold shortcomings, came closest to providing the education the government expected the schools to give. Pupils in these schools totalled roughly 70 per cent of those in the age group eligible to attend, which still represents a huge change for the Indian population in less than thirty years.[119]

EVALUATING EDUCATION POLICY

Canada's educational obligations to Indians stemmed first from the fact that Indians were legally wards of the state, and second from the contractual commitments under the treaties. But expectations on either side with respect to schools never were spelled out in any detail and, as shown above, this left a great deal of latitude for government and Indians to develop widely differing assumptions about what the educational obligations entailed. The assumptions of each side were rooted in previous experience with Indian schools, and government policies developed after the treaties within a particular political and social climate.

*Financial Cost*

There were constant allegations that the cost to the Canadian treasury of Indian schools, particularly in the prairie West, was excessive. The reason is at least partly evident from table 6.1.

If, for the sake of argument, there were 3,000 treaty Indian children of school age in Manitoba and the districts of Alberta, Assiniboia, and Saskatchewan, the per-pupil cost of schooling them would be roughly one hundred dollars for the year in question.[121] The government formula for day schools was twelve dollars per pupil to a maximum of $300 (twenty-five pupils). Had the government committed only to day schools (a common view of what its treaty commitment entailed), and paid only according to this formula, the basic cost to the system would have been $36,000[122] (along with the relatively minor costs of inspectors, very occasional medical attendance, and small periodic contributions toward building or equipment costs). Moreover, this grant of $300 per school would have approached what the North-West Territories government paid to support white rural schools, which likely would have fit with public expectations of reasonable cost.

However, the total cost for Indian schools in Manitoba and the North-West Territories exceeded the combined total expenditures on all items

Table 6.1 Expenditures for Indians in Manitoba and the North-West Territories, 1904–05[120]

| Expense | Cost (percentage of total) |
| --- | --- |
| Major items | |
|   Day, boarding, and industrial schools | $301,823,67 (34.69) |
|   Supplies for destitute and working Indians | $173,118.41 (19.9) |
| General expenses | |
|   Annuities | $144,705.00 (16.63) |
|   Agricultural supplies and livestock | $62,477.48 (7.18) |
| Total expenditure | $869,980.95 |

for Native peoples in British Columbia, central Canada, and maritime Canada. As the government believed that day schools were ineffective, it invested heavily in the more expensive boarding and industrial schools. Boarding schools had average costs in excess of one hundred dollars per pupil, while industrial schools had average costs of $155 to $270 per pupil, which made them the target of critics who charged excessive cost with little appreciable benefit. Yet the government could argue that these schools considerably exceeded the expense anticipated at the time of the treaties in order to accelerate and intensify the educational experience of Indian children. In a sense, the policy front-loaded the expense of educating children to hasten the day when Indians would be self-supporting, enfranchised, and no longer public charges. By contrast, day schools provided not a glimmer of hope that these goals would be achieved. The question of whether the expenditure on boarding and industrial schools was wise and actually benefitted the children was an altogether different matter.

### The Nature, Purpose, and Common Problems of White and Indian Schools

Basic numeracy and literacy remained essential goals of public education throughout 1870 to 1905. Equally important was the goal of producing socialized, responsible, and independent adults. But the nature of the schools also was affected by centralization of administration, standardization of curricula, professionalization of teaching, and imposition of strict discipline and coercion, all within a context of increasing nativist

intolerance of ethnic (or "racial"), linguistic and religious difference that
so transformed public education during this period. Eliminating difference was a major, and widely accepted, objective.

Corporal punishment was often harsh, and was employed in both
white and Indian schools. "Spare the rod and spoil the child" was a commonly cited proverb.[123] Punishment and ridicule for speaking a language
other than English (or, in some cases, French) was a common and distressing experience for Indian and immigrant children. Adults, whether
Indian or immigrant, were not thought to be assimilable; schools were to
extinguish alien cultural traits in children and inculcate the values and
outlook of the dominant culture. All children must be subject to this
process: the provinces and territories adopted truancy laws requiring
children to attend school, even against their parents' wishes.[124]

The federal government soon amended the Indian Act in 1894, providing "regulations ... to secure the compulsory attendance of [Indian]
children at school." It also provided "for the arrest and conveyance to
school, and detention there, of truant children and of children who are
prevented by their parents or guardians from attending." Parents or
guardians who "fail, refuse or neglect to cause such children to attend
school" were subject to fines or imprisonment upon conviction. Justices
of the peace and Indian agents were empowered to commit Indian children under age sixteen to an industrial or boarding school, "there to be
kept, cared for and educated" up to age eighteen.[125] In law, then, schools
were becoming more like prisons, or at least like government reformato-
ries to house and redeem recalcitrant youth. Interestingly, this truancy
provision was not much questioned when the bill was discussed in the
House of Commons; the chief concern raised was whether the section
might necessitate even more schools and thus increase the "enormous
sacrifice of money" already spent on Indian education.[126]

Though it assumed the power, the government never fully implemented the provision, at least in the period to 1905. Indian resistance to
schools remained strong on several reserves. As annual reports of school
officials attest, in some cases referred to above, many Indians could and
did refuse to send their children to any school; they also could and did
retrieve their children from boarding and industrial schools.

Officials believed that boarding schools for Indians derived at least
partly from a superior model of education long used for whites: the elites
of Britain and Canada often sent their children to white boarding
schools which they themselves had in many cases attended. But such
schools were far better funded and staffed than Indian schools, and were

not compulsory. Another model was that of white public institutions, including industrial schools, for orphaned, abandoned, and delinquent children.[127] In the 1880s and 1890s, experts deemed such institutions more likely than available family settings to reform troubled or disadvantaged white children, give them manual training, and instil discipline and the habits of good health. It was, notes Sutherland, a part of the process of bringing order into an industrializing and urbanizing society; new laws were introduced to circumscribe and "improve" behaviour, especially of the lower classes.[128]

Such notions were part of the rationale behind Indian boarding schools. Government officials and missionaries often thought of the Indian population as a lower class in need of improvement and discipline. Schooling was intended "to fit them [Indian pupils] into the lower echelons of the new economic order."[129] Such misguided and racist paternalism might have been rendered more palatable in its day had the schools been better funded, staffed, and equipped. Instead, they have been criticized for not meeting the children's nutritional and other physical needs, and also for being hazardous to Indian health, though white schools everywhere, especially in poorer areas, were also notorious for spreading diseases. It is arguable that boarding schools anywhere often did not, and probably could not, meet the children's emotional and relational needs. Thus, up to a point, the problems of Indian schools were common, considered in context.[130] The boarding school model itself has also been revealed as fundamentally flawed wherever it has been adopted, as has since been seen in other cases across Canada, the United States, and Ireland.[131]

## Problems Specific to Indian Schools

Despite sharing many of the characteristics and failings of white schools of the day, Indian schools also faced some problems that were unique, or nearly so. Comparing Indians' school experience with that of immigrants, for example, only goes so far. The majority of non-English-speaking immigrants came from Europe, which, despite its linguistic, denominational, social, and cultural diversity, was still comprised of a cultural and social nexus that was fundamentally Christian and that mostly accepted the forms of school and discipline found in Canada. Such immigrants had left one cultural region and arrived in another in which their old culture had less legitimacy. Indians, by contrast, were at home, in a place where they believed their culture had legitimacy and in which they found their identity. They did not teach or discipline their children in the European way, and mostly abhorred corporal punishment. Learning was not simply acquired in a formal classroom, but absorbed as life experience from relatives, peers, and honoured elders. Learning to hunt, trap, fish, identify useful plants, and survive on the land in all seasons, or to understand one's place in the cultural context, were learned in family and community. Education was holistic and engaged the spiritual, natural, and verbal realms.[132] The Indian approach to education also suited the needs of a people for whom conditions were expected to continue much as they always had; it mostly did not prepare children for a rapidly changing world in which they would require skill sets different from those of their parents and elders. Indian leaders had recognized the need for some change when they embraced the idea of schools during the treaty negotiations. From an Indian perspective, the government ideally would have prepared children to adapt in a manner that did not alienate them from their heritage; they did not understand at first that such alienation was precisely its objective.

### The Government's Obligation

Did the government fail in its wardship and treaty obligations with respect to education? Viewed from over a century later, the overpowering evidence from the crushed spirits and ruined lives of thousands of survivors of boarding schools, and the evidence of thousands of others who did not survive, is that it did. That evidence cannot be controverted.[133]

The purpose here is not to rehearse that tragic story, but to contextualize the government's policies. The values of the late nineteenth century were far removed from those of the late twentieth or early twenty-first centuries. The government understood its educational treaty obligation to be to enable the Indians to assume a role in the wider society as independent, responsible individuals. Day schools could not achieve that goal. Coming alongside the Indians to help them preserve their cultures would have been viewed as a waste of public funds and a betrayal of the needs of these public wards. The treaty commitment was to provide a transformative education that would meet the needs of a progressive, mostly agricultural community. Doing so would require an approach that was systematic, aggressive, and, increasingly, compulsory.

The federal government likely did not understand its treaty commitment to mean taking full financial responsibility for Indian education. It had partnered with various Christian denominations since the beginning with respect to Indian education in central and eastern Canada. At no point in Ontario, for example, had government paid the entire cost for Indian education; Christian denominations picked up a large portion. Indeed, up to the 1870s all governments had always been parsimonious with respect to educational expenditure. None ever anticipated paying the whole cost of education for any white community; they provided grants, but local ratepayers helped to build, equip, and maintain a school, and to hire and pay a teacher. Indians, of course, would not have to pay, but the denominations were expected to pick up a significant portion of the cost and responsibility in return for the opportunity to proselytize. It is almost certain that the governments that negotiated the treaties thought federal educational costs per school in the West would parallel rather than exceed those of Indian schools in Ontario, Quebec, and the Maritimes.

The government's industrial school model incorporated aspects of the day's advanced educational thinking. Robert M. Stamp notes that, from the time of confederation, there were increasing demands in the white community "for a more practical approach to Canadian education." In rural areas, this translated into demands for more agricultural education. One authority in Ontario called in 1880–81 for "elementary education … so directed as to prove of practical value as a basis" for an agricultural career. Many of the rural population regarded "book learning" with scorn. By the 1890s in central and eastern Canada, the agricultural curriculum in rural schools was expanding, and included garden plots and fields for instructional purposes. Given these prevailing ideas about what rural schools should teach, inclusion of farm, garden, and manual skills training in Indian industrial and boarding schools made sense.

Were the government's educational goals hampered by stingy pay for teachers? In fact, at the beginning of the twentieth century, average annual salaries for elementary school teachers in Canada who were graduates of normal schools were $400 for men and $300 for women. The $300 that the DIA had paid day school teachers since the 1880s may have seemed reasonable in this context; the problem was that many schools boards wanted to hire teachers, and the remoteness and intercultural challenges of living and teaching on reserves made it difficult for Indian schools to compete for competent staff. The government would have had to pay a considerable premium to recruit and retain better teachers, which in turn would have opened it to further opposition and press charges of extravagance.[134]

*Criticism*

J.R. Miller, having critically examined the entire history of Indian boarding schools in Canada, concludes they "simply did not work economically or academically. Period."[135] They failed, he points out, in one major
goal: to make Indians self-sufficient and no longer a burden on the federal treasury. Nor did they produce Indians who spoke, wrote, and read
English fluently; who were more competent farmers than those who had
never attended school; or who were able to manage a skilled trade in
competition with whites. Experiments with the outing system, in which
older students were sent to work with white farmers or as domestics,
also failed.[136] The reasons Miller cites for the schools' failure include too
much emphasis on child labour and too little on academic study; too
many underqualified teachers and teachers unprepared for the isolation
or cross-cultural and linguistic challenges of reserves; inappropriate curriculum; reading cultural differences as shortcomings and weaknesses;
inadequate funding; physical, sexual, and emotional abuse and excessive
punishment at the hands of missionary administrators and teachers.
Milloy further mentions poor morale, and notes that physical, sexual,
and emotional abuse also occurred at the hands of other students.[137]
Generally, major scholars view Indian schools as the opposite of the safe,
secure environment essential for learning and personal growth for many,
if not most, pupils.

Reports on the schools from pupils who attended them in this period
are scarce. One helpful study is based on several interviews with Cree
elders from north-central Alberta who attended Blue Quills Boarding
School, Red Deer Industrial School, Whitefish Lake Day School, Goodfish
Lake Day School, or Saddle Lake Day School from 1899 to 1923. When
asked about positive experiences, all agreed they liked the academic side
of learning, and several wished there had been more of it. Some liked
learning practical skills. Most noted friendships with children from different tribes or reserves. A couple mentioned some nuns who showed
love to the students.

But recollection of negative experiences needed no prompting. The
elders reported homesickness, lack of freedom, emotionally cold institutions, social distance between students and staff, and the military discipline that required them to rise every day without exception at five in the
morning and follow a rigid schedule. Worse, they reported deliberate
humiliation, instilled fear, and brutal, irrational, and sadistic punishments. One elder recalled counting 128 strappings administered by a

nun to a boy for speaking Cree. Children could be shackled or tied down and beaten, but sometimes other pupils were expected to hold the victim down. Emotions still were raw decades afterward.[138] One impression is that the repressive brutality got even worse after 1905.

On the other hand, one also must acknowledge the conclusion of historian Elizabeth Churchill, who examined schooling on the Tsuu T'ina reserve from the 1880s through the 1930s. She notes the abuse and other shortcomings of the schools, but affirms that her evidence "demonstrate[s] that Tsuu T'ina formal education was an overwhelming success in producing a group of adept workers who formed a sub-class of wage-earning labourers." She finds that the schooling helped a younger generation of Tsuu T'ina deal with new conditions in the post-treaty era. Adaptation and modernization could mean rethinking what it meant to be Indian and Tsuu T'ina, and to be agents of that change, not merely victims. Churchill's view is that many Indian graduates of the schools were able to make a living in a variety of ways.[139]

Pauline Dempsey has mainly positive memories of her time attending St Paul's Anglican Indian Residential School on the Kainai reserve between 1934 and 1942. But beyond her own direct experience, she also mentions the reportedly remarkable effectiveness of one of her mother's teachers, Miss Beth Wells, at the school in the very early twentieth century. Wells apparently was academically sound, and taught with love and kindness. There were about twenty girls who were influenced by her in the six years that she was at St Paul's, during which time "she moulded these girls into the future social leaders of the reserve while their husbands all became chiefs and leaders." Esther S. Goldfrank wrote of these women in the 1930s that they were "the most progressive women of their generation – and the most ambitious."[140] The education transformed their lives, and the lives of other members of their tribe, by enabling them both to be comfortable with white society and to adapt their traditional culture to changing circumstances. These girls did not cease to be Indian, but neither did they disparage their education. Thus, while acknowledging the traumatic experience that the schools imposed on many children, it is nevertheless reasonable to observe that at least some students had reason for positive memories.[141]

Moreover, the DIA's goals became more modest with the passing of time, as Sifton acknowledged in 1904 when he spoke disparagingly of distributing "over the whole band a moderate amount of education and intelligence." And, from the government perspective, at least some progress was being made. In 1906, Agent J. Batty at Saddle Lake remarked he was pleased to find that "the majority of the younger people speak, read and write English, and their dress and general appearance is [sic] very creditable."[142] After 1900 in Canada, a new approach to education, called "the Macdonald-Robertson Movement," promoted the idea of more manual training: according to Sutherland, by "1903 there were forty-five fully qualified manual training teachers in Canada, half of them native Canadians ... training over 700 boys each week."[143] Some industrial school instruction was having a positive effect.

Still, the basic approach to Indian education changed little. Titley points out that even as late as 1922, when the High River industrial school closed, neither the government nor the teachers and administrators were willing to examine why these schools failed: there was "no fundamental questioning of the premise that education should drive a wedge between young and old, and that it should alienate children from their parents and everything they stood for."[144] Officials and teachers persuaded themselves that good parents would want their children transformed so they could have a chance at success in white society, while resistant parents were holding their children back. There was a racist element in this colonialist policy, but it was also a product of the rise of reform in the wider, increasingly liberal and individualistic, society; and of the conviction that government-backed professionals in a variety of fields knew better than parents what was best for children.

Given the model it chose to adopt to fulfill its moral, legal, and treaty obligations, modern critics of the government argue it assumed responsibility for providing qualified teachers, adequate equipment and learning materials, appropriate and healthful learning and living environments, adequate and balanced diets, good medical care for those who became ill, funds to enable students to devote more time to their studies and less to farming, industrial, or domestic skills, and so on, as well as safety from abuse – and that it failed at this responsibility. Politics, however, is the art of the possible, and this would have been an unrealistic and unachievable ideal. In its day, critics mostly accused the government of doing too much, not too little.

Also sad was the fact that the society that now surrounded the Indians also looked down on them. The schools were deeply flawed, but they did not operate in a vacuum. The government claimed that it wanted all Indians to be enfranchised and assimilated, but most whites disagreed and would never treat them as equals. Prejudice ran too deep, and Indians felt it every time they were badly treated by agents or farm instructors on reserves, or by farmers and ranchers for whom they worked, or by police, or by people in towns and cities. In all that emphasis on creating farmers, carpenters, and shoemakers in industrial schools, it was never made clear that most officials assumed these workers would work on reserves; occasional rhetoric aside, few thought Indians could or should compete with white skilled workers. For the expectations of industrial, or even boarding, schools to have been realized, there would have to have been a wholesale upheaval in social attitudes toward Indians, and neither government nor educational officials made any effort in that direction. What, after all, did industrial school graduates have to look forward to beyond the boundaries of the reserves?

Hon. David Mills, MP, Bothwell, Ontario, minister of the interior and superintendent general of Indian Affairs, took a hard line on Indian expenditures and thwarted David Laird's efforts to treat Indians more generously and sympathetically. Library and Archives Canada, Topley Studio fonds/PA-026513 (MIKAN 3508662).

Sir John A. Macdonald, prime minister 1867–73 and 1878–91,
was also superintendent general of Indian Affairs 1878–87. He
began with some sympathy for Native peoples, but his experience
after 1878, and the North-West Rebellion of 1885, turned him
to a harder line. Library and Archives Canada/Harold Daly
fonds/C-021290 (MIKAN 3192008).

Hon. Edgar Dewdney, MP, Assiniboia East, North-West Territories, and minister of the interior 1888–92, is pictured here in 1889. As Indian commissioner (1879–88), he greatly influenced Sir John A. Macdonald's Indian policy before himself becoming the superintendent general of Indian Affairs (1888–92). Library and Archives Canada, Topley Studio fonds/PA033695 (MIKAN 3214887).

Hayter Reed, pictured here in 1897, served as an Indian agent before becoming Indian commissioner (1888–93) and deputy superintendent general (1893–97). He is now much derided for policies restricting Indians' access to mechanized farming equipment. Library and Archives Canada/ Topley Studio fonds/PA-212538 (MIKAN 3431042).

Frank Tried to Flay and George Left Hand sowing seed at the North Camp of the Siksika reserve, 1880s. What's in a picture? Often used to illustrate Hayter Reed's policy of denying farm equipment to Indians, broadcast seeding like this was in fact common on both white and Indian farms at this time. Only in the early 1890s did the Brandon experimental farm demonstrate seeding equipment suited to Canadian prairie circumstances. Glenbow Museum Archives NA-127-1.

A caravan of hay racks on the Kainai reserve, hauling hay to the Cochrane ranch around 1905. The Kainai had sufficiently large and reliable hauling and freighting capacity that they became important players in the economy around the reserve, even forcing down rates paid to white freighters. Glenbow Museum Archives NA-451-6.

Titled "Deserted Indian Village," this illustrates the Indian winter dwellings very common in the Saddle Lake and Edmonton agencies; at other times of the year, Indians often travelled off reserve for traditional hunting, fishing, and gathering. Provincial Archives of Alberta B 13.

St Joseph's Industrial School (also known as Dunbow or High River school), pupils, and staff, in the 1890s. The school already had numerous outbuildings and was a large-scale operation. Glenbow Museum Archives NA-2172-7.

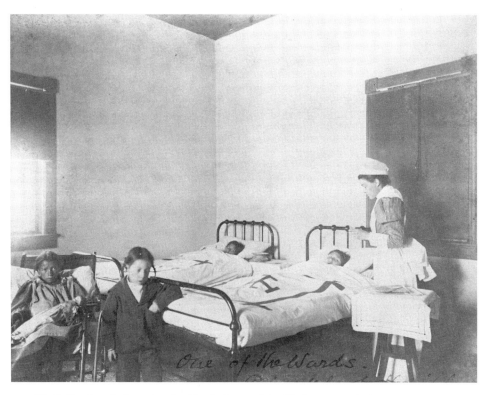

The Indian hospital ward at the North Camp of the Siksika reserve before 1900. Generally the government provided a subsidy for building and operating reserve hospitals, but the religious denominations usually assumed responsibility for staffing them in the early years. Glenbow Museum Archives NA-1773-14.

Passpasschase's Cree/Metis band signed an adhesion to Treaty 6;
their reserve covered much of present-day south Edmonton, but
the government secured a surrender by dubious means in the
1880s. Glenbow Museum Archives NA-579-13.

Tahnocoach, Sioux wife of NWMP Constable George Pembridge
and niece of Chief Sitting Bull, photographed at Fort Walsh,
1878. Some NWMP officers found Indian wives and stable
relationships. Glenbow Museum Archives NA-935-1.

NWMP Constables Fred Young and G.B. Moffatt with a Kainai man
at Fort Walsh, 1879. NWMP officers were not often photographed
out of uniform in this period; the buckskin outfits were likely
intended to demonstrate a relaxed relationship with Indians.
Glenbow Museum Archives NA-136-2.

An NWMP officer and Indian scouts, Fort Macleod, 1894. The NWMP found Indian scouts invaluable in tracking criminals (from horse thieves to murderers) and maintaining peace in the southern prairies. Glenbow Museum Archives NA-2646-5.

A completed Blood Sun Dance Lodge, Kainai reserve, 1893. Indians resisted attempts to prohibit the dance ceremonies, wherein their identities were deeply rooted and renewed. The NWMP in Alberta before 1905 mostly confined themselves to trying to eliminate the self-torture parts of the ceremonies. Glenbow Museum Archives NA-668-37.

# 7

# "A National Crime"?
# The Problem of Indian Health

In October 1903, Indian Commissioner David Laird drew the government's attention to disturbing mortality rates among the treaty Indians of western Canada. While tubercular diseases remained the most serious and persistent problem, epidemics of influenza, whooping cough, scarlet fever, measles, and pneumonia, along with some cases of smallpox, had swept across much of the region in 1902–03. Of agencies Laird especially noted, the hardest hit in the district of Alberta were Saddle Lake (causes unspecified), the Siksika reserve (measles), and the Kainai reserve (smallpox): "In short, the mortality is so great in some of the principal bands ... that, in spite of the fact that the birth-rate among our Indians is generally greater than that of the average European countries, which is about 3.60 per cent, if it continues, their bands must at no distant day become nearly extinct." He noted that the Piikani reserve, with a birth rate of 4.76 per cent, had thirteen more deaths than births; the Kainai reserve, with a 3.60 birth rate, had fifty-five more deaths than births; and the Siksika reserve, with a 3.80 birth rate, had sixty-six more deaths than births. The causes remained a mystery to Laird, because Indians were "better clad and housed than formerly, good doctors are in attendance, and sanitary precautions are being increased." That is, mortality and morbidity remained high despite public health measures deemed appropriate for the day that had been in place since the 1890s. There were some signs of hope among other bands: population gains in Alberta agencies included Saddle Lake (net of six, despite ten deaths in April and May alone), Hobbema (twenty-seven), Stoney Nakoda (eight), and Edmonton (twenty-six), while the Tsuu T'ina "about held their own."[1]

Deputy Superintendent General Frank Pedley could muster little sympathy. He offered a then-popular social Darwinist analysis: many Indians had not adapted to the reserve environment, "the process of selection under the law of 'survival of the fittest' seems to be still in operation," and they suffered from an "inborn weakness, an idiosyncracy of constitution" that made them especially vulnerable to disease.[2] Such an attitude no longer satisfied the public. Clifford Sifton, the minister of the Interior and superintendent general of Indian Affairs, facing politically sensitive health crises in both his immigration and Indian responsibilities, overruled Pedly, took Laird's concerns to heart, and decided to try a fresh approach. In 1904, he appointed Dr Peter Henderson Bryce as medical officer in his departments. Sifton was responding first to growing public concern about immigrants carrying disease to Canada, and second to the shocking reports of high levels of disease and mortality among Canada's Indians. He directed Bryce to devote about two-thirds of his time to politically charged immigration-related health problems, and the remaining third to inspecting reserves. He was to supervise and improve "the medical attendance and the sanitary arrangements on the various Indian reserves." The doctors attending the Indians were good, remarked Sifton, but needed a supervising medical authority.[3]

Bryce was a remarkable appointment. He had been secretary of the Ontario Board of Health since its inception in 1882, and was devoted to development of public health measures.[4] He was energetic, insightful, opinionated, and published his ideas and findings frequently, often to the embarrassment and irritation of his political superiors. Ultimately, his vigorous advocacy cost him his job, as governments were reluctant to make the commitment to Indian health that Bryce believed was medically and morally essential. Out of this experience, in 1922 he published *The Story of a National Crime: Being an Appeal for Justice to the Indians of Canada*.[5] Most of his impact is beyond the scope of this book, but his early reports reflect both the health of Canada's Indians to 1905, and also the assumptions of the public health movement that was transforming how Canadians regarded government responsibilities with respect to health and medical matters. Moreover, Bryce's claim that the government's record with respect to Indian health was "a national crime" has subsequently become fairly orthodox in Indian and scholarly writing on the subject.[6]

While still with the Ontario Board of Health, Bryce wrote to the deputy superintendent general in October 1903, the same month that Laird wrote from the West. He was concerned by the spread of contagious diseases on Ontario Indian reserves, and wanted better organization in the medical service and modern methods to combat disease. Writing to

Sifton, the deputy was just as dismissive of Bryce's ideas as he had been about Laird's concerns, pointing out the likely high costs and adding that the DIA "is doing as well as can be expected for the Indians."[7] Sifton hired Bryce anyway.

The new medical officer complained in his first annual report, from October 1905, that data submitted by the DIA's agents and doctors in the field were neither up to standard nor complete.[8] Nevertheless, Bryce determined that the Indian mortality rate was lowest in Quebec (22.2 per 1,000), but almost twice as high in Manitoba and the North-West Territories (42.6 per 1,000).[9] Of the bands reporting in the district of Alberta for 1904–05, the Cree of Saddle Lake were remarkably healthy, with a mortality rate of just 1.3 per 1,000; by contrast, the Cree of Hobbema had a rate of 50.3, and the Piikani had a rate of 70.7 – the highest in Canada. There seemed no obvious explanation as to why some bands' mortality rates were below that of the white population, while Bryce considered others of the same culture and similar environment "decimating."[10] Why, for example, did the Piikani have such a high rate of tuberculosis in a dry and healthy part of the country that, in the medical opinion of the day, should have been an ideal place to send tubercular patients to recover? There could also be substantial year-to-year variation, as the statistics for Saddle Lake Laird cited for 1902–03 and Bryce cited for 1904–05 indicate. Bryce was anxious to investigate many matters.

## WHAT CHANGED? WHAT HAD NOT CHANGED?

Why all this belated attention to Indian health and mortality? Historians such as Maureen Lux argue correctly that health conditions on the western reserves had been dreadful for a quarter-century before Laird wrote of his concerns to Sifton. James Daschuk claims that the nadir of Indian health lay in the late 1880s, though neither politicians nor public opinion then were much exercised about it.[11] Why did a few years affect the response so much? Why did the effort expended over the decade and a half before 1905 seem to make so little difference to Indian health?

The first question is readily answered: these years coincided with major breakthroughs in medicine, resulting in a dramatic increase in the size and force of the public health movement. Between the mid-1870s and about 1900, advances in the techniques of scientific research enabled the discovery and study of "germs" and confirmed them to be the cause of various diseases. For most diseases, effective pharmaceutical treatment remained in the future. However, the importance of government-imposed regulations guided by health-care professionals to ensure such things as municipal and hospital sanitation, quarantines to control diseases, and education to encourage personal hygiene became apparent. Urban slums, long viewed as repositories of disease, now were perceived to be an explicit danger. Reformers demanded action on many fronts, from urban planning to inspection of school children by doctors, nurses, and dentists.

This contrasts sharply with earlier approaches. Notions of "sanitary reform" had been incorporated into early public health legislation in mid-century to deal with health crises in industrial slums in Great Britain, continental Europe, and the United States, but there was little system, force, or understanding behind them. British North America had followed suit, but the reality was that colonial governments only got involved when there was some kind of epidemic disease and usually dismantled their efforts once the crisis passed. Otherwise, in the 1860s and 1870s, it was up to municipalities, churches, and families to deal with health matters affecting citizens and immigrants.[12]

It was this model that underlay the government's thinking about how to approach Indian health care. As noted above, when Canada's Indian legislation was amended after confederation, it provided for chiefs-in-council to take primary responsibility for reserve health care in a manner similar to white municipal councils. This too was intended to prepare Indians for enfranchisement. That was part of the Indian Act, the framework within which government officials negotiated the clauses dealing with health matters in Treaty 6:[13] in accepting these clauses, the government guaranteed that in future it would carry out its pre-existing fiduciary-like responsibilities. No one in the 1870s could have conceived of the health-care commitment that later evolved.

The government also approached health care and famine relief for Indians with the same assumptions that hampered its approach to farming and schooling. In white society, children were seen as refractory potential adults who had to be disciplined, educated, and encouraged if they were to become responsible adults. It was far from a perfect system, but it more or less worked because a social consensus underpinned it. Whites thought that as wards of the state, Indians similarly needed to be directed and prodded toward responsible citizenship, but Indians did not agree as to the methods and ends. There was a disjunction between how policies were conceived and how they were received. For example, the government believed that reducing rations would cause Indians to work harder to feed themselves and their families, as men were expected to do in white communities. Yet the simple reality was that starving Indians could not work harder. And there was more to it: the government policy focused on individuals, playing against Indians' community values. Indian communities were often demoralized, and came to believe that the government owed them food and clothing in a way that white communities were not and did not. The story was sometimes similar with other health measures: Indians, with some exceptions, did not improve housing or sanitation at least in part because demands that they do so came across as critical of their values and way of life. Cultural insensitivity seems to have been endemic among politicians and within the bureaucracy.

At least one other issue underlay government assumptions: the value-laden belief that Indians were inherently more susceptible to disease than whites, reinforcing white notions of Indian inferiority and their own superiority. While the same diseases affected everyone, the effect was disproportionately greater among Indian communities. Whites had built up some resistance to these diseases over hundred of generations in Europe; Indians in the Americas had been devastated after white contact by those same diseases. Some historians, such as Lux, argue that reserve Indians did not have any endemic susceptibility to epidemic and contagious diseases, and that the obscenely high morbidity and mortality on reserves resulted from people weakened by starvation and the government's failure to live up to its treaty obligations with respect to health care and famine relief. Undoubtedly, the government tended to be somewhat fatalistic, and could and should have done more. Yet Indians did not have to be on reserves to contract these diseases: they were afflicted repeatedly and devastatingly before the treaties even when the bison and other food sources remained viable. They suffered on the reserves too, no matter what the government did. As Laird noted in 1903, even improvements in medical care, diet, housing, and hygiene seemed to make little difference to mortality rates. Also, whether a band maintained a large measure of traditional lifestyle or adapted to more settled farming and ranching was not a reliable predictor of its health. The conundrum of Indian health seemed intractable.

## THE ORIGINS OF INDIAN HEALTH POLICY

It is well to review the government commitment with respect to Indian health care. Its legal and moral responsibility to Indians as wards of the state predated and framed the treaties. The health clauses in Treaty 6 stipulate a part of what that responsibility was understood to entail. For instance, "a medicine chest shall be kept at the house of each Indian Agent for the use and benefit of the Indians, at the discretion of such Agent." There was also the provision that if they were "overtaken by any pestilence, or by a general famine," the Queen, when so advised by the Indian agent and at the discretion of the responsible minister, would grant assistance deemed "necessary and sufficient to relieve the Indians from the calamity that shall have befallen them."

While these clauses were generalized to apply to all the numbered treaties, they were requested and granted in a particular context. Memories of the measles and scarlet fever epidemic of 1865,[14] the smallpox outbreak of 1869–70, and the starvation among the Cree in 1870–71 and 1873–74 remained vivid. No one in the 1870s thought the government could prevent such periodic catastrophes, but Indians did expect it to respond with sympathy and significant mitigating relief. The medicine chest was a reactive (not preventive) measure, much as the Hudson's Bay Company had made available from its trading posts. One account asserts that in the late nineteenth century, "the 'medicine chest' represented the embodiment of medical services available through the agent."[15] In the 1870s, these were very limited.

Given the DIA's staffing situation in 1876 and 1877, the treaty provisions literally meant that 1.5 medicine chests were available for the future district of Alberta, one for the Treaty 7 agent and one for the Treaty 6 agent that was shared between Alberta and Saskatchewan. With time that would change, and by 1905 there were five agents for Treaty 7 and three for the Alberta portion of Treaty 6. Yet, general medical care by 1905, or even by the early 1880s, had expanded considerably beyond that provided from agents' houses. The meaning of the medicine chest and emergency aid changed after the 1870s: first the government expanded the number and locations of physicians available to respond to Indian health issues; and, second, it later introduced preventive public health measures. The urgency of these changes was intensified by starvation and declining health conditions of Indians on the reserves. These were far more dire and intractable than anyone had contemplated at the time of the treaties. In the 1870s, the government paid NWMP surgeons, as part of their contracts, to attend Indians, and by the early 1880s, contrary to the myths often perpetuated in the literature, the government began to contract with other physicians to look after Indian needs.[16]

Sir John A. Macdonald, during an 1881 House of Commons discussion of the high cost of Indian administration, remarked: "Of course the system is expensive, especially in feeding the destitute Indians. But it is cheaper to feed them than to fight them, and humanity will not allow us to let them starve." Macdonald also remarked, defending against opposition charges of excessive government generosity, that in order to prevent Indians from congregating at food supply depots "they have only been fed on half rations, and we have been so severe upon the Indians in this regard that we have on several occasions received remonstrances from the medical men in the vicinity of these points, stating that the food was insufficient to support them."[17] The government thus was both aware and willing to admit that its policies endangered Indian health. It also construed this as tough love, believing fewer rations would goad Indians to work at agriculture to feed themselves. Instead, the results included starvation, susceptibility to disease, and people too weak to work. Did the treaties obligate the government to feed Indians for however long they were unable to support themselves? Or was the government morally obligated to pressure Indians into becoming responsibly self-sustaining?

Shortage of food was not the only issue. In his 1883 report on agencies in the western portion of Treaty 6, Agent W. Anderson commented, "the majority of deaths during the year have been from consumption ... This is owing, in a great extent, to their want of clothing which is really lamentable. Many of the children going naked and some adults being barefooted in the dead of winter. All this is caused by the disappearance of the buffalo and other game from which they formerly obtained their covering and lodges. The latter are now made of very thin cotton, and are utterly inadequate to protect them from this severe winter climate." He also noted that the HBC had formerly supplied Indians with coffins, and they now expected the government to do likewise, something over which Anderson had no authority: "This has caused much bitter feeling and complaints against me, as they cannot understand that I have no power to procure such things for them."[18] The government believed that Indians should work to earn money to pay for their clothing, and presumably coffins. Indian health suffered and anger mounted.

Alma Favel-King contends the Treaty 6 elders believed that the Queen undertook to "look after them in the manner in which they had looked after themselves. First Nations' holistic concept and understanding of health led to a broad interpretation of this agreement." It follows, she asserts, that there is "a treaty right to health," which by the latter half of the twentieth century came to mean accessible and available health benefits and services at the primary, secondary, and tertiary levels. By contrast, Favel-King derisively dismisses the federal government's position (which for decades rejected any such interpretation of the treaties) as limited to a requirement to provide "the equivalent of a first aid kit." At best, she argues, even today the government provides health care on the basis of "humanitarian principles," rather than from recognition of it as a treaty right.[19] She contends that the Indian model of holistic health means "the physical, emotional, mental and spiritual aspects of a person being in balance and harmony with each other as well as with the environment and other beings." The western medical model, by contrast, "has perpetuated the concept of health as being 'the absence of disease.'"[20]

Favel-King was addressing the situation of the 1990s, and it is uncertain to what extent the elders' views on the original meaning of the treaties' medical provisions are filtered through the perspectives of the mid- and late twentieth century. It is more certain that neither government officials nor Western medicine could have conceived of this kind of holistic approach in the 1870s. From their perspective, the only thing truly new about the health provisions of Treaty 6 – the medicine chest and discretionary emergency relief – was their inclusion in the treaty, which probably reduced the government's discretionary powers regarding medical assistance and relief.

The DIA's records for the years prior to 1876 demonstrate it had long understood that it had a legal and moral responsibility for wards of the state. It provided for some medical attendance upon Indians people in central, eastern, and western Canada, and undertook vaccination programs for smallpox. It also provided relief to Indians, Metis, and whites in the face of the locust-induced famine in Manitoba in the 1870s. In other words, everyone received medical care and relief on a reactive basis, in response to outbreaks of disease or other need, in an era when public health and preventive measures (apart from vaccination) were not employed anywhere in Canada. Government medical services were never limited to the medicine chest after 1876, but were supplemented, as necessary, by doctors (where available) on retainer to respond to needs as they arose – again, a service that predated Treaty 6. It must be acknowledged, however, that both wardship and the medical profession of the day implied a strongly paternal approach to medical treatment as with other aspects of Indian life, and tended to dismiss Indian solutions to injury and disease.[21]

Several of the treaties, including 6 and 7, were negotiated during a serious economic depression; economy, even parsimony, was the watchword of the government in every area. Moreover, many whites were envious that Indians received a level of care not available to most. Sick or injured Canadians typically paid out of pocket for medical care, when available or affordable – which it often was not in remote towns or rural areas. Alexander Morris, who negotiated Treaty 6, argued that everywhere in Canada there were "the poor, the blind and lame," and "the poor whites have as much reason to be helped as the poor Indian; they must be left to the charity and kind hearts of the people." It behoved the prosperous among them to "help your unfortunate brothers." The social expectation was that individuals, families, and religious or other organizations would offer charity to the needy; doing so was not the state's responsibility. Indians, however, might respond that the health provisions of the treaties were part of a negotiated compensation for access to their land and therefore did not constitute a "hand-out."[22]

It was not the cost of the medicine chest per se that worried government, but the cost and concomitant expectations of medical attendance for widespread medical problems, and the costs of famine or epidemic relief as these became general instead of isolated emergencies.[23] In the most literal sense, the government did fulfill its treaty obligation with respect to the medicine chest. In 1887, for example, Inspector of Agencies and Reserves Alex McGibbon noted, "each agency is supplied with a medicine chest. These are replenished as occasion requires, so that a constant supply of useful medicines is kept on hand for cases of sickness among the Indians. In this connection, I noticed that each agent has been furnished with a very good doctor's book, on the treatment of all kinds of diseases."[24] Arguably, the agents were as informed and supplied as traders had been at HBC posts.

Finally, with respect to general observations, Laurie Meijer Drees comments, "the history of Indian health care is very much linked to trends within Euro-Canadian society, rather than an exception to them."[25] She notes that the attitudes of missionaries and government officials to Indian health at any given point reflected accepted social values. It is futile to expect that the public and officials of the 1870s and 1880s would have a now-modern understanding of diseases and how to respond to them; they had only the understanding of their era, and must be judged within that framework. That still leaves considerable latitude for critical evaluation.

Before confederation, Canada's impoverished and indigent had been
dealt with mainly under poor laws that favoured institutions such as
workhouses and orphanages as a solution. However, from the 1840s,
townships in Canada West were permitted to provide some public support to such people. That is, the primary or front-line public response
was to be local or community based. A similar mentality carried forward into the confederation agreement. Health care fell to the provincial governments under the constitution, but in practice mostly remained
a local responsibility. Hugh Shewell notes, "welfare relief ... was not a
readily accepted function of the state in the middle to late nineteenth
century, especially in North America."[26] The federal government had
no department devoted to health matters until after World War I.[27] The
battles over public health measures to prevent disease in the later nineteenth century were mostly intraprovincial. Ontario established the first
provincial board of health in 1882, but took several years to grant it
effective powers, and other provinces only gradually followed its lead.
Not until 1898 did the North-West Territories Council pass an ordinance providing for the appointment of medical health officers and sanitary inspectors, a measure that underlay Alberta's first public health
laws in 1905 and 1907. Even after legal establishment, provincial health
boards and inspection were often underfunded, their legislation was
under-enforced, and large portions of the public resented and resisted
their measures. It took many years to establish a professional, political,
and social consensus about such policies.[28] It is therefore unsurprising
that confusion and inconsistency often seemed to constrain the early
establishment of patterns of health care for Canada's Indians. On top of
this, the federal government in the late nineteenth century had no desire
either to create a medical establishment or to incur any great expense,
which, together with the racist and paternalistic views of the day with
respect to Indians, led to rather disorganized, ad hoc responses to their
health concerns.

THE EARLY TREATY PERIOD

Epidemic disease was the major exception to the rule of localized
response in the 1870s, for it potentially constituted a danger to the whole
community and could not be addressed solely by local authorities,
whether in municipalities or on reserves. Responding to reports of the
"almost superstitious terror" with which western Indians looked upon
smallpox, Superintendent General David Mills appointed Dr Daniel

Hagarty, an Ontario physician, as "resident Medical Superintendent of the North West," charged mainly with ensuring that the Indian population of the region was vaccinated as soon as possible. The appointment was a result of a smallpox outbreak the previous summer in Keewatin, which had only been confined by the vigorous response of the Manitoba and federal governments. He was struck not only by the "dismay" the outbreak occasioned, but by "the expenditure of a very large amount of money, a considerable proportion of which (in the panic and excitement attending the visitation) was, it is feared, extravagantly, if not uselessly expended."[29] This illustrates perfectly the government's reactive and penny-pinching approach to a health crisis. Mills was moved by the "harrowing" stories of the tragic impact of this illness on the Indian population, but he was even more moved by the desire to control future expenditure. Hagarty, he said, was appointed "to protect the Indians hereafter against the ravages of this disease, and to prevent the large expenditure entailed upon the country by its periodic visitations, not to mention the loss occasioned by the interruption of the Indian trade."[30] However, having a permanent medical officer to supervise administration of health measures among Indians, and implementation of public health measures, was not on the horizon for any Canadian government in the 1870s.

In the North-West Territories when the treaties were negotiated, there were few, if any, qualified physicians apart from the handful who were medical officers (or sometimes veterinarians) with the North-West Mounted Police. The first such officer to serve Indians in the future Alberta was Richard Barrington Nevitt, who arrived as a NWMP surgeon in 1874; he received half his salary from the Indian Branch. He was hired at age twenty-four with his medical training incomplete, although he eventually returned to Ontario and completed his degree in 1882. During his time in the West, Indians, Metis, and many others availed themselves of his services and medications. Apparently the first fully qualified physician in the region was Dr George Kennedy who, like Nevitt, was a NWMP medical officer at Fort Macleod.[31]

Reporting on his own first year's activities in the west in 1879, Indian Commissioner Edgar Dewdney concluded that there was no reason to continue Hagarty's appointment: "There are now distributed over the North-West several experienced medical men, some of them in the Mounted Police Force, drawing pay for the special purpose of attending to the Indians." He also noted that there were medicine chests at Battleford, complete with instructions.[32] Dewdney exaggerated the supply of medical expertise available. In 1880, Norman Macleod, Indian agent for Treaty 7, observed that the lack of medical help was "much felt amongst the Indians, as it is only in the neighborhood of the police posts that they can obtain any assistance, and being now settled on their reservations they cannot even have this. There are many serious cases which might be cured, or greatly alleviated, if advice was at hand to which they could have recourse. Pulmonary complaints and affections of the bowels are prevalent."[33] N W M P officials contended the same year that "a hospital or infirmary" should be established on reserves,[34] but little notice was taken of the recommendation, likely because of the expense and difficulty in securing even minimally qualified medical and nursing staff.[35]

The small NWMP hospital at Fort Macleod endeavoured to treat Indians as well as police officers, though it could address only a fraction of the total need. In 1881, despite treatment, an epidemic of whooping cough proved fatal to "a large number of children." Dr George Allan Kennedy, a NWMP surgeon, noted increased Indian demand for his services, greater faith in his practice, and requests for medication. He added, "in surgery they are still tenacious of their own practices, and rightly so too, for many of them understand the subject pretty well and not unfrequently [sic] obtain results which would be creditable even to our own ... surgery."[36] Indians were highly capable of treating conditions with which they were familiar using medications derived from natural sources,[37] but rarely were these effective for the settler-imported epidemic diseases that thrived on reserves. At Whitefish Lake, for example, Sam Bull recalled that the "medicine man" had dealt with cases of "external bleeding," "internal hemorrhage, inflammation and gangrene." In general, he had a high success rate, "and few cases were lost." Bull claimed that the medicine man had wrought a cure in some cases when the white doctor had given up. He resented whites' dismissive attitude to Indian medical knowledge.[38]

Smallpox was fairly effectively controlled in this period among vaccinated populations; nevertheless, there was some Indian and white resistance to the procedure, and cases recurred from time to time into the early twentieth century.[39] More serious in the early years of reserve life were measles, scarlet fever and the related erysipelas, and whooping cough. These diseases often were susceptible to some control with proper care, but periodically reached epidemic proportions, frequently carrying off children and the elderly. In 1886–87, for example, a measles epidemic affected almost every reserve in the district of Alberta.

Most devastating of all was tuberculosis, then usually called consumption or pulmonary phthisis, and the allied disease called scrofula (or glandular tuberculosis), which killed or affected thousands of whites and hundreds of Indians each year, though its incidence was far higher on reserves than elsewhere.[40] One study contends that the soaring incidence of diseases like tuberculosis resulted from a conjunction of "radical social, spiritual, and ecological disruptions," including crowded housing, inadequate resources, and boarding schools, combined with the construction of the Canadian Pacific Railway, which facilitated "the spread of people and pathogens to the west," particularly European immigrants who often "harboured the tubercule bacillus."[41]

Tuberculosis indeed provides a good example of why confusion surrounded the development of public health policy. Only in 1882 did a German physician, Roland Koch, prove that a particular bacillus was responsible for the disease. But even then, many physicians refused to believe it was contagious, viewing it as the result of "constitutional peculiarities" that were often inherited, and as generally incurable. (This was widely accepted as an explanation as to why it was prevalent among Indians.) A medical consensus that tuberculosis was contagious was only reached around the turn of the twentieth century, and a recognized medical cure was not developed until 1944.[42]

## THE INFLUENCE OF THE PUBLIC HEALTH MOVEMENT

The public health movement sought to use the recent understanding of communicable disease to improve living and working environments, promote sanitary habits, and pressure governments to legislate preventive measures. It also was influenced by the professionalization of health services, creating a pool of experts who wanted to shape policy for the public good.[43] Moreover, the public health movement was part of a social purity movement that tended to link science and morality; the moral and physical health of a society were held to be closely linked. Put another way, according to Meijer Drees, "disease, dirt and degradation were all related."[44] Indian health was believed to linger behind "primarily because Indian people lacked the necessary moral development." Bryce himself claimed that the "difference in moral development [of the Indian people], with its accompanying lagging behind in material advancement," was the major factor in their poor health.[45]

The movement's ideas were adopted by the DIA, and from the early 1890s were formalized into an annual health circular to all agents,[46] who in turn responded in their annual reports by indicating how the recommendations to improve the reserves and Indian health were being met. Implicitly, an unkempt reserve or home was as much a moral failing as a health risk. As early as the mid-1880s the DIA enjoined Indian agents to ensure that Indians were keeping their homes, and the areas and buildings around them, clean.[47] In spring, garbage was to be gathered up and burned. Houses were to be swept regularly, and whitewash and lime applied to control germs. Early houses, often built according to white instruction, were usually small, poorly ventilated one- or two-room structures of log and mud with thatched or sod roofs. In fairness, such abodes also were typical first homes for early homesteaders, and the DIA encouraged Indians over the years to upgrade or rebuild them, much as white farmers were doing. Emphasis lay on getting Indians to settle down in fixed, rather than temporary, abodes. Though often disease infested, these houses were somewhat warmer during the bitterly cold winters. Their materials were also more readily available than the animal hides needed for traditional Indian lodges; the latter were wearing out and could not easily be replaced, given the demise of the bison and relative scarcity of other game animals.[48] Heating and cooking fires created smoky interiors, especially in non-traditional housing.[49] Such conditions almost certainly worsened pulmonary and eye problems. Overcrowding and inadequate clothing further compromised health on reserves.

This experience led at least some Indians to romanticize life before the reserves. Mike Mountain Horse, a Kainai, contends that frequent moving, healthy diet, and an active outdoor life had resulted in excellent health, generally speaking, for Indians. He claims that diseases such as colds or pneumonia were practically unknown: "the early Indian's open air life, his staple foods, and his constant exercise, built up for him a constitution able to withstand any strain and hardship imposed on it during the time of a natural life span." Indians died from accidents, old age, battle, or clan feuds, but rarely from disease.[50] Educating and "civilizing" Indians resulted in less outdoor exercise, less resistance to diseases such as tuberculosis, and previously unknown tooth decay.[51]

On the reserves, it is true that all bands suffered from numerous diseases. However, there is a widespread belief, paralleling Mountain Horse, that the small bands who continued a traditional lifestyle of hunting, gathering, fishing, and trading, who lived in teepees as much as possible, and who undertook little or no farming fared best and were healthiest. By contrast, those who settled with little opportunity to pursue a traditional lifestyle and diet, who lived in close quarters in houses or lodges, and who engaged in farming are often said to have had a higher incidence of disease. These perceptions are not reliable, despite their appearance in official reports, some Indian memoirs, and some scholarly literature. The population tables for Treaty 6 in chapter 3 in this book show that among the less-settled bands population declined noticeably over the post-treaty period, with one or two exceptions where it remained stable or grew marginally. The perception of health may be wishful thinking, or it may have arisen because these bands were not regularly visited or carefully monitored by officials and/or did not request medical aid. Treaty 6 bands that grew in population over the period were more settled and agriculturally successful, such as the Saddle Lake, Blue Quill, James Seenum, and Samson bands. Treaty 7 bands appear to fit the stereotype more closely, but were also much less successful in farming during these years, and therefore in providing for themselves a properly balanced diet, than were settled bands in Treaty 6.[52]

PERSPECTIVES FROM THE AGENCY AND BAND LEVELS

It is impossible, given space limitations, to examine the health of each band in each year. A snapshot from annual reports of agents for 1888–89 – often frustratingly vague or medically uninformed – may help to illustrate not only differing rates or perceptions of illness, but the typical attitudes that shaped those reports.

In the Saddle Lake agency in the northeast of the district, the agent reported that among the mostly settled Saddle Lake band in 1888 "very little [serious] sickness" had occurred, but a mild winter in 1888–89 was thought to have increased "petty illness, especially among children." The small Wahsatanow band, which did little farming, suffered two deaths despite otherwise good health; the agent believed that because there were few children, "the band will pass away with the present generation." The settled Whitefish Lake band experienced a serious outbreak of scrofula. The Beaver Lake band led "a more active life than Indians engaged in agricultural pursuits," and "their health has been good throughout the year, and it has not been necessary to provide medical attendance." The tiny Lac la Biche band reported no health problems,[53] while the Chipewyan band at Heart Lake, forty miles north-east of Lac la Biche, appeared to be experiencing health problems that the agent attributed to excessive intermarriage within the band, but he hoped that situation was being addressed.[54]

In the Edmonton agency, health was reported as good, epidemic disease was reported as absent, and the doctor was only called to make four visits. The agent, William C. DeBalinhard, barely referred to health issues.[55] Agency bands grew by fourteen members during the year.

In the Peace Hills agency, the inspector noted that the agent's effort to encourage fishing at nearby Pigeon Lake "had a beneficial effect upon the health of the Indians." Over all, Indians in this agency were said to enjoy good health, to have benefitted from medical attendance, to give increased attention to cleanliness, and to "appreciate the issue of soap during the past year." The exception was the Sharphead Stoney band, where unspecified illness prevailed.[56] Agency bands grew by 115 in 1889.

In contrast with the Treaty 6 bands, those in Treaty 7 suffered more dramatic population losses. In 1889, the Treaty 7 population fell by 160 (3.2 per cent), to 4,893.[57] The agents' reports are frustratingly unhelpful with respect to health issues. J.C. Cornish, reporting on the Tsuu T'ina and Stoneys, stated they had "been carefully attended medically throughout the year by Dr N.J. Lindsay, who has won their confidence, and consequently improved their condition in this respect very much." Sanitary measures were also widely adopted. The Kainai suffered most of all – there was much illness and many children died of whooping cough, "notwithstanding they had all the medicine necessary." On the Siksika reserve, "the missionaries have been doing their utmost in attending to sick Indians," Lindsay visited monthly from Calgary, and 240 Indians were vaccinated for smallpox. On the Piikani reserve, Agent A.R. Springett reported generally good health, and that births exceeded deaths in the previous twelve months.[58]

A study of the Tsuu T'ina by Elizabeth Churchill details some health care in this period and what the medicine chest had come to mean in effect. In addition to smallpox vaccinations, she notes, "the Indian Agent distributed patent medicines to the Tsuu T'ina from the time of their first settlement at the Fish Creek Reserve in 1883. These medicines most often were cough syrup and eye drops provided for childhood ailments but patent medicines were also distributed to Chief Bullhead and other adults in the band." These medications were the same as could be purchased by the white population. During an influenza outbreak in 1890, the entire band was placed on the sick list.[59]

By the turn of the twentieth century, the DIA had more effectively systematized its reporting, though agents often seemed to be plugging standard responses into a template. They also wished to paint as positive a picture as the facts permitted. Thus, Indian health was usually reported as good or improving; medical attention was always beneficial; and Indians were evaluated on their cleanliness, both personal and communal. The available information is far from comprehensive, but it permits some useful conclusions. In this light, it is instructive to consider the picture that emerged by the end of the territorial period, in 1905.

The agent reported that the population of the Siksika reserve was 842, with "no serious epidemic illness." Yet in almost the same breath, reflecting the still-widespread conviction that tuberculosis was not contagious and therefore not epidemic, he noted that some had succumbed to "pulmonary ailments, which lurk in the system of many of these people." Houses were not entirely sanitary, were often too small for their residents, and lacked sufficient ventilation. Many chose to live in tents during the summer, which probably was beneficial. At the north end of the reserve from 1895 was a small Anglican-sponsored hospital with a resident doctor (Dr William Rose) and nurses, and Dr James D. Lafferty of Calgary regularly attended the reserve as well. Construction of the hospital was assisted by a small government grant to cover interior plastering and masonry work; the government also provided an annual subvention toward expenses. Other costs were paid by the Anglican church and its women's auxiliary. The inspector of agencies, J.A. Markle, was pleased to report that the DIA only had to contribute $1,000 per year to the institution, which in 1904–05 treated ninety-nine in-patients, 316 out-patients, provided medication for 317 persons "for various ailments," and also treated school children 213 times.[60]

The Kainai reserve in 1905 had a population of 1,204 and reported no epidemic diseases and generally "satisfactory" health. There was a Roman Catholic hospital, established and staffed by the Grey Nuns in 1893 and intended to serve the Piikani and Siksika reserves as well, which admitted 275 patients in 1904–05. The government contributed $2,500 toward construction costs, along with a small subvention for furnishings. Later, it paid the nuns' salaries and covered operating costs, which was more generous support than that offered to the hospital on the Siksika reserve. Again, the "open-air life in tents" possible for most of the year proved highly beneficial. Houses were being improved with respect to ventilation, light, and cleanliness, with encouraging results.[61]

On the Piikani reserve (population 599), health was "good," consumption was "their greatest trouble," and the outdoor life and exposure to "the pure air and sunshine cure" was "a great health restorer." The Tsuu T'ina (population 205) also reportedly enjoyed good health. The agent believed that the gradual reduction of rations of beef and flour since 1897 had a positive impact as, having to farm to produce more food, "they now get more exercise and have something to live for." The Stoney (population 652) were said to enjoy good health, "with the exception of a few old cases of scrofula and consumption, the latter disease claiming some children who have succumbed during the year."[62] It is difficult to believe that these reports were about the same peoples whose mortality rates so distressed Laird and Bryce. One can consider the reports of agents and inspectors either to be absurdly optimistic, or to reflect the larger condition on reserves since, after all, not all Indians were sick or dying. Understanding the true state of affairs requires both perspectives.

In the Treaty 6 area, the Saddle Lake band (now incorporating the Blue Quill band) with a population of 247 apparently had good health and sanitation, reasonably healthy dwellings and environment, and "satisfactory" medical attendance. The James Seenum band (population 331) near Whitefish and Goodfish lakes enjoyed good health except for "some chronic cases of scrofula, and a mild form of varioloid"; the latter, a form of smallpox, was kept to two houses by strict quarantine. No health issues were reported for the Lac la Biche (population ten), Chipewyan (population eighty), or Beaver Lake (population ninety-four) bands, all of whom still made their living in traditional ways.[63]

The Enoch band (population 126) in the Edmonton agency reportedly had good sanitary measures and medical attendance, "but so widespread is the taint of scrofula and consumption that both remedial and preventive measures seem to make but little impression on the death rate." Similarly, the Michel band (population ninety-four) had "prevalent" consumption and a high death rate, though "their way of living and sanitary observance and surroundings are much the same as prevail among their white neighbours." The Alexander (population 189), Joseph (population 146), and Paul (population 157) bands reportedly fared better than the others, with good health, a vigorous outdoor life, and little need for medical attendance.[64]

The report for the Hobbema agency grouped the bands together (population 655), and claimed health was "fairly satisfactory." Proper ventilation and allocation of more space per person in new buildings, proper garbage disposal, ensuring uncontaminated drinking water, a greater proportion of vegetables in the diet, and care to ensure the proper condition of meat consumed were all promoted. Every effort was made to care for those with consumption and to prevent the spread of the disease. Yet, reported Agent W.S. Grant, "the social habits are such that the Indian customs are conducive to the spread of throat diseases. These customs we are continually contending against; and shall continue to do so until the end of the chapter."[65]

These reports contain no sense of urgency or crisis. High levels of certain diseases were accepted as a persistent norm. The agents seem rather wearied, almost inured to the suffering, convinced that if Indians would alter their behaviour, improve their living conditions, adopt clean habits, and work to provide themselves with healthy balanced diets the disease problem would be resolved. There still was no known cure for consumption,[66] but its spread might well have been inhibited through more aggressive quarantine and sanitation. Epidemic and contagious diseases also affected white and Metis communities – typically less intensely, but with higher incidence in poorer and less sanitary areas such as working-class districts in Montreal or Toronto. That these districts posed a threat to the rest of society was an accepted fact and, linked with humanitarian motives, spurred the reform and public health movements of the day. Reserves, certainly those in Alberta, were more isolated and in 1905 seemed a less pressing concern.[67]

### BRYCE'S REPORTS

Bryce, a seasoned public health campaigner, took a different view and his 1905 report contrasts those of Indian agents. There was little excuse, in his view, for a national mortality rate of 3.47 per cent among the Indian population, which across the country had increased by only 174 persons in the previous year. Simply by lowering the mortality rate to 2 per cent, "there would be an additional 2,000 added through lives saved annually." Public health measures had lowered white rates in Canada and England "much below" that figure, and there was no reason they should not do the same for Indian rates.[68]

In his more comprehensive and considered report of 1906, Bryce claimed that some of Canada's highest Indian mortality rates occurred among the Nizitapi (8.18 per cent) and in the Edmonton area (8.64 per cent), and concluded that they could not be accounted for by climate or geography. The problem had several causes, including not knowing how to live properly in houses; introduction of infection into small, crowded homes; presence of sputum on floors, walls, and other surfaces of homes; sending infected children into schools (especially boarding and industrial schools, often "over-crowded and ill-ventilated"); return of infected children from the schools to their homes; and Indian habits of visiting the sick, visiting others while sick, and expectorating freely.[69]

Efforts to treat diseased Indians in their homes were "generally found useless," meaning that the best option was treatment in a hospital or sanatorium. This likely would be too costly for government and bureaucrats to stomach, so Bryce favoured tents or some other "simple 'Home'" that could house several patients on the reserves where they could be "supplied with food from the band's funds or rations." Some plan for patient supervision and care would need to be effected, and he had several suggestions that amounted to adapting public health measures and training workers for reserve service.[70] There seemed to be hope for improvement, but these would run into officialdom's brick walls of entrenched conservatism and parsimony.

This is not to say that the DIA had not been investing in more medical care. In 1896 it had a half-dozen medical officers spread across the West, and by 1904 it had twenty-six.[71] In the early years, the medical officers were physicians on contract to the department for specified, and part-time, services. Most also had private practices in nearby cities or towns, and often had other contracts with entities such as the CPR or the NWMP. Sometimes they invested in hospitals, clinics, or even non-medical businesses. In an era before medical insurance plans, when most people could not afford their fees, that was how doctors were able to make ends meet. DIA contracts were, for those with the right connections, highly desired patronage. The government also paid an unspecified number of nurses to work in the hospitals on reserves.

### SCHOOLS AND HEALTH

Boarding schools have often been viewed as laboratories for the production of disease.[72] In 1894, Joseph Martin, a Liberal member of Parliament from Winnipeg, detailed for the House of Commons the dreadful mortality rate of Qu'Appelle Industrial School graduates, demanding, "what is the object of educating these children, if it costs their lives to educate them? It is not worth while spending $233,000 for the purpose of killing them." Referring to the schools generally, he asserted, "unless the pupils become citizens, and are improved by the schooling they get, they are of very little use to the community; and so far as I can judge by the report, they nearly all die shortly after they come out."[73] Duncan Campbell Scott, national supervisor of Indian schools, estimated in 1912 that half the children who entered the schools "did not live to benefit from the education which they had received therein."[74] A significant portion of the responsibility for this appalling record must lie with schools and the federal government. Too often there was an absence of supervision of school building plans and construction: siting might be bad, plans incompetent or non-existent, materials poor, construction amateur, and funding inadequate. Recommended renovations, expansions, or upgrades were continually deferred due to lack of resources.[75] Teachers and missionaries, especially if male, found themselves carrying out or supervising maintenance, repairs, and renovations for which they often were untrained and unpaid, and their expenses were not always reimbursed. Too frequently schools were poorly planned and ventilated, difficult to heat, overcrowded, and inadequately furnished. All of these things contributed to the possibility of an unhealthy environment. Moreover, while the government set dietary and clothing regulations, cash-strapped schools could not always meet expectations. Pupils reported being hungry, diets were sometimes unbalanced, and occasionally food – particularly meats, fish, and unpasteurized milk – was served after it had started to go bad.[76]

The government issued medical regulations in 1894, but they, too, were not well enforced. New pupils were supposed to be inspected before admission, but so few Indians were willing to give up their children to boarding and industrial schools that school officials accepted even ill children for the government grant they could generate. Dormitories were frequently overcrowded and, while some schools had infirmaries for more seriously ill students, many petty illnesses circulated freely. Standards of cleanliness varied by school. By the end of the 1880s most schools were visited fairly regularly by doctors on government retainers, and a few had a nurse on staff, which helped control or even cure many diseases. But, as noted above, tuberculosis remained an intractable problem. The best control was to separate the victims from the rest of the population, but because they were often contagious before they were symptomatic and diagnosed, they readily transmitted the disease to others.

So it was that extraordinary mortality rates were reported. In his 1907 report, Bryce pointed out that a sample study showed that 24 per cent of pupils who entered boarding schools between 1888 and 1905 in supposed good health died either at the school or within three years of leaving.[77] In another study, Churchill reports that between 1893 and 1909 some fifty-four pupils – thirty-six boys and eighteen girls – attended the boarding school on the Tsuu T'ina reserve. Nineteen boys died before adulthood, and eight girls died "either prior to or shortly after their graduation," which is a 50 per cent mortality rate overall.[78] It is not clear to what extent schools were responsible for all these deaths. First, not all new students were in good health, despite what the certificates said; as mentioned above, school officials colluded with doctors to maximize admissions and concomitant government grants. Second, not all pupils remained at school with no outside contact for the entire time they were registered. It was a reserve school; pupils' homes were readily accessible; parents could and did visit, despite being discouraged from doing so. Many pupils ran away and were returned. Others were claimed by their parents for periods of varying length, including holidays at some schools. At any of these points, students could contract disease from or spread disease to those at home on reserves. Third, when they left school, they returned to reserves often rife with malnutrition and disease. Fourth, it was common for boys to leave school by age twelve, so they had several years after leaving school in which to contract fatal diseases and die "before adulthood." Thus, the schools are by no means the whole story with respect to the prevailing mortality rates. They are perhaps better viewed as part of a feedback loop of disease in Indian communities. Some parents brought their children home when they became ill at school, while others only sent their children to school when they became ill at home, apparently in hope that they might be better fed and nursed back to health while away.[79] Yet another consideration is that the time the children spent in school often was quite limited. In the case of the Tsuu T'ina school cited above, boys evidently spent on average less than two years in school during the period in question, though girls stayed somewhat longer.[80] It seems unlikely that the high mortality rate can be attributed entirely to their short time in school. How far such attendance figures can be generalized is uncertain, but it is not unreasonable to suppose that similar conditions prevailed on many Alberta reserves.

When Bryce's reports generated controversy about the schools in the years after 1905, school and church officials tended to either dismiss or attempt to explain away criticism. Proposals to close schools which Bryce contended fomented disease were met with anger from these officials, and with finger pointing – particularly to inadequate government funding, bad reserve conditions, and Indians' alleged susceptibility to whites' diseases.[81] The denominations had invested much human, spiritual, emotional, and financial capital in the educational and missionary endeavour over several decades, and had become vested interests.

CONCLUSION

When the government negotiators agreed to the medical and health provisions in Treaty 6, they had no idea how the terms would be interpreted
within just a few years. They imagined the government could guide
Indians through a short transitional period on the reserves that would
enable them to function fully as self-supporting individuals in wider
society. They would feed themselves in a reliable, healthy, and balanced
manner, similarly to white farmers of the day. If all went well, outbreaks
of pestilence and famine would be rare, and perhaps things of the past.
The policy embodied in the Indian Act envisaged reserves and extended
families as the levels at which everyday health issues would be addressed,
as municipalities and families were in white society. In this task, the
medicine chest and professional medical assistance when available
would help Indians address problems that could not be managed individually or locally.

The reality was much different. For a variety of reasons, life on reserves
or in boarding and industrial schools generated high rates of disease and
mortality. The government soon found that famine relief was not emergency relief but an ongoing necessary and regular obligation. Even when
the government tried to cut rations, it faced a continuing expectation
that it would feed the elderly, orphaned, disabled, and sick. Health crises
were no longer rare and exceptional.

In the late nineteenth century, the developing understanding of how
disease spread created not only hope for dealing with problems more
effectively, but also new expectations of what the government could and
must do about them. Whether on reserves or in the wider society, the rise
of the public health movement demanded a leadership role for, and
extensive intervention by, government and professionals. This in turn
heightened the tendency to look down on traditional practices, dismissed
as folk medicine, and the determination to replace them with "scientific
medicine."[82]

As with agriculture and education, Indians did not have a unified
response to federal health initiatives. Not all wanted – and some resisted
– modern medical practices, whether smallpox vaccination, hospitals, or
medications. Many preferred traditional healing practices, which could
be fairly effective, and – significantly – were culturally understood. They
would often choose either, or both, Western and traditional medicine, as
it suited them. Interventionist Western practices were often insensitive to

patient needs or wishes, and carried inferences of moral disapproval of Indian ways. With the best intentions, officials expected that "nursing matrons on the reserves and in the hospitals" had duties beyond caring for the sick, to teaching "Indian women and children the basics of home-making and moral living, both seen as important to overall health." Patients were isolated, which both tore them from their families and their communities and led to indoctrination about how to live "cleaner and purer lives" when recovered. Despite their humane purposes, it often seemed as if federal and medical officials could not help but create an aura of cultural critique in health care.[83]

The government's response to the ongoing health crisis was half-hearted, though it certainly changed over time. It is best comprehended in the context first of the government's reactive approach at the time of the treaties, and second of the spread and transformation of active and mandated public health measures in the succeeding decades. To these latter measures, reaction of both whites and Indians was decidedly mixed. The federal government was slower than Ontario in taking up public health measures, but it did not lag as far behind as some of the provinces. It nevertheless worsened the health crisis by contributing to malnourishment through the limited, unbalanced diet in its relief pro-grams, through attempts to coerce Indians by cutting back rations, and by failing to give boarding schools the funds to adequately feed and clothe pupils. It did not insist on its specified better school health mea-sures, and mishandled isolation for pupils with contagious disease by acting with cultural disregard and inadequate funding. It told Indians they should build better, bigger, well-ventilated homes, but provided lim-ited encouragement and direction to do so. Officials' outlook seems to have been constrained by the workhouse and self-help mentality, as well as pressure to contain costs.

The mortality and morbidity rates of the last two decades of the nine-teenth century may have marked a low point in Indian health, "the direct result," in Daschuk's opinion, "of economic and cultural suppression."[84] Yet it is by no means clear that new practices and more professionals in Indian health care, and the advent of public health advocates like Bryce, who publicized the shortcomings of the system, resulted in improvement in the early twentieth century. One study claims that Indian health con-tinued to worsen until the 1940s, after which mortality rates began to decline somewhat. However, while epidemic disease declined, it gave way to chronic disease: cardiovascular and pulmonary disease, arthritis, obesity, and diabetes rates remain unacceptably high among Canada's

Indian population. So does the mortality rate. Infectious diseases also remain far more prevalent among Canada's Indians than among the general population.[85] Others have looked to racism, colonialism, unemployment, and underemployment as at least partial explanations,[86] but the linkages are not entirely persuasive.

Recent studies by anthropologists suggest "indigenous groups [anywhere in the world] get into trouble when they abandon their traditional diets and active lifestyles for Western living." Indians had adapted physiologically over time to a particular diet and lifestyle. Assumptions that they would have had health conditions similar to whites if the average white diet had been available in sufficient quantity and balance may thus be somewhat flawed, even simplistic.[87]

One of the ironies of the situation is that Indians only agreed to the treaties on the understanding that they would be able to continue their traditional hunting and gathering lifestyle. (The government agreed, subject to certain conditions.) It may be that their health would have been better had they been able to do so to a greater extent. The matter of the evolving limitations upon that lifestyle is the subject of the next chapter.

# 8

# Indians' Hunting and Fishing Rights

Despite all the public attention given in recent decades to Native peoples' lands disputes and the unhappy legacy of boarding schools, no topic has been the focus of more litigation than hunting and fishing rights. According to one study, in the 1990s alone, there were eighty hunting cases and seventy-three fishing cases reported in Canadian courts, and many more in lower courts were likely left unreported. Eighty-two of these cases went to appeal, and eleven reached the Supreme Court of Canada.[1] The constitutionalization of Indian treaty rights, including hunting and fishing, in the 1980s contributed to increased litigation, not least because provinces sought to defend their constitutional right to regulate hunting and fishing, environmentalists sought to limit these activities, and sport and business interests sought to prevent the curtailment of what they perceived as their rights.[2] Native people are more assertive about their rights now that they are grounded in the constitution, but the frequency of legal recourse also reflects the difficulty governments have in determining their jurisdiction and duty within a context of shifting social attitudes, varying political pressures, and evolving messages from the courts. Furthermore, the gestation of the issues before the courts in the contemporary era largely occurred in the nineteenth century. Matters affecting hunting and fishing rights in the district of Alberta to 1905 shed some light on this process.

The Robinson Superior and Robinson Huron Treaties of 1850 established that Indians would be allowed "the full and free privilege to hunt over the territory now ceded by them, and to fish in the waters thereof as they have heretofore been in the habit of doing," except for lands sold · or leased under the law of the province of Canada.[3] In explaining this provision, Commissioner W.B. Robinson commented that, having been granted reserves and the right to hunt and fish, Indians could not claim the government had taken away their traditional means of supporting themselves, and therefore would have no claim to additional support.[4] The expectation that permitting Indians to continue to subsist at least partially through their traditional hunting and gathering, and thus not become public charges, would be important in subsequent treaties. It also reflected Indians' desire to retain their traditional patterns of living for as long as possible.

Hunting and fishing rights were not included in the written text of Treaties 1 and 2, but Lieutenant Governor Adams Archibald acknowledged during the negotiations that much of the land to be surrendered was likely unsuited to agriculture and noted, "till these lands are needed for use you will be free to hunt over them, and make all the use of them which you have made in the past."[5] Indians had raised the issue of maintaining their traditional lifestyle, Archibald had made an oral promise, and a provision along these lines was added to each of the subsequent numbered treaties of the 1870s.

Lieutenant Governor Alexander Morris reported that the Indians at the Treaty 6 negotiations feared "they would be compelled to live on the reserve wholly, and abandon their hunting" outside the reserve, as had been the case in the United States. He quickly reassured them. The treaty provided that "said Indians, shall have right to pursue their avocations of hunting and fishing throughout the tract surrendered ... subject to such regulations as may from time to time be made by Government of her Dominion of Canada," except for lands required for settlement, mining, lumbering, or other purposes. Although it omitted fishing, the article in Treaty 7 was the same.[6] However, the context of the Treaty 7 negotiations was rather different, because a few months earlier the territorial government had legislated restrictions on bison hunting, which Indian Commissioner David Laird noted in his opening remarks at the treaty negotiation. The Indians likely objected to the new law, as at the next meeting he assured them that it was their "privilege to hunt all over the prairies," provided "they did not molest settlers and others in the country."[7] To the Indian population of the region, such a clause was a sine qua non of any treaty – which is not to say both sides understood it in the same way.

Plainly, the government intended the treaty provision to persuade Indians that the adjustment to reserve life would be gradual; that hunting, fishing, and gathering would be permitted so long as the land was not required for other purposes; and that these practices would be regulated. It seems clear, as noted in the Robinson treaty cases, that the provision was also intended to minimize the need to issue rations during the transition to self-sufficiency.[8] Both sides fervently hoped that resources – animals, birds, fish, and plants – would be plentiful. In the 1870s, neither fully realized how quickly white settlement in the prairie region would alter, or complicate access to, the seemingly vast traditional hunting and fishing areas, or how inadequate resources would prove to be to meet the unprecedented demand following the demise of the bison.

Nor did the two sides realize the extent to which their perspectives on resources and their management differed.[9] Federal officials believed they had made a promise with limitations: the right to hunt and fish off reserve in the traditional manner, subject to government regulation and not on land needed for white use. They likely intended it to support Indians during the transition to a settled life, and to gradually diminish in importance thereafter. Indians, by contrast, believed they had received a promise of a perpetual, perhaps untrammelled, right to hunt, fish, gather, and trap, supplemented by whatever they could produce from their reserve lands. Officials appear to have thought the right meant hunting and fishing for personal or band nutritional needs. At least some Indians thought the right included a commercial component, as they had traded or sold meat, fish, berries, and other products to white and Metis customers for many years before the treaties.

The first attempt to regulate hunting on the prairies was the abortive ordinance of the North-West Territories Council in 1877 to curtail the bison hunt.[10] Indians of the central and western prairies, as well as missionaries, Hudson's Bay Company officials, and the North-West Mounted Police, had demanded a measure along these lines for some years. As with so many issues, it was not a straightforward matter. Under the Canadian constitution, regulations for hunting game fell to the provinces. The federal government had ultimate authority in the North-West Territories until 1905, but in 1875 it had passed the North-West Territories Act, under which in October 1876 it appointed a local government known as the North-West Territories Council. The federal government devolved to this council responsibility for regulating the bison hunt, a matter ideally informed and shaped by local expertise. The council did so in March 1877, having consulted extensively with interested whites and Metis, but apparently not with Indians. However, hunting and fishing rights were part of the treaty agreement between Indians and the federal government; it was questionable whether the power to regulate Indians in this respect could simply be passed off unilaterally by the government to the council.[11]

In any event, under the 1877 ordinance, mass slaughter of bison was prohibited, as was hunting them for sport or for "their tongues, choice cuts or peltries." A closed season on cows was imposed from 15 November to 14 August, along with an absolute prohibition on killing calves under two years of age. Indians, both treaty and non-treaty, were exempt from the regulations between 15 November and 14 February, as was any person "in circumstances of pressing necessity" who needed to "satisfy his immediate wants." Opposition to the measure from Metis bison hunters was immediate,[12] while Indians were divided. Native people had advocated for hunting restrictions since the early 1870s, so the government probably thought they would support the legislation. What officials apparently did not understand was that Indians very likely wanted restrictions on commercial and sport hunting by others, not on their own ability to hunt. The case demonstrates well-intentioned legislation passed without sufficient consultation with all significant stakeholders and without the preparatory groundwork for acceptance.[13] Whether it was this opposition that led to repeal of the ordinance in 1878 is unclear, and indeed is a moot point: all ordinances passed by the first council in 1877 were found to be inoperative due to ineptitude in wording of the North-West Territories Act.[14] By the time any compromise successor legislation might have been proposed, it was far too late. By 1879, bison in Canada were all but extinct and other game animals were increasingly scarce.

When in 1883 the territorial government passed an ordinance to regulate and restrict hunting in general, it exempted treaty Indians hunting for personal rather than commercial purposes. By then, authorities had concluded that the local government did not have the power to restrict Indians' treaty rights to hunt.[15] Traditional hunting provided food, clothing, shelter, and tools. It also had a deep cultural and religious significance: game animals were given by the Creator, and also had spirits with which one might relate. Finally, Indians had also traditionally used the fruits of hunting, fishing, and gathering to barter or trade for other goods, although this now was forbidden under the ordinance.[16] Whether justifiably or not, many settlers believed Indians abused their "privileges" (treaty rights) and overhunted. Settlers often expected to be able to supplement their diets by hunting, and resented the Indian exemptions. The rather elitist sport-hunting community also opposed traditional Indian hunting, as well as anyone who commercialized the sale of game (for example, meat or trophy heads), or who killed female or young animals, as Indian hunters allegedly did.[17] In 1889, responding to a public climate that was increasingly hostile toward Indian advantage with respect to hunting, the territorial legislature repealed the exemption. The federal government promptly disallowed that change – a formal, if belated, recognition that under the treaties only the Government of Canada could legislate restrictions on Indian hunting.[18]

Any appearance of a victory for Indian hunting rights was short lived. In 1890, the federal government, without discussion with treaty Indians, amended the Indian Act to permit the superintendent general of Indian Affairs to declare that Indians identified by the government would be subject to provincial or territorial game laws when hunting off reserve.[19] The legislation occasioned not a word of debate as it passed through the House of Commons.[20] Any animals or birds on a reserve could be killed at any time for food or personal, but not commercial, use. Provincial and territorial authorities had pressed for the implementation of this legislation, as had fish and game associations and rod and gun clubs from Calgary, Lethbridge, Edmonton, Red Deer, and Fort Macleod. They accused Indians of the reckless slaughter of game and of taking eggs and killing young birds, and claimed their own interest was "the protection of game." Lawrence Vankoughnet, the deputy superintendent general, told his minister that "while alleging that they have no wish to interfere with any Treaty rights of the Indians," these groups really desired that Indian hunters be "placed on the same footing as white hunters." In fact, lobbyists proposed that the government should restrict Indians to their reserves during the hunting season – so much for equal footing. From Indians' perspective, the federal government was caving in to pressure to criminalize their traditional way of life, which, as they saw it, the treaties had guaranteed.[21] Effective 1 January 1894, the federal government placed many territorial Indians under the jurisdiction of territorial game laws; in the district of Alberta, affected bands included the Michel and Enoch la Potac bands in the Edmonton agency, all bands in the Hobbema agency, and the Tsuu T'ina, Siksika, Piikani, and Kainai. A year later, the Stoney Nakoda of Treaty 7 were added, delayed only because they were active hunters and officials had feared their response. The remaining bands in the Edmonton and Saddle Lake agencies were added effective 1 July 1903.[22]

The most intense white agitation about Native hunting was directed at the Stoney Nakoda – not because they depended more on hunting than did other bands, but because they were highly skilled hunters whose interests conflicted most directly with those of sport hunters, and of conservationists in and around the Rocky Mountains National Park. From their base in the Bow River Valley, the Stoney Nakoda traditionally ranged as far west as Golden, British Columbia, south as far as Crowsnest Pass, into the Kananaskis and foothills country, and north to the Kootenay Plains. This was the prime area that attracted rich big-game trophy hunters from eastern Canada, the United States, Britain, and Europe, and they and local outfitters found that the Indians were serious competition. They alleged that the Stoney Nakoda harvested mountain sheep to sell trophy heads to tourists or, just as bad (though inconsistent with previously expressed concerns), that they were eating the sheep and leaving the salable heads to rot. They were said to hunt on horseback, in a crowd, with dogs – as if whites did not. James Brewster, a Banff outfitter, claimed in 1905 that the Indians shot animals indiscriminately, while a colleague, Philip Moore, added colourfully that "an Indian of the Stoney tribe is an incomparable hunter, patient & tireless & they seldom miss a shot ... They clean the country like a rake."[23] Although the DIA concluded that most of the propaganda was misinformation and exaggeration, it backed away from what it believed would be a losing battle to try to counter it publicly.

Indians objected to the new policy as an infringement on their treaty right to hunt and gather. The government maintained that the restrictions were in their best interests, that officials at the treaties had insisted on the government's right to regulate hunting, and that hunting exemptions for Indians were no longer tenable. The government not only placed the Stoney Nakoda under territorial game laws in 1895, but also directed the NWMP to enforce the hunting and trapping ordinances within the boundaries of the Rocky Mountains National Park.

In 1902, the government complicated the situation by expanding the national park's boundaries.[24] This pleased a growing legion of alpinists, tourists and associated businesses, and sport hunters, and was thought essential to manage the eastern Rockies' watershed that was vital to the ranches, farms, irrigation projects, and growing towns and cities downstream.[25] As before, the affected Stoney Nakoda were simply informed of the change. From a legal perspective, as the government interpreted the treaties, consultation was unnecessary: the affected area was Crown land outside of the Stoney Nakoda reserve. The situation, however, was not so simple. As noted previously, the government had accepted that the reserve was mostly unsuited to agriculture, and much of it was not even high-grade grazing land. In the 1880s and 1890s, it had encouraged the

Stoney Nakoda to exercise their treaty right to hunt in their traditional areas because doing so was one way they could sustain themselves and incur less of a welfare burden. Enclosing much of the traditional hunting grounds within a national park gave more clout to those who opposed Stoney Nakoda hunters. In 1904, the park superintendent, Howard Douglas, complained that the Stoney Nakoda ignored territorial law and closed seasons. Soon, he predicted, "this vast tract of mountain land, abounding in all that is required for the sustenance of wild animals, will be deserted, unless the Indians are compelled to remain on their reserves. Laws are of no use unless they are enforced." But he was aware of the sensitivity of the situation: "We need to apply the laws more forcibly than we have, without creating any adverse sentiment."[26] That was a conundrum for the government, but with public sentiment behind total closure of the park to hunting, pressure on the Stoney Nakoda was about to increase. Those who wanted to curtail the Stoney Nakoda from hunting in the region further argued that doing so would hasten their settling and assimilation.[27]

Also complicating the issue was the fact that since 1889 the Stoney Nakoda had been pressing a case with Ottawa to expand their reserve. In the 1890s, Indian Commissioner A.E. Forget had accepted their request for fifty-five additional square miles. However, the DIA needed the approval of the Department of the Interior, which controlled the land in question, and the case was lost in bureaucratic red tape until it was renewed in 1901 with Laird's encouragement. However, much of the best land near the reserve was tied up in grazing leases granted to influential ranchers, and the park's new boundaries in 1902 enclosed most of the remaining land that might have been suitable to meet the Stoney Nakoda claim.[28]

There also is the question of fisheries. Though a relatively marginal matter for most Indians in Treaty 7, fisheries were of considerable importance for those in Treaty 6, where freshwater fish constituted an important part of many bands' diet. The Constitution Act, 1867 gave exclusive control of fisheries, oceanic and inland, to the federal government, where it remained until 1930.[29] The question thus fell under the jurisdiction of the Department of Marine and Fisheries, which was far less inclined than the DIA to consider Indians' rights. The DIA argued that some waters ought to be set aside exclusively for Indians, and that they should be exempt from Marine and Fisheries regulations. Hayter Reed commented in 1889 that it was wrong that "grumbling on the part of a few local white and half-breed fishermen should be allowed to affect the

question of keeping faith with the Indians with regard to Treaty stipulations, or to interfere with their contributing towards their own support
and to a corresponding extent relieving the whole country of the burden
of their maintenance, when nothing of graver impact than a license fee is
in question."[30]

Both sides had some valid points. The DIA understood that not only
did Indians under the treaties have, and insist upon, a right to use fisheries "for their own consumption, sale and barter" (if subject to government regulations), but that under the Indian Act they were to be free
from taxation, which included license fees. At the same time, Marine and
Fisheries noted that overfishing of some waters by Indians and Metis, as
well as whites, had led to severe depletion of the stocks; hence the desir-
ability of regulation. Shortages of fish, as well as game shortages, were
noted a number of times in Indian agents' annual reports in the 1880s
and 1890s.

A major concern was that Indian fishers allegedly took large quantities
of whitefish and other stock when the fish came to shallow waters near
shore to spawn, thus severely impairing the reproductive cycle. Marine
and Fisheries officials tried to impose a closed season, but did not have
the personnel to enforce it with any consistency, and Indians resisted the
regulations in any event. The department achieved more success by prohibiting the sale of fish taken during the closed season to non-Natives,
which resulted in a somewhat reduced take. The inspector of fisheries for
Manitoba and the North-West Territories, Alexander McQueen, noted
in his report for 1890:

Indians have been deluded into the idea that they had a legal right,
under treaty stipulations, to fish during the close season; but a late
decision of the Department of Justice has set this matter at rest.
The Minister [of Justice], after fully reciting the terms of the several treaties, concludes by saying: "The regulations are binding
upon the Indians there to the same extent as they are binding upon
the other subjects of Her Majesty. The close seasons, created by the
regulations, apply to the Indians, subject to the proviso contained
in section 5 of the [Fisheries] Act [1889]; and the Indians have no
right of fishing without license or during the spawning season, or
on the spawning grounds, as provided for by that section."

McQueen went on to suggest that an immediate full imposition of the
regulations might cause "privation and trouble," and recommended a

gradual implementation in which the government would allow fishing for personal consumption, provide equipment to encourage fishing in deeper waters, and educate Indians about "the necessity of protecting the fish in their own interest."[31] Marine and Fisheries did step up enforcement, appointing a separate inspector of fisheries for the territories, F.C. Gilchrist, in 1891, along with the aid of the NWMP. By 1892 the department added overseers of fisheries, which in practice meant double duty for forest rangers, homestead inspectors, and at least one Indian agent (at Peace Hills), whose task included destroying fixed nets and weirs that were placed out of season or were otherwise illegal.

The catch in the North-West Territories was much greater than most people have since realized. From July 1891 to June 1892, for example, it amounted to just under 20 million pounds, including almost 11.5 million of whitefish and eight million of pike. The recommended daily fish ration for Indians was four per man, two per woman, one per child, and two per dog. The total take of whitefish was 190,000 pounds at Lac Ste Anne and White Whale Lake (Wabamun), and 120,000 pounds at Pigeon Lake.[32] Still, the restrictions proved controversial and created hardship. The catch in 1892 was the largest for some years, as enforced regulations lessened takes.

Superintendent General T. Mayne Daly suggested in 1894 that free licenses be issued to the affected Indians that would restrict fishing during the closed season to those who had no other means to support themselves, for their own consumption only. Better to allow them to feed themselves, opined Daly, than to incur the expense of the government having to feed them, which would "confirm them in the most pernicious habit of dependence upon the Government."[33] That year, as a result of this negotiation, free licenses were issued to a number of agencies, including Edmonton and Hobbema. Under these licenses, some Indians profited from sale of fish to whites. In 1895, Marine and Fisheries returned to a more restrictive approach, issuing free licenses for domestic consumption only.

Additional factors beyond government regulations affected the take of fish. By the mid-1890s, for example, Marine and Fisheries was perplexed about a massive die-off of fish in Whitefish Lake and Saddle Lake in Alberta, and at other locations in Saskatchewan and Assiniboia; after investigation, it appeared that the situation was at least partly due to a prolonged period of severe drought that lowered water levels beyond anything in memory. In southern Alberta, to cite another case, construction of irrigation works "brought the trout face to face with a new and serious danger." Although the government passed legislation to require fishways and other alterations to benefit the fish, the irrigation lobby succeeded in having it suspended. If action were not taken, warned the department, "the ground fisheries of the mountain streams ... will be entirely ruined."[34] Fish were always a minor, though not entirely negligible, part of the Indian diet in the region, so problems had a less severe impact than in Treaty 6.

What can be concluded about this tangled topic of hunting and fishing rights? As with other aspects of the treaties, each side had its own impression of what they had agreed to, mainly because of differing cultural perceptions and imperfect linguistic comprehension. On the Indian side, the memories of elders in the late twentieth century were consistent. Lazarus Roan, of Treaty 6, claimed that in the treaty negotiations, "not one animal was given to the white man, not one piece of timber was given to the white man, not even the grass." John Buffalo of the Ermineskin reserve contended that only arable land was to be alienated to whites, and they "were not to take the game animals, the timber, nor the big lakes – that was for the Indians' means of survival." He believed that the whites had stated, "we are not taking your animals," but had gone on to profit from the sale of hunting and fishing licenses: "They make money from these; that is not what they promised us; those are things they took right out of our hands."[35] Lazarus Wesley of the Stoney Nakoda stated that in 1877 the government had said, "the fish and buffalo are ours ... our major right was to hunt but we lost that right." The editors of a major book on Treaty 7 state: "All of the bands that accepted the treaty thought they would be able to continue 'to use' all of the territory on which they had traditionally lived by hunting and fishing."[36] On the government side, a reasonable reading of the English-language treaty texts, and of the negotiators' recorded oral comments, reflect officials' effort to make it clear that Indians' right to hunt and fish was conditional: as lands were settled, or used for mining or harvesting timber, they would no longer be available to Indian hunters. The negotiators consistently stated that Indian hunting and fishing would be subject to government regulation. It appears that this did not register with most Indians. Underlying both these positions, of course, was the fact that Indians hoped they could maintain their traditional lifestyle in some form indefinitely, while the government hoped it would be replaced sooner than later.[37]

There is another major line of argument on this subject: the moral and legal responsibility of the Canadian government for Indians. That is, by imposing a dependency or wardship status on Indians, a status that pre-dated the treaties under British-Canadian law, the government (and all Canadians) also took on some responsibility for their welfare. This rela-tionship is partially defined in, but is not limited by, the provisions of the treaties. Notes Dale Gibson in a private communication, "Even if there had been no bad faith and no negligence on the part of its representa-tives, the Government of Canada was caught in a massive conflict of interest between its role as negotiator for non-Aboriginal Canadians and its *legally enforceable* fiduciary duty toward its Aboriginal wards." This conflict of interest appears as much in the development of policy with respect to hunting and fishing rights, as in any area of administration of Indian affairs. The government is obligated to fulfil promises undertaken in the treaties, and these promises – at least since 1982 – are held to be constitutionally guaranteed and not merely amendable contractual obli-gations. But in a wardship relationship, in which Indians were legally regarded as minors, the government also had no requirement to negoti-ate with the minors about actions taken on their behalf (and generally it did not on most matters in the period under study). Yet it seems clear that the fiduciary-like obligation to promote or act in Indians' best inter-ests often lost out in matters of hunting and fishing rights to the interests of the more powerful white community, at least in the late nineteenth century. More recently, constitutionally guaranteed Indian rights have been held to have primacy over the rights and interests of commerce or white individuals.[38] This position has been fully developed mainly since the entrenchment of Indian rights in the 1982 constitution and in a series of subsequent court decisions. It explains little, however, of how matters were understood prior to 1905, when Indians' best interests seem to have been defined rather differently.

Brian Calliou argues that the law of 1890, which permitted delegation of federal powers or responsibilities concerning traditional Indian hunt-ing and fishing to lower levels of government, amounted to an abroga-tion of the "constitutional obligation to look out for the interests" of the Indian beneficiaries. This amounted to a breach of "fiduciary-like duties."[39] Note that provincial jurisdiction over natural resources, including wildlife, was upheld by the courts in 1886. In addition, the *St Catharine's Milling and Timber* ruling of 1887 appeared to weaken Indian rights with respect to resources as well as land, and probably encouraged the government to take a harder line on Indian issues. It is true that the territories did not have provincial status and remained under federal jurisdiction, but the federal government chose to leave such matters to the local government, at least partly because there was a growing demand from influential whites to restrict Indian rights. To supporters of Indian rights, this shows that federal authorities lacked the spine to insist upon the primacy of Indians' treaty rights. Apparently, fairness and the interests of dependent Indians were thought to be found in treating them as one of many roughly equal interest groups. From the perspective of the federal authorities in the 1890s, there was a kind of stand off: an acknowledged federal moral, legal, and constitutional responsibility for Indians ran up against a confirmed provincial constitutional power (to legislate concerning wildlife), which the federal government, for political reasons, assigned to the territorial government. The federal government was not willing to assert its authority in the territories and override local legislation on behalf of its wards. Not until 1932 were Indian rights successfully asserted in the courts.[40]

From one perspective, the federal government had an obligation under the treaties to ensure that Indians would have primacy in exploiting fish and game resources. Calliou contends that, notwithstanding territorial and later provincial game laws, responsibility to uphold Indian interests fell to the federal government, and treaties were entered into "under which they were assured that their traditional livelihoods would be protected." The federal government's unilateral delegation of powers to regulate Indian hunting and fishing to the territorial and provincial governments impaired Indians' ability "to exercise their rights promised by the Queen's representatives."[41]

This argument can only be sustained if it can be shown that the federal government promised in the treaties, or negotiations, to protect Indians' traditional way of life. In Treaties 1 to 7, it did not.[42] It intended Indians to give up their traditional lifestyle. It encouraged hunting and fishing in the interim mainly for economy – ammunition and fishing gear were cheaper than rations.[43] It only promised freedom to continue to hunt and fish as long as whites did not otherwise require lands outside the reserves. It made no promise to give primacy to Indian hunters and fishers except on reserve lands, where the right was exclusive. As seen, from the arrival of the NWMP in 1874, the old commons with its privileged or priority access was lost, replaced by a policy of equal access for all. Under the treaties, the federal government retained the power to regulate off-reserve hunting and fishing; arguably, it chose to regulate by accepting that territorial game laws applied to Indians, thereby treating them equally under the law. Arguably, regulation was needed to preserve the very resources to which Indians wanted access. Furthermore, federal

officials believed that hunting, fishing, and gathering reinforced the traditional values and lifestyles that federal policy aimed to replace; therefore, limiting those practices would encourage adaptation to agriculture
and a settled lifestyle that were deemed to be in Indians' best long-term
interests. In that sense, the federal government believed it was fulfilling,
not failing, its moral and legal responsibility. In delegating powers to
the territorial government, it applied the principle that everyone should
be regulated equally under the law with respect to fish and game management; it was not thereby derogating from its responsibility under
the treaties.[44]

It now remains to look more broadly at the ways in which the government sought to impose Canadian law and justice upon Native peoples in
the West, and at Native peoples' response.

# The Queen's Law:
# Indians, the North-West Mounted Police,
# and the Justice System

In recent years, the North-West Mounted Police and the courts have been portrayed as perpetrators of a series of heinous or irresponsible criminal acts carried out against prairie Native peoples.[1] Doubtless those who implemented Canada's Indian policies would be appalled to learn of how their actions and motives have been construed. While some incidents and aspects of policy certainly merit condemnation, arguably, taken as a whole, the record was rather mixed.

Only a decade after the North-West Rebellion, the NWMP and many whites remained skittish about the potential for Native unrest. Resentment lay close to the surface in many Native communities. They vividly remembered their treatment in 1885, to say nothing of the post-rebellion hard line the government took and the NWMP enforced. Disease, starvation, and abusive attitudes by some authorities persisted on reserves and in schools.

Yet circumstances had dramatically changed over that same decade. Increased white settlement in the district of Alberta resulted in Indians becoming a distinct minority, making open resistance seem futile, if not self-defeating. Moreover, the police were not viewed by Indians only as agents of repression – they often negotiated space for Indians when the government and the public wanted strict policies, and were frequently more inclined than Department of Indian Affairs officials to work with them. Many bands had at least a residue of respect for the NWMP. All this is illustrated by a conjunction of three tragic episodes in the mid-1890s, a useful starting point to assess the evolving relationship of the police, justice system, and Indians.

The first incident occurred at the south camp of the Siksika reserve on 4 April 1895, when Scraping High murdered Frank Skynner, issuer of rations, at the latter's home. The details of the story vary, but all accounts agree that Scraping High was distraught over his only son's illness and death, possibly a result of disease contracted at school. He had desperately sought extra rations for his seriously ill child, only to be rudely refused by Skynner. After killing Skynner, he fled into the bush where police and other Indians tracked him down. He resisted arrest, fired at his pursuers, and finally was himself shot.[2]

The second incident began in October 1895 in the district of Saskatchewan, when Sgt Colin Colebrook arrested Kitchi-Manito-Waya (Almighty Voice) for killing a steer owned by a settler. (Kitchi-Manito-Waya claimed, according to some accounts, that his father owned the steer.) He escaped from the Duck Lake prison, but Colebrook tracked him down. Kitchi-Manito-Waya warned Colebrook to back off or he would shoot, and when the officer approached he shot him through the heart and once again escaped. Occurring only a decade after the North-West Rebellion, and following many signs of Indian dissatisfaction with restrictive government policies, these incidents caused many people to believe that the region was on the brink of a widespread Native uprising.[3]

Kitchi-Manito-Waya was still evading capture, almost certainly with the aid of sympathetic Indians and Metis, when the third incident occurred on the Kainai reserve in Alberta. Si'k-Okskitsis (Charcoal) murdered Nina'msko'taput-sikumi (Medicine Pipe or Medicine Pipe Man) on 30 September 1896 for conducting an affair with his wife Anu'-tsis-tsis-aki (Pretty Wolverine Woman). Being cuckolded in any society is humiliating, but Nina'msko'taput-sikumi taunted Si'k-Okskitsis, believing he would not do anything about it. On top of everything, Nina'msko'taput-sikumi and Anu'tsis'tsis'aki were cousins, and their affair violated a strong social taboo. Having caught the pair *in flagrante delicto*, Si'k-Okskitsis executed his tormentor with a rifle shot through the eye. Under traditional Kainai customs he would have been a hero for this act, but he was now under the Queen's law. He thus believed that, when caught, he would likely be executed for murder.

Yet Si'k-Okskitsis also perceived the situation through the traditional belief system of the Kainai. According to Hugh Dempsey, in preparation for his coming death, he desired "to kill an important person whose spirit would announce his coming, and then kill Pretty Wolverine Woman and himself so that their spirits would travel together and she would eternally be his slave."[4] He initially proved inept at this, failing to locate and kill Mékaisto (or any important chief) and shooting but only slightly wounding a white farm instructor, Edward McNeill. The NWMP, under Superintendent Sam Steele, tracked down and surrounded Si'k-Okskitsis and his wives, mother-in-law, and children (all of whom he had forced to accompany him) on the Kainai timber limit near the United States border. But Si'k-Okskitsis and most of his family slipped through the cordon and escaped on stolen NWMP horses. In fact, despite being seriously ill with tuberculosis and frequently near starvation, Si'k-Okskitsis eluded the NWMP and Indian scouts at least five times in ensuing weeks. Eventually the family was able to get away from him, and he headed alone toward the Piikani reserve. NWMP officer W.B. Wilde followed, and Si'k-Okskitsis shot him and escaped on his horse. Having killed his "important person," he had only now to execute his wife and then himself.[5] He returned to the Kainai reserve, and was betrayed by his brothers (who had been pressured by the NWMP) and captured; he tried to commit suicide in custody, but failed. He was convicted of murder, and was hanged in March 1897.[6]

In May 1897, Kitchi-Manito-Waya and two companions were finally tracked down near the One Arrow reserve in Saskatchewan. They managed to seriously wound an incautious inspector and a sergeant, and killed another officer and a civilian special constable. Eventually, the police brought in heavy field guns and pounded the Native position until Kitchi-Manito-Waya and his companions were dead.[7]

The deaths of Si'k-Okskitsis and Kitchi-Manito-Waya in 1897 enabled Western society – whites, NWMP, and, interestingly, most Indians – to heave a sigh of relief, though not for the same reasons. By most accounts, whether viewed as criminal or aberrant, Scraping High, Si'k-Okskitsis, and Kiktchi-Manito-Waya were seen as dangerously disturbing individuals, though each had some local or family support. The police and whites generally viewed Indians, both individually and as a society, as at best semi-civilized and susceptible to reverting to their "wild nature." They feared that the actions of a criminal few might incite the unstable many.[8] The longer the criminals eluded arrest, and the more their would-be captors demonstrated ineptitude in the pursuit, the more rebellion seemed possible. The public viewed the NWMP's power as lying in its record of apprehending criminals quickly and maintaining order; the longer criminals remained at large, the more the force's reputation would be undermined. It is scarcely surprising, therefore, that the force attempted to cover up the most embarrassing aspects of the bungled affairs.[9]

It seems possible, for example, that the original charges against Kitchi-Manito-Waya concerning cattle killing would not have stood up in court. Accounts differ widely concerning who owned the steer in question. While in custody, Kitchi-Manito-Waya may have been frightened by a police officer telling him he could be hanged if convicted of cattle killing, and so he escaped through a unlocked prison door. John Jennings explains Kitchi-Manito-Waya's anxiety to escape custody somewhat differently: his grandfather's health had been seriously compromised during incarceration following the North-West Rebellion, and his father had been jailed for six months' hard labour for theft only days before Kitchi-Manito-Waya killed the cow. Jennings believes that his last stand symbolized "protest against the inevitability of the new era against the coercion of the Police and the Indian Department [and] against the systematic destruction of Indian culture."[10]

With respect to Si'k-Okskitsis, the police almost certainly could have captured him through negotiation without incident, but they fired on him first, let him slip through their lines with most of his family and escape on police horses, and approached him aggressively and incautiously. In both cases, preparation and a modicum of prudence could have avoided most of the casualties.

Going beyond the matter of police ineptitude, Dempsey argues Steele and Si'k-Okskitsis inhabited very different worlds and did not comprehend one another. Born in 1856, Si'k-Okskitsis grew up with the values of a horse-mounted bison-hunter/warrior culture, untrammelled by external boundaries and restrictions. These values did not translate well to the reserve, to agriculture, or to being dominated by whites, whether government officials or police officers. Equally important, he grew up in a world inhabited by spirits, incomprehensible to men such as Steele – the majesty of the British empire and of British law and order had no place for, or patience with, "superstition."[11]

But at least one other point of interest arises from these three incidents: in all of them, many Indians supported the police in seeking to apprehend the different suspects. Dempsey observes that Si'k-Oskitsis's fellow Kainai and Piikani were frightened by his behaviour (which they saw as possessed, unpredictable, and threatening), to the extent that they slept in apprehension and even left their small ranches to reside together in villages: "They did not like to feel so helpless and afraid, so when the chance came to put an end to Charcoal's freedom, the Bloods volunteered willingly. This was not done to please the Mounted Police, nor to help the white man; it was simply a matter of self-preservation. They did not hate Charcoal; they feared him for what he had become."[12]

Dempsey notes that the Piikani, also very much afraid, did not turn out in support of the search, so the self-preservation theory does not explain everything.[13] And there is more to it. For one thing, many of the Kainai who volunteered had worked for the NWMP in the past. For another, helping the police apprehend Indian criminals was a treaty obligation.[14] Dempsey further explains that Si'k-Okskitsis was part of the Choking band, composed of outsiders and disturbers among the Kainai who were tolerated but not much liked up to 1896.[15] They longed for the old days and ways, and did not readily accept that agriculture, ranching, and restriction were the future. The Kainai, like many Indians, thus were not united in their views of the police or of whites. These mixed views had a context well beyond the experience of 1885 and after.

## IMPOSING LAW AND JUSTICE

When the NWMP arrived in the western prairies in 1874, it (and, by extension, the Canadian government) assumed that one system of British-Canadian law applied equally to all, whether Indian, Metis, or white.[16] Its initial successes depended on its visible, equitable application. Because it worked mostly in Indians' immediate interests, they readily embraced it. Within a relatively short space of time, whiskey traders ceased to be a serious problem, battles between tribes ended, and the prairies became much safer.

The NWMP was initially given extraordinary powers, what Jennings terms "a legal tyranny." At first, officers had the power to arrest, prosecute, judge, and carry out any sentence; this changed for more serious crimes with the creation of the Supreme Court of the North-West Territories in 1886, but the police continued to dispose of significant numbers of minor cases through 1905.[17] Such powers could have been subject to great abuse, but they appear to have been exercised with fairness and restraint most of the time. Cases could be dealt with quickly and cheaply, without long stays in custody before trial and without the associated legal costs of lawyers and hearings and the like. Besides, Indians had little previous experience with the British legal system, and so had little framework for criticism. The system at first seemed more or less reasonable and effective, and so it was widely accepted.

The distribution of the NWMP in the early years indicates where trouble was anticipated, whether from liquor smugglers or from Indians themselves; it also reflects the larger, influential – and sometimes fearful

– white population in the south, the greater likelihood of interracial friction, and the resultant significant political pressure to have a police presence. In 1881, for example, all of the NWMP personnel in the future
district of Alberta were found in the Treaty 7 area, at Fort Macleod
(thirty-four), Blackfoot Crossing (fifteen), Calgary (eight), and the Kainai
reserve (two); more than ninety additional personnel were located at
Fort Walsh, just to the east. None was listed as centred in the western
section of Treaty 6.[18] By 1883, some twenty-six worked out of Fort
Saskatchewan, but 175 were in the south, mainly at Fort Macleod and
Calgary. By 1887, there were nearly 1,000 men in the NWMP; of these,
268 were in the Treaty 7 area and eighty-nine were at Fort Saskatchewan.
Finally, in 1905, there were forty-six working out of Fort Saskatchewan
and 166 in southern Alberta.[19] The NWMP was an active and regular
presence in the lives of the Indians of the Treaty 7 area, where detach-
ments were found on or near most reserves. By contrast, patrols were
much less frequent in the western portion of Treaty 6, where sometimes
the only visible police presence for Indians in a given year consisted of
officers attending the annuity payments.

The NWMP was the most visible, but by no means the only, means by
which justice was imposed on the prairie region. Shelley A.M. Gavigan,
in *Hunger, Horses, and Government Men*, demonstrates that the justice
system, although a serious imposition upon Indian cultures, was more
flexible and fair than it has often been represented to be, and indeed that
Indians took advantage of it to achieve their goals. She finds that the
police and the court system often mediated between the hard line advocated by politicians, senior DIA officials, and the public on the one hand,
and Indians on the other. Still, Sarah Carter contends that the Indian
residents of the plains deserve as much of the credit for strategies to
maintain the peace as do "the actions of a handful of police."[20]

How did the North-West Rebellion affect relations between police
and Indians? Blair Stonechild and Bill Waiser assert that, by 1885,
Indians had gone from respecting the NWMP to hating it.[21] Such may
have been the case in the district of Saskatchewan, but at least for the
Indians of Alberta, "hatred" appears to put the case rather too strongly.
A workable relationship had developed between Indians and police
because Indians perceived the NWMP as mostly fair in applying the law.
The police also employed Indians, because of their knowledge of the
land, languages, and local customs, in a variety of roles, which arguably
resulted in a measure of cooperation and mutual respect.[22] Certainly it
did not help that relationship when the police were expected to support

or enforce unpopular DIA policies, such as cutting back the rations to which many Indians believed they were entitled under the treaties when they were going hungry. As seen, white attitudes toward Indians hardened as a result of the North-West Rebellion and its troubling antecedents of Native unrest and confrontation with authorities. In these challenging circumstances, nevertheless, the NWMP sometimes buffered government officials' more extreme ideas about Indians; the government sometimes ignored some NWMP officers' more extreme ideas in turn; and sometimes the judicial system saved the situation. In the same manner, often moderate Indian leaders were able to ameliorate situations that radicals among them tried to exacerbate. Thus when crises arose, as in 1895–97, Indians and police could sometimes recognize a common interest and work together.[23]

How well did the system work to achieve justice and fairness? The Star Child case of 1881 is suggestive. In 1879, near Fort Walsh, NWMP Constable Marmaduke Graburn was murdered; the suspect was a young Indian named Star Child. It seems likely that after the murder Star Child had slipped into the United States with other Siksika, but when they returned to Canada in 1881 the NWMP heard first that he was with the Siksika, and then that he had gone to the Kainai reserve near Fort Macleod. He was armed, indicated that he would resist arrest, and was said to be strongly supported by other Indians. Two constables arrested him in May as some chiefs restrained his fellows, and he was brought to a jury trial in October, which was presided over by former NWMP Commissioner James F. Macleod, now a stipendiary magistrate, and Superintendent L.N.F. Crozier, who by virtue of his office was also a justice of the peace. The principal witness was an Indian who stated that Star Child had confessed to the crime, claiming that killing the officer was a reaction to being struck by the constable. But another witness apparently stated that boasting about such activities was common, and "that it was possible that Starchild, especially as he was only a boy, might have lied and said he killed Grayburn [sic]." After deliberating for twenty-four hours, the jury was not persuaded beyond a reasonable doubt that Star Child was guilty, and recommended acquittal. Commissioner A.G. Irvine commented in his annual report that Star Child, "as a matter of course, received a fair and impartial trial, such as is afforded to the humblest of Her Majesty's subjects in every portion of the realm." He appears to have believed that Star Child was guilty as charged, but accepted the verdict.[24]

The case is fascinating on several levels. It was the first murder of a NWMP officer, and any police force regards the murder of one of its own as the most serious of crimes. It was extremely important that such a crime be seen to be solved and the criminal punished. The public was worked up and wanted a guilty verdict. Yet Macleod meticulously charged the jury members to consider only the evidence before them, to disregard anything they had heard about the case outside the court, and "to get rid of prejudice on account of the murdered man being a white man and the prisoner being an Indian." Having said all that, when the jury actually recommended acquittal, Macleod was unhappy. This, he argued, was the first case of an officer being murdered in the North-West Territories since the police arrived in 1874, and if Star Child was guilty and yet acquitted, "the Indians would have nothing but contempt of the whiteman's law and no settler's life would be safe." But the jury stuck to its view that the evidence presented was not conclusive and Macleod accepted the verdict. E.H. Maunsell, a jury member, claimed that in light of a widespread demand for vengeance the decision to acquit required more courage than a conviction.[25] It was a remarkable demonstration of justice, and the lesson that the law would be administered fairly was not lost on Indians.

Even more important, this was not an isolated case. Jennings points out that in 1879 only sixteen Indians were arrested and only four convicted in all of the North-West Territories, as opposed to the eighteen whites (out of a smaller population) being charged with liquor infractions alone. In succeeding years, arrests of Indians remained relatively low, and convictions lower; most offenses related to either horse stealing or liquor. Jennings states that up to 1881, "not only was Indian crime, other than horse stealing, almost non-existent, but practically all convictions for horse stealing resulted from Indian help." In 1882, overall crime rates rose sharply with the advent of the Canadian Pacific Railway, its construction gangs, and settlers and entrepreneurs. Nevertheless, Indian crime rates remained low while white crime rates continued to be much higher. Though they were a majority of the population in the territories, Indians constituted only 20 per cent of arrests in 1882, 10 per cent in 1883, and 8 per cent in 1884. Very few Indian arrests were for killing cattle, despite howls from ranchers, and Jennings concludes that although they were at the verge of starvation, Indians were mostly "scrupulous about other men's property."[26]

Nevertheless, the NWMP believed it was sitting on a powder keg. It pointed out each year the risks associated with Indians' continued starvation. It was convinced that despite a veneer of peaceable behaviour, the Siksika, Kainai, and Piikani were "notably wild and warlike, three numerically strong and savage tribes." In 1882, Irvine wrote, "It must be remembered that these Indians have led a lawless and roving life, that they have been accustomed from infancy to regard other men's cattle and horses as fair plunder, and that the habits of a lifetime are not easy to unlearn." He also predicted the CPR's arrival would mean that a period of gradual adjustment to whites would become a time of abrupt confrontation.[27] Despite the consistently low levels of actual Indian crime, the police generally portrayed the situation as an uneasy peace preserved only by their presence and judicious actions.

In 1883, 386 cases went to trial in the territories, of which twenty-five were Indians tried in Alberta (at Fort Macleod and Calgary). All were heard by NWMP officers, or by former officer Macleod. About one-third were charges of cattle killing, and another three or four were for horse stealing. Two were for possession of liquor, one was for attempting to escape from prison, and others involved larceny, stabbing, shooting, causing a disturbance, and gambling. Eight of the twenty-five cases were dismissed outright. Sentences upon conviction were mostly small, from a ten-dollar fine for gambling, to a few days or weeks in jail for other offenses, to six months for horse stealing or cattle killing. Sentences were harsher for a couple of repeat offenders, who received two years for cattle killing or horse stealing. Star Child, who had the misfortune to appear before Macleod on a charge of stealing horses, was the exception and received four years at Stony Mountain Penitentiary.[28]

In fairness, the statistics probably under-report the crime rate. Indians were not always forthcoming in turning over others to the authorities, and while police tracked down quite a few suspects, many more got away. Sometimes they were hidden by family and friends on reserves, but likely more often they took refuge among relatives on reserves south of the international boundary. In November 1885, for example, Wind Bellows, a Kainai, allegedly murdered his wife and later took refuge with the South Piegan.[29]

### HORSE RAIDING

Horse raiding, criminalized as theft with the advent of the police and the settlement frontier, had long been a source of intertribal conflict and a means of proving one's manhood. In a bison-hunting and nomadic society, horses were invaluable not only for chasing down game, but also as beasts of burden, particularly when moving camp. Wealth was frequently measured in the number of horses owned, and dowries were often paid in horses, as were certain kinds of debts. Horses were one of the few possessions that the plains peoples sought, and flaunted, in numbers well beyond immediate hunting or work requirements. Accumulating horses was one way individuals could stand out and win prestige. Horse raiding was not a criminal activity among the plains tribes, but if it was a kind of sport, it was one that carried a high risk. It could lead to injury or death, and even escalate to outright warfare.[30]

The values of the horse and bison culture inevitably became less relevant with the near-extermination of the bison, the move to reserves, and the advent of white ranching and the settlement frontier. Maintaining large herds of horses had less of an economic basis on reserves, but the deep cultural attachment not only to possessing horses, but also to appropriating them from others, did not quickly disappear. In the 1870s and early 1880s, horse raiding remained a sublimated form of warfare, and when young men spoke of going to war, they usually meant raiding horses. White-owned horses were also considered fair game, although the latter had a different understanding of the activity and expected the police to protect their property, whether cattle (supposedly usually killed for food) or horses. Other factors further complicated the picture. For one thing, Canadian Indians raided south of the international boundary and American Indians raided north of it. Canadian Indians often stole horses to take into the United States to sell for liquor restricted from them in Canada. For another thing, some white and Metis people, often in cooperating "gangs," engaged in what the police deemed professional horse stealing, and contrived in many cases to have blame laid upon Indians. From its arrival in the West, the NWMP understood that if intertribal peace, as well as good relations with incoming settlers and ranchers, were to be maintained, horse stealing would have to end. What had been acceptable, even approved, behaviour was now to be criminalized.

At first, the police moved cautiously. Experts disagree on when moderation turned to more active coercion and punishment – in the early 1880s, or from 1885[31] – but to start, police seized stolen horses, returned them to their owners, and reproved the offenders. By the early or mid-1880s, pressure from settlers, ranchers, government officials, and Americans led to more severe punishments on the order of imprisonment for six months to two years, particularly for repeat offenders. One officer reported, concerning the sending of war parties to raid horses:

This horse stealing on the part of the younger men is doing an incalculable amount of harm throughout the camp. Setting aside

the complications it may, at any time, give rise to with the United
States Government, it unsettles them greatly. If one man succeeds
in evading arrest, the others are thus prompted to copy him and
so doing is considered a signal sign of personal bravery that invariably meets with universal approbation.

Thus a large number of the Blood Indians are becoming professional horse-thieves, and though their operations are carried on,
for the greater part, south of the international boundary line, it
cannot be said to be universally the case, and war parties often
visit distant portions of our Territories, solely for the purpose of
horse stealing.

That our Indians can, with the utmost ease, procure strong alcoholic drink in the United States is unquestionably the fact. This
proves a powerful incentive towards the continuance of these
southern migrations, as does the fact that they receive aid, most
willingly proffered, in their criminal practices from their blood
relations, the South Piegans (also of the Blackfoot Nation) ... In
addition to this, our Indians go over to the United States to purchase ammunition. They can and do get any quantity of it from
American traders, who appear to be specially equipped for the
purpose of making such sales.[32]

Thus horse raiding was more than sport, war, or a way to prove manhood and honour. It became part of a kind of underground economy,
and a possessor of horses could trade the animals for items prohibited or
restricted in Canada (e.g., alcohol or, especially after 1885, ammunition), for other goods, for other assistance, or to repay debts. Such economic activities would not have been government approved, but they
were more culturally acceptable, more profitable, and a lot more fun
than the hard and discouraging work of farming.

Cross-border raids created special problems for the NWMP because
the government expected international complaints to be given a higher
priority. It was exasperating for both the police and the Canadian Indians
that under Canadian law American horses rounded up in Canada were
to be returned to their American owners, because there was no reciproc-
ity in this regard. At the same time, farmers and ranchers demanded that
the NWMP recover their missing horses from Indians; upon investigation, the police often found that the animals in fact had been lost through
theft by whites or Metis, or through their owners' carelessness. Nevertheless, by the mid-1880s some farmers and ranchers slept near their

horses to prevent theft, and after 1886 the police introduced a system of
regular patrols in the southern plain and boundary areas, which significantly curtailed horse theft.[33]

It is sometimes forgotten that Indians themselves tried to stop the
horse raiding and warfare. Continuing raids, mostly by young men,
across the international border between the Kainai from Canada and the
Assiniboine and Gros Ventres in Montana led Indians sometimes to kill
one another as well as steal horses. Mékaisto approached Indian Agent
William Pocklington, a former NWMP officer, in March 1887 to suggest
that the tribes concerned be permitted to meet to create a peace treaty. In
a unique example of international cooperation between the tribes, and
between the DIA, the NWMP, and the Montana-based military, a peace
treaty between the tribes was reached in Montana in June 1887. It neatly
bypassed the complications of inter-government diplomacy. It also was a
considerable risk for Mékaisto, who estimated that as many as half of
the Kainai were opposed to such a treaty. Yet it was effective, and became
a basis for lasting friendship between the Kainai and the American
Assiniboine.[34]

THE PASS SYSTEM

One of the most controversial government policies introduced after the
1885 rebellion was the pass system, which required Indians who wished
to leave their reserve to obtain from their agent a signed pass granting
permission to do so.[35] The system was designed to enhance government control, to encourage Indians to attend to agricultural labour
and animal husbandry, and to minimize confrontation between Indians
and whites. In 1883, Deputy Superintendent General of Indian Affairs
Lawrence Vankoughnet had suggested it as a way to address "the indis-
criminate camping of Indians in the vicinity of towns and villages in the
North-West." Such Indians, in the view of authorities, allegedly were
enabled at least in their laziness, and at worst in moral laxity (drinking,
gambling, prostitution). Irvine strongly objected to Vankoughnet's proposal, telling the minister, "such a system would be tantamount to a
breach of confidence with the Indians generally, inasmuch as from the
outset the Indians had been led to believe that compulsory residence on
reservations would not be required of them, and that they would be at
liberty to travel about for legitimate hunting and trading purposes. This
concession largely contributed to the satisfactory conclusion of the
treaty with the Blackfeet, and I am sure that your decision in the matter,

namely, that discretionary power, according to circumstances, should be vested in the officers of police, was wise and sound." Indian Commissioner Edgar Dewdney also commented that a pass system would violate the treaties.[36]

Sensible as this advice was, it was trumped by the events of 1885 and, according to F. Laurie Barron, by subsequent prodding from Hayter Reed to implement strict and controlling policies. Sir John A. Macdonald, exasperated by the rebellion, told Vankoughnet in August 1885, "As to the disloyal bands this [pass system] should be carried out in consequence of their disloyalty. The system should be introduced in the loyal Bands as well and the advantage of the change pressed on them. But no punishment for breaking bounds could be inflicted and in case of resistance on the grounds of Treaty right should not be insisted upon."[37] In other words, he knew the proposed policy violated treaty rights and could have no basis in law; yet he contended that rebellion extinguished the treaty right of those bands involved, and hoped that most Indians would buy the argument that the policy was for their benefit and not be bold enough to insist upon their treaty rights. Macdonald presumed guilt prior to any court decisions, that rebellion could erase treaty commitments, and that the alleged actions of a few could justify attempting to set aside the rights of the many.

Thereafter, writes Carter, Indians "who wished to leave their reserves were required to obtain passes from the agent or farm instructor declaring the purpose of their absence, the length of absence, and whether or not they had permission to carry arms."[38] This illegal policy gave agents great power over the Indians as individuals, and was used to prevent parental visits to Indian schools and to discourage off-reserve gatherings for events such as the sun dance or collective action such as protesting government policies. It was justified by claims that it would facilitate Indians' advancement and civilization, and was ultimately for their own good. The government hoped, moreover, that it would allay potential settlers' fears about coming to a West lately troubled by rebellion.[39]

How did the pass system work in practice? In 1887, a new commissioner, L.W. Herchmer, seems to have been more sympathetic to it than his predecessor, although he implied it often was not much enforced. He complained, "the rapid settlement of the country in the vicinity of these [Nizitapi] tribes, and the system of allowing the Indians off their reserves, practically when they please, together with their being permitted to carry arms (mostly of repeating pattern) is liable sooner or later to result in serious trouble, involving not only the cattle business in the West, but the settlers." The bad winter of 1886–87, which had been disastrous for ranchers and farmers, had been equally disastrous for wildlife. Herchmer concluded that inasmuch as there were no longer animals for Indians to shoot, they could be required to leave their rifles on the reserves. He also hoped that more of them would turn from hunting to farming under the changed circumstances.

The authorities had various means to enforce the pass system. Police could charge an Indian who was off reserve without a pass under the Vagrancy Act; Indians returned to reserves by police often would see their rations cut by agents as punishment; and other privileges might be withheld. NWMP Superintendent McIlree at Calgary even ordered that Tsuu T'ina were to be sent back to the reserve, "pass or no pass." The police knew that Indians were unlikely to take the matter to court.

The NWMP was particularly anxious to stop Indian off-reserve movement in the border regions, to halt raids into American territory. Patrols throughout the region discouraged horse theft and cattle killing, but now the police arranged for aid from Indian scouts, who were "attached to the patrols and so far have done very good service, being invaluable as trailers [trackers], and able and willing to travel excessive distances in an almost incredible space of time." Herchmer wanted to hire more, not only to assist police patrols, but also to "strengthen the good understanding between the Indians and Police. On several occasions this summer these scouts arrested members of their own tribes." The only problem with Indian scouts was their "tendency ... to serve a short time and then return home, which is not always convenient." They were a bargain for the NWMP, as they provided their own horses while the police provided arms and saddles and paid them twenty-five dollars per month.⁴⁰ The patrol system, supplemented by these scouts, removed much of the economic incentive from horse raiding and therefore reduced movement off the reserve, while it increased the likelihood of arrest for engaging in illegal activities.⁴¹

By 1888, Herchmer recommended even more restriction over Indian movement off reserves, allowing them, when they visited towns, to remain for only a limited period to conduct trade. The police nevertheless remained cautious about enforcement. For example, Inspector R. Burton Deane at Lethbridge noted that most of the Kainai who visited the town "behaved themselves well. Some few came to work, and work well." Any who came to engage in prostitution of Indian women, were sent back to the reserve when discovered. He continued:

Others come with all sorts of plausible pretexts to account for being off their reserve without a pass. Some do not appear to think a pass necessary at all. One Indian produced a pass which was exactly a year old, and therewith was quite content. Some of them seem to be aware that in point of law they have as much right to roam about the country as white men, and that confinement to a reserve was not one of the provisions of their treaty. It thus behooves the police to be very careful in handling them, to avoid being compelled to take back water, in case of an Indian's asserting his right to freedom of action, and maintaining it.[42]

By the 1890s, Indians generally created few problems for the police. For the most part, Indian crime remained minor. Indians usually did not challenge the pass system directly, but seem to have tolerated it most of the time and ignored it the rest of the time. The Tsuu T'ina, for example, regularly obtained passes. One study claims that in one month, July 1896, some twenty-nine passes were issued to Tsuu T'ina individuals: fourteen to visit friends and relatives, or to attend a sun dance; five for wolf hunting; three to trade in Calgary; four for buying, trading, and selling horses; and the remainder for other kinds of work. There is no reason to think this month unusual, and the pass system was largely a means of tracking Indians – a pro-forma means of social control, but one rather easily evaded.[43] The police were rarely rigid in enforcing it, but could be persistent. Inspector G.E. Sanders of the Calgary detachment reported in 1902: "From a police point of view, the Indians are easily managed, and obey our orders willingly ... We order them back to their reserves when found without passes." In 1905, he noted, "we cannot always do this, as sometimes nearly all the Indians from the three reserves near Calgary come into town to attend the fair and race meeting, [and] on these occasions we let them alone."[44] An interesting case arose in 1905 when the agent for the South Piegan reservation in Montana asked the agent for the Kainai in Alberta not to issue more than two passes per month for Kainai who wished to visit their Montana relatives, as the South Piegan lived in extreme poverty and had difficulty feeding the visitors.[45]

Some police thought their task would be easier if agents issued fewer passes. The agents retorted that if they did not issue passes, Indians would leave the reserves anyway. Indians had come to understand that the police frequently had neither the personnel nor the will to enforce the policy with any rigour.[46] The relationship between Indians and police on this matter was mostly one of practical accommodation. The N W M P accepted that it was expected to enforce the system on behalf of the government, and many police believed the policy was an appropriate expedient that helped manage a potentially difficult situation as the white settlement population became dominant and pervasive in the region. Indians tolerated the policy, but did not accept it, for the pass system was one of their more bitterly resented memories of this period and a clear violation of their understanding of the treaties.[47]

## ALCOHOL AND PROHIBITION

From their earliest days in the territories, a constant and significant, if Sisyphean, task for the police, and for Indian agents, was stopping the flow of alcohol to Indians. Keeping alcohol off reserves was a promise made from Treaty 1 through Treaty 6.[48] There appears to be no such provision in Treaty 7,[49] despite the fact that the N W M P first made its reputation in ending the activities of Fort Whoop-Up and other whiskey traders' posts in the future Treaty 7 area after 1874, and were praised by Indian leaders and whites for so doing.[50] Yet prohibition was no more likely to work with Indian communities than it would later across the country. Those who profited from selling alcohol to Indians troubled themselves but little about the resultant problems, which included public and family violence, worsened eating habits, enhanced vulnerability to disease, impoverishment, and abandonment of farming and other responsibilities.

Unable to impose complete prohibition, the police made examples of some in hope that others would take heed. For example, in 1887 they heard that Calf Shirt, a minor Kainai chief, had brought whiskey in from Montana and announced he would defy any attempt to arrest him. The police would not let such a challenge go, and promptly arrested Calf Shirt, found five Indians who testified he had been in possession of alcohol, and sent him to the local jail for a month of hard labour. This, along with the arrest and similar sentencing of Good Rider for cattle killing, was believed to "have had a very good effect on the Bloods." However, a little later three Kainai, named Wolf, Bird, and Piegan, were arrested for drunk and disorderly conduct near Lethbridge and also sentenced to a month's hard labour; much to the annoyance of the police, the woman who obtained the alcohol for them refused to divulge her source and claimed she had found it in the bush.[51] So much for the good effect of the Calf Shirt case.

The key to understanding police objectives with respect to matters such as minor crime and morality in any society is control and management, not eradication. One way the police dealt with illicit liquor sales to Indians was to hire Indians to help stop the traffic.[52] By the end of the period under consideration, levels of alcohol-related crime among Indians were fairly minor and within social levels of tolerance. The commissioner's reports by this time provided only summary statistics of crime, since the number of offenses had climbed dramatically over the previous quarter-century as the district was settled. For perspective, 823 whites were convicted for drunk and disorderly conduct in the territories/new provinces in 1904–05, while sixty-nine Indians were convicted for drunkenness off reserve, and twenty-nine for the offense on reserve. Seventy-eight persons were convicted of selling alcohol to Indians, up by sixteen over the previous year. Still, Commissioner A. Bowen Perry contended, "the nefarious traffic has been kept under control."[53] Inspector Sanders thought that a decline in convictions for selling liquor to Indians in his district was due to "the Indian's displaying more cunning in concealing his source of supply." Inspector P.H.C. Primrose at Macleod thought an apparent decline there resulted from the incorporation of the town and its determination to enforce its own bylaws rather than continuing to employ the N W M P to expose the true levels of activity. In a backhanded compliment, Primrose commented that Indians were much more inclined to pay fines than were whites by court-imposed deadlines, and continued, "If it were not for his great passion for liquor or an occasional theft of a horse, or the killing of an animal for beef, the Indian would give little trouble."[54] Indeed, of 400 men held in the Calgary guardroom during the year, twenty-three were Indian; and of thirty-one women, four were Indian.[55] Crime, the police had come to realize, was much more endemic among whites than among Indians.

The police preferred to sentence Indians convicted of possessing alcohol, or of public drunkenness, to the greater deterrent of prison terms rather than fines. Some Indians learned that the courts might be more lenient and appealed their sentences. This angered Perry, who wanted the government to ban this legal right: "The Indians are wards of the Government, and I would strongly recommend that no right of appeal should be [granted] except with the consent of the Superintendent General of Indian Affairs." That this attitude was not unique was reflected in a statement by NWMP officer Sam Steele, who after arresting some Indians at a sun dance, commented with astonishing arrogance, "They were wards and we were officers of the Crown, therefore there was no chance of a miscarriage of justice."[56]

## SUPPRESSION OF THE SUN DANCE

The sun dance, or thirst dance, was another area of attempted social control that generated much friction between Indians and whites.[57] This endeavour engaged missionaries, government officials, and the NWMP from the mid-1880s onward. Usually held in the summer, the dance was, for plains and parkland Indians, a deeply spiritual event that took place over several days and nights, or sometimes weeks; it involved the entire band, and frequently members of more than one reserve. One Indian, Greasy Forehead, told a department official in 1898 that the "Sun Dance was part of his body and could not be given up."[58] Its deepest mysteries were not much understood by whites, most of whom failed to appreciate its significance and the prairie Indians' profound attachment to it. Whites who witnessed the ceremony were typically aghast at the torture to which frenzied young men submitted themselves. Captain R. Burton Dean was not unusual in stating he had once seen a dance on the Kainai reserve in his early days in the West (1889), and he never wanted to see one again: "All such exhibitions as this could only have the effect of keeping alive the primeval homicidal and criminal instincts of the native."[59] He provided a more extended comment in his annual report for 1889, in which he dismissed the event as a "form of entertainment" that "serves no useful purpose whatever." He witnessed half a dozen young men undergo the self-torture, which involved ritualized piercing and rending of the skin and flesh on the breast during ecstatic dancing, some of them in his opinion being shamed into it. He thought it brought out "all the bad qualities of the Indians": "It feeds the naturally cruel nature of the spectators, it panders to the lust of both sexes, and unsettles the marital relations of the Indians themselves; and last, though not least, it acts as an incentive to the triumphant participant to evince a courage to which he is far from feeling in the commission of some lawless act."[60] Ahenakew, by contrast, while noting that the practice was more common among the Nizitapi than the Cree, thought it amounted to mortification of the flesh, which Christians had long practiced. It was not, in his view, "the making of a brave" so much as it was seeking the compassion of *Ma-ni-to* and subordinating oneself to his will.[61]

Governments feared that the dances would be an excuse for various bands and tribes to conspire together against them. They also saw that attendees were neglecting their farming responsibilities, including the daily care of their animals.[62] Missionaries feared the dance because it renewed Indian religious convictions and undermined months or even years of effort to bring their charges to Christian faith and practice. Believing that the ceremonies involved a return to primitivism, officials and educators saw them as vitiating their efforts to "civilize" and acculturate Indian children. Moreover, as with the potlatch in British Columbia coastal societies, giving away property was contrary to the acquisitive, individualist, and capitalist ethic the government wanted to inculcate in the Indian population. The federal government first moved in 1884 to outlaw the potlatch, a ceremonial giving away or even destruction of large amounts of goods to enhance one's status, in British Columbia by amending the Indian Act;[63] on the prairies, it was left to Indian agents and the NWMP to try to discourage the sun dance in other ways. The pass system, for example, was sometimes used to prevent off-reserve gatherings for the dance. There were, nonetheless, limits as to what they could do. On one occasion, in 1893, the Indian agent at Hobbema, D.L. Clink, destroyed a sun dance lodge at a nearby Metis settlement on the Battle River and arrested some Native leaders. Cree from Saddle Lake, Hobbema, and Stony Plain had participated along with the Metis. The DIA informed Clink that he had exceeded his authority, and that his impression that the so-called Potlatch Law gave him power to act in this way was incorrect.[64] Finally, in 1895, the government further amended the Indian Act to prohibit those aspects of the sun dance related to giving away property or money or to physical torture. But fear of a hostile Indian reaction led the DIA and NWMP to take a cautious approach to enforcement.[65]

In retrospect, neither the DIA nor the police were especially rigorous, for each recognized that Indians were deeply committed to the ceremony. Officials and the NWMP hoped that if they hampered it around the edges they could be seen to be taking at least some of the action whites demanded. Each year officials and police reported hopefully that the sun dance was on its last legs. In 1888, the year before Deane was repulsed by elements of torture that he witnessed in the dance, Reed claimed, "the sun dances are going more and more out of fashion and becoming less objectionable in their character." He reported that Isapo-Muxika tried to discourage them. Yet, almost annually, impressive numbers still turned out for the dances. In 1886, the hundreds of lodges that were erected on the Bow River flats on the Siksika reserve are a case in point. Moreover, in 1887, Indians prayed at the sun dance for rain to end a serious drought; rain quickly followed, which, as Reed sourly acknowledged, greatly enhanced the reputation of the medicine men "among the superstitious."[66] Deane's previously noted report from 1889 shows the dance continued through the 1880s alive and well. Even when chiefs like Isapo-Muxika and Mékaisto (perhaps under pressure from officials) verbally discouraged the dances or declined to attend, the dances still went on, for they were associated with vows of individuals and did not require the sanction of the chiefs. Whites failed to appreciate this aspect of Indian social structures.

During the 1890s, pressures to discourage the dances increased. In 1898, for example, Deane noted that the Kainai had been permitted to dance, provided they did not give away property or hold the event on Sundays.[67] Yet on the same reserve in 1902 the sun dance lasted five weeks during which, according to the agent, "all work ceased." On the Hobbema reserve, where normally the Methodist and Roman Catholic Indians lived fairly separate lives, the sun dance that same summer united them for a few days. The agent reported that they "saw no incongruity in returning to their ancient rites and ceremonies ... combining the prayers of the Church with pagan ceremonies, and making pagan vows and keeping them with Christian fortitude. This is an Indian characteristic, and worth studying."[68]

Revealing, however, was the report of Indian Commissioner David Laird for 1902, in which he stated, "a vigorous effort was made during the year to suppress illegal dancing on most of the reserves." The policy was most successful in Manitoba and the eastern territories, but less so in Alberta: "On the Blood reserve ... I am sorry to say, a sun dance was held which was largely attended." He claimed that the actual dance was for only three days, though Indians camped at the site for about a month. Not only was "much valuable time ... wasted when they ought to be occupied with their hay-making," but Laird suspected, without offering proof, that "immorality, gambling and other such evils were practiced." There was no evidence that anything illegal had transpired, as also was the case with a dance on the Piikani reserve in the same month. Still, Laird believed that the practices must be stamped out, because "the farming instructor, the teacher and the missionary cannot accomplish much among people who give themselves for weeks together to the excesses of a heathen celebration."[69]

The police were disinclined to be as rigorous in stamping out the dances as the DIA desired. They periodically laid charges when blatant violations of the law occurred, but Keith Regular claims they often "turned a blind eye to many Indian religious and social festivities." Four Indians near Fort Macleod received suspended sentences in 1903 for giving away twelve horses, a blanket, and other items at a ceremony; in 1904 there were but two convictions in the territories, and after that there were no reports of convictions in the annual reports. Regular concludes that the police had come to prefer "pacification as opposed to oppression," desiring "to promote amicable relations between the aboriginal and white races."[70]

In 1898, the NWMP attempted to mediate a dispute between Indian Agent James Wilson and his Kainai charges concerning dances. The case illustrates how on occasion the police could buffer the insensitivity of an agent bent on strict enforcement of the law. Mékaisto wanted to hold a Medicine Pipe Society meeting and initiation ceremony; Wilson was opposed because he understood it to entail giving away property, illegal under the Indian Act. In the course of discussions, Mékaisto was led to believe that he would be arrested if he proceeded. Puzzled and angry, the elderly chief went to Deane to determine if his understanding was correct. Deane spent an afternoon sorting out the facts of the case. He found that both women and men were eligible to be members of the Medicine Pipe Society, which was prestigious, restrictive in its membership, and secretive in its practices. Members were elected, and a payment was required. Apparently the wife of Heavy Shield recently had believed herself to be near death and vowed that if she recovered she would seek membership in the society by purchasing a medicine pipe (one of only fifteen). When she regained her health, she sought to fulfil her vow. One of Mékaisto's wives had such a pipe, which she was willing to sell for a customary fifteen horses.

Mékaisto was president of the society, and proposed calling a meeting to consider the matter. The proceedings would involve four dances over eleven days. Wilson was displeased, because the meeting would disrupt haying time and he understood it to be a "give away" ceremony. Deane had some sympathy for Wilson, but knew that any police actions must be legally defensible. He thought the proposed payment could be regarded either as a thank-offering from the point of view of Indian religion, or as an initiation fee to a secret society (not unknown among whites). He concluded that either way, "no court would hold that the

Indian Act had been infringed." So Deane made a proposal: if the Kainai would give up having a sun dance that year, he would intercede with the agent to "pass on this one occasion out of consideration for 'Red Crow' and his advanced age."[71] Allowing the Medicine Pipe dance to proceed in this way would appear to have been a common-sense solution, but Wilson was enraged, and wrote to the Indian commissioner: "The spectacle of a Police officer meeting with Indians and even encouraging them to 10 days of such pagan ceremonies, at which as many as 50 head of horses, besides blankets, quilts, guns, etc. exchange hands at one such dance, and this sanction granted with the knowledge that it was against the wishes of the Department, is surely bad enough, but the effect upon the reserve requires to be seen to be understood."[72]

Attitudes of the public to such matters were changing more rapidly than those of Indian agents and missionaries. In the last decade of the territorial period, Indians were confronted with whites' contradictory attitudes toward their dances and ceremonies. Many whites now saw Indians as a curiosity rather than a threat, and sometimes invited them to hold dances and ceremonies to entertain celebrity visitors, as well as the public at various fairs and exhibitions. DIA officials and missionaries were infuriated at such official recognition and approval of the very ceremonies they had expended so much effort (with so little success) to extirpate. But the business communities and Indians both saw an opportunity for profit, as the colourful dances and seemingly exotic music and singing now were popular entertainment. By the early twentieth century, the Siksika and the Tsuu T'ina had participated in the Calgary Inter-Western Exhibition. In 1903, Indians were encouraged to stage a "sham fight" to show they had not forgotten "the art of war and scalpery." Tsuu T'ina Agent McNeill denounced the effort "to turn the Sarcees into a Circus troop or some kind of 'wild west show' just to entertain some of the residents of the Town." In 1904, to McNeill's horror, a Tsuu T'ina police scout who had recently been Christianized and married in the church was found painted up and taking a leading role in "pagan" dances in Calgary. No higher official approval of the dances could have been offered than what essentially were command performances presented when the Marquis of Lansdowne toured the West in 1899, Governor General Lord Minto and his wife in 1900, and the Duke of York in 1901. When Rev H. Gibbon-Stocken complained to Minto about his watching the "scene of picturesque barbarity," the governor general dismissively replied that he considered the dances "harmless."[73]

## NATIVE WOMEN AND THE NWMP

At a conference in Calgary in the 1970s, James Gray delivered a paper entitled "Sex and the Single Settler." His main point was that in the writings of historians of western Canada, lusty, healthy, single young white men seem to have behaved like monks, betraying little interest in the opposite sex until united in marriage with a suitable white woman and the blessing of a Christian clergyman. Gray set out to explode this myth, publishing his findings about a randy population of men in *Red Lights on the Prairies*.[74] In Gray's portrayal of the prairie West, brothels and prostitutes thrived on the fringes of every prairie city and town, constituting a continual problem for conflicted authorities and police forces, who officially tried to eliminate the problem but more often tried to manage it, and who were periodically discovered to be clients themselves. Rod Macleod relates one incident when the NWMP went to raid a brothel and found among the clientele a couple of their colleagues who claimed, unconvincingly, to be conducting an undercover investigation on their own time.[75]

Historians, among others, have often found much to snigger at in such stories, which play against the stereotype of the police as a morally upright force that sought to represent and impose a higher, more principled form of Christian behaviour, not least with respect to women. It was widely held in white society that women occupied a usually domestic and private sphere different from the public sphere occupied by men. This meant normally that women's distinctive gifts and roles were seen as within the family, where they had a special responsibility to transmit Christian social and moral values. Stable families, along with the church, were held to be the rock upon which society's moral foundations were secured. Within this sphere, women were to be specially honoured. Sexual intercourse, a subject rarely if ever discussed in public, was expected to be confined to the marital bed. A principal goal of Christian missionaries since early contact with Indians had been to persuade the latter to adhere to monogamous life-long marriage in a nuclear family, which they and officials saw as a sure sign of civilization and Christianization. It was not an easy sell, for Indians had different values and ideas of family structures that they believed made more sense in their traditional culture.[76]

No amount of moralizing could eliminate physical urges, and wide discrepancies opened between the officially encouraged behaviour and reality. Desire manifested in relationships that ranged from those of mutual consent and/or genuine affection to commercial transactions to abusive situations. Prostitution, like gambling and the alcohol trade, fell under the class of moral problems and criminalized behaviours that needed to be managed. The NWMP, according to S.W. Horrall, consistently "looked upon prostitution as a necessary evil which, given the basic urges of human nature, would never be eradicated. In fact ... prostitution provided an outlet for those men who were unable to control themselves, and made them less likely to prey upon the respectable women in society." Horrall also observes, "police records clearly identify prostitutes as belonging to a morally inferior class," but also, "the officers who wrote most of the reports considered themselves morally superior."[77]

Under Canadian criminal law, operation of a brothel, or being found in one, was an indictable offense that carried up to a year in jail upon conviction. But the police usually proceeded under the less severe vagrancy provisions of the law; one definition of a vagrant was a person who "being a common prostitute wanders in the fields, public streets or highways and does not give a satisfactory account of herself." Conviction of a misdemeanour under this provision could result in a fine of fifty dollars, six months in jail, or both.[78] However, in the 1870s and 1880s the police rarely brought charges against prostitutes or brothels, except for a very few in connection with CPR construction camps. Horrall observes, "in the male-dominated frontier settlements prostitution appears to have been openly tolerated." Police records show no complaints about it, and indeed, "the rank and file of the force were some of the prostitutes' best customers."[79]

Horrall specifically excludes the prostitution of Indian and Metis women from his study, since the police "regarded [them] in quite a different light."[80] However, the general view of the police on prostitution was also part of the framework within which they viewed Indian and Metis prostitution, a framework also shaped by the larger relationship the NWMP and government had with Indians and Metis. Furthermore, police could go several years without encountering a white woman, and it is scarcely surprising that some of them formed relationships with Indian and Metis women. As early as 1879, Laird, then lieutenant governor, told Macleod, "Reports are brought to me that some of your officers are making rather free with the women [near Fort Walsh]. It is to be hoped that the good name of the Force will not be hurt through too open indulgence of that kind, and I sincerely hope that Indian women will not be treated in a way that hereafter will give trouble." While Macleod denied there was "a regular brothel" at Fort Walsh, the substance of the reports apparently was accurate.[81] Considering the situation across Alberta, however, there is not much evidence that in the early years Indian women were found in brothels, and it is also noteworthy that police reports show that Indians believed to be engaging in prostitution in towns like Lethbridge or Calgary were usually required to return to their reserves rather than being prosecuted.

The police in the 1870s and 1880s were not entirely separated from a society that shared many continuities with the fur-trade era. Earlier fur traders had – usually mutually consensual – sexual liaisons with Indian women. Some were of the one-night-stand variety, but many others led to marriage according to the custom of the country, for love or affection, and/or for useful alliances, forming long-term relationships and families. But often, men put aside their Indian or Metis wives and families when white women became available – a well-known example was that of D.W. Davis, a former whiskey trader and Canadian agent for interests at Fort Benton. In 1887, Davis married a white school teacher from Ontario just as he was about to become the Conservative M P for Alberta; at the same time, he apparently divorced his first wife, a sister of Chief Mékaisto named Revenge Walker, with whom he had four children.[82] Sargent Frank Fitzpatrick reported that a few police "did fall for the charms of these sometimes pretty maidens and married them Indian fashion. In some cases they retained them as their lawful wives but in other cases, just as in civilised parts of our country, they discarded them without much further thought."[83]

There appears to be little evidence that Indians saw anything inappropriate in most of these relationships, so long as they were conducted with mutual respect or to mutual advantage, for they largely fit a pattern in Indian society.[84] In one sense this also fit with behaviours in white society that, while officially disapproved, were widely tolerated in certain circumstances. But it was never so simple a matter. That the police exploited their position of authority in these relationships, inasmuch as disempowered Indians were legally wards of the state and the police had influence over their welfare, can hardly be denied.[85] Perhaps the situation was much the same in the fur trade era, in which Hudson's Bay Company officials took advantage of their position.[86] Certainly, these behaviours reflected a disjunction between the high-minded purposes of the monogamous morality of Christian civilization and British-Canadian law, and the day-to-day reality of human character and circumstance; though it seems that such inconsistency was understood and, insofar as there was mutual consent, did not much concern Indians, and is not much commented upon, if at all, in the few available Indian memoirs and recollections.

Some police evidently enjoyed socializing with Indians in other ways, even participating in their dances. They also invited Indian and Metis women to police-sponsored dances at their posts, though without them there would have been a significant gender imbalance at these events, as white women were scarce in the early years. This sometimes has been regarded as evidence of their desire to be open and friendly to Native peoples as part of the acculturating process. But at least some of the police had carnal rather than elevating purposes in mind.[87]

Too often, consent and good will did not prevail. There were those among the police and government officials who engaged in sexual encounters with Indian and Metis women who had no interest in the women as persons, viewing them only as sources of gratification. Andrew Graybill claims that at least some of the police "physically or sexually abused aboriginal women"; though he provides little evidence, such behaviour probably occurred in a variety of these relationships, and likely was rarely reported let alone addressed.[88] In a few cases, some officials and police abused their positions of authority, requiring Native women to submit to intercourse in return for food for themselves and their families – unconscionable behaviour under any circumstance, but even worse when Indians were starving as a result of government policy.

The police, and presumably the government officials, paid a price for their lust: in 1886, a member of Parliament charged that the NWMP's reports showed that 45 per cent of officers had been treated for venereal disease.[89] In 1881, George A. Kennedy, the NWMP physician at Fort Walsh, reported:

A feature in the medical history of the past year, and one that is very much to be regretted is the introduction of *syphilis* among the men. This has already played great havoc, and still more serious consequences are to be feared if some means be not devised to prevent the spread of the disease. It was brought over from the other side of the line by the Cree and Assiniboine camps on their return here a year ago last fall. In the present state of the Indians it is practically impossible to define the limits of the disease and effect a quarantine, but if new cases occur as frequently as they have been doing of late, some such decisive action *must* be taken. At the best, however, it is a subject surrounded with difficulties.

Kennedy listed seventeen cases of gonorrhoea, eleven of syphilis, and two of chancre, usually associated with syphilis. He also treated 447 cases of disease among the Indians, of which eleven were gonorrhoea and nine were syphilis. At Fort Macleod, where Kennedy also served, he treated five cases of gonorrhoea.[90] It is possible that in the period up to about 1882, venereal disease contracted by members of the NWMP in the western territories came mostly from contact with Indian and Metis women.[91] However, with the CPR's construction, and the growth of cities and towns in the 1880s and 1890s, many white prostitutes were available to police and government officials, so the high rates of sexually transmitted diseases should not be attributed solely to such interaction.[92]

The rank-and-file and the commissioned officers of the NWMP took advantage of the opportunities for a variety of liaisons in the early years; it appears that these frequently could be consensual relationships that did not necessarily violate social norms for the period. It is arguable that police attitudes stemmed more from class than race prejudice: that is, certain behaviours were viewed as normal for lower classes, regardless of ethnicity. In fact, police appear to have been less inclined to prosecute Native women for prostitution than white women, and to have tried other ways to discourage Native prostitution in towns and cities. There was some sensitivity, at least among government officials and senior police officers, about how treatment of Native women might affect Native-white relations more generally. It may also have been the case that pressure from missionaries to discourage Native prostitution shaped police enforcement policy.

That said, undeniably some officials and police took advantage of their positions to require sexual favours from those placed under them. That these behaviours on the part of an unknown minority of officers and officials constituted abuse of authority cannot be disguised or excused among them any more than abuse can be excused in the schools.[93] Both government and police were supposed to represent a new and higher order of things. Such behaviour can hardly have caused the Indians and Metis to think highly of the blessings of Christian and British civilization. For a few, however, liaisons became stable relationships that survived even when the officers retired from the force and turned to farming or other occupations.

## CONCLUSION: A VERY MIXED RECORD

Primrose commented in 1905 "on the amenableness of the Indians to law, as compared to a great many white men." By this time, Indians appeared to present no collective threat to the larger community. The role of the NWMP with respect to them was to accompany officials to annual treaty payments, maintain the pass system, return truant children to school, minimize Indian prostitution near cities and towns or railway construction gangs, and to prevent Indians from selling goods to whites without the permission of their agent. Occasionally horse raiding persisted, as when seven young Kainai started to take horses from Mormon settlements in southern Alberta and dispose of them to purchasers (who professed ignorance of the horses' origins) in British Columbia. (The thieves had all attended industrial schools, which, as Primrose noted, "does not speak well."[94]) Over all, the police role with respect to Indians had become numbingly routine; their focus had moved to other problems, and comments on Indian issues constituted only a small portion of their annual reports.

Were the police an instrument of fundamental injustice? The charges relate mainly to government policies and the police role in implementing or supporting them. Harring and Ennab hold that the NWMP and the courts disregarded rights at the post-rebellion 1885 trials, mistranslated the treaties, committed fraudulent acts, tried to suppress traditional cultures, imposed an authoritarian legal order, and committed violence against Indians and Metis.[95] To this list must be added the poor treatment of Native women, and the enforced restrictions on hunting and fishing rights, which Indians believed violated the treaty agreements.

The first charge relates to the trials and imprisonment of many, and execution of some, Indians following the 1885 North-West Rebellion (see chapter 4 in this book). It seems undeniable that very few Indians committed murder; even if some later commentators might believe the cases to be a sort of justifiable homicide, the death penalty in the context of the day, when hanging was the norm upon conviction for murder, may have been deserved. But those accused, whether found guilty or not, deserved as a matter of right a fair trial, which they did not receive even by the standards of the day. Also indefensible was the fact that a disproportionately large number of treaty Indians were charged and tried, while Metis defendants were few considering their central responsibility for the events. This might have resulted from the fact that Indians were more numerous and spread across the prairie region, and were thus perceived as a threat by whites at a time when the government wanted to be perceived as taking a firm line on law and order. Nevertheless, the number of arrests was excessive, and the charges and the trials were fundamentally flawed and unjust. Note, however, that while members of the

NWMP in 1885 were agents of the government in carrying out arrests, providing security, and representing state control, the government orchestrated the trials and the courts conducted them.

The second and third charges relate to translation issues at the treaties (see chapters 1 and 2 of this book), and the effectual bison-hunting ordinance of 1877 (see chapters 2 and 8 of this book); neither was particularly a police issue. The fourth charge relates to the suppression of the sun dance, and the fifth to imposition of the illegal pass system (see above). As I further acknowledge below, the police were generally unhappy with both government policies, and enforcement was less than rigorous, but there is no question that they imposed them.

To return to the justice system, the trials of 1885 were arguably atypical examples of how it functioned. The evidence appears to indicate that Indians charged with offences over the whole post-treaty period, both before and after 1885, were generally fairly treated. The system was far from perfect, but, as a rule, Indian convictions for both major crimes and lesser misdemeanours had to result from evidence, often from fellow Indians. If the evidence was not forthcoming, the charges were dismissed. It is telling that Indian leaders on a number of occasions located criminals and turned them over to police. Quite a few Indians were employed by the police and developed a good working relationship with the force. Indian leaders often worked with police to solve crimes, not only because it was a treaty obligation, but also because criminals and drunkards destabilized their societies and undermined their sense of security.

None of this is to contend that police and Indians embraced one another with affection. The police had to enforce laws or policies that were at best dubious and at worst illegal, such as the prohibition on dances or the pass system. They appear rarely to have interfered directly with the sun dance, at least in Alberta, and instead left that area of control more to the Indian agents, with an understanding that what they regarded as the most objectionable elements should be minimized.[96] The police gradually accepted their obligation to enforce the pass system, despite their belief that it was illegal; by the end of the period they took it for granted and somewhat irregularly and arbitrarily enforced it. For their part, much as Indians resented the limitations imposed by the pass system, they seemed to tolerate it when they could not evade it. The police also had to enforce the game laws occasionally, and many Indians resented controls on what they regarded as their treaty right to hunt and fish off reserve. The NWMP presence also provided the framework within which government could impose starvation, truancy laws, and other disciplinary measures on Indians as part of its coercive plan of acculturation. Police officers often pointed out the injustice and likely consequences of such measures, but accepted that it was their duty to enforce them.

The police rationalized this system because they saw themselves as part of the great imperial scheme to impose the majesty of the Queen's justice on the Indians of the frontier, to bring order out of wilderness chaos, and to bring Indians to appreciate the blessings of the new regime of peace, order, and good government.[97] Indians could not fully embrace the police, because they knew that under the new system they could not be viewed as equals in their own land. The police represented a society that fundamentally believed Indians could never be whites' full equals, and that at the best they could exhibit a veneer of civilization which, if scratched, would inevitably reveal a wild underlying nature. The police would always be condescending as they wore masks of respect.[98] Many whites did not even try to cover their contempt and fear. Indians were wards of the state, and they were not allowed to forget it.

An authority on policing, Jonny Steinberg, writes, "The consent of citizens to be policed is a precondition of policing."[99] Perhaps "citizens" might be modified to "a people" in the case of the Indians of the West. At the beginning there was, arguably, consent and trust. Not all was advantageous to Indians in the 1870s, as the police permitted whites equal access to lands and resources. Yet they did benefit from ending the whiskey trade and intertribal warfare, and in the early stages the NWMP was reasonably fair in administering the law and acting as a buffer between Indians and whites. But trust began to be eroded by events such as the Bull Elk affair, by the events of 1885, and by the state's use of the police to enforce policies that were probably illegal, certainly racist, and decidedly contrary to the Indian understanding of treaty commitments. Some officers' physical and sexual abuse of Indians, especially women, contributed to this process and besmirched the force's reputation. However, the events and consequences of the North-West Rebellion of 1885, the advent of the railway, and the expansion of the settlement frontier also demonstrated the growing power disparity in favour of the Canadian state. By the mid-1890s, as the cases of Scraping High, Kitchi-Manito-Waya, and Si'k-Okskitsis demonstrate, the state's power to impose its version of law and order could not be seriously challenged – nor was there, by this time, much will for confrontation. Most Indians were inclined to tolerate that which could not be changed.

Such Indian memoirs as are available about the period to 1905 generally do not reflect much indignation about the NWMP. Some ignore the police, others are neutral, and yet others are warm in their praise. Mike Mountain Horse, despite some criticism of the NWMP's handling of the Si'k-Okskitsis episode, is almost effusive, and concludes, "what really made the Red Man adopt principles and laws foreign to them was that these laws were administered with such bravery, fairness and honour on the part of the administrators [NWMP] that the respect of the Indians was completely won. These were qualities which the Indians loved, admired and from their viewpoint, [the police] had always practiced."[100] Rose-coloured glasses in retrospect, perhaps. But at least for some, despite some significant flaws, the overall record could still be viewed positively.

# Postscript

You know what they say. If at first you don't succeed, try the same thing again ... For an individual, one of the definitions of insanity is doing the same thing over and over again in the same way and expecting different results. For a government, such behaviour is called... policy.

Thomas King[1]

Looking back at the first quarter-century of the post-treaty era, there is much truth in King's witticism. Broad policy goals, and the methods employed to implement them, changed slowly, at best, over that time. It is useful, then, to ask, what remained constant and what changed in the second quarter-century of reserve life in Alberta. In the early 1920s, Deputy Superintendent General Duncan Campbell Scott reported, "the principal [on-reserve] occupations of the Indians of Alberta are farming and stock-raising. Almost all the reserves in the settled districts of the province had large herds of horses and cattle."[2] Less than two decades after provincehood, and nearly fifty years since the treaties, many Alberta Indians were apparently fulfilling at least some of the government's original objectives. The goal had not changed, but Indians had made a significant advance toward it compared to where they were in 1905. It is not clear to what extent this development was due to the maturation of a new generation of farmers who were graduates of school training in agriculture. However, new strains of grain, modern equipment, and the advent of dryland farming techniques contributed enormously to enable the Siksika, Kainai, Piikani, and Tsuu T'ina reserves to produce significant wheat and oats crops, mostly a hopeless cause before 1905. In contrast to the Treaty 7 region, in the 1920s the Treaty 6 reserves produced little wheat, but modest quantities of oats. All these reserves produced some root crops and wild hay. At the same time, across the Treaty 6 and 7 portions of Alberta, Indian horse culture persisted, with over

13,000 head – more than twice the number of cattle. This may have been because "land rentals" (cattle grazing leases) to whites generated sizeable income for the Siksika, Kainai, Hobbema, and Edmonton agencies. As was the case in 1905, all agencies continued to generate a great deal of their income through off-reserve wage labour. By this time, however, the Siksika reserve supplanted the Kainai as the most productive in Alberta.

Population had mostly stabilized by the 1920s; the sharp decline of the early years had been arrested. However, since the activities of farming and raising livestock lay principally with a minority of the reserve population as farm size and mechanization increased, economic necessity took greater numbers of Indians off the reserves for longer and longer periods of time. To an even greater extent than had been the case in the first quarter-century of reserve life, reserves could not provide an economic base for all Indians. The nature of farming had changed vastly since the signing of the treaties in the 1870s, but the straightjackets of the treaty terms (especially respecting reserves) and of the Indian Act discouraged flexibility and fresh responses.

With respect to education, in the 1920s six day schools remained on the reserves of the former district of Alberta[3] with a total enrolment of over 160 but average daily attendance of under eighty, or less than 50 per cent. All the industrial schools had been closed by this time, but there were ten boarding schools in the Treaty 6 and 7 area,[4] with a total enrolment of over 570 and average attendance of over 500, or roughly 88 per cent. Almost all Indian children of school age were registered in a school. Boarding schools, some now off-reserve, provided the educational experience for most of them. Scott observed, "the policy to-day is to care for all capital expense at Indian residential schools whenever funds can be found for the purpose. This releases the finances of the missionary societies and orders ... for better instruction, food and clothing." Thus the division of financial responsibility was clearer. The government was also trying to improve classrooms in day schools, and – at last – to secure better-qualified teachers by paying higher salaries.[5] None of this should obscure the fact that schooling for many pupils was, if anything, more disorienting, harsh, and abusive than in the earlier period.[6]

There was much continuity in Indian policy, in large part because the deputy superintendent general from 1913 to 1932 was Scott, who had joined the DIA in 1880, and whose very conservative ideas were rooted in the late territorial period. It is evident that he did not much like or respect Indians, and under his influence administration was even more centralized and controlling than before. For example, in the 1920s the government still was trying, with very limited success, to eradicate the sun dance.[7] Health problems persisted in at least some Indian schools.[8] But the government also began to exercise its powers more extensively to keep Indian children in school for longer periods, until they were seventeen or even eighteen years of age, powers that exceeded those in the white school system.[9] Early attempts to form an Indian organization to challenge increasingly restrictive and repressive amendments to the Indian Act, and to help Indians obtain a fair hearing for grievances, among other things, were actively discouraged by the DIA and the police, and went nowhere. Meaningful political organization, embodied in the Indian Association of Alberta, would have to wait until after World War II.[10]

The government argued that its policies had, on the whole, enjoyed some success by the 1920s. According to Scott, "the Indians as a class are now self-supporting. This Department of necessity occupies the same position with reference to indigent Indians as the municipalities at large to the ordinary destitute among the white population, and our total expenditure for all these purposes is moderate."[11] Most Indian children were experiencing a formal school education and were returning to reserves that were adapting to modern farming, where housing was both upgraded and permanent, and where off-reserve income was mostly generated from working for, or marketing to, whites rather than from traditional hunting, fishing, trapping, or gathering.[12] The government had been correct in its assessment that the traditional lifestyle simply could not sustain Indians of the prairie and parkland region over the long term. But a significant change from the earlier period was that a smaller proportion of Indians could sustain themselves entirely on the reserves; inexorably, more and more were drawn off-reserve for longer and longer periods of time. The government's goal of Indians as fully enfranchised, self-supporting, and assimilated citizens remained as elusive as ever: Indians mostly remained determinedly attached to their distinctive identities and cultures within the Canadian state.

# Reflections

"In the beginning," wrote John Locke, "all the world was America." Thus, comments Patricia Seed, did Locke relegate Native peoples to the past: "Native Americans would disappear because their communal ownership of property represented an earlier stage of human development that could only and inevitably be replaced by individual possession and farming."[1] The over-arching narrative that came to frame and justify British imperial policy, particularly as it concerned indigenous peoples across the empire, rested on certain fixed assumptions. Among the most important of these, especially in North America, was that Native peoples were inherently indifferent to, or incapable of, real work to make the land productive; that God intended the land of the earth to be occupied, claimed, and worked by people able, and willing, to maximize productivity; that such productivity could best be realized by individual ownership of land; and that Indians, having failed to do this, also had failed to make a real claim upon the land. The Native way represented a dark past; the European way represented a bright future.

Certain assumptions and practices framed the process of acquiring the land from Indians. Among the most important of these were that ultimate title resided in the Crown, that Indians must be persuaded (through a treaty process) to surrender their aboriginal title to use of the land, and that the Crown had a legal and moral responsibility to aid them during the transition to modernity. And modernize they must: they could not be permitted to impede progress. If they were to survive, they had to modernize. That Indians were subjects of the Crown and (after 1870) subject to Canadian laws and policies did not result from the treaties. Rather, the treaties were negotiated in light of the Crown's ultimate title, and of Canada's existing Indian legislation and policies. The government's goal in all of this was to ensure a process of peaceful agricultural white settlement, and integration of the region into the transcontinental Canadian economy. Indians' interests were not unimportant, but were decidedly secondary.

Farmers were deemed real workers who legitimized their claim to the land by enclosing it, and benefitting themselves and others from the prosperity they generated from intensively "improving" it. While Indians, by contrast, were widely believed to have a deep-seated aversion to such labour, government policy was based on the assumption that they, or at least their children on the reserve and at school, could be taught the habits of independent acquisitive capitalist individualism and hard work. In this way, they would legitimize a claim to a portion of the soil on the reserves and ready themselves for full-fledged responsible citizenship. Government policy was supposed to benefit Indians, but was an exercise in coercive social engineering that was slow to show success and quick to generate harm and mistrust.

The early reserve years in the district of Alberta illustrate the extent to which Indian and settler cultures had not really shared a mutual understanding from the beginning. They also show how Indian resistance and realities on the ground forced the government to modify some of its administrative methods, and to accept that its intended timing for achieving its goals would have to expand. Nevertheless despite appearances, the underlying assumptions and purposes of the government's policy actually changed but little during the period to 1905 (or, for that matter, in the next quarter century).

Evidence both from the period and from elders since that time establishes that Indians perceived the treaty process quite differently from the government. They did not know about the Indian Act or other legislation that lay behind the treaties, and believed that the treaties were the only agreement between themselves and the Crown. The elders took it for granted that the treaties were about sharing land, not about selling it. The treaty documents and the process surrounding them were about forming a relationship of mutual respect in which Indians would be supported as necessary in return for allowing whites to access their homeland. They were about giving Indians space to retain and adapt their cultures to change, not about erasing Indian identity. While the government in the 1870s saw reserves as temporary places of transformation, Indians saw them as permanent safe places for their cultures in an inevitably alien sea of settlers.

The government believed that most Indians would – and indeed wanted to – learn to farm on the reserves, preferably as individuals. Indians sought out many other options, either out of preference or out of realism, and produced mixed economies that frequently were extensively intertwined with nearby settlers, ranches, and towns. They found, especially in the early years, that they could derive additional income as well as some of the necessities of life from traditional activities (hunting, fishing, trapping, gathering), or (as settler farmers also often found) from paid labour to supplement often inadequate or unreliable farm income. That did not equate with individual independence for all: a few Indian farmer/ranchers prospered, but many did not, and most Indians depended heavily on government rations throughout the period. At the outset, as noted, Indians tended to believe that farming would supplement traditional activities, while the government expected that it would become the principal activity of most reserve residents.

Agricultural potential varied enormously from reserve to reserve, and (especially with respect to weather, pests and the like) from year to year. Indian farmers faced the limitations imposed by crops unsuited to the regions, distance from markets, and other factors that hindered success, but their early experience prepared them to take advantage of improved strains, technology, and transportation after 1905, and many did much better in that period.

Indians wanted a commitment to education in the treaties, but likely believed that the schools would be similar to what they had experienced before the treaties: local, non-compulsory, and adaptable to patterns of Indian life. The government, by contrast, could not conceive of schools in that way, for even in the 1870s it intended them to be institutions for social engineering, for transforming recalcitrant youth into productive citizens with common values, and for instilling skills necessary for a kind of life that would differ significantly from that in which adult Indians had been raised. Given this mismatch of purposes, conflict was inevitable. Day schools did not attract Indian children, suffered from low enrolment and poor attendance, and were far too slow in effecting the government's desired transformation (especially with the added pressures resulting from the unexpected, sudden collapse of traditional means of subsistence). The result was the mostly unhappy, alienating, and tragic experiment with industrial and boarding schools intended to accelerate the process.

The government's tendency from the beginning was administrative centralization and close supervision, along with increasing restriction on

Indians' lives. It was seen in the schools, as compulsory attendance began to be enforced, though that happened more strongly after 1905 than before. It was seen, too, in the efforts to limit Indian movement off reserves, particularly (though not only) through the pass system. The government also tried, with little success in Alberta, to stamp out traditional activities such as the sun dance; it had a bit more success with horse raiding. Indians had a mixed relationship with the NWMP, which early on ensured intertribal peace, halted the whiskey trade, and tried to maintain an even-handed administration of the law. But as time went on, it was expected to enforce increasingly restrictive government policies. The NWMP's responsibilities had also expanded to deal with non-Indian crime, ethnic tensions, and some urban as well as rural policing, so its task became more diffuse and managing Indians became less important. Moreover, the force never overcame its inherent prejudice toward, and sense of superiority to, Indians.

By the end of the period, the government had been forced to accept that dealing with Indians was going to be a permanent, not a temporary, issue. Yes, some had learned to farm, most had settled on reserves, and many had been to school. Subject to government control and management, they had even become "domesticated" – they now produced ceremonies and war dances in their finery for royal visitors and attenders of fairs and rodeos, sold handicrafts, and seemed to present no threat to larger society. The recent past, and supposed "primitivism" and "savagery" (perceived by the early twentieth century as exotic), had become a source of amusement, and of profit for Indians and non-Indian business people alike. Indians had ceased to be fearsome.

But beneath that veneer lay a resentful and confined Indian society that suffered still from high morbidity and mortality, whose children increasingly were taken from homes to abusive school situations, where reserve life was not providing full opportunity or meaning for many. For all the fine talk of civilization and assimilation, government policies based on the assumption that Indians were legally minors ensured that they did not have the variety of opportunities open to them that whites did. Yet the broad goals of government policy remained mostly fixed: civilization through settlement agriculture, education, acquisition of an individualist capitalist ethic, Christianization, and ultimately assimilation. Too often Indian policy continued to be administered by people who had low regard for Indians and their potential, and to whom it would never have occurred either to undertake serious self-examination of policy failures or to consult with the victims of those policies about how improvement might be effected. Out of these early decades of stress and tragedy, nevertheless, emerged most of the Indian leaders who would develop the confidence and skills to open a different chapter in the story of Indian-settler relations, as they began to shape a challenge to the era of government domination and insist that their voices be heard, particularly after World War II.

# Federal Politicians and Civil Servants, 1867–1905

## PRIME MINISTERS AND PARTY AFFILIATIONS

| | |
|---|---|
| Sir John A. Macdonald | 1867–73 (Liberal-Conservative) |
| Alexander Mackenzie | 1873–78 (Reform/Liberal) |
| Sir John A. Macdonald | 1878–91 (Liberal-Conservative) |
| Sir John J.C. Abbott | 1891–92 (Liberal-Conservative) |
| Sir John S. Thompson | 1892–94 (Liberal-Conservative) |
| Sir Mackenzie Bowell | 1894–96 (Liberal-Conservative) |
| Sir Charles Tupper | 1896 (May–July) (Liberal-Conservative) |
| Sir Wilfrid Laurier | 1896–1911 (Liberal) |

## SUPERINTENDENTS GENERAL OF INDIAN AFFAIRS

| | |
|---|---|
| H.L. Langevin (also Secretary of State of Canada) | 1867–69 |
| Joseph Howe (also Secretary of State for the Provinces) | 1869–73 |
| Thomas N. Gibbs (also Secretary of State for the Provinces) | 1873 (June) |
| Sir Alexander Campbell (also Minister of the Interior) | 1873 July–November) |
| David Laird (also Minister of the Interior) | 1873–76 |
| David Mills (also Minister of the Interior) | 1876–78 |
| Sir John A. Macdonald (also Minister of the Interior)* | 1878–87 |
| Thomas White (also Minister of the Interior)* | 1887–88 |
| Sir John A. Macdonald, *acting* (also Minister of the Interior)* | 1888 (May–September) |
| Edgar Dewdney (also Minister of the Interior) | 1888–92 |
| Thomas Mayne Daly (also Minister of the Interior) | 1892–96 |

Hugh John Macdonald (also Minister of the Interior)     1896
                                                        (May–July)
Clifford Sifton (also Minister of the Interior)         1896–1905
Frank Oliver (also Minister of the Interior)            1905–11

\* Sir John A. Macdonald ceased to be minister of the interior in October 1883. Sir David Lewis Macpherson (1883–85), and then Thomas White (1885–88), succeeded him in that department. White only became the superintendent general of Indian affairs in October 1887. Following White's sudden death in April 1888, Macdonald became acting minister of both departments.

### DEPUTY SUPERINTENDENTS GENERAL OF INDIAN AFFAIRS

| | |
|---|---|
| W. Spragge | 1862–73 |
| Lawrence Vankoughnet | 1874–93 |
| Hayter Reed | 1893–97 |
| James A. Smart | 1897–1902 |
| Frank Pedley | 1902–13 |

### INDIAN COMMISSIONERS

| | |
|---|---|
| J.A.N. Provencher | 1873–76 |
| David Laird | 1876–79 |
| Edgar Dewdney | 1879–88 |
| Hayter Reed | 1888–93 |
| Amédée Emmanuel Forget | 1893–98 |
| David Laird | 1898–1909 |

# Indian Reserve Land Gains/Exchanges/Surrenders in the District of Alberta to 1 September 1905

## CATEGORY 1: LAND EXCHANGES, ACQUISITIONS, AND ERROR CORRECTION

In 1883 the Blackfoot (Siksika), Blood (Kainai), and Sarcee (Tsuu T'ina) formally surrendered land assigned them under Treaty 7, and each signed a new treaty agreement specifying the reserves that they had chosen.[1]

In 1885 the government paid David James Cochrane $3,500 for sixty-two acres of improved land that properly belonged on the Blood reserve.[2]

In 1885 the government paid Angus Macdonald $200 for ten acres of improved land on the Passpasstayo (Passpasschase; also referred to as the Two Hills Band of Cree Treaty Indians) reserve.[3]

In 1886 the government corrected an error made in the 1883 treaty with respect to a portion of the land that was to be included in the Blood reserve, with a simple land exchange.[4]

In 1887 the government purchased ten acres of improved land, added to the Whitefish Lake (James Seenum) reserve, for $400.[5]

## CATEGORY 2: LAND SURRENDERS FOR PURPOSES OF RAILWAYS OR ROADS

In 1891 the Samson and Ermineskin bands assented to a road allowance for the Calgary and Edmonton Railway, amounting to roughly forty-three and sixty acres, respectively.[6]

In 1900 the Sarcee surrendered a sixty-foot wide road allowance across part of their reserve.[7]

In 1901 the Bobtail band surrendered 1.54 acres for a road allowance.[8]

In 1902 the Enoch band surrendered 9,113 acres in connection with a road allowance.[9]

CATEGORY 3: OUTRIGHT LAND SURRENDERS

Surrender of Passpasschase Reserve #136, 1888.[10] Interest on profits realized from sale to be paid out to signatories and their descendants "forever."

In 1892 an agreement was reached with the Enoch reserve to accept into membership the former members of the Passpasschase band, and in return to receive a share of the payout from the sale of land.[11]

In 1889 the Bloods (Kainai) agreed to a surrender of 440 acres.[12]

In 1892 the Blackfoot agreed to surrender their Castle Mountain timber limit, the interest from the proceeds to be paid to the members of the tribe and their descendants.[13]

In 1897 the Sharphead (Stoney) band surrendered their reserve #141, 42.4 square miles, which they had not occupied for some years, the proceeds to be shared with the various bands with which former members now lived.[14]

In 1903 the Michel band surrendered 7,800 acres along its west side, interest to be paid to band members.[15]

# Notes

In citing works in the notes, the following abbreviations have been used:

| | |
|---|---|
| RG 10 | Record Group 10 (DIA, at NAC) |
| CSP | Canada. Parliament. *Sessional Papers* |
| DCB | *Dictionary of Canadian Biography* |
| *Debates* | Canada. House of Commons. *Debates* |
| NAC | National Archives of Canada |
| PAA | Provincial Archives of Alberta |
| PAC | Public Archives of Canada (see NAC) |

Titles of annual reports located in the *CSP* are abbreviated as follows:

| | |
|---|---|
| Agriculture | Department of Agriculture |
| DIA | Department of Indian Affairs |
| Fisheries | Department of Marine and Fisheries |
| Interior | Department of the Interior |
| Militia | Department of Militia and Defence |
| NWMP | North-West Mounted Police |
| SSP | Secretary of State for the Provinces |

## PROLOGUE

1 This approach differs diametrically from Michael Asch's 2014 *On Being Here to Stay*, which rests on the premise that the treaties embodied a common understanding. See also J.R. Miller, review of *Canadian Historical Review*, by Asch, 96 (Mar. 2015): 109–12.

2 Darwin, *After Tamerlane*, 340.

3  On the notion of environment as determinative, see Diamond, *Guns, Germs, and Steel*, parts 1 and 2; Diamond, *The World Until Yesterday*, 19.

4  McKay, "The Liberal Order Framework"; Brownlie, "A Persistent Antagonism."

5  Todorov, *The Conquest of America*, ch. 3; Greenblatt, *Marvellous Possessions*, 9.

6  See Spicer, *Cycles of Conquest*, 4–8.

7  Ibid., 6.

8  Dickason, in a book review, *Journal of American History*, Dec. 1991, 1104. I am indebted to Donald Smith for bringing this to my attention. While many officials undoubtedly had good intentions, it would be futile to deny that many others were corrupt, cruel, and repressive.

9  Ultimately far more valuable to the HBC was the grant of a fixed number of sections in each township in the fertile belt, and land around its trading posts. Martin, *"Dominion Lands" Policy*, ch. 1. To explain why the dominion government had to borrow the sum, in 1869 its budgetary revenue was $12.9 million, its budgetary expenditure was $17.9 million, and its direct debt was $112.2 million. Urquhart and Buckley, *Historical Statistics of Canada*, 197–204. The £300,000 (or approximately $1.5 million) equalled roughly 11.68 per cent of its revenues.

10 The region was called the North-Western Territory from 1870 to 1875. It became the North-West Territories under the North-West Territories Act of 1875, and in 1906 the area excluded from the new provinces of Alberta and Saskatchewan (1905) was renamed the Northwest Territories. See Zaslow, *The Opening of the Canadian North*, 13–14.

11 NAC, Sir John A. Macdonald Papers, letterbook 8, 8–11, Macdonald to Edward Watkin, 27 March 1865.

12 The text of the petition may be found in CSP, 1872, #22, 33–34 (see headnote in bibliography). Nee-ta-me-na-hoos's Cree name is found in Dempsey, *Maskepetoon*, 174.

13 As early as 1863, Wikaskokiseyin reportedly went to Edmonton to inquire whether reports that the HBC had sold the lands and were about to give up the fort were in fact true. Thus Indians were aware, at least in a general way, of the negotiations that had begun in England in 1857 concerning the renewal of the HBC lease. Dempsey, *Maskepetoon*, 177.

14 Morris, *Treaties*, 169.

15 All Christie quotations found in Morris, *Treaties*, 169–70.

16 The most thorough treatment of this subject is Ronaghan, "The Archibald Administration in Manitoba."

17  Miller, *Compact, Contract, Covenant*, 32–33; Ray, Miller, and Tough, *Bounty and Benevolence*, 99.

18  While the issue of translation is raised frequently in connection with the treaties (Christie was to be involved in the negotiation of Treaty 6), no one appears to question the adequacy of Christie's English version of the Indians' concerns in the 1871 petition.

19  Pryke, "Archibald," 33; Ronaghan, "Archibald Administration."

20  *CSP*, 1872, #22 (Indian Branch, Secretary of State for the Provinces), 3–35.

CHAPTER ONE

1  Olive P. Dickason points out the underlying assumption that "the British, by simply setting foot in North America, had acquired title to Indian lands." In 1887, in *St Catherine's Milling v. The Queen*, the Judicial Committee of the Privy Council ruled, "there has all along been vested in the Crown a substantial and paramount estate, underlying the Indian title." Dickason, *Canada's First Nations*, 318; Isaac, *Aboriginal Law*, 29; see also Saywell, *The Lawmakers*, 118–21; Elliott, "Aboriginal Title," 57–58.

2  In 1874, for example, Governor General Lord Dufferin referred to Indians generally as "subjects of the Canadian Government," and also as subjects of the Queen; in effect they were one and the same. Dufferin, *Speeches and Addresses*, Speech of 28 August 1874.

3  Excellent works of great insight along these lines have been produced by, for instance, J.R. Miller, A.J. Ray, and Aimée Craft.

4  Ray, Miller, and Tough, *Bounty and Benevolence*, ch. 1 contains an excellent overview of this relationship.

5  Such, at least, seems to be the consensus of historians such as Ray, Miller, Friesen, and numerous others; the view arguably is challenged by Daschuk, *Clearing the Plains*, ch. 1–5, in which the HBC is not a benign force in the increasingly chaotic situation facing Indians of the plains prior to 1870.

6  Creighton, "Macdonald, Confederation, and the West," 233–34; Waite, *Life and Times of Confederation*, 307–08.

7  Manitoba Act, 33 Vict. [1870], ch. 3. On this episode, see Flanagan, *Metis Lands in Manitoba*, 29–43; Ens, "Hybridity," 241–43. For a useful analysis of the language of the Manitoba Act relating to matters of aboriginal title, see Miller, *Compact, Contract, Covenant*, 144–45.

8  Of course, retaining control of Crown lands allowed the federal government great freedom, largely unhampered by provincial interests, to assign reserves in Manitoba for the Indians of Treaty 1 in 1871.

9  They (especially the French Catholic Metis) also enjoyed powerful political support in Quebec; Indians of the West never enjoyed any such support, within or outside the region, in the period to 1905.

10 Over time, and especially since 1982, the treaties have come to have a far greater significance than the Canadian government seems to have intended in the 1870s.

11 Dempsey, *Red Crow*, 13–14. Daschuk, in *Clearing the Plains*, 24–26, notes that an even more serious outbreak may have occurred in the 1730s, though in the absence of Europeans it was not well documented. On the outbreak in the 1770s and 1780s, see Daschuk, ch. 2.

12 Daschuk, *Clearing the Plains*, chs. 1–5.

13 Morris, *Treaties*, 245.

14 I intentionally use the American spelling rather than the Canadian "Peigan" because the individual involved was from Montana Territory.

15 Dempsey, *Crowfoot*, 59–60.

16 Ibid.; Dempsey, *Red Crow*, 13–14. The smallpox epidemic was not confined to the Indian population, and John Foster notes it also hit whites and Metis hard: "two-thirds of the Metis [in the St Albert district] would become ill; half of these would die." Such was the devastation that three new cemeteries were established. Foster, "The Metis and the End of the Plains Buffalo in Alberta," 68–70. See also Daschuk, *Clearing the Plains*, ch. 6.

17 Ray claims, "Buffalo were still plentiful in the Edmonton area in the early 1870s," but the basis for this assertion is far from clear. He notes that the HBC recorded 10,729 hides for 1870, obtained in the parkland/grassland area. According to Ray, most of these hides came from the Swan River district, which was very distant from Edmonton; at the same time, he claims, "in contrast to the situation around Edmonton, buffalo were scarce in Saskatchewan and absent in Manitoba," even though, according to Ray's maps, the latter areas were part of the Swan River Trading District. At any rate, Ray's reports of plenty conflict directly with reports by Indians, and by Chief Factor William J. Christie, concerning severe shortages in the northern parkland/grassland region. Ray, *The Canadian Fur Trade in the Industrial Age*, 23, 24, 27–28; see Dempsey, *Maskepetoon*, ch. 12; Brink, *Imagining Head-Smashed-In*, ch. 9.

18 On the spread of smallpox, particularly among the Cree, see Butler, *Great Lone Land*, 367–73.

19 *CSP*, 1873, #23, 3.

20 There was some question as to whether the 1867 constitution gave the Canadian parliament the power to create a new province, so the British

settled that matter with retroactive legislation in 1871 (Constitution Act, 1871, 34–35 Vict., ch. 28, which authorized the creation of additional provinces out of territories not included in any province). Other actions of the Canadian government in the newly acquired North-West Territories were not at issue, however. The British had formally extended the rule of Canadian law to the HBC territories in acts in 1803 and 1821; see Rich, *The Fur Trade and the Northwest*, 194–95, 239–41. Note that the British North America Act, 1867, was renamed in 1982 as the Constitution Act, 1867; I most often follow the latter usage. Below, I discuss the claim of some Indian leaders that neither the British nor the HBC had legitimate title to the land they transferred to Canada. For now, I will relate the story based on the Canadian government's belief that it had secured a legitimate ultimate title to the land, though this belief did not deny that Indians also had rights. Tough, "Aboriginal Rights," is a useful introduction to issues relating to the transfer of the HBC territories from the perspective of the rights of Indians.

21  Statutes of Canada, 1869, ch. 3, reprinted in Owram, *The Formation of Alberta*, 24–26.

22  Statutes of Canada, 1871, ch. 16. On this subject in general, see Thomas, *The Struggle for Responsible Government*, chs. 1–3; Thomas refers to the 1871 version as the North-West Government Act.

23  Dempsey, *Firewater*, 124. The Mackenzie government strengthened this when it passed a federal law in 1874 prohibiting the importation of "intoxicating liquors" into the North-Western Territory; 37 Vic., ch. 7.

24  Butler, *Great Lone Land*; Macleod, "Butler," 142–44. This also was in fulfillment of government instructions to Archibald of 4 August 1870 that he investigate and report fully on conditions in the North-Western Territory. Oliver, *The Canadian North-West*, 2: 974–75 (E.A. Meredith, undersecretary of state for the provinces, to Archibald).

25  CSP, 1885, #116 (Papers and Correspondence in Connection with Half-breed Claims and other matters relating to the North-West Territories), 1–2; Petition from John Fisher and ten others to Lieutenant Governor Alexander Morris, 5 May 1873; Reply, 4 June 1873. The petition acknowledges the annexation of the region to Canada, and also accuses the government of making "bright promises" to both the Metis and the Indians of Treaties 1 and 2 that have not been kept.

26  The standard work is Martin's 1938 *"Dominion Lands" Policy*. The federal government's attempt in the late summer and fall of 1869 to begin the square survey even before the transfer of land shows that its intent to pursue this policy predated the 1871 act. On Treaty 1, see Hall, "'A Serene

Atmosphere'?" Apparently there was some Native resistance to surveyors and settlers in 1870; Morris, *Treaties*, 25–26.

27  Dempsey, *Big Bear*, 56–57.

28  Reference to Oliver, *The Canadian North-West*, part 2.

29  Ruthless wolf hunters and pelt traders; see below.

30  This account is derived from Dempsey, *Firewater*, ch. 8 (citation quoted at 117), which strikes me as making the most sense of the conflicting evidence surrounding this tragedy. Still useful is Sharp, *Whoop-up Country*, ch. 4, which carries the story through the failure to bring the murderers to justice.

31  Horrall, "Sir John A. Macdonald and the Police Force," 192. Parliament had passed an act in May to authorize the force. Useful on the whiskey trade generally is Berry, "Fort Whoop-up and the Whiskey Traders," 21–25.

32  Horrall, "Sir John A. Macdonald and the Police Force," 180–82; Macleod, *The North-West Mounted Police*, 8–12; Morton, "Cavalry or Police," 6–9.

33  In 1860, a road also linked Fort Benton with the Columbia River system to the west. Owing to a decline in the fur trade, the fort was sold by the American Fur Company in 1865 to the US Army.

34  Dempsey, *Firewater*, 113.

35  Ibid., 90.

36  Dempsey, *Firewater*, 135–47, puts a human face to the tragedy. On the notion of Indians as sub-human, see Seed, *American Pentimento*, ch. 7.

37  Dempsey, *Firewater*, 114–15.

38  Horrall, "Sir John A. Macdonald and the Police Force," 194–200; Macleod, *The North-West Mounted Police*, 16–18.

39  Rees, *Arc of the Medicine Line*, prologue; Wilson, *Frontier Farewell*, ch. 12; Dormaar, *Alberta's 49th Parallel*, 7–9. Tupper, a former premier of Nova Scotia, was a prominent minister in the Macdonald cabinet.

40  Wilson, *Frontier Farewell*, 191–93. The portion of the border that would form the southern boundary of the future Alberta was surveyed in July and August 1874.

41  Rees, *Arc of the Medicine Line*, 299; Wilson, *Frontier Farewell*, 198. While some Metis were employed on the project, often providing transport for supplies, there is no indication that Indians were offered employment.

42  LaDow, *The Medicine Line*; McManus, *The Line which Separates*.

43  Promotion of immigration, later widely associated with the Interior Department, remained under the Department of Agriculture for another two decades.

44  Mayfield, "The Interlude," 19–20. Theodore Binnema believes that this may push the evidence too far; in a private communication, he

acknowledges Indians were legally subjects of the Crown at this stage, but believes it is not clear that the western Indians were yet wards of the state.

45 Mayfield, "The Interlude," 18, 24.

46 Ibid., 20–21.

47 See chapter 9 in this book.

48 Cited in Mayfield, "The Interlude," 23. This seems to contradict the evidence of elders that the N W M P sought and received permission from the Nizitapi to stay only the winter of 1874–75. See Treaty 7 Elders et al., *The True Spirit and Original Intent of Treaty 7*, 135. It is possible that the different understandings arose from problems with translation, as would occur in 1877 at the Treaty 7 negotiations. Mayfield provides an alternative account that might explain the elders' evidence: "a number of traders had been circulating rumors to the effect that the Mounted Police would remain in the area only for the winter, leaving again in the spring." On a different matter, Irene Spry contends that the coming of the N W M P to impose law and order "had one effect that is seldom recognized: the Indians were no longer to be permitted to keep intruders out of their country by force." The problem with this assertion is that the Indians had long since lost that ability when faced with well-armed intruders (e.g., whiskey traders, wolfers, and Metis bison hunters). Spry, "The Great Transformation," 29; see, for example, Gavigan, *Hunger, Horses, and Government Men*, 209n29.

49 Mayfield, "The Interlude," 26–28.

50 The early history of the Department of Indian Affairs is outlined in Hodgetts, *Pioneer Public Service*, ch. 13. Hodgetts takes the story to 1880. For a list of holders of the office of Minister of the Interior and Superintendent General of Indian Affairs, see appendix 1 in this book. For the record, from 1867 to 1873 the secretary of state for the provinces also was superintendent general of Indian affairs: H.L. Langevin (1867–69); J. Howe (1869–73); T. Gibbs (1873).

51 See chapter 3 in this book.

52 Its full title was An Act to Amend and Consolidate the Laws Respecting Indians. A very brief account, which should be used with caution, is Leslie, "The Indian Act."

53 *Debates*, 1875, 397 (1 March 1875); 499–500 (4 March 1875). Mackenzie agreed with comments "as to the high character of many of the Indians, especially in the West. A more peaceable and orderly population it was difficult to have, and many of them were men of great intelligence and learning." He was referring to the Indians of western Ontario, not to those of the North-West Territories. The government thought that it had done due

diligence in consulting with those Indians it thought capable of providing informed comment and consent, whose views could be understood to represent the interests of all Canadian Indians. On the contemporary notion that the Indians of Ontario and Quebec were superior to those elsewhere in Canada, see Anderson and Robertson, *Seeing Red*, 54.

54 Milloy, "The Early Indian Acts," 145–47; Scott, "Indian Affairs, 1850–1867," 351–58; Leighton, "The Development of Federal Indian Policy," chs. 1–7.

55 John Tobias notes that the legislation of 1850 "established the precedent that non-Indians determined who was an Indian and that Indians would have no say in the matter." Tobias, "Protection, Civilization, Assimilation," 41–42. A recent revisionist discussion of the matter is Binnema, "Protecting Indians' Lands."

56 *Historical Development of the Indian Act*, 23–26.

57 Ibid., 26–29; Miller, *Skyscrapers*, 138–43; Milloy, "The Early Indian Acts," 147–50. Note that fifty-acre farms were a common size for viable farming (if a bit smaller than average) in central Canada in the 1850s. On viewing Indians' refusal to embrace enfranchisement as an act of resistance, see Dyck, *What Is the Indian 'Problem,'* 52.

58 Leighton, "The Development of Federal Indian Policy," 344, 545.

59 *Historical Development of the Indian Act*, 52–54; Tobias, "Protection, Civilization, Assimilation," 43; *Debates*, 1869, 83–85 (27 April 1869); Milloy, "The Early Indian Acts," 151–52. By contrast, a non-Indian woman who married an Indian man gained Indian status: the "marrying-in" provision. These regulations followed the then-accepted premise that a woman's identity derived from her father (if single) or husband (if married). Respecting the blood-quantum provision, Binnema in a personal communication noted he believes it was never actually enforced in the period under review. During the debate on the measure, Dorion suggested – apparently with some support – that intermarriage between Indians and whites should be encouraged, as it "would tend to raise the character of the whole tribe." It is unclear how he could square this with the provision that Indian women who married white men, and their children, would lose status. On the extensive opposition to this 1869 act from Ontario Indians, see Sherwin, *Bridging Two Peoples*, 75–76.

60 Ray, Miller, and Tough, *Bounty and Benevolence*, 52–54; Owram, "White Savagery," 36–37.

61 *Historical Development of the Indian Act*, 60; CSP, 1876, #9, xii–xiii; and see (on Vankoughnet) Leighton, "A Victorian Civil Servant at Work," 113–14; Shewell, "*Enough to Keep Them Alive*," 36. After extensive exposure

to Native people, Morris, a commissioner for Treaties 3 to 6, and supposedly one of the most sympathetic white officials, still characterized them in 1880 as a "helpless population" who were "wards of Canada"; *Treaties*, 295–96. Laird's comments say much about the frame of mind of one of the chief negotiators of Treaty 7.

62  Tobias, "Protection, Civilization, Assimilation," 44.

63  Ibid., 45.

64  Ibid., 44, 45–46. In 1880, the Indian Act was amended to make the elective system mandatory.

65  The assumptions of British policy had passed into American law. In 1831, Chief Justice John Marshall observed that Indians "are in a state of pupilage. Their relation to the United States resembles that of a ward to his guardian." Cited in Washburn, *The Indian and the White Man*, 121. On the question of wardship and trusteeship generally, see Green, "Trusteeship and Canada's Indians"; also useful is Harper, "Canada's Indian Administration," which discusses wardship and guardianship.

66  Ray, Miller, and Tough, *Bounty and Benevolence*, 52–54, address the matter of the legal connection of the "social and economic responsibilities of the pre-1870 company [HBC] for livelihood to the legal title of First Nations" at the negotiations covering the transfer agreement respecting HBC lands. The point is interesting and important if Indians were not regarded as subjects at the time of the transfer; if they were subjects, the point becomes moot, inasmuch as the government in any event had a legal and moral responsibility. Doug Owram notes that in the early 1870s Canadian officials and travellers assumed the Indians of the West were wards of the state, but he also remarks, "it was a guardianship, not a permanent childhood." Owram, "White Savagery," 36–37.

67  37 Vict., ch. 21 [1874]. (An Act to Amend Certain Laws respecting Indians, and to Extend Certain Laws, relating to Matters Connected with Indians to the Provinces of Manitoba and British Columbia.) Section 12 applied to the North-Western Territory 31 Vict., ch. 41 (1868), 32–33 Vict., ch. 6 (Gradual Enfranchisement Act, 1869), and the 1873 Act (36 Vict., ch. 4) creating the Department of the Interior. Surveying of some reserves was not completed until the mid-1880s.

68  The treaties of the 1870s and official documents related to their negotiation were published by Morris in his 1880 *The Treaties of Canada with the Indians*. Treaties, surrenders, and adhesions for all of Canada were published by the government as *Indian Treaties and Surrenders from 1680 to 1902* in three volumes (vols. 1 and 2 in 1891 and vol. 3 in 1912). A modern scholarly survey is Miller's *Compact, Contract, Covenant*. Background to the

treaties, as well as a detailed treatment of Treaty 6, which is relevant to this study, may be found in Ray, Miller, and Tough, *Bounty and Benevolence*.

69 Ray, Miller, and Tough, *Bounty and Benevolence*, address this subject exhaustively; see also Ray, *Telling It to the Judge*, 69–70. This is a vital matter with respect to Indian understanding of the treaty process; I do not dwell extensively on it, first because others have done it so well; and second because I do not believe that embracing the forms of negotiation of the fur-trade era necessarily reveals much about underlying government assumptions and purposes, which are the focus of this book.

70 A helpful summary of the treaties of 1851 (Fort Laramie) and 1855 in the United States, in which Blackfoot Indians participated, may be found in Wissler and Kehoe, *Amskapi Pikuni*, 32–38.

71 Seed, *American Pentimento*, 126–29.

72 Ibid., 21–25. Note that by the nineteenth century some prairie Indians put great stock in written agreements to which their signatures were attached; see Dempsey, *Maskepetoon*, 92–93. That is, well before the treaties of the 1870s they understood the fundamental importance to white officials of the written document.

73 "Conquest" refers to British victory over the French in 1759–60 and the outcome of the Peace of Paris in 1763; there is no conquest with reference to Indians. Useful on the law of treaties as it stood prior to the entrenchment of Native rights in the 1982 Constitution (and therefore as understood in the period addressed in this book) is Green, "Legal Significance of Treaties Affecting Canada's Indians." Seed, *American Pentimento*, 23–24, points out that the Indians considered the French to have offered gifts for access to the land (exchange), and not to have purchased it; they could not have transferred to the English something they never owned. European perceptions were very different.

74 Cumming and Mickenberg, *Native Rights in Canada*, 39; an usufructuary title protected "the Indians in the *absolute use and enjoyment of their lands*," although they also had no right to alienate the lands to any party but the Crown "in whom the ultimate title was … considered as vested" (citation from 1887 St Catherine's Milling case; emphasis by Cumming and Mickenberg). This opinion held until the 1973 Calder case. See Ray, *An Illustrated History of Canada's Native People*, 336–37; Miller, *Compact, Contract, Covenant*, 254–55; and Bartlett, *Indian Reserves and Aboriginal Laws in Canada*, 72–86. Usufructuary title also has been described as a right of occupation. On the evolution in the 1870s and 1880s of different politicians' ideas about Indian land title in Canada, see Cottam, "Indian Title as a 'Celestial Institution.'"

75 Oliver, *The Canadian North-West*, 2: 937–46; Miller, *Compact, Contract, Covenant*, 70. The Order-in-Council of 23 June 1870, sec. 14, stipulated, "any claims of Indians to compensation for lands required for purposes of settlement shall be disposed of by the Canadian government in communication with the Imperial Government."

76 Overhunting of the bison had indeed been noticeable since the 1840s, but the situation was critical by the late 1860s and early 1870s. See Dempsey, *Maskepetoon*, ch. 12.

77 Morris, *Treaties*, 285, 302–13; Miller, *Compact, Contract, Covenant*, 108–18; Ray, Miller, and Tough, *Bounty and Benevolence*, 35–44. Note that the 1850 treaties used the word "privilege," not "right"; the 1862 treaty referred to "rights and privileges in respect to the taking of fish."

78 Taylor, "Canada's Northwest Indian Policy," 5.

79 Morris, *Treaties*, 17. Robinson also told them that they would receive less because they could hunt and fish, which their brethren in the midst of southern Ontario farmland and settlement were precluded from doing. Robinson was disingenuous in his valuation of the land, knowing that it was mineral wealth, not agricultural potential, that white entrepreneurs sought.

80 Wissler and Kehoe, *Amskapi Pikuni*, 34–37.

81 By Treaties 6 and 7, Canadian land provisions per Indian head of family (640 acres) were far more generous than the American treaties; clothing provisions for Canadian Indians were restricted to chiefs and subordinate chiefs, but without time limitation; annuities were smaller, but given to all individuals indefinitely; the government had much more control than in the United States. By 1876 and 1877, Native Americans had seen incursions on their reserve lands without compensation or negotiation, which made the land guarantees in the Canadian treaties very important. Canadian reserves were much smaller than the American Blackfoot reserve, but Canadian Indians had the right to hunt, fish, trap, and roam off reserve on unoccupied lands (see chapter 8 in this book).

82 *CSP*, 1872, #22 (SSP, Indian Branch), 6, Howe to W.M. Simpson, S.J. Dawson, and Robert Pether, 6 May 1871. Howe also noted that he was informed that before Confederation in Ontario and Quebec, "the highest price paid for the finest lands has seldom, if ever, exceeded four dollars per head per annum." This amounted to twenty dollars per family of five, far in excess of Howe's instruction. He would not necessarily have seen this as an inconsistency, because he appears to have assumed that land in central Canada was inherently more valuable than that in the West. He instructed the commissioners to pay according to the value, in agricultural potential, of the land.

83 Lord Dufferin remarked in 1874 that, as governor general, "I am but representing the wishes of the Local Canadian Government, and following the instruction of the Imperial authorities." Dufferin, *Speeches and Addresses*, 157.

84 On this subject generally, see Miller, "Victoria's 'Red Children,'" 1–23; Craft, *Breathing Life into the Stone Fort Treaty*, ch. 5; Abley, *Conversations with a Dead Man*, 129 (on metaphor). Of course, the word government is itself a translation, and it is arguably uncertain what the original Indian speaker(s) had in mind. For examples, see Morris, *Treaties*, 60, 61, 74, 86.

85 Seed, *American Pentimento*, 25–26, writes, "negotiations and signings of land treaty purchases often included elements of indigenous ceremonies ... During these formalized treaty purchase negotiations, Englishmen participated in Native American rituals to guarantee their power to bind the natives to the surrender of land, despite the native peoples' own understandings of the agreements they had concluded. The incorporation of native ceremonial devices did not create bilaterally binding agreements." She also notes, "the incorporation of native rituals into the discussions did not mean that natives had any greater control over the terms." The written text had priority over the spoken word. An alternate reading of the evidence is in Kelly, "Three Uses of Christian Culture," 357–84.

86 In addition to evidence noted above, see Anderson and Robertson, *Seeing Red*, 22.

87 Erasmus, *Buffalo Days and Nights*, 240.

88 Miller has identified six references by white officials to God or to the Great Spirit in the negotiation of Treaties 1 through 7 (*Compact, Contract, Covenant*, 160–61, 329n14), and attaches considerably more meaning to them than I do. Some in fact follow the conclusion of the treaty negotiations (for example, at each of Fort Carlton and Fort Pitt with Treaty 6), and are in the nature of "may God bless you, give you wisdom and prosper you," a common and casual benediction (definitely *not* an invocation) in white society. Alternatively, there is a pro-forma mention at Treaty 7 of the Great Spirit who made everything, and from whom the Queen derived her authority, after which the deity disappears from the government's discourse.

89 Taylor, "Canada's Northwest Indian Policy," 5. On Treaty 1, see Hall, "'A Serene Atmosphere'?"; Friesen, "Magnificent Gifts"; Miller, *Compact, Contract, Covenant*; Ronaghan, "The Archibald Administration," ch. 32. The Indian perspective is very well conveyed in Craft, *Breathing Life into the Stone Fort Treaty*.

90  See map 6. Another map that dramatically illustrates the difference between the Canadian and American reserve models appears in Dickason, *Canada's First Nations*, 299.

91  *CSP*, 1872, #22, 27–32, esp. 28–29. Indians had insisted that these promises be itemized in written form.

92  Carter, *Aboriginal Peoples*, 121–23. As confirmation that the government would have provided various kinds of assistance, see Morris, *Treaties*, 66, where Morris affirmed at the Treaty 3 negotiations that the government would help Indians begin agriculture, and adds, "if you had not asked it the Government would have done it all the same."

93  Morris, *Treaties*, 338–39; and see Laird's comments in *CSP*, 1876, #9 (Interior), vi–vii.

94  Morris, *Treaties*, 288–89.

95  Hall, "'A Serene Atmosphere'?," 349, 351.

96  Only males over age twenty-one could receive title to a homestead and qualify as heads of households.

97  Lambrecht, *The Administration of Dominion Lands*, 24–25; Morris, *Treaties*, 29.

98  *CSP*, 1872, #22, 28. On the Selkirk Treaty, see Ray, Miller, and Tough, *Bounty and Benevolence*, ch. 2; Miller, *Compact, Contract, Covenant*, 132.

99  Settlement and agriculture were intended to transform Indian culture. In addition, however (following the ideas of Seed in *Ceremonies of Possession*), from the perspective of the British tradition, settling and farming were crucial to legitimizing Indian possession and land title. As later events show, Indians' failure to settle and improve all of their reserve lands provided fuel for those who would claim that unimproved lands were surplus to Indian needs, and that Indian title to such lands was not legitimate.

100  Miller, *Compact, Contract, Covenant*, 169; Miller suggests that there may have been more ceremony at Treaties 1 and 2 than was reported. Ray, Miller, and Tough note, with respect to Treaties 1 to 3, that "Indian chiefs were well informed about land and resource issues, both in terms of their own needs and of the values that Whites placed on them." *Bounty and Benevolence*, 69–70. Note that the annuities for Treaties 1 and 2 were increased to the Treaty 3 levels in 1875.

101  Ray, *Canadian Fur Trade in the Industrial Age*, 32.

102  References for this paragraph all may be found in Morris, *Treaties*, ch. 5.

103  Ibid., 327–28.

104  Ibid., 49, 65, 74.

105 Note that Morris's comment was made three years prior to the 1876 Indian Act, underlining that this legal distinction was of long standing.

106 Ibid., 50, 69. In fact, in 1875 a group of Metis was allowed to renounce their Metis rights and assume Indian status under Treaty 3; see "Adhesion by Halfbreeds of Rainy River and Lake," 12 September 1875, in Cumming and Mickenberg, *Native Rights in Canada*, 319–20. The adhesion of the Lac Seul Indians to Treaty 3 in 1874 marked the first occasion on which Indians who had not been part of a treaty negotiation were allowed to join subsequently, setting a precedent for future treaties; see Cumming and Mickenberg, *Native Rights in Canada*, 320–21. On the adhesions to Treaty 6 (which continued as late as 1956), see Chalmers, "Treaty No. Six," 24–25.

107 This matter is expounded in Ray, Miller, and Tough, *Bounty and Benevolence*, 106–13. I believe, however, that there is room for disagreement when these authors accuse Morris of being less than truthful in his discussions with Indians about land issues; I think Morris's position was in line with the view of the Canadian government, and I believe it is supported by Morton's general argument in *A History of the Canadian West to 1870–71*, ch. 11. It is a somewhat complex issue that cannot be rehearsed here. See also Oliver, *The Canadian North-West*, 939.

108 See, for example, Morris, *Treaties*, 205; Ray, Miller, and Tough, *Bounty and Benevolence*, ch. 7.

109 Miller, *Compact, Contract, Covenant*, 172. Miller speculates that this sweeping language had not been part of the oral agreement. Nevertheless, Morris did state, "the treaty was interpreted to them [Indians] carefully" before it was signed; *Treaties*, 178.

110 Miller, *Compact, Contract, Covenant*, 173–75; Ray, Miller, and Tough, *Bounty and Benevolence*, ch. 8.

111 The notion of supplanting is described as a widespread historical phenomenon in Day, *Conquest*, especially ch. 4.

CHAPTER TWO

1 Virtually all of Treaty 8 lay outside territorial Alberta and did not become part of the province of Alberta until 1905, so it remains beyond the compass of this study. The discussion excludes Indians at points like Frog Lake and Cold Lake as a result.

2 Friesen, *Canadian Prairies*, 133; Dempsey, *Maskepetoon*, 224–27.

3 Wilson, *Frontier Farewell*, 99, 210, 213; Friesen, *Canadian Prairies*, 133–35.

4  See Talbot, *Negotiating the Numbered Treaties*, chs. 7–9. The government position, of course, was that it was responsibly negotiating a new treaty each year (1873–75), addressing areas most pressing to the settlement process.

5  Report of Charles Bell, March 1874, cited in McQuillan, "Creation of Indian Reserves," 382–83.

6  Starvation had been a persistent problem for decades. A.J. Ray notes that even before 1821 there had occurred serious game shortages occasioned by "ruinous fur trading competition" in that period. Starvation years were recorded in fur trade records with considerable frequency from the 1820s. Ray, *Telling It to the Judge*, 11; Dempsey, *Maskepetoon*, 24, 31, 102, 131, 143–44, 148–49, 155, 157, 209–10, 217, 230, 231; Daschuk, *Clearing the Plains*, chs. 1–5. What was new in the 1870s was the intensity of the events, and the bleak prospects for any recovery of game, particularly bison.

7  Friesen, *Canadian Prairies*, 143; Morris, *Treaties*, 172. In 1874 and 1875, the Geological Survey employed a large diamond drill to test for mineral deposits along the proposed Pacific railway route; at Fort Carlton, for example, it drilled to a depth of 175 feet. It was this survey activity that the Cree halted. See Zaslow, *Reading the Rocks*, 116. On the stoppage of the telegraph line construction, see Ronaghan, "Three Scouts and the Cart Train," 12–14.

8  Morris, *Treaties*, 173–75. McDougall's actual figure was 3,976, but the basis for such precision is unclear.

9  Ibid., 351–67; Carter and Hildebrandt, "A Better Life with Honour," 246–47. Other important accounts of the negotiation of Treaty 6 include Ray, Miller, and Tough, *Bounty and Benevolence*, ch. 9; and Erasmus, *Buffalo Days and Nights*, ch. 14. Talbot, *Negotiating the Numbered Treaties*, 96–111, provides an account very sympathetic to Morris. On subsequent adhesions, see Dempsey, *Maskepetoon*, 230–31.

10  Morris, *Treaties*, 182–83, 197–98.

11  Lee, "The Importance of the Sacred Pipe Ceremony," 111–12; Ray, Miller, and Tough, *Bounty and Benevolence*, 133. Christie and McKay, whose experience with the Cree and the ceremonies of the fur trade was supposed to be extensive, likely shaped Morris's understanding of the ceremony. Talbot, *Negotiating the Numbered Treaties*, 104, is persuaded that Morris had a good idea of the significance of the pipe ceremony.

12  Carter and Hildebrandt, "A Better Life with Honour," 251; Morris, *Treaties*, ch. 12.

13  Ray, Miller, and Tough, *Bounty and Benevolence*, 131–32.

14  On Erasmus, see Spry, "Introduction," ix–xxxii; Payne, "Erasmus, Peter." He had an unusually high level of education in English (and Greek) for

the day, as well as extensive experience with plains cultures and their languages.

15 Carter and Hildebrandt, "A Better Life with Honour," 351. Indians thoroughly understood the central importance of the written text in the treaty process; even at Treaty 1 they had demanded that the oral promises not included in the written text of the treaty be put in writing.

16 Cited in Chalmers, "Treaty No. Six," 24.

17 Erasmus, *Buffalo Days and Nights*, 244. This outburst, among other things, demonstrates that Poundmaker was able to grasp, from Erasmus's translation, the fundamental idea about the limitations embodied in the government offer concerning reserves.

18 Ibid., 245.

19 Carter and Hildebrandt, "A Better Life with Honour," 352–53; Wilson, *Frontier Farewell*, 172.

20 Morton, *A History of the Canadian West*, 821.

21 On the other hand, the HBC may also have been colouring, if not outright manipulating, the evidence to support its case. The company's governors told their officials who were to testify at the hearings that "our great object before the Committee ... will be to shew [*sic*] that all our regulations for the administration of the country and the conduct of our trade have been such as were calculated to protect the Indians and prevent their demoralization, and that, as far as can be reasonably expected, we have been successful." Cited in den Otter, "The 1857 Parliamentary Inquiry," 145. No Native person was asked to testify.

22 Morris, *Treaties*, 358; Erasmus, *Buffalo Days and Nights*, 250, 253–54. Ray raises questions (*Telling It to the Judge*, 72, 83) concerning the reliability of Erasmus's memoirs because the latter was old when they were produced, and because they were written down by a journalist who interviewed him. However, arguably they constitute a lucid account and were mostly consonant with and even corroborated by other contemporary evidence. Of course, questions of reliability can apply equally to the evidence of aged elders, and to evidence of Indians during the treaty negotiations as recorded by journalists.

23 Price, *The Spirit of the Alberta Indian Treaties*, 105. The only Cree views in Price from the future district of Alberta are from the Hobbema area, which did not take part in the treaty negotiations but took a later adhesion. The evidence of these elders might therefore be considered more second-hand than that of elders from tribes who participated in the negotiations.

24 These misunderstandings were, in fact, common in exchanges between cultures. Lutz, in *Makúk*, 10–11, 22–23, calls them "transformational

exchanges." What one side thought it was giving was not what the other received. Another example might be annuity payments, which whites construed as contractual obligations and a kind of business expense, but which Indians construed as an annual symbolic renewal of a promise of a kinship relationship.

25  Atkin, *Maintain the Right*, 107–08; Robb, "David Laird," 578; Treaty 7 Elders et al., *The True Spirit and Original Intent of Treaty 7*, 76; Titley, *The Indian Commissioners*, 40–43.

26  Robb, "David Laird," 579–80.

27  That is, the first person to hold the office independently; since 1870 the lieutenant governor of Manitoba also had been the lieutenant governor of the North-Western Territory – first Adams Archibald (1870–72) and then Alexander Morris (1872–76). From 1876 to 1905, the region had a separate lieutenant governor.

28  Robb, "David Laird," 580, quoting Lewis H. Thomas.

29  Ibid., 581.

30  Macleod, "James Farquharson Macleod," 673.

31  Ibid.

32  Dempsey, *Crowfoot*, 103–04.

33  Morris, *Treaties*, 266–67, citing reports from the Toronto *Globe*.

34  Ibid., 253; and see Armstrong, *The River Returns*, 37–38. Vital Grandin, bishop of St Albert, was in Fort Macleod and region in the early summer of 1876 and reported that a plague of locusts had destroyed the vegetation from the Red Deer River south to Fort Benton; it seems not to have occasioned much distress among the Native population, however, and by the time of Treaty 7 the region seems to have largely recovered. Dempsey, "A Letter from Bishop Grandin," 8–11.

35  Mayfield, "The Interlude," 35.

36  Morris, *Treaties*, 32. So much for any notion that the commissioners thought that they were dealing with Indians as equals at the treaty talks.

37  Carter and Hildebrandt, "A Better Life with Honour," 258.

38  Denny, *The Law Marches West*, 106–07. Denny may not have been aware that the Cree band headed by Bobtail was there seeking an adhesion to Treaty 6; see Morris, *Treaties*, 256–57, 260, 361–62.

39  Morris, *Treaties*, 257–58. The issue of land security was important to them, because in the United States, Indian lands could be taken by an act of Congress, and this indeed had been done several times with respect to the formerly very large Blackfoot Reservation in Montana and to the Sioux reservation in eastern Montana and the Dakotas. Freedom to hunt off the reserve was the opposite of US policy.

40 Laird operated from the assumption that the Queen already ruled the area, not that she sought to rule it; and because all of them already fell under the Queen's jurisdiction, both the Indian and white populations were brothers (though not equals).

41 The reference was to an ordinance of the North-West Territories Council enacted that spring to restrict the bison hunt. The language, of course, is figurative; it is improbable that the Queen had even heard of the ordinance in question.

42 Morris, *Treaties*, 267–69.

43 Ibid., 257, 268, 368–71.

44 Ibid., 289.

45 Ibid., 270–71.

46 Ibid., 370.

47 Ibid., 270–71; Dempsey, *Crowfoot*, 99.

48 Morris, *Treaties*, 258, 271. Some status Indians and recent interpreters understand this exchange differently than Laird, viewing the laughter of the assembled chiefs as being directed at him, not at Medicine Calf. Dempsey, *Crowfoot*, 100n8. Also see Treaty 7 Elders et al., *True Spirit and Original Intent of Treaty 7*, 252–53, which does not view Laird's words as intended humour but as an "outrageous suggestion that the Blackfoot pay for the protection that the police were offering them." In fact, the subsequent exchanges in 1877 suggest both that Laird was not serious because he never followed up the suggestion, and that the chiefs were much less offended by Laird's humour than later commentators.

49 Morris, *Treaties*, 258. For an excellent discussion of the background to this subject, see Mayfield, "The Interlude," 21–39. See also Carter and Hildebrandt, "A Better Life with Honour," 242–44.

50 Dempsey, *Crowfoot*, 97–107. More details on the interpreters may be found in Treaty 7 Elders et al., *True Spirit and Original Intent of Treaty 7*, 19–22; and in the second part of this chapter. On L'Heureux as an interpreter, see also Huel, "Jean L'Heureux," 11–12.

51 Morris, *Treaties*, 275.

52 Ibid, 368–74. Note that the treaty text, which was read to the assembled chiefs by their own chosen translator, referred to mining, despite later assertions of elders that the subject was never mentioned. For more details, see the second part of this chapter.

53 Record Group 10, vol. 3,695, 14,942 [mfm. Reel 10,122], Scollen to Major Irvine, 13 April 1879; Dempsey, *Crowfoot*, 105.

54 Dempsey, "Isapo-Muxika," 442–45; Dempsey, *Crowfoot*.

55 Dempsey, "Isapo-Muxika," 443.

56 Dempsey, *Crowfoot*, 101–07; Treaty 7 Elders et al., *True Spirit and Original Intent of Treaty 7*, 244–45, 295–96.

57 Dempsey, "Mékaisto," 718; Dempsey, *Red Crow*, ch. 8; Hungry Wolf, *The Blood People*, 236–55.

58 Dempsey, *Red Crow*, 91.

59 An example of the Nizitapi actions that produced this reputation occurred in 1866 when a group of 200 went to Fort Pitt to trade; they forced their way in to the fort, and seized a number of items from the five men occupying it. On their way from the fort they encountered a party of HBC men returning from the hunt with meat provisions, fired at them, and took eight horses and "whatever they wished from the carts." While the HBC men escaped injury, the Nizitapi soon afterward shot and wounded a company clerk. McTavish of the HBC commented, "no cause is assigned for those acts, but it is feared the Blackfeet have made up their minds to be troublesome and are likely to commit more acts of violence." *CSP*, 1867–68, #19 (Return to an Address from the House of Commons, dated 18 November 1867; for Correspondence, Report of Proceedings and other documents, in possession of the Government relative to Hudson's Bay Territory), 16, Mactavish to Thomas Fraser, 31 July 1866. On Scollen, see Huel, "Constantine Scollen," 10–18.

60 Morris, *Treaties*, 247–49. On Scollen's missionary work among the Kainai, see Dempsey, "Sotai-na (Rainy Chief)," 661–62. Wilton Goodstriker in *The True Spirit and Original Intent of Treaty 7* is too dismissive of Scollen, who spent time with the Kainai in 1876–77, and who became close to and respected by Rainy Chief. Scollen did not, despite Goodstriker's assertion, state that the Nizitapi wanted a treaty; he was clear that it was he, and the settlers, who thought a treaty desirable. He did, however, state that they were "expecting to have a mutual understanding with the Government, because they have been told of it by several persons." See also Huel, *Proclaiming the Gospel*, 51–52.

61 Morris, *Treaties*, 252.

62 Carter and Hildebrandt contend that Laird was inconsistent at Blackfoot Crossing, mentioning the passing of a law to protect the buffalo, and shortly thereafter stating that they likely would be destroyed. Still, both were true: the law was passed with good intentions, but his traversal of the country allowed him to see for himself the reality of the crisis. Carter and Hildebrandt, "A Better Life with Honour," 259.

63 Mayfield, "The Interlude," 32.

64 Ibid., 30–31.

65 Dempsey, *Red Crow*, 91; Treaty 7 Elders et al., *True Spirit and Original Intent of Treaty 7*, 74.

66 Snow, *These Mountains Are Our Sacred Places*, 20–21, 24; Hamilton, *From Wilderness to Statehood*, 185–87. On the Baker (or Marias) Massacre, see Wilson, *Frontier Farewell*, 77–78; Sharp, *Whoop-up Country*, 149; McManus, *The Line Which Separates*, 70–71.

67 Snow, *These Mountains Are Our Sacred Places*, 24.

68 Treaty 7 Elders et al., *True Spirit and Original Intent of Treaty 7*, 73–74; Dempsey, *Crowfoot*, 97. Crowfoot had, in Dempsey's word, "spurned" Sitting Bull's attempt to unite the tribes, though he did confer with the Sioux chief, much to the consternation of white officials. See *Crowfoot*, ch. 8.

69 Mayfield, "The Interlude," 28.

70 Treaty 7 Elders et al., *True Spirit and Original Intent of Treaty 7*, 74–75.

71 Snow, *These Mountains Are Our Sacred Places*, 23–25, ch. 3.

72 Treaty 7 Elders et al., *True Spirit and Original Intent of Treaty 7*, 276–77.

73 For example, Henderson, "Interpreting *Sui Generis* Treaties"; Venne, "Understanding Treaty 6."

74 Tosh, *Pursuit of History*, 295, 311.

75 Wertsch, "Collective Memory," 118, 123–24. Put another way, one kind of truth may take precedence over another.

76 Tosh, *Pursuit of History*, 312–13; Friedman, "Fractious Action," 223–67.

77 Tosh, *Pursuit of History*, 313. An excellent case study is Wicken, *Colonization*.

78 "Partial" in two senses: a portion or fraction of; and conveying a particular bias.

79 Dempsey, *Always an Adventure*, 97, 368–69; Wicken, *Colonization*, 240.

80 After 1880 Morris's *Treaties* also was widely available, and later elders' comments reflect familiarity with that text.

81 Treaty 7 Elders et al., *True Spirit and Original Intent of Treaty 7*, 67–68.

82 Ibid., 68–69.

83 Ibid., 77, 78, 81; Snow, *These Mountains Are Our Sacred Places*, 29. The sentiments in the words attributed to Laird are not wholly consonant with what survives of his remarks either at the treaty talks or in documents he wrote; I would like to know more about when these words were spoken, and whether the translation from English to the relevant Native language (perhaps Cree when he was dealing with Stoneys) was accurate. On the use of Cree with the Stoneys, see Treaty 7 Elders et al., *The True Spirit and Original Intent of Treaty 7*, 130–33.

84 Price, *Spirit of the Alberta Indian Treaties*, 105, 108.

85 Ibid., 128–38.

86 Treaty 7 Elders et al., *True Spirit and Original Intent of Treaty 7*, 77.

87 Cited in Carter and Hildebrandt, "A Better Life with Honour," 261–62. However, see n52 above.

88 Treaty 7 Elders et al., *True Spirit and Original Intent of Treaty 7*, 79, 145.

89 On these treaties, see Hamilton, *From Wilderness to Statehood*, 177–84, 189–91; Sharp, *Whoop-up Country*, 142–43, 145; St Germain, *Indian Treaty-Making Policy*, 17, 30–31; Daschuk, *Clearing the Plains*, 91, 225n96.

90 Sealey, "Jerry Potts," 858–59.

91 Wilson, *Frontier Farewell*, 96–97.

92 Dempsey, "Jerry Kiaayo ko'-si," 16. Touchie, in *Bear Child*, 227–28, attributes the problem to alleged inconsistencies in Laird's speech with respect to the buffalo (see n48 above), and claims Kiaayo ko'-si "either did not understand – or he chose not to lie," and in any case did not translate what Laird said. In my judgment, this unduly stretches the evidence, and ignores other evidence about Kiaayo ko'-si's translating abilities at the treaty talks.

93 Treaty 7 Elders et al., *True Spirit and Original Intent of Treaty 7*, 19–21.

94 Ibid., 21. By 1877, Bird had spent much of his time for fifty years among the Nizitapi, and was married into the tribe and integrated with them. At the time of his death, according to a personal communication from Binnema, he was regarded on the Blackfoot Reservation as a Piikani. He spoke French and English as well as five Native languages. Wilson, *Frontier Farewell*, 178.

95 Treaty 7 Elders et al., *True Spirit and Original Intent of Treaty 7*, 21–22; Huel, "Jean L'Heureux"; Kennedy, "A Map and Partial Manuscript of Blackfoot Country," 7–8. Huel provides evidence that L'Heureux was both gay and a pedophile. The DIA paid him for some years in the 1880s to act as an interpreter, and as a recruiter for the Dunbow industrial school, until his "eccentricities" led to his dismissal in 1891.

96 Treaty 7 Elders et al., *True Spirit and Original Intent of Treaty 7*, 22; a more critical Stoney assessment of McDougall's Cree skills is at 132, but it does not explain why the Cree themselves appear to have been much less critical. Scollen later claimed that the quality of interpretation had been poor, and that he had recommended suitable interpreters but had been ignored; Record Group 10, vol. 3,695, Scollen to Irvine, 13 April 1879.

97 Treaty 7 Elders et al., *True Spirit and Original Intent of Treaty 7*, 76, 81. See also Wilson, *Frontier Farewell*, 178–79. It may be that the Stoney Nakoda and possibly Tsuu T'ina, who were more comfortable in Cree than in Blackfoot, necessitated some discussion in Cree. Some Blackfoot

speakers may have misconstrued this as interpreters using Cree because they did not know sufficient Blackfoot. Indeed, the missionaries preached to, and freely interacted with, the Stoney Nakoda in Cree, which many of them evidently understood.

98  Hungry Wolf and Hungry Wolf, *Indian Tribes of the Northern Rockies*, 53; Snow, *These Mountains Are Our Sacred Places*, 34–41. McDougall also arranged, with Chiniki's cooperation, to have all three bands assigned reserves near his Morleyville mission, which the Stoneys considered to be Chiniki territory; Bearspaw's and Kichipwot's bands traditionally had occupied lands well south and north, respectively, of Chiniki's.

99  Snow, *These Mountains Are Our Sacred Places*, 34–36.

100  Treaty 7 Elders et al., *True Spirit and Original Intent of Treaty 7*, 80.

101  Ibid., 25–28; Carter and Hildebrandt, "A Better Life with Honour," 262–63. Kiaayo ko'-si has become "several" in Goodstriker's account.

102  Morris, *Treaties*, 258–59, 270–73.

103  Treaty 7 Elders et al., *True Spirit and Original Intent of Treaty 7*, 82. Freedom from taxation was a provision of the Indian Act (sec. 64–65) granting an exemption from taxes on real or personal property on reserves, and was not included in any treaty. See Boswell, "'Civilizing' the Indian," 90; Bartlett, "Taxation," 581, 584–85.

104  Morris, *Treaties*, 270, 272. Such a positive reaction to colonizers who brought peace, especially through ending internecine intertribal warfare, was very common in many parts of the world; see Diamond, *The World until Yesterday*, 148–49.

105  Treaty 7 Elders et al., *True Spirit and Original Intent of Treaty 7*, 71. I have chosen to follow this account of the memory of the elders. Another account provides a recollection of Pemmican's advice, and if this is accurate, Isapo-Muxika's speech was heavily influenced by that of Pemmican; see Dempsey, *Crowfoot*, 101–02.

106  Treaty 7 Elders et al., *True Spirit and Original Intent of Treaty 7*, 72–73.

107  Dempsey, *Red Crow*, 97.

108  Ibid., 98–101.

109  Wilson, *Frontier Farewell*, 180. Conrad also was a signatory of Treaty 7.

110  Dempsey, *Always an Adventure*, 134.

111  Ray, *Telling It to the Judge*, 78–80, 83.

112  Even today when individuals enter into contracts or arrangements with basic understanding of issues and plenty of expert advice, subsequently questions arise that ideally would have been clarified in advance; the problem is vastly complicated when the arrangements are between different legal systems and cultures.

113 Treaty 7 Elders et al., *True Spirit and Original Intent of Treaty 7*, 67–69. As to the treaties being unalterable documents, Tobias notes that Cree leaders Little Pine, Piapot, and Big Bear believed that "the treaties were inadequate and that revisions were necessary." Tobias, "Canada's Subjugation of the Plains Cree," 524.

114 If Dempsey is a reliable guide, Indians seem never to have made important treaties among themselves for purposes other than temporary relief from warfare, so it is understandable that a peace treaty was the model that was in their minds when it came to treaties with Canada. On the varieties of Indian treaties, see *Maskepetoon*, 170–72.

115 DIA Annual Report, 1882, 171–72; and see Wilson, *Frontier Farewell*, ch. 7. On horse stealing, see chapter 9 in this book.

116 Brown, *Big History*, 75–80. On these matters, see chapter 5 in this book.

117 Hall, "A Serene Atmosphere," 341, 349. See also Seed, *American Pentimento*, 126, 129.

118 This is very different from the notion of invoking God for a common purpose in the treaties.

119 *CSP*, 1872, #22, 9. See also discussion of Treaty 3 in chapter 1 in this book.

120 Morris, *Treaties*, 353, 369; Treaty 7 Elders et al., *The True Spirit and Original Intent of Treaty 7*, 233. Concerning the white understanding, Gibson in a private communication notes, "the common law view was that, unless expressly stated to the contrary, ownership of the surface of land or water includes a vast inverted spatial pyramid extending, so far as occupation or use was possible, down to the centre of the earth and upwards to the heavens. It is hardly surprising that Aboriginal people did not understand or share that perception."

121 In the United States, the treaties were between the president and Senate on the one hand, and Native Americans on the other. Native Americans were judged incapable of transacting their own business affairs, and were not regarded as having title to land in fee simple. Furthermore, in 1831 the Supreme Court ruled that the Cherokee Nation was "a domestic dependent nation" – a decision with widespread ramifications. Many American politicians believed that the process of Senate ratification of treaties with Native Americans as independent nations was a "farce," leading to termination of the practice in 1871. Washburn, *Red Man's Land*, 65–69; St Germain, *Indian Treaty-Making*, 13–20. Richard White, in contrast, contends that post-1871 agreements with Native Americans amounted to treaties in all but name; *Railroaded*, 60–61.

122 This insight is courtesy of Theodore Binnema in personal communication.

123 In fairness, while officials clearly knew that Indians had the legal right to appeal issues under the treaties and the Indian Act to the courts, they took measures to try to ensure that this did not happen.

124 Miller, "Compact, Contract, Covenant," 66–72; Miller, *Compact, Contract, Covenant*, ch. 1–2.

125 This point is made persuasively in den Otter, "1857 Parliamentary Inquiry."

126 Friesen, "Magnificent Gifts," 47. The notion could be put more accurately as "commissioners appeared to the Natives to accept." Indian perception ought not to be equated with white understanding.

127 For a broad discussion of the changing ways in which Canada's Indians perceived this relationship with the Queen in the late nineteenth century, and the ways in which whites came to use the idea to try to manipulate them, see Miller, "Victoria's 'Red Children.'"

128 See chapter 5 in this book. Note that Indians had engaged successfully in agriculture, mostly as a supplement to hunting and gathering, in the future north-western Ontario and Manitoba; they sometimes even profited by selling their surplus to the HBC. While this was well to the east of the future Alberta, it (along with the example of Indian farmers in central Canada) persuaded whites that prairie Indians could learn to farm. See Moodie and Kaye, "Indian Agriculture in the Fur Trade Northwest," 171–83.

129 Some contend that the bison remained sufficiently abundant in the mid-1870s to provide a meaningful alternative, and that there were those, like the Stoney Nakoda in the foothills and the Cree and Stoneys north of the North Saskatchewan River, who had more varied food resources that could have sustained them. (Thanks to Donald Smith for pointing this out.) But my reading of the evidence is that from the early 1870s the Indians under discussion here were very worried about the sustainability of their traditional food supply in both parklands and plains, that some of them were facing starvation in some years, and that sufficient bison were only more or less reliably available in American territory, which was increasingly closed to them.

130 Morris, *The Treaties of Canada with the Indians*, 169–70. They asked about "the intention of the Canadian Government in relation to them." In 1875 the reference was to the government and the "Great Chief," as well as to the "Great Queen." Ibid., 173–75.

131 Ibid., 210–11.

132 Saywell, *The Office of Lieutenant Governor*, ch. 1, esp. 14–15.

133 Creighton, *John A. Macdonald*, vol. 2, ch. 3; Stacey, *Canada and the Age of Conflict*, vol. 1, 19–30; Smith, *The Treaty of Washington*. The

argument of modern Indians amounts to this: since Canada did not have treaty-making power, and since Indians were sovereign at the time of negotiating the treaties, the negotiation therefore had to have been between them and the Queen (British Crown), and the British had the power to bind their colony Canada to the agreed-upon provisions.

134 One way to appreciate the different nature of international treaties and treaties negotiated with Indians is that the former are mostly adhered to (or abandoned) voluntarily, while the latter were enforceable at law in the Canadian courts even prior to the constitutional entrenchment of Indians' rights in 1982. See also Henderson, "Interpreting *Sui Generis* Treaties" (for a radical Native perspective); Borrows and Rotman, "The *Sui Generis* Nature of Aboriginal Rights."

135 *CSP*, 1869, #25 (Report of Delegates appointed to negotiate for the acquisition of Rupert's Land and the North-West Territory), 5–10, Lord Kimberley to C.B. Adderley, 27 October 1868; Adderley to Kimberley, 1 December 1868. There is some ambiguity about how reserves were understood at this time, and a tendency to assume retrospectively that they might have looked similar to those created in the 1870s. Yet in 1857 at the parliamentary inquiry most parties, including HBC officials, appeared to assume that the best policy would be to remove Indians from the arable or fertile lands that white farmers would soon settle, and to have them remain on the northern fringes of the territory until they were "civilized" enough to mingle with the settler community. There is no indication of how this sweeping policy might have been implemented. It also is far from clear how this policy could be reconciled with the equally common view that Indians needed to pursue agriculture as part of the civilizing process. See den Otter, "The 1857 Parliamentary Inquiry," 160–63, 167.

136 *CSP*, 1869, #25, 36–7, Sir F. Rogers to Sir S.H. Northcote, 3 April 1869, and Memorandum of 22 March 1869. Useful on the transfer are Ray, Miller, and Tough, *Bounty and Benevolence*, ch. 4; and Morton, *History of the Canadian West*, 842–52. There is no evidence that the Canadian government subsequently consulted with Britain on the treaties.

137 Note that this practice was not universal; witness British practice in Australia, British Columbia, and elsewhere.

138 All citations in this paragraph from Ray, Miller, and Tough, *Bounty and Benevolence*, 60–61.

139 *CSP*, 1871, #23 (SSP, Indian Branch), 3–4. The proposals of HBC officials in 1857 raise significant questions about the company's beneficence and wisdom.

140  Carter and Hildebrandt, "A Better Life with Honour," 237.

141  Morris, *Treaties*, 274–75. The requirement to abide by the laws of the Great Mother surely meant different things to the commissioner and Indians. Anderson and Robertson, in *Seeing Red*, 4, claim, "the treaty system … effectively stripped Aboriginals of the vast majority of their lands at the end of a gun barrel or with the implied threat of violence. This amounted to naked military conquest." They offer no evidence for this statement.

142  One recent work, referring to a 1983 article by Tobias, maintains, "Tobias' work made it impossible for researchers to take the self-serving professions of government treaty negotiators and other officials at face value." Ray, Miller, and Tough, *Bounty and Benevolence*, 208. My reading of Tobias found little evidence to support this assertion, certainly for the period through 1877. Indeed, Tobias demonstrates that those who had negotiated the treaties subsequently tried to persuade "the government [to] act quickly to establish reserves and honour the treaties." See Tobias, "Canada's Subjugation of the Plains Cree," 518–48; quotation on 525. Talbot, *Negotiating the Numbered Treaties*, ch. 9, makes an extremely persuasive case in this regard for Morris. On Laird, post-treaty, see Titley, *The Indian Commissioners*, 52–61. Treaty 7 Elders et al., *True Spirit and Original Intent of Treaty 7*, 251–56, is critical of Laird; I respond to these criticisms in chapter 4 and elsewhere in this book.

143  Morris, *Treaties*, 296–97.

### CHAPTER THREE

1  *CSP*, 1880, #4 (Interior), xii. Macdonald likely was reflecting the sentiments of Alexander Morris, who wrote in 1880, "the provisions of these treaties must be carried out with the utmost good faith and the nicest exactness." Morris, *Treaties*, 285.

2  Miller, *Compact, Contract, Covenant*, 155. To this list, add "corrupt": see Daschuk, *Clearing the Plains*, chs. 6–9.

3  *CSP*, 1880, #4, 77; 1881, #14 (DIA), 81.

4  See discussion in chapter 1 in this book.

5  The exception was Macdonald, who gave up the Ministry of the Interior in 1883 but remained superintendent general until 1887 (see appendix 1 in this book). The general point remains, however: as prime minister, Indian Affairs was hardly his principal focus.

6  For a listing of deputy superintendents general, see appendix 1.

7 I frequently acknowledge parsimony in expenditures on Native peoples. However, parsimony extended to government employees as well. According to a major study, DIA officers were "often underpaid, ill-clothed and badly housed." The same complaints arose from the NWMP, where officers received "low pay, bad accommodation, insufficient replacements for worn uniforms and poor meals." Leighton, "The Development of Federal Indian Policy," 556; Sowby, "Macdonald the Administrator," 106.

8 The same might be said of the outcome of Vankoughnet's tour of the west in 1883; see CSP, 1884, #4 (DIA), x (Report of Superintendent General).

9 For a listing of Indian commissioners, see appendix 1. The standard work on this subject is Titley, *The Indian Commissioners*; see also Titley, *The Frontier World of Edgar Dewdney*. Note that Wemyss Mackenzie Simpson was named commissioner in 1871, but his tenure was short and his brief different.

10 Titley, *The Indian Commissioners*, 207.

11 CSP, 1879, #7 (Interior), 64 (Laird to Macdonald, 11 November 1878), and 84; 1880, #4 (Interior), 101–02. There also was one agent, Col A. McDonald, for Treaty 4. The principal work on this is Looy, "The Indian Agent and His Role," esp. 122.

12 CSP, 1880, #4, 101.

13 CSP, 1881, #14 (DIA), 95–96, 124–25; see also CSP, 1880, #4, 99.

14 CSP, 1906, #27 (DIA), part 2, 159–64; this figure refers to the district of Alberta, not to the number in the enlarged province from September 1905.

15 Note that in some years inspectors of agencies doubled as inspectors of Indian schools; but often there were officials appointed only as inspectors of Indian schools, usually separate persons for Roman Catholic and Protestant schools.

16 Daugherty and Madill, *Indian Government*, 6, chs. 1–2.

17 Ibid., 12.

18 Ibid., 30, 36, ch. 3.

19 Ibid., 70. See also Pettipas, *Severing the Ties that Bind*, 72–73.

20 Niemi-Bohun contends, "the percentage of absences [on annuity distribution lists] typically ranged between 8 and 21 per cent." Niemi-Bohun, "Colonial," 93n57.

21 I elaborate on these points in succeeding chapters.

22 CSP, 1882, #6 (DIA), 113–14.

23 *Census of the Three Provisional Districts of the North-West Territories, 1884–5*, 3, 10–11. The *Census* used the English/French terms

"Indians / Sauvages" and "Half-Breeds / Métis"; I have chosen Indians and Metis as the less offensive in modern usage.

24 *Report of the Fourth Census of Canada, 1901,* 5, 393.

25 I discuss this matter in more detail in chapter 4.

26 According to the Saddle Lake Cree Nation website (www.saddlelake.ca), in 1902 the government forced an amalgamation of four bands or tribes that would be known as IR 125: Onchaminahos (Little Hunter), James Seenum, Blue Quill, and Wasatnow. This is not mentioned in the relevant departmental annual reports (though see table 3.6), and administratively government officials continued to report the bands separately, though they noted some population movement between them. The Wasatnow band merged with the Blue Quill band in 1894 owing to a small and declining population. According to the website, "the bands did not find [the amalgamation agreements] suitable for very long. Dissatisfaction with the results of the merger broke out only a few years after signing."

27 Added to the Native population of Alberta when it became a province was much, though not all, of the Treaty 6 population of the Onion Lake Agency (Onion Lake, Cold Lake, and Frog Lake), given as 930 souls; CSP, 1906, #27 (DIA), part 2, 78. The northern half of the new province encompassed most of Treaty 8 of 1899, the total population of which was given by the department as 3,308. CSP, 1906, #27, part 2, 90.

CHAPTER FOUR

1 *CSP,* 1878, #10 (Interior), xv (Annual Report of the Minister).

2 One study maintains that Macdonald was engaged in many aspects of administration in his departments, often addressing these matters late into the evening. He personally supervised nearly all civil service appointments and other patronage. See Sowby, "Macdonald the Administrator," 2–9, 103, ch. 6.

3 Gwyn, *Nation Maker,* vol. 2, 399, 417, 419.

4 *Debates,* 1880, 1991 (5 May 1880). On the origin of the Indian quotation, see Gwyn, *Nation Maker,* 423fn. A frustrated Macdonald, just after the conclusion of the North-West Rebellion in 1885, expressed these views more crudely: "we cannot change the barbarian, the savage, into a civilised man." *Debates,* 1885, 3119 (6 July 1885).

5 *Debates,* 1881, 1427 (17 March 1881); 1882, 1186 (27 April 1882).

6 Clothing was not a treaty obligation, apart from that provided for chiefs and headmen. But traditional Indian clothing derived from hunting and trapping was no longer sufficiently available, resources to purchase

clothing from whites were scarce, and lack of proper clothing hampered many everyday activities.

7  Record Group (RG) 10, vol. 3695, 14,942 (reel 10,122), Scollen to Irvine, 13 April 1879. That is, from very early on the Indians understood the spirit of the treaty to encompass more than the written terms.

8  Dempsey, *Crowfoot*, 108–09; Dempsey, *Red Crow*, 103–04. The mild winter and absence of snow melt left water levels so low that surveyor W.F. King reported fording the North Saskatchewan River with his carts at Edmonton in April 1878, a very rare event. *CSP*, 1879, #7 (Interior), appendix 4, 17.

9  Dempsey, *Crowfoot*, 112; Stanley, *The Birth of Western Canada*, 226; Beal and Macleod, *Prairie Fire*, 65; *CSP*, 1877, #11 (Interior), xii, xxxvi.

10  Dempsey, *Crowfoot*, 112; Dempsey, "The Starvation Year," 6–12. The starvation years are vividly portrayed in Daschuk, *Clearing the Plains*, ch. 7.

11  RG 10, file 15,266 (reel 101,220, Dewdney to Col Dennis, 22 July 1879); file 16,142, Laird to Dewdney, 28 August 1879.

12  RG 10, (reel 10,122), file 15,142, Confidential Report, 6 August 1879.

13  Beal and Macleod, *Prairie Fire*, 61–62, 72. Recall that during the Treaty 6 negotiations, the commissioners spoke against the idea that Indians should be fed by the government every day, and Indian leaders firmly stated that such was not their intent: they wanted rations for the first three years of settlement on the reserves, and thereafter only in emergencies. At no point in 1876 or 1877 did Indian leaders indicate that they expected ongoing daily rations from the government as a price for signing the treaties; they almost certainly could not have imagined that it might become necessary.

14  There is at least a partial parallel with the three-year trial period for white homesteaders. While homesteaders did not receive government assistance, they were supposed to create a viable farm within three years, after which they could receive title to their land. Dyck calls the government policies "coercive tutelage"; for a definition and examination, see *What Is the Indian 'Problem,'* 24, ch. 6.

15  *CSP*, 1879, #7 (Interior), 59–63; year ending 30 June 1878. There also was some distribution of flour, tea, and potatoes to the Stoney bands in Treaty 7.

16  *CSP*, 1879, #7, 64 (Laird report, November 1878).

17  *CSP*, 1879, #7 (Interior), 5–6. See also Titley, *The Indian Commissioners*, 57–58.

18  Titley, *The Indian Commissioners*, 66–67. The standard biography is Titley, *The Frontier World of Edgar Dewdney*. A useful discussion of the evolution of government policy in this period is Dyck, "The Administration of Federal Indian Aid," 28–37. On the establishment and failure of the

home farm system, see Carter, *Lost Harvests*, 81–94. See also chapter 6 of this volume.

19  RG 10, (reel 10,122), file 15,266, Dewdney to Col Dennis, 22 July 1879.

20  This was an accepted Biblical principle; see I Thess. 2:9; II Thess. 3:8–10.

21  Dempsey, *Crowfoot*, 112–15; Dewdney provided a detailed report in CSP, 1880, #4 (Interior), 76–104; Sowby, "Macdonald the Administrator," 190–91. See also Titley, *Frontier World*, 39–45.

22  Dempsey, *Crowfoot*, ch. 11.

23  CSP, 1881, #14 (DIA), 102–03; on Stewart, see RG 10, (reel 20,211), file 14,875. He was fired in 1881 for incompetence (poor accounting for use of resources) and extravagance. See Tyler, "A Tax-Eating Proposition," 40–44. At Edmonton and Fort Saskatchewan by 30 June 1879, some 3,700 pounds of flour, 1,038 pounds of pemmican, and 2,100 pounds of pounded meat had been distributed; much more by the end of the year, and even more in the first part of 1880. Stewart had added in small quantities of raisins, sugar, and chocolate, to which the Ottawa authorities took umbrage. "A Tax-Eating Proposition," 36, 44.

24  CSP, 1882, #6 (DIA), 84.

25  *Debates*, 1882, 1,186 (27 April 1882). Mills argued that Indians had become "pensioners upon the Public Treasury," fed and clothed by the government, but "doing little or nothing for themselves. Now, I believe a barbarous population like the Indians may very easily be made wholly dependent upon the Government." Sowby contends that starving Indians did not stimulate more work, but increased dependency upon the government for food and clothing. Sowby, "Macdonald the Administrator," 23.

26  Dyck, "The Administration of Federal Indian Aid," 50–58. Dyck also details several other examples of bureaucratic incompetence.

27  McQuillan, "Creation of Indian Reserves," 391–92 (citing Hayter Reed, 1883).

28  Cited in Price, *The Spirit of the Alberta Indian Treaties*, 116.

29  Hanks and Hanks, *Tribe under Trust*, 14. On similar tactics used to enhance the size of Indian families to increase annuities and rations, see Dempsey, *Charcoal's World*, 9–10. The Liberal opposition in 1881 charged rampant annuities fraud, amounting to thousands of extra claims each year; see *Debates*, 11 March 1881, 1348–54.

30  Taylor, *Standing Alone*, 30. Adolf and Beverly Hungry Wolf assert that after the signing of Treaty 7, "members from all divisions [of the Blackfoot nation] continue[d] to go back and forth across the border for some years,

to collect treaty goods and payments." Hungry Wolf and Hungry Wolf, *Indian Tribes of the Northern Rockies*, 13.

31  *CSP*, 1881, #14 (DIA), 85–86.

32  On this, see Miller, *Compact, Contract, Covenant*, 97–99.

33  *CSP*, 1879, #7 (Interior), 195–96. The cost of provisions and initial treaty payments (gratuities) for Treaty 7 was just under $73,000. Ibid., 206–07.

34  *CSP*, 1881, #14 (DIA), 88–89 (concerning payments at Fort Macleod, 1880).

35  Stanley, *Birth of Western Canada*, 270.

36  Titley, *Edgar Dewdney*, ch. 3.

37  Morris, *Treaties*, 369–70; Dempsey, *Crowfoot*, 104; Larmour, *Laying down the Lines*, 37.

38  The government began to survey in 1878, but that work was rendered fruitless by Indians' change of mind. Larmour, *Laying down the Lines*, 38.

39  Dempsey, *Red Crow*, 108–10. In 1883, the Kainai, Tsuu T'ina, and Siksika formally surrendered the reserve set out in the 1877 treaty in favour of the new ones. The Siksika moved somewhat south because the route for the CPR would have run through their original lands. See Larmour, *Laying down the Lines*, 38. Dempsey, in *Always an Adventure*, 375–76, notes the reduction in the figures for the Kainai who received annuities, from 3,542 in 1882 to 2,589 in 1883, when the reserve was actually surveyed; his research did not explain the discrepancy, but it clearly led to a smaller reserve.

40  Details of the 1883–84 revisions of the land provisions of Treaty 7 may be found in Canada, *Indian Treaties and Surrenders*, vol. 2., 128–38. See also Armstrong et al., *The River Returns*, 326–27. Former Indian Agent R.N. Wilson regarded these new reserve delineations as amounting to another treaty with the Siksika, Kainai, Piikani, Stoney Nakoda, and Tsuu T'ina. See Wilson, *Our Betrayed Wards*, 2–3.

41  Snow, *These Mountains*, 32–38.

42  Ibid., 39–41. See also Larmour, *Laying down the Lines*, 39. A different perspective, no less critical, is found in Treaty 7 Elders et al., *The True Spirit and Original Intent of Treaty 7*, 167–70.

43  Larmour, *Laying down the Lines*, 41–43.

44  McQuillan, "Creation of Indian Reserves," 387. On the other hand, Dempsey is persuaded that "skulduggery" lay behind the survey of the Kainai reserve; *Always an Adventure*, 376–77. Note that the government's apparent slowness in surveying reserves was mostly due to its struggle to survey enough land in Manitoba and the eastern North-West Territories to

maintain an orderly process of white settlement. Many other surveyors were occupied with establishing the CPR's route.

45 The name was spelled in several ways (e.g., Papaschase, Paspaschase); the band also was known as the Pahpastayo band, or sometimes by the translation "Woodpecker." See Tyler, "A Tax-Eating Proposition," 30n18. Unless otherwise indicated, the material that follows on the Passpasschase issue derives from Tyler's work, ch. 2. Also useful are Sanders, "The Expropriation of Indian Reserve Lands," 153–66; and *South Edmonton Saga*, 15–24. (Thanks to Robert Davidson for bringing this reference to my attention.) A brief account from an Indian perspective is Dion, *My Tribe, The Crees*, 183–84.

46 Melanie Niemi-Bohun, "Colonial Categories and Familial Responses," 73n5, notes that the straggler category encompassed "Native individuals who did not reside with or belong to a designated band at the time [the band] entered treaty, and … individuals or groups who initially refused to enter treaty." She contends that the Edmonton Stragglers were overwhelmingly female.

47 The government began to seek surrenders of reserve lands in the 1880s (Passpasschase), and the process gradually intensified over the next two or three decades (see appendix 2 for the period to 1905). In most cases, Indians were resistant and insistent upon their rights, determined to protect their reserves as far as possible, so the government had to manipulate the process to secure surrenders. See also n116 and n117 below.

48 An excellent brief discussion is in Abley, *Conversations with a Dead Man*, 140.

49 On this movement, see Ens, *Homeland to Hinterland*, 111–22. Agriculture in Red River had been perilous and uncertain, with many partial or total crop failures owing to pests, drought, frost, primitive technology, and crops not always suited to the region. By contrast, the bison hunt proved somewhat more reliable and was, as one writer observes, "essential for the survival of the people of the Red River Settlement and the success of the fur trade economy." Sprenger, "The Métis Nation," 115–30. In the settlements in the future Alberta, agriculture was probably as reliable as in Red River in the 1860s and bison were more readily accessible.

50 Giraud, *The Métis in the Canadian West*, vol. 2, ch. 33. A useful twenty-first century view of Metis settlements, rather dismissive of Giraud, is Ray, *Telling It to the Judge*, chs. 6–7. Ray testified on behalf of the Metis in court cases, and argued for a somewhat decentered, much enlarged definition of a Metis community.

51 Dickason, "Metis," 201; Devine, "Les Desjarlais," 152; Devine, *The People Who Own Themselves.*

52 Beal, Foster, and Zuk, *The Métis Hivernement Settlement*, 13–14. The authors note that Metis who had come from outside the region to trap and hunt bison and even winter there, "risked depredations not only from bands of the Blackfoot Confederacy but from Assiniboine and possible Cree bands with whom they did not have kin relations."

53 On the relative infrequency of intermarriage between outsiders and the Nizitapi, see Wissler and Kehoe, *Amskapi Pikuni*, 31–32.

54 Beal, Foster, and Zuk, *The Métis Hivernement Settlement*, chs. 2–3; Metis Association of Alberta et al., *Metis Land Rights in Alberta*, 18–20; Baldwin, "Wintering Villages of the Metis Hivernants"; Jamieson, "The Edmonton Hunt," 10–18.

55 Beal, Foster, and Zuk, *The Métis Hivernement Settlement*, 102. The petition, and Laird's response, appear in CSP, 1885, #116 (Papers and Correspondence in connection with Half-breed Claims and other matters relating to the North-West Territories), 22–23. Useful for contextualizing the situation in the 1870s are Niemi-Bohun, "Colonial Categories and Familial Responses"; Ens, "Hybridity."

56 CSP, 1885, #116, 23.

57 Ibid., 11–17.

58 Ens, "Metis Ethnicity," 164.

59 Ibid.

60 Ens, "Hybridity," 236–37, 242–43.

61 CSP, 1877, #11 (Interior), xxxiii–xxxv. See also Niemi-Bohun, "Colonial Categories and Familial Responses," 83–84.

62 CSP, 1877, #11, xxxvii–xxxviii.

63 This story is recounted in CSP, 1885, #116, 31 (30 September 1878); 39–40 (15 November 1878, and comments); 1882, #18 (Interior), 15 February 1882. Dennis (1820–1885) headed the survey party when Riel stopped it in 1869; but he had some subsequent experience in the West as a surveyor, and thus some exposure to the Metis. He was appointed deputy minister by Macdonald in November 1878, and retired at the end of 1880. See Read, "John Stoughton Dennis," 244–46. Note that the Lac la Biche band was not the only one made up largely of Metis.

64 43 Vict., ch. 28 (7 May 1880), sec. 14; Dickason, "Metis," 203. On the origins of the Metis conception of aboriginal title and land rights, see Metis Association of Alberta et al., *Metis Land Rights*, 69–73. Tom Pocklington makes the useful point that the extinction of such aboriginal rights as the

Metis of the North-West Territories had was accomplished by the government unilaterally rather than by negotiation and treaty; the same was true for how the Metis would be compensated (with land). Pocklington, *The Government and Politics of the Alberta Metis Settlements*, 6.

65 A good starting point is Beal and Macleod, *Prairie Fire*.

66 *CSP*, 1885, #116, 42–44.

67 *CSP*, 1882, #18 (Interior), 15 February 1882.

68 *CSP*, 1885, #116, 93–96 (Remarks on the Condition of the Half-breeds of the North-West Territories, 20 December 1878); and see Sowby, "Macdonald the Administrator," 137–38. The division into two classes of Metis is supported by Morris, *Treaties*, 294–95, and Giraud, *The Métis in the Canadian West*, vol. 2, ch. 33. See also Flanagan, *Riel and the Rebellion*, 76–77. Ray, *Telling It to the Judge*, 106–09, largely rejects the typology of Metis and their settlements portrayed by Giraud and, by implication, Dennis. Without debating the matter, my point is that Dennis's was a representative and influential view in his day, and underlay official government views of the western Metis in the late nineteenth century.

69 *CSP*, 1885, #116, 90–92. Davin's report may be found in Early Canadiana Online. Milloy states that Davin was "the first to make a link between anticipated disorder and the utility of a residential school system." But the idea originated with Dennis, arising at least as much from concern about the Metis as about the Indians. Milloy, *A National Crime*, 31.

70 Miller, *Shingwauk's Vision*, 101–02.

71 Flanagan, *Riel and the Rebellion*, 77–78.

72 A point made in 1879 in the *Saskatchewan Herald*; quoted in Beal and Macleod, *Prairie Fire*, 62–63.

73 Cited in Beal and Macleod, *Prairie Fire*, 74–75. See also Stonechild and Waiser, *Loyal till Death*, 46–47.

74 Beal and Macleod, *Prairie Fire*, 78.

75 *CSP*, 1882, #18 (Interior), pt. 3, 50–55 (report from L.N.F. Crozier); Stanley, *Birth of Western Canada*, 278; Dempsey, "The Bull Elk Affair," 2–9.

76 Dempsey, *Crowfoot*, 142–45; DIA Annual Report, 1882, 168–69 (C.E. Denny).

77 Ibid., 279–80; Beal and Macleod, *Prairie Fire*, 81–85.

78 See, e.g., Beal and Macleod, *Prairie Fire*, 279–80.

79 On some of these issues, see James Dempsey, "Persistence of a Warrior Ethic," especially 4–6. Dempsey notes that as "the old nomadic ways ... were now suppressed ... religion [and ritual] became the main avenue left

for the males to follow to retain their dignity and find relief from the dull and oppressive reserve life. It also became a consolation at a time when one-half of many Plains bands were carried off by epidemics."

80  Dempsey, *Crowfoot*, ch. 8.

81  The seminal work on this is Tobias, "Canada's Subjugation," 519–48. Dempsey, *Big Bear*, is useful, but was completed too early to benefit from Tobias's work. On Big Bear's political activity, see Beal and Macleod, *Prairie Fire*, ch. 4. The proposed 1885 meeting of chiefs is central to Stonechild and Waiser's explanation of why almost all Cree chiefs declined to join cause with Riel in *Loyal till Death*, chs. 3–5.

82  Stonechild and Waiser, *Loyal till Death*. The source of the title of the book is found at page 176, in a letter of 10 April 1885 by the Hobbema chiefs to Indian Commissioner Dewdney, promising that they would "have nothing to do with the insurgents," and that they would fulfil their treaty promises to the Queen and "remain loyal till death."

83  Sprague, *Canada and the Métis*. Ens has argued that the movement of Metis west and north was more a product of pursuit of economic and other interests than of displacement from their lands in Manitoba. Ens, *Homeland to Hinterland*; see also Flanagan, *Metis Lands in Manitoba*.

84  Dempsey, *Crowfoot*, 118–24.

85  Almost everything about the rebellion, its causes and outcome, Metis land rights, Riel, and the involvement of Indians has been contested in the historical literature. The best introduction to these events is Beal and Macleod, *Prairie Fire*. Especially useful on the matter of Indian involvement is Stonechild and Waiser, *Loyal till Death*. If somewhat dated in interpretation, the works of Stanley (*The Birth of Western Canada* and *Louis Riel*) remain immensely informative. Note that the Frog Lake site was incorporated into the new province of Alberta in 1905.

86  This is documented in Stonechild and Waiser, *Loyal till Death*.

87  On Strange, see Macleod, "Introduction," xi–xxi; Macleod, "Strange, Thomas Bland," 981–82; McCullough, "Gunner Jingo," 2–9.

88  Beal and Macleod, *Prairie Fire*, 208.

89  CSP, 1886, #4 (DIA), xlvi. See Rowand, "The Rebellion at Lac la Biche," 1–9.

90  Beal and Macleod, *Prairie Fire*, 209–12; Waddell, "The Honorable Frank Oliver," 127. See also Breen, "'Timber Tom,'" for an insightful analysis of the excitement at Edmonton and Calgary.

91  Beal and Macleod, *Prairie Fire*, 212.

92  Ibid., ch. 15.

93  Stonechild and Waiser, *Loyal till Death*, 175–76.

94  Beal and Macleod, *Prairie Fire*, 234–35; Stonechild and Waiser, *Loyal till Death*, 173–74; Rowand, "Rebellion at Lac la Biche"; Stanley, "Indian Raid at Lac la Biche," 25–27.

95  Stonechild and Waiser, *Loyal till Death*, 176.

96  Dempsey, *Crowfoot*, ch. 15; Dempsey, *Red Crow*, ch. 14; Dempsey, "Blackfoot Peace Treaties," 22. Dempsey views the situation differently than do Stonechild and Waiser, claiming that Crowfoot by 1885 was suspicious of the government and that "he would [have] liked to have joined with the Cree insurgents," only being prevented by Red Crow's opposition and by his belief that the rebellion was doomed to failure. See Dempsey, "The Bull Elk Affair," 8–9. If so, Lacombe and the government officials were correct in their assessment of Crowfoot. John Jennings, "The Plains Indians and the Law," 65, argues that the fact that rebellion did not break out in the Treaty 7 area "was primarily due to the work of the Mounted Police." This, not unexpectedly, also was the view of Cecil E. Denny, former NWMP superintendent in the area, who was recalled in 1885 to secure the peace in the Treaty 7 area; see Denny, *The Law Marches West*, ch. 25. These concerns notwithstanding, Macdonald later told the House of Commons that Crowfoot was "not only a great chief but a great man." *Debates*, 1887, 1110, 17 June 1887.

97  See Beal and Macleod, *Prairie Fire*, ch. 16–17.

98  Stonechild and Waiser, *Loyal till Death*, 193, 214–37.

99  Reed's arbitrary list of loyal and disloyal bands is to be found in Stonechild and Waiser, *Loyal till Death*, 254–60. In the Saddle Lake agency, he declared only the James Seenum and Blue Quill bands loyal; all the Edmonton agency bands he declared "unsettled" and undeserving of credit, apart from a few individual cases; the same remarks applied to the Ermineskin, Samson, and Bobtail Cree in the Hobbema agency, while he deemed the Muddy Bull Cree and Sharphead Stoney, and the Treaty 7 Indians, loyal.

100  *CSP*, 1887, #6 (DIA), 106–07. Cattle on the reserves were killed for food in 1885 on a greater scale than normally permitted, because of food shortages resulting from failure to plant and cultivate reserve farms during the rebellion.

101  The pass system is discussed more fully in chapter 9.

102  Gwyn, *Nation Maker*, 14, 42, 414–33, 489–90, 529.

103  *Debates*, 1872, 507–08 (12 June).

104  *Debates*, 1885, 1484 (30 April 1885). In fairness, Mills focused his opposition to Indians having the vote on the fact that, apart from those enfranchised under the law, they were wards of the state, legally minors,

who contributed nothing in taxes and could not own their land in the sense that whites owned land; see 1485. This was a time when property ownership, or renting property of a set minimum value, was held among whites to be a crucial qualification for eligibility to vote. On the matter of the franchise for Indians, see Dickason, *Canada's First Nations*, 263–64; Smith, "Aboriginal Rights a Century Ago," 4.

105 *Debates*, 1885, 1487 (30 April 1885); 1574–76 (4 May 1885). Note that in 1880 Morris had expressed opposition to any "premature enfranchisement" of the Indians of the North-West Territory. Morris, *Treaties*, 288.

106 The Liberals remained convinced that granting the vote to Indians who had not been enfranchised and given up their Indian status as wards of the state was simply wrong, and used their majority under Laurier in 1898 to repeal the provision. See Gwyn, *Macdonald*, vol. 2, 420; Dickason, *Canada's First Nations*, 264. Another example of this distinction was the Indian Advancement Act of 1884, intended to strengthen municipal institutions on the reserves; it did not apply to the North-West, but was aimed at Indians of Ontario and British Columbia; see Dickason, 263–64.

107 Hall, "The Half-Breed Claims Commission," 1–2; Hatt, "The North-West Rebellion Scrip Commissions," 189–204; Flanagan, "Comment on Ken Hatt," 205–09; Niemi-Bohun, "Colonial Categories," 79–81; Ens, "Hybridity," 243–46. In 1900, the government granted scrip to Metis children born in the North-West Territories between 1870 and 1885. Tyler, "A Tax-Eating Proposition," 106.

108 Hatt, "The North-West Rebellion Scrip Commissions," 196.

109 *CSP*, 1886, #45, 2. Many in 1885 were from the Michel band, near St Albert, and several were from the Edmonton Stragglers, which included some from the Passpasschase band.

110 *Bulletin*, 4 July 1885, cited in Tyler, "A Tax-Eating Proposition," 84.

111 Hatt, "The North-West Rebellion Scrip Commission," 197.

112 *CSP*, 1887, #7 (Interior), xix–xx; Tyler, "A Tax-Eating Proposition," 86–87, 90–102. Burgess's statement masked what had been a huge political problem over the summer of 1886, and the fact that the pressure for government to restrict discharges had come from agents on the ground, who were witnesses to the chaos.

113 Tyler, "A Tax-Eating Proposition," 88.

114 Ibid., 89–90.

115 *CSP*, 1887, #7, 79; 1886 #4 (Interior), xlv–xlvii; Sanders, "The Queen's Promises," 110.

116 This paragraph is derived from Tyler, "A Tax-Eating Proposition," chs. 3–4. In 2008 the Supreme Court of Canada rejected a land claim by

descendants of the Passpasschase band, mainly because the 500-member band "waited too long to launch a civil lawsuit, and ... they are now barred from doing so by Alberta's statute of limitations." *Edmonton Journal*, 4 April 2008, A3, A16.

117  See appendix 2 in this book. On land surrenders, see Martin-McGuire, "First Nation Land Surrenders." Additional surrenders in Alberta prior to provincehood included Sharphead IR 141 at White Whale Lake (1897), and fourteen square miles of the Enoch/Stony Plain IR 135 (1902). As was the case with the surrender of the Passpasschase reserve, both appear to have been procedurally (and therefore legally) dubious. A good case study of Indian resistance to departmental efforts to secure a surrender is Irwin, "No Means No," 165–83. The surrenders of the Siksika, Kainai, and Tsuu T'ina reserves in 1883 were part of a land exchange for new reserves, and so fall into a different category than the outright surrender of the Passpasschase reserve.

118  The remaining reserves were surveyed in 1885 (Edmonton agency) and 1886 (Saddle Lake agency). By this time the surveyors understood the necessity of negotiating, in the company of the Indian agent, with the chief and other leading members of each band, in selecting the desired land. Larmour, *Laying down the Lines*, 41–43.

### CHAPTER FIVE

1  *CSP*, 1903, #27 (DIA), 151. This notion was not new. For example, in 1881, William Paterson, Liberal member of Parliament for Brant, observed, "some of the Indians are sufficiently advanced to grow crops, which argues a certain amount of civilization, and consequently a certain amount of manhood. My view of the Indian question is that any particle of manhood in Indians should be encouraged, and not repressed." *Debates*, 1881, 1426–27, 17 March 1881.

2  Or, implicitly, to be descended from those who did. Many of Canada's elite saw their heritage as rooted in the soil, and their values and culture as shaped by that fact.

3  Tobias, "Protection, Civilization, Assimilation"; Miller, *Skyscrapers*, 139–43, 256, 281.

4  Carter, *Lost Harvests*, 15; also Carter, "We Must Farm to Enable Us to Live," 103–26.

5  See, for example, Loo, *States of Nature*, ch. 1.

6  Lutz, *Makúk*, 251. Lutz points out that these occupations were deemed work when undertaken by whites. In 1873, the Toronto *Globe* offered

the view that "a man cannot be both a hunter and a farmer"; cited in Anderson and Robertson, *Seeing Red*, 43. For a discussion of the deep medieval and early modern origins of English class and gendered notions of hunting, and the idea that "hunting was not work," see Seed, *American Pentimento*, 50–55, 128–31.

7 Baker, *Agricultural Revolution*, 8. See also Pagden, *Peoples and Empires*, 138–39. In 1972, Marshall Sahlins challenged the view that farming gave people more leisure time than hunting in his essay, "The Original Affluent Society." Useful on contemporary Canadian anthropological perspectives is Owram, "White Savagery," 24–34.

8 Baker, *Agricultural Revolution*, 38. This can be too simple a distinction; there is plenty of evidence of hunting/gathering societies, including North American plains cultures, using fire, for example, to try to influence or control nature. Still, agricultural societies go much farther in that direction.

9 *CSP*, 1899, #14, xxi.

10 Fully functioning CPR transcontinental service did not commence until 1886.

11 Lutz, *Makúk*, 23–24, calls this layering of traditional and modernized capitalist economies "moditional economies," noting that generally speaking the latter did not entirely replace the former, whether in Indian or white society.

12 A useful introduction to the cost to whites of setting up homesteads is Dick, "Estimates of Farm-Making Costs."

13 Carter, *Lost Harvests*. A complementary comparative study of US and Canadian policy is Bateman, "Talking with the Plow," 211–28. On Hayter Reed (1849–1936), see Titley, *The Indian Commissioners*, ch. 5; Russell, *How Agriculture Made Canada*, 223–24.

14 One study, conversely, argues that Reed "brought good judgement and a well-developed sense of duty to his work," and was a man of "extraordinary ability and qualification." Sowby, "Macdonald the Administrator," 26, 109.

15 Cited in Baker, *Agricultural Revolution*, 5, 8–9. While Baker finds the approach of Westropp and his ilk to be problematic, in fairness, recent anthropological studies of societies in Southeast Asia and the Pacific Islands suggest a fairly regular pattern in the movement from loosely organized tribes to more complex political organizations. They found, "the most successful models were those that prohibited the skipping of steps during a society's rise, with each one passing sequentially through all the stages of increasing complexity." Curry, "On the Origin of Societies," 16, notes, "Cultural evolution is a lot like biological evolution ... You

don't start with a sundial and move straight to a wristwatch. There are a lot of small steps in between." In a sense, then, Reed may have been on to something, but without the sophistication, sensitivity, or time to apply the ideas appropriately to the situation. Moreover, the Canadian government's approach to cultural evolution and modernization was to accelerate it through management and control, which likely did not apply in the Asian or Pacific cases. See also Byfield, *The Great West before 1900*, 88.

16 Daschuk, in *Clearing the Plains*, 173, argues that ranchers lobbied to deny cattle to reserve Indians because selling cattle to the government to feed them was profitable.

17 See n18 below and discussion later in this chapter.

18 *CSP*, 1892, #14 (DIA), 193–85; 1893, #14, xxxii–xxxiii, 48–49. The Sarcee agency included both the Tsuu T'ina and Stoney Nakoda, and listed 105 cows and one bull. Note that the government had provided cattle to Treaty 7 reserves in the early 1880s; see, for example, *CSP*, 1882, #6 (DIA), 116–18 (T.P. Wadsworth to Superintendent General, 1 December 1881); McQuillan, "Creation of Indian Reserves," 390–91. Russell, *How Agriculture Made Canada*, 222, points out that some stock-raising occurred on reserves east of Alberta in the 1880s, but the numbers were small and were in the context of mixed farming.

19 Hall, *Clifford Sifton*, vol. 1, 125–26.

20 Beaudoin, "What They Saw," 31–40. Daschuk, *Clearing the Plains*, describes the effect of highly variable climate and weather conditions in the nineteenth century.

21 Morris, *The Treaties of Canada with the Indians*, 194, 206, 217, 218–19; Carter, *Lost Harvests*, 57.

22 See chapter 4 in this book.

23 Morris, *The Treaties of Canada with the Indians*, 194, 262, 268. According to Morris, "the Stonies are the only Indians adhering to this treaty who desired agricultural implements and seed ... The Blackfeet and Bloods asked for nothing of this kind; they preferred cattle."

24 Baker, *Agricultural Revolution*, 388, 392.

25 Dyck, *What Is the Indian 'Problem'*, ch. 5, argues a somewhat different case. He believes that the treaty negotiators, both government and Indian, were in much closer agreement, and that in the immediate post-treaty era there was an opportunity to establish self-supporting and self-governing Indian communities; however, the opportunity was lost owing to government ineptitude, especially after 1885 when it responded to the North-West Rebellion with "a repressive system of reserve administration" that

was fundamentally contrary to the treaty arrangement. I view the evidence differently, but Dyck's case is well-researched and influential.

26 *Debates*, 1879, 1685–86 (26 March 1879).

27 See, for example, Macdonald's comments in his annual report for 1883 in *CSP*, 1884, #4 (DIA), 52.

28 *Debates*, 1887, 1102–04 (17 June 1887). For other stunning statements about how Indians should have been thankful even for food rations of poor quality, see *Debates*, 1885, 3319 (11 July 1885), and 3341 (13 July 1885). Bannerjee and Duflo in *Poor Economics*, 185, note that Victorians viewed the poor as characteristically "impatient and unable to think far enough ahead." They saw them "as essentially different people, whose innate inclination toward shortsighted behavior is what keeps them poor." Thus Indians were doubly disadvantaged, by race and by class.

29 The best study is Mabindisa, "The Praying Man."

30 Erasmus, *Buffalo Days and Nights*, 189–90; Mabindisa, "Steinhauer," 412–33.

31 Barrett letter of 17 December 1875, printed in *Christian Guardian*, 10 May 1876; reproduced in Smith, "Elizabeth Barrett," 21–22.

32 Morris, *The Treaties of Canada with the Indians*, 191, 238; Erasmus, *Buffalo Days and Nights*, 260–61.

33 Grant, *Ocean to Ocean*, 175–76. Useful introductions to the early years of Fort Victoria (later renamed Pakan) are Ironside and Tomasky, "Development of Victoria Settlement"; Ironside and Tomasky, "Agriculture and River Lot Settlement"; Hurt, "The Victoria Settlement"; Melyncky, *A Veritable Canaan*.

34 Milloy, *A National Crime*, 53. The most substantial attempt at agriculture in the future Alberta probably was at Fort Edmonton, where by 1850 the HBC produced good crops of barley and potatoes, but where the growing season was too short for available strains of wheat to succeed; Thomas, "A History of Agriculture on the Prairies to 1914," 34. In the future Manitoba and northwestern Ontario, some Indians had succeeded in agriculture, even on a limited commercial basis, but this appears to have had little if any influence on those of the future Alberta; see Moodie and Kaye, "Indian Agriculture in the Fur Trade Northwest," 83. See also Russell, *How Agriculture Made Canada*, ch. 8, who argues for extensive Indian prairie agriculture before the treaties, though little of his evidence pertains to future Alberta.

35 In *Treaties*, 290, Morris notes Laird had claimed that the Whitefish Lake band in 1877 "raised enough [on their farms in 1877] ... to maintain

themselves without going to hunt." This does not appear to be consistent with other evidence.

36  An exception may have been the Michel band; see below.

37  Beaver Lake is just southeast of Lac la Biche, and Heart Lake somewhat further northeast.

38  The jury is still out on this; see chapter 7 in this book.

39  CSP, 1906, #27 (DIA), 128–29, 163–64.

40  Such land was not evenly distributed across the agency, which also had bodies of water and wetlands.

41  CSP, 1906, #27 (DIA), 131–32, 165–66. A useful look at the early years of adapting to reserve life is Titley, "Transition to Settlement." The relevant bands were Ermineskin, Samson, and Muddy Bull, all mainly Cree. A Stoney band, the Sharphead, had been located near present-day Ponoka, but was devastated by disease in 1889 and 1890, and was disbanded in the latter year, surviving members mostly joining the Paul band in the Edmonton agency; see Dempsey, *Indian Tribes of Alberta*, 52–53.

42  CSP, 1887, #6 (DIA), 238–39, 248–49; 1896, #14 (DIA), 88–91, 245–51, 325–27; 1906, #27 (DIA), part 2, 138–47.

43  CSP, 1906, #27 (DIA), 162. On Victoria Callihoo, see MacEwan, *Métis Makers of History*, 144–47. Members of this very independent population so disliked government interference in their lives that they tried twice (in 1931 and 1949) to give up their status and take control of their reserve; they finally succeeded in 1958, when they legally ceased to be Indian. See Dempsey, *Indian Tribes of Alberta*, 97–98.

44  CSP, 1896, #14 (DIA), 326–27, 384–407, 442–75; 1906, #27 (DIA), 77–79.

45  Marchildon, Pittman, and Sauchyn, "The Dry Belt and Changing Aridity," 31–35.

46  Through protective tariffs, a transcontinental all-Canadian railway, and aggressive settlement of the prairie west, the government intended to develop a transnational economy integrating all regions; in this scheme the West was intended to produce foodstuffs and raw materials, and to consume manufactures that would be produced mainly in Ontario and Quebec.

47  Useful on this topic is Dempsey, "The Fearsome Fire Wagons," 55–69, 298–99. The DIA negotiated on Indians' behalf. Snow observes that the CPR offered one dollar per acre for its line through the Stoney Nakoda reserve; the DIA valued the land at $2.50 per acre, and the compromise reached in 1889 was $1.25. See Snow, *These Mountains Are Our Sacred Places*, 45, 61.

48  See maps in Breen, *The Canadian Prairie West and the Ranching Frontier*, 31, 44–46.

49 The most recent study is Regular's *Neighbours and Networks*. Regular's bibliography is thorough and largely precludes the need to list other works here. One useful exception, focused on the Siksika experience, is Jobson, "The Blackfoot Farming Experiment." Another is Churchill, "Tsuu T'ina," which in part examines the economic and social interaction of the Tsuu T'ina with Calgary and the surrounding region.

50 Voisey, *Vulcan*.

51 Ibid., 113–15; he observes, "the long hours of summer sunshine and the strong prevailing winds of southern Alberta have the capacity to evaporate more water than the region receives in rainfall." On the variety and fertility of soils, see 119–22.

52 Ibid., 23, and chs. 4 and 5.

53 *CSP*, 1906, #27 (DIA), part 2, 136–48.

54 Ibid., 136–37. By way of comparison, in 1880 the Mi'kmaw of Nova Scotia had better housing than Alberta Indians in 1905; most families lived in frame homes by the early twentieth century. Wicken, *The Colonization of Mi'kmaw Memory and History*, 197–98.

55 Dempsey, *Red Crow*, 108–09, 113–14. A good introduction is Dempsey, "The Story of the Blood Reserve," 27–36.

56 *CSP*, 1881, #14 (DIA), 85.

57 *CSP*, 1882, #6 (DIA), xxiv, 118.

58 Ibid., xxv.

59 Dempsey, "The Story of the Blood Reserve," 33; Magzul, "The Blood Tribe," 292–93; Regular, *Neighbours and Networks*, 13–14.

60 *CSP*, 1882, #6 (DIA), xxiv–xxv. In 1881 it was already clear that the Kainai intended to settle in clan groupings at various points on the reserve.

61 Dempsey, *Red Crow*, 110–14, and ch. 12; *CSP*, 1882, #6 (DIA), xxxi. Concerning fences, Denny noted in his report for 1883 that the Indians would cut rails and build fences in the summer, only to use the rails as fuel in the winter; for that reason, he asked the department to supply wire fencing materials. *CSP*, 1884, #4 (DIA), 78.

62 Carter, *Lost Harvests*, 84–94, 102–08.

63 *CSP*, 1882, #6 (DIA), xxvi–xxviii.

64 Ibid., 121–22.

65 Dempsey, "The Story of the Blood Reserve," 33; *CSP*, 1886, #4 (DIA), 73–74. The Indians harvested 7,000 bushels of potatoes (storing 1,500 bushels in root cellars for seed), 1,000 bushels of turnips, and fifty bushels of carrots. By contrast, that same year there was no reported harvest of wheat or barley, and only 117 bushels of oats, on the Kainai reserve. There

were 1,250 horses, all privately owned, among a reported population of 2,310; *CSP*, 1886, #4 (DIA), 72, 206–07, 214–15.

66  Dempsey, "The Story of the Blood Reserve," 33. Surveyor John Nelson, according to Wilson, "employed Indians for the greater part of the work and reported that they did very well and made excellent line men." *CSP*, 1893, #14 (DIA), 84.

67  *CSP*, 1894, #14 (DIA), 345–48.

68  *CSP*, 1886, #4 (DIA), 72–73. Those named were Striped Dog, Good Young Man, Running Wolf, Bull Young Man, Many Pas, Many White Horses, Three Bulls, Running Crane, Bear's Child, Never-Goes-Out, Three Persons, Eagle Shoe, Heavy Gun, Bull Shield, Day Chief, Calf Child, and High Sun.

69  *CSP*, 1886, #4 (DIA), 72.

70  *CSP*, 1894, #14 (DIA), 346. Wilson noted that in 1893 it was so dry that much of the seed planted in Indian gardens never germinated, and that grain crops barely returned seed grain. He had hopes that an irrigation experiment in the agency garden could be more widely implemented on the reserve. *CSP* 1895, #14 (DIA), 87.

71  By "drought," I mean insufficient precipitation to permit successful agriculture given the crops and techniques available at the time, rather than a period of less precipitation than normal for the region. Given that it was normally a dry climate, it might be better to think of years of sufficient rainfall as the exception to the rule. This is illustrated in Wilson's 1897 report:

> The spring of 1895 had been cold and backward, and the rains late in coming, consequently crops were late and in a good many cases frozen before they were thoroughly ripe, which made the yield small and grain poor. Potatoes were a very fair crop, and the Indians had a good supply for winter use and sufficient for seed this spring [1896]. The season of 1896 opened late, and, although growth was good for some time, the warm dry weather of June killed all our grain, and there will be a complete failure this season of all cereal crops and garden produce.

*CSP*, 1897, #14 (DIA), 155.

72  *CSP*, 1888, #15 (DIA), 97–98, 181–82, 206–07, 216–17. In 1891, for example, 543 steers and cows were slaughtered for beef on the Kainai reserve. The slaughter was contracted to Cochrane & Co, and to P. Burns; 241 hides were given to the Indians to make footwear and the like, and the remainder were sold to the contractors for $2 each. *CSP*, 1893, #14 (DIA), 133. Kainai men employed at the facility were paid $13 per month. RG 10 (reel 10,122), file 14,875, T.P. Wadsworth to Dewdney, 14 August 1884. Wadsworth noted that Isapo-Muxika wanted the same pay for men on the Siksika reserve.

73  *CSP*, 1897, #14 (DIA), 156.
74  Dempsey, "The Story of the Blood Reserve," 33. According to Superinten-
     dent General T.M. Daly, the cattle given to the Piikani and the Kainai were
     "Polled Angus, or Aberdeens." *Debates*, 1894, 4848 (22 June 1894).
75  *CSP*, 1897, #14 (DIA), 157. Wilson also had purchased six pure-bred
     shorthorn bulls to assist the band in upgrading the stock.
76  Taylor, *Standing Alone*, 31; see also DIA, *Annual Report* for 1883, 83.
77  *CSP*, 1894, #14 (DIA), 406–07. The Tsuu T'ina and Stoney Nakoda made
     over $1,670 from beef sales, over $2,000 from furs and hunting, and over
     $1,400 from labour and freighting, and were economically the most suc-
     cessful in the Treaty 7 region in 1893.
78  Taylor, *Standing Alone*, 31; *CSP*, 1906, #27 (DIA), part 2, 140.
79  *CSP*, 1906, #27, 167–68.
80  *CSP*, 1906, #27, part 2, 138–39.
81  Ibid., 141.
82  Ibid., 148.
83  The wealth was not necessarily evenly distributed; see n125 below.
84  *CSP*, 1906, #27 (DIA), 167. A useful discussion of government rationing
     policy may be found in Regular, "Red Backs and White Burdens," 21–27,
     80–84.
85  Fraser Taylor, *Standing Alone*, 31–32.
86  For health issues, see chapter 7 in this book. Good maps of the reserve are
     in Regular, *Neighbours and Networks*, 14, 16, 25. The 1881 population
     figure is taken from *CSP*, 1882, #6 (DIA), xxiv; that for 1889 from *CSP*,
     1890, #12 (DIA), 238; and that for 1904 from *CSP*, 1906, #27 (DIA), part
     2, 79. According to Regular, 17, the Kainai population bottomed out at
     1,128 in 1911, remained stable for a couple of decades, and then began to
     recover very slowly. Not all of the decline was due to mortality. In 1896,
     for example, the agent reported an overall decline from the previous year
     of eighty-nine. However, eighty-one Indians elected to leave the treaty for
     other reserves, a "larger proportion" of whom went to the South Piegan
     agency in Montana. The agent noted sixty-five births (twenty-nine girls
     and thirty-six boys) and fifty-seven deaths during the year, for a net natural
     increase of eight. Unquestionably, most of the deaths resulted from disease
     – the agent referred particularly to consumption, scrofula, and syphilis.
     I have not attempted to reconcile the agent's figures, which are in *CSP*,
     1897, #15 (DIA), 155. A more systematic study of population changes
     on reserves in this period remains to be undertaken.
87  Regular, *Neighbours and Networks*, 28–33; and see Taylor, *Standing
     Alone*, 31.

88  Regular, *Neighbours and Networks*, 74–75.
89  Ibid., 79–86.
90  Ibid., 88–100.
91  Ibid., ch 4. The $12,000 represents wages paid by the company to "several hundred" Blood workers, and does not include amounts earned by labour on individual farms.
92  Good introductions to the early history of irrigation in Alberta are den Otter, *Irrigation in Southern Alberta*, and Armstrong et al., *The River Returns*, ch. 6. See also *CSP*, 1906, #27 (DIA), 114–16, 167–68; Samek, *The Blackfoot Confederacy*, 63, 72–74, 78–79; Mitchner, "William Pearce"; Stotyn, "The Bow River Irrigation Project," ch. 1.
93  *CSP*, 1897, #14 (DIA), 156. The agent also reported that some male Indians worked for white settlers "and usually earn good wages for themselves."
94  Regular, *Neighbours and Networks*, 166.
95  Ibid.
96  See, for example, Regular, *Neighbours and Networks*, 167–68.
97  *CSP*, 1906, #27 (DIA), 114–16, 167–68.
98  *CSP*, 1884, #4 (DIA), x–xi. Here Macdonald is following Denny's report, but Denny's more general expression of "not many years ago" becomes "less than half a decade."
99  *CSP*, 1906, #27 (DIA), 113; Jobson, "The Blackfoot Farming Experiment," 21; Jobson, "The Blackfoot and the Rationing System," 16.
100 Jobson, "The Blackfoot Farming Experiment," 15–18.
101 In addition to Markle's report, referenced in n97, see Hanks and Hanks, *Tribe under Trust*, 29–34; Dempsey notes in *Always an Adventure*, 134, that Crowfoot "was strongly against the introduction of ranching." On his experience of 1877–78, see chapter 2 in this book. Chapter 1 of Hanks and Hanks is a useful introduction to the adaptation to reserve life, and of active resistance to farming, among the Siksika; and see Jobson, "The Blackfoot Farming Experiment," 20. Note that in 1890 Edgar Dewdney complained, especially of the Siksika and Piikani, that "in the Blackfeet country we have to ration almost every man, woman and child, for they are the most helpless and unprogressive of all the Indians." *Debates*, 1890, 2170 (18 March 1890).
102 Magnus Begg, an Indian agent, reported Isapo-Muxika's death to the commissioner, stating: "Crowfoot before he died thanked everyone connected with the Dept for their kindness to him, he also sent a message to Mr Dewdney [then superintendent general] thanking him for his kindness

and wishing him to continue the same to his people." Begg noted that the Indians were "quiet, but feel the loss very much, and so do I, as I know it will be impossible to get another Indian that will even gain half the control over the Indians he had." RG 10, reel T1,460, vol. 1,027, 66–67, Begg to Commissioner, 27 April 1890.

103　4,272 pounds of bacon, 113,032 pounds of flour, 5,540 pounds of beans, and 682.5 pounds of tea.

104　*CSP*, 1906, #27 (DIA), 112–13, 168–70.

105　Jobson, "The Blackfoot Farming Experiment," 21; Jobson, "The Blackfoot and the Rationing System," 16.

106　Jobson, "The Blackfoot Farming Experiment," 23–30. On the irrigation matter, see Armstrong et al., *The River Returns*, 156.

107　Jobson, "The Blackfoot Farming Experiment," 23.

108　*CSP*, 1906, #27 (DIA), 112–13, 168–70.

109　*CSP*, 1906, #27 (DIA), 138–39, 165–66; part 2, 136–48. Dempsey notes that from 1882 to 1885 the Peigans had been strongly encouraged to grow potatoes, producing 6,700 bushels in 1885, before a glutted market that generated no profit "discouraged and disillusioned" them. Dempsey, "One Hundred Years of Treaty 7," 25.

110　*CSP*, 1906, #27 (DIA), 152–53; Churchill, "Tsuu T'ina," 70. The short frost-free period was determined by altitude more than latitude.

111　Churchill, "Tsuu T'ina," 85. They also sold potatoes to the NWMP at Calgary. Macdonald had a less sanguine view of the Tsuu T'ina: they were, he asserted, "the least promising" of the Treaty 7 bands, mostly as a result of the proximity to Calgary, which he believed facilitated indolence and prostitution. See *CSP*, 1884, #4 (DIA), lii.

112　Churchill, "Tsuu T'ina," 87–88.

113　Ibid., 120.

114　*CSP*, 1906, #27 (DIA), 166–7; Churchill, "Tsuu T'ina," 85–87.

115　Churchill, "Tsuu T'ina," 131–37, 247.

116　Ibid., 241. An interesting sidelight concerning white-Indian relations on the Tsuu T'ina reserve is that apparently language learning was almost all one-way, with the Indians learning English (but creating a reserve form of the language). Churchill (261–66) claims, "no missionaries ever mastered the Tsuu T'ina language."

117　*CSP*, 1899, #14 (DIA), 167.

118　This is explored further below in chapter 8.

119　*CSP*, 1906, #27 (DIA), 154, 172; Regular, "Red Backs and White Burdens," 106.

120  *CSP*, 1906, #27 (DIA), 153–54, 160–61.

121  Ibid., 154; Regular, "Red Backs and White Burdens," 145. With respect to income levels and food shortages, it seems likely that wild game and fish were underreported and undervalued, so the situation may not have been as bad as suggested. All indications are that the health of the Stoney Nakoda was the best among the Treaty 7 Indians.

122  Dempsey, "One Hundred Years of Treaty 7," 24.

123  See chapter 8 in this book.

124  Armstrong et al., *The River Returns*, 330–33.

125  Any date chosen as an end-point for a historical study is arbitrary, and the picture necessarily incomplete. To provide but one snapshot of how the situation evolved by the early twenty-first century, Lorenzo Magzul, in a 2009 article that addresses the ability of the Kainai to adapt to climate change, makes the point that of the almost 352,000 acres on the reserve, just over 180,000 (51 per cent) were cultivated, and another 55,600 acres were leased to sixty-one white farmers. About 80 per cent of the land was privately held by about 10 to 12 per cent of the people; the remainder was held communally and administered by the band council. This socio-economic division was a source of friction. Most of those who did not own land lived in tribe-administered rental housing in town sites such as Standoff, or in nearby white communities. The 2001 Statistics Canada figure of 3,850 persons living on the reserve is contested by the council, which estimates the actual population as between 6,000 and 7,000 because of a constant flow off and on to the reserve. Although the Blood Tribe Lands Department claims that agriculture is the reserve's economic base, Magzul points out that not one of 915 adults surveyed by Statistics Canada in 2001 "reported agriculture as an occupation." Thus at best only a very small fraction of the tribe engaged in agriculture. Magzul, "The Blood Tribe," 295–96, shows that the band continues to have "low educational levels, a high unemployment rate, lower levels of income, a shortage of housing, and only a few of the people depend on the land for their livelihood." The government's 1905 vision for the Indians appears hopelessly unrealistic, although the extent to which this was to be the case could not have been appreciated at that time. Modern machinery, agricultural techniques, and crop strains make farming possible on a scale unimagined in 1905, but the government would not have conceived that the vast majority of people would become effectively landless and rootless.

CHAPTER SIX

1 Peterson, *Tell It Slant*, 193. Dyck, *What Is the Indian 'Problem'*, 32, puts it slightly differently: "History is replete with examples of those attempting to do good not recognizing the real, cumulative results of their actions."

2 Judt, *Reappraisals*, 72.

3 White attitudes on the subject also were coloured by their prejudices toward Indians generally.

4 Sutherland, *Children in English-Canadian Society*, 7, 9–11.

5 Ibid., ch. 1; Parr, *Labouring Children*; Bagnell, *The Little Immigrants*; Parker, *Uprooted*.

6 Sutherland, *Children in English-Canadian Society*, 16–21.

7 Milloy, *A National Crime*, 54, cites the two provisions, but makes nothing of the differences between them. J.R. Miller, *Shingwauk's Vision*, 99, claims, "a provision was inserted in each of the seven treaties signed in the 1870s promising a school on their reserve 'whenever the Indians shall desire it.'" This passes over the clause giving the government discretionary authority; and in any case, the provision in Treaty 7 was different. Tkach, "Alberta Catholic Schools," 24, acknowledges the significance of the change, but does not explore it very far. A radical pro-Indian reading of the education clauses and treaty commitments is Henderson, "Treaties and Indian Education"; while his views are forcefully argued and merit acknowledgement, he and I differ in how we interpret the evidence. A useful survey of the historiography of the issue is Trevithick, "Native Residential Schooling in Canada," 49–86.

8 That is, day and boarding schools; industrial schools were not contemplated in the treaties. On the Indian role in construction of schools, see n28 and n29 below.

9 Different school acts were required for Canada East and Canada West.

10 Johnson, *A Brief History of Canadian Education*, ch. 5–6; Audet, "Education in Canada East and Quebec," 174–75.

11 Bemount, "Minority Religious Education Rights in Alberta," 9.

12 Though these schools are now commonly referred to as residential schools, the government during this period referred to them most often as boarding schools, a term I will also use. During this period, broadly speaking, industrial schools taught academics, agriculture, domestic, and trade skills, and aimed to train to higher levels; while boarding schools focused on academic, domestic, and agricultural skills.

13 Milloy, *A National Crime*, 16–17. Note that the linkage of church and formal education, and the notion that priests also could be schoolmasters, has roots deep in medieval England; see Ackroyd, *The History of England*, vol. 1, 371–72.

14 Wilson, "The Ryerson Years," 215.

15 The Constitution Act, 1867, sec. 91 (24).

16 Miller, *Shingwauk's Vision*, chs. 2–4.

17 Indians were not alone in being singled out by race for separate treatment; black people in Ontario had a separate school system, for example, though the story is more complex. See Walker, "African Canadians," 159–60.

18 Milloy, *A National Crime*, 16–21.

19 Ibid., 12–13. Anderson and Robertson, *Seeing Red*, 51, contend, "Indigenous people were held to be human – but at a vaguely substandard level." The same racism was found in the United States; see Hoxie, *A Final Promise*, 189, 193–95.

20 Milloy, *A National Crime*, 14–19. Still, many Canadian politicians in the 1870s and 1880s remarked that many Ontario Indians were as literate as many whites, and considered them highly intelligent; see below. These Indians were the products of the very schools the same leaders claimed were ineffective.

21 *CSP*, 1892, #14 (DIA), xv; calculation of percentages is mine. Dewdney claimed in 1889 that more Indian children attended school in the North-West Territories than in Ontario or Quebec; *Debates*, 1889, 1174 (10 April 1889). The figures in the 1892 report mean that almost 6,000 school-age Indian children were not even registered at school in 1891.

22 Sutherland, *Children in English-Canadian Society*, 166. It is likely that a higher percentage of white children than of Indian children enrolled. The earliest attendance figure given for Alberta is for the province in 1905, when average daily attendance was 55.1 per cent of enrolled pupils. Urquhart and Buckley, *Historical Statistics of Canada*, series 5, 1–20, 589. However, the first report of Alberta's Department of Education gave the average school attendance in 1905 as 51 per cent of enrolled pupils. Annual Report of the Department of Education of the Province of Alberta, 1906, 12–13.

23 Lupul, "Education in Western Canada before 1873," 254–55; Nix, "McDougall, George Millward," *DCB*, vol. 10, 471–72; Sieciechowicz, "Steinhauer, Henry Bird," *DCB*, vol. 11, 848–50; Huel, "Lacombe, Albert," *DCB*, vol. 14, 573–77; Snow, *These Mountains Are Our Sacred Places*, 18–19; Tkach, "Alberta Catholic Schools," chs. 2–3; Hochstein, "Roman

Catholic Separate and Public Schools in Alberta," 11–12; Sparby, "History of the Alberta School System," 21; Friesen, "John McDougall," 11–12.

24  CSP, 1885, #116e (Papers and Correspondence in Connection with Half-breed Claims and Other Matters Relating to the North-West Territories), 9–11; 1879, #7 (Interior), 57; Sparby, "History of the Alberta School System," 22, 24. The best account of the school at Whitefish Lake is Mabindisa, "The Praying Man," 433–64.

25  Huel, *Proclaiming the Gospel*, 51–52. As late as 1869, Methodist teacher Adam Snyder conducted twice-daily classes among Cree children while they were with their families on the bison hunt. Mabindisa, "The Praying Man," 441–42.

26  Smith, "Elizabeth Barrett," 23. Chief Pakan recalled Barrett's tenure as a teacher with great fondness, remembering, "all the good she did for us. Our children loved her for all her acts of kindness ... and our women looked upon her with affection." Quoted in *Regina Leader* 15 October 1886; reference courtesy D.B. Smith.

27  CSP, 1877 #11 (Interior), xxxiii (Dickieson to the Minister of the Interior, 7 October 1876). The materials referred to could have meant contributing desks, textbooks, and other educational materials, as well as construction materials. Dickieson's comments notwithstanding, Morris in his report noted "the universal demand for teachers," which might have meant that the chiefs strongly endorsed the provision for education. Morris, *Treaties*, 194.

28  CSP, 1880, #4 (Interior), 102. Under the Indian Act of 1876, sec. 63, one of the duties of the chief or chiefs in council on a reserve was to construct and repair schoolhouses, so Dickieson's interpretation of the education provision in Treaty 6 was understandable. What Indians understood of these responsibilities is less clear. By the time the government considered the matter of local government for the prairie tribes in the 1880s, it had largely concluded that they were not yet capable of self-government.

29  Morris, *Treaties*, 185–86, 194, 205, 217. The verb, both here and in the treaty text, was "maintain," not "construct" or "provide." As will be seen below, it appears that most day schools were built by the Indians themselves, or by the religious denominations with Indian labour, sometimes with partial government financial support. Boarding schools were often built with Indian labour, but were more complex and costly, and so were subsidized by denominations and government and usually had at least some professional oversight. Still, this apparently was not always the case and without consistent expert design, oversight, or quality control, the

results were highly variable. Industrial school buildings were primarily, but
not always completely, financed by the government.

30 Morris, *The Treaties of Canada with the Indians*, 269. Ahenakew, *Voices
of the Plains Cree*, 92, is explicit that Indians at the Treaty 6 negotiations
understood the education clause to mean provision of a day school on
each reserve. This does not explain why some bands asked for boarding
schools, or why numerous parents sent their children to boarding schools
even when day schools were available nearby.

31 *CSP*, 1880, #4 (Interior), 102.

32 Treaty 7 Elders et al., *The True Spirit and Original Intent of Treaty 7*, 219;
see also 159–61. Very useful on the Indians' methods of educating children
prior to schools is Carr, "A Historical Survey of Education."

33 Price, *The Spirit of the Alberta Indian Treaties*, 120.

34 A sample curriculum may be found in *CSP*, 1896, #14 (DIA), 347–51.

35 On the costs of industrial schools, see n58 and n107, below.

36 House of Commons, *Debates*, 1896, 2394–97 (1 October); 1897, 4076
(14 June); 1899, 7490–93 (14 July). Aspects of the internal government
debate on the costs of Indian education are discussed in Milloy, *A National
Crime*, 62–75.

37 Neither was an industrial school as the government would define them
after 1884.

38 *CSP*, 1880–81, #14 (DIA), 91, 308–09; 1879, #7 (Interior), 24–26. The figures given for St Albert are for 1880, while those for Lac la Biche are for
1878, because no figures were provided for 1880. Early reporting was
more irregular, and probably less reliable, than in later years. An outline of
the early history of the Lac la Biche school is in Tkach, "Alberta Catholic
Schools," 72–74.

39 *CSP*, 1885, #116e (Papers and Correspondence in Connection with Half-
breed Claims and Other Matters Relating to the North-West Territories),
12–17 (Bishop Vital Grandin, St Albert, to David Laird, Superintendent
General, 5 April 1875); 1881, #14 (DIA), 91.

40 *CSP*, 1880–81, #14 (DIA), 98–99.

41 Ibid., 7–8. Ironically, the government began active development of day
schools at the same time in Nova Scotia; it appears that no boarding
schools were proposed. Wicken, *The Colonization of Mi'kmaw Memory
and History*, 46–49.

42 The government paid $300 for teachers in charge of up to forty-two
pupils, and $400 for those with classes exceeding forty-two (rare, if ever, in
Alberta). Religious denominations were free to supplement these rates, but
most could not afford to do so. Macdonald admitted that, while bilingual

teachers were desirable, "for $300 you cannot get a man who speaks English and Indian as well." *Debates*, 1885, 3343 (13 July 1885).

43  A useful perspective on this is Banerjee and Duflo, *Poor Economics*, 72.

44  It was a major cultural shift for both Indian and white societies in the nineteenth century to view regular school attendance as the great priority for children.

45  In addition to the major studies by Miller and Milloy, Titley provides a short overview of government policy with respect to Indian education in *A Narrow Vision*, ch. 5. An insightful treatment of reasons for the failure of day schools is Kozak, "Education and the Blackfoot," ch. 4.

46  *CSP*, 1889, #16 (DIA), ix–xiii.

47  In a curious exception to prevailing DIA opinion, Protestant school inspector J. Ansdell MacRae offered favourable, extended comments on day schools; his freedom to express views at variance with those of his superiors was evidently curtailed, and his reports thereafter consisted of nothing but sterile statistical material. See *CSP*, 1891, #18 (DIA), 66–67.

48  Kozak, "Education and the Blackfoot," 6, 8, 61–62.

49  *CSP*, 1890, #12 (DIA), 70–76. In 1891, the agent reported that most of the band had been discharged from the treaty, leaving "now fourteen souls only, of whom the majority are children." *CSP*, 1892, #14 (DIA), 75. The discrepancy in figures from the other report is not explained. The usual per-pupil grant was provided for treaty children who were enrolled at a school.

50  *CSP*, 1893, #14 (DIA), 196.

51  *CSP*, 1891, #18 (DIA), 55–56, 65–66. Attendance at white schools was not very good either. As lieutenant governor of the North-West Territories, Dewdney reported that in the summer term of 1886 (1 April to 31 October), 2,553 students were registered in white schools, but only 669 (26 per cent) attended for one hundred days or more. Assuming that a disproportionate number of these lived in towns, villages, and cities, average attendance at rural schools likely was much lower. *CSP*, 1887, #7 (Interior), part 4, 4.

52  The government still did not class the St Albert school as an industrial school, despite its many similarities to such schools.

53  *CSP*, 1892, #14 (DIA), 105. There was no report from the Catholic school inspector for any Alberta schools in *CSP*, 1891.

54  The Sharphead Indians suffered terribly from disease in 1889–90, the reserve was about to be closed, and they merged mostly with the Paul band in the Edmonton agency.

55  *CSP*, 1891 #18 (DIA), 54, 66.

56  *CSP*, 1892, #14 (DIA), 77, 97–101, 105–06.

57  See *CSP*, 1891, #18 (DIA), 230–35.

58  Miller, *Shingwauk's Vision*, 103–04; Milloy, *A National Crime*, 44; *CSP*, 1885, #3, l. Drawing wider conclusions based on the experience of the Qu'Appelle school is Gresko, "White 'Rites' and Indian 'Rites,'" 163–81, 220–23. The government initially budgeted around $9,000 or $9,500 for each of the three new industrial schools; and it decided belatedly to provide $1,500 for the St Albert school, which was in effect an industrial school that already had a hospital and numerous other buildings to operate, and that depended almost entirely upon whatever funds Grandin could raise. *Debates*, 1883, 1377 (22 May 1883).

59  *CSP*, 1884, #4 (DIA), xlvi (Report of Superintendent General).

60  Titley, "Indian Industrial Schools in Western Canada," 141.

61  Miller, *Shingwauk's Vision*, 100–04; Milloy, *A National Crime*, ch. 3.

62  *CSP*, 1884, #4 (DIA), xi. The government was either ignorant of, or chose to disregard, Indian provisions for dealing with orphaned children.

63  *CSP*, 1886, #4 (DIA), 76–78.

64  Milloy, *A National Crime*, 70; *CSP*, 1891, #18 (DIA), xii; Titley, "Dunbow Indian Industrial School," 98. Titley states (99) that according to an 1887 government report, the Siksika declined to send their children to the school mainly because they did not want their children to "resemble the white people."

65  *CSP*, 1884, #4 (DIA), 104.

66  The religious affiliation of the band and reserve school was a major determinant of what industrial school a child would attend. Occasionally the annual census of Indians included information about those known to be missing at the time of counting (usually at annuity payments), and this information could include which school off-reserve children attended. For example, in 1889, eight of the Michel band reportedly attended the High River Industrial School; four of the Enoch band attended Morleyville, and two attended St Albert. The figures are by no means always complete or reliable. *CSP*, 1890, #12 (DIA), 237–38.

67  Mortality rates from consumption on the reserves typically were much higher.

68  Indian health, both in schools and on reserves, is discussed more fully in chapter 7. The figures cited are from Titley, "Dunbow Indian Industrial School," 101. Of the other students, one was transferred and seventy-nine were discharged. Of the latter group, eight could not be traced, forty-nine were considered to have attended the school too briefly to have had much

benefit, sixteen were deemed to be doing very well, and six were deemed to be doing fairly well.

69  Claude's report is at *CSP*, 1891, #18 (DIA), 106–09.

70  *CSP*, 1891, #18 (DIA), 139; 1892, #14 (DIA), 91.

71  *CSP*, 1890, #12 (DIA), 85.

72  *CSP*, 1892, #14 (DIA), 84; RG 10 (reel T1,460), vol. 1,027 (Magnus Begg to Indian Commissioner [summer 1890].)

73  Ibid., 107.

74  *CSP*, 1890, #12 (DIA), 85–86; 1892, #14 (DIA), 107.

75  *CSP*, 1891, #18 (DIA), 60–61.

76  Mountain Horse, *My People The Bloods*, 5, 6. Mountain Horse's memory is not always accurate. Here he refers to a day school, but he also claims to have attended St Paul's Anglican boarding school. He says he enrolled in 1893 when he was six, but he was born in 1888, and he says he was one of the first pupils enrolled in the school, which was founded in 1889. See also 15–18, and Dempsey, "Introduction," v.

77  *CSP*, 1891, #18 (DIA), 58; and see 1890 #12 (DIA), 81.

78  *CSP*, 1906, #27 (DIA), part 2, 26–27. These schools were Bull's Horn (Kainai agency), Goodfish Lake and Saddle Lake (Saddle Lake agency), St Joseph's and White Whale Lake (Edmonton agency), and Samson (Hobbema agency). A seventh, the Louis Bull School (Hobbema), closed in March 1905 due to lack of enrolment.

79  *CSP*, 1906, #27 (DIA), 419–34; R. Bird, "Schooling in the Paul Band," 34–40.

80  *CSP*, 1906, #27 (DIA), 413.

81  Kozak, "Education and the Blackfoot," ch. 3.

82  Milloy, *A National Crime*, 81–82; Titley, "Indian Industrial Schools," 140; Scott-Brown, "The Short Life of St. Dunstan's," 41–49.

83  *CSP*, 1899, #14 (DIA), 287–99.

84  Mountain Horse, *My People The Bloods*, 108–09.

85  Scott-Brown, "The Short Life of St. Dunstan's," 45; Dempsey, "Native Peoples and Calgary," 29–30.

86  Scott-Brown, "The Short Life of St. Dunstan's," 48.

87  Ibid., 46; *CSP*, 1906, #27 (DIA), 430–31. Hogbin's figures differ from Markle's; he claimed forty-one pupils at the start of the year, and twenty-seven at the end (1904–05). *CSP*, 1906, #27 (DIA), 344.

88  Scott-Brown, "The Short Life of St. Dunstan's."

89  These funding problems are rehearsed in Fox, "The Failure of the Red Deer Industrial School."

90  Titley, "Red Deer Industrial School," 58. Sadly, this directive seems to have been honoured more in the breach than in the observance throughout the boarding school system.

91  Milloy, *A National Crime*, 78, 134, 140–41; Titley, "Red Deer Industrial School," 59; Miller, *Shingwauk's Vision*, 324; *Edmonton Journal*, 29 June 2010, A1–2 ("Forgotten Aboriginal Children will Be Honored"; the story concerned a cemetery on the grounds of the former Red Deer Industrial School in which there appear to be unmarked graves for "dozens" of Indian children; see also *Journal*, 1 July 2010, A1, A3, "Children's Spirits Finally Set Free"). The death rate cited is not conclusive proof that the diseases were contracted at the school, though they may have been. In the early years, there was not always careful inspection of prospective pupils and some arrived carrying diseases such as consumption; rates of disease were also high, and living conditions and diet often poor, in the bands to which the graduates returned. Health, diet, and medical care at the school were also far from optimal. See also Bird, "Schooling," 46–56.

92  *CSP*, 1906, #27 (DIA), 347–49.

93  Ibid., 428–30. For Markle, how clearly and loudly Indian children responded to questions was a major factor in his evaluation of a teacher's the success. Milloy, *A National Crime*, 82, notes that the Red Deer school was criticized for its dated facilities in 1908.

94  Fox, "The Failure of the Red Deer Industrial School," 34, 40, 51–53, 110–12.

95  Titley, "Red Deer Indian Industrial School," 66.

96  Enrolment was limited by the size of the government grant.

97  *CSP*, 1906, #27 (DIA), 427–28. The history of the school is outlined in Titley, "Dunbow Indian Industrial School."

98  *CSP*, 1906, #27, 353.

99  Ibid., 352–53. Mangolds were a beet with a large yellow root, often grown as cattle feed.

100  St Joseph's Industrial School closed in 1922. Miller, *Shingwauk's Vision*, 113–14, 320, 329, 456n53; Milloy, *A National Crime*, 44, 51, 82, 225; Lux, *Medicine that Walks*, 108.

101  *Debates*, 1894, 22 June 1894, 4871.

102  Most critics focused on what they deemed excessive cost for too little benefit; rarely did they mention the schools' serious institutional failings. For the schools as academic failures, see Miller, *Shingwauk's Vision*, 166–67; on the policy changes, see Hall, "Clifford Sifton and Canadian Indian Administration," 133–38; Milloy, *A National Crime*, 72; and Enns, "But What Is the Object of Educating These Children," 101–23.

103 *CSP*, 1906, #27 (DIA), 307–08.
104 Such reward techniques were common for generations in white schools as well.
105 *CSP*, 1906, #27 (DIA), 407.
106 *CSP*, 1906, #27 (DIA), part 2, 8. The school generated over $900 in other revenue, leaving a deficit of over $670. Of the eleven Indian boarding schools in the district of Alberta, only two broke even on the year's operations: Ermineskin (Hobbema) and Peigan Protestant (which received over 40 per cent of its income from the Church of England). *CSP*, 1906, #27 (DIA), part 2, 6–17.
107 Average per-student costs for the three industrial schools were $270.01 (Calgary), $155.56 (Red Deer), and $227.51 (St Joseph's). Author's calculation, from *CSP*, 1904–05, #27 (DIA), part 2, 27–29, 44–45, 427.
108 *CSP*, 1906, #27 (DIA), 421.
109 Ibid., 422.
110 Ibid., 126.
111 Tkach, "Alberta Catholic Schools," 70.
112 *CSP*, 1906, #27 (DIA), 338–39, 419–20.
113 Maximum number qualifying for government grant, 1905: Kainai Anglican, fifty; Kainai RC, thirty; Siksika RC, twenty-five; Siksika Anglican, fifty; Piikani Anglican, thirty; Piikani RC, twenty-five; Tsuu T'ina, fifteen; Stoney Nakoda (McDougall Orphanage), forty. For the record, maxima in Treaty 6 schools were eighty at St Albert RC, forty-five at Blue Quill RC, and fifty at Erminskin RC. *CSP*, 1906, #27 (DIA), part 2, 48–51. Schools had capacities ranging from roughly 30 to 100 per cent larger than the government-imposed maximum enrolments allowed.
114 *CSP*, 1906, #27 (DIA), 335–36, 424.
115 *CSP*, 1906, #27 (DIA), 305–06, 425. Bryant (1794–1878) was a prolific American poet and long-time editor of the *New York Evening Post*; the poem may be found at www.poemhunter.com/poem/the-prairies. It would have been more interesting had Markle probed the pupils' response to the poet's portrayal of Indian history and Indian-white relations.
116 *CSP*, 1906, #27 (DIA), 303–04, 310–11, 433–34.
117 *Debates*, 1904, 6946–56, 18 July 1904.
118 The census category is sixteen to twenty, so it is unclear how many of the general population fell into the sixteen to eighteen category.
119 A certain number of Alberta Indian children were sent to schools out of the district. Another minor point: a few boarding schools, such as the Old Sun school on the Siksika reserve, had several children aged three to five

who were too young to qualify for a government grant. Why they were admitted, and what sort of schooling they received, is unknown.

120 Calculated from *CSP*, #27 (DIA), part 2, 165–66. No breakdown is provided for Alberta alone, though there is no reason to believe that the proportions of expenditure would have been significantly different.

121 The assumed number of children is likely close to the actual figure.

122 Assuming, highly improbably, something close to 100 per cent enrolment and attendance.

123 Adapted from Prov. 13:24. On social acceptance of corporal punishment to discipline children, see Sutherland, *Children in English-Canadian Society*, 18, 101, 138. Axelrod also provides useful context in "No Longer a 'Last Resort,'" 262–66.

124 Sparby, "A History of the Alberta School System," 76–77, notes that compulsory attendance laws had been enacted in Ontario in 1871, and in the North-West Territories in 1888, though effective enforcement took some years. See also Sutherland, *Children in English-Canadian Society*, 93, 159–60, 168–69, 212–13.

125 57–58 Vict., ch. 32, sec. 11 [1894], subsequently incorporated into the Indian Act. By way of comparison, the 1892 school ordinance of the North-West Territories was much less strict: parents had to ensure that their children between the ages of seven and twelve attended school for a minimum of twelve weeks per year, at least six of which had to be consecutive. There also were stipulations concerning truancy: violations of either provision could result in a fine of one dollar for the first offence, and two dollars for each subsequent offense; there was no provision for imprisonment. NWT Ordinance #22 of 1892, sec. 188–89, 191–93.

126 *Debates*, 9 July 1894, 5551–53; the concern was raised by James McMullen, Liberal MP for Wellington North, Ontario.

127 These institutions are discussed in Sutherland, *Children in English-Canadian Society*, especially chs. 7–9. A useful case study is Robertson, "Heartbreak in Huronia."

128 Sutherland, *Children in English-Canadian Society*, 96.

129 Titley, "Red Deer Indian Industrial School," 55; also see Bird, "Schooling in Paul Band," 75–79.

130 Miller, *Shingwauk's Vision*, 289–90, acknowledges, but does not explore, the failings of white boarding institutions.

131 See, for example, *Edmonton Journal*, "Decades of Rape, Torture at Hands of Church," 21 May 2009, A16. In January 2011, *Christianity Today* reported that between 1950 and 1990 many (white) children of missionaries were abused while in attendance at boarding schools run by the US

Presbyterian Church in Asia and Africa, and at least fifty more in such schools in Senegal run by New Tribes Mission. See also Zylstra, "When Abuse Comes to Light."

132  An excellent discussion of these issues is in Miller, *Shingwauk's Vision*, ch. 1. Avoidance of corporal punishment was not absolute. Mountain Horse, in *My People The Bloods*, 9, recalls, "on rare occasions an Indian child of teen age was punished. In winter time a naughty youth was taken out, stripped naked, and rolled around in deep snow, and the snow kicked in his face." Such punishment in a later period would have been denounced as abusive. See Carr, "A Historical Survey of Education in Early Blackfoot Indian Culture," which addresses corporal discipline in the broad context of how Indians educated their children.

133  As starting points, consider the works of Miller and Milloy, as well as the evidence compiled by the Truth and Reconciliation Commission of the early twenty-first century.

134  Stamp, "Education and the Economic and Social Milieu," and "Evolving Patterns of Education," 290–336. Note that future Prime Minister R.B. Bennett received $160 in New Brunswick in 1887, his first year of teaching with a second-class certificate, a qualification equivalent to, or better than, that of most teachers in Indian schools. Waite, *In Search of R.B. Bennett*, 8. Payment of teachers in boarding and industrial schools was determined within a different budgetary structure.

135  Miller, *Shingwauk's Vision*, 168.

136  On "outing," see Miller, *Shingwauk's Vision*, 164, 253–57. The practice, however, appears to parallel modern work experience courses.

137  Milloy, *A National Crime*, 111, 129–41; and see Titley, *The Indian Commissioners*, 162–63. Older students abusing younger ones was a problem in boarding schools of all kinds.

138  Bull, "Indian Residential Schooling," 57–72. This survey is based on interviews with ten elders who volunteered to tell their stories. The interviewees frequently named names and schools, but Bull suppressed them.

139  Churchill, "Tsuu T'ina," 10, and chs. 5 and 6.

140  Dempsey, "My Life in an Indian Residential School," 25–26. In fairness, Dempsey also notes (24–25) that she and other students experienced some physical and verbal punishment at school, but she seems to have considered it within normal boundaries for the day, and much less severe than reports she heard about what went on at the Roman Catholic boarding school.

141  Mountain Horse recalled the principal at St Paul's, Rev Frank Swainson, with great affection. Apparently Swainson was able to overlook the high

spirits and pranks of the children, was generous to them and their parents, and provided Christmas presents for them. Mountain Horse notes that during World War I he and other former pupils who had enrolled in the Canadian Army, took the time to seek out Swainson, who had retired to England. Swainson conducted the school in English, but conducted church services in Blackfoot "so that we might more easily assimilate the teachings relative to the great God of the white man." Swainson's forceful and respected character led many Indians to adopt Christianity. *My People The Bloods*, 16–18.

142  *CSP*, 1906–07, #27 (DIA), 175.
143  Sutherland, *Children in English-Canadian Society*, 183. Sutherland does not break the figures down by province, or suggest where the Indian instructors picked up their expertise. Other positive examples of industrial school outcomes are related by Dion, *My Tribe the Crees*, 156–57. Of St Joseph's, he wrote that it "became one of the greatest institutions of its time and it turned out many really good men and women during its short span of activity."
144  Titley, "Dunbow Indian Industrial School," 113.

CHAPTER SEVEN

1  *CSP*, 1904, #27 (DIA), 237–38.
2  Regular, "Red Backs and White Burdens," 16.
3  *Debates*, 1904, 6960–63 (19 July 1904); on Bryce's immigration responsibilities, see 7,283 (21 July 1904).
4  *The Canadian Encyclopedia*, vol. 1, 291. Useful material on Bryce and Indian health is found in Kelm, *Colonizing Bodies*; and Lux, *Medicine That Walks*.
5  Ottawa, 1922.
6  Typical are the views of Kelm and Lux, cited above; see also Daschuk, *Clearing the Plains*. A Indian perspective may be found in Favel-King, "The Treaty Right to Health," 120–29.
7  Titley, *A Narrow Vision*, 83.
8  *CSP*, 1906, #27 (DIA), 271–78.
9  The death rate for all Canadians in 1904 was 1.35 per cent; in Quebec it was 1.84; in Montreal, notoriously high in white Canada, it was 2.34. By way of comparison, the death rate for Nova Scotia's Mi'kmaw in 1905 was 3.32 Urquhart and Buckley, *Historical Statistics of Canada*, 42–43, series B 82–91 and B 82–99; Wicken, *The Colonization of Mi'kmaw Memory and History*, 191–94.

10  Ibid.

11  Lux, *Medicine that Walks*; Daschuk, *Clearing the Plains*.

12  Good introductions include Rosen, *A History of Public Health*, chs. 6 and 7; Cassel, "Public Health in Canada," 278–80; Canadian Public Health Association, "This Is Public Health."

13  The assumptions about band or tribal councils having local municipal-like responsibilities went mostly unspoken by officials in 1876, though as seen previously, there is evidence that the officials were familiar with the Indian Act. If that were the case, then the officials' assumption would have been that minor health matters were a local responsibility, and the larger issues (epidemics, famine) fell to the government. The medicine chest's purpose, then, would have been to provide medications and ameliorative aid to address situations that could not be resolved successfully in local or traditional ways.

14  On this, see Dempsey, *Maskepetoon*, 186. On the history of disease and starvation among the Indians of this region, long predating confederation, see Daschuk, *Clearing the Plains*, chs. 1–5; and Ray, "Diffusion of Diseases."

15  Waldram et al., *Aboriginal Health in Canada*, 154. The major proactive exception to this was the HBC's effort long prior to 1870, and the government's after 1870, to vaccinate all populations to try to control the spread of smallpox.

16  *CSP*, 1884, #4 (DIA), 85.

17  *Debates*, 11 March 1881, 1351.

18  *CSP*, 1884, #4 (DIA), 73. Limited as Anderson's appreciation of the causes of tuberculosis might have been, he was correct to note that inadequate clothing and housing exacerbated the conditions in which the disease thrived.

19  Favel-King, "The Treaty Right to Health," 120–21. The idea of the first-aid kit is witty and memorable, but it also is an unfair caricature of what the government was actually doing in the late nineteenth century, however inadequate its response may appear in retrospect.

20  Ibid., 125.

21  Lux, *Medicine That Walks*, is replete with examples. However, the fact that Indians readily availed themselves of medical services whenever a doctor was available, and also where Catholic nuns ran hospitals or infirmaries, suggested to whites (who believed their medicine to be founded on scientific principles) that Indians found white medicine and medical knowledge to be valuable and probably in some respects superior.

22  Lux, *Medicine That Walks*, 26–27. Note that by the later 1870s Morris's principles were already set aside and the government had begun to assume

responsibility for looking after elderly and disabled Nizitapi while the tribes hunted bison in Montana. For a recollection of how health issues were addressed on the frontier at the time of the treaties, see McDougall, "Pioneer Life in the 1870s," 26.

23 The treaty provisions raised Indian expectations and limited government discretionary power.

24 *CSP*, 1888, #15 (DIA), 187. Among Indian complaints in 1884 was a failure to deliver the promised medicine chests; the government had been dilatory. Lux, *Medicine That Walks*, 52.

25 Meijer Drees, "Reserve Hospitals and Medical Officers," 153.

26 Shewell, *"Enough to Keep Them Alive,"* 30.

27 The main federal expertise in the medical field for some time after 1867 resided in the Department of Agriculture, charged with preventing outbreaks of diseases affecting farm animals from entering Canada, with tracking and preventing epidemic diseases such as bubonic plague from reaching Canadian shores, and with minimizing the impact when they did. Responsibility for Indian health fell to Indian Affairs, but it took years for the department to determine what that responsibility entailed and how to address it.

28 A useful discussion is Sutherland, "To Create a Strong and Healthy Race," 361–93; Sutherland, *Children in English-Canadian Society*, part 2. I also have benefitted from reading a manuscript by Eagle, "The Evolution of the Canadian Welfare State," chs. 1 and 3.

   Among the Indians of the West were some who resisted vaccination programs and others who welcomed them; some who welcomed white doctors, medicines, and health measures and others who ignored or resisted them. No more than in white society was the response to the new ways uniform. See Mountain Horse, *My People the Bloods*, 4–5.

29 *CSP*, 1878, #10 (Interior), xi–xii. For another case of reactive response to disease, see *CSP*, 1876, #9 (Interior), 37–38 (measles outbreak). Daschuk, *Clearing the Plains*, 105, 112–13; the doctor's name is sometimes "Hagerty" in the documents.

30 *CSP*, 1878, #10 (Interior), xi.

31 Hagarty was directed to reside in Winnipeg and devote his efforts to Manitoba Indians to ensure that all were vaccinated. See *CSP*, 1879, #7 (Interior), 13; 1881 #14 (DIA), 125; Dempsey, *Frontier Life*, xi–xxii, xvi; Neatby, "The Medical Profession in the North-West Territories."

32 *CSP*, 1880, #4 (Interior), 102. Dewdney also said he would send a separate memorandum to the DIA about how he thought medical attendance should be provided for Indians, but this has not been found. It may also be

that, at a time when government contracts were greatly valued by physicians, he did not wish to continue giving patronage to a Liberal appointee.

33  *CSP*, 1881, #14 (DIA), 100.

34  *CSP*, 1881, #3 (NWMP), 15.

35  In the period under review, there were far fewer trained nurses than physicians in Canada: in 1901, there were 280 nurses, compared to 5,442 physicians. Urquhart and Buckley, *Historical Statistics of Canada*, 44, series B
114–15. This is not broken down by region or province. For some reason
the 1901 census did not provide compiled statistics on occupation, which
were provided in 1891 and 1911, so they have to be calculated separately.
A rough calculation by Mary Munk, genealogical consultant at Library
and Archives Canada, in a personal communication suggests that in the
district of Alberta in 1901 there were some thirty-one nurses, as compared
to twenty-three doctors, five surgeons, and twenty physicians (it is unclear
whether there was any overlap in these categories). The 1891 census lists
"nurses and midwives" as a category within "domestic and personal services" (rather than "professionals") under occupations, and lists twelve in
total for the North-West Territories (given as one male and nine females
over fifteen years of age, and two females under fifteen). It is not clear
whether any Indian midwives are included in this total. *Third Census of
Canada*, vol. 2, table 12, 183. As late as 1890 even Calgary, the largest
urban centre in Alberta, had but one trained nurse. McNeil, "Women of
Vision and Compassion," 18–19.

36  *CSP*, 1882, #18 (Interior), 30. Kennedy (1858–1913) for a short time was
responsible for an area 150 miles north from the international boundary,
and approximately the same distance east from the foothills of the Rockies.
In addition to looking after the needs of one hundred NWMP officers and
another one hundred townspeople and settlers, he was expected to look
after the Kainai and Piikani reserves. See Lampard, *Alberta's Medical
History*, 114–31. On Indian surgery, see Luxton, "Stony Indian Medicine,"
109–11.

37  Good discussions are in Lux, *Medicine That Walks*, ch. 2; and Waldram et
al., *Aboriginal Health in Canada*, ch. 5. Ahenakew, *Voices of the Plains
Cree*, 98, is less sanguine than many, including Lux and Favel-King, about
the efficacy of Indian medical knowledge. Burnett, "The Healing Work and
Nursing Care of Aboriginal Women," contends that the importance of
healing work and traditional knowledge among Indians, and especially
women, during the early years of contact and white settlement has been
consistently undervalued, and that mutual sharing of healing knowledge
between Indian women and whites (such as missionary wives) constituted

an important cultural exchange. Indian perspectives include Dion, *My Tribe the Crees*, 4–7; Hungry Wolf, *The Blood People*, 180–89; and Mountain Horse, *My People The Bloods*, 66–69, 103–04.

38 Bull, "100 Years at Whitefish Lake," 9–10. On the healing abilities of medicine men, see also Denny, "Blackfoot Medicine Men," 9–12.

39 Decker, "Smallpox along the Frontier," 92–118. Most smallpox in this period appears to have entered Canada from the United States, and affected white and Metis populations much more than Indian reserves. Bryce noted in 1905 that this outbreak at the turn of the century affected thousands in the North-West Territories, but few cases occurred among Indians, while Metis were severely affected. *CSP*, 1906, #27 (DIA), 277. On resistance, see *CSP*, 1882, #6 (DIA), lx; many other examples are found in agents' reports. See also Sutherland, *Children in English-Canadian Society*, 41–42.

40 On tuberculosis generally in Canada, see Wherrett, *The Miracle of the Empty Beds*; McCuaig, *The Weariness, the Fever, and the Fret*. Waldram et al., *Aboriginal Health in Canada*, 61, make the point that tuberculosis was commonly reported among Indians from the early seventeenth century. Luxton, *Stony Indian Medicine*, 111, reports one case of a Stoney Indian who recovered from tuberculosis under care of his medicine man after white treatment failed.

41 Waldram et al., *Aboriginal Health in Canada*, 62. Advancing beyond most previous discussions of the disease is Daschuk's *Clearing the Plains*, which distinguishes different kinds and histories of tuberculosis, and is particularly informative about bovine tuberculosis, which infested reserve populations from the meat and unpasteurized milk of infected cattle.

42 McCuaig, *The Weariness, the Fever, and the Fret*, 4.

43 Sutherland, *Children in English-Canadian Society*, ch. 3.

44 Meijer Drees, "Reserve Hospitals and Medical Officers," 154. Pagden, *Peoples and Empires*, 140, notes that by the 1880s, "cleanliness was not only next to godliness, it was one of the defining marks of civilization."

45 Meijer Drees, "Reserve Hospitals and Medical Officers," 160.

46 Lux, *Medicine That Walks*, 194; Milloy, *A National Crime*, 89.

47 For example, in 1887 the superintendent general reported, "the preservation of the health of the Indians generally throughout the Dominion has engaged the careful attention of the Department; full instructions have been sent to the Indian agents as to the sanitary measures to be adopted." *CSP*, 1887, #6 (DIA), xii.

48 See, for example, *CSP*, 1881, #14 (DIA), 98 (report of Agent Norman T. Macleod, Treaty 7).

49 Dion, *My Tribe The Crees*, 4, notes the teepees of the "Bush Crees" were deliberately smoke-filled to drive off the clouds of mosquitoes in the region, so there were traditional and practical reasons in many cases for smoke-filled dwellings. Mountain Horse, *My People The Bloods*, 105, contends teepees were better ventilated than log huts or tents.

50 Mountain Horse, *My People The Bloods*, 104. The evidence Daschuk provides in *Clearing the Plains*, chs. 1–5, does not corroborate this disease-free perspective.

51 Mountain Horse, *My People The Bloods*, 105.

52 This subject cries out for systematic scholarly investigation.

53 Daschuk, *Clearing the Plains*, 165, reports 160 disease-related deaths at Lac la Biche in 1886–87, apparently based on reports in the *Saskatchewan Herald*, but these likely cannot have been deaths among local treaty Indians, if only because the band never was anywhere near that large. Perhaps the total included Metis.

54 *CSP*, 1890, #12 (DIA), xxix, 71–76.

55 *CSP*, 1890, #12, 78–79, 292.

56 Ibid., xxix, 77, 283.

57 Ibid., xxix.

58 *CSP*, 1890, #12, 81–87. Dr Neville James Lindsay was the first physician in Calgary (1883), and had contracts to serve the Siksika, Tsuu T'ina, and Stoney Nakoda reserves, the High River Industrial School, the NWMP, and the CPR labour force in addition to maintaining his private practice. He managed to visit each of the reserves and the school once a month for eleven years. Lampard, *Alberta's Medical History*, 42–49.

59 Churchill, "Tsuu T'ina," 110, 131–32. Disease also hampered work on the reserve, as did the fact that after a death in any house, the dwelling had to be torn down and replaced, and relatives and friends did not work during the mourning period.

60 Meijer Drees, "Reserve Hospitals and Medical Officers," 164–69; Lux, *Medicine That Walks*, 117, notes that despite the hospital's "excellent work," it "had little impact on the death rates on the reserve."

61 On the Kainai hospital, see Meijer Drees, "Reserve Hospitals and Medical Officers," 155–58; *Debates*, 1893, 2094 (9 March 1893; T.M. Daly). Also with respect to medical care at this time, former NWMP officer R. Burton Deane recalled in his memoirs that Dr Mewburn in Lethbridge became celebrated among the Kainai and Siksika after operating to cure a man of goitre, and apparently he offered his services free of charge to the Indians (and was never compensated by the DIA). According to Deane, "the Indians grew to have a blind faith in him and

brought him all sorts of cases." Deane, *Mounted Police Life in Canada*, 47–48.

62  1905 data from *CSP*, 1906, #27 (DIA), 112, 114, 139, 152, 153, 169–70.

63  Ibid., 149–52.

64  Ibid., 126–29.

65  Ibid., 130–31. On the issue of meat, Grant wrote: "It has ... been noteworthy that meat a white man could not possibly eat, has no visible ill effects upon an Indian after eating it. Be that as it may, every inducement is held out to prevent consumption of polluted meat as food."

66  Useful on this matter is Hogan, "Climate, Calgary and Tuberculosis," 519–23.

67  Lux, *Medicine That Walks*, 129, argues that fear of disease spreading from reserves to the wider population was important in shaping policy, but most of her evidence is post-1905. McCuaig, *The Weariness, the Fever and the Fret*, 152, notes that by the interwar period Indians were regarded as "a reservoir of infection" and a threat to the wider community. Donald Smith posed the question of whether working with Indians was risky for whites, such as teachers and government employees (private communication). I have found little evidence on the subject.

68  *CSP*, 1906, #27 (DIA), 278. Mortality rates for Canada as a whole are given as 1.62 per cent in 1901, and 1.3 per cent in 1905; Urquhart and Buckley, *Historical Statistics of Canada*, 42, series B 89.

69  *CSP*, 1906–07, #27 (DIA), 274–76.

70  Ibid., 276–84.

71  Meijer Drees, "Reserve Hospitals and Medical Officers," 158–59. By 1927, there were ninety-seven medical officers to care for Indians in the prairie provinces. Meijer Drees does not indicate what proportion were employed in Alberta.

72  Lux, *Medicine That Walks*, ch. 3; Milloy, *A National Crime*, ch. 5. There appears to be no study comparing mortality in Indian and white boarding schools, where rates could also be appalling. For example, the Woodlands Memorial Garden in New Westminster, British Columbia, was established to remember some 3,000 children (and some staff) who died at the Woodlands and nearby Essondale institutions between 1920 and 1958.

73  *Debates*, 22 June 1894, 4872–74. Martin was referring to the entire Indian education budget for the North-West Territories. See also Enns, "'But What Is The Object of Educating These Children,'" 101–23.

74  Cited in Milloy, *A National Crime*, 51. Scott was referring to all Indian boarding schools, not specifically those in Alberta.

75  Ontario set standards on such matters for its schools from as early as 1883, but they were not adopted elsewhere for many years; and when

adopted were not rigorously enforced in Ontario or anywhere else in Canada during the period under examination. See Sutherland, *Children in English-Speaking Canada*, 40–41.

76  On these matters, see Milloy, *A National Crime*, 78–88, 116–17, 124; Miller, *Shingwauk's Vision*, 290–97, 301–08.

77  Milloy, *A National Crime*, 91. Milloy calculates that the premature death rate may have been as high as 42 per cent. Lux, *Medicine That Walks*, 122–23, calculates the figures differently, stating, "of the 1,537 students with records, 35 per cent were either sick or dead."

78  Churchill, "Tsuu T'ina," 235.

79  Bryce's 1907 report led to a debate about whether disease originated more on reserves or in schools; see Lux, *Medicine That Walks*, 125–37. Gresko, "White 'Rites' and Indian 'Rites,'" 174–75, notes that Indians "often allowed only the female, sick, and orphaned to attend industrial institutions." See also Fox, "The Failure of the Red Deer Industrial School," 55–56.

80  Churchill, "Tsuu T'ina," 264.

81  Lux, *Medicine That Walks*, 127–28.

82  Waldram et al., *Aboriginal Health in Canada*, 96–100.

83  Meijer Drees, "Reserve Hospitals and Medical Officers," 174–76.

84  Daschuk, *Clearing the Plains*, ch. 9, 186.

85  Bourassa, "Colonization," 220–21. Among infectious diseases, tuberculosis remains a scourge for Indians, with a rate in 2003 of 43 per 100,000 people, versus a rate for whites of 1.5 per 100,000.

86  Bourassa, "Colonization," especially 221–22.

87  Gibbons, "The Evolution of Diet," 52.

CHAPTER EIGHT

1  Calliou, "Losing the Game," 1. I am indebted to this work for stimulating much of what follows, even if I disagree with some of Calliou's interpretation of the evidence. See also Calliou, "The Supreme Court of Alberta," 135–42. Two excellent treatments of many of the issues are Irwin, "Not Like the Others," and Binnema and Niemi, "Let the Line Be Drawn Now." A useful sketch of the legal background is found in Gulig, "We Beg the Government." A sampling of legal opinion and judgments from a much later period sheds some light on how these matters are regarded in retrospect; see Zlotkin, "Post-Confederation Treaties," 328. An excellent culturally contextualized case study is Wicken, *The Colonization of Mi'kmaw Memory and History*.

2  See, for example, Snow, *These Mountains Are Our Sacred Places*, 76–78.

3  Morris, *Treaties*, 303, 306.

4  Ibid., 19. See also Miller, *Compact, Contract, Covenant*, 116. One obvious fact requires emphasis: Indians might continue to hunt, fish, and gather outside reserves, but now they did so on land to which the Crown had full, unimpaired title, and which it could choose itself, or authorize others, to develop and "improve." Robinson did not address what Indian expectations of government might be should the traditional means of support fail.

5  Morris, *Treaties*, 29. Note the significant difference between what Morris said in 1871 and Robinson said in 1850: the former envisaged a time when lands used for traditional purposes would be taken up by whites; the latter appears to have expected that the lands would be available indefinitely. Expectations concerning long-term land use were different in each case. For a discussion of these matters in Treaties 1 and 2, see Friesen, "Grant Me Wherewith to Make My Living," 143–47.

6  Morris, *Treaties*, 183, 218, 353, 369.

7  Ibid., 257, 269–70; see also Treaty 7 Elders et al., *The True Spirit and Original Intent of Treaty 7*, 242–43.

8  Before confederation, Canadian policy had been to persuade Indians to grow their own food and regard hunting and fishing as a supplement. Sowby, "Macdonald the Administrator," 22.

9  Calliou, "Losing the Game," abstract, asserts, "First Nations had entered into treaties under which they were assured that their traditional livelihoods would be protected." I do not believe this conclusion is justified by either the language of the treaties or by the recorded comments of the treaty commissioners, or even by the reports of Indian elders I have seen. Daschuk, *Clearing the Plains*, notes the desperate shortages of traditional means of sustenance prior to the treaties; all parties to the treaties knew that the traditional way of life was no longer sustainable on its own. Dyck, *What Is the Indian 'Problem'*, 28, suggests that persistence of Indian hunting and fishing was part of a pattern of resistance to "coercive tutelage," albeit one necessitated by practical need.

10  "An Ordinance for the Protection of the Buffalo," *Ordinances of the Lieut.-Governor and Council of the North-West Territories*, 22 March 1877. This episode is described in Stanley, *The Birth of Western Canada*, 218–23; Harring, *White Man's Law*, 257–62; Calliou, "Losing the Game," 14–15; also see *Debates*, 1877, 993–95 (16 March 1877).

11  Dale Gibson, in a private communication, notes, "the Council's power to regulate such matters was legally valid, but it did so only as an instructed delegate of the Government of Canada."

12  In addition to sources in n10 above, see Giraud, *The Métis in the Canadian West*, vol. 2, 416–18.

13  Moreover, according to Lacombe, Indian bands did not trust one another to obey the bans, making effective enforcement improbable; see *Debates*, 1877, 993–95 (16 March 1877).

14  Thomas, *The Struggle for Responsible Government*, 77. The 1877 Ordinance was repealed by Ordinance No. 3 of 2 August 1878.

15  If the local government in 1883 did not have the power to restrict Indian hunting rights under the treaties, presumably it did not have that right in 1877 either, but the 1878 repeal of the 1877 ordinance precluded that matter being raised at the time. It is clear in retrospect that only the federal government had the power to act, but to have done so would have been a unilateral alteration of the treaties, as indeed happened in the 1890s. The issue is a good example of how poorly the government thought through issues affecting the West generally, and Indians in particular.

16  Calliou, "Losing the Game," 23–25, 148; Ordinance No. 8 of 1883 ("An Ordinance for the Protection of Game"), sec. 19: "The provisions of this Ordinance shall not apply to Indians in any part of the Territories, with regard to any game actually killed for their own use only, and not for purposes of sale or traffic."

17  This is outlined in Calliou, "Losing the Game," 32–44; also see Binnema and Niemi, "Let the Line Be Drawn Now," 729–34. Hunters considered profiting from organized sport hunting to be legitimate, as it was governed by legislated take limits; profiting from selling meat or other animal parts would encourage excessive pressure on the animal resources.

18  Calliou, "Losing the Game," 15.

19  53 Vic., ch. 29, sec. 10 (which became sec. 133 of the Indian Act): "The Superintendent General may, from time to time, by public notice, declare that, on and after a day therein named, the laws respecting game in force in the Province of Manitoba or The Western Territories, or respecting such game as is specified in such notice, shall apply to Indians within the said Province or Territories, as the case may be, or to the Indians in such parts thereof as to him seems expedient."

20  *Debates*, 1890, 4903–05, 14 May 1890.

21  Calliou, "Losing the Game," 3, 16, 18–19, 118–42, 152–53, 164–66.

22  Ibid., appendices A, B, C; Binnema and Niemi, "Let the Line Be Drawn Now," 729. Useful for understanding fish and game associations is Colpitts, "Fish and Game Associations in Southern Alberta."

23  Calliou, "Losing the Game," 104–18; Calliou, "The Supreme Court of Alberta," 138–42; Snow, *These Mountains Are Our Sacred Places*, 46–47,

59; Loo, *States of Nature*, 44; Dempsey, *Indian Tribes of Alberta*, 53–54; Regular, "Red Backs and White Burdens," 103–14, 116, 137–47.

24 See map 5.

25 *CSP*, 1903, #25 (Interior), part 5, 6.

26 *CSP*, 1904, #25 (Interior), part 7, 6; 1905, #25, part 5, 6.

27 Binnema and Niemi, "Let the Line Be Drawn Now," 725.

28 Snow, *These Mountains Are Our Sacred Places*, 65–68.

29 The Constitution Act 1867, sec. 91.12. The main exception in Treaty 7 was the Stoney Nakoda, who fished Devil's Lake (Lake Minnewanka) in the Rocky Mountains National Park; this fishery is noted in Armstrong et al., *The River Returns*, 41–42, 220–22. My discussion of the fisheries matter leans heavily on Irwin, "Not Like the Others," 242–46. While the federal government ultimately had power over everything in the North-West Territories until 1905, regulation of fisheries was different from that of hunting – the former being a federal power administered by a bureaucracy throughout Canada and the latter being a provincial power and thus without a comparable national bureaucracy and legal framework. The fisheries issue put two federal departments, the DIA and Marine and Fisheries, at odds with one another. Note that Brian J. Smith, "The Historical and Archaeological Evidence," makes a case for fishing being more important to bison hunters than has been previously acknowledged.

30 Cited in Friesen, "Grant Me Wherewith to Make My Living," 151. On the fishing crisis in the mid-1880s and its exacerbation by commercial fishing, see Daschuk, *Clearing the Plains*, 150.

31 *CSP*, 1891, #8A, *Supplement No. 1 to the Annual Report of the Department of Fisheries. Fisheries Statements and Inspectors' Reports for the Year 1890*, 160–61. On the matter of fisheries as the question affected Indians in Manitoba, see Friesen, "Give Me Wherewith to Make My Living," 147–51.

32 *CSP*, 1893, #10 (Fisheries), part 2, v, 117; #10A, xi, 149. Note that at Pigeon Lake, whites and Metis took 84,000 pounds and Indians from Peace Hills agency took 36,000 pounds.

33 Quotations from Irwin, "Not Like the Others," 244–45.

34 *CSP*, 1895, #11A (Fisheries), App. #12, North-West Territories, 346–49, 361. The warning apparently had little effect, or the regulations were ignored, because for the next several years departmental reports note the worsening conditions for trout.

35 Price, *The Spirit of the Alberta Indian Treaties*, 116, 119–20, 125.

36 Treaty 7 Elders et al., *The True Spirit and Original Intent of Treaty 7*, 90, 93, 95–96, 105, 137.

37 In British Columbia the restrictions on Indian hunting, trapping, and fishing were more extensive, as whites expected to control these activities and most Indians had no recognized treaty rights in the period under review; see Lutz, *Makúk*, 20, and chs. 6 and 7.

38 Treaty 7 Elders et al., *The True Spirit and Original Intent of Treaty 7*, 307–08; Calliou, "Losing the Game," 97–104 and conclusion. The major study of the subject is Rotman, *Parallel Paths*, esp. ch. 4. A more accessible introduction is Bartlett, *Indian Reserves and Aboriginal Lands in Canada*, ch. 11–12; and see Mainville, *Overview of Aboriginal and Treaty Rights*, ch. 3.

39 Calliou, "Losing the Game," 91; Harring, *White Man's Law*, 262–63.

40 Calliou, "Losing the Game," 90–97, 143–47. The 1932 case was *R. v. Wesley*.

41 Calliou, "Losing the Game," abstract, 165–69.

42 The language of Treaty 8 (1899) is even more detailed, but along much the same lines as previous treaties; its text may be found in Canada, *Indian Treaties and Surrenders*, vol. 3 (1912), 290–93. My reading differs from that of Calliou, "Losing the Game," 20–21, 141–43. Despite this, Laird apparently had to be more liberal in his offer in Treaty 8 (see Fumoleau, *As Long As This Land Shall Last*, 84–85). Likely, the restrictive policies of the 1880s and 1890s in the southern territories caused the Treaty 8 Indians to fear that such policies would apply to them – a matter that became a real sticking point. Laird verbally reiterated the government's right to legislate on the subject, but then proceeded to promise "they would be as free to hunt and fish after the treaty as they would be if they never entered into it."

43 See, as one example, Dewdney's comment in *CSP*, 1892, #14 (DIA), xix: "By following this course a saving to the country is effected, and the Indians are saved from the demoralization which would attend their being fed in idleness."

44 Calliou, "Losing the Game," provides an overview of how evolving law, court decisions, and the 1982 constitution have led in recent decades to a very different legal situation with respect to Indians' hunting and fishing rights. In this book, I am concerned with attempting to understand the situation up to 1905; I think that there is a tendency to read the past through the lens of the present.

CHAPTER NINE

1 Harring, *Native People in Nineteenth-Century Canadian Jurisprudence*, ch. 11. His examples are as follows: (1) disregarding rights at trial, namely the post-rebellion 1885 trials of Indians; (2) mistranslating treaties, namely

the suggestion that poor translation at Treaties 6 and 7 was at least in part a deliberate act to mislead Indians; (3) fraudulent acts, namely the 1877 buffalo ordinance and its 1878 repeal; (4) prohibiting exercise of tribal cultures, namely the efforts to suppress the sun dance; and (5) imposing an authoritarian legal order, namely the imposition of the legally dubious pass system. The first three have been addressed previously; the remaining two will be addressed below. Another study also portrays the period as one of unrelieved violence perpetrated against the Indians of western Canada: Ennab, "Rupturing the Myth of the Peaceful Western Canadian Frontier." As is evidenced in this chapter, and elsewhere, I read the record quite differently.

2 *CSP*, 1896, #15 (NWMP), 6, 129; Dempsey, *Charcoal's World*, 40–41. I have been unable to determine Scraping High's Blackfoot name. The Toronto *Globe* used the Skynner murder as a basis for a fear-mongering article on brewing trouble among the Siksika, generating a debate in the House of Commons; see *Debates*, 1895, 3874–905 (4 July 1895).

3 Hanson, "Kitchi-Manito-Waya," *DCB*, 12, 497–98. On the Kitchi-Manito-Waya incident, see Jennings, "The North West Mounted Police and Indian Policy," ch. 8; Lee, "Almighty Voice and His Stories"; Smith, *Long Lance*, 112–13; Atkin, *Maintain the Right*, 292–93, 295–97; Berton, "The Legend of Almighty Voice," 209–33. See also Kennedy (Ochankugahe), *Recollections of an Assiniboine Chief*, 81–85.

4 Dempsey, "Si'k-Oskitsis," *DCB*, 12, 970; Dempsey, *Charcoal's World*, 81. Useful Native perspectives on Charcoal may be found in Mountain Horse, *My People The Bloods*, 119–31; Hungry Wolf, *The Blood People*, 279–82.

5 Dempsey, *Charcoal's World*, 112, 142, 147.

6 Ibid., ch. 15–18. The trial's report is found in the *North-West Territories Law Reports* for 1897, and is reproduced in Macleod, "The Problem of Law and Order in the Canadian West," 171–75.

7 Hanson, "Kitchi-Manito-Waya," 498–99; Macpherson, *Outlaws of the Canadian West*, 118–29.

8 Dempsey, *Charcoal's World*, 86; Regular, "Red Backs and White Burdens," 70–74.

9 Dempsey, *Charcoal's World*, 74–76.

10 Jennings, "The North West Mounted Police and Indian Policy," 337–38. Jennings contends that Indians had an almost pathological fear of being jailed.

11 Dempsey, *Charcoal's World*, 28–29, 60, ch. 12; and see Macleod, *NWMP and Law Enforcement*, 145–46.

12 Dempsey, *Charcoal's World*, 73–74.

13  Ibid., ch. 11.

14  Morris, *The Treaties of Canada with the Indians*, 355, 371. An identical provision in both treaties stated that the Indians agreed to "assist the officers of Her Majesty in bringing to justice and punishment any Indian offending against the stipulations of this treaty, or infringing the laws in force in the country so ceded."

15  Dempsey, *Charcoal's World*, 14, 74, 107.

16  Neither the police nor the government had any conception of the existence of Indian customary law; in any event, only Canadian law was deemed legitimate.

17  Jennings, "The Plains Indians and the Law," 58; Macleod, *The North-West Mounted Police and Law Enforcement*, 35–37; Macleod and Rollason, "Restrain the Lawless Savages" 159–60.

18  *CSP*, 1882, #18 (NWMP), 8–9, 12. The commissioner requested an increase from 293 to 500 men, of which he proposed placing 200 in "Blackfoot country" and twenty-five in an outpost of Calgary at Edmonton. Certainly some NWMP had previously been located at Fort Saskatchewan, where on 20 December 1879 the first convicted murderer was hanged in the area that became Alberta. A Cree man, Ka-Ki-Si-Kutchin (Swift Runner), had admitted to murdering and cannibalizing his wife, mother, brother, and six children; the Cree communities had earlier exiled him. Gavigan, *Hunger, Horses, and Government Men*, 59–63; Pruden, "Swift Runner's Last Walk," *Edmonton Journal*, 18 September 2011, C3.

19  *CSP*, 1884, #12 (NWMP), 21; 1888, #28 (NWMP), 96–97; 1906, #28 (NWMP), part 2, 4–6.

20  Carter, *Aboriginal People and Colonizers*, 127–30; Gavigan, *Hunger, Horses, and Government Men*.

21  Stonechild and Waiser, *Loyal Till Death*, 171.

22  Many Indian leaders tried to uphold the treaty commitment to obey the law.

23  In many ways, Dempsey's study of Charcoal is a case study in these matters.

24  *CSP*, 1882, #18 (Interior), 25; Martin, "Macleod at Law," 43, 45–46.

25  Jennings, "The Plains Indians and the Law," 59–61. Maunsell's recollection of the incident is published in Dempsey, "The West of Edward Maunsell," 2: 23–24. On one occasion, F.W.G. Haultain, a prominent lawyer and later premier of the North-West Territories, argued in a case that a white man ought not to be convicted on the uncorroborated testimony of an Indian; Macleod, the presiding magistrate, took umbrage, and "remarked rather warmly that it was the first time it had ever been suggested in his Court that an Indian was not as worthy of credibility as a white man, and he

hoped it would be the last." With respect to the case in question, Macleod accepted the Indian's story as true, though "it subsequently transpired that there was not a word of truth in it." Deane, "The Story of Joe Bush," 13.

26 Jennings, "The Plains Indians and the Law," 61–62. Another telling case: a few days after arriving at Fort Macleod in 1879, Dewdney noted in his diary that he "attended trial of Indians for killing cows, no evidence, dismissed." This was during a time of appalling starvation among the Indians. Dempsey, "The Starvation Year," 8. Macleod and Rollason, "Restrain the Lawless Savages," provide a careful statistical analysis. Martin, "Macleod at Law," 47, 55, contends that in the period 1882–88 Indians, unsurprisingly, were much more likely than whites to be convicted of horse theft. They were also more likely to plead guilty, while whites retained counsel. But horse theft constituted only a fraction of the cases brought to courts.

27 CSP, 1882, #18 (Interior), 10–12. Daschuk, *Clearing the Plains*, chs. 7–8, demonstrates that there was ample reason to think Indian unrest was both legitimate and dangerously high.

28 CSP, 1884, #12 (Interior), 12–13, appendix A; Jennings, "The Plains Indians and the Law," 60–61. Many cases were tried at Fort Walsh and Medicine Hat, outside Alberta, but most of these related to white labour matters in conjunction with construction of the CPR. Interestingly, no cases appear to have been tried in the Treaty 6 portion of the district of Alberta. Concerning the incarceration of Star Child, Denny said, "We are well rid of him, as he has been a disturbing element in the camp." CSP, 1884, #4 (DIA), 79. That said, Star Child subsequently must have been viewed as largely rehabilitated, because he became a scout for the NWMP; Dempsey, "The West of Edward Maunsell," 2: 25.

29 CSP, 1886, #8 (NWMP), 6–7.

30 Hubner, "Horse Stealing and the Borderline," 281–85. Also useful are Elofson, *Frontier Ranching*, ch. 9; Elofson, *Cowboys, Gentlemen & Cattle Thieves*, 113–14.

31 The various views are discussed in Hubner, "Horse Stealing," 285–86.

32 CSP, 1886, #8 (NWMP), 6. One source claims that a mange epidemic in 1881 killed about half of the Piikani horses, "making younger warriors more eager to raid enemy camps." Hungry Wolf and Hungry Wolf, *Indian Tribes of the Northern Rockies*, 13.

33 Macleod, *The NWMP and Law Enforcement*, 27, 44–45; CSP, 1885, #153 (NWMP), 14–19; 1886, #8, 5–6. Also useful on horse stealing is Samek, *The Blackfoot Confederacy*, 153–55. On the patrol system, see Monaghan, "Mounties in the Frontier."

34 Dempsey, "Final Treaty of Peace," 8–16; Dempsey, *Red Crow*, ch. 16.

35 Barron, "The Indian Pass System in the Canadian West," 25–42; Sowby, "Macdonald the Administrator," 182–88. Sowby claims that a pass system was advocated in 1882 to control trans-border activity, but was quickly dropped. Informative on how the system functioned between 1896 and 1911 is Regular, "Red Backs and White Burdens," 19–21, 75–80, 115.

36 *CSP*, 1885, #153 (NWMP), 6; Sowby, "Macdonald the Administrator," 185. Irvine went on to point out that for "the social evil" (prostitution) complained of in association with these encampments "the white man is solely to blame." The idea of the pass system was probably derived from the United States, which had adopted such a system in the 1870s. Graybill, *Policing the Great Plains*, 45. However, in the United States, Indians received very large reservations and agreed under the treaties to reside upon them; in Canada, Indians accepted smaller reserves only on the understanding that they would be free to come and go from them.

37 Sowby, "Macdonald the Administrator," 182; and see Barron, "Indian Pass System," 30 and 40n26.

38 Carter, *Aboriginal People and Colonizers of Western Canada*, 162–63; Sowby, "Macdonald the Administrator," 186; Smith, *Liberalism, Surveillance and Resistance*, 60–73. Graybill, *Policing the Great Plains*, 43, claims that the Indian Act justified the pass system, but does not explain why.

39 Barron, "The Indian Pass System," 30. Miller, *Skyscrapers*, 258–60, contends that the pass system was not always enforced in the later 1880s, and that by 1893 it was "virtually a dead letter," as a result of native defiance and of NWMP refusal in the 1890s to enforce an illegal policy. However, there is plenty of evidence that the pass system persisted and was variably enforced until at least 1905. Agents also tried to control movement by withholding rations to limit unapproved off-reserve excursions. See, for example, *CSP*, 1886, #4 (DIA), 74.

40 *CSP*, 1888, #28 (NWMP), 7–17, 46; Sowby, "Macdonald the Administrator," 186.

41 Some Indian chiefs were becoming exasperated with the continual disturbing effects of horse raiding, and sometimes other crimes, on reserves, and from time to time turned over troublesome individuals to the NWMP; see, for example, *CSP*, 1888, #28, 48.

42 *CSP*, 1889, #17 (NWMP), 9, 68; Barron, "The Indian Pass System," 35. Deane noted in his memoirs, "as it happened, our 'bluff' was never 'called' by the Indians, who invariably did as we wanted them to do." *Mounted Police Life in Canada*, 262–63.

43 Churchill, "Tsuu T'ina," 81–84, 134–35.

44 *CSP*, 1903, #28 (NWMP), 42; 1906, #28 (NWMP), 52.

45 Samek, *The Blackfoot Confederacy*, 63. Samek, 155–56, acknowledges that by 1905 the pass system could not be properly enforced on either side of the international border.

46 Regular, "Red Backs and White Burdens," 77.

47 The NWMP's annual reports from the 1890s onward have plenty of evidence of the police enforcing the policy, often under the umbrella of vagrancy law. See also Carter, *Aboriginal People and Colonizers of Western Canada*, 163–64; Harring, *White Man's Law*, 266. Harring considers the pass system to be "structured" and "institutionalized ... lawlessness." On the persistence of the pass system into the 1950s, see Dyck, *What Is the Indian "Problem,"* 21.

48 "Within the boundary of Indian Reserves ... no intoxicating liquor shall be allowed to be introduced or sold," and laws passed for this purpose "shall be strictly enforced." Treaty 1, in Morris, *The Treaties of Canada with the Indians*, 315.

49 Morris, *The Treaties of Canada with the Indians*, 353 (Treaty 6), 368–71 (Treaty 7).

50 Sharp, *Whoop-up Country*, ch. 3, 5.

51 *CSP*, 1888, #28 (NWMP), 49, 59.

52 Samek, *The Blackfoot Confederacy*, 153. This was approved in 1889.

53 *CSP*, 1906, #28 (NWMP), 7–8, 10. The ninety-eight Indian convictions constituted about 10.6 per cent of all cases, slightly less than the percentage of Indians in the population of the district of Alberta in 1905.

54 Ibid., 44, 65.

55 *CSP*, 1906, #28, 49. The other males were classified as follows: Whites, 319; Half-breeds, 28; Lunatics, 27; Negroes, 2; Chinamen, 1. Other females were: Whites, 7; Half-breeds, 14; Lunatics, 6. Three Indians were truant boys who were returned to their schools. (Terms as in original.)

56 Perry and Steele cited in Regular, "Red Backs and White Burdens," 98–99; and Dempsey, *Charcoal's World*, 99. See also Regular's discussion of the alcohol problem at "Red Backs and White Burdens," 43–48, 96–103.

57 See Pettipas, *Severing the Ties that Bind*; Waldram, Herring, and Young, *Aboriginal Health in Canada*, 119–21; Titley, *A Narrow Vision*, ch. 9; Regular, "Red Backs and White Burdens," 27–38, 84–96, 152–62. Useful explanations of the dance are in Mandelbaum, *The Plains Cree*, 183–99; Jenness, *The Sarcee Indians of Alberta*, ch. 6. A perceptive Indian account is Dion, *My Tribe the Crees*, 36–42. Most sources, including Pettipas, Mandelbaum, and Dion, see the sun and thirst dances as basically the same, but Ahenakew, *Voices of the Plains Cree*, 46–49, distinguishes between them. Dion, 41–60, also describes at least ten other dances,

situating them in the religious life of the Cree. Also helpful are Mountain Horse, *My People The Bloods*, 57–65, 72–74; Hungry Wolf, *The Blood People*, 20–44. Pettipas, 68, argues that so far as the Cree were concerned at the Treaty 6 discussions, the government promised "their cultural autonomy was not a point of negotiation." Instead, "the treaties were guarantees that they could continue to live in their territories according to their customary ways and that they would receive assistance in establishing an alternate economic base. Judging from Morris's words, there was no reason to believe that there would be interference in their daily lives." Of course, that would mean that the government had undertaken not to interfere in religious ceremonies and dances. By contrast, I contend that the discussions at the treaty negotiations conveyed a very different message, so I do not find Pettipas's conclusion persuasive; I do agree that nothing was said directly about restricting dances or other religious ceremonies.

58 Regular, "Red Backs and White Burdens," 54.
59 Deane, *Mounted Police Life in Canada*, 83–85.
60 *CSP*, 1890, #13 (NWMP), 42.
61 Ahenakew, *Voices of the Plains Cree*, 94–95.
62 Ibid., 95, points out that every year Indians took time off from their farming duties on long pilgrimages to visit Catholic shrines without complaint from officials.
63 Pettipas, *Severing the Ties that Bind*, 87–93 (re: sec. 114 of the Indian Act). Americans had banned Indian religious ceremonies in 1883; Seed, *American Pentimento*, 175.
64 Pettipas, *Severing the Ties that Bind*, 104.
65 Ray, *Illustrated History of Canada's Native Peoples*, 230–34; Pettipas, *Severing the Ties that Bind*, 95–96, 107–11; Titley, *A Narrow Vision*, 166–67.
66 *CSP*, 1889, #16 (DIA), 131; 1890, #12 (DIA), 172; Dempsey, *Crowfoot*, 199–200. Reed saw the rainfall as a coincidence; but it is likely that Christians in their churches who also prayed for rain would have seen it as a divine answer to prayer.
67 *CSP*, 1899, #15 (NWMP), 27. Oddly, this source refers to "Sioux dances," but contextually the meaning is likely sun dances.
68 *CSP*, 1903. #27 (DIA), 129, 151.
69 Ibid., 188–89.
70 Regular, "Red Backs and White Burdens," 92–93.
71 *CSP*, 1899, #15 (NWMP), 27. Mékaisto told Deane that he was "too old to give up his own prayers, and would not do so." He did say, "he liked the christians' [*sic*] prayers, but he liked the Indians' prayers too."

72 Cited in Regular, "Red Backs and White Burdens," 88.

73 On these matters, see the extended discussion in Regular, "Red Backs and White Burdens," 38–43, 152–62.

74 Gray, *Red Lights on the Prairies*.

75 Macleod, *The NWMP and Law Enforcement*, 127. The zealous officers were duly charged by the commissioner under the Police Act. Lutz, *Makúk*, 179–81, argues (at least for the British Columbia experience), "Prostitution may describe the relationship that non-aboriginal men thought they were engaged in, but it is unlikely that it accurately describes the relationship as viewed by participating aboriginal women. Within the context of the sale of sex, what was sold was not the same as what was purchased."

76 The principal study is Carter, *The Importance of Being Monogamous*. See also Regular, "Red Backs and White Burdens," 48–54. The women discussed in this paragraph would have been regarded as "respectable," and therefore needing protection, while those engaged in the sex trade were thought of as exploitable lower-class women with very different values.

77 Horrall, "The (R)NWMP and Prairie Prostitution," 106, 125. He adds that the officers "would have included many other westerners in the same class as prostitutes, including most of their own men."

78 Ibid., 107.

79 Ibid., 108. Horrall adds, "prostitutes were off-limits to commissioned officers," who were supposed to behave like "gentlemen."

80 Ibid., 126n5.

81 Atkin, *Maintain the Right*, 131–32. Who provided this information, and the nature of it, is not clear.

82 Carter, *The Importance of Being Monogamous*, 70–71. Carter sees this sort of thing as a discontinuity with the past, noting increasing unease among "non-Aboriginal communities" with cross-cultural marriages, and a tendency to desert "Aboriginal spouses." Yet this same behaviour was thoroughly documented for the fur-trade era by Jennifer Brown and Sylvia Van Kirk. A very helpful summary of these issues is in A. Prentice et al., *Canadian Women*, 15–29, ch. 6. For a contemporary (1886) comment on the relationships between Indian women and white men, see Gray, *Red Lights on the Prairies*, 219–20. Carter comments on the differences between what she terms "the marriage laws of the Aboriginal peoples" and those of whites in "Complicated and Clouded," 152–55. On Davis, see Stacey, "D.W. Davis," 1–11.

83 Ibid., 132.

84 See, for example, Mandelbaum, *The Plains Cree*, 146–50.

85 Those who argue that, regardless of what the government view of Indian status under the law might have been, Indians regarded themselves as independent entities and therefore free agents, logically cannot accept this line of reasoning.

86 It would, however, be wrong to deny the agency of those Indian women who sought such liaisons, insofar as they had some freedom of choice.

87 Carter, *Capturing Women*, 173–75; Atkin, *Maintaining the Right*, 131–32.

88 Graybill, *Policing the Great Plains*, 39. The evidence is most thoroughly reviewed by Carter in *Capturing Women*, ch. 5. Carter, 180–81, cites one case of public physical abuse by a NWMP officer, Superintendent W.D. Jarvis, who assaulted his Indian wife, evidently at least in part because of his ignorance of local customs and complete misreading of her actions on one occasion. Jarvis was dismissed from the NWMP as a result of his disgraceful actions. His great mistake was that his action was very public; private domestic abuse was rarely noted, let alone prosecuted, in this era. With respect to abuse by government officials, see Carter, *Capturing Women*, 182; and Daschuk, *Clearing the Plains*, 113, 152–54, 185.

89 Carter, *Capturing Women*, 167–68.

90 *CSP*, 1882, #18 (Interior), 29, 31–32, 34.

91 None of the sources consider the possibility that any disease could have spread from the police to the women.

92 Daschuk seems to imply this. Daschuk, *Clearing the Plains*, 113, 152–54, 185.

93 A later era would describe these behaviours as part of rape culture.

94 *CSP*, 1906 (NWMP), #28, 60, 65. Primrose successfully argued for the young offenders to be incarcerated locally, rather than at Stony Mountain Penitentiary.

95 Harring, *Native People in Nineteenth-Century Canadian Jurisprudence*, ch. 11; Ennab, "Rupturing the Myth of the Peaceful Western Canadian Frontier."

96 It is, perhaps, telling that the sun dance issue was often addressed more regularly and extensively in the DIA annual reports than in NWMP reports.

97 Dempsey, *Charcoal's World*, 162.

98 Graybill, *Policing the Great Plains*, 15, sees the NWMP as condescending, rather than bearing animosity, toward Indians. On the notion that Indians possessed at best a very thin veneer of civilization, see the speech of Prime Minister Macdonald, *Debates*, 1885, 3118–19 (6 July 1885). On police attitudes, see Regular, "Red Backs and White Burdens," 70–75.

99 Quotation from *Thin Blue*, cited in *Time*, 11 March 2013, 33.

100  Mountain Horse, *My People The Bloods*, 106–07. Men like Mountain Horse and Ahenakew perhaps represent a rather benign, even positive, attitude toward the whites that an embittered younger generation of Indians may not share. Mountain Horse, for example, was born in 1888 and educated in an Indian school on the Kainai reserve and at the Calgary industrial school, and exhibits none of the alienation or bitterness that most accounts of the schools suggest that he should have felt.

### POSTSCRIPT

1  King, *The Inconvenient Indian*, 94.
2  Information in the following two paragraphs derives from CSP, 1924, #24 (DIA).
3  Louis Bull, Samson, Pakan (Goodfish Lake), Saddle Lake, Sarcee, Stony; Saddle Lake was Church of England, and the rest were Methodist.
4  Macleod (C.E., Kainai), Standoff (R.C., Kainai), Cluny (Crowfoot, R.C.; Siksika), Gleichen (Old Sun, C.E., Siksika), St Albert (R.C.), Hobbema (Ermineskin, R.C.), Brocket (Piikani, R.C.), Brocket (Piikani, C.E.), Blue Quills (Saddle Lake, R.C.), Whitefish Lake (C.E.).
5  The government also undertook to pay the expenses of Indian students qualified to attend high schools, colleges, and universities in Canada, considerably expanding its vision of its responsibility for Native education from what it had been before 1905.
6  See Miller, *Shingwauk's Vision*; Milloy, *A National Crime*; and see n9, below.
7  Titley, *A Narrow Vision*, ch. 9.
8  Ibid., 87–88.
9  Ibid., 91–92. Unhappily, more rigorous enforcement of truancy laws and moving some schools farther from the reserves seems to have coincided with increasingly oppressive attitudes and practices in the schools, with now well-known tragic consequences.
10  Titley, *A Narrow Vision*, 101–09; Meijer Drees, *The Indian Association of Alberta*, ch. 2, esp. 11–12.
11  Total expenditure for destitute Native peoples in Manitoba, Saskatchewan, Alberta, and the North-West Territories was $264,500 in 1923; for all medical expenses, by contrast, it was about $185,000. The government also still contributed modest amounts for implements, tools, livestock, seed, and the like, almost fifty years after the treaties. CSP, 1924, #14 (DIA), 7, 68. Scott's statement was a significant modification of what the government had understood "self-supporting" to be in the

1870s and 1880s: permanent government responsibility for the indigent, provision of housing, assumption of secondary and post-secondary education costs, and other expenses went far beyond the arrangements envisaged in the earlier era.

12 About 95 per cent of Alberta Indian revenue generated from hunting and trapping was from the Treaty 8 area. No band in the Treaty 6 and 7 area generated as much from such sources as it earned in other occupations.

### REFLECTIONS

1 Seed, *American Pentimento*, 158.

### APPENDIX TWO

1 For land surrenders through 1902, most page references are to Canada, *Indian Treaties and Surrenders from 1680–1902*, vols. 1 and 2 (1891), and 3 (1912). Tribal/band names as in original documents. A useful survey, though not comprehensive, is Martin-McGuire, "First Nation Land Surrenders on the Prairies."

For the Blackfoot chosen reserves under Treaty 7, see Canada, *Indian Treaties and Surrenders*, 2: 128–31. For the Blood, see 2: 132–35. For the Sarcee, see 2: 136–38.

2 Canada, *Indian Treaties and Surrenders*, 2: 158–59.

3 Ibid., 2: 159–60.

4 Ibid., 2: 194–95.

5 Ibid., 2: 212–13.

6 Ibid., 3: 26–29.

7 Ibid., 3: 301–03.

8 Ibid., 3: 346–47.

9 Ibid., 3: 349–50; Martin-McGuire, "First Nation Land Surrenders on the Prairies," 253–56.

10 Canada, *Indian Treaties and Surrenders*, 2: 266–67.

11 Ibid., 3: 118–19; Martin-McGuire, "First Nation Land Surrenders on the Prairies," 244–46.

12 Canada, *Indian Treaties and Surrenders*, 3: 3–5.

13 Ibid., 3: 91–93.

14 Ibid., 3: 216–17; Martin-McGuire, "First Nation Land Surrenders on the Prairies," 246–47.

15 Canada, *Indian Treaties and Surrenders*, 3: 385–87.

# Bibliography

With very few exceptions, references to various departmental annual reports, including Indian Affairs, are to those published in the *Sessional Papers*. However, the Department of Indian Affairs reports also were printed separately, and are available at www.collectionscanada.gc.ca/databases/indianaffairs. This may cause some confusion for interested readers, because the department reports are listed by the reporting year, while CSP reports are listed by the year in which the report was introduced into Parliament and printed as a sessional paper; thus, for example, the 1883 DIA report was published in the 1884 CSP. Pagination should, however, be the same.

## PRIMARY SOURCES

Ahenakew, Edward. *Voices of the Plains Cree*. Ed. Ruth M. Buck. Regina: Canadian Plains Research Center, 1995.

Alberta, Government of. *Annual Report of the Department of Education of the Province of Alberta, 1906*. Edmonton: Government Printer, 1907.

Budd, Rev. Henry. *The Diary of the Rev. Henry Budd, 1870–1875*. Ed. Katherine Pettipas. Vol. 4. Winnipeg: Manitoba Record Society Publications, 1974.

Bull, Sam. "100 Years at Whitefish 1855–1955." Whitefish, United Church, 1956.

Butler, William Francis. *The Great Lone Land: An Account of the Red River Expedition and Other Travels and Adventures in Western Canada*. Edmonton: Hurtig, 1968 [1872].

Canada. *Indian Treaties and Surrenders from 1680 to 1902*. 3 vols. Ottawa: Queen's Printer, 1891 [vols. 1 & 2] and King's Printer, 1912 [vol. 3]. Reprint, Toronto: Coles Publishing, 1971.

Canada. Parliament. *Sessional Papers* (CSP), 1867–1910, 1924.

Deane, Captain R. Burton. *Mounted Police Life in Canada: A Record of Thirty-One Years' Service*. London: Cassell, 1916. Reprint, Toronto: Coles Publishing, 1973.

– "The Story of Joe Bush." Ed. William M. Baker. *Alberta History* 40, no. 4 (Autumn 1992): 3–15.

Dempsey, Hugh A., ed. "The Final Treaty of Peace [1887]." *Alberta Historical Review* 10, no. 1 (Winter 1962): 8–16.

– *Frontier Life in the Mounted Police: The Diary Letters of Richard Barrington Nevitt*, NWMP *Surgeon 1874–78*. Vol. 18. Calgary: Alberta Records Publication Board, Historical Society of Alberta, 2010.

– "A Letter from Bishop Grandin [July 1876]." *Alberta Historical Review* 21, no. 1 (Winter 1973): 8–11.

– "The Starvation Year: Edgar Dewdney's Diary for 1879." Pts. 1 and 2. *Alberta History* 31, no. 1 (Winter 1983): 1–12; 31, no. 2 (Spring 1983): 1–15.

– "To Fort Benton and Return, 1873: Diary of the Rev. George McDougall." *Alberta History* 54, no. 2 (Spring 2006): 7–17.

– "The West of Edward Maunsell." Pts. 1 and 2. *Alberta History* 34, no. 4 (Autumn 1986): 1–17; 35, no. 1 (Winter 1987): 13–26.

Dempsey, Pauline. "My Life in an Indian Residential School." *Alberta History* 59, no. 2 (Spring 2011): 22–27.

Denny, Sir Cecil E. *The Law Marches West*. Toronto: J.M. Dent, 1972 [1939].

– "Blackfoot Medicine Men." *Alberta History* 55, no. 1 (Winter 2007): 9–12.

Dion, Joseph F. *My Tribe the Crees*. Ed. Hugh A. Dempsey. Calgary: Glenbow Museum, 1979.

Dufferin, Lord. *Speeches and Addresses of the Right Honourable Frederick Temple Hamilton, Earl of Dufferin*. Ed. Henry Milton. London: John Murray, 1882.

Dust, William, and George H. Buck. "William Scollen: Alberta Pioneer School Band Teacher." *Alberta History* 58, no. 4 (Autumn 2010): 11–17.

Erasmus, Peter. *Buffalo Days and Nights: Peter Erasmus as Told to Henry Thompson*. Ed. Irene Spry. Calgary: Fifth House, 1999.

Government of Canada. *Census of Canada, 1880–81*, 4 vols. Ottawa: MacLean, Roger & Co, 1882.

– *Census of Canada, 1890–91*. Ottawa: S.E. Dawson, 1892.

– *Census of the Three Provisional Districts of the North-West Territories, 1884–5*. Ottawa: Maclean, Roger & Co, 1886.

– *Constitution Acts, 1867 to 1982, The*. (Consolidation, 2001). Ottawa: Department of Justice, 2001.

– *Report of the Census of Population and Agriculture of the Northwest Provinces, 1906.* Ottawa, 1907.

– *Report of the Fourth Census of Canada, 1901.* Ottawa, 1902.

– *Statutes of Canada, 1868–1905.*

Grant, Rev. George M. *Ocean to Ocean: Sandford Fleming's Expedition through Canada in 1872.* Edmonton: Hurtig, 1967 [1872].

Grant, John Francis. *A Son of the Fur Trade: The Memoirs of Johnny Grant.* Ed. Gerhard J. Ens. Edmonton: University of Alberta Press, 2008.

Kennedy, Dan (Ochankugahe). *Recollections of an Assiniboine Chief.* Ed. James R. Stevens. Toronto: McClelland and Stewart, 1972.

Lieut.-Governor and Council of the North-West Territories. *Ordinances of the Lieut.-Governor and Council of the North-West Territories, 1877, 1878, 1883.*

Macleod, R.C., ed. *Reminiscences of a Bungle by One of the Bunglers; and Two Other Northwest Rebellion Diaries* [by Lewis Redman Ord, Richard Scougall Cassels, and Harold Penryn Rusden]. Western Canada Reprint Series. Edmonton: University of Alberta Press, 1983.

McDougall, Annie. "Pioneer Life in the 1870s." *Alberta History* 46, no. 3 (Summer 1998): 25–27.

McDougall, John. *Opening the Great West: Experiences of a Missionary in 1875–76.* Intro. by J. Ernest Nix. Calgary: Glenbow-Alberta Institute, 1970.

Morris, Alexander. *The Treaties of Canada with the Indians, Including the Negotiations on Which They Were Based, and Other Information Relating Thereto.* Toronto: Belfords, Clarke, 1880.

Morton, W.L. *Manitoba: The Birth of a Province.* Manitoba Record Society Publications, vol. 1. Altona, MN: D.W. Friesen, 1965.

Mountain Horse, Mike. *My People the Bloods.* Ed. Hugh A. Dempsey. Calgary: Glenbow Alberta Institute; Standoff, AB: Blood Tribal Council, 1979.

Oliver, E.H., ed. *The Canadian North-West: Its Early Development and Legislative Records.* 2 vols. Ottawa: Government Printing Bureau, 1915.

Owram, Douglas R., ed. *The Formation of Alberta: A Documentary History.* Calgary: Alberta Records Publication Board, Historical Society of Alberta, 1979.

Public Archives of Canada, Manuscript Division. *Preliminary Inventories for Record Groups 10 (Indian Affairs) and 15 (Department of the Interior).* Ottawa: Public Archives of Canada, 1951, 1957.

Robertson-Ross, Patrick. "Reconnaisance of the North West Provinces and Indian Territories of the Dominion of Canada, and Narrative of Journey across the Continent through Canadian Territory to British Columbia and

Vancouver Island." [1872] *Canadian Sessional Papers* 1873, 9 (Militia): 107–27.

Ross, Donald. "Early Farming in Edmonton." *Alberta History* 59, no. 3 (Summer 2011): 24–25.

Strange, Thomas Bland. *Gunner Jingo's Jubilee.* Ed. R.C. Macleod. Western Canada Reprint Series. Edmonton: University of Alberta Press, 1988 [1893].

Washburn, Wilcom E., ed. *The Indian and the White Man.* Documents in American Civilization Series. New York: Anchor Books, 1964.

Wilson, R.N. *Our Betrayed Wards: A Story of "Chicanery, Infidelity and the Prostitution of Trust."* Montreal: Osiris, 1973 [1921].

SECONDARY WORKS

Abel, Kerry, and Jean Friesen, eds. *Aboriginal Resource Use in Canada: Historical and Legal Aspects.* Winnipeg: University of Manitoba Press, 1991.

Abley, Mark. *Conversations with a Dead Man: The Legacy of Duncan Campbell Scott.* Madeira Park, BC: Douglas & McIntyre, 2013.

Ackroyd, Peter. *The History of England.* Vol. 1, *Foundation.* London: Macmillan, 2011.

Alberta Federation of Metis Settlement Associations, Daniel R. Anderson, and Alda M. Anderson. *The Metis People of Canada: A History.* Alberta Federation of Metis Settlement Associations and Syncrude Canada Ltd: [197-].

Anderson, Mark Cronlund, and Carmen L. Robertson. *Seeing Red: A History of Natives in Canadian Newspapers.* Winnipeg: University of Manitoba Press, 2011.

Anderson, Raoul. "Agricultural Development of the Alexis Stoney." *Alberta Historical Review* 20, no. 4 (Autumn 1972): 16–20.

Armstrong, Christopher, Matthew Evenden, and H.V. Nelles. *The River Returns: An Environmental History of the Bow.* Montreal: McGill-Queen's University Press, 2009.

Arthur, George. "The North American Plains Bison: A Brief History." *Prairie Forum* 9, no. 2 (Fall 1984): 281–89.

Asch, Michael. *On Being Here to Stay: Treaties and Aboriginal Rights in Canada.* Toronto: University of Toronto Press, 2014.

Atkin, Ronald. *Maintain the Right: The Early History of the North West Mounted Police, 1873–1900.* Toronto: Macmillan, 1973.

Audet, Louis-Philippe. "Education in Canada East and Quebec: 1840–1875." In Wilson, Stamp, and Audet, *Canadian Education,* 167–89.

Axelrod, Paul. "No Longer a 'Last Resort': The End of Corporal Punishment in the Schools of Toronto." *Canadian Historical Review* 91, no. 2 (June 2010): 261–85.

– *The Promise of Schooling: Education in Canada, 1800–1914.* Toronto: University of Toronto Press, 1997.

Axtell, James. *Natives and Newcomers: The Cultural Origins of North America.* New York: Oxford University Press, 2001.

Baker, Graeme. *The Agricultural Revolution in Prehistory: Why Did Foragers Become Farmers?* Oxford: Oxford University Press, 2006.

Baker, William M., ed. *The Mounted Police and Prairie Society, 1873–1919.* Regina: Canadian Plains Research Center, 1998.

– "Superintendent Deane of the Mounted Police." *Alberta History* 41, no. 4 (Autumn 1993): 20–26.

Baldwin, Douglas O. *Teachers, Students and Pedagogy: Selected Readings and Documents in the History of Canadian Education.* Markham, ON: Fitzhenry & Whiteside, 2008.

Baldwin, Stuart J. "Wintering Villages of the Metis Hivernants: Documentary and Archaeological Evidences." In Métis Association of Alberta, *The Métis and the Land.*

Bannerjee, Abhijit V., and Esther Duflo. *Poor Economics: A Radical Rethinking of the Way to Fight Global Poverty.* New York: Public Affairs, 2011.

Barron, F. Laurie. "The Indian Pass System in the Canadian West, 1882–1935." *Prairie Forum* 13, no. 1 (Spring 1988): 25–42.

Barron, F. Laurie, and James B. Waldram, eds. *1885 and After: Native Society in Transition.* Regina: Canadian Plains Research Center, 1986.

Bartlett, John. *Bartlett's Familiar Quotations.* Revised 15th ed. Boston: Little, Brown, 1980.

Bartlett, Richard H. *Indian Reserves and Aboriginal Lands in Canada: A Homeland.* Saskatoon: University of Saskatchewan Native Law Centre, 1990.

Bateman, Rebecca B. "Talking with the Plow: Agricultural Policy and Indian Farming in the Canadian and U.S. Prairies." *Canadian Journal of Native Studies* 16, no. 2 (1996): 211–28.

Beal, Bob, and Rod Macleod. *Prairie Fire: The 1885 North-West Rebellion.* Edmonton: Hurtig, 1984.

Beal, R.F., J.E. Foster, and Louise Zuk. "The Metis Hivernement Settlement at Buffalo Lake, 1872–1877." Edmonton: Department of Culture, Alberta Government: Historic Sites and Provincial Museum Divisions, 1987.

Beaudoin, Alwynne B. "What They Saw: The Climatic and Environmental Context for Euro-Canadian Settlement in Alberta." *Prairie Forum* 24, no. 1 (Spring 1999): 1–40.

Behiels, Michael D., and Reginald C. Stuart, eds. *Transnationalism: Canadian-United States History into the 21st Century*. Montreal: McGill-Queen's University Press, 2010.

Bemount, Stephen Louis. "Minority Religious Education Rights in Alberta: A Study of the Governance and Financial Issues in the Provision of Separate Schooling within the Public System." PhD diss., University of Alberta, 2007.

Berger, Carl. *The Sense of Power: Studies in the Ideas of Canadian Imperialism, 1867–1914*. Toronto: University of Toronto Press, 1970.

Bernier, Jacques. *Disease, Medicine and Society in Canada: A Historical Overview*. Historical Booklet no. 63. Ottawa: Canadian Historical Association, 2003.

Berry, Gerald L. "Fort Whoop-up and the Whiskey Traders." In *The Pioneer West*, 21–25. Alberta Historical Review reprints, no. 1. Calgary: Historical Society of Alberta, 1969.

Berton, Pierre. *The Last Spike: The Great Railway, 1881–1885*. Toronto: McClelland and Stewart, 1971.

– "The Legend of Almighty Voice." In *The Wild Frontier: More Tales from the Remarkable Past*, 209–33. Toronto: McClelland and Stewart, 1978.

– *The National Dream: The Great Railway, 1871–1881*. Toronto: McClelland and Stewart, 1970.

Binnema, Theodore. *Common and Contested Ground: A Human and Environmental History of the Northwestern Plains*. Toronto: University of Toronto Press, 2004 [2001].

– "Protecting Indian Lands by Defining *Indian*: 1850–76." *Journal of Canadian Studies/Revue d'études canadiennes* 48, no. 2 (Spring 2014): 5–39.

Binnema, Theodore, Gerhard Ens, and R.C. Macleod, eds. *From Rupert's Land to Canada: Essays in Honour of John E. Foster*. Edmonton: University of Alberta Press, 2001.

Binnema, Theodore, and Susan Neylan, eds. *New Histories for Old: Changing Perspectives on Canada's Native Pasts*. Vancouver: University of British Columbia Press, 2007.

Binnema, Theodore, and Melanie Niemi. "'Let the Line Be Drawn Now': Wilderness, Conservation, and the Exclusion of Aboriginal People from Banff National Park in Canada." *Environmental History* 11, no. 4 (October 2006): 724–50.

Bird, Ruby. "Schooling in the Paul Band, 1893–1923." MA thesis, University of Alberta, 1978.

Blackfoot Gallery Committee, The. *The Story of the Blackfoot People: Niitsitapilsinni*. Richmond Hill: Firefly Books, 2013.

Boon, T.C.B. "Henry Budd." *DCB*, 10, *1871–1880*, 108–09.

Borrows, John, and Leonard I. Rotman. "The *Sui Generis* Nature of Aboriginal Rights: Does It Make a Difference?" *Alberta Law Review* 36, no. 1 (1997): 9–45.

Boswell, Marion Joan. "'Civilizing' the Indian: Government Administration of Indians, 1876–1896." PhD diss., University of Ottawa, 1978.

Bourassa, Carrie. "Colonization, Racism and the Health of Indian People." *Prairie Forum* 29, no. 2 (Fall 2004): 207–23.

Boyer, Pascal, and James V. Wertsch, eds. *Memory in Mind and Culture.* Cambridge: Cambridge University Press, 2009.

Bradford, Tolly. "A Useful Institution: William Twin, 'Indianness,' and Banff National Park, c. 1860–1940." *Native Studies Review* 16, no. 2 (2005): 77–98.

Breen, David H. *The Canadian Prairie West and the Ranching Frontier, 1874–1924.* Toronto: University of Toronto Press, 1983.

– "'Timber Tom' and the North-West Rebellion." *Alberta History* 19, no. 3 (Summer 1971): 1–7.

Brink, Jack W. *Imagining Head-Smashed-In: Aboriginal Buffalo Hunting on the Northern Plains.* Edmonton: Athabasca University Press, 2008.

Brown, Cynthia Stokes. *Big History: From the Big Bang to the Present.* New York: New Press, 2007.

Brown, Desmond. "Ambiguous Authority: The Development of Criminal Law in the Canadian North-West and Alberta." In Connors and Law, *Forging Alberta's Constitutional Framework*, 25–60.

Brown, Jennifer S.H. *Strangers in Blood: Fur Trade Company Families in Indian Country.* Vancouver: University of British Columbia Press, 1980.

Brownlie, Robin Jarvis. "A Persistent Antagonism: First Nations and the Liberal Order." In *Liberalism and Hegemony: Debating the Canadian Liberal Revolution*, ed. Jean-François Constant and Michel Ducharme, 298–321. Toronto: University of Toronto Press, 2009.

Buckley, Helen. *From Wooden Ploughs to Welfare: Why Indian Policy Failed in the Prairie Provinces.* Montreal: McGill-Queen's University Press, 1992.

Bull, Linda R. "Indian Residential Schooling: The Native Perspective." MEd thesis, University of Alberta, 1991.

Burley, Edith I. *Servants of the Honourable Company: Work, Discipline, and Conflict in the Hudson's Bay Company, 1770–1879.* Toronto: Oxford University Press, 1997.

Burnett, Kristin. "Aboriginal and White Women in the Publications of John Maclean, Egerton Ryerson Young, and John McDougall." In Carter et al., *Unsettled Pasts*, 101–22.

– "The Healing Work and Nursing Care of Aboriginal Women: Female Medical Missionaries, Nursing Sisters, Public Health Nurses, and Female Attendants in Southern Alberta First Nations, 1880–1930." PhD diss., York University, 2006.

Byfield, Ted, ed. *The Birth of the Province, 1900–1910*. Alberta in the 20th Century, vol. 2. Edmonton: United Western Communications, 1992.

– *The Great West before 1900*. Alberta in the 20th Century, vol. 1. Edmonton: United Western Communications, 1991.

Calliou, Brian Louis. "1899 and the Political Economy of Canada's North-West: Treaty 8 as a Compact to Share and Peacefully Co-exist." In Payne, Wetherell, and Cavanaugh, *Alberta Formed, Alberta Transformed*, 300–31.

– "Losing the Game: Wildlife Conservation and the Regulation of First Nations Hunting in Alberta, 1880–1930." LLM thesis, University of Alberta, 2000.

– "The Supreme Court of Alberta and First Nations Treaty Hunting Rights: Federalism and Respect for 'the Queen's Promises.'" In *The Alberta Supreme Court at 100: History and Authority*, ed. Jonathan Swainger, 133–57. Edmonton: University of Alberta Press and the Osgood Society for Canadian Legal History, 2007.

Canada. Department of Justice. "Canada's Court System." http://www.justice. gc.ca.eng/csj-sjc/ccs-ajc/pdf/courten.pdf.

Canada. Indian and Northern Affairs. *Historical Development of the Indian Act*. 2nd ed. Ottawa: Treaties and Historical Research Centre, P.R.E. Group, Indian and Northern Affairs, 1978.

Canada. Privy Council. Public Archives of Canada. *Guide to Canadian Ministries since Confederation, July 1, 1867–April 1, 1973*. Ottawa: Public Archives of Canada, 1974.

*Canadian Encyclopedia, The*. 2nd ed., 4 vols. Edmonton: Hurtig, 1988.

Canadian Public Health Association. "This Is Public Health: A Canadian History." 2011. http://www.cpha.ca/en/programs/history/book.aspx.

Carr, Kevin James. "A Historical Survey of Education in Early Blackfoot Indian Culture and Its Implications for Indian Schools." MEd thesis, University of Alberta, 1968.

Carter, Sarah. *Aboriginal People and Colonizers of Western Canada to 1900*. Toronto: University of Toronto Press, 1999.

– *Capturing Women: The Manipulation of Cultural Imagery in Canada's Prairie West*. Montreal: McGill-Queen's University Press, 1997.

– "'Complicated and Clouded': The Federal Administration of Marriage and Divorce among the First Nations of Western Canada, 1887–1906." In Carter et al., *Unsettled Pasts*, 151–78.

– *The Importance of Being Monogamous: Marriage and Nation Building in Western Canada to 1915*. Edmonton: University of Alberta Press, 2008.

– *Lost Harvests: Prairie Indian Reserve Farmers and Government Policy*. Montreal: McGill-Queen's University Press, 1990.

– "The Missionaries' Indian: The Publications of John McDougall, John Maclean and Egerton Ryerson Young." *Prairie Forum* 9, no. 1 (Spring 1984): 27–44.

– "Two Acres and a Cow: 'Peasant' Farming for the Indians of the Northwest, 1889–97." In Miller, *Sweet Promises*, 353–77.

– "'We Must Farm to Enable Us to Live': The Plains Cree and Agriculture to 1900." In *The Prairie West as Promised Land*, ed. Douglas Francis and Chris Kitzan, 103–26. Calgary: University of Calgary Press, 2007.

Carter, Sarah, Lesley Erickson, Patricia Roome, and Char Smith, eds. *Unsettled Pasts: Reconceiving the West through Women's History*. Calgary: University of Calgary Press, 2005.

Carter, Sarah, and Walter Hildebrandt. "A Better Life with Honour: Treaty 6 (1876) and Treaty 7 (1877) with Alberta First Nations." In Payne, Wetherell, and Cavanaugh, *Alberta Formed, Alberta Transformed*, 236–68.

Cassel, Jay. "Public Health in Canada." In *The History of Public Health and the Modern State*, ed. Dorothy Porter, 276–312. Atlanta, GA: Editions Rodopi R.V., 1994.

Chalmers, John W. "Education behind the Buckskin Curtain: A History of Native Education in Canada." Edmonton: Author, 1970.

– "Treaty No. Six." *Alberta Historical Review* 25, no. 2 (Spring 1977): 23–27.

Child, Alan H. "The Ryerson Tradition in Western Canada, 1871–1906." In *Egerton Ryerson and His Times*, ed. Neil McDonald and Alf Chaiton, 279–301. Toronto: Macmillan, 1978.

Chinook Country Historical Society, The, ed. *Remembering Chinook Country: Told and Untold Stories of Our Past*. Calgary: Detselig, 2005.

Chumak, Sebastian. *The Stonies of Alberta*. Calgary: The Alberta Heritage Foundation, 1983.

Churchill, Elizabeth. "Tsuu T'ina: A History of a First Nation's Community, 1890–1940." PhD diss., University of Calgary, 2000.

Clapperton, Jonathan. "Naturalizing Race Relations: Conservation, Colonialism, and Spectacle at the Banff Indian Days." *Canadian Historical Review* 94, no. 3 (September 2013): 349–79.

Cocker, Mark. *Rivers of Blood, Rivers of Gold: Europe's Conquest of Indigenous Peoples*. New York: Grove Press, 1998.

Colpitts, George W. "Fish and Game Associations in Southern Alberta, 1907–1928." *Alberta History* 42, no. 4 (Autumn 1992): 16–26.

Connors, Richard, and John M. Law, eds. *Forging Alberta's Constitutional Framework*. Edmonton: University of Alberta Press, 2005.

Cottam, S. Barry. "Indian Title as a 'Celestial Institution': David Mills and the *St Catherine's Milling* Case." In *Aboriginal Canada: Historical and Legal Aspects*, ed. Kerry Abel and Jean Friesen, 247–65. Winnipeg: University of Manitoba Press, 1991.

Craft, Aimée. *Breathing Life into the Stone Fort Treaty: An Anishinabe Understanding of Treaty One*. Saskatoon: Purich Publishing, 2013.

Creighton, Donald. *John A. Macdonald: The Old Chieftain*. Toronto: Macmillan, 1955.

– *John A. Macdonald: The Young Politician*. Toronto: Macmillan, 1952.

– "Macdonald, Confederation, and the West." In *Towards the Discovery of Canada: Selected Essays*, 229–42. Toronto: Macmillan, 1972 [1967].

Cumming, P.A., and Neil H. Mickenberg, eds. *Native Rights in Canada*. 2nd ed. Toronto: The Indian-Eskimo Association of Canada in association with General Publishing Co, 1972.

Curry, Andrew. "On the Origin of Societies." *Discover*, April 2011, 16.

Daschuk, James. *Clearing the Plains: Disease, Politics of Starvation and Loss of Aboriginal Life*. Regina: University of Regina Press, 2013.

Darwin, John. *After Tamerlane: The Global History of Empire since 1405*. London: Allen Lane, 2007.

Dawson, Bruce. "The Roots of Agriculture: A Historiographical Review of First Nations Agriculture and Government Indian Policy." *Prairie Forum* 28, no. 1 (Spring 2003): 99–115.

Day, David. *Conquest: How Societies Overwhelm Others*. New York: Oxford University Press, 2008.

*Edmonton Journal*. "Decades of Rape, Torture at Hands of Church." 21 May 2009, A16.

Decker, Jody. "Smallpox along the Frontier of the Plains' Borderlands at the Turn of the Twentieth Century." In Binnema and Neylan, *New Histories for Old*, 91–118.

Dempsey, Hugh A. *Always an Adventure: An Autobiography*. Calgary: University of Calgary Press, 2011.

– *Big Bear: The End of Freedom*. Vancouver: Douglas & McIntyre, 1984.

– "The Blackfoot Indians." In Morrison and Wilson, *Native Peoples*, 381–413.

– "Blackfoot Peace Treaties." *Alberta History* 54, no. 4 (Autumn 2006): 22–26.

– "The Bull Elk Affair." *Alberta History* 40, no. 2 (Spring 1992): 2–9.

– *Charcoal's World: The True Story of a Canadian Indian's Last Stand*. Calgary: Fifth House, 1998.

- *Crowfoot: Chief of the Blackfeet.* Edmonton: Hurtig, 1972.
- "1870: A Year of Violence and Change." In Payne, Wetherell, and Cavanaugh, *Alberta Formed, Alberta Transformed*, 208–34.
- "The Fearsome Fire Wagons." In Dempsey, ed., *The CPR West: The Iron Road and the Making of a Nation*, ed. Hugh A. Dempsey, 55–69. Vancouver: Douglas & McIntyre, 1984.
- *Firewater: The Impact of the Whisky Trade on the Blackfoot Nation.* Calgary: Fifth House, 2002.
- *Indian Tribes of Alberta.* Rev. ed. Calgary: Glenbow Museum, 1997.
- "Introduction." In Mountain Horse, *My People the Bloods*, v–xi.
- "Isapo-Muxika." DCB, 11, *1881–1890*, 442–45.
- "Jerry Potts: Plainsman." Occasional Paper no. 2. Calgary: Glenbow-Alberta Institute, 1966.
- *Maskepetoon: Leader, Warrior, Peacemaker.* Victoria: Heritage House, 2010.
- "Mékaisto." DCB, 12, *1881–1890*, 717–19.
- "Native Peoples and Calgary." In *Centennial City: Calgary, 1894–1994*, ed. Donald B. Smith, 25–35. Calgary: University of Calgary, 1994.
- "One Hundred Years of Treaty 7." In *One Century Later: Western Canadian Reserve Indians since 1877*, ed. Ian A.L. Getty and Donald B. Smith, 20–30. Vancouver: University of British Columbia Press, 1978.
- *Red Crow: Warrior Chief.* Saskatoon: Western Producer Prairie Books, 1980.
- "Si'k-Oskitsis." DCB, 12, *1881–1890*, 970.
- "Smallpox: Scourge of the Plains." In *Harm's Way: Disasters in Western Canada*, ed. Anthony Rasporich and Max Foran, 15–40. Calgary: University of Calgary Press, 2004.
- "Sotai-na (Rainy Chief)." DCB, 10, *1871–1880*, 661–62.
- "The Story of the Blood Reserve." *Alberta Historical Review* 1, no. 3 (November 1953): 27–36.
Dempsey, Hugh A., and Lindsay Moir. *Bibliography of the Blackfoot.* Native American Bibliography Series, no. 13. Lanham, MD: Scarecrow Press, 1989.
Dempsey, James. "Little Bear's Band: Canadian or American Indians?" *Alberta History* 41, no. 4 (Autumn 1993): 2–9.
- "Persistence of a Warrior Ethic among the Plains Indians." *Alberta History* 36, no. 1 (Winter 1988): 1–10.
Dempsey, Pauline. "My Life in an Indian Residential School." *Alberta History* 59, no. 2 (Spring 2011): 22–29.
den Otter, A.A. "The 1857 Parliamentary Inquiry, the Hudson's Bay Company, and Rupert's Land's Aboriginal People." *Prairie Forum* 24, no. 2 (Fall 1999): 143–69.

– *Irrigation in Southern Alberta, 1882–1901.* Occasional Paper no. 5. Lethbridge: Whoop-up Country Chapter, Historical Society of Alberta, 1975.

Devine, Heather. "Les Dejarlais: The Development and Dispersion of a Proto-Métis Hunting Band, 1785–1870." In Binnema, Ens, and Macleod, *From Rupert's Land to Canada,* 129–58.

– *The People Who Own Themselves: Aboriginal Ethnogenesis in a Canadian Family, 1660–1900.* Calgary: University of Calgary Press, 2004.

Diamond. Jared. *Guns, Germs, and Steel: The Fates of Human Societies.* New York: W.W. Norton, 1997.

– *The World until Yesterday: What Can We Learn from Traditional Societies?* New York: Viking, 2012.

Dick, Lyle. "Estimates of Farm-Making Costs in Saskatchewan, 1882–1914." *Prairie Forum* 6, no. 2 (Fall 1981): 183–201.

Dickason, Olive P. "Aboriginals: Metis." In Magosci, *Encyclopedia of Canada's Peoples,* 70–79.

– *Canada's First Nations: A History of Founding Peoples from Earliest Times.* 2nd ed. Toronto: Oxford University Press, 1997.

– "Metis." In Magosci, *Aboriginal Peoples of Canada,* 189–213.

*Dictionary of Canadian Biography* (DCB). 16 vols. Toronto: University of Toronto Press, 1966–2014.

Dormaar, Johan F. *Alberta's 49th Parallel: A Natural & Historical Journey.* Lethbridge: Lethbridge Historical Society, 2009.

Dougherty, Wayne, and Dennis Madill. *Indian Government under Indian Act Legislation 1868–1951.* Ottawa: Treaties and Historical Research Centre, Research Branch, Corporate Policy, Dept. of Indian and Northern Affairs Canada, 1980.

Dreisziger, N.F. "The Canadian-American Irrigation Frontier Revisited: The International Origins of Irrigation in Southern Alberta, 1885–1909." Canadian Historical Association *Historical Papers* 1975: 211–29.

Dyck, Noel. "The Administration of Federal Indian Aid in the North-West Territories, 1879–1885." MA thesis, University of Saskatchewan, 1970.

– *What Is the Indian "Problem": Tutelage and Resistance in Canadian Indian Administration.* St. John's: Institute of Social and Economic Research, Memorial University of Newfoundland, 1991.

Eagle, John Andrew. "The Evolution of the Canadian Welfare State: Origins to 1984." Unpublished manuscript in possession of Margaret Eagle, Edmonton.

Elliott, David W., ed. *Law and Aboriginal Peoples of Canada.* 2nd ed. North York: Captus Press, 1994.

Elofson, Warren M. *Cowboys, Gentlemen & Cattle Thieves: Ranching on the Western Frontier*. Montreal: McGill-Queen's University Press, 2000.

– *Frontier Cattle Ranching in the Land and Times of Charlie Russell*. Montreal: McGill-Queen's University Press, 2004.

English, John. *The Decline of Politics: The Conservatives and the Party System, 1901–20*. Toronto: University of Toronto Press, 1977.

Ennab, Fadi Saleem. "Rupturing the Myth of the Peaceful Western Canadian Frontier: A Socio-Historical Study of Colonization, Violence, and the North West Mounted Police, 1875–1905." MA thesis, University of Manitoba, 2010.

Enns, Richard A. "'But What Is the Object of Educating These Children, if It Costs Their Lives to Educate Them?': Federal Indian Education Policy in Western Canada in the Late 1800s." *Journal of Canadian Studies/Revue d'études canadiennes* 43, no. 3 (Fall 2009): 101–23.

Ens, Gerhard J. *Homeland to Hinterland: The Changing Worlds of the Red River Metis in the Nineteenth Century*. Toronto: University of Toronto Press, 1996.

– "Hybridity, Canadian Indian Policy, and the Construction and 'Extinguishment' of Metis Aboriginal Rights in the Nineteenth Century." In Wunder and Kinbacher, *Reconfigurations of Native North America*, 236–51.

– "Métis." In Wishart, *Encyclopedia of the Great Plains*, 584–85.

– "Metis Ethnicity, Personal Identity, and the Development of Capitalism in the Western Interior: The Case of Johnny Grant." In Binnema, Ens, and Macleod, *From Rupert's Land to Canada*, 161–77.

Favel-King, Alma. "The Treaty Right to Health." In *The Path to Healing: Report of the National Round Table on Aboriginal Health and Social Issues*, 120–29. Ottawa: Royal Commission on Aboriginal Peoples, Minister of Supply and Services, 1993.

Ferguson, Niall. *Civilization: The West and the Rest*. New York: Penguin, 2011.

Fisher, Robin. "The Border and First Nations History: A Canadian View." In Behiels and Stuart, *Transnationalism*, 32–43.

Flanagan, Thomas. "Comment on Ken Hatt, 'The North-West Rebellion Scrip Commissions, 1885–1889.'" In Barron and Waldram, *1885 and After*, 205–09.

– "From Indian Title to Aboriginal Rights." In Knafla, *Law & Justice*, 81–100.

– *Metis Lands in Manitoba*. Calgary: University of Calgary Press, 1991.

– *Riel and the Rebellion: 1885 Reconsidered*. 2nd ed. Toronto: University of Toronto Press, 2000.

Flannery, Tim. *The Eternal Frontier: An Ecological History of North America and Its Peoples*. New York: Atlantic Monthly Press, 2001.

Foster, John E. "The Métis: The People and the Term." *Prairie Forum* 3, no. 1 (Spring 1978): 79–90.

– "The Metis and the End of the Plains Buffalo in Alberta." In *Buffalo*, ed. John E. Foster, Dick Harrison, and I.S. MacLaren. Alberta Nature and Culture series. Edmonton: University of Alberta Press, 1992, 61–77.

– "The Plains Metis." In Morrison and Wilson, *Native Peoples*, 414–43.

– "Wintering, the Outsider Adult Male and the Ethnogenesis of the Western Plains Métis." In Binnema, Ens, and Macleod, *From Rupert's Land to Canada*, 179–92.

Fox, Uta Hildemarie. "The Failure of the Red Deer Industrial School." MA thesis, University of Calgary, 1993.

Friedman, Jeff. "Fractious Action: Oral History-Based Performance." In *Thinking about Oral History: Theories and Applications*, ed. T. Charlton, Lois E. Myers, and Rebecca Sharpless, 223–67. Lanham, MD: Altamira Press, 2009.

Friesen, Gerald. *The Canadian Prairies: A History*. Toronto: University of Toronto Press, 1984.

Friesen, Jean. "Alexander Morris." *DCB*, 11, *1881–1890*, 608–15.

– "Grant Me Wherewith to Make My Living." In Abel and Friesen, *Aboriginal Resource Use*, 141–55.

– "Magnificent Gifts: The Treaties of Canada with the Indians of the Northwest, 1869–76." *Transactions of the Royal Society of Canada* V, no. 1 (1986): 41–51.

Friesen, John W. "John McDougall: Spirit of a Pioneer." *Alberta Historical Review* 22, no. 2 (Spring 1974): 9–17.

Fumoleau, René, OMI. *As Long As This Land Shall Last: A History of Treaty 8 and Treaty 11, 1870–1939*. Toronto: McClelland and Stewart, 1973.

Gavigan, Shelley A.M. *Hunger, Horses, and Government Men: Criminal Law on the Aboriginal Plains, 1870–1905*. Vancouver: University of British Columbia Press, for the Osgoode Society for Canadian Legal History, 2012.

Geiger, John Grigsby. "River Lot Three: Settlement Life on the North Saskatchewan." *Alberta History* 44, no. 1 (Winter 1996): 15–25.

Getty, Ian A.L., and Antoine S. Lussier, eds. *As Long as the Sun Shines and Water Flows: A Reader in Canadian Native Studies*. Vancouver: University of British Columbia Press, 1983.

Gibbons, Ann. "The Evolution of Diet." *National Geographic* 236, no. 3 (September 2014): 30–61.

Gibbons, Kenneth M., and Donald C. Rowat, eds. *Political Corruption in Canada: Cases, Causes and Cures*. Toronto: McClelland and Stewart, 1976.

Gibson, Dale, and Lee Gibson. *Substantial Justice: Law and Lawyers in Manitoba 1670–1970*. Winnipeg: Peguis, 1972.

Giraud, Marcel. *The Métis in the Canadian West*. Vol. 2. Trans. George Woodcock. Edmonton: University of Alberta Press, 1986.

Graham-Cumming, G. "Health of the Original Canadians, 1867–1967." *Medical Services Journal, Canada* 23 (February 1967): 115–66.

Granatstein, J.L. *Yankee Go Home? Canadians and Anti-Americanism*. Toronto: HarperCollins, 1996.

Gray, James H. *Red Lights on the Prairies*. Saskatoon: Fifth House, 1995 [1971].

Graybill, Andrew. *Policing the Great Plains: Rangers, Mounties, and the North American Frontier, 1875–1910*. Lincoln: University of Nebraska Press, 2007.

Green, L.C. "Legal Significance of Treaties Affecting Canada's Indians." *The Anglo-American Law Review* 1 (1972): 119–35.

– "Trusteeship and Canada's Indians." *Dalhousie Law Journal* 3, no. 1 (May 1976): 104–35.

Greenblatt, Stephen. *Marvelous Possessions: The Wonder of the New World*. Chicago: University of Chicago Press, 1991.

Gresko, Jacqueline. "White 'Rites' and Indian 'Rites': Indian Education and Native Responses in the West, 1870–1910." In *Western Canada: Past and Present*, ed. A.W. Rasporich, 163–81, 220–23. Calgary: McClelland and Stewart West, 1975.

Gulig, Anthony G. "'We Beg the Government': Native People and Game Regulation in Northern Saskatchewan, 1900–1940." *Prairie Forum* 28, no. 1 (Spring 2003): 81–98.

Gwyn, Richard. *John A.: The Man Who Made Us*. Vol. 1, *1815–1867*. Toronto: Random House, 2007.

– *Nation Maker: Sir John A. Macdonald*. Vol. 2, *1867–1891*. Toronto: Random House Canada, 2011.

Hall, Anthony J. "*The St Catherine's Milling and Lumber Company versus the Queen*: Indian Land Rights as a Factor in Federal-Provincial Relations in Nineteenth-Century Canada." In Abel and Friesen, *Aboriginal Resource Use*, 267–86.

Hall, David J. "Alexander Mackinnon Burgess." DCB, 12, *1891–1900*, 140–41.

– "Clifford Sifton and Canadian Indian Administration, 1896–1905." *Prairie Forum* 2, no. 2 (1977): 127–51.

– *Clifford Sifton*. Vol. 1, *The Young Napoleon, 1861–1900*. Vancouver: University of British Columbia Press, 1981.

– *Clifford Sifton*. Vol. 2, *A Lonely Eminence, 1901–1929*. Vancouver: University of British Columbia Press, 1985.
– "The Half-Breed Claims Commission." *Alberta History* 25, no. 2 (Spring 1977): 1–8.
– "'A Serene Atmosphere'? Treaty 1 Revisited." *Canadian Journal of Native Studies* 4, no. 2 (1984): 321–58.
Hamilton, James McClellan. *From Wilderness to Statehood: A History of Montana*. Portland, OR: Binfords & Mort, 1957.
Hanks, Lucien M., Jr, and Jane Richardson Hanks. *Tribe under Trust: A Study of the Blackfoot Reserve of Alberta*. Toronto: University of Toronto Press, 1950.
Hanson, S.D. "Kitchi-Manito-Waya." *DCB*, 12, *1891–1900*, 497–98.
Harper, Allan G. "Canada's Indian Administration." *America Indigena* 6, no. 4 (October 1946): 297–314.
– "Canada's Indian Administration: Basic Concepts and Objectives." *America Indigena* 5, no. 1 (April 1945): 119–32.
– "Canada's Indian Administration: The Treaty System." *America Indigena* 7, no. 2 (April 1947): 129–48.
Harring, Sydney L. "'There Seemed to Be No Recognized Law': Canadian Law and the Prairie First Nations." In Knafla and Swainger, *Laws and Societies*, 92–126.
– *White Man's Law: Native People in Nineteenth-Century Canadian Jurisprudence*. Toronto: University of Toronto Press, Osgood Society for Canadian Legal History, 1998.
Hatt, Ken. "The North-West Rebellion Scrip Commissions, 1885–1889." In Barron and Waldram, *1885 and After*, 189–204.
Henderson, James (sákéj) Youngblood. "Interpreting *Sui Generis* Treaties." *Alberta Law Review* 36, no. 1 (1997): 48–96.
– "Treaties and Indian Education." In *First Nations Education in Canada: The Circle Unfolds*, ed. Marie Battiste and Jean Barman, 245–61. Vancouver: University of British Columbia Press, 1995.
Hochstein, Sister L.A., F.C.J. "Roman Catholic Separate and Public Schools in Alberta." MEd thesis, University of Alberta, 1954.
Hodgetts, J.E. *Pioneer Public Service: An Administrative History of the United Canadas 1841–1867*. Toronto: University of Toronto Press, 1955.
Hogan, C.B. "Climate, Calgary and Tuberculosis (c. 1900)." In Lampard, *Alberta's Medical History*, 519–23.
Horrall, S.W. "The (Royal) North-West Mounted Police and Prostitution on the Canadian Prairies." *Prairie Forum* 10, no. 1 (1985): 105–27.

– "Sir John A. Macdonald and the Police Force for the Northwest Territories." *Canadian Historical Review* 53, no. 2 (June 1972): 179–200.

Hoxie, Frederick E. *A Final Promise: The Campaign to Assimilate the Indians, 1880–1920*. Lincoln: University of Nebraska Press, 1984.

Hubner, Brian. "Horse Stealing and the Borderline: The NWMP and the Control of Indian Movement, 1874–1900." *Prairie Forum* 20, no. 2 (Fall 1995): 281–300.

Huel, Raymond. "Albert Lacombe." *DCB*, 14, *1911–1920*, 573–77.

– "Constantine Scollen: The Forgotten Missionary." *Alberta History* 59, no. 4 (Autumn 2011): 10–18.

– "Father Lacombe, the Oblate Missions, and the Western Treaties." *Alberta History* 59, no. 9 (Spring 2011): 2–10.

– "Jean L'Heureux: A Life of Adventure." *Alberta History* 60, no. 4 (Autumn 2012): 9–16.

– *Proclaiming the Gospel to the Indians and the Métis*. Edmonton: University of Alberta Press, 1996.

– "Western Oblate History: The Need for Reinterpretation." *Western Oblate Studies* 3, 13–39. Edmonton: Western Canadian Publishing, 1994.

Hungry Wolf, Adolf. *The Blood People: A Division of the Blackfoot Confederacy. An Illustrated Interpretation of the Old Ways*. New York: Harper & Row, 1977.

Hungry Wolf, Adolf, and Beverly Hungry Wolf. *Indian Tribes of the Northern Rockies*. Skookumchuck, BC: Good Medicine Books, 1989.

Hurt, Leslie J. "The Victoria Settlement: 1867–1922." Occasional Paper no. 7. Edmonton: Alberta Culture, Historical Resources Division, Historic Sites Service, June 1979.

Ironside, R.G., and E. Tomasky. "Agriculture and River Lot Settlement in Western Canada: The Case of Pakan (Victoria), Alberta." *Prairie Forum* 1, no. 1 (April 1976): 3–18.

– "Development of Victoria Settlement." *Alberta Historical Review* 19, no. 2 (Spring 1971): 20–29.

Irwin, Robert. "No Means No: Ermineskin's Resistance to Land Surrender, 1902–1921." *Canadian Journal of Native Studies* 23, no. 1 (2003): 165–83.

– "Not Like the Others: The Regulation of Indian Hunting and Fishing in Alberta." In Connors and Law, *Forging Alberta's Constitutional Framework*, 237–65.

Isaac, Thomas. *Aboriginal Law: Commentary, Cases and Materials*, 3rd ed. Saskatoon: Purich Publishing, 2004.

Jamieson, Frederick C. "The Edmonton Hunt." *Alberta Historical Review* reprints no. 1, *The Pioneer West*, 10–18. Calgary: Historical Society of Alberta, 1969.

Jenness, Diamond. *The Sarcee Indians of Alberta*. Canada, Department of Mines and Resources, National Museum of Canada, Bulletin no. 90, Anthropological Series no. 23. Ottawa: King's Printer, 1938.

Jennings, John Nelson. "The North West Mounted Police and Indian Policy, 1874–1896." PhD diss., University of Toronto, 1979.

– "The Plains Indians and the Law." In *Men in Scarlet*, ed. Hugh Dempsey, 50–65, 213–14. Calgary: Historical Society of Alberta, n.d.

Jobson, Valerie. "The Blackfoot and the Rationing System." *Alberta History* 33, no. 4 (Autumn 1985), 13–17.

– "The Blackfoot Farming Experiment 1880–1945." MA thesis, University of Calgary, 1990.

Johnson, F. Henry. *A Brief History of Canadian Education*. Toronto: McGraw-Hill, 1968.

Johnson, J.K., ed. *The Canadian Directory of Parliament, 1867–1967*. Ottawa: Public Archives of Canada, 1968.

Judt, Tony. *Reappraisals: Reflections on the Forgotten Twentieth Century*. New York: Penguin, 2008.

Kelly, Brendan. "Three Uses of Christian Culture in the Numbered Treaties, 1871–1921." *Prairie Forum* 33, no. 2 (Fall 2008): 357–84.

Kelm, Mary-Ellen. *Colonizing Bodies: Aboriginal Health and Healing in British Columbia, 1900–50*. Vancouver: University of British Columbia Press, 1998.

Kennedy, Margaret. "A Map and Partial Manuscript of Blackfoot Country." *Alberta History* 62, no. 3 (Summer 2014): 5–14.

King, Thomas. *The Inconvenient Indian: A Curious Account of Native People in North America*. Anchor Canada, 2013.

Klassen, Henry C. *A Business History of Alberta*. Calgary: University of Calgary Press, 1999.

Knafla, Louis A. "From Oral to Written Memory: The Common Law Tradition in Western Canada." In Knafla, *Law & Justice*, 31–77.

– "Introduction: Laws and Societies in the Anglo-Canadian North-West Frontier and Prairie Provinces, 1670–1940." In Knafla and Swainger, *Laws and Societies*, 1–47.

– ed. *Law & Justice in a New Land: Essays in Western Canadian Legal History*. Toronto: Carswell, 1986.

Knafla, Louis A., and Jonathan Swainger, eds. *Laws and Societies in the Canadian Prairie West, 1670–1940*. Vancouver: University of British Columbia Press, 2005.

Kozak, Kathryn. "Education and the Blackfoot: 1870–1900." MA thesis, University of Alberta, 1971.

LaDow, Beth. *The Medicine Line: Life and Death on a North American Borderland.* New York: Routledge, 2001.

Lambrecht, Kirk N. *The Administration of Dominion Lands, 1870–1930.* Regina: Canadian Plains Research Center, 1991.

Lampard, Dr Robert. *Alberta's Medical History: "Young and Lusty, and Full of Life."* Red Deer: Author, 2008.

– *Five Celebrated Early Surgeons of Southern Alberta, 1874–1913.* Occasional Paper no. 43. Lethbridge: Lethbridge Historical Society, 2006.

Larmour, Judy. *Laying down the Lines: A History of Land Surveying in Alberta.* Calgary: Brindle & Glass, 2005.

Lee, David. "Almighty Voice and His Stories." *Native Studies Review* 10, no. 2 (1995): 57–76.

Lee, Gordon. "The Importance of the Sacred Pipe Ceremony." In Price, *Spirit of the Alberta Indian Treaties,* 111–12.

Lee, Richard, and Richard Daly, eds. *The Cambridge Encyclopedia of Hunters and Gatherers.* Cambridge: Cambridge University Press, 1999.

Leighton, James Douglas. "The Development of Federal Indian Policy in Canada, 1840–1890." PhD diss., University of Western Ontario, 1975.

– "A Victorian Civil Servant at Work: Lawrence Vankoughnet and the Canadian Indian Department." In Getty and Lussier, *As Long as the Sun Shines,* 104–19.

Leslie, John F. "The Indian Act: An Historical Perspective." *Canadian Parliamentary Review* 25, no. 2 (Summer 2002): 23–27.

Loo, Tina. *States of Nature: Conserving Canada's Wildlife in the Twentieth Century.* Vancouver: University of British Columbia Press, 2006.

Looy, Anthony Jacobus. "The Indian Agent and His Role in the Administration of the North-West Superintendency, 1876–1893." PhD diss., Queen's University, 1977.

Lovisek, Joan A. "Algonquians/Subarctic." In Magosci, *Aboriginal Peoples of Canada,* 98–128.

Lupul, David. "The Bobtail Land Surrender." *Alberta History* 26, no. 1 (Winter 1978): 29–39.

Lupul, Manoly R. "Education in Western Canada before 1873." In Wilson, Stamp, and Audet, *Canadian Education,* 241–64.

Lussier, Antoine S., and D. Bruce Sealey. *The Other Natives: The-les Métis.* Vol. 1, *1700–1885,* and vol. 2, *1885–1978.* Winnipeg: Manitoba Métis Federation Press and Editions Bois-Brûlés, 1978.

Lutz, John Sutton. *Makúk: A New History of Aboriginal-White Relations.* Vancouver: University of British Columbia Press, 2008.

Lux, Maureen K. *Medicine that Walks: Disease, Medicine, and Canadian Plains Native People, 1880–1940.* Toronto: University of Toronto Press, 2001.

Luxton, Eleanor G. "Stony Indian Medicine." In *The Developing West: Essays on Canadian History in Honor of Lewis H. Thomas*, ed. John E. Foster, 101–21. Edmonton: University of Alberta Press, 1983.

Mabindisa, Isaac Kholisile. "The Praying Man: The Life and Times of Henry Bird Steinhauer." PhD diss., University of Alberta, 1984.

MacEwan, Grant. *Métis Makers of History*. Saskatoon: Western Producer Prairie Books, 1981.

MacGregor, James G. *Father Lacombe*. Edmonton: Hurtig, 1975.

– *A History of Alberta*. Edmonton: Hurtig, 1972.

MacInnes, T.R.L. "History of Indian Administration in Canada." *Canadian Journal of Economics and Political Science* 12 (February–November 1946): 387–94.

Mack, D.B. "George Munro Grant." *DCB*, 13, *1901–1910*, 403–09.

Macleod, R.C. "Canadianizing the West: The North-West Mounted Police as Agents of the National Policy, 1873–1905." In *Essays in Western History in Honour of Lewis Gwynne Thomas*, ed. Lewis H. Thomas, 101–10. Edmonton: University of Alberta Press, 1976.

– "Introduction." In Strange, *Gunner Jingo's Jubilee*, xi–xxii.

– *The NWMP and Law Enforcement 1873–1905*, Toronto: University of Toronto Press, 1976.

– "James Farquharson Macleod." *DCB*, 12, *1891–1900*, 672–75.

– "The Problem of Law and Order in the Canadian West, 1870–1905." In *The Prairie West to 1905: A Canadian Sourcebook*, ed. Lewis G. Thomas, 132–216. Toronto: Oxford University Press, 1975.

– , ed. *Swords and Ploughshares: War and Agriculture in Western Canada*. Edmonton: University of Alberta Press, 1993.

– "Thomas Bland Strange." *DCB*, 15, *1921–1930*, 981–82.

Macpherson, M.A. *Outlaws of the Canadian West*. Edmonton: Lone Pine, 1999.

– "William Francis Butler." *DCB*, 13, *1901–1910*, 142–44.

Macleod, R. C, and Heather Rollason Driscoll. "Natives, Newspapers and Crime Rates in the North-West Territories, 1878–1885." In Binnema, Ens, and Macleod, *From Rupert's Land to Canada*, 249–69.

– "'Restrain the Lawless Savages': Native Defendants in the Criminal Courts of the North West Territories, 1878–1885." *Journal of Historical Sociology* 10, no. 2 (June 1997): 157–83.

Magosci, Paul Robert, ed. *Aboriginal Peoples of Canada: A Short Introduction*. Toronto: University of Toronto Press, 2002.

—, ed. *Encyclopedia of Canada's Peoples*. Toronto: University of Toronto Press/Multicultural Society of Ontario, 1999.

Magzul, Lorenzo. "The Blood Tribe: Adapting to Climate Change." *Prairie Forum* 34, no. 1 (Spring 2009): 289–309.

Mainville, Robert. *An Overview of Aboriginal and Treaty Rights and Compensation for Their Breach*. Saskatoon: Purich Publishing, 2001.

Mandelbaum, David G. *The Plains Cree: An Ethnographic, Historical, and Comparative Study*. Regina: Canadian Plains Research Center, 1979.

Marchildon, Gregory P., Jeremy Pittman, and David J. Sauchyn. "The Dry Belt and Changing Aridity in the Palliser Triangle, 1895–2000." *Prairie Forum* 34, no. 1 (Spring 2009): 31–44.

Marino, Mary C. "Siouans." In Magosci, *Aboriginal Peoples of Canada*, 251–63.

Martin, Chester. *"Dominion Lands" Policy*. Toronto: Macmillan, 1938.

Martin, Fred V. "Alberta Métis Settlements: A Brief History." In Connors and Law, *Forging Alberta's Constitutional Framework*, 345–89.

Martin, Roderick G. "Macleod at Law: A Judicial Biography of James Farquharson Macleod, 1874–1894." In *People and Place: Historical Influences on Legal Culture*, ed. Jonathan Swainger and Constance Backhouse, 37–59. Vancouver: University of British Columbia Press, 2003.

Martin-McGuire, Peggy. *First Nations Land Surrenders on the Prairies, 1896–1911*. Ottawa: Report for Indian Claims Commission, 1998.

Maundrell, C.R. "Indian Health, 1867–1940." MA thesis, Queen's University, 1941.

Mayfield, Barbara. "The Interlude: The North-West Mounted Police and the Blackfoot Peoples, 1874–1877." In Baker, *The Mounted Police*, 17–40.

– "The North-West Mounted Police and the Blackfoot Peoples, 1874–1884." MA thesis, University of Victoria, 1979.

McCuaig, Katherine. *The Weariness, the Fever, and the Fret: The Campaign against Tuberculosis in Canada, 1900–1950*. Montreal: McGill-Queen's University Press, 1999.

McCullough, A.B. "Gunner Jingo: Thomas Bland Strange, 1831–1935." *Alberta History* 48, no. 1 (Winter 2000): 2–9.

McKay, G.A. "Climate Change and the Canadian Economy." In *Essays on Meteorology and Climatology: In Honour of Richmond W. Longley*, ed. K.D. Hage and E.R. Reinelt, 151–69. Edmonton: Department of Geography, University of Alberta, 1978.

McKay, Ian. "The Liberal Order Framework: A Prospectus for a Reconnaissance of Canadian History." *Canadian Historical Review* 81, no. 4 (December 2001): 617–45.

McLaren, John, Hamar Foster, and Chet Orloff, eds. *Law for the Elephant, Law for the Beaver: Essays in the Legal History of the North American West*. Regina: Canadian Plains Research Center, 1992.

McLeod, Neal. *Cree Narrative Memory: From Treaties to Contemporary Times*. Saskatoon: Purich Publishing, 2007.

– "Plains Cree Identity: Borderlands, Ambiguous Genealogies and Narrative History." *Canadian Journal of Native Studies* 20, no. 2 (2000): 437–54.

McManus, Sheila. *The Line which Separates: Race, Gender, and the Making of the Alberta-Montana Borderlands*. Edmonton: University of Alberta Press, 2005.

McNab, David. "The Colonial Office and the Prairies in the Mid-Nineteenth Century." *Prairie Forum* 3, no. 1 (Spring 1978): 21–38.

McNeill, Eileen M. "Women of Vision and Compassion: The Foundation of Health Care in Calgary." *Alberta History* 50, no. 1 (Winter 2002): 17–25.

McQuillan, D. Aidan. "Creation of Indian Reserves on the Canadian Prairies 1870–1885." *The Geographical Review* 70, no. 4 (October 1980): 379–96.

Meijer Drees, Laurie. *The Indian Association of Alberta: A History of Political Action*. Vancouver: University of British Columbia Press, 2002.

– "Reserve Hospitals and Medical Officers: Health Care and Indian Peoples in Southern Alberta, 1890s–1930." *Prairie Forum* 21, no. 2 (Fall 1996): 149–76.

Melnycky, Peter. *A Veritable Canaan: Alberta's Victoria Settlement*. Edmonton: Friends of Victoria Historical Society, 1997.

Métis Association of Alberta, The. *The Métis and the Land in Alberta: Land Claims Research Project, 1979–80*. Edmonton: The Métis Association of Alberta, 1980.

Métis Association of Alberta, The, Joe Sawchuk, Patricia Sawchuk, and Teresa Ferguson. *Metis Land Rights in Alberta: A Political History*. Edmonton: The Métis Association of Alberta, 1981.

Miller, J.R. "Aboriginals: Introduction." In Magosci, *Encyclopedia of Canada's Peoples*, 1–14.

– *Canada and the Aboriginal Peoples 1867–1927*. Historical Booklet no. 57. Ottawa: Canadian Historical Association, 1997.

– *Compact, Contract, Covenant: Aboriginal Treaty-Making in Canada*. Toronto: University of Toronto Press, 2009.

– "Compact, Contract, Covenant: The Evolution of Indian Treaty-Making." In Binnema and Neylan, *New Histories for Old*, 66–91.

– "Denominational Rivalry in Indian Residential Education." *Western Oblate Studies* 2, ed. R. Huel. Lewiston: Edwin Mellen Press, 1992.

– "Introduction." In Magosci, *Aboriginal Peoples of Canada*, 3–37.

– Review of M. Asch, *On Being Here to Stay* (2014), in *Canadian Historical Review*, 96:1 (Mar. 2015), 109–11.

– *Shingwauk's Vision: A History of Native Residential Schools.* Toronto: University of Toronto Press, 1996.
– *Skyscrapers Hide the Heavens: A History of Indian-White Relations in Canada.* 3rd ed. Toronto: University of Toronto Press, 2000.
– ed. *Sweet Promises: A Reader on Indian-White Relations in Canada.* Toronto: University of Toronto Press, 1991.
– "Victoria's 'Red Children': The 'Great White Mother' and Native-Newcomer Relations in Canada." *Native Studies Review* 17, no. 1 (2008): 1–23.
Milloy, John S. *A National Crime: The Canadian Government and the Residential School System, 1879 to 1986.* Winnipeg: University of Manitoba Press, 1999.
– "The Early Indian Acts: Developmental Strategy and Constitutional Change." In Miller, *Sweet Promises,* 145–54.
– "'Our Country': The Significance of the Buffalo Resource for a Plains Cree Sense of Territory." In Abel and Friesen, *Aboriginal Resource Use,* 51–70.
Milne, Brad. "The Historiography of Métis Land Dispersal." *Manitoba History* 1995: 30–41.
Mitchner, E. Alyn. "William Pearce: Father of Alberta Irrigation." MA thesis, University of Alberta, 1966.
Mittelstadt, David. "Calgary's Early Courts: Establishing Our Justice System." In Chinook Country Historical Society, *Remembering Chinook Country,* 197–206.
Monaghan, Jeffrey. "Mounties in the Frontier: Circulation Anxieties and Myths of Settler Colonial Policing in Canada." *Journal of Canadian Studies/Revue d'études canadiennes* 47, no. 1 (Winter 2013): 122–48.
Moodie, D. Wayne, and Barry Kaye. "Indian Agriculture in the Fur Trade Northwest." *Prairie Forum* 11, no. 2 (Fall 1986): 171–83.
Morris, Ian. *Why the West Rules – For Now: The Patterns of History, and What They Reveal about the Future.* Toronto: McClelland and Stewart, 2010.
Morrison, R. Bruce, and C. Roderick Wilson, eds. *Native Peoples: The Canadian Experience.* 2nd ed. Toronto: McClelland and Stewart, 1986.
Morse, Bradford W., ed. *Aboriginal Peoples and the Law: Indian, Metis and Inuit Rights in Canada.* Ottawa: Carleton University Press, [1985] 1991.
Morton, Arthur S. *A History of the Canadian West to 1870–71, Being a History of Rupert's Land (The Hudson's Bay Company's Territory) and of the North-West Territory (Including the Pacific Slope).* 2nd ed. Ed. Lewis G. Thomas. Toronto: University of Toronto Press, 1973 [1939].
Morton, Desmond. "Cavalry or Police: Keeping the Peace on Two Adjacent Frontiers, 1870–1900." In Baker, *The Mounted Police,* 3–16.

Morton, W.L. "Clio in Canada: The Interpretation of Canadian History."
    *University of Toronto Quarterly* 15, no. 3 (April 1946): 227–34. Reprinted
    in *Approaches to Canadian History*, ed. Carl Berger, 42–49. Toronto:
    University of Toronto Press, 1967.
– *The Critical Years: The Union of British North America, 1857–1873*.
    Toronto: McClelland and Stewart, 1964.
Naylor, R.T. *Canada in the European Age, 1453–1919*. Vancouver: New Star
    Books, 1987.
Neatby, Hilda. "The Medical Profession in the North-West Territories." In
    Shortt, *Medicine in Canadian Society*, 165–88.
Nichols, Roger I. "Do Borders Matter in Native American History? An
    American Perspective." In Behiels and Stuart, *Transnationalism*, 21–31.
– *Indians in the United States and Canada: A Comparative History*. Lincoln:
    University of Nebraska Press, 1998.
Niemi-Bohun, Melanie. "Colonial Categories and Familial Responses to Treaty
    and Metis Scrip Policy: The 'Edmonton and District Stragglers,' 1870–88."
    *Canadian Historical Review* 90, no. 1 (March 2009): 71–98.
Nigol, Paul C. "Discipline and Discretion in the Mid-Eighteenth-Century
    Hudson's Bay Company Private Justice System." In Knafla and Swainger,
    *Laws and Societies*, 150–82.
Nix, James Ernest. "George Millward McDougall." *DCB*, 10, *1871–1880*,
    471–72.
Oswalt, Wendell H. *This Land Was Theirs: A Study of Native Americans*.
    7th ed. New York: McGraw-Hill Higher Education, 2002.
Owram, Douglas Robb, ed. *The Formation of Alberta: A Documentary
    History*. Calgary: Alberta Records Publication Board, Historical Society of
    Alberta, 1979.
– *Promise of Eden: The Canadian Expansionist Movement and the Idea of
    the West, 1856–1900*. Toronto: University of Toronto Press, 1980.
– "White Savagery: Some Canadian Reaction to American Indian Policy,
    1867–1885." MA thesis, Queen's University, 1971.
Pagden, Anthony. *Peoples and Empires: A Short History of European
    Migration, Exploration, and Conquest from Greece to the Present*. New
    York: Modern Library, 2001.
Painter, Nell Irvin. *The History of White People*. New York: W.W. Norton,
    2010.
Palmer, Howard, with Tamara Palmer. *Alberta: A New History*. Edmonton:
    Hurtig, 1990.
Papaschase Historical Society. *South Edmonton Saga*. Edmonton: Papaschase
    Historical Society, 1984.

Payne, Michael. "Erasmus, Peter." *DCB*, 16. http://www.biographi.ca/en/bio/
erasmus_peter_16E.html.

Payne, Michael, Donald Wetherell, and Catherine Cavanaugh, eds. *Alberta
Formed, Alberta Transformed.* Vol. 1. Edmonton: University of Alberta
Press, 2006.

Peterson, Eugene H. *The Pastor: A Memoir.* New York: HarperOne, 2011.

– *Tell It Slant: A Conversation on the Language of Jesus in His Stories and
Prayers.* Grand Rapids: Eerdmans, 2008.

– *Under the Unpredictable Plant.* Grand Rapids: Eerdmans, 1992.

Pettipas, Katherine. "Introduction." In Budd, *The Diary of the Rev. Henry Budd.*

– *Severing the Ties that Bind: Government Repression of Indigenous Religious
Ceremonies on the Prairies.* Winnipeg: University of Manitoba Press, 1994.

Pocklington, T.C. *The Government and Politics of the Alberta Metis
Settlements.* Regina: Canadian Plains Research Center, 1991.

Prentice, Alison, Paula Bourne, Gail Cuthbert Brandt, Beth Light, Wendy
Mitchinson, and Naomi Black. *Canadian Women: A History.* 2nd ed.
Scarborough, ON: Nelson, Thomson Learning, 2004.

Preston, Richard A. "Patrick Robertson-Ross." *DCB*, 11, *1881–1890*, 758–60.

Price, Richard, ed. *The Spirit of the Alberta Indian Treaties* [Treaties 6, 7, 8].
Montreal: Institute for Research on Public Policy and Indian Association of
Alberta, 1979. (Also 3rd ed., Edmonton: University of Alberta Press, 1999.)

Pruden, Jana G. "Swift Runner's Last Walk." *Edmonton Journal*, 18 September
2011, A1–2, C3.

Ray, Arthur J. *The Canadian Fur Trade in the Industrial Age.* Toronto:
University of Toronto Press, 1990.

– "Diffusion of Diseases in the Western Interior of Canada, 1830–1850." In
Shortt, *Medicine in Canadian Society*, 45–73.

– *I Have Lived Here since the World Began: An Illustrated History of
Canada's Native People.* Toronto: Lester Publishing, 1996.

– *An Illustrated History of Canada's Native People.* Rev. and expanded ed.
Toronto: Key Porter Books, 2010.

– *Telling It to the Judge: Taking Native History to Court.* Montreal: McGill-
Queen's University Press, 2011.

Ray, Arthur J., Jim Miller, and Frank J. Tough. *Bounty and Benevolence: A
History of Saskatchewan Treaties.* Montreal: McGill-Queen's University
Press, 2000.

Read, Colin. "John Stoughton Dennis." *DCB*, 11, *1881–1890*, 244–46.

Rees, Tony. *Arc of the Medicine Line: Mapping the Word's Longest
Undefended Border across the Western Plains.* Vancouver: Douglas &
McIntyre, 2007.

Regular, W. Keith. *Neighbours and Networks: The Blood Tribe in the Southern Alberta Economy, 1884–1919*. Calgary: University of Calgary Press, 2009.

– "'Red Races and White Burdens': A Study of White Attitudes towards Indians in Southern Alberta, 1896–1911." MA thesis, University of Calgary, 1985.

Reiter, Robert A. *The Law of Canadian Indian Treaties*. Edmonton: Jura Analytica Publishing, 1995.

Rich, E.E. *The Fur Trade and the Northwest to 1857*. Toronto: McClelland and Stewart, 1967.

Robb, Andrew. "David Laird." *DCB*, 14, 1911–1920, 578–81.

Robertson, Heather. "Heartbreak in Huronia." *Canada's History* October–November 2013: 28–32.

Ronaghan, Allen. "Another Father of Confederation?" *Prairie Forum* 24, no. 2 (Fall 1999): 269–76.

– "The Archibald Administration in Manitoba, 1870–1872." PhD diss., University of Manitoba, 1986.

– "The 9th Quebec Voltigeurs." *Alberta History* 42, no. 2 (Spring 1994): 10–15.

– "Three Scouts and the Cart Train." *Alberta History* 25, no. 1 (Winter 1977): 12–14.

Rosen, George. *A History of Public Health*. Expanded ed. Baltimore: The Johns Hopkins University Press, [1958] 1993.

Rotman, Leonard Ian. *Parallel Paths: Fiduciary Doctrine and the Crown-Native Relationship in Canada*. Toronto: University of Toronto Press, 1996.

Rowand, Evelyn. "The Rebellion at Lac la Biche." *Alberta Historical Review* 21, no. 3 (Summer 1973): 2–9.

Russell, Peter A. *How Agriculture Made Canada: Farming in the Nineteenth Century*. Montreal: McGill-Queen's University Press, 2012.

Sahlins, Marshall. *Culture in Practice: Selected Essays*. New York: Zone Books, 2000.

St Germain, Jill. *Indian Treaty-Making Policy in the United States and Canada, 1867–1877*. Toronto: University of Toronto Press, 2001.

Samek, Hana. *The Blackfoot Confederacy, 1880–1920: A Comparative Study of Canadian and U.S. Indian Policy*. Albuquerque: University of New Mexico Press, 1987.

Sanders, Douglas. "The Queen's Promises." In Knafla, *Law & Justice*, 101–27.

Sanders, G. "The Appropriation of Indian Reserve Lands and the Creation of a Non-status Population." In Métis Association of Alberta, *The Métis and the Land*.

Sanders, Harry M. *The Story behind Alberta Names: How Cities, Towns, Villages and Hamlets Got Their Names*. Calgary: Red Deer Press, 2004.

Sandlos, John. *Hunters at the Margin: Native People and Wildlife Conservation in the Northwest Territories*. Vancouver: University of British Columbia Press, 2007.

Saywell, John T. *The Lawmakers: Judicial Power and the Shaping of Canadian Federalism*. Toronto: University of Toronto Press, 2004.

– *The Office of Lieutenant Governor*. Toronto: University of Toronto Press, 1957.

Schissel, Bernard, and Terry Wotherspoon. *The Legacy of School for the Aboriginal People: Education, Oppression, and Emancipation*. Don Mills: Oxford University Press, 2003.

Scott, Duncan Campbell. "Indian Affairs, 1840–1867." In *Canada and Its Provinces*, ed. Adam Shortt and Arthur G. Doughty, 331–62. Vol. 5. Toronto: Publishers' Association of Canada, 1913.

– "Indian Affairs, 1867–1912." In *Canada and Its Provinces*, ed. Adam Shortt and Arthur G. Doughty, 593–626. Vol. 7. Toronto: Publishers' Association of Canada, 1913.

Scott-Brown, Joan. "The Short Life of St Dunstan's Calgary Indian Industrial School, 1896–1907." *Canadian Journal of Native Education* 14, no. 1 (1987): 41–49.

Sealey, D. Bruce, and Antoine S. Lussier. *The Métis: Canada's Forgotten People*. Winnipeg: Manitoba Métis Federation Press, 1975.

– "Statutory Land Rights of the Manitoba Metis." In Lussier and Sealey, *The Other Natives*, vol. 2, 1–11.

Sealey, D.B. "Jerry Potts." DCB, 11, *1891–1900*, 858–59.

Seed, Patricia. *American Pentimento: The Invention of Indians and the Pursuit of Riches*. Minneapolis: University of Minnesota Press, 2001.

– *Ceremonies of Possession in Europe's Conquest of the New World, 1492– 1640*. Cambridge: Cambridge University Press, 1995.

Sharp, Paul F. *Whoop-up Country: The Canadian-American West, 1865–1885*. Helena: Historical Society of Montana, 1955.

Sherwin, Allan. *Bridging Two Peoples: Chief Peter E. Jones, 1843–1909*. Waterloo: Wilfrid Laurier University Press, 2012.

Shewell, Hugh. *"Enough to Keep Them Alive": Indian Welfare in Canda, 1873–1965*. Toronto: University of Toronto Press, 2004.

Shortt, S.E.D., ed. *Medicine in Canadian Society: Historical Perspectives*. Montreal: McGill-Queen's University Press, 1981.

Sieciechowicz, Krystyna Z. "Henry Bird Steinhauer." DCB, 11, *1881–1890*, 848–50.

Smandych, Russell C. "The Exclusionary Effect of Colonial Law: Indigenous Peoples and English Law in Western Canada, 1670–1870." In Knafla and Swainger, *Laws and Societies*, 127–49.

Smith, Brian J. "The Historical and Archaeological Evidence for the Use of Fish as an Alternate Subsistence Resource among Northern Plains Bison Hunters." In Abel and Friesen, *Aboriginal Resource Use*, 35–49.

Smith, Donald B. "Aboriginal Rights a Century Ago: The St Catharines Milling Case of 1885 Hardened Attitudes toward Native Land Claims." *The Beaver* 67, no. 1 (February/March 1987): 4–15.

– "Aboriginal Rights in 1885: A Study of the St Catharines's Milling or Indian Title Case." In Macleod, ed., *Swords and Ploughshares*, 21–44.

– "Elizabeth Barrett." *Alberta History* 46, no. 4 (Autumn 1998): 19–28.

– "Color Conscious: Racial Attitudes in Early 20th Century Calgary." In Chinook Country Historical Society, *Remembering Chinook Country*, 119–32.

– *Long Lance: The True Story of an Impostor*. Toronto: Macmillan, 1982.

– "Macdonald's Relationship with Aboriginal Peoples." In *Macdonald at 200: New Reflections and Legacies*, ed. P. Dutil and R. Hall, 58–93. Toronto: Dundurn, 2014.

– *Mississauga Portraits: Ojibwe Voices from Nineteenth-Century Canada*. Toronto: University of Toronto Press, 2013.

– "The Original Peoples of Alberta." In *Peoples of Alberta: Portraits of Cultural Diversity*., ed. Howard Palmer and Tamara Palmer, 50–83. Saskatoon: Western Producer Prairie Books, 1985.

– "The Steinhauer Brothers: Education & Self-Reliance." *Alberta History* 50, no. 2 (Spring 2002): 2–10.

Smith, Goldwin. *The Treaty of Washington*. Ithaca: Cornell University Press, 1941.

Smith, Keith D. *Liberalism, Surveillance and Resistance: Indigenous Communities in Western Canada, 1877–1977*. Edmonton: Athabasca University Press, 2009.

Snow, Chief John. *These Mountains Are Our Sacred Places: The Story of the Stoney Indians*. Toronto: Samuel Stevens, 1977.

Sowby, Joyce Katharine. "Macdonald the Administrator: Department of the Interior and Indian Affairs, 1878–1887." MA thesis, Queen's University, 1984.

Sparby, Harry Theodore. "A History of the Alberta School System to 1925." PhD diss., Stanford University, 1958.

Sprague, D.N. *Canada and the Métis, 1869–1885*. Waterloo: Wilfrid Laurier University Press, 1988.

Sprenger, H.S. "The Métis Nation: Buffalo Hunting vs. Agriculture at Red River Settlement." In Lussier and Sealey, *The Other Natives*, vol. 1, 115–30.

Spry, Irene M. "Aboriginal Resource Use in the Nineteenth Century in the Great Plains of Modern Canada." In Abel and Friesen, *Aboriginal Resource Use*, 81–92.

- "The Great Transformation: The Disappearance of the Commons in Western Canada." In *Man and Nature on the Prairies*, ed. Richard Allen, 21–45. Canadian Plains Studies 6. Regina: Canadian Plains Research Center, 1976.
- "Introduction." In Erasmus, *Buffalo Days and Nights*, ix–xxxii.

Stacey, Beverley A. "D.W. Davis: Whiskey Trader to Politician." *Alberta History* 38, no. 3 (Summer 1990): 1–11.

Stacey, C.P. *Canada and the Age of Conflict*. Vol. 1, *1867–1921*. Toronto: Macmillan, 1977.

Stanley, G.F.G. "Alberta's Half-Breed Reserve Saint-Paul-des-Métis 1806–1909." In Lussier and Sealey, *The Other Natives*, vol. 2, 75–107.

- "As Long as the Sun Shines and the Water Flows: An Historical Comment." In Getty and Lussier, *As Long as the Sun Shines*, 1–26.
- *The Birth of Western Canada: A History of the Riel Rebellions*. Toronto: University of Toronto Press, 1960 [1939].
- "Indian Raid at Lac la Biche." *Alberta History* 24, no. 3 (Summer 1976): 25–27.
- *Louis Riel*. Toronto: Ryerson, 1963.

Steckmesser, Kent Ladd. *The Westward Movement: A Short History*. New York: McGraw-Hill, 1969.

Stevenson, Allyson. "'Men of Their Own Blood': Metis Intermediaries and the Numbered Treaties." *Native Studies Review* 18, no. 1 (2009): 67–90.

Stewart, Gordon T. *The Origins of Canadian Politics: A Comparative Approach*. Vancouver: University of British Columbia, 1986.

Stonechild, Blair. "The Indian View of the 1885 Uprising." In Miller, *Sweet Promises*, 259–76.

Stonechild, Blair, and Bill Waiser. *Loyal Till Death: Indians and the North-West Rebellion*. Calgary: Fifth House, 1997.

Stotyn, Keith. "The Bow River Irrigation Project 1906–1949." MA thesis, University of Alberta, 1982.

Sutherland, Neil. *Children in English-Canadian Society: Framing the Twentieth-Century Consensus*. Waterloo: Wilfrid Laurier University Press, 2000 [1978].

- "'To Create a Strong and Healthy Race': School Children in the Public Health Movement, 1880–1914." In Shortt, *Medicine in Canadian Society*, 365–93.

Swainson, Donald. "Canada Annexes the West: Colonial Status Confirmed." In *The Prairie West: Historical Readings*, ed. R. Douglas Francis and Howard Palmer, 120–39. Edmonton: Pica Pica Press, 1985.

Talbot, Robert J. *Negotiating the Numbered Treaties: An Intellectual & Political Biography of Alexander Morris*. Saskatoon: Purich Publishing, 2009.

Taylor, Fraser. *Standing Alone: A Contemporary Blackfoot Indian* [Pete Standing Alone]. Halfmoon Bay, BC: Arbutus Bay Publications, 1989.

Taylor, Leonard John. "Canada's Northwest Indian Policy in the 1870s: Traditional Premises and Necessary Innovations." In Price, *The Spirit of the Alberta Indian Treaties*, 3–7.

– "The Development of an Indian Policy for the Canadian North-West, 1869–79." PhD diss., Queen's University, 1975.

– "Two Views on the Meaning of Treaties Six and Seven." In Price, *Spirit of the Alberta Indian Treaties*, 9–45.

Taylor, M. Scott. "Buffalo Hunt: International Trade and the Virtual Extinction of the North American Bison." Cambridge, MA: National Bureau of Economic Research, Working Paper 12,969. http://www.nber.org/papers/w12969.

Thomas, Lewis Herbert. "A History of Agriculture on the Prairies to 1914." *Prairie Forum* 1, no. 1 (April 1976): 31–45.

– *The Struggle for Responsible Government in the North-West Territories, 1870–97*. Toronto: University of Toronto Press, 1956.

Titley, Brian. "Dunbow Indian Industrial School: An Oblate Experiment in Education." *Western Oblate Studies* 2, ed. R. Huel, 95–113. Lewiston: Edwin Mellen Press, 1992.

– "Fate of the Sharphead Stoneys." *Alberta History* 39, no. 1 (Winter 1991): 1–8.

– *The Frontier World of Edgar Dewdney*. Vancouver: University of British Columbia Press, 1999.

– "Hayter Reed and Indian Administration in the West." In Macleod, *Swords and Ploughshares*, 109–47

– *The Indian Commissioners: Agents of the State and Indian Policy in Canada's Prairie West, 1873–1932*. Edmonton: University of Alberta Press, 2009.

– "Indian Industrial Schools in Western Canada." In *Schools in the West: Essays in Canadian Educational History*, ed. Nancy M. Sheehan, J. Donald Wilson, and David C. Jones, 133–53. Calgary: Detselig Enterprises, 1986.

– *A Narrow Vision: Duncan Campbell Scott and the Administration of Indian Affairs in Canada*. Vancouver: University of British Columbia Press, 1986.

– "Red Deer Indian Industrial School: A Case Study in the History of Native Education." In *Exploring Our Educational Past: Schooling in the North-West Territories and Alberta*, ed. Nich Kach and Kas Mazurek, 55–72. Calgary: Detselig Enterprises, 1992.

– "Transition to Settlement: The Peace Hills Indian Agency, 1884–1890." In *Canadian Papers in Rural History*, ed. Donald H. Akenson, 175–94. 8 vols. Gananoque: Langdale Press, 1992.

Tkach, Nicholas. "Alberta Catholic Schools: A Social History." Edmonton: Publication Services, Faculty of Education, University of Alberta, 1983.

Tobias, John L. "Canada's Subjugation of the Plains Cree, 1879–1885." *Canadian Historical Review* 64, no. 4 (December 1983): 518–48.

– "Protection, Civilization, Assimilation: An Outline History of Canada's Indian Policy." In Getty and Lussier, *As Long As the Sun Shines*, 39–55.

Todorov, Tzvetan. *The Conquest of America: The Question of the Other.* Trans. Richard Howard. Norman: University of Oklahoma Press, [1984] 1999.

Tosh, John. *The Pursuit of History.* Rev. 3rd ed. London: Longman, 2002.

Touchie, Rodger D. *Bear Child: The Life and Times of Jerry Potts.* Surrey, BC: Heritage House, 2005.

Tough, Frank J. "Aboriginal Rights versus the Deed of Surrender: The Legal Rights of Native Peoples and Canada's Acquisition of the Hudson's Bay Company Territory." *Prairie Forum* 17, no. 2 (Fall 1992): 225–50.

– "Fisheries Edonomics and the Tragedy of the Commons: The Case of Manitoba Inland Commercial Fisheries." York University, Department of Geography Discussion Paper Series no. 33, 1987.

Treaty 7 Elders and Tribal Council, with Walter Hildebrandt, Sarah Carter, and Dorothy First Rider. *The True Spirit and Original Intent of Treaty 7.* Montreal: McGill-Queen's University Press, 1996.

Trevithick, Scott. "Native Residential Schooling in Canada: A Review of the Literature." *Canadian Journal of Native Studies* 18, no. 1 (1998): 48–86.

Trigger, Bruce. *Natives and Newcomers: Canada's 'Heroic Age' Reconsidered.* Montreal: McGill-Queen's University Press, 1985.

Truth and Reconciliation Commission of Canada. *Interim Report.* Winnipeg: Truth and Reconciliation Commission of Canada, 2012.

Turner, Allan R. "Wikaskokiseyin, Abraham [Sweetgrass]." DCB, 10, *1871–1880, 702.*

Tyler, Kenneth James. "A Tax-Eating Proposition: The History of the Passpasschase Indian Reserve." MA thesis, University of Alberta, 1979.

Tyman, John Langton. *By Section, Township and Range: Studies in Prairie Settlement.* Brandon, MB: Assiniboine Historical Society, 1972.

Urquhart, M.C., and K.A.H. Buckley, eds. *Historical Statistics of Canada.* Toronto: Macmillan, 1965.

van Herk, Aritha. *Mavericks: An Incorrigible History of Alberta.* Toronto: Penguin, 2001.

Van Kirk, Sylvia M. "The Development of National Park Policy in Canada's Mountain National Parks, 1885 to 1930." MA thesis, University of Alberta, 1969.

– *"Many Tender Ties": Women in Fur Trade Society, 1670–1870.* Winnipeg: Watson & Dwyer, 1980.

Venne, Sharon. "Understanding Treaty 6: An Indigenous Perspective." In *Aboriginal and Treaty Rights in Canada: Essays on Law, Equity, and Respect for Difference,* ed. Michael Asch, 173–207, 267–69. Vancouver: University of British Columbia Press, 1997.

Voisey, Paul. *Vulcan: The Making of a Prairie Community.* Toronto: University of Toronto Press, 1988.

von Drehle, David. "The Case against Summer Vacation." *Time,* 2 August 2010, 36–42.

Waddell, William S. "The Honorable Frank Oliver." MA thesis, University of Alberta, 1950.

Waiser, Bill. "Too Many Scared People: Alberta and the 1885 North-West Rebellion." In Payne, Wetherell, and Cavanaugh, *Alberta Formed, Alberta Transformed,* 270–98.

Waite, P.B. *The Life and Times of Confederation, 1864–1867: Politics, Newspapers, and the Union of British North America.* Toronto: University of Toronto Press, 1962.

– *In Search of R.B. Bennett.* Montreal: McGill-Queen's University Press, 2012.
– "Thomas White." *DCB,* 11, *1881–1890,* 919–21.

Waldram, James B., D. Ann Herring, and T. Kue Young. *Aboriginal Health in Canada: Historical, Cultural, and Epidemiological Perspectives.* Toronto: University of Toronto Press, 1995.

Ward, Donald. *The People: A Historical Guide to the First Nations of Alberta, Saskatchewan, and Manitoba.* Fifth House, 1995.

Walsh, Brian J., and Sylvia C. Keesmaat, *Colossians Remixed: Subverting the Empire.* Downers Grove, IL: IVP Academic, 2004.

Washburn, Wilcomb E. "The Moral and Legal Justifications for Dispossessing the Indians." In *Seventeenth-Century America: Essays in Colonial History,* ed. James Morton Smith, 15–32. Chapel Hill: University of North Carolina Press, 1959.

– *Red Man's Land / White Man's Law: A Study of the Past and Present Status of the American Indian.* New York: Charles Scribner's Sons, 1971.

Wherrett, George Jasper. *The Miracle of the Empty Beds: A History of Tuberculosis in Canada.* Toronto: University of Toronto Press, 1977.

White, Richard. *Railroaded: The Transcontinentals and the Making of Modern America.* New York: W.W. Norton, 2011.

Wicken, William C. *The Colonization of Mi'kmaw Memory and History, 1794–1928.* Toronto: University of Toronto Press, 2012.

Wilson, C. Roderick. "Myths and Realities: An Overview of the Plains." In Morrison and Wilson, *Native Peoples*, 375–80.

Wilson, Garrett. *Frontier Farewell: The 1970s and the End of the Old West.* Regina: Canadian Plains Research Center, 2007.

Wilson, J. Donald. "The Ryerson Years in Canada West." In Wilson, Stamp, and Audet, *Canadian Education*, 214–40.

Wilson, J. Donald, Robert M. Stamp, and L.-A. Audet, eds. *Canadian Education: A History.* Toronto: Prentice-Hall, 1970.

Wise, S.F., and R. Craig Brown. *Canada Views the United States: Nineteenth-Century Political Attitudes.* Toronto: Macmillan, 1967.

Wishart, David J., ed. *Encyclopedia of the Great Plains.* Lincoln: University of Nebraska Press, 2004.

Wissler, Clark, and Alice Beck Kehoe, with Stewart E. Miller. *Amskapi Pikuni: The Blackfeet People.* Albany: SUNY Press, 2012.

Wolvengrey, Arok. "On the Spelling and Pronunciation of First Nations Languages and Names in Saskatchewan." *Prairie Forum* 23, no. 1 (Spring 1998): 113–25.

Wood, Patricia K. "Calgary and the Tsuu T'ina Nation: The Early Years, 1877–1887." In Chinook Country Historical Society, *Remembering Chinook Country*, 133–39.

Woywitka, Anne B. "Waugh Homesteaders and their School." *Alberta History* 23, no. 1 (Winter 1975): 13–17.

Wunder, John R. "Indigenous Colonial Treaties of North America in Comparative Perspective." In Wunder and Kinbacher, *Reconfigurations of Native North America*, 13–31.

Wunder, John R., and Kurt E. Kinbacher, eds. *Reconfigurations of Native North America: An Anthology of New Perspectives.* Lubbock: Texas Tech University Press, 2009.

Yellowhorn, Eldon. "Algonquians/Plains." In Magosci, *Aboriginal Peoples of Canada*, 82–97.

Zaslow, Morris. *The Opening of he Canadian North 1870–1914.* Toronto: McClelland and Stewart, 1971.

– *Reading the Rocks: The Story of the Geological Survey of Canada, 1842–1972.* Ottawa: Energy, Mines and Resources, and Information Canada, 1975.

Zylstra, Sarah Eckhoff. "When Abuse Comes to Light." *Christianity Today* 58, no. 2 (March 2014): 44–47.

# Index